ENCYCLOPAE

OF

BIRMINGHAM

CITY

PUBLISHING

First published in Great Britain by
Britespot Publishing Solutions Limited
Chester Road, Cradley Heath, West Midlands B64 6AB.

October 2000

Dedicated to all Bluenoses everywhere!!

ISBN 0-9539288-0-2

Cover design : Britespot Publishing Solutions Limited

Print and Production: Cradley Print & Design,
Chester Road, Cradley Heath, Warley,
West Midlands, B64 6AB

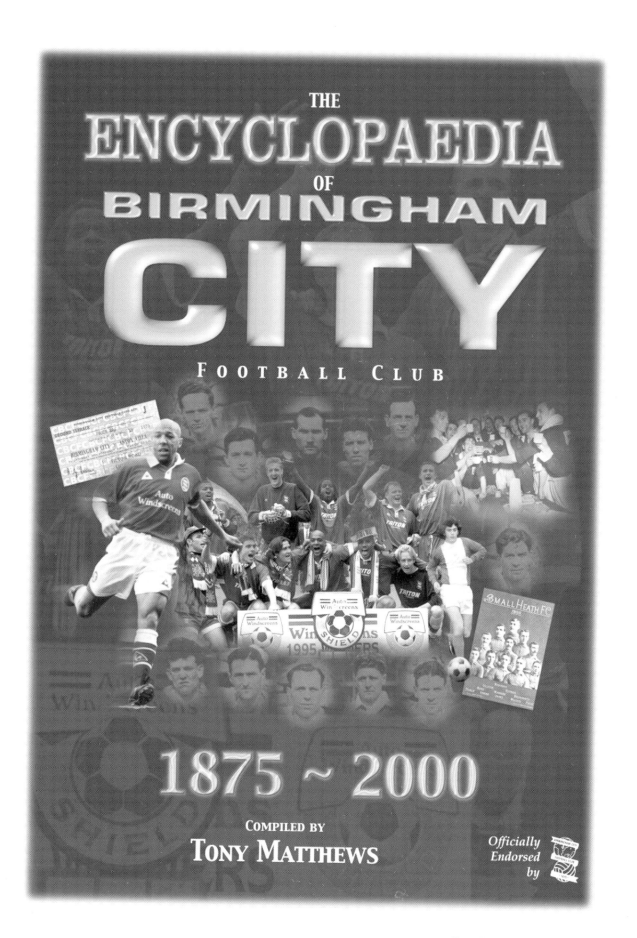

THE
ENCYCLOPAEDIA
OF
BIRMINGHAM
CITY
FOOTBALL CLUB

1875 ~ 2000

COMPILED BY
TONY MATTHEWS

Officially Endorsed by

by Tony Matthews

britespot
PUBLISHING SOLUTIONS LIMITED

ACKNOWLEDGEMENTS

So many people have contributed in some small way to making this Encyclopaedia what it is - a terrific publication. But I must say a special 'thank you' to three supporters who have certainly assisted far more than they perhaps realise, namely Roger Baker, Dave Drage and Dafydd Williams.

They all helped me enormously with the compilation of my Blues book The Complete Record of the club, published in 1989 and up-dated in 1995, and then Roger and Dave assisted me greatly when I compiled the Birmingham City Who's Who, published in between, in 1991.

The information contained in those three books has certainly boosted the content of this lastest publication with Dave adding several more 'vital' statistics to the files.

Also I have to say a big thank you to Ivan Barnsley, author of the Birmingham City 'Heroes in Action' books who gave me permission to use extracts from his works as well as several photographs contained therein. Also thank you sincerely to Roy Smiljanic, who has supplied some excellent photographs including shots of St Andrew's.

And I cannot fail to mention the many people, young and old, who have been extremely helpful in supplying snippits of information, some verbal, some written, as well as loaning me old programmes, postcards, cigarette cards, trade-cards, photographs, scrapbooks etc....a big thank you to one and all, namely: Dave Allan, Sam Bagnall, Bert Batt, Tim Beddow, John Blakemore, Jim Cadman, Peter Cocks, Ted Collier, Millicent and Walter Davies, Fred Evans, Liz Harvey, Alan Hatton, Andrew Henry, Lindon Hodgetts, Patrick Houlihan, Charles Jackson, Roger Kedwards, Paul Kelly, Barry Lankester (former BBC TV presenter), Nick Mansell, Jean Meeries, Keith Munnings, Phil Nend, Charlie Poultney, John Quickenden, Bob Rock, Keith Rowbottom, Clive Shaw, Harold Sherriff, Mick Sherry, Mike Shirley, Phil Smith (Media Options/Koala), John Swift, David Sword, Mick Talbot, John Tandy, Paul Turner, Brian Tynings and Jim Yeomans, plus quite a few AFS members all over the country whose odd fact and figure here and there have all come in useful!

Also thank you to Tim Beech, Carl Chinn, Paul Franks and Stuart Linnell (from Radio WM), to Bill Howell and Colin Tattum (of the Sports Argus/Birmingham Mail) and to David Instone (from the Express & Star).

I also acknowledge the assistance afforded to me by the picture libraries of both the Birmingham Post & Mail and the Express & Star (Wolverhampton).

Thank you, too (and 'sorry') to my long-suffering wife Margaret, who once again has had to put up without me whilst I've been sat at the computer hour after hour, tip-tapping away, and also thumbing through pages of reference books, programmes and magazines, checking and re-checking the statistics and stories.

And last but by no means least I give a sincere thank you to Dave Ethridge at Contact Colour, and to everyone who has worked hard on the book at Cradley Digital Imaging (Cradley Print/Britespot Publishing), Paul Burns, Richard Wood, Claire Bennett, Lee Mason and especially to Stuart Hardie and even moreso to Roger Marshall for agreeing to publish the book after other companies had turned the offer down.

INTRODUCTION

I have attempted to make this Encyclopaedia of Birmingham City Football Club as comprehensive as possible, utilising all the statistical information available which I have obtained from various sources over the past 12 years. I started compiling this book, in a manner of speaking, at the same time I began putting together The Complete Record of Birmingham City in 1988-89, and following that publication I have continually been adding to my collection of Blues facts and figures. As a result I have finally brought out this 256-page, 175,000-word encyclopaedia covering in detail the 125-year history of one of the biggest clubs in the country!

All the great players - and a few of the not so great - who have represented the club down the years are all featured in this book. Blues' full playing record in the various League and Cup competitions is covered in depth. There is an international section listing the honours won by Blues players past and present along with details of the club's top appearance-makers and champion goalscorers, attendance figures, sendings-off, Blues' managers, St Andrew's (Blues' head-quarters since 1906), substitutes, transfers, nicknames, European football and much, much more....plenty to keep you occupied during the winter months and certainly enough information to enable you to get your friends and colleagues talking Blues down the pub and club.

I have tried to cover everything on Birmingham City Football Club and for the record I have in most cases called the club Blues rather than Small Heath Alliance, Small Heath or Birmingham City.

Over the past year or so, through various local newspapers and radio channels, I have continually asked supporters (young and old, male and female) for information regarding Birmingham City football Club. As a result literally hundreds of statistics have flooded in along with scores of fond memories, many points of view, some sobering thoughts and a great deal of general news of the Blues. Whether supplied verbally, by letter, fax or E-mail it has all been fed into the system and as a result I feel I have put together a bumper book, perhaps one of the best ever done (statistically) on a major football club.

I have tried to cram as much into this book as I possibly could. I just hope I haven't missed too much, but if I have, I would dearly love to hear from you so that my records can be updated and/or amended in readiness for the next 'big book' on Blues. With so many facts and figures, statistics, listings and features condensed in this publication I feel sure there will be a discrepancy, a small error, a spelling mistake, even a missing player, a word, a club, somewhere down the line. I am only human, like every one else, and even the great writers of the past made the odd mistake here and there....missed out something which should have been included, got a year, a date wrong. Please accept my apologies if something is amiss. I have, with the assistance of several willing helpers, tried to ensure that everything in this book is factual, up-to-date and precise in every detail.

Birmingham City is a big, big club...a sleeping giant so they say! Unfortunately the team has yet to play in the Premiership. In fact, the last time Blues appeared in the top flight of British football was back in season 1985-86. But surely a place with the Manchester Uniteds, Arsenals and Liverpools of this world isn't too far away. Twice denied a play-off final place in recent years, Blues' chance to pit their wits at Old Trafford, Anfield, Highbury and such likes will surely come again. Let's hope it's sooner rather than later. The club's dedicated fans deserve success. They have still to cheer on a League Championship winning side or celebrate a major Cup triumph at Wembley. The Football League Cup (1963), the Leyland DAF Trophy (1991) and the Auto-Windscreen Shield (1995) have all been won but the team from St Andrew's hasn't claimed a big prize...yet.

St Andrew's is now one of the country's finest all-seater stadiums. And there is no doubt that if Blues are winning, then the support they can generate is tremendous with an average turnout of 25,000 guaranteed at every home game. One feels that if - or should that be when - Blues get into the Premiership, the ground capacity would have to be increased to accommodate the 40,000 regulars who want to watch them beat the elite!

Wishful thinking? Not really...Blues will be back.

ABANDONED MATCHES

Snow at St Andrew's groundsman giving the thumbs down.

- The first recorded game to be abandoned involving Blues was during the 1881-82 season - a friendly against Darlaston All Saints. Blues led 8-0 at half-time and scored another eight goals in the opening fifteen minutes of the second period before the referee called a halt to the proceedings, declaring it 'no contest' with the scoreline reading 16-0!
- On 26 August 1882 Blues were leading Walsall Town 4-3 at home in another friendly encounter when the referee called a halt to the proceedings after 70 minutes due, it is believed, to the extreme heat as several players complained of being exhausted.
- A third home friendly against Wolverhampton Wanderers on 26 January 1884 was called off through bad light with the visitors leading 1-0.
- Blues were 4-0 down to Aston Villa in a friendly in January 1898 when the referee abandoned the game due to the weather.
- On 9 March 1899 Blues were leading Leek 2-1 in a friendly before the weather caused a 76th minute abandonment.
- Blues' were beating Manchester City 1-0 in an away League match on 10 January 1903 when bad light caused the game to be abandoned in the 83rd minute. Blues lost the re-scheduled fixture 4-0!
- The Lord Mayor of Birmingham Charity Cup Final between Aston Villa and Blues in 1905 was abandoned after 50 minutes through bad weather with Villa 1-0 ahead. The game was declared a draw and each club held the trophy for six months.
- In the 36th minute of Blues' home game with Nottingham Forest on 22 February 1908, a gust of wind blew the roof off one of the stands, causing the game to be abandoned with the scores level at 1-1. Blues won the 'reply' 1-0 five weeks later.

- The Aston Villa-Blues Charity Football Festival friendly at Villa Park in March 1909 was abandoned due to bad weather during the second half with the hosts 2-1 ahead.
- Fog caused the 70th minute abandonment of Blues' home League game with Leicester City on 16 December 1933 with the visitors 2-1 in front. Blues won the re-arranged fixture 3-0 in late March.
- The Blues-Sheffield Wednesday League match on 22 February 1936 was called off after 36 minutes through snow with the home side 1-0 ahead. Blues went on to win the replayed game 4-1.
- On 15 February 1958 Blues were holding Manchester City to a 1-1 draw at Maine Road when the game was abandoned in the 40th minute through fog. The re-arranged fixture also ended 1-1.
- On 10 January 1959 the Blues v Middlesbrough third round FA Cup-tie at Ayresome Park was abandoned through snow after an hour's play with the scores level at 1-1. Fifteen days later Blues won the replay 1-0.
- On 25 February 1963, after weeks of harsh weather, the Blues v Bury long-delayed FA Cup 3rd round tie was abandoned at half-time because of a frozen and dangerous pitch. Blues were leading 1-0 in front of 19,287 freezing spectators! The tie eventually took place again on 5 March (after a total of 14 postponements plus that abandonment) and ended all-square at 3-3. Bury won the replay 48 hours later by 2-0.
- The Texaco Cup match between Newcastle United and Blues at St James' Park on 28 November 1974 was abandoned through bad light after 110 minutes play with the scores level at 1-1. A week later Newcastle won the re-staged fixture 3-1 to go through into the next round 4-2 on aggregate.
- Blues travelled to play Crystal Palace in a friendly at Selhurst Park in August 1981. The game was abandoned after 70 minutes when the floodlights failed. Palace were leading 1-0 at the time.

ABBOTT, Walter

Born in Small Heath in 1877 and signed from Rosewood Villa, inside-left Walter Abbott scored on his senior debut for Blues in an 8-0 Test Match victory over Manchester City in April of 1896. Three years later he was transferred to Everton (July 1899) and remained at Goodison Park for nine years, helping the Merseysiders win the FA Cup in 1906 and finish runners-up the following season. After more than 300 games for the Toffeemen (37 goals scored) he returned 'home' to Blues in July 1910, retiring the following May. Abbott - a powerful, strong-running forward - netted 66 goals in just 85 first team appearances during his two spells at the club, and he still holds the seasonal individual scoring record for Blues with a total of 42 goals in the 1898-99 campaign, including five in a League match v Darwen. In fact, Abbott was the country's top-marksman that season with 34 League goals. Capped once by England (at centre-half against Wales at Wrexham in 1902 despite playing his club football in the forward-line), Abbott also starred for the Football League on four occasions. He was forced to retire with a knee injury and later worked at the Longbridge car factory. He died in Birmingham in February 1941.

ACCRINGTON STANLEY

Blues never met Accrington Stanley in a major competition before the Lancashire club lost its Football League status in 1962, having been a member since 1921. The 'first' Accrington club (without Stanley) existed from September 1878 to January 1896, playing in the Football League for the first five seasons: 1888-93.

Players with both clubs include: W Aveyard, H Bodle (player & manager of Stanley), R Crawshaw, H Deacon, H Gayle, S Lynn, HC Randle (Blues reserve), H Riley, WH Smith (Stanley player-coach), JW Williams.

AC CESENA

Blues played AC Cesena in an Anglo-Italian Cup-tie on 13 December 1995 at St Andrew's. A crowd of 7,813 saw Blues win the game 3-1 with goals by Louie Donowa (32 minutes), Jonathan Hunt (76) and Steve Claridge (87).

ADEBOLA, Dele

Adebola in action against Port Vale

Nigerian international striker Dele Adebola, a powerful, forceful player, was top-scorer for Crewe Alexandra in 1996-97, helping them reach the Nationwide League Division One for the first time in the club's history. Scouts (and managers) from all over the country took note of his achievements and in February 1998, having taken his tally of goals to 46 in 152 appearances for the Gresty Road club, Adebola was snapped up by Trevor Francis for £1 million. He became an instant hit with the St Andrew's fans as he rattled in five more goals in his first five outings for Blues. Born in Lagos, Nigeria on 23 June 1975, he stands 6ft 3ins tall and weighs 12 st 8lbs. And his pace, power and sheer strength, his ability in the air and on the ground (he has a tremendous left foot) makes Adebola a fearsome opponent. Indeed. most defenders know they've been in a game after facing him. A hamstring injury interrupted the second half of the 1998-99 campaign but he still managed 17 goals and the following season he again did the business when helping Blues reach the First Division play-offs for the second time running. Adebola, who has scored some 30 goals in more than 100 appearances for Blues was all set to leave St Andrew's for the Spanish club Las Palmas in a £1.2 million deal in July 2000 but the transfer fell through on medical grounds..

ADEY, George

Born in Handsworth in 1869, George Adey played as a wing-half and inside-forward for Blues, making 79 appearances and scoring two goals. A player with strength, skill and stamina, he joined the club from Stourbridge in 1898 and left for Kettering Town in 1902. He was a very popular with the latter club.

ADMISSION PRICES

Match ticket (Blues v Villa) 1977

When Blues first entered the Football League in 1892, the general charge for admission to a home game varied from one old penny to 6d (3p). The 6d entrance fee remained as the minimum charge until just after the First War when it was increased to one shilling (5p) for the 1919-20 season. Over the next 22 years that shilling (bob) admission price stayed in force, but for the 1942-43 Wartime campaign it went up to 1s. 3d (7p). From then on the increase to the minimum entrance fee and highest admittance charge, have both gradual......four shillings (20p) by the early 1950s, rising to 4s.6d (23p) and up to 5s (25p) by 1960-61. It was 6s (30p) in the mid '60s, then 10s (50p) in the late 1960s and 25 years ago the entrance fee had risen to £1.00. Thereafter it rose steadily: £1.50 up to £2.00 and then to £2.50 by 1980 and since all-seater stadia has been with us the cheapest adult admission price to St Andrew's has risen dramatically.

Here is a conservative guide to the dearest adult admission prices to St Andrew's over the last ten years:

Season	Terraces	Seats
1990-91	£4.50	£10.00
1991-92	£5.00	£10.00
1992-93	£6.00	£12.00
1993-94	£8.50	£13.00
1994-95	-	£14.00
1995-96	-	£15.00
1996-97	-	£17.00
1997-98	-	£18.00
1998-99	-	£22.00
1999-2000	-	£24.00

- The Family Season Ticket/match ticket was introduced during the mid-1990s.
- And occasionally there are concessions/allowances (reduced seat prices) for certain matches (League and Cup).

SEASON TICKETS

A late 1880s ground season ticket to watch Blues cost the supporter 3s (15p) - in those days a club used to play between 15 and

20 home matches per season. When they entered the Football League in 1891 - 92 the average price for a season ticket was 5s (25p).

At the turn of the century (1900-01) the price had risen to 10s (50p) and in the first season after the Great War (1919-20) a season ticket at St Andrew's was priced at 15s (75p).

Over the next 20 years or so the overall price rose slowly - in 1930 supporters paid 30s a time (£1.50); in 1934 it had risen to £2 per season ticket and just before League Football was suspended in 1939 the cost had climbed to three guineas (£3.15).

Immediately after World War Two, the admission charge had reached £4 a time; it was £5 ten years later (in 1956) and in 1960 the average price of a season ticket was £8.

Between 1961 and 1974 season ticket prices went up slowly - from £9 to £10 to £12 to £15 to £18 and for the 1974-75 campaign fans at St Andrew's were paying upwards of £20, plus an extra £6 for five cup matches and £17 (plus £5) in the main stand.

The 1977-78 season ticket prices ranged from as low as £10 (for juniors)to as high as £45 (adults)...and if you wanted a reserved car parking place you had to pay an extra £12.

In 1979-80, the price for an adult of a Blues season ticket (in the main stand) was around the £60 mark (this was the norm up and down the country for the majority of the First Division club). And since then the general cost of a season ticket has risen steadily, from £50 (terraces) and £100 (seats) in 1984-85, from £55/£120 with four years, quickly rising to around the £85/£150 mark in 1990. Season tickets rose rapidly - £150/£200, then £220 in 1993-94 (for an adult in the main stand) upwards of £250 and in season 1999-2000 the dearest season tickets at St Andrew's were priced at £300 plus.

COMPLIMENTARY TICKETS

For football League matches, the visiting club can normally claim in the region of 40 complimentary tickets - 25 for the use by the players, managers and coach and the remainder for the Director etc. However, there is no set limit on how many complimentary tickets the home club can issue.

AGE

Trevor Francis

OLDEST PLAYERS

Dennis Jennings (born on 20 July 1910) was 39 years, nine months and 17 days old when he played his last game for Blues on 6 May 1950 against Wolves in a First Division encounter at Molineux. The Wanderers won 6-1.

Prior to Jennings, the previous 'oldest' Blues League player had been Frank Womack, aged 39 years, 207 days. When he left Blues in March 1951 (still registered as a player) Jennings was fast approaching his 41st birthday.

Gil Merrick was 37 years,

eight months and eight days old when he played his last first team game for Blues on 3 October 1959.

YOUNGEST PLAYERS

Trevor Francis (born in Plymouth on 19 April 1954) was just 16 years, four months and 16 days old when he made his first team debut for Blues as a substitute away to Cardiff City on 5 September 1970.

AGE CONCERN

Former Blues defender Alex Leake was 40 years of age when he was named as England's reserve in 1912 while serving with Burnley.

Goalkeeper Billy George is the oldest player to make his senior debut for Blues - aged 37 in September 1911 (v Barnsley).

Steve Bruce was almost 36 when he joined Blues from Manchester United in the summer of 1996.

When he left St Andrew's in March 1970 manager Stan Cullis was approaching his 54th birthday while Sir Alf Ramsey was 58 years of age when he left the club.

The oldest player to oppose Blues in a League game has been Stanley Matthews of Stoke City, who was aged 48 years, nine months and 29 days when he set up two goals in the Potters' 4-1 Second Division victory at The Victoria Ground on 30 November 1963.

AGGREGATE SCORE

- Blues beat Derby County 7-0 on aggregate in a two-legged League Cup-tie in October 1983.
- A two-legged FA Cup 6th round clash with Bradford (P.A.) in March 1946 went in favour of Blues 8-2 on aggregate.
- Aston Villa beat Blues 7-0 on aggregate (2-0 and 5-0) in a two-legged League Cup-tie in September/October 1988.
- After drawing 4-4 on aggregate with Barcelona in the two-legged semi-final of the Inter Cities Fairs Cup in October/November 1957, Blues were defeated 2-1 in the 'replay' to effectively lose the tie 6-5 overall.
- The Luxembourg part-timers from FC Union St Gilloise were ousted from the ICFC by Blues 8-4 on aggregate in the two-legged semi-final which was played during October/November 1959.
- Thirteen goals were scored in Blues' two-legged ICFC second round clash with Boldklub Copenhagen in November/December 1960. Blues drew 4-4 in Denmark and then won the return game 5-0 at St Andrew's to go through 9-4 on aggregate.

AINSCOW, Alan

A Lancastrian, born in Bolton in July 1953, Alan Ainscow, an efficient, hardworking midfielder, served Blues for three seasons (July 1978 - August 1981) during which time he made 125 appearances and scored 22 goals. He started out with Blackpool and won England youth caps as a teenager before leaving Bloomfield Road for St Andrew's. He was a key members of Blues' promotion-winning side of 1980 and went on to amass more than 500 League appearances during an excellent career which also saw him serve with Barnsley (on loan), Wolverhampton Wanderers, Blackburn Rovers and Rochdale. He also played for Eastern FC in Hong Kong in 1983 and for Horwich RMI after leaving Spotland in 1990.

Alan Ainscow

AIRDRIEONIANS

Blues met the Scottish club in a Festival of Britain game at St Andrew's on 7 May 1951. A crowd of almost 8,000 saw an eight-goal thriller go in favour of the visitors by 5-3. Right-winger Johnny Berry scored twice for Blues.

Players with both clubs include: J Conlon, A Garrett, M Good, J Inglis, W Main, R McRoberts, RG Thomson.

ALDERSHOT (also Town)

Blues have never met the Shots at League, FA Cup or League Cup level.

Blues have only played the Shots once - in the Leyland DAF Trophy at The Recreation Ground on 28 November 1989 when only 1,148 spectators bothered to turn up to see the home side win quite comfortably by 3-0.

At the time this was Blues' lowest attendance (at home or away) for a competitive game since 1914.

Players with both clubs include: K Bertschin, S Claridge, D Howitt, AP Needham, WR Robb, F White (Shots guest), S Wigley.

Also: Jim Smith (Shots player, Blues manager).

ALLEN, George

Came into the Blues' side on a regular basis following the tragic death of Jeff Hall in 1959. He developed into a solid, strong-tackling left-back who appeared in 165 games for the club before joining Torquay United in January 1962. Born in Small Heath in January 1932, Allen was an amateur with Coventry City before signing for Blues, initially in 1952, turning professional in November of that same year. Allen later he assisted non-League side Bideford Town (1965-66).

ALTRINCHAM

Blues were sensationally defeated 2-1 at St Andrew's by Altrincham of the Gola League in a third round FA Cup-tie on 14 January 1986. A disappointing crowd of just 6,636 watched a mediocre Blues side (bottom of the First Division at the time and without a win in 17 games) carry over their dismal League form into Cup action. Robert Hopkins scored Blues' consolation goal. David Seaman was the Blues' goalkeeper while his counterpart between the Altrincham posts was Jeff Wealands, who had previously been at St Andrew's!

Players with both clubs include: F Carrodus, J Fall, M McCarrick, H Riley, W Smith, J Wealands, D Weston.

AMATEURS

Over the years several amateur footballers have played for Blues at senior level, among them two fine goalkeepers Horace Bailey and Chris Charsley, and a splendid full-back Walter Corbett.

Bailey and Corbett represented England at both amateur and senior levels while Charsley also played for full England international side. Bailey and Corbett also represented Great Britain in the 1908 Olympic Games soccer tournament.

Two amateur caps for goalkeeper Stan Hauser

Amateur right-winger Billy Harvey was another senior England international who toured South Africa with the FA party in 1920 and managed Blues in 1927-28, while goalkeepers Stan Hauser (2 caps) and Ken Tewksbury (4 caps between 1929-31) and Jack Slater (2 caps: 1928-30) also played for England at amateur level.

Don Dearson (4 caps, 1932-34) and George Edwards (one cap, 1938) both appeared in amateur internationals for Wales before signing for Blues.

- Two FA Amateur Cup semi-finals have been staged at St Andrew's - in 1967 and 1969.
- Blues played the famous Corinthians amateur side four times between 1922 and 1926.

ANCONA

A crowd of around 1,500 saw Blues beat Ancona 2-1 away in the Anglo-Italian tournament in November 1995. Edwards scored Blues' first goal on 29 minutes and their second came courtesy of an own-goal by Ancona defender Davide Tenoni four minutes later. Mario Sesia reduced the deficit early in the second half.

This was surrounded by controversy when it was alleged that 'home' coach Massimo Cattiatori had suffered a fractured jaw during a fight in the tunnel. Blues defender Liam Daish and player-coach David Howell immediately faced extradition over the incident but after Daish was suspended from the competition, the Italian prosecutor decided - at that stage - to take no further action! However, the incident was never closed and in May 2000 - four-

11

and-a-half years later - Michael Johnson, who initially was not thought to be involved, and Liam Daish, were advised by the PFA and Blues to plead guilty (by letter) to the charge of assault. Howell appeared to escape any action whatsoever.

ANDERSON, George

Outside-left George 'Nosey' Anderson, fast and incisive, scored 10 goals in 80 first team outings for Blues. Born in Sunderland in 1881, and a trialist with his local side Sunderland Albion, he was signed in 1905 from Sunderland Royal Rovers. He spent four years with the club before going on to appear in almost 100 games for Brentford whom he served from August 1909 until the summer of 1912.

ANGLO-ITALIAN CUP

ANGLO·ITALIAN
INTER·LEAGUE CLUBS COMPETITION 1972
SPECIAL TWO-MATCH EDITION
BIRMINGHAM CITY v LANEROSSI, WEDNESDAY, JUNE 7/72
BIRMINGHAM CITY v SAMPDORIA, SATURDAY, JUNE 10/72

Brochure front cover: 1971-72.

Blues have taken part in this competition on four separate occasions.

In 1971-72 they played Lanerossi Vicenza at home and away, drawing 0-0 in Italy and winning 5-3 at St Andrew's when Bob Latchford scored twice. They also lost 2-1 away to Sampdoria, but won the return fixture 2-0 yet only finished in fourth position in the 'English' group and so failed to qualify for the Final.

In 1992-93 they beat Sunderland 1-0 at Roker Park and drew 3-3 at home with Cambridge United in preliminary round matches before entering the international stage.

Here they beat AS Bari 1-0 at home, defeated Cesena 2-1 in Italy, shared the points in a 1-1 draw at St Andrew's with Ascoli Calcio before losing 3-0 away to Lucchese. Only 139 hardy souls paid entrance money to watch the latter game - the lowest ever crowd for a Blues' first team game.

The following season (1993-94) Blues failed to get beyond the preliminary stage, losing 2-0 at Stoke and drawing 2-2 at home to Wolves, when the turn out was just 2,700 - the lowest at St Andrew's for a senior game since December 1910. Substitute Adam Wratten, coming off the bench, scored both Blues goal that evening...this being his only first team appearance for the club.

Blues' next venture into this competition came in 1995-96 when,

after losing 3-2 at home to Genoa, they made good progress with two fine victories in Italy over Perugia 1-0 and Ancona 2-1, plus a 3-1 home triumph over Cesena. This brought Blues a home draw against rivals West Bromwich Albion who, after a 2-2 draw, won the penalty shoot-out 4-1 to go forward into the English Final v Port Vale.

'The Battle of Ancona' in November 1994 was surrounded by controversy when Italian coach Massimo Cattiatori suffered a fractured jaw during a fight in the tunnel. (See under Ancona).

When Genoa visited St Andrew's in September 1995, the attendance of 20,340 was the largest for any game since the competition started up again in the 1990s, other than the Wembley Final.

Bob Latchford, with three goals, is Blues' top scorer in this competition.

This is Blues' full record in the Anglo-Italian Cup competition:

Venue	P	W	D	L	F	A
Home	9	4	4*	1	21	15
Away	8	4	1	3	7	9
Totals	17	8	5	4	28	24

*Includes one game lost on penalties (to WBA).

ANGLO-SCOTTISH TOURNAMENT

Blues played in this competition twice - in 1977-78 and 1979-80.

In the former campaign (based in Group 'A') Blues drew 1-1 away with both Plymouth Argyle and Bristol Rovers before defeating Bristol City 1-0 at St Andrew's. Unfortunately they failed to qualify for the next round.

Two years later Blues again failed to proceed beyond the group stage after losing 4-0 at home to Bristol City, drawing 1-1 at Home Park with Plymouth and defeating Fulham 5-0 at Craven Cottage.

Keith Bertschin scored three ASC goals, Trevor Francis netted two.

Blues' record in the Anglo-Scottish Cup:

Venue	P	W	D	L	F	A
Home	3	2	0	1	6	4
Away	3	0	3	0	3	3
Totals	6	2	3	1	9	7

AP LEAMINGTON
(also Lochheed & Town)

There has always been a close relation between Blues and the Leamington club with numerous friendlies taking place regularly, and there have also been several Blues players associated with the non-League club, among them: S Bayley, C Brazier, D Carr, E Edwards, D Jennings, GS Moore.

APPEARANCES

Lists of the top appearance-makers in the various competitions for Blues (substitute appearances have been included in the respective players' totals):

FOOTBALL LEAGUE
491	Frank Womack
485	Gil Merrick
414	Joe Bradford
409	Johnny Crosbie
401	Ken Green

382	Dan Tremelling
365	Trevor Smith
358	Harry Hibbs
351	Malcolm Beard
339	Malcolm Page
332	Ray Martin
331	Percy Barton
329	Frank Wigmore
323	George Liddell
306	Garry Pendrey

FA CUP

56	Gil Merrick
35	Ken Green
35	Trevor Smith
33	Jeff Hall
31	Joe Bradford
30	Fred Harris
30	Harry Hibbs
29	Malcolm Page
28	Percy Barton
27	Gordon Astall
26	George Briggs
26	Frank Wigmore
25	Malcolm Beard
24	Jimmy Cringan
24	Peter Murphy
24	Frank Womack

23	Johnny Crosbie
23	George Morrall
23	Nat Robinson
23	Cyril Trigg

FOOTBALL LEAGUE CUP

24	Malcolm Beard
23	Garry Pendrey
19	Trevor Francis
19	Ray Martin
17	Joe Gallagher
17	Roger Hynd
17	Bob Latchford
15	Colin Green
14	Kevin Dillon
14	Malcolm Page
12	Trevor Smith
11	Bertie Auld

INTER-CITIES FAIRS CUP

17	Trevor Smith
17	Brian Farmer
17	Johnny Watts
15	George Allen
14	Dick Neal
12	Johnny Schofield
11	Johnny Gordon

Trevor Smith

Gil Merrick

13

Ken Green

11	Mike Hellawell
11	Brian Orritt
10	Gil Merrick
9	Eddie Brown
8	Gordon Astall
8	Harry Hooper
8	Graham Sissons

OTHER COMPETITIONS

19	Jim Hagan
14	Garry Pendrey
14	Bob Hatton
12	Malcolm Page
11	Alan Campbell
10	Joe Gallagher
11	Tony Want
10	Gordon Taylor
8	Trevor Francis
9	Dave Latchford

ALL MAJOR COMPETITIONS

551	Gil Merrick
515	Frank Womack
445	Joe Bradford
443	Ken Green
432	Johnny Crosbie
430	Trevor Smith
405	Malcolm Beard
395	Dan Tremelling
388	Harry Hibbs
374	Ray Martin
360	Garry Pendrey
355	Frank Wigmore
349	Percy Barton

345	George Liddell
335	Joe Gallagher
329	Trevor Francis
324	George Briggs
312	Fred Harris
306	Nat Robinson

FIRST WORLD WAR

92	Frank Womack
87	Jack Whitehouse
84	Bill Ball
68	Albert Gardner
50	Ernie Edwards

SECOND WORLD WAR

176	Arthur Turner
166	Don Dearson
164	Dennis Jennings
164	Gil Merrick
111	Ray Shaw
108	Jock Mulraney
95	Cyril Trigg
92	Fred Harris

EVER PRESENTS

Goalkeeper Nat Robinson holds the record for most ever-present campaigns for Blues - four. Billy Ollis, Dan Tremelling and Fred Wheldon all had three full seasons.

Here is a list of Blues' ever presents in a League season:

- 1892-93 (22 games) T. Hands, W. Ollis, G.F. Wheldon,
- 1893-94 (28 games) E.J. Devey, T. Hands, W. Ollis, G.F. Wheldon,
- 1894-95 (30 games) W. Purves, W. Ollis
- 1895-96 (30 games) G.F. Wheldon
- 1896-97 (30 games) A. Leake
- 1897-98 (30 games) W.A. Abbott, T. Dunlop
- 1898-99 (34 games) W.A. Abbott, A. Leake, S. E. Walton
- 1899-00 (34 games) A. Archer, A. C. Robinson, S.E Wharton
- 1900-01 (34 games) A. Archer, W. Wigmore
- 1901-02 (34 games) A.C. Robinson
- 1902-03 (34 games) A.Goldie
- 1904-05 (34 games) A.H. Green, A. C. Robinson, F. Stokes
- 1905-06 (38 games) A.C. Robinson
- 1906-07 (38 games) W. J. Beer, B. H. Green, W. H. Jones
- 1911-12 (38 games) F. Womack
- 1914-15 (38 games) A. Gibson, W. R. Robb
- 1919-20 (42 games) A.R. Tremelling
- 1923-24 (42 games) A.R. Tremelling
- 1924-25 (42 games) A.R. Tremelling
- 1927-28 (42 games) A. Leslie
- 1932-33 (42 games) H. Booton, T. Grosvenor
- 1933-34 (42 games) A.F. Calladine
- 1935-36 (42 games) F. Harris
- 1949-50 (42 games) G.Merrick
- 1950-51 (42 games) A. Atkins, J. Berry, G. Merrick
- 1952-53 (42 games) K. Green
- 1961-62 (42 games) M. Beard, M. Hellawell
- 1962-63 (42 games) T. Hennessey
- 1964-65 (42 games) W. Foster
- 1966-67 (42 games) J. Herriot
- 1967-68 (42 games) B. Bridges, F. Pickering

- 1969-70 (42 games) R. Martin
- 1971-72 (42 games) A. Campbell, R. Hynd, R. Latchford
- 1972-73 (42 games) R. Latchford
- 1976-77 (42 games) T. Francis, T. Hibbitt
- 1977-78 (42 games) K. Bertschin, T. Francis
- 1979-80 (42 games) L.C. Curbishley
- 1980-81 (42 games) D. Langan
- 1983-84 (42 games) P. Van Den Hauwe
- 1984-85 (42 games) W. Wright
- 1985-86 (42 games) D.Seaman
- 1989-90 (46 games) T Matthewson
- 1990-91 (46 games) T Matthewson
- 1991-92 (46 games) N Gleghorn
- 1994-95 (46 games) I Bennett

FACTS

Including Wartime football, goalkeeper Gil Merrick made a total of 713 first team appearances for Blues and full-back Frank Womack 607.

Merrick also made a club record 145 consecutive League and FA Cup appearances for Blues between April 1949 and March 1952 (136 coming in the Football League).

Another goalkeeper Dan Tremelling fell two short of that record, making 132 consecutive first team appearances (126 in the Football League) between May 1923 and October 1926. He surpassed another 'keeper's feat, Nat Robinson, whose record of 115 consecutive first team appearances was set between September 1899 and September 1903.

Striker Bob Latchford made over 100 consecutive appearances for Blues during the early 1970s while colleague Trevor Francis amassed 100 between April 1976 and September 1979.

The following players (all linked in some way with Blues) are currently lying in the top 20 all-time Football League appearance-makers with these tallies:

Mick Mills 652
Colin Todd 639
Frank Worthington 625
Howard Kendall 610
Jim Montgomery 608

ARCHER, Arthur

Arthur Archer was a teak-tough defender who appeared in 170 League and Cup games for Blues (three goals scored) over a period of five years from 1897, helping them win promotion in 1901. Born in Derby in 1874, he joined Blues from Burton Wanderers and on his departure in 1902 he signed for New Brompton (now Gillingham) and later assisted QPR, Norwich City, Brighton & Hove Albion and Millwall

Arthur Archer

ARMSTRONG, Ken

A very useful central defender, tall, a shade better in the air than on the ground, Ken Armstrong played in 69 games for Blues between August 1984 and February 1986. Born in Bridgnorth in January 1959, his early career was spent with Kilmarnock, Southampton and Notts County and he cost Blues £60,000 when moving from Meadow Lane. He left St Andrew's for Walsall in a £10,000 deal was forced to retire in November 1986 after breaking an ankle during his first training session with the Saddlers!

ARSENAL (Royal, Woolwich)

Blues' playing record with the Gunners:

FOOTBALL LEAGUE

Venue	P	W	D	L	F	A
Home	55	29	13	13	108	66
Away	55	4	16	35	37	109
Totals	110	33	29	48	145	175

FA CUP

	P	W	D	L	F	A
Home	3	2	0	1	7	3
Away	3	1	2	0	6	4
Totals	6	3	2	1	13	7

LEAGUE CUP

	P	W	D	L	F	A
Away	1	0	0	1	1	4

WARTIME

	P	W	D	L	F	A
Home	1	0	0	1	0	1
Away	2	2	0	0	5	1
Totals	3	2	0	1	5	2

'Goal' for Bob Hatton in the 3-1 home win over Arsenal in September 1974

The first League game between Blues and Arsenal was staged at Muntz Street in October 1893. Blues came out on top, winners by 4-1 with Fred Wheldon scoring twice in front of 3,000 spectators.

Blues later completed the double over the Gunners, winning by the same score in London in March when Wheldon was again on target along with future Arsenal player Caesar Jenkyns.

By beating Arsenal 4-1 (away) in March 1894 Blues clinched second spot in the Division 2 table for that season.

Blues were beaten 6-1 and 5-0 by Arsenal in London in April 1903 and March 1906 respectively - and each time it was their heaviest defeat of the season.

Arsenal moved to Highbury in 1913 and Blues' first visit there saw them lose 1-0 in a Second Division match on 22 November of that year.

Blues lost 5-2 at Highbury in November 1921 and 3-0 on the last day of the 1925-26 season.

The Gunners won 4-2 at St Andrew's in September 1930, doubled up over Blues in 1932-33 and won 5-1 at Highbury in September 1934. Then over 50,000 fans saw Blues gain revenge with a 3-0 home win in February 1935.

The first meeting at League level after World War Two was at Highbury in November 1948 when 62,000 fans saw the Gunners win 2-0.

Seven years later at St Andrew's, Blues won 4-0 with Noel Kinsey (2), Eddie Brown and Gordon Astall on target in front of 35,765 fans.

Ten goals were scored in the two League games in 1956-57. Blues won 4-2 at home but lost 4-0 away. And in March 1958 it was Blues 4 Arsenal 1 at St Andrew's. Another 4-1 home win for Blues followed in April 1959 and it was 3-0 to Blues a year later also at St Andrew's.

Bunny Larkin scored twice in that 4-1 victory in 1959 which was one of Blues' best performances of the season.

Blues lost both League games 4-1 in 1963-64 and crashed to two more defeats the following season (2-3 at home and 3-0 away).

When Blues beat Arsenal 3-1 at St Andrew's in September 1974, Bob Hatton scored twice, one great header past Gunners' 'keeper Jimmy Rimmer.

In January 1977 a six-goal thriller at St Andrew's ended all square at 3-3, Trevor Francis notched a hat-trick for Blues and Malcolm MacDonald did likewise for Arsenal.

Blues' initial meeting with the Gunners at competitive level was in the FA Cup on 16 January 1892 when a first round tie ended in a 5-1 victory for Blues at Muntz Street in front of 4,000 spectators. Jack Hallam and Fred Wheldon both scored twice for Blues.

A crowd of just 6,234 at St Andrew's saw Blues relegated to the Second Division after a 1-0 defeat at the hands of Arsenal in May 1986.

A crowd of 67,872 saw Blues win a 6th round FA Cup encounter by 3-1 at Highbury in March 1956, on their way to Wembley. Gordon Astall netted with a tremendous header in this tie from Roy Warhurst's pin-point cross.

And in March 1968, after a 1-1 draw at Highbury, Blues knocked Arsenal out of the FA Cup in the 5th round with a 2-1 home victory thanks to a brace from Barry Bridges in front of 51,586 fans.

The last time Blues met the Gunners at competitive level was in the League Cup in October 1997 when Arsenal won 4-1 at Highbury. Tony Hey scored for Blues in front of 27.097 spectators.

Players with both clubs include: J Aston, J Bloomfield, W Blyth, C Buchan (Blues wartime guest), A Chaplin, T Dark (associate Schoolboy), P Gorman, E Hapgood (Blues guest), CB Hare, P Howard, WM Hughes (guest), CAL Jenkyns, G Johnston, HE King, A Limpar, DJ Madden, A Miller, F Mitchell (guest), I Rankin, JG Roberts, D Seaman, JH Southam (guest), L Thompson, C Wreh, C Whyte, N Winterburn (Blues junior).

Also: Pat Beasley (Arsenal player, Blues manager), Bruce Rioch (Blues player, Arsenal manager), Leslie Knighton (manager of both clubs), Albert Lindon (Blues player, Arsenal scout).

ARTHUR STREET

Blues' first ground was a strip of wasteland in Arthur Street, Small Heath near to the sight where St Andrew's was to be built. They played here for one season - 1875-76 - before moving to Ladypool Road, Sparkbrook.

Blues' first-ever game (as Small Heath Alliance) was staged on the Arthur Street pitch in November 1875 against Holte Wanderers from Aston. The game ended 1-1.

AS BARI

The Italian side met Blues in an Anglo-Italian international Stage Group 'A' encounter at St Andrew's on 11 November 1992. A crowd of 4,970 saw Blues win the game 1-0 with a Mark Cooper goal.

AS ROMA

Blues met the Italian giants over two-legs in the Fairs Cup Final of 1961.

The first game was staged at St Andrew's on 27 September and a crowd of just over 21,000 saw Blues held to a 2-2 draw, Mike Hellawell and Bryan Orritt the home scorers.

A fiery second leg in Rome took place a fortnight later on 11 October and in front of 50,000 fans Blues succumbed to a 2-0 defeat to lose the final 4-2 on aggregate.

Match summary:

Venue	P	W	D	L	F	A
Home	1	0	1	0	2	2
Away	1	0	0	1	0	2
Totals	2	0	1	1	2	4

ASCOLI CALCIO

On 8 December 1992, Blues were held to a 1-1 draw at St Andrew's by Ascoli in an Anglo-Italian International stage cup-tie. A crowd of just 3,963 witnessed the game in which Simon Sturridge scored for Blues.

ASHINGTON

There have been no competitive games between Blues and Ashington, but one player who did serve with both clubs was full-back E Ashurst.

ASHURST, Elias

A strong, well-built and resilient full-back, born in Willington in December 1901, Eli Ashurst was secured by Blues from Stanley United in January 1922, having previously starred for Ashington and Shildon FC. He scored once in 70 games during his stay at St

Andrew's that ended in the summer of 1926 when he retired through illness. Sadly Ashurst died in December 1927, three weeks before his 27th birthday. His brother Billy played for West Bromwich Albion, Notts County and England.

ASTALL, Gordon

Regarded by many as the finest outside-right ever to don a Blues shirt, Gordon Astall netted 67 goals in 271 appearances for the club following his £14,000 transfer from Plymouth Argyle in October 1953. He found the net in both his international outings for England and helped Blues win promotion from the second Division and reach the FA Cup Final in successive seasons: 1954-55 and 1955-56. Fast and direct, he loved to hug the touch-line and could whip in some devastating crosses on the run. As well as making goals for his colleagues, he also scored some marvellous ones himself. He moved to Torquay United on leaving St Andrew's in July 1961, retiring two years later. Born in Horwich in September 1927, Astall had trials with Bolton Wanderers before signing as a professional for Plymouth in 1947. He now lives in Torbay, Devon.

Gordon Astall

ASTON UNITY

The only major game between the two clubs was a first round FA Cup-tie on 15th October 1887 which resulted in a comprehensive 6-1 home win for Blues.

Players with both clubs include: E Bailey, H Williams.

ASTON VILLA

Blues' playing record against Aston Villa:

FOOTBALL LEAGUE

Venue	P	W	D	L	F	A
Home	48	20	12	16	74	68
Away	48	12	13	23	60	82
Totals	96	32	25	39	134	150

FA CUP

Home	2	0	1	1	0	4
Away	1	0	0	1	0	1
Totals	3	0	1	2	0	5

LEAGUE CUP

Home	3	1	0	2	3	4
Away	3	0	1	2	0	6
Totals	6	1	1	4	3	10

SIMOD CUP

Away	1	0	0	1	0	6

WARTIME

Home	7	4	1	2	11	10
Away	8	1	2	5	7	18
Totals	15	5	3	7	18	28

Blues first met Aston Villa on 27 September 1879 in what was billed as a 'friendly' match at Muntz Street. Blues registered a 1-0 victory that led to the Villa players claiming that the pitch was only suitable for pot holing!

The first League tussle took place on 1 October 1894 and in front of a sun-drenched 20,000 crowd at Villa's Wellington Road ground in Perry Barr, Blues lost 2-1. The return game on Blues' soil on 20 October finished all square at 2-2, Dennis Hodgetts equalising for Villa from the penalty spot and Fred Wheldon (with Blues' first ever penalty) and Jack Hallam had given their side a 2-1 lead.

Blues registered their first League win over Villa on 16 September 1905 (2-0 at Muntz Street).

A crowd of 40,000 saw Blues win 3-1 at Villa Park in January 1906 to complete the double over their arch-rivals, having claimed a 2-0 success at Muntz Street earlier in the season.

The first 'second City' local derby at St Andrew's was played on 19 January 1907 and in front of a near 50,000 crowd it was Villa who took the honours with a 3-2 victory.

The League game between Blues and Villa in October 1925 produced six goals. Villa were leading 3-0 on their own ground with time running out fast. Hundreds of fans in the 55,000 crowd were already making their way home when Blues produced a devastating finish, scoring three times late on to earn a point.

Walker and Dorrell, York and Kirton had blitzed the Blues defence in the first-half. Walker scored twice before the break and Capewell added a third halfway through the second half as Blues wilted under pressure. But then, amazingly, Joe Bradford made it 3-1 on 79 minutes; two minutes later he scored again and with the referee ready to blow the final whistle, the Villa goalkeeper Cyril Spiers conceded an own-goal for the equaliser. As he went for the ball he slipped and in trying to recover he only succeeded in knocking the ball into the unguarded net.

Billy Walker scored two penalties in Villa's 3-0 home win over Blues in March 1923 and Blues' full-back Stan Lynn netted from the spot in each of the local derbies against his former club Villa in 1963-64.

Fred Harris made a goalscoring debut for Blues against Aston Villa at St Andrew's in 1934 and two years later Cyril Trigg

17

Kenny Burns scoring for Blues against Villa at St Andrew's in 1976.

appeared in his first senior game for Blues in the second city local derby.

The last pre Second World War League encounter between Blues and Villa took place in March 1939. A crowd of almost 41,000 saw Johnny Martin score a hat-trick in Villa's 5-1 win on home soil.

In December 1948, a crowd of 61,632 saw Jackie 'Jack-in-the-box' Stewart run rings round the Villa defence to score twice in Blues' 3-0 win at Villa Park.

Trevor Smith skippered Blues for the first time when they defeated FA Cup holders Villa 3-1 at St Andrew's in August 1957. This was Blues' first home win over their arch-rivals for 19 years and over 50,000 spectators saw it.

After going a goal down Blues stormed back to beat relegation-threatened Villa 4-1 at St Andrew's in December 1958, Scotsman Alex Jackson scoring twice in this his only derby game!

In October 1960 Gerry Hitchens became the first player to score a hat-trick in post-war Blues-Villa derbies when he achieved the feat in Villa's 6-2 win.

The first Second Division meeting between the clubs took place on 7 October 1967. Blues won 4-2 at Villa Park, Barry Bridges (2), Geoff Vowden and Malcolm Beard (penalty) scoring in front of 49,984 fans.

After Villa had spent time in the Second and Third Divisions they got back to serious League action with Blues in 1975-76. The game at Villa park ended in a 2-1 defeat for Blues, but at St Andrew's, in front of 46,251 fans, goals by Terry Hibbitt (a superb 25 yarder), Kenny Burns and Trevor Francis, earned Blues a 3-1 victory.

The last League meeting between the two clubs was in December 1987 when a brace by Garry Thompson gave Villa a 2-1 victory at St Andrew's.

Two of Blues' heaviest League defeats have come against Aston Villa - 7-3 at Perry Barr in September 1895 and 6-2 at Villa Park in October 1960.

In September 1968, in front of some 40,500 fans at St Andrew's, the Blues v Villa Second Division game was goalless with 25 minutes to play. Then Blues turned up the heat to overpower their rivals

to the tune of 4-0 with goals from Jimmy Greenhoff, Johnny Vincent, Phil Summerill and Geoff Vowden.

Two goals by Wayne Clarke and another by Steve Whitton gave Blues a handsome 3-0 win at Villa Park in March 1986 - the last time the teams met in the top flight of English football! The crowd was a meagre 26,294!

Blues doubled the admission price for their home FA Cup-tie against Aston Villa in March 1901 - and the public showed its disapproval by staying away as only 18,000 fans turned up instead of the estimated 25,000.

The first FA Cup meeting between Blues and Villa was played at Muntz Street on 5 November 1887 - the same day that Buffalo Bill Cody took his famous Wild West Show to Aston Lower Grounds (Villa's home ground). A crowd of 12,000 saw Blues hammered 4-0 by their arch-rivals while 5,000 spectators cheered on the Indians and cowboys three miles away!

Blues' only League Cup win over Villa came in the first leg of the 1962-63 Final at St Andrew's (3-1). A crowd of 31,580 saw Blues firmly get a grip on the trophy with a fine performance and they duly took the prize after holding Villa to a 0-0 draw in the return leg in front of almost 38,000 fans. Ken Leek (2) and Jimmy Bloomfield scored for Blues in the initial game.

In this same competition Villa beat Blues 5-0 at home in September/October 1988, taking the tie 7-0 on aggregate after their 2-0 victory at St. Andrew's

Blues were also hammered 6-0 at Villa Park in a Simod Cup-tie in November 1988 when the attendance was under 8,400. Villa led 5-0 at the interval.

On 12 January 1946 Villa were held to a 2-2 draw by Blues in a Football League (South) game at Villa Park before 63,280 fans. This was the highest attendance Blues played in front of during either the Great War or the Second World War, other than the crowds that attended the two FA Cup semi-final matches against Derby County in March 1946.

In the drawn game at Villa Park, Neil Dougall equalised for Blues five minutes from time after Harry Parkes had missed a penalty for the home side.

In the return game a week later, Blues won 3-1 in front of 40,000 spectators - and they went on to pip Villa by just 0.206 of a goal to win the League (South) championship that season.

Blues played Villa on April 1940 in a 'farewell' (benefit) game for legendary goalkeeper Harry Hibbs. Blues won 2-1 in front of 15,000.

Blues beat Villa 5-2 in the Lord Mayor of Birmingham Charity Cup at St Andrew's in September 1908. During the second-half Villa were awarded a penalty which Harry Hampton took only to shoot straight at the Blues' 'keeper Jack Dorrington. The ball rebounded to Joe Bache, but as he was about to shoot he was felled inside the area by Frank Womack, the Blues full-back, resulting in a second spot-kick. Again Hampton fired directly at Dorrington, who this time held the ball before clearing his lines.

In a pre-season friendly at Perry Barr in August 1889, Football Alliance side Blues beat Football League runners-up Aston Villa 4-0.

An audience of around 23,000 saw Blues beaten by Aston Villa 6-3 in a Central League game at Villa Park in 1928. The big crowd turned out to see the debut of the home club's new signing, Tom 'Pongo' Waring, who celebrated by scoring a hat-trick!

Blues played Aston Villa at Villa Park in a 'Football League Founders Day' centenary match on 13 April 1988. Blues lost 5-2.

Joe Bradford made most appearances for Blues in derby matches against Villa (23). He also scored most goals - eight. Johnny Crosbie had 19 outings against the enemy!

Twelve players - Des Bremner, Alan Curbishley, Cammie Fraser, David Geddis, Tony Hateley, Mark Jones, Stan Lynn, Charlie Phillips, John Sleeuwenhoek, Peter Withe, Colin Withers and Ron Wylie - all played in second city derby matches for both clubs.

Brian Little signed for Blues from Aston Villa on 3 July 1979 subject to a medical report...72 hours later the deal was called off!

Players with both clubs include: J Allen (Blues guest), B Anstey, WC Athersmith, M Beard, N Blake, J Bradford (Villa trialist), D Bremner, FC Buckley, F Carrodus, F Chapple, G Charles, C Charsley (guest), WS Corbett, F Cornan, A Coton (Villa trialist), LC Curbishley, W Devey, H Dobson, H Edgley, E Eyre, S Fox (on associate schoolboy forms with Villa), F Foxall, JC Fraser, W Freeman, D Geddis, W George, H Hampton, CB Hare, R Harper, A Hateley, JB Higgins, T Hockey, D Hodgetts, R Hopkins, LR Jenkins, MA Jones, JM Kearns, MI Kendall, F Kerns, A Leake, AE Lindon, I Linton, G Lunn, S Lynex (Villa trialist), S Lynn, A McClure, R Martin, CH Millington, A Morley, D Mortimer, A Mulraney, JA Murray, C Phillips, A Phoenix, K Poole, A Rees, B Rioch, P Robinson, K Rogers, L Sealey (Blues N/C), FH Shell (Blues reserve), J Slueenwhoek, B Small, K Tewkesbury, R G Thomson, JE Travers, AS Turner, A Vale, G Vowden, C Wallace, S Webb, T Weston, G F Wheldon, JM Wilcox, P Withe , C Withers and R Wylie (also coach at Villa).

Also associated: Villa players H Edgley, C Wallace and T Weston (1916-19) and then F Broome, G Cummings, G Edwards, R Iverson, A Massie and F Moss (1939-45) all guested for Blues during the two World Wars. Bob Brocklebank (Villa player, Blues manager), Ron Saunders (manager of both clubs), Keith Bradley and Nigel Spink (Villa players, Blues coaches), Don Dorman (Blues player and scout, Villa scout), Harry Parkes (Villa player and Director of both clubs), Doug Ellis (Director with both clubs - appointed by Blues in 1967 - also Villa Chairman), Peter Doherty (Blues guest, Villa chief scout), Graham Leggatt (Blues player, assistant-trainer/coach with Villa), Keith Leonard (Villa player, Blues coach), Ray Shaw (Blues player & coach, Villa trainer &

physio), Bill Shorthouse (coach/trainer at both clubs), Keith Smith (lottery staff both clubs).

NB - Giant goalkeeper Billy George made 399 senior appearances and one for Blues (to bring up the round 400). He was trainer at St Andrew's when in an emergency he replaced Horace Bailey for the League game against Barnsley in September 1911 at the age of 37....the oldest player to make his debut for Blues!

ATHERSMITH, Charlie

One of the game's fastest wingers, certainly in the last decade of the nineteenth century, Charlie Athersmith reigned supreme on his day with only Billy Bassett of West Bromwich Albion, comparable to him for speed and ability. A great touchline player, he centred with pin-point accuracy but was penalised several times for straying offside, so eager was he to get forward! He spent ten excellent years at Villa Park during which time he won five League championship medals (1894, '95,'97,'99 and 1900) and two FA Cup winners medals (1895 and '97). He also won 12 England caps and in 1896-97 won every honour in the game as Villa captured the coveted League and Cup double. It is reported that during one game (v Sheffield United) the rain was so severe that Athersmith borrowed an umbrella from one of the spectators to shield himself as he ran up and down the wing. After scoring 86 goals in 310 appearances for Villa he went on to have more than 100 outings for Blues.

Born in Bloxwich on 10 May 1872 Athersmith attended Walsall Road School and played for Bloxwich Wanderers, Bloxwich Strollers and Unity Gas Depot before joining Villa in February 1891. He moved to Birmingham in June 1901 and was Grimsby Town's trainer from June 1907 to May 1909. Soon after leaving St Andrew's he went on an authorised tour of Germany and was suspended for his troubles! He died at Shifnal on 18 September 1910.

ATKINS, Arthur

Born in Tokyo (where his parents ran a business) in February 1925, centre-half, strongly built with sound heading ability, Arthur Atkins was recruited from Paget Rangers in August 1948 and went on to appear in 105 first-class games for Blues before leaving St Andrew's for Shrewsbury Town in June 1954. He was a key member of Blues' 1951 FA Cup semi-final side. Atkins died in Good Hope Hospital, Sutton Coldfield on 7 January 1988.

ATKINS, Ian

During a fine career, midfielder Ian Atkins made over 550 League appearances while playing for Shrewsbury Town, Sunderland, Everton, Ipswich Town, Blues, Colchester United and Cambridge United. Born in Sheldon on 16 January 1957, he finally arrived at St Andrew's in March 1988, initially on loan, signing permanently in a £50,000 transaction the following month. A very effective player, he stayed with Blues until 1990, making 117 appearances and scoring nine goals. He then became player-manager at Layer Road. He was appointed Blues' assistant-manager in 1991-92 before taking over as player-boss at The Abbey Stadium, later becoming assistant at Sunderland, team manager of Doncaster Rovers and later boss of Northampton Town and Chester City, resigning from the latter club after relegation to the Football Conference in May 2000. The following month he took over the reins at Third Division Carlisle United.

ATTENDANCES

Full house at St Andrew's

Blues' average home League attendances from 1892 to date:

SEASON	AVERAGE
1892-93	2,181
1893-94	2,928
1894-95	6,440
1895-96	6,233
1896-97	4,526
1897-98	5,633
1898-99	5,588
1899-1900	5,176
1900-01	5,558
1901-02	13,058
1902-03	17,411
1903-04	11,386
1904-05	14,441
1905-06	11,868
1906-07	15,315
1907-08	15,473
1908-09	10,607
1909-10	8,921
1910-11	13,764
1911-12	13,052
1912-13	15,157
1913-14	17,411
1914-15	11,315
1919-20	22,880
1920-21	31,244
1921-22	27,967
1922-23	25,328
1923-24	20,395
1924-25	22,547
1925-26	21,649
1926-27	24,372
1927-28	21,646
1928-29	23,406
1929-30	22,193
1930-31	21,275
1931-32	23,380
1932-33	20,044
1933-34	24,718
1934-35	22,795
1935-36	22,955
1936-37	22,432
1937-38	25,452
1938-39	26,434
1946-47	32,462
1947-48	36,467
1948-49	38,821
1949-50	34,310
1950-51	24,728
1951-52	24,570
1952-53	20,046
1953-54	22,594
1954-55	21,002
1955-56	33,828
1956-57	32,582
1957-58	29,647
1958-59	26,893
1959-60	26,880
1960-61	25,751
1961-62	23,587
1962-63	22,559
1963-64	21,996
1964-65	19,714
1965-66	14,398
1966-67	19,798
1967-68	28,083
1968-69	26,008
1969-70	24,028
1970-71	24,164
1971-72	32,337
1972-73	36,663
1973-74	33,048
1974-75	30,854
1975-76	28,002
1976-77	28,338
1977-78	23,910
1978-79	20,164
1979-80	20,427
1980-81	19,248
1981-82	17,116
1982-83	15,880
1983-84	14,106
1984-85	12,522
1985-86	10,899
1986-87	7,426
1987-88	8,576
1988-89	6,289
1989-90	8,558
1990-91	7,030
1991-92	12,399
1992-93	12,328
1993-94	14,378
1994-95	16,941
1995-96	18,054
1996-97	17,556
1997-98	18,708
1998-99	20,794
1999-2000	22,103

HOW THE RECORD CROWD AT ST ANDREW'S HAS BEEN BROKEN:

32,000 Blues v Middlesbrough FL 26.12.1906
35,940 Arsenal v Sheffield Wednesday FAC SF 23.3.1907

49,950 Blues v Aston Villa FL 19.1.1907
60,017 Blues v West Ham United FL 27.12.1920
66,544 Leicester City v Portsmouth FAC SF 17.3.1934
67,341 Blues v Everton FAC 11.2.1939

ATTENDANCE FACTS & FIGURES

- Blues' best seasonal average at League level has been 38,821 in 1948-49.
- The lowest average home gate at St Andrew's is 6,289, set as recent as 1988-89.
- Blues' average home attendance dropped by over 30,000 in 16 years - from 36,663 in 1972-73 to 6,289 in 1988-89.
- Over a period of twelve years covering six peacetime seasons - 1936-37 to 1948-49 - the average League crowd at St Andrew's rose steadily each term from 22,432 to a record 38,821.
- The biggest crowd a Blues team has ever played in front is 98,982, for the 1956 FA Cup Final v Manchester City at Wembley.
- There were 90,368 fans present for the 1931 FA Cup Final v West Bromwich Albion, 80,407 witnessed the 1946 FA Cup semi-final replay against Derby County at Maine Road and 76,663 saw Blues win the Auto Windscreen Shield at the Empire Stadium in 1995.
- The initial FA Cup semi-final clash at Hillsborough between Blues and Derby County in March 1946 was attended by 65,013 spectators and a combined total of 145,420 fans assembled for those post-war both semi-final encounters.
- Over 140,000 fans saw the two FA Cup semi-final games between Blues and Blackpool in March 1951 - 70,066 at Maine Road and 70,114 at Goodison Park. Record receipts of £13,475 were taken at Maine Road.
- A crowd of 75,000 saw the Barcelona-Blues Inter-Cities Fairs Cup clash at the Nou Camp stadium in May 1960.
- For the FA Cup-tie at Chelsea in 1931, the attendance at Stamford Bridge was 74,365 - and another 6,000 fans were locked outside. This is the biggest attendance for game in this competition involving Blues other than for a semi-final or final itself.
- The biggest League attendance at St Andrew's has been that of 60,250 for the Blues v Aston Villa local derby on 23 November 1935.
- The lowest-ever crowd to watch a competitive game at St Andrew's is 1,000 v Blackpool, Division Two, on 27 November 1909 and also v Burnley in the same Division on 28 February 1910. Just under 1,500 fans saw the League game with Chesterfield in April 1909.
- The lowest League crowd for a Blues home game is 500 for the visit to Muntz Street of Crewe Alexandra on 6 December 1893. Just 800 fans saw the visit of Darwen on 14 September 1896 and only 600 attended the game at home to Manchester City on 19 April 1897.
- Only 139 paying customers witnessed the Lucchese v Blues Anglo-Italian Cup tie in Italy on 16 December 1992 - the lowest ever crowd to witness a Blues first team game at competitive level.
- There were just 821 hardy supporters in attendance in London when Charlton played Blues in the Full Members Cup in November 1986.
- Only 200 spectators saw the Middlesbrough Ironopolis v Blues League game on 25 November 1893 and there were just 500 fans

present for the Gossop v Blues Second Division fixture on 19 September 1914.
- Barely 1,000 supporters attended each of the following six away Second Division games involving Blues - at Northwich Victoria on Christmas Eve 1892, at Burslem Port Vale on 25 March 1893 and again on 25 September 1893, at Lincoln on 11 November 1893, at Rotherham on 23 March 1894 and at Luton on 11 March 1899.
- Since the Second World War Blues' lowest League crowd has been 4,026 for the visit of Swindon Town on 18 April 1989 (Division 2).
- The lowest crowd in the First Division during the 1925-26 season was that of 3,977 for the Blues v Notts County clash at St Andrew's.
- And a decade later, the 5,729 turn out for the Blues v Middlesbrough League game at St Andrew's was again the lowest in the First Division for the whole of the 1934-35 season.
- The 3,443 attendance figure for the Blues-Macclesfield League Cup encounter at St Andrew's in September 1998 was the lowest for a major League or Cup game at the ground for 65 years (since 1913 when 3,000 fans saw the Grimsby Town League match).
- In the Anglo-Italian Cup competition of 1995-96, crowds of 1,500 saw Blues' two games in Italy against Perugia and Ancona.
- The near 22,000 average home League attendance for Blues in 1999-2000 was the best at St Andrew's for 20 years.
- A record crowd of 27,445 witnessed Carlisle United's draw 2-2 with Blues in a third round FA Cup-tie at Brunton Park in January 1957.
- For Blues' next home game after the record attendance had been set at St Andrew's, the crowd dropped by 42,000 to 25,000 for the visit of Grimsby Town for a League Division One game.
- The record attendance (to date) at The Alfred McAlpine Stadium, Huddersfield is 18,775 for the visit of Blues on 6 May 1995.
- Only 6,256 fans saw Shrewsbury beat Blues 1-0 in the last League game at St Andrew's in 1990-91. Three weeks later 40,000 supporters cheered Blues to victory over Tranmere Rovers in the Leyland DAF Final at Wembley. And then for the first home game after that Wembley triumph (v Bury on 17 August 1991) the turnout was just 9,033!
- A crowd of 63,820 saw the Aston Villa v Birmingham City League South game at Villa Park in January 1946. And 56,615 spectators were at St Andrew's for the Blues v Charlton clash the following month. These were the two biggest attendances (outside the FA Cup games v Derby in 1946) that Blues played in front of during the Second World War.

AULD, Bertie

Left-winger Bertie Auld, besides being a great crowd pleaser, was also a player with a fiery temper and during his professional career was sent-off half-a-dozen times. A classy performer on his day, possessing good ball skills, determination and powerful shot, he joined Blues for £15,000 from Celtic in April 1961 and immediately appeared in that season's Fairs Cup Final against AS Roma. Two years later he helped Blues win the League Cup and went on to score 31 goals in 147 appearances for the club before returning to Parkhead in January 1965 for £12,000. Born in Glasgow in March 1938, Auld played for Dumbarton on loan during his first spell at Celtic and after his second he went on to assist Hibernian, later becoming a coach at Easter Road. He managed Partick Thistle (twice), Hibs, Hamilton Academical and Dumbarton in later years. With Celtic, whose manager Jock Stein converted him into a midfielder on his return to Parkhead, Auld gained a European Cup winners medal, two League championship medals, three Scottish Cup and four League Cup winners medals. He also helped the Bhoys win the World Club Championship and played for his country on three occasions, as well as representing the Scottish League.

Auld getting in a left-foot shot.

AUTOGLASS TROPHY

Blues played two preliminary round matches in this competition in season 1991-92, losing them both - 3-1 at Stoke City and 1-0 at home to Walsall.

Paul Tait scored Blues' only goal in this tournament!

Record:

Venue	P	W	D	L	F	A
Home	1	0	0	1	0	1
Away	1	0	0	1	1	3
Totals	2	0	0	2	1	4

AUTO-WINDSCREEN SHIELD

On 23 April 1995 Blues won the Auto Windscreen Shield final at Wembley, beating Carlisle United 1-0 in the final with an extra-time 13th minute 'sudden death' goal by Paul Tait from Ricky Otto's chipped pass. A crowd of 76,663 saw that triumph when Blues, under the guidance of manager Barry Fry, fielded this side: Ian Bennett; Gary Poole, Gary Cooper; Mark Ward, Dave Barnett, Liam Daish; Jonathan Hunt, Steve Claridge, Kevin Francis (Louie Donowa), Ricky Otto, Peter Shearer (Paul Tait).

En-route to the final Blues knocked out Peterborough United (a) 5-3 (thanks mainly to a hat-trick from Jonathan Hunt); Walsall (h) by 3-0 (two goals coming from Peter Shearer); Gillingham (h) also by 3-0 in round three; Hereford United (h) 3-1 in front of 22,352 fans; Swansea City (h) by the narrowest of margins, 3-2 after extra time 'sudden death' in the Southern Area semi-final, and Leyton Orient by 4-2 on aggregate (1-0 at home, 3-2 away) in the Southern Area Final, when over 24,000 fans attended the game at St Andrew's. The Portuguese blond midfielder Rui Esteves made his debut for Blues in the latter game but walked off the pitch complaining that the challenges were tough and vigorous! (He didn't play for the club again)!

Blues' 100 per-cent record in the AWS is:

Venue	P	W	D	L	F	A
Home	6	6	0	0	16	5
Away	1	1	0	0	5	3
Neutral	1	1	0	0	1	0
Totals	8	8	0	0	22	8

Steve Claridge top-scored with four goals; Jonathan Hunt, Peter Shearer and Paul Tait each netted three times.

AWAY FROM HOME

IT'S JOY DAY FOR STUBBS AND HOOPER
by Tom Duckworth

Nottingham Forest 1 Birmingham City 7

Trust a Blues-Forest game to provide shocks. Blues gained ample revenge for their crushing 5-0 Cup defeat by Forest at Leicester by hammering the Nottingham side in a goal rush at the City Ground. No doubt about Blues' superiority on this occasion. Only in the first half an hour, during which they took the lead through Dwight, were Forest in the picture. Once they had equalised through Stubbs in the 32nd minute, it was Blues all the way.

Newspaper cutting from 7-1 win at Forest in 1959.

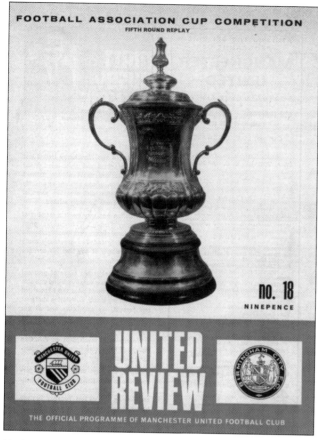

Match programme from the Manchester United v Blues FAC replay in 1969 which ended in a 6-2 defeat for the Brummies!

Over the years Blues, when playing away from home, have recorded some excellent wins as well as producing some fine performances that haven't necessarily earned them a victory.

They have also lost heavily on their travels in both League and in the various Cup competitions they've participated in.

Here are details of some big wins and heavy defeats over the years:

AWAY WINS

7-0 v Northwich Victoria (League) January 1894
7-0 v Stoke City (League) January 1998
7-1 v Torquay United (FA Cup) January 1956
7-1 v Nottingham Forest (League) March 1959
7-1 v Oxford United (League) December 1998
7-3 v Leicester City (League) April 1934
6-0 v Northwich Victoria (League) December 1892
6-1 v Walsall (League) October 1896
6-1 v Southend United (FAC) January 1957
6-1 v Sunderland (League) April 1958
6-2 v Leicester Fosse (FA Cup) October 1891
6-2 v Burton Wanderers (League) February 1897
6-2 v Burton Swifts (League) September 1898
6-2 v Leicester City (League) December 1976

Blues also won 5-4 at Portsmouth in August 1966 (Division 2). Other impressive away performances include two FA Cup semi-final wins over Sunderland, 2-0 at Elland Road in 1931 and 3-0 at Hillsborough in 1956, and two Wembley victories in the 1991 Leyland DAF Trophy Final and the 1995 Auto Windscreen Shield Final.

AWAY DEFEATS

1-9 v Sheffield Wednesday (Alliance) December 1889*
1-9 v Newton Heath (Alliance) April 1890
1-9 v Sheffield Wednesday (League) December 1930
0-8 v Derby County (League) November 1895
0-8 v Newcastle United (League) November 1907
2-8 v Rotherham County (War) December 1916
0-7 v Hull City (League) December 1909
0-7 v Huddersfield Town (League) October 1913
1-7 v Sunderland (League) December 1894
1-7 v Huddersfield Town (League) April 1911
1-7 v Sheffield United (League) February 1923
1-7 v Blackburn Rovers (League) April 1925
1-7 v Burnley (League) February 1962
2-7 v Wolverhampton W. (League) January 1896
0-6 v Wednesbury Old A. (FA Cup) December 1881
0-6 v Bootle (Alliance) April 1890
0-6 v Bolton Wanderers (League) December 1955
0-6 v Tottenham Hotspur (FA Cup) April 1967
0-6 v Sheffield United (League) December 1969
0-6 v Norwich City (League) April 1970
0-6 v Crystal Palace (League) March 1987
0-6 v Aston Villa (Simod Cup) November 1988
1-6 v Sunderland Albion (Alliance) October 1889
1-6 v Blackburn Rovers (League) April 1963
1-6 v Tottenham Hotspur (League) October 1963
1-6 v Plymouth Argyle (League) September 1965
2-6 v Stafford Road (FA Cup) November 1882
2-6 v Crewe Alexandra (Alliance) February 1890
2-6 v Manchester United (FA Cup) February 1969

* Blues fielded only ten players in this game.

AWAY FACTS

- Blues lost a 12-goal thriller by 7-5 in a First Division League at Blackburn in September 1929.
- Blues have also suffered away disappointment in two Wembley FA Cup Finals - in 1931, beaten by West Bromwich Albion and in 1956, defeated by Manchester City).
- Blues have been beaten in four FA Cup semi-finals as well - in 1886 (4-0 to West Bromwich Albion), in 1957 (2-0 to Manchester United), in 1972 (3-0 to Leeds United) and in 1975 (1-0 by Fulham after a 0-0 draw).
- Blues' heaviest away defeat in the League Cup has been 5-0 at Tottenham in October 1986 and Villa Park in October 1988.
- Blues were denied a place in the 1958 Inter Cities Fairs Cup Final when they lost their semi-final replay in neutral Basle to Barcelona. And it was also away from home, against the same Spanish opposition that Blues lost the 1961 Fairs Cup Final on aggregate, Barcelona winning 4-1 in the Nou Camp after a 0-0 draw at St Andrew's.
- With the help of a 2-1 first leg semi-final win in Italy over Inter Milan, Blues went through to the 1961 Fairs Cup Final, but after being held 2-2 at home by AS Roma, they travelled to Rome and lost the second leg 2-0, thus going down 4-2 on aggregate.
- Blues' best away record in a complete League season was achieved in 1984-85 when they claimed 13 victories and one draw from 21 Second Division encounters.
- In 1919-20 they won 10 and drew five of their 21 matches, finishing third in the First Division table.
- In 1947-48 Blues won 10 and drew three of their 21 Second

Division away matches.

- In 1892-93 - the club's first season in the Football League - Blues won seven and drew one of their 11 fixtures when clinching the Second Division championship. The following season they won nine and lost four of their 13 matches on opponents' soil.
- Blues won only one of their 19 away games in the Second Division of 1909-10 and had to apply for re-election!
- In 1932-33 Blues also won one and drew eight of their 21 away matches and in 1949-50 again only one away win was achieved.
- Relegated from the First Division in bottom spot in 1978-79, Blues lost 19 times away from St Andrew's - a club record. They won their last match at QPR 3-1.
- In contrast Blues lost 16 out of 21 away games in 1926-27 and had the same record in 1938-39 when relegated from the top flight.
- In 1963-64 they suffered 17 away defeats (winning the other four) and in 1975-76 they also lost 17 times on their travels.
- In 1947-48 Blues went 15 away League games without defeat - a club record.
- Between 1980 and 1982 Blues set another club record when failing to win any of their 32 away League matches.
- In 1897 Blues ran up a sequence of nine successive away wins in the Football League - a record.

Jack Badham

AYR UNITED

Blues' playing record against the Scottish club:

TEXACO CUP

Venue	P	W	D	L	F	A
Home	1	1	0	0	3	0
Away	1	0	1	0	0	0
Totals	2	1	1	0	3	0

A crowd of 12,327 saw Blues win the first leg of a second round Texaco Cup-tie against Ayr at St Andrew's on 17 September 1974 when Kenny Burns scored twice. The return leg a fortnight later attracted under 5,000 fans and it ended goalless. Gary Allen made his only appearance for Blues in the game in Scotland.

Players with both clubs include: J Crosbie, G Getgood, J

BADHAM, Jack

A well-built, sinuous and versatile defender, Jack Badham served Blues for 23 years, occupying, in fact, eight different outfield positions but clearly preferring that of full-back! He joined the club as an amateur in 1934, signed full-time professional forms in 1946 and left for Stourbridge in 1957, later managing Moor Green. He made 190 senior appearances for the club and scored two goals. Born in Birmingham in January 1919, he helped Blues win promotion to the First Division in 1948 and 1955 but sadly missed the 1956 FA Cup Final, Johnny Newman being preferred instead.

Badham, who was a big favourite with the supporters, died in his native Birmingham in January 1992.

BAILEY, Dennis

London-born striker Dennis Bailey, quick and decisive, netted 25 goals in 93 appearances for Blues following his £90,000 transfer from Crystal Palace in August 1989. A lively forward and devout Christian, he was on Schoolboy forms with Watford and after playing for non-League Barking, Fulham (on a non-contract basis) and Farnborough he signed for Palace in December 1987, a month after his 22nd birthday. He had two separate loan spells with Bristol Rovers before and during his time at St Andrew's and on leaving Blues he signed for Queens Park Rangers for a fee of £150,000 in June 1991, having gained a Leyland DAF Trophy winners' medal. He later had loan spells with Watford, Charlton Athletic and Brentford and became a Gillingham player in 1995 and later served with Lincoln City.

BAILEY, Horace

Goalkeeper Horace Bailey made 53 appearances for Blues between September 1910 and April 1913 when he announced his retirement. Born in Derby in July 1881 he played for the Rams, Ripple Athletic, Leicester Imperial, Leicester Fosse and Derby County (again) before moving to St Andrew's. Despite being on the small side he was a very capable 'keeper, unmatched in versatility and won five senior and eight amateur international caps for England. He also gained a Gold Medal in the 1908 Olympic Games when representing Great Britain and in that same year (1908) conceded 12 goals in a League game while playing for Leicester Fosse against Nottingham Forest. After quitting football he worked as a rating officer for the Midland Railway Company. Bailey died in Biggleswade in August 1960.

BARCELONA (CF)

Programme for the match at St Andrew's and the front cover of the programme from return leg of the 1960 Final in Barcelona.

- Joe Lane, a 1920s Blues centre-forward, coached with Barcelona in the 1924-25 season.
- Blues played a friendly in Barcelona against CD Europa (won 6-1) during their summer tour of 1923.

BARKAS, Ned

Barkas shaking hands with the Albion skipper Tommy Glidden before the start of the 1931 FA Cup Final.

Blues met Barcelona five times in the Inter-Cities Fairs Cup competition over a period of nineteen months: October 1957 to May 1960.

On 23 October 1957 Blues defeated the Spanish giants Barcelona in the first leg of the Fairs Cup semi-final in front of 31,000 fans at St Andrew's

Having made progress through the group stage Blues were full of confidence on the night and won a cracking contest 4-3. Eddie Brown put Blues ahead with a cheeky goal in the second minute but Tejada equalised soon afterwards following a raid down the Blues' left flank.

In the 18th minute Evaristo put the visitors in front only for Bunny Larkin to set up an equaliser for Bryan Orritt. Before the cheering had died down Villaverde scored a brilliant goal to make it 3-2 to Barcelona, but incredibly Blues drew again level two minutes later when Gordon Astall's free-kick was clipped on by Brown for Peter Murphy to head in at the far post. And it was Murphy who struck again on 62 minutes, firing home the winner with a long range shot which 'keeper Ramallets never saw!

The return leg in the Nou Camp stadium three weeks later (mid-November) went in favour of Barcelona by 1-0 in front of 60,000 fans. That meant a replay in the St Jacob Stadium, Basle, Switzerland on 26 November and despite a battling performance in front of 20,000 fans Blues lost 2-1, Murphy their scorer.

The 1960 Fairs Cup Final was also played over two legs. The first meeting took place at St Andrew's on 29 March when a crowd of 40,524 witnessed a tedious 0-0 draw. Barcelona then won the return leg in Spain on 4 May by 4-1 to the delight of their fans in the 75,000 crowd. Harry Hooper was the Blues marksman.

This Blues' record against the Spanish giants:

Venue	P	W	D	L	F	A
Home	2	1	1	0	4	3
Away	2	0	0	2	1	5
Neutral	1	0	0	1	1	2
Totals	5	1	1	3	6	10

- Emilio Aldecoa Gomez, capped as a substitute by Spain against the Republic of Ireland in May 1948, helped Barcelona win their domestic League championship in 1951-52 and 1952-53. He was chief coach at St Andrew's under manager Gil Merrick in the early 1960s. He died in Spain in September 1999.

Ned Barkas skippered Blues in the 1931 FA Cup Final. A tough tackling defender, both authoritative and influential, he actually began his career as a centre-forward. Born in Northumberland in November 1902 he played for a variety of intermediate teams in the north-east of England including South Shields, prior to joining Norwich City as an amateur in 1920. However, he quickly returned 'home' to play for Bedlington Town and in 1921, signed professional forms for Huddersfield Town. He spent seven years at Leeds Road before transferring to St Andrew's for £4,000 in December 1928. He went on to score nine goals in 288 appearances for Blues over the eight-and-a-half years before leaving being re-united with his former manager Leslie Knighton at Chelsea. Just before the War Barkas returned to the Midlands to become player-manager of Solihull Town. He played spasmodically during the hostilities for two works teams and died in Little Bromwich in April 1962.

BARNET

There has been no League or Cup action as yet between Blues and Barnet.

Players with both clubs include: S Barnes, D Barnett, K Bertschin, M Bodily, G Bull, C Charley, K Dearden, P Harding, D Howell, J Hunt, R Huxford, K Lowe, G Poole, D Regis, ET Watkins, R Willis.

Also associated: Barry Fry (manager of both clubs), Ed Stein (player & coach at Barnet), David Howells (coach at both clubs). Fry guided Barnet into the Football League as GM Vauxhall Conference champions in 1992.

Gary Bull (with 20 goals) is Barnet's record scorer in League competition in a season (1991-92).

When he was manager of Barnet, Barry Fry once said: "It was like living with a double-decker bus on your head. When I left it was like it had been driven off."

BARNSLEY

Blues' playing record against the Tykes:

FOOTBALL LEAGUE

Venue	P	W	D	L	F	A
Home	28	15	7	6	47	28
Away	28	11	7	10	42	42
Totals	56	26	14	16	89	70

PLAY-OFFS

Venue	P	W	D	L	F	A
Home	1	0	0	1	0	4
Away	1	1	0	0	2	1
Totals	2	1	0	1	2	5

FA CUP

Venue	P	W	D	L	F	A
Home	2	0	1	1	0	2
Away	3	1	1	1	5	6
Totals	5	1	2	2	5	8

WARTIME

Venue	P	W	D	L	F	A
Home	3	3	0	0	12	1
Away	3	0	1	2	5	7
Totals	6	3	1	2	17	8

Nicky Eaden

Blues lost 7-2 at Barnsley in a League game in January 1899 - their heaviest defeat at the hands of the Tykes. Dick Jones scored a hat-trick for Barnsley.

Blues crashed to a 5-1 defeat at Barnsley in September 1909 yet the following the season they turned the tide by winning 3-2 on the same ground!

Barnsley doubled up over Blues in 1911-12 and as FA Cup holders the following season they came to out on top at Oakwell (3-1)

but lost 1-0 at St Andrew's.

Harry Hampton scored twice on his debut when Blues won 5-0 at Barnsley on St Valentine's Day 1920. Percy Barton also scored a rare goal in this game.

In the first season after World War Two Barnsley did the double over Blues and they began they 1947-48 campaign with a 3-2 win at St Andrew's before Blues finally broke the sequence with a 1-0 victory at Oakwell in December, Harold Boodle the scorer.

In 1950-51 Blues won both League games against the Tykes 2-0 and the following year doubled up again with a couple of 2-1 victories and repeated the act in 1952-53 with two 3-1 successes.

After a loan period without meeting each other Blues drew 0-0 at home with Barnsley in 1984-85 but won 1-0 away when David Geddis was on target.

In October 1988 an eight-goal thriller at St Andrew's resulted in a 5-3 defeat for Blues - and amazingly all eight goals were scored by different players, three coming in the space of three minutes in the second-half (56-59).

On 2 September 1995 Blues won 5-0 at Barnsley, scoring all their goals in the second-half of a First Division match. It was their biggest away win for 36 years; both Michael Johnson and Ken Charley made their debuts and Barnsley had two players sent-off - goalkeeper David Watson and defender Charlie Bishop.

In May 2000, Blues were hammered 4-0 at home by Barnsley in the Nationwide League Division One play-off semi-final first leg in front of almost 27,000 fans. For the return encounter at Oakwell, with around 3,500 Bluenoses cheering them in the capacity 19,050 crowd, Blues salvaged some pride with a battling 2-1 victory only to lose the tie 5-2 on aggregate and so miss out on a Wembley visit for the second season running.

Players with both clubs include: A Ainscow, T Aylott, S Barrowclough, J Beresford, N Brunskill, L Burkinshaw (guest), K Burns, H Cope (Blues reserve), F Cornan, S Davies, J Deakin, N Eaden, D Geddis, B Green, I Hendon, P Howard, A Johnson, A Jones, DB Latchford, AE Lindon, K Miller, A Phoenix, H Powell, AN Rawson, A Rees, W Ronson, A Saville, D Speedie, BJ Taylor, L Thompson (amateur), JE Travers, W Wardle.

BARROW

Blues' playing record against Barrow:

LEAGUE CUP

Venue	P	W	D	L	F	A
Home	1	1	0	0	5	1
Away	1	0	1	0	1	1
Totals	2	1	1	0	6	2

Blues met Barrow in the 1962-63 League Cup competition and coasted to an easy aggregate victory. Jimmy Harris scored twice in the 5-1 win at St Andrew's.

Players with both clubs include: W Clark, N Doherty, T Farnell, K Lowe, E Purdon, J Robertson, AH Sheldon (Blues reserve), G Smith, CG Spencer (Blues reserve), J Wealands (also coach), P Withe

Also: Fred Pentland (Blues player, Barrow manager), Norman Bodell (Blues coach & scout, Barrow coach & manager).

BARTON, Percy

Born in London in August 1895 and a former butcher's boy, Percy Barton developed into an exceptionally fine international

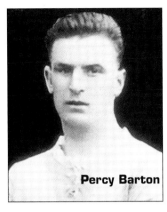

Percy Barton

footballer who could perform equally as well in both full-back and both wing-half positions as well as centre-forward, gained seven full caps for England. He starred for a handful of London-based non-League clubs before joining Blues in January 1914 and spent 15 years at St Andrew's during which time he scored 13 goals in 349 appearances, helping Blues win the Second Division championship in 1921. On 13 November 1920 he amazed the 40,000 St Andrew's crowd by scoring with a 30-yard header in a 4-1 win over Wolves. A strong, determined and positive footballer, Barton always enjoyed a battle and was sent-off four times during his career, three dismissals coming whilst at St Andrew's.

In August 1929 he moved to Stourbridge, announcing his retirement in 1933. Barton, who guested for Tottenham Hotspur during the First World War, died in October 1961.

BEARD, Malcolm

Malcolm Beard

After scoring 32 goals in 405 senior appearances for Blues, the ever-reliable Malcolm Beard played in six games for rivals Aston Villa before quitting League soccer in June 1972. A splendid wing-half - born in Cannock on 3 May 1942 - Beard joined Blues as a junior in 1957, turning professional in May 1959. He moved to Villa Park in July 1971 and rounded off his career with Atherstone United in 1973. Joining the World Sporting Academy in 1974 he took a coaching spell in Saudi Arabia and on his return to England became a scout with Blues, later holding the position of chief scout at Villa Park. Beard was named coach at Middlesbrough in 1987; he did similar job with Portsmouth in 1990 and was appointed Villa's reserve team manager in 1997.

At the start of his career after gaining an England Youth international cap as a teenager, Beard helped Blues reach the final of the Inter-Cities Fairs Cup in 1961 and won a League Cup prize in 1963 at Aston Villa's expense. He had the misfortune to be sent-off in his last League game for Blues against Millwall at The Den in December 1970.

BEASLEY, Pat

Pat Beasley

Born in Stourbridge in July 1913, Pat Beasley was a left-half or outside-left with Stourbridge, Arsenal (1931-36 and as a Wartime guest in 1945-46), Huddersfield Town (1936-45) and Fulham (1945-50). He first went into management with Bristol City in 1950 whilst still a player and finally hung up his boots in 1952 at the age of 39. He was appointed joint-manager of Blues (with Arthur Turner) in January 1958 and remained at St Andrew's until May 1960 when he handed over the reins to Gil Merrick. In season 1960-61 Beasley scouted for Fulham and after managing Dover Athletic for three seasons, up to 1964, he retired to live in Chard, Somerset. He won one full England cap and collected two League championship medals with Arsenal (1934 and 1935) followed by an FA Cup winners runners-up medal with Huddersfield in 1938. As manager he guided Bristol City to the Second Division title in 1950 and the Third Division (South) championship in 1955. Beasley died in Taunton in February 1986.

BEAU BRUMMIE CLUB

The Beau Brummie Club - for diehard Blues' supporters - was officially opened in August 1966 and on one of the early away trips the organisers arranged for a bar and disco to be on board to accompany the fans on their journey to and from the game!

BEER, Billy

Wing-half Billy Beer was both a player and manager of Blues. Born near Chesterfield in January 1879, he was an amateur with Sheffield United before joining Chesterfield Town. He returned to Bramall Lane as a professional in 1898 and four years later moved

Billy Beer

to Blues for £700 (with Charlie Field). A very skilful footballer, he spent eight years at the club, retiring in May 1910 after scoring 35 goals (over 20 of them penalties) in 250 appearances. On leaving St Andrew's he became a sheep farmer in Australia, returning to England in 1920 to take over a pub. In May 1923 he was appointed manager of Blues, a position he held until March 1927 when he resigned despite receiving a massive vote of confidence from the board. Beer died in March 1941.

BELL, Willie

Willie Bell took over from Freddie Goodwin as Blues' manager in September 1975, staying in office for two years before handing over his duties to Sir Alf Ramsey. A Scotsman, born in Johnstone in September 1937, Bell was a full-back for Queens Park (Glasgow), Leeds United (1960-67), Leicester City and Brighton & Hove Albion (as player-coach under Freddie Goodwin). He retired to become Goodwill's senior coach at St Andrew's in August 1970. On leaving Blues in 1977 he took charge of Lincoln City but in October 1978 he quit his job at Sincil Bank to join an American-based religious sect. He went over to the States to coach the Campus Crusade of Christ team, aiming to convert sportsmen to Christianity. He later became soccer coach at the Liberty Baptist College in Virginia.

Willie Bell

BENEFIT & TESTIMONIAL MATCHES

Dressing line-up prior to Dave Latchford's Testimonial match in 1979: left to right - Bob Hatton, George Smith, Terry Hibbitt, Pat Howard, Barry Bridges, Gordon Taylor, Bob Latchford, Garry Pendrey, Dave Latchford (with mascot), John Connolly, Joe Gallagher Jimmy Calderwood and Keith Bertschin.

Programme from 1912 when a team of ex-Aston Villa players (the Old Villans) took on a side made up of former Blues players (Old Heathens) at Villa Park in a Charity game.

Over the years several Blues players have been granted either a benefit or testimonial match and these include the following: Malcolm Beard (1969 v International XI whom Blues beat 12-8), Kevan Broadhurst (1986 v Aston Villa), Chris Charsley (1890 v Aston Villa), Ted Devey (1895 v Aston Villa), James Elliott (1896 v Aston Villa), Winston Foster (1971 v Plymouth Argyle, away), John Frain (v Aston Villa 1996), Joe Gallagher (1981 v Aston Villa, Blues lost 3-6), Ian Handysides (1988 Blues v Manchester United), Harry Hibbs (1940 v Aston Villa), Sammy Holmes (1895 v Walsall), Caesar Jenkyns (1893 v WBA), Dave Latchford (1979 v ex-Blues XI), Alex Leake 1898 v WBA - a game Blues won 8-3), Ray Martin (171 v Wolves, Blues lost 3-4), Harry Morris (1892), Malcolm Page (1977 v Ex-Blues XI), Garry Pendrey (1979 v West Bromwich Albion, Blues won 4-0), Billy Pratt (1901 v Select XI), Johnny Schofield (1967 v ex-Blues XI), Trevor Smith (1964 v Distillery), Fred Speller (1893 v Darwen), Eddie Stanley (1889 v Past XI), Frank Stokes (1910), Paul Tait, Billy Walton (1897 v Aston Villa), Sid Wharton (1903: English players v Scottish players), Fred Wheldon (1894 v WBA)), James Whittall, Frank Worthington (Blues XI v Ron Atkinson's Select XI) and Ron Wylie (1970 v Manchester City).

- A crowd of almost 8,000 (paying £45,000 in receipts) attended John Frain's testimonial match v Aston Villa in May 1996. Brian Little played for the visitors - his first game in 10 years - and he helped his side to a comfortable 6-0 win.

- Blues defender Frank Stokes never even played in his benefit match in 1910 - he played for the second team on the same day!
- A crowd of over 12,000 attended Paul McGrath's testimonial match at Villa Park when Blues were the visitors in May 1995. Gareth Hall (Chelsea) had a trial for Blues in this match.
- A crowd of 6,762 attended St Andrew's to say 'thank you' to Frank Worthington in September 1991 when a Blues XI played Ron Atkinson's Select XI in a benefit match for the former Blues striker who had left the club nine-and-a-half years earlier.
- Blues played Kidderminster Harriers in Richard Forsyth's benefit match in August 1995 (won 4-1).
- The Plymouth Argyle and former Blues defender Winston Foster had his testimonial match against Blues at Home Park in March 1971.
- And ex-Blues centre-half and team manager Arthur Turner's testimonial match was between Stoke City and Blues at Oxford United's Manor Ground in October 1972.
- Brighton played Blues in a testimonial match for Geoff Sidebottom in May 1972 and six years later Blues took a side to Weymouth for a similar game for Stuart Morgan.
- Tommy McLaren (Port Vale) had his testimonial match against Blues at Vale Park in October 1978 and the following month Blues drew 2-2 at Newport County's Somerton Park in a testimonial for Ken Saunders.
- Also in August 1995 Blues took a team to Coventry City for Brian Borrows' testimonial and drew 1-1 in front of 6,036 fans.
- Blues played a Memorial Match for the late Jeff Hall against an All Star XI in September 1959 (lost 1-5).
- Blues goalkeeper Gil Merrick guested for Coventry City in George Mason's Testimonial match in 1952.
- Blues took a team to Harborne Lynwood for a benefit match in aid of James Whittall in 1917 (2-2 draw). In 1968 Corby Town's Alex Stenhouse had his testimonial match against Blues and Barry Williams of Worcester City also elected to have his testimonial match against Blues at St George's in 1981.
- In May 1974 a combined WBA/Aston Villa side played a combined Blues/Wolves side in a testimonial for the Baggies' defender Ray Wilson at The Hawthorns.
- In 1947 a combined Birmingham XI (seven Blues players and four from Aston Villa) played Coventry City at Highfield Road in a testimonial match for Dick Bayliss.
- An International XI played a Midland All-Stars team at St Andrew's on 22 March 1967 in a match arranged for the Tony Allden testimonial fund. Allden was struck by lightning while playing for local non-League side Highgate United. He died soon afterwards.
- Newport County's Keith Saunders had his testimonial match against Blues at Somerton Park in November 1978 (2-2) and a month earlier Blues visited Port Vale for Tommy McLaren's testimonial (won 1-0).
- Former Villa goalkeeper Geoff Sidebottom, then of Brighton & Hove Albion, had his testimonial against Blues in May 1972.
- Ron Saunders who managed both Aston Villa and Blues, had a testimonial match at Villa Park in May 1980 when Blues beat Villa 3-2.
- The respective testimonial matches for Andy Needham (Aldershot) and Jimmy McCafferty (Weymouth) were both against Blues in May 1981
- Following the Ibrox Park disaster, Blues met Aston Villa in a fund-raising friendly game at Villa Park on 30 April 1902. The game ended 1-1, Bob McRoberts scoring for Blues.

- On 29 April 1903 Blues were beaten 3-2 by West Bromwich Albion at The Hawthorns in a benefit game in aid of the Warwickshire County Cricket Club.
- The Lord Mayor's Prisoner of War Fund encounter between Coventry City and Blues at Highfield Road in November 1916 ended in a 3-3 draw.
- Four months later, in March 1917 Blues beat West Bromwich Albion 3-1 at Muntz Street in a Sportman's Motor Ambulance Fund encounter. And a similar game took place two months later when Blues won 1-0 on Baggies' soil.
- In May 1919 Blues played two Birmingham County FA Charity matches. They won them both, 2-1 at Aston Villa and 3-2 at Coventry City.
- On 17 January 1921 Blues drew 1-1 with Aston Villa in the Lord Mayor's Unemployment Fund match .
- After the Birmingham pub bombings in November 1974, St Andrew's staged a friendly match between a Midlands XI and an international XI managed by Joe Mercer.
- Blues played Poole Town in a match to mark the non-League club's centenary in January 1981.
- On Easter Monday in April 1912, an ex-Aston Villa XI met an old Blues XI in a Charity match at Villa Park. A crowd of 3,000 witnessed the 4-4 draw.

BENNETT, Ian

Goalkeeper Ian Bennett - born in Worksop in October 1971 - was a junior with Queens Park Rangers before joining Newcastle United in 1989. He failed to make the breakthrough at St James' Park and was released on a free transfer in March 1991 when he signed for Peterborough United. He played more than 80 games for Posh before moving to Blues for £325,000 in December 1993. A fine shot-stopper, Bennett suffered with injuries during the late 1990s (he only played in 23 games in 1999-2000) but he has still managed to amass well over 250 senior appearances for Blues whom he helped win the Second Division title and Auto Windscreen Shield in 1994-95. That same season he also kept 27 clean sheets out of the 62 first class matches he played in.

BERRY, John

Johnny Berry was forced to retire following the Munich air disaster of February 1958. Born in Aldershot in June 1926, he joined Blues as a professional in 1944 (recommended to the club by Fred Harris) and remained at St Andrew's until August 1951 when Manchester United secured his services for £25,000 (signing him to replace Jimmy Delaney). A dashing outside-right he scored six goals in 114 first team outings for Blues, helping them win the Second Division title in 1948. At Old Trafford, he was a star performer in the famous Busby Babes side and won three First Division championship medals and an FA Cup runners-up medal in the space of five years. He also gained four full England caps and represented his country at 'B' team level as well as playing for the Football League side. Berry scored 43 goals in 273 games for United and after that tragic air crash he returned to Aldershot to help run the family sports shop. He died in Farnham in 1995.

Aston Villa goalkeeper Joe Rutherford dives at the feet of Johnny Berry during the League game at St Andrew's in April 1950

BERTSCHIN, Keith

Keith Bertschin in action against Leicester City

Striker Keith Bertschin, born in Enfield in August 1956, played for Barnet and Ipswich Town before joining Blues for £135,000 in July 1977. He went on to score 41 goals in 141 appearances during his time at St Andrew's which ended in August 1981 when he transferred to Norwich City for £200,000. A hard working player, strong in the air, Bertschin later served with the NASL club Jacksonville Teamen (on loan), Stoke City, Sunderland, Walsall, Chester City, Aldershot, Solihull Borough, Evesham United, Barry Town, Tamworth, Worcester City and Hednesford Town. He helped Ipswich win the FA Youth Cup in 1975, Sunderland the Third Division championship in 10988 and Barry Town the Welsh Cup in 1994. He was capped three times by England at Under-21 level and actually scored with his first kick in English League soccer - a header as a substitute for Ipswich against Arsenal at Highbury in April 1976. Bertschin netted over 150 goals in senior football.

BIRMINGHAM & DISTRICT LEAGUE

Blues' reserve side spent 24 seasons playing in the Birmingham & District League between 1893 and 1923. They fulfilled a total of 788 matches and secured 1,576 points.

Blues' 'A' team had three seasons in the BDL (1957-60), playing 110 games.

BIRMINGHAM EXCELSIOR

In season 1883-84, Blues were knocked out of the FA Cup in the first round by rivals Birmingham Excelsior. After a 1-1 draw at Muntz Street, Excelsior won the replay 3-2 at the Aston Lower grounds. Excelsior repeated the act the following season, ousting Blues again in the first round, this time by 2-0.

Blues' record against Excelsior:

FA CUP

Venue	P	W	D	L	F	A
Home	1	0	1	0	1	1
Away	2	0	0	2	2	5
Totals	3	0	1	2	3	6

Players with both clubs include: J Bodenham, W Harrison

BIRMINGHAM ST GEORGE'S

Blues' playing record against St George's:

FOOTBALL ALLIANCE

Venue	P	W	D	L	F	A
Home	3	1	1	1	6	8
Away	3	0	0	3	5	10
Totals	6	1	1	4	11	18

Blues' only victory was a 3-2 success on the opening day of the 1889-90 season in front of 2,000 fans at Muntz Street.

St George's won a nine-goal thriller by 5-4 in November 1890. Will Devey and Jack Hallam both scored twice for Blues.

Players with both clubs include: W Harrison, D Hodgetts

BIRMINGHAM SENIOR CUP

Blues first entered this competition in 1878-79, losing in the opening round 1-0 to Calthorpe on 9 November.

Their first victory followed on 25 October 1879 when they beat Wednesbury Old Athletic 2-1 away.

In 1881-82 Blues beat Aston Clifton 7-2 in the first round but lost by the same score to Wednesbury old Athletic in the next round.

On 1 December 1883 Blues whipped Dudley 11-0 at home in a second round tie but went out at the next hurdle to Walsall Swifts after a replay.

A 10-3 home win over Sandwell in October 1885 was followed by a 3-1 replay defeat at the hands of their old rivals Wednesbury Old Athletic five weeks later.

Blues reached the semi-final stage for the first time in 1886-87 after knocking out Stafford Road 7-0, Coseley 13-0 and Derby Junction 1-0 (at the second attempt - they won the initial game 4-0 but the opposition submitted a protest). Blues then met Long Eaton Rangers in the semis but after a 2-2 draw at the Lower grounds (Aston) they were defeated 2-0 at Muntz Street.

That 13-0 victory over Coseley on 11 November 1886 is still the biggest win ever recorded by a Blues first team at competitive level.

Over the next few seasons Blues did nothing at all in the competition, but in 1894-95 they again reached the last four after ousting Burton Swifts 5-4 and Wolves 3-2 (after a 3-3 draw). But they failed to make the final, losing 3-2 in front of 5,000 fans at Molineux in the semis.

Two years later Blues went to Molineux for a second round tie and crashed 8-2 to the Wanderers.

After more disappointment and a few more heavy defeats in 1904-05 Blues at long last got into the Birmingham Senior Cup Final. They knocked out rivals Aston Villa 3-1 away in the first round, defeated Stourbridge 6-1 at home in the semis before overpowering West Bromwich Albion 7-2 in the final at Muntz Street on 20 February in front of almost 8,500 spectators.

The Blues team was: Robinson; Glover, Stokes; Beer, Wigmore, Dougherty; Tickle, Green, Jones, Windridge and Field.

The scorers were Jones (3), Windridge (3) and Field.

The following season, as holders of the trophy, Blues decided to put out their reserve side and went on to reach the final again only to lose 3-1 to Aston Villa in front of an 11,000 crowd on 24 February.

Since then Blues, like several other leading Midlands clubs, have fielded their reserve team (second XI) in the competition and they have done extremely well at times.

Blues won six more finals - 5-3 v Wolves in 1907, 2-0 v Stoke's first team in 1915, 3-0 v Stoke reserves in 1920, 5-1 v Stoke reserves again in 1921 and 2-1 v Wellington Town in 1922. Their 1-0 victory over Aston Villa as recent as 1983 was gained when both clubs put out strong first teams after the reserves had done the spade-work in the earlier rounds!

Blues' second XI has regularly participated in the Birmingham Senior Cup since the late 1940s to date, but it was mainly first-team players who starred in the 1983 final when Blues conjured up a 1-0 victory over Aston Villa. Ian Handysides scored the all-important goal in front of 11,763 fans at St Andrew's. And the Blues team for this game included goalkeeper Tony Coton, defenders Noel Blake, Byron Stevenson, Jim Hagan and Kevan Broadhurst, striker Mick Harford and of course match-winner Handysides.

Nine years later, in April 1992, and fielding a team that included four YTS players and seven teenagers, Blues were beaten by VS Rugby of the Beazer Homes League 3-0 in the Final at The Hawthorns, home of West Bromwich Albion. Graham Potter, Dean Peer, Ian Atkins and David Foy played in the Blues side that night.

In May 1996, after the reserves had battled through the previous rounds, Blues, with a line-up of mainly first-team players, beat

Aston Villa 2-0 in the Senior Cup Final before a meagre turn out of only 1,773 fans at St Andrew's. Jason Bowen (32 minutes) and Ricky Otto (42) scored the goals. The game, though, boiled over towards the end and four players were sent-off, three from Blues, John Cornforth, Ian Jones and Paul Peschisolido, along with Villa's Ben Petty.

Official programme for the 1983 Senior Cup Final at St Andrew's

BLACKBURN ROVERS

Blues' playing record against Rovers:

FOOTBALL LEAGUE

Venue	P	W	D	L	F	A
Home	45	28	8	9	89	50
Away	45	7	8	30	61	118
Totals	90	35	16	39	150	168

FA CUP

Home	1	1	0	0	3	0
Away	1	1	0	0	2	1
Totals	2	2	0	0	5	1

LEAGUE CUP

Home	2	1	1	0	2	1
Away	1	0	0	1	0	2
Totals	3	1	1	1	2	3

Blues heaviest defeat against Blackburn came in January 1895 when they crashed 9-1 on Rovers' soil. In goal for Blues was Wednesbury-born Charlie Partridge while Tilson Pritchard made his only appearance for the club at right-back. Two players - Ted Killean and Harry Chippendale - both scored hat-tricks for Rovers.

When they returned to the First Division for the 1903-04 season Blues beat Rovers 2-1 at home and drew 1-1 at Ewood Park; the following season Rovers were defeated twice: 2-0 at Muntz Street and 4-1 at home, when Billy Jones netted twice, once from the penalty spot.

In November 1905 Blackburn gained revenge when they whipped Blues 5-1 at home but were on the receiving end of a 3-0 defeat on Blues' soil in late April 1906.

In the early 1920s Blues and Rovers played out four 1-1 draws in five starts before Blackburn slammed Blues 7-1 at Ewood Park in front of just 3,000 spectators in April 1925. This wasn't a happy game for Blues left-back Jack Jones who conceded a penalty and an own-goal and was responsible for two more Rovers' goals.

Over a period of eighteen months there were two 4-4 draws involving Blues and Rovers in League competition - both at Ewood Park. The first in January 1926 saw Joe Bradford score a hat-trick for Blues and then in September 1927 Bradford netted all his side's goals in another thrilling encounter.

A 12-goal thriller at Ewood Park in September 1929 saw Rovers take the points with a 7-5 victory. Syd Puddefoot netted four times for the home side while Joe Bradford scored a hat-trick for Blues while Johnny Crosbie claimed the other two. And Bradford was again a thorn in Rovers' defence when he scored all his side's goals as Blues beat Blackburn 4-1 at St Andrew's in February 1931.

Bradford simply loved playing against Blackburn - he scored a total of 29 goals for Blues against the Lancashire club.

Fred Harris scored twice (one a real beauty) hen Blues beat Rovers 4-1 at St Andrew's in February 1936 - having netted once in a 2-1 win at Ewood park earlier in the season.

The first post second World War League meeting between the clubs saw Blues win 3-2 at St Andrew's in October 1950 (Division 2) when Cyril Trigg netted a cracker in front of 25,000 fans.

Blues had an excellent 4-1 win at Blackburn in April 1952 when Tommy Briggs scored twice and when Blues gained promotion to the top flight in 1954-55 they beat Rovers 3-1 at home and drew 3-3 away.

On the last day of the 1959-60 season - a week before the FA Cup Final - Blues beat finalists Rovers 1-0 at St Andrew's with a goal by Johnny Gordon.

In April 1963 Blackburn beat Blues 6-1 in a League game at Ewood Park - a week after Blues had crashed 6-3 at home to Blackpool!

Already relegated Blues drew 5-5 with Blackburn Rovers in a ding-dong First Division match at St Andrew's in April 1965. Malcolm Beard, playing out of position at inside-left, was the star performer for Blues, scoring a hat-trick in the space of seven second-half minutes, this after Blues had trailed 5-3 with time running out The attendance of 8,877 was the lowest of the season.

Steve Whitton's goal gave Blues their first League win over Rovers in the 1980s - 1-0 at St Andrew's in September 1987.

Both FA Cup-ties between the clubs took place in the 1930s, while the two League Cup clashes were played in 1994-95. Blues were quoted at 400-1 to win the League Cup this season - before they met Premiership side Rovers and their £27 million worth of players including the England striking duo of Alan Shearer and Chris Sutton.

Mike Newell (before joining Blues) was Rovers' top-scorer in 1992-93, gained a Premiership championship medal in 1994-95 and then scored a hat-trick in the European Champions League in 1995-96. In 1999 he had a spell in non-League football with Doncaster Rovers!

Players with both clubs include: A Ainscow, JM Beattie, J Beresford, T Briggs, JH Burton, C Calladine, AW Clarke, H Cope (Blues reserve), J Crisp (Blues reserve), RO Evans, H Gayle, J Glover, W Guest, W Halsall, CW Jones (Rovers' trialist), R Jones, H Kendall (Rovers player-manager), A Kennedy, A Miller, A Mulraney (Rovers guest), AP Needham, M Newell, F Okenla (trialist), FB Pentland, F Pickering, M Rathbone, G Robertson, WH Smith, D Speedie, PM Starbuck, G Taylor.

Also: Jim Smith (manager of both clubs), Jackie Bestall (Blackburn manager, Blues coach/chief scout), Sid Evans (Blues player, Rovers trainer), Norman Bodell (Blues coach, scout, Rovers coach).

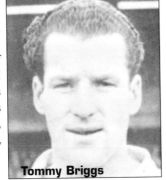
Tommy Briggs

BLACKPOOL

Blues' playing record against The Seasiders:

FOOTBALL LEAGUE

Venue	P	W	D	L	F	A
Home	37	20	8	9	88	50
Away	37	7	8	22	31	62
Totals	74	27	16	31	119	112

FA CUP

	P	W	D	L	F	A
Home	1	0	0	1	0	1
Neutral	2	0	1	1	1	2
Totals	3	0	1	2	1	3

LEAGUE CUP

	P	W	D	L	F	A
Home	1	1	0	0	4	2
Away	3	0	1	2	2	5
Totals	4	1	1	2	6	7

Both Johnny McMillan and Bob McRoberts scored five goals apiece when Blues beat Blackpool 10-1 in a League game at Muntz Street in March 1901. Some reports state that McMillan only netted twice but further investigation has revealed that equalled McRoberts' tally of five.

There was an own-goal and two penalties (one scored) when Blues beat Blackpool 5-1 at Muntz Street in April 1903.

The joint lowest attendance for a League game at St Andrew's, just 1,000 spectators, saw the Blues v Blackpool encounter in November 1909 (the visitors won 2-1).

Eighteen months later, in April 1911, a crowd of 13,000 on the same ground saw Blues win 2-0.

Andy Smith netted with a smashing penalty as Blues beat the Seasiders 3-0 at St Andrew's in November 1914. And in the first League game between the clubs after the Great War, in October

Blues' 'keeper Johnny Schofield dives across his six-yard box to cut out a cross during Blackpool's emphatic 6-3 win at St Andrew's in April 1963.

1919, Blues again came out on top, winning 4-2 at St Andrew's with Jack Elkes netting a superb goal.

Blackpool were one of the best teams in the country in the early 1950s and when Blues got into the First Division in 1955-56 they lost both matches to the Seasiders.

Blues followed a smart 4-2 home victory over Blackpool at St Andrew's in December 1958 by completing the double in 1959-59 (2-1 at home, 1-0 away) and two fine goals by Mick Hellawell gave Blues a narrow home win in December 1960.

Blackpool beat Blues 6-3 at St Andrew's in a First Division game in April 1963 and later that year, in November, Blues won 3-2 on the same ground. In March 1964 it was 3-0 to the Seasiders at Bloomfield Road and Blues lost by the same score at St Andrew's seven months later. And when Blackpool won 3-1 at home in March 1965 it made it 24 goals in five matches between the two clubs.

When Blues gained promotion in 1971-72 they beat Blackpool 2-1 at home in their 36th match, Bob Latchford and Trevor Francis the scorers.

A crowd of more than 18,000 saw Blues defeat Blackpool 7-1 at St Andrew's on New Year's Eve 1994. This was Blues' best win at any level for 35 years (since their 7-1 win at Nottingham Forest in 1959). And in fact it was their best home victory in the League for 40 years (since knocking over Liverpool 9-1 in 1954). They went to the top of the Second Division table as a result of this victory.

The two FA Cup semi-final clashes between Blues and Blackpool in March 1951 attracted a total of more than 140,000 spectators. Just over 70,000 witnessed the goalless draw at Maine Road when Jackie Stewart hit the Blackpool post late on and there were 70,114 present to see the Seasiders win the replay at Goodison Park 2-1.

Bob Hatton scored a hat-trick in Blues' 4-2 League Cup second round replay victory over Blackpool at home in October 1973. Hatton later scored 22 goals for the Seasiders in 1977-78 but couldn't prevent them from losing their Second Division status.

Players with both clubs include: G Ablett, A Ainscow, F Barber, R Booth, T Carter, H Crossthwaite, P Doherty (Blues guest), A Evans, R Forsyth, B Green, P Hart, R Hatton, C Kirby, JC Lane, JW Morfitt, A Mulraney (trialist), M Newell, FB Pentland, F Pickering, J Quinn, CL Richards, TE Robinson, W Ronson, G Rowett, L Sealey (Blues N/C), R Sbragia, S Sturridge, C Trigg (guest), A Wallace, W Wardle.

Also: Major Frank Buckley (Blues player, Blackpool manager), Fred Davies (coach at both clubs).

BLAKE, Noel

Powerful centre-half Noel Blake was born in Jamaica in January 1962. He came over to England as a youngster and after leaving school joined Sutton Coldfield Town. He signed for Walsall in 1978 and then became a professional with Aston Villa the following year. A loan spell with Shrewsbury Town preceded his transfer to St Andrew's in September 1982 for £55,000 and over the next two years Blake scored five goals in 96 appearances for Blues. He left the club for Portsmouth in August 1984 for £150,000 and four years later he was recruited by Leeds United for £175,000. He spent three seasons with Stoke City and after a loan spell with Bradford City he joined Dundee. He later became player-coach, then manager of Exeter City

BLOOMFIELD, Jimmy

Jimmy Bloomfield

Jimmy Bloomfield was a playmaking inside-forward, who served with Brentford and Arsenal before joining Blues in November 1960. He scored 31 goals in 147 appearances during his time at St Andrew's, gaining a League Cup winners' prize in 1963, having played in the Fairs Cup Final two years earlier.

He returned to his former club Brentford in June 1964 and after spells with West Ham United and Plymouth Argyle he was appointed player-manager of Leyton Orient in March 1968. He then had six years in charge of Leicester City (1971-77) before serving a second term in the hot seat at Orient. He ended his footballing days as a scout with Luton Town (1981-83). Born in Kensington in February 1934, Bloomfield was capped by England at Under-23 level and also represented the Football League. He led both Leicester and Orient to FA Cup semi-finals. Bloomfield, whose son David works for the FA, died of a heart attack in Chingford, Essex in April 1983

BODLE, Harold

Harold Bodle

Once a miner in his native Doncaster, inside-forward Harold Bodle was a bag of tricks, a fine footballer with an eye for goal. Born in October 1920, he had trials for Doncaster Rovers and Bradford Park Avenue before joining Rotherham United in May 1938. Blues paid £2,000 for his signature in November of that year and he remained at St Andrew's until March 1949 when he signed for Bury. Bodle scored 36 goals in 110 League and Cup outings for Blues and he also scored over 30 times in more than 80 Wartime appearances for the club as well as guesting for his former clubs Doncaster and Rotherham. He helped Blues win the Football League South championship in 1946 and the Second Division title in 1948. After Bury he assisted Stockport County and Accrington Stanley and after retiring in 1959 he became manager at Peel Park, retaining office for a year. From 1962 to 1964 he was in charge of non-League Burton Albion and in later life ran a post office in Burton and Derby.

BOLDKLUB COPENHAGEN

Two goals apiece by Johnny Gordon and Jimmy Singer earned Blues a 4-4 draw in Denmark against Boldklub Copenhagen in a second round first leg Inter-Cities Fairs Cup-tie on 23 November 1960.

In the second leg on 7 December, former Everton forward Jimmy Harris made his debut for Blues - and scored in the 48th minute - as the Danish side were hammered 5-0 in front of almost 22,500 fans. There were only hardy supporters 2,500 present at the first leg.

SUMMARY

Venue	P	W	D	L	F	A
Home	1	1	0	0	5	0
Away	1	0	1	0	4	4
Totals	2	1	1	0	9	4

BOLTON WANDERERS

BIRMINGHAM CITY v BOLTON W.

Shirts: Royal Blue, Shorts: Royal Blue   Shirts: White   Shorts: Black

FOOTBALL LEAGUE DIVISION TWO

(M&B)

Referee:
Mr. D. Wallace
(Swindon)

Linesmen:
Mr J. R. Davies
Yellow Flag

Mr. G. E. Flint
Red Flag

Birmingham City		Bolton W.
1	Jim HERRIOT	Eddie HOPKINSON 1
2	Colin GREEN	John RITSON 2
3	Bobby THOMSON	Sid FARRIMOND 3
4	Ron WYLIE	Gareth Williams 4
5	Fred PICKERING	Arthur MARSH 5
6	Malcolm BEARD	David HATTON 6
7	Jimmy GREENHOFF	Terry WHARTON 7
8	Johnny VINCENT	Freddie HILL 8
9	Bob LATCHFORD	John MANNING 9
10	Trevor HOCKEY	Roy GREAVES 10
11	Phil SUMMERILL	Gordon TAYLOR 11

Programme centre spread showing Pickering at No. 5 for Blues v Bolton in 1968

Blues' playing record against the Wanderers:

FOOTBALL LEAGUE

Venue	P	W	D	L	F	A
Home	50	26	13	11	90	57
Away	50	6	15	29	47	108
Totals	100	32	28	40	137	165

FA CUP

Venue	P	W	D	L	F	A
Home	3	2	0	1	6	5

The first League meeting between the two clubs took place on 8 September 1894 when Blues won 2-0 at Muntz Street (Fred Wheldon scoring both goals). Blues also won the away game that season by 2-1.

Blues lost 4-0 at Burnden Park in January 1902 and were crushed 5-2 at Muntz Street in March 1906 before they came good with a couple of fine wins in 1906-07, 4-2 at home and 3-2 away, Billy Beer scoring from the penalty spot in the former.

The first two clubs to be relegated from the First Division for a third time were Blues and Bolton Wanderers who went down together for that third drop in 1907-08.

Bolton won a Second Division fixture by 5-1 at home in December 1910, but then the Wanderers had to beat Blues at St Andrew's on the final day of that season to capture the championship. They lost 2-1 and the crown went to West Bromwich Albion instead, Bolton taking the runners-up spot.

When Blues joined the Wanderers in the top flight in 1921-22 the teams drew 1-1 at St Andrew's while Blues won 2-1 at Bolton, thanks to a brace from Joe Bradford.

FA Cup holders Bolton won 3-0 on Blues' soil in September 1923 and the following season they repeated that scoreline to a tee at Burnden Park!

In April 1927 Blues beat Bolton 6-1 at home, Johnny Crosbie scoring twice. But on Boxing Day 1928, Bolton gained sweet revenge by defeating Blues 6-2 at Burnden Park, Blues having beaten the Wanderers 2-0 at St Andrew's just 24 hours earlier!

In March 1932 Bolton claimed a 5-1 home win over Blues and in the last pre-war season of 1938-39 they completed the double, winning 2-0 at St Andrew's and 3-0 at Burnden Park.

The first three 1940s League confrontations all ended 0-0, in October 1948, March 1949 and October 1949.

They next two saw Bolton wins, the second a rasping 6-0 score-line at Burnden Park on December 1955 when England centre-forward Nat Lofhouse scored four times.

In April 1956, Blues warming nicely up for their FA Cup Final clash with Manchester City, beat Bolton 5-2 at St Andrew's. Visiting defender Johnny Wheeler conceded two own-goals.

Four years later, in March 1960, it was Bolton's turn to register a 5-2 win, also at St Andrew's. They were 3-0 up at half-time and three goals were scored in the first four minutes of the second-half, two by Blues.

Blues were minus four central defenders, Winston Foster, Dave Robinson, Brian Sharples and John Sleeuwenhoek for the home League game with Bolton on 25 March 1969 and as a last resort manager Stan Cullis chose centre-forward Fred Pickering to occupy the centre-half berth. He played superbly well, Blues won 5-0 and Phil Summerill scored a hat-trick!

Neil Whatmore

In February 1971, sixteen year-old Trevor Francis scored all Blues' goals in their 4-0 victory over Bolton at St Andrew's.

Bob Taylor scored after just 18 seconds for Bolton in their 3-1 home League win over Blues in September 1998.

Blues were 3-1 up on Bolton in a League game at The Reebok Stadium in September 1999 but Graham Hyde was sent-off after conceding a last minute penalty (for deliberate hand-ball) and the Wanderers salvaged a point with the resulting penalty (3-3). The Holdsworth twins, David (Blues) and Dean (Bolton) played against each other in this game.

The Wanderers won a thrilling FA Cup-tie 4-3 at Muntz Street in 1893-94 in front of 7,000 spectators.

Players with both clubs include: G Astall (trialist), S Charlton, A Evans, P Fitzpatrick, T Grosvenor, W Halsall (amateur), R Hansbury, R Hatton, CW Jones (trialist), FW Jones (trialist), A Kennedy, W McCafferty, J McDonough, J Millington (Blues reserve), T Morgan, I Rankin, J Sheridan, B Small, S Storer, P Tait (Bolton trialist), G Taylor, N Whatmore (four spells with Bolton), F Worthington

Also: Barry Fry (Bolton player, Blues manager), Bruce Rioch and Colin Todd (Blues players, Bolton managers).

BOND, Benny

Benny Bond

Frail-looking left-winger but nevertheless a very useful one who scored 13 goals in 85 appearances for Blues between 1926 and 1932 before a serious knee injury forced him into early retirement. Born in Wolverhampton in August 1904, Bond played for a number of local non-League clubs before signing amateur forms at St Andrew's, turning professional in the same year (1926). He died in Wolverhampton in March 1972.

BOND, John

John Bond

A solid full-back with West Ham United (1949-66) and Torquay United, making a total of 428 League and Cup appearances, John Bond was coach to Gillingham and manager of Bournemouth, Norwich City, Manchester City Burnley and Swansea City before taking charge at St Andrew's in January 1986, replacing Ron Saunders. He stayed with Blues until May 1987 after failing to produce the goods. He then became assistant-boss of Shrewsbury Town, moving up to manager at Gay Meadow in 1991 and remaining there for two years, quitting after the Shrews

had failed to make the play-offs. He later became coach at Wigan Athletic (1999-2000).

Bond, who was born in Colchester in December 1932, represented the Football League and toured South Africa with the FA in 1956. He won a Second Division championship medal with the Hammers in 1958 and collected an FA Cup winners medal six years later. As a manager he guided Norwich to promotion from Division Two and to the 1975 League Cup Final. After that he lifted Bournemouth up from the Fourth Division (as runners-up) before taking Manchester City to the 1981 FA Cup Final.

BOOTLE

Blues' playing record against Bootle:
FOOTBALL LEAGUE

Venue	P	W	D	L	F	A
Home	1	1	0	0	6	2
Away	1	1	0	0	4	1
Totals	2	2	0	0	10	3

FOOTBALL ALLIANCE

Venue	P	W	D	L	F	A
Home	3	2	1	0	13	4
Away	3	1	1	1	2	7
Totals	6	3	2	1	15	11

The two League matches took place in the Second Division in 1892-93 and Jack Hallam scored a hat-trick in Blues' 6-2 win at Muntz Street.

When Blues defeated Bootle 7-1 at home in an Alliance match in March 1891 Fred Wheldon claimed a hat-trick.

Bootle's only win over Blues was a 6-0 triumph at home in April 1890.

Players with both clubs include: A Goldie, T Jones

BOOTON, Harry

Right-back Harry Booton from Annesley Colliery, scored twice in 162 League and Cup games for Blues. He arrived at St Andrew's as a 23-year-old from Shirebrook FC in April 1929 and remained with the club until February 1936 when he signed for Luton Town. He ended his career with Atherstone in 1939 before becoming a landlord of the Market Inn, Swadlincote, Derbyshire.

A strong, determined player, somewhat laxadazical in his approach, Booton was the crooner in the dressing room - with an awful voice! He died in Uxbridge in October 1976.

BORUSSIA DORTMUND

Blues met the German Bundesliga side in a friendly match at St Andrew's on 31 October 1957 - to officially 'switch on' the club's recently erected floodlights. A crowd of 45,000 witnessed the 3-3 draw with Bryan Orritt (2) and Alex Govan scoring for Blues.

BOURNEMOUTH (AFC)

Blues' playing record against the Cherries:
FOOTBALL LEAGUE

Venue	P	W	D	L	F	A
Home	5	0	3	2	1	3
Away	5	2	0	3	7	9
Totals	10	2	3	5	8	12

LEAGUE CUP

Home	1	0	0	1	0	1
Away	1	0	1	0	1	1
Totals	2	0	1	1	1	2

The first League meeting between Blues and the Cherries produced six goals Bournemouth winning 4-2 at Dean Court on 1 January 1988.

Amazingly Blues have yet to beat the Cherries at St Andrew's! Their first win came at Dean Court in October 1988 when John Frain's goal separated the two teams.

The two League Cup games were played in August/September 1990.

Players with both clubs include: T Aylott, J Birch, S Claridge, R Cooke, J Coxford, H Evans, B Farmer, D Givens, W Hutchinson (Blues reserve), H Isherwood, R Jones, RE Keating, D Langan, DJ Madden, T Morgan, P Moulden, TE Pike, J Randle, CL Richards, CJ Russell, P Shearer, D Regis, DJ Singer, AW Smith, D Smith, W Trelfall, HL Turner (reserve), JC Whitehouse.

Also: John Bond and Leslie Knighton (managers of both clubs), Fred Davies (Cherries goalkeeper, Blues coach).

BOYD, Len

Len Boyd, who was born in Plaistow, London on 11 November 1923 and played in the same School team as another Birmingham City player, Ken Green, and skippered Blues to promotion from the Second Division in 1954-55 and then led them in the 1956 FA Cup Final.

After playing as an amateur for Ilford and spending a couple of years serving in the Royal Navy, Boyd made 80 first-class appearances for Plymouth Argyle - the Pilgrims having spotted his undoubted talents while he was playing as an inside-forward in Malta.

Len Boyd

Boyd, tall, composed with a long stride, took time to settle down at Home Park, but then, as his confidence grew, he made rapid strides. So much so that after being converted into a right-half by Argyle manager Jack Tresadern, a splendid display for the Pilgrims at St Andrew's prompted the Midland club to take more interest!

Consequently, in January 1949, Boyd wrote his name in Plymouth Argyle's history books by becoming the club's first five-figure transfer when he joined Blues for £17,500. The whole of the transfer negotiation, in fact, had been kept secret from the press and public until the forms were completed.

Boyd enjoyed bringing the ball out of defence into attack, driving his forwards before him with one of those imperious waves of the hand which were to become his trademark. He took over from Fred Harris in the Blues half-back line, allowing Harris to switch to left-half in place of Frank Mitchell. He retained the number four berth, practically unchallenged until retiring in May 1956, soon after Blues had lost that season's FA Cup Final.

Capped by England 'B', Boyd was undoubtedly a fine player, a hard-worker who made 282 appearances for Blues (14 goals scored). On leaving St Andrew's he had a brief spell as a player with Hinckley Athletic and was later coach and chief scout with Redditch United.

BRADFORD, Joe

Joe Bradford is arguably the best marksman Blues have ever had - his record proves that beyond all doubt - 267 goals in 445 appearances for the club. A dynamic centre-forward, he was rated the best in his position during the mid-1920s and indeed he went on to win a total of 12 England caps as well as representing the Football League. Born in a picturesque Leicestershire village in January 1901, Bradford scored goals galore in junior football, including 13 in one match before having unsuccessful trials with both Aston Villa and Derby County. He finally left his local side Peggs Green Victoria to sign professional forms for Blues in February 1920, for what was to prove a bargain price of just £125 (£100 down and £25 when he had made his League debut). Groomed in the reserves he became an established first team player at St Andrew's in 1921-22, having appeared in just four games the previous season when Blues won the Second Division championship. Able to shoot with both feet and head a ball as strong as some players could kick it, he was a fearless centre-forward, afraid of no one and a player who simply loved scoring goals! In fact, in September 1929 Bradford netted 11 times in eight days! He scored a hat-trick when Blues beat Newcastle United 5-1, claimed a five-timer for the

Joe Bradford

Football League in a 7-2 victory over the Irish League and notched another treble when Blues lost 7-5 away at Blackburn. In all, he cracked in 17 goals during that month alone!

He found the net in the 1931 FA Cup Final (v West Bromwich Albion) and, he finished up as either top-scorer or joint top scorer for Blues eleven seasons running - 1921-22 to 1932-33. He left St Andrew's in May 1935 to join Bristol City after receiving an emotional send-off from the fans in his farewell game on the last day of that season when Everton won 3-2 on Blues' soil. He later became a publican and also ran a successful shop in Sutton Coldfield. Bradford died in Birmingham in September 1980, aged 79.

BRADFORD CITY

Blues' playing record against the Bantams:

FOOTBALL LEAGUE

Venue	P	W	D	L	F	A
Home	10	6	4	0	13	4
Away	10	3	4	3	10	13
Totals	20	9	8	3	23	17

FA CUP

Venue	P	W	D	L	F	A
Home	1	1	0	0	1	0

WARTIME

Venue	P	W	D	L	F	A
Home	3	2	1	0	8	3
Away	3	2	1	0	7	3
Totals	6	4	2	0	15	6

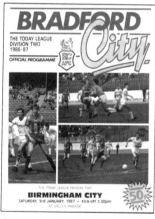

Programme from Bradford-Blues game in January 1987

Bradford City, as Second Division champions, replaced Blues in the top flight for the 1908-09 season.

The first League game between the two clubs took place in April 1922 when Blues won 2-0 in Yorkshire. But then, after completing the double with a 1-0 win at St Andrew's, Blues had to wait 64 years and four months before they met the Bantams again in the Football League! This time they defeated them 2-1, also at home in August 1986, with both goals coming from the former Aston Villa midfielder Dennis Mortimer, one of them a real beauty! The return at Bradford in January ended goalless.

In October 1987 Blues lost 4-0 at Valley Parade and after two draws they gained some revenge with a 1-0 home win in April 1989, courtesy of John Frain's goal.

Blues completed the double over City in 1991-92, winning 2-0 at home and 2-1 away.

When Bradford gained promotion to the Premiership in 1998-99 they won 2-1 at The Pulse Stadium (Valley Parade) but lost by the same score at St Andrew's.

Players with both clubs include: N Blake, K Broadhurst (Bradford trialist), J Conlin, T Farnall, W Gildea, H Graham, S Harland, E Harvey, T Hockey, R Huxford, E Islip, K Leek, JS McMillan, M Newell, I Rankin, A Scriven, C Shutt, B Small, JT Smith, B Squires, P Tomlinson, GB Waddell, WB Walker, R Woolhouse (Blues reserve).

Also: Major Frank Buckley and Jack Peart (Blues players, City managers), Bob Brocklebank (manager of both clubs), Colin Todd (Blues player, City assistant-manager), Ken Oliver (coach with both clubs).

BRADFORD (Park Avenue)

Blues' playing record against Park Avenue:

FOOTBALL LEAGUE

Venue	P	W	D	L	F	A
Home	8	4	1	3	16	11
Away	8	2	2	4	7	19
Totals	16	6	3	7	23	30

FA CUP

Venue	P	W	D	L	F	A
Home	1	1	0	0	6	0
Away	1	0	1	0	2	2
Totals	2	1	1	0	8	2

LEAGUE CUP

Venue	P	W	D	L	F	A
Away	1	1	0	0	1	0

WARTIME

Venue	P	W	D	L	F	A
Home	3	2	0	1	5	2
Away	3	1	1	1	4	4
Totals	6	3	1	2	9	6

Blues lost 5-0 to Park Avenue in March 1910 and 5-1 in December 1913 - both games in Yorkshire.

In May 1947 Blues beat Bradford 4-0 at St Andrew's when Harold Bodle netted twice in front of 23,000 plus spectators.

Seven goals were scored on the same ground six months later when Blues won 4-3, Frank Mitchell slotting home a penalty, and in April 1948 when Blues triumphed 2-1 at Park Avenue, Mitchell again netted from the spot.

This was the last time the teams met at League level, Avenue eventually lost their place in 1970.

The two FA Cup games were played in 1945-46, Blues romping to an easy 8-2 aggregate victory over Park Avenue in a quarter final round tie. Almost 20,000 fans saw the first leg and a crowd of 49,858 packed into St Andrew's for the second when three players, Jock Mulraney, Harold Bodle and Neil Dougall all netted twice.

Players with both clubs include: J Hall (Park Avenue trialist), T Handley, AW Hartwell, HB Houghton, JW Morfitt, K Tewksbury.

BREMNER, Des

Between September 1979 and September 1984, the hard-working midfield play of Des Bremner was always evident in the Villa side. He made 227 League and Cup appearances for the club, scored 10 goals and created several more for his colleagues. After that he gave Blues excellent service, making almost 200 appearances for the St Andrew's club up to August 1989 when he joined Fulham on a free transfer. Later, for three months at the end of that season (March-May 1990) he served Walsall. A Scotsman, born in Aberchider, Kirkcaldy on 7 September 1962, he moved to Villa Park from Hibernian for £250,000 (plus Joe Ward) and won a League Championship medal in 1981 and European Cup and Super Cup prizes soon after. Capped once by Scotland at senior level and nine times by the Under-23s, Bremner assisted Stafford Rangers after Walsall and is the oldest player ever to appear in a League game for the Saddlers: aged 37 years 240 days v Bristol City, May 1990.

- Des Bremner's brother Kevin spent 14 years in football (1978-92). During that time he played for the Scottish side Keith, Colchester United, Blues (1982), Wrexham, Plymouth Argyle, Millwall, Reading, Brighton & Hove Albion, Peterborough United, Shrewsbury Town and Dundee. He scored over 150 goals and in 1982-83 he netted against reading for three different clubs - Wrexham, Plymouth and Millwall. He also served with Colchester and Blues during that same campaign.

Des Bremner

BRENTFORD

Blues' playing record against the Bees:

FOOTBALL LEAGUE

Venue	P	W	D	L	F	A
Home	14	7	3	4	25	13
Away	14	8	2	4	19	15
Totals	28	15	5	8	44	28

FA CUP

Home	1	0	0	1	1	3

LEYLAND DAF TROPHY

Home	1	1	0	0	2	1
Away	1	1	0	0	1	0
Totals	2	2	0	0	3	1

WARTIME

Home	1	1	0	0	1	0
Away	1	0	0	1	1	2
Totals	2	1	0	1	2	2

Blues first met the Bees at League level in season 1935-36 (Division 1). A crowd of 25,000 saw Blues win 2-1 at home and 20,000 attended Griffin Park to witness the return game that Blues again won 1-0.

Seymour Morris scored Blues' first goal after just 45 seconds in their 4-0 home win over the Bees in March 1937 and Frank White notched four goals when Blues eased to a 5-1 victory at St

Andrew's in December 1938.

Peter Murphy scored twice in Blues' 3-1 home victory in December 1952 and on the last day of that season at Griffin Park goals by Jackie lane and Murphy enabled Blues to complete the double with a 2-1 scoreline.

Six different players found the net when Blues beat Brentford 5-1 at home in October 1953 and after the return encounter that season (when the Bees won 2-0 at Griffin Park) it was another 45 years before the next game - a 1-0 victory for Blues in London (September 1989).

Brentford had Kevin Godfrey sent-off after just 10 minutes of the League game at St Andrew's in December 1990 but still beat Blues 2-0. After the game 200 City fans demonstrated after the match with chants of 'Mackay out'.

Mark Ward scored for both sides when Blues beat Brentford 2-1 at Griffin Park in October 1994.

Blues 3-1 aggregate victory over the Bees in the Southern Area Final of the 1990-91 Leyland DAF trophy ensured a trip to Wembley for the first time in 35 years.

In April 1995 a crowd of over 25,000 saw Blues beat the Bees 2-0 at St Andrew's in a vital promotion match. Kevin Francis and Liam Daish netted the goals.

Players with both clubs include: GT Anderson, GE Anderson, D Bailey, J Bloomfield, F Chapple, F Clack, G Cooper, K Dearden, R Fenton, R Ferris (amateur), C Field, N Forster, D Geddis, N Gleghorn, J Goodwin, M Grainger, G Hall (Blues trialist), HE King, W McCafferty, S Marsh, Sam Morris (Blues reserve), A Mulraney (guest), G Parris, FB Pentland (player & coach with Bees), W Quinton, MJ Regan, DT Richards, R Taylor, ET Watkins, D Williams, P Williams.

Programme front from Leyland DAF Trophy Southern Area Final 1st leg.

BRIBERY

In November 1913, prior to Blues' home League game with Grimsby Town, full-back Frank Womack was approached by a man who offered him £55 guineas (£57.75) to help 'fix' the result of the match so that it would end in a draw. Womack immediately informed the club who in turn contacted the police. A trap was set, the culprit arrested and charged and he was later found guilty and given a six-month prison sentence at the local County Assize Court. The game itself finished in a 2-1 win for Grimsby!

BRIDGES, Barry

A sprint champion at School, Barry Bridges carried his athleticism onto the football pitch where he starred as a dashing utility forward for Chelsea after initially acting as understudy to Jimmy

Greaves (he got into the side when Greaves moved to AC Milan). Bridges was transferred to Blues for £55,000 in May 1966 and went on to score 46 goals (some of them beauties) in 104 games in two seasons at St Andrew's, helping Blues reach the semi-final of both the FA Cup and League Cup. He left Blues for Queens Park Rangers in August 1968 and later assisted Millwall (1970), Brighton & Hove Albion (1972), Highlands Park in South Africa, St Patrick's in Ireland, where he was player-manager and Sligo Rovers also as manager, before entering non-League soccer in 1979. He became a hotelier in Brighton after quitting football in the mid 1980s. Born in a village near Norwich in April 1941, Bridges won Youth Cup and League Cup prizes with Chelsea; he gained four England caps at senior level and also represented his country at Schoolboy and youth teams levels as well as playing for the Football League XI. In an excellent career he amassed a fine record of 215 goals in 567 League appearances.

BRIERLEY HILL ALLIANCE

Blues' playing record against the Alliance:
FA CUP

Venue	P	W	D	L	F	A
Home	1	1	0	0	6	2

Fred Wilkes scored a hat-trick in this 1891-92 Cup win by Blues.

Players with both clubs include: W Bidmead, J Glover, JB Higgins, CW Jones, JW Kidd, MA Lane, CH Millington, A Phoenix, G Robertson, A Scriven, AR Smith, HL Turner (Blues reserve), W Wigmore, HR Yarnold (Blues reserve)

BRIGGS, George

Scorer of a goal every three games for Blues (107 in 324 appearances) out-side-right George Briggs was a player at St Andrew's for ten years, from December 1923 until July 1933, when he moved to Plymouth Argyle, later assisting St Austell before retiring in 1937. Born in Wombwell, Yorkshire in May 1903, he joined Blues from non-League club Denaby Main (with Aubrey Scriven in a deal worth £400). A short, stocky red head with great determination he was tried in every forward position before settling down on the right wing. A big favourite with the support-ers, he played in the 1931 FA Cup Final and was one of the best players on that rain-soaked Wembley sur-face. Briggs died in his native Yorkshire.

George Briggs

BRIGGS, Tommy

Tommy Briggs (no relation to George) was a sturdy, well built centre-forward who was one of the finest marksmen in the country during the late 1940s and early 'fifties. Born in Chesterfield in November 1923, he started his career with Plymouth Argyle and after doing extremely well with Grimsby Town (from 1947) he joined Coventry City for close on £20,000 in January 1951. Blues acquired his signature nine months later and he went on to net 23 goals in just 52 outings before leaving St Andrew's for Blackburn Rovers in a £15,000 deal in December 1952. Briggs returned to Blundell Park in March 1958 and after serving as player-manager with Glentoran (1959-61) he left football to work for a radio and TV company in Grimsby where he died in February 1984. Briggs won one England 'B' cap and in all scored 286 League goals in only 390 appearances - a terrific record. He once struck seven goals for Blackburn when they beat Bristol Rovers 8-3 in February 1955 and, in fact, is one of only four players to have notched seven goals in a League game.

BRIGHTON & HOVE ALBION

Brighton drew 1-1 at St Andrew's in May 1983 and here Blues' striker Mick Ferguson is challenged in the air by Albion defenders Steve Walford (left) and Steve Foster.

Blues' playing record against the Seagulls:
FOOTBALL LEAGUE

Venue	P	W	D	L	F	A
Home	7	3	3	1	11	8
Away	7	1	2	4	4	12
Totals	14	4	5	5	15	20

FA CUP

Home	1	1	0	0	3	0
Away	1	0	1	0	0	0
Totals	2	1	1	0	3	0

LEAGUE CUP

Home	1	1	0	0	2	0
Away	2	1	0	1	1	2
Totals	3	2	0	1	3	2

FULL MEMBERS CUP

Away	1	1	0	0	3	0

Blues first met Albion at League level in 1980-81 (Division 1). On 13 September the teams fought out a 2-2 draw at The Goldstone Ground and then in the return fixture at St Andrew's in February Blues won 2-1 with Tony Evans and Alan Curbishley (later to join Brighton) the goalscorers.

In March 1982 Mick Harford scored the only goal of the game at St Andrew's and Tony Rees netted twice when Blues won 2-0 at home in February 1987.

However, Blues' fans will not easily forget the day they saw Brighton win 4-0 at Hove in December 1988.

Leading Albion 2-0 at St Andrew's in April 1995, Blues then had Gary Cooper sent-off for two yellow cards. The Seagulls gained the initiative, dominated the game and took advantage of the extra man to edge in front by 3-2, only for Mark Ward to net a late penalty and so salvage a point for Blues at 3-3.

The last two League Cup encounters were in season 1996-97 when Blues won 2-0 at home and 1-0 away.

And there were under 3,800 fans present when Blues won 3-0 at Hove in the Full Members Cup in October 1986.

Players with both clubs include: A Archer, S Barnes, JW Bradford (Blues reserve), K Bremner, B Bridges, F Buckley, LC Curbishley, M Dennis (Albion trialist), T Evans, M Ferguson, J Hall, WJ Hastings, F Hawley, CG Henderson, FW Hoyland, J James (amateur), A Jones, MA Jones, WH Jones (also Albion trainer), A Kennedy, D Mortimer, P Moulden, IJ Muir, WR Mumford, A Murray, F Okenla (trialist), GM O'Reilly, G Parris, F Pickering (Albion trialist), S Small, S Storer, SE Sykes, F Worthington, WA Wragg.

Also: Freddie Goodwin (manager of both clubs), Willie Bell (Albion player-coach, Blues manager), George Dalton (Blues trainer, Albion player).

BRISTOL CITY

Blues' playing record against the Robins:

FOOTBALL LEAGUE

Venue	P	W	D	L	F	A
Home	23	11	8	4	40	25
Away	23	7	5	11	20	30
Totals	46	18	13	15	60	55

FA CUP

Home	2	2	0	0	5	2

LeagueCup

Home	1	1	0	0	2	1
Away	1	0	1	0	0	0
Totals	2	1	1	0	2	1

ANGLO-SCOTTISH CUP

Home	2	1	0	1	1	4

Blues first met Bristol City at League level in 1902-03 (Division 2). After a 1-1 draw away from home Blues won the return fixture 2-0, both goals coming from Jimmy Windridge.

A First Division match at St Andrew's on the last day of the 1907-08 season (25 April) saw relegated Blues crash to a 4-0 defeat.

At the end of the 1954-55 season Blues left the Second Division for the First while the Robins rose from the Third Division (S) into the Second.

When the teams met again in 1965-66 Bristol completed the double over Blues but revenge was quick and at St Andrew's in October 1966 Blues won 4-0 with Geoff Vowden and Dennis Thwaites among the scorers.

On Boxing Day 1967, a crowd of 40,429 at St Andrew's saw Blues beat City 4-1 to stay on top of the Second Division table.

The Robins came to St Andrew's in January 1990 and won 4-0 - their best victory of the 16 achieved over Blues so far.

Five goals were scored in the first half when Blues beat Bristol City 4-2 in a see-saw match at St Andrew's in November 1998.

Players with both clubs include: W Bennett (Blues reserve), R Blackmore (apprentice), J Bradford, I Brown, T Carter, F Chapple, F Clack, M Cooper, JM De Souza, E Dolan, L Donowa, R Dryden, G Emmanuel, P Fitzpatrick, C Gordon, M Harford, F Hawley, J Hick (Blues reserve), A Johnson, M Kuhl, JH Kearns, J Leonard, FR McGurk, P Mardon, WR Meacock, TJ Morgan, M Prudhoe, D Rennie, A Scriven, C Shutt, B Squires (trialist), G Wallis (Blues reserve).

Also: Frank Barlow, (Robins' assistant manager, Blues coach), Pat Beasley and Terry Cooper (City player-managers, Blues managers), Joe Devlin (Blues player, City scout), Chic Bates (City player, Blues assistant-manager, coach), Peter Doherty (Blues guest, Bristol City manager).

NB - Terry Cooper is Bristol City's oldest-ever player, aged 40 years, 86 days in 1984.

Louie Donowa

BRISTOL ROVERS

Blues' playing record against the Pirates:

FOOTBALL LEAGUE

Venue	P	W	D	L	F	A
Home	6	3	3	0	10	6
Away	6	0	5	1	6	7
Totals	12	3	8	1	16	13

LEAGUE CUP

	P	W	D	L	F	A
Home	2	2	0	0	4	1
Away	3	2	0	1	4	5
Totals	5	4	0	1	8	6

ANGLO-SCOTTISH CUP

	P	W	D	L	F	A
Away	1	0	1	0	1	1

The first League game between Blues and Rovers was played on 17 October 1953 (Division Two) when a crowd of 35,164 at Rovers' Eastville Stadium witnessed a 1-1 draw. Ted Purdon scored for Blues.

The initial encounter at St Andrew's followed on 6 March 1954 when 25,300 fans again saw the teams play out a 1-1 draw. Skipper Len Boyd was on target for Blues on this occasion.

Blues' first win over Rovers was achieved on 25 August 1954 - by 2-1 at St Andrew's when Noel Kinsey and Ken Rowley found the net in front of 26,000 fans.

Steve Claridge scored in both games for Blues in 1994-95 - in the 2-0 home win and in the 1-1 away draw.

Blues beat Rovers in both legs of their League Cup-tie in 1999-2000 - winning 2-0 at home and 1-0 at The Memorial Ground.

Players with both clubs include: D Bailey, J Barratt, S Barrowclough, T Carter, J Daws, R Dryden, G Emmanuel, T Farnall, C Gordon, P Hendrie, CT Jones, J Jones, F Kerns, TJ Morgan, Sam Morris (reserve), G Pendrey, WW Peplow, N Platnauer, E Purdon, J Roach, W Robertson, CJ Russell, MA Smalley, J Smith, WB Stevenson, R Stubbs, MR Thomas, HL Turner (reserve), SP Wallington, H Wassell, FJ Wilcox.

Also: Terry Cooper (Rovers player & manager, Blues manager), Tony Taylor (Rovers player, Blues coach).

BROADHURST, Kevan

Kevan Broadhurst

Kevan Broadhurst gave Blues superb service both as a solid central defender and also as a hard working midfielder. He spent eleven years at St Andrew's, first as an apprentice (from June 1975) and then as a professional (from March 1978). Once he had established himself in the side his performances stood out and he was selected to play for the England under 21 side v Holland in Alkmaar, but the match was postponed through snow and ice and he never got another chance. Sadly, a series of niggling and prolonged knee and ankle injuries forced him to retire prematurely in March 1986 following a brief but interesting loan spell with Walsall. Born in Dewsbury, Yorkshire in June 1959, he had unsuccessful trails with Bradford City before moving to St Andrew's. He scored 10 goals in 173 appearances for Blues to where he returned as youth coach in September 1993 after managing Knowle and playing for Sherwood Celtic. He later stepped up to become assistant-joint manager of Blues just prior to Barry Fry's arrival when he reverted back to youth team coach, combining that position with a playing role for Sherwood Celtic.

BROCKLEBANK, Bob

A former pupil at Woodhouse Secondary School, North Finchley, London, Bob Brocklebank was an excellent pre-war inside-forward with Finchley FC, Middlesex County Boys, Aston Villa (1929-36) and Burnley. He was nicknamed the 'Toff' at Villa Park because of the extent of his education and culture was then something of a rarity among professional footballers. Born the fifth of a family of eight, he managed Birmingham City from October 1949 to October 1954 having previously been in charge at Chesterfield (from 1945). After leaving St Andrew's he became scout-coach with West

Bob Brocklebank

Bromwich Albion (1954-55) and then managed Hull City (1955-61) and Bradford City (1961-64) before retiring to Brixham where he died in September 1981. He took Blues to the 1951 FA Cup semi-final and produced stars like Trevor Smith, Johnny Schofield and Jeff Hall and signed the likes of Eddie Brown, Tommy Briggs, Noel Kinsey, Roy Warhurst, Len Boyd, Gordon Astall and Alex Govan. In fact, it was Brocklebank who built Blues' promotion-winning side of 1955 and the FA Cup Final team of 1956, yet amazingly during his five-year reign as Blues boss he sold, transferred or released practically three full teams!

1. Robertson (to Stoke), Quinton (Brentford), Blake (Gillingham), Dougall (Plymouth), McDonnell (Coventry), Ferris (Worcester), Berry (Manchester United), Brennan (Fulham), Purdon (Sunderland), Capel (Nottingham Forest), Wardle (Barnsley).

2. Robinson (trialist 'keeper), Dorman (Coventry), McKee (Gillingham), Evans (Bournemouth), Duckhouse (Northampton), Smith (Blackburn), Goodwin (Brentford), Daily (Exeter), Briggs (Blackburn), Bodle (Bury), Roberts (Shrewsbury).

3. Quinton (Brentford), Southam (Northampton), Slater (York), Jordan (Sheffield Wednesday), Higgins and O'Hara (Hereford United), Havenga (Luton) and Laing (Watford) plus a number of reserves including Hughes, Sweeney, Lloyd, Kersey, Kernick and Rothwell.

BROWN, Eddie

Eddie Brown

As a youngster Eddie Brown wanted to join the church but he was persuaded not to by a football-mad clergyman and as a result developed into a very useful if somewhat unorthodox centre-forward, going on to have a very interesting professional career which spanned 16 years. Born in Preston in February 1926, Brown - after deciding against the cloth - signed for his home town club at Deepdale in 1948. He switched to Southampton in 1950 and Coventry City in 1952. He left Highfield Road for St Andrew's in October 1954 and went on to score 90 goals in 185 appearances for Blues whom he helped win promotion from the Second Division and reach the 1956 FA Cup Final. A fast raiding striker, extremely mobile and forever dangerous in and around goal, Brown joined Leyton Orient in January 1959 and later assisted Scarborough, Stourbridge, Bedworth (as player-manager) and Wigan Athletic. He finally retired in 1964 and became a schoolteacher and during his ten years as games master at Preston Catholic School he discovered future Liverpool star Mark Lawrenson. Famous for running away and shaking hands with a corner flag after scoring a goal, Brown now describes himself as sublimely retired and enjoys a round of golf twice a week.

BRUCE, Steve

Centre-half Steve Bruce spent two seasons with Blues - June 1996 to July 1998 - making 84 appearances and scoring three goals. All this after he had starred in more than 425 senior games for Manchester United, winning medals galore at Old Trafford, including three Premiership titles, two FA Cup Final victories, two League Cup triumphs and success in the European Cup Winners Cup. Born in Corbridge in December 1960, Bruce started his professional career with Gillingham in 1978 and made over 230 appearances for the Kent club before joining Norwich City in 1984. A further 180 games were added to his impressive with the Canaries before his £800,000 transfer took him to Old Trafford in 1987. On leaving St Andrew's Bruce became player-manager of Sheffield United but in June 1999 he was lured away from Bramall Lane to take over at Huddersfield Town. A terrific competitor in every aspect of defensive play, clearly emphasised by the many scars he has on his head!

BUCKLEY, Alan

Although he spent only one season at St Andrew's (October 1978 to July 1979) striker Alan Buckley clearly showed at times what a fine marksman he was, netting eight goals in 29 appearances for Blues. Born in Mansfield in April 1951, he started out with Nottingham Forest and then gave Walsall splendid service over a number of years, accumulating more than 200 senior goals for the Saddlers in his two spells at Fellows Park either side of his time with Blues. His first commenced in August 1973 and his second ended in 1986 during which time he had twice been team manager (1979-81 and 1982-86).

He left League football for a short while and played for Stourbridge and Tamworth, but then, after managing Kettering Town, he returned to the big time to take over as boss of Grimsby Town (June 1988). At the time of his arrival the Mariners were a struggling Fourth Division side, but Buckley's experience and know-how saw promotion gained to the Second Division in double quick time and as a result he was pulled away from Blundell Park by West Bromwich Albion in 1994. Unfortunately he failed to do the business at the Hawthorns and in May 1997 he rejoined Grimsby Town, leading them to a Wembley double in 1998 when they lifted the Auto Windscreen Shield and clinched promotion by winning the Second Division play-off final before losing his job in 2000.

Alan Buckley

BUCKLEY, Major Franklin Charles

Major Frank Buckley was connected with football for 53 years. One of five brothers, he was born in Urmston, Manchester in November 1882 and soon after leaving School he enlisted in the Army (1898). He served in the Boer War and in the summer of 1903, aged 22, he joined Aston Villa as a defender. Unfortunately he failed to make the grade at Villa Park and in July 1905 moved south to Brighton & Hove Albion. In August 1907 he switched to Manchester United and after a spell with Manchester City he was recruited by Blues (July 1909), He stayed at St Andrew's until to August 1911, making 56 appearances and scoring four goals. He then played for Derby County (until July 1914) and Bradford City (briefly) before retiring as a player towards the end of the First World War, having served with the 17th Middlesex Regiment (known as the Footballers' battalion). He became a Commanding Officer, attaining the rank of Major in 1918.

Whilst with Derby, Buckley gained his only England cap (v Ireland in 1914) having helped County win promotion to the First Division two years earlier. In March 1919, he became manager of Norwich City, retaining that post until May 1920 when he left football briefly to become a Commercial Traveller in London. In July 1923 the Major returned to the game as Blackpool's manager and after four years at Bloomfield Road, he went to Molineux, taking over the manager's hot seat there in June 1927. Over the next seventeen years Buckley transformed Wolves from a mediocre Second Division side into a very useful First Division outfit. They won the Second Division championship in 1932, reached the FA Cup Final in 1939 and won the Wartime League Cup in 1942. He introduced some great players to League football, among them Stan Cullis, Jimmy Mullen, Dennis Westcott and Billy Wright. Buckley left Wolves in March 1944. He managed Hull City for two years (1946-48) and then spent five seasons (to the summer of 1953) as boss of Leeds United, bringing the great John Charles into the football arena. After leaving Elland Road, Buckley managed Walsall until retiring in June 1955. As a player he was an attack-minded centre-half who tackled hard but fair. Known as the 'Iron Major' Buckley was unequivocal, progressive, ambitious and voluble. His ideas were freely communicated to the local and national press. He was totally against the use of the white football and it was he who advocated the numbering of players' jerseys for the benefit of supporters. Buckley died in Walsall on 22 December 1964 - still enjoying his football.

BUMPHREY, Jim

A useful wing-half from Morpeth in Northumberland (born in 1885) Jim Bumphrey scored six goals in 143 appearances for Blues between August 1908 and July 1915, when he returned nearer home to sign for Durham City. He died in Durham

BURKINSHAW, Laurie

Known simply as 'Lol', Burkinshaw was a skilful outside-right who had a good record with Blues - 12 goals in 75 appearances, made between August 1919 and June 1922. Born in Kilnhurst (Sheffield) in December 1893, he played for Mexborough Town, Sheffield Wednesday, Rotherham Town, Kilnhurst FC and Stalybridge Celtic before moving to St Andrew's. He helped Blues win the Second Division championship before transferring to

Laurie Burkinshaw

Halifax Town, later assisting one of his former clubs, Mexborough Town. He guested for Barnsley during the War and died in Mexborough in 1969.

BURNLEY

Blues' playing record against the Clarets:

FOOTBALL LEAGUE

Venue	P	W	D	L	F	A
Home	37	20	6	11	63	44
Away	37	4	9	24	36	76
Totals	74	24	15	35	99	120

FA CUP

Home	2	1	0	1	1	2
Away	2	0	0	2	2	5
Totals	4	1	0	3	3	7

LEAGUE CUP

Away	1	0	0	1	2	3

WARTIME

Home	1	1	0	0	2	0

Blues first met Burnley in the Football League on 13 October 1894. A crowd of 5,000 saw the Lancastrian side win 3-1 at Turf Moor but Blues gained revenge in the return clash at Muntz Street when Fred Wheldon gave them a 1-0 victory.

In February 1910 the joint lowest League attendance at St Andrew's, just 1,000 spectators, saw Blues beat Burnley 2-1 in a Second Division match.

In April 1912, top of the table, Burnley were hammered 4-0 by Blues at St Andrew's in front of 35,000 fans. Centre-forward Arthur Reed scored twice on his Blues debut.

On 27 August 1921, a crowd of 40,000 saw Blues lose 3-2 at home to Burnley in their first Division One game for 13 years. Jack Elkes scored both Blues goals.

When Burnley whipped Blues 7-1 in a League game at St Andrew's in April 1926, their centre-forward Louis Page scored six

Vince Overson

goals - the most by a home or indeed by a visiting player on Blues' territory. Three of his goals (numbers 4, 5 and 6) came inside three minutes during the second half after Dan Tremelling had conceded an own-goal. Page is the only Burnley player to have ever scored a double hat-trick. It was a pity that only 16,616 fans saw this achievement.

This is Blues' joint heaviest home defeat of all time, equalled by West Bromwich Albion in April 1960.

Two-and-a-half years later, in November 1928, Burnley beat Blues 6-3 at Turf Moor and this time Page scored just twice!

After 16 years without meeting each other at League level Burnley inflicted upon Blues their first defeat in seven years when they won 2-0 at St Andrew's on 7 September 1946! Blues also succumbed 1-0 at Turf Moor later in the season.

Blues registered their first win over Burnley for more than 26 years when they triumphed by 2-0 at St Andrew's in December 1956.

In September 1961 Burnley won 6-2 at St Andrew's, making it 11 goals 'against' for Blues in successive home games following their 5-1 defeat at the hands of Leicester a fortnight earlier.

Five months later at Turf Moor Burnley again went to town at Blues' expense, hammering them 7-1 in the return fixture.

The following season (September 1962) Burnley were crushed 5-1 by Blues at St Andrew's. Flame-haired right-winger Mick Hellawell boosted his England prospects with two smartly taken goals as well as having a hand in those scored by Jimmy Bloomfield and Peter Bullock.

For the League game at Turf Moor in October 1971 Blues fielded, for the first time in a senior competitive game, a loan player - full-back Tommy Carroll from Ipswich Town. The result was a 1-1 draw.

In September 1975 Burnley lost 4-0 at St Andrew's and 1-0 at Turf Moor as they slithered into the Second Division and when the teams met again, in December 1979, Frank Worthington played a blinder by scoring both goals in Blues' 2-0 home win.

A crowd of 47,760 saw Burnley beat Blues 3-2 at Turf Moor in a pulsating 6th round FA Cup-tie in March 1935.

The Wartime game between the clubs in September 1939 was a Second Division fixture played before the outbreak of fighting and was subsequently declared null and void.

Players with both clubs include: W Abbott, P Barnes, R Crawshaw, J Devine, L Donowa, N Dougall, R Fenton, J Kelly, J Gallagher, J Gayle, N Gleghorn, B Green, R Hansbury, S Harland, A Leake, JL Loughran, T McMinn, IJ Muir, F Okenla (trialist), V Overson, A Saville, D Sonner, N Whatmore, M Yates.

Also: Bob Brocklebank and Harry Storer (Burnley players, Blues managers), John Bond (manager of both clubs), Chris Woods (Burnley player, Blues coach).

BURNS, Kenny

Scotsman Kenny Burns could play anywhere and often did! He started off as a dominant centre-half but then became a top-notch centre-forward, scoring plenty of goals. He also turned out in midfield, inside-forward, as an emergency full-back and an occasional winger! Born in Glasgow in September 1953, Burns was on Schoolboy forms at Ibrox Park before joining Blues as an apprentice in 1970, turning professional the following year. He stayed at St Andrew's for six more years, netting 53 goals in 204 first team appearances.

He joined Nottingham Forest for £150,000 in July 1977 and was immediately made captain by manager Brian Clough. He then moved to Leeds United for £400,000 in October 1981, switched to Derby County in March 1984 (after two loan spells at the Baseball Ground) and ended his League career in England with Barnsley. He then had a spell in Sweden with IF Elfsborg (1986) before touring the non-League scene with Sutton Town (as player-manager), Stafford Rangers, Grantham Town, Heanor Town, Gainsborough Trinity, Ilkeston Town (player-coach), Oakham United (player-coach) and Telford United (assistant-manager). Capped 20 times by Scotland at senior level and twice by the Under-23s, Burns won the European Cup twice with Forest and also gained League championship and League Cup winners medals during his time at The City Ground under Brian Clough's management. He was voted PFW 'Footballer of the Year' in 1978. On quitting football Burns worked for a furnishing company in Nottingham before becoming a publican in Stoke-on-Trent in the mid-1990s.

Kenny Burns

BURTON SWIFTS

Blues' playing record against the Swifts:

FOOTBALL LEAGUE

Venue	P	W	D	L	F	A
Home	7	6	0	1	20	7
Away	7	6	1	0	20	6
Totals	14	12	1	1	40	13

FA CUP

Venue	P	W	D	L	F	A
Home	1	1	0	0	4	2

FOOTBALL ALLIANCE

Venue	P	W	D	L	F	A
Home	1	1	0	0	3	1
Away	1	0	0	1	3	6
Totals	2	1	0	1	6	7

Defender Edwin Jolly starred on the wing for Blues, scoring twice and making two more goals when they beat the Swifts 6-1 at Muntz Street in a Second Division game in September 1893

BURTON UNITED

Blues' playing record against United:

FOOTBALL LEAGUE

Venue	P	W	D	L	F	A
Home	1	1	0	0	2	0
Away	1	1	0	0	1	0
Totals	2	2	0	0	3	0

These two League games were played in 1902-02 - and Bob McRoberts scored Blues' winning goal at Burton.

Players with both clubs include: J Preston, A Tinkler, S Webb

BURTON WANDERERS

Blues' playing record against the Wanderers:

FOOTBALL LEAGUE

Venue	P	W	D	L	F	A
Home	1	1	0	0	3	2
Away	1	1	0	0	6	2
Totals	2	2	0	0	9	4

FA CUP

Venue	P	W	D	L	F	A
Home	3	3	0	0	20	3
Away	1	0	1	0	1	1
Totals	4	3	1	0	21	4

Walter Gadsby scored two goals, had a third disallowed and laid on one for his colleague when making his debut for Blues in a 6-2 win at Burton in February 1897. Two weeks later Blues won the return fixture 3-2 to complete the double.

Blues whipped the Wanderers 9-2 and then 9-0 in home FA Cup ties in the 1880s. In the second game both Ted and Will Devey scored fourtimers, while Stanley netted four goals in the 9-2 victory.

Players with both clubs include: A Archer, E Devey, W Devey, J Preston

BURY

Blues' playing record against the Shakers:

FOOTBALL LEAGUE

Venue	P	W	D	L	F	A
Home	32	16	5	11	50	39
Away	32	10	4	18	36	54
Totals	64	26	9	29	86	93

FA CUP

Venue	P	W	D	L	F	A
Home	2	0	1	1	4	7
Away	1	0	0	1	0	2
Totals	3	0	1	2	4	9

LEAGUE CUP

Venue	P	W	D	L	F	A
Home	1	1	0	0	3	2
Away	1	0	1	0	1	1
Totals	2	1	1	0	4	3

Blues first met the Shakers at League level in season 1895-96 and what a cracking game it was! A crowd of 6,000 at Bury saw Blues win 5-4 with both Fred Wheldon and Jack Jones scoring twice. Blues also won their home game that season by 1-0 to complete the double.

Blues' 5-0 home victory over Bury in October 1904 turned out to be their best in the League that season.

Blues' last League game - and indeed their last win - at Muntz

Street was against Bury on 22 December 1906. A crowd of 10,000 saw the 3-1 victory.

By coincidence Blues' first League defeat at St Andrew's was at the hands of Bury on 16 September 1907, the Shakers winning 1-0.

Over the Christmas period of 1914 Blues again completed the double over Bury by winning 1-0 at home and 3-1 away. They repeated that feat in 1920-21 with a 1-0 success at Gigg Lane followed a week later by a resounding 4-0 victory at St Andrew's when Johnny Crosbie netted twice.

George Briggs found the net twice when Blues won 4-1 at home in April 1925 and it was two-goal Joe Bradford who earned Blues a couple of 3-2 wins at Bury in March 1928 and at St Andrew's twelve months later.

There was no action in the 1930s, but in December 1946 Blues beat the Shakers 3-0 in a mud-bath at St Andrew's. Ted Duckhouse, Neil Dougall and George Edwards were the scorers that day.

When Jeff Hall made his League debut for Blues in the 3-3 draw at home to Bury on 20 January 1951, he conceded a first-half penalty (scored by Billy Griffiths). Blues got a spot-kick themselves in the 55th minute, netted by Cyril Trigg. Ex-Brummie star Harold Bodle scored Bury's first goal.

On 18 December 1965 Ronnie Fenton became the first substitute to score for Blues in a League game, doing so against Bury in a 4-0 win at St Andrew's. Goalkeeper Jim Herriot was the player he replaced!

Blues beat Bury 4-2 at Gigg Lane in December 1998 with Paul Furlong scoring twice.

The bad weather that gripped Britain during the winter of the

Billy Rudd

45

1962-63 season caused the postponement of the Blues-Bury 3rd round FA Cup tie no fewer than 14 times and there was also one abandonment as well before Blues eventually went out of the competition after a replay.

Blues' 4-3 aggregate League Cup semi-final win over Bury in 1963 took them through to the Final.

In 1962-63 Blues met Bury four times in cup football.

Players with both clubs include: J Acquaroff (Blues guest), P Barnes, J Beckford, H Bodle, W Bradbury, F Carrodus, J Cringan (trialist), JM De Souza, G Farrell, J Firth, P Fitzpatrick, A Godden, P Howard, D Howitt, FW Hoyland, J Kelly, DB Latchford, T Matthewson, J Paskin, W Rudd, B Small, W Smith, D Sonner, G Taylor, D Wassall, JM Williams.

Also: Dan Tremelling (Blues player, Bury assistant-trainer), Jeff Wealands (Bury coach)

CALDERWOOD, Jimmy

Converted from a creative midfielder into a useful overlapping right-back Scotsman Jimmy Calderwood scored five goals in 159 appearances for Blues during his nine years at St Andrew's. Born in Glasgow in February 1955, he joined Blues' groundstaff in the summer of 1971 and signed professional forms the following year. A loan spell with Cambridge United preceded his departure from the club in July 1980. Later played in Holland with Willem II, Roda JC, SC Heracles, Den Ham and SC Cambuur as well as being assistant-manager of FC Zwolle and Leewaardon. He retired as a player in 1990. Calderwood gained one Under-23 cap for his country.

CALLADINE, Charlie

Born in Derbyshire in January 1911, wing-half Charlie Calladine was signed by Blues from Scunthorpe United in May 1930 on the platform of Doncaster railway station. Described as being quick and cunning, he made 127 senior appearances for Blues (four goals scored) before transferring to Blackburn Rovers in February 1936. He later assisted Guildford City before retiring during the Second World War. He died in Matlock in October 1983.

CAMBRIDGE UNITED

Blues' playing record against United:

FOOTBALL LEAGUE

Venue	P	W	D	L	F	A
Home	4	1	1	2	2	6
Away	4	2	0	2	5	3
Totals	8	3	1	4	7	9

ANGLO-ITALIAN CUP

Home	1	0	1	0	3	3

LEYLAND DAF TROPHY

Home	1	1	0	0	3	1

The first time Blues met United was in season 1979-80 (Division 2). They won 1-0 at home (Steve Lynex on target) but lost 2-1 away.

After winning 1-0 at Cambridge in August 1990 (thanks to a Nigel Gleghorn goal) Blues then lost the return fixture 3-0 at St Andrew's five months later.

A crowd of 9,429 saw Blues beat United 3-1 at St Andrew's in the Southern Area semi-final of the Leyland DAF Trophy in 1990-91 to set up a two-legged Area Final clash with Brentford.

Just over 3,000 hardy supporters witnessed the six-goal thriller in the Anglo-Italian Cup at St Andrew's in September 1992.

Steve Claridge

On Boxing Day 1994 a best of season crowd at St Andrew's of 20,098 saw Blues held to a 1-1 draw by United in a League game.

Players with both clubs include: I Atkins (United player-manager), K Bowker, G Bull, J Calderwood, S Claridge, L Daish, K Dearden, R Hansbury, J Hunt, R McDonough, G Poole, D Preece, G Rowett, M Sale, GS Scott.

Also: Ian Atkins (Blues player, United manager), Lil Fuccillo (United player, Blues coach).

CAMKIN, W.A. 'Bill'

Bill Camkin was handed the title of honorary managing-Director of Birmingham (City) football club in September 1939, a position he held unopposed until November 1944 (with the last few years also seeing him acting as the club's secretary). Together with trainer George Blackburn (the former Aston Villa player) he oversaw quite a successful period in Blues' history. The team did very well in Regional League and Cup matches under his guidance. After Ted Goodier had succeeded him as team boss he remained on the Board before ill-health forced him into retirement in 1952. His son, John was a well-known journalist who later became a Director with Coventry City. The Camkin Cup competition was introduced for local Midland clubs in the 1950s.

CAMPBELL, Alan

Alan Campbell

When Scottish midfielder Alan Campbell was on song so too were Blues! With his long black hair, he was the hub of the engine-room and besides grafting hard and long he also had the knack of finding space from where he created and scored some excellent goals. Born in Arbroath in January 1948, he moved south to join Charlton Athletic in 1964, turning professional at The Valley early in 1965. Blues signed him in October 1970 and he spent five-and-a-half years at St Andrew's during which time he scored 14 goals in 210 senior appearances, helping the club win the Second Division title in 1972. In March 1976 he switched to Cardiff City and later played for Carlisle United before returning to the Midlands to assist Redditch United, Olton Royal and Highgate United, the latter as assistant-manager (1989-90).

CAPTAINS

Steve Bruce

Full-back Ned Barkas skippered Blues to their first Wembley Cup Final in 1931. Right-half Len Boyd followed him 25 years later, but it was centre-half Trevor Smith who was the first skipper to lift a major prize for the club, doing so after Aston Villa had been defeated in the two-legged League Cup Final of 1963.

Vince Overson walked up the 39 steps to Wembley's Royal Box to receive the Leyland DAF trophy after Blues' 3-2 win over Tranmere Rovers in 1991 and skippering the side to victory in the Auto-Windscreen Shield Final at the same venue in 1995 was Irishman Liam Daish.

In 1969-70 defender Garry Pendrey became the club's youngest skipper in major League and Cup competitions at the age of 20 years, six months.

Over the years several other players have had the honour of being captain of Birmingham City football club, among them (in A-Z order) Gary Ablett (1990s), Steve Bruce, Frank Buckley (1910-11), Kenny Burns, Liam Daish (1990s), Don Dearson, Will Devey (1888-91), Billy Edmunds (the club's first official team captain in 1875), Joe Gallagher, Archie Gemmill, Ken Green, Stan Harland, Fred Harris (the club's first post Second World War captain), Terry

Garry Pendrey was only 20 when he captained Blues

Hennessey, Arthur James (1878-85), Caesar Jenkyns, Howard Kendall, George Liddell, Alec McClure (who skippered both the first and second teams), Ray Martin, Dick Neal, Billy Ollis, Vince Overson, Malcolm Page, Garry Pendrey, Dai Richards (late 1930s), Colin Todd, Tony Towers, Cyril Trigg, Roy Warhurst, Johnny Watts and Ron Wylie (FA Cup semi-final in 1968).

● Walter Green regularly captained Blues' second XI during the 1880s.

Liam Daish (right) skippering Blues against Oldham Athletic at Boundary Park in December 1995. The Latics' captain is Ian Snodin and the referee Steve Baines (ex-Walsall).

47

CARDIFF CITY

Blues' playing record against the Bluebirds:

FOOTBALL LEAGUE

Venue	P	W	D	L	F	A
Home	27	15	8	4	42	23
Away	27	9	2	16	30	43
Totals	54	24	10	20	72	66

FA CUP

Venue	P	W	D	L	F	A
Home	1	1	0	0	5	2

WARTIME

Venue	P	W	D	L	F	A
Home	1	1	0	0	3	2
Away	1	0	0	1	2	5
Totals	2	1	0	1	5	7

The first game between Blues and Cardiff ended in a 2-1 home victory for the Welsh side in September 1920.

Blues' goalkeeper Dan Tremelling saved a 70th minute penalty taken by Cardiff City's usual reliable Len Davies in a crucial First Division League game at St Andrew's in May 1924. Cardiff had to win this last match of the season by any score to become champions. They could only draw 0-0 and so missed out on capturing the title by 0.024 of a goal, Huddersfield Town retaining the trophy.

Blues' first League win over Cardiff finally arrived in September 1924 when they triumphed 2-1 at St Andrew's, Joe Bradford scoring twice.

As FA Cup holders Cardiff doubled up over Blues in 1927-28 but

George Hicks scored two splendid goals against Cardiff in 1928.

Blues quickly gained revenge with a 4-1 victory at Ninian Park in December 1928 when George Hicks struck home two beauties.

A vital promotion clash in April 1948 attracted a crowd of 52,880 to St Andrew's where Blues beat Cardiff 2-0 - on their way to the Second Division championship.

In season 1951-52 Blues and Cardiff again battled it out hammer and tongue for promotion from the Second Division. This time it was the Welsh side who eventually got there, pipping Blues for the runners-up spot on goal-average, both teams finishing on 51 points, two behind the champions Sheffield Wednesday.

Ken Leek scored twice on his senior debut for Blues in a 3-0 home win over Cardiff City in December 1961.

As usual Stan Lynn buried a penalty when Blues beat Cardiff 4-2 at home in November 1965 and later in the season at Ninian Park, Geoff Vowden's two goals earned Blues a 3-1 victory and the double over the Welsh side.

Trevor Francis made his Football League debut for Blues as a substitute against Cardiff on 5 September 1970 at Ninian Park. Blues lost 2-0.

In the return fixture that season Francis was on target in Blues 2-1 win at st Andrew's.

Blues completed the double over Cardiff in season 1979-80 (Division 2), winning both matches by 2-1.

When Blues won 1-0 at Ninian Park on 28 December 1994 it was their sixth successive victory on the road. Ricky Otto scored the only goal.

Blues' 5-2 third round FA Cup win over the Bluebirds was in January 1974 when the two 'Bobs' Hatton and Latchford each scored twice in front of 22,435 fans at St Andrew's.

Players with both clubs include: J Bowen, JH Burton, A Campbell, J Cornforth, E Curtis, S Davies, G Edwards (also Director of Cardiff), A Evans, SJ Evans, G Farrell, R Hansbury, P Harding, R Hatton, D Hill, G Johnston, RE Keating, N Kinsey, A Legg, S Lynex, AA Millard, E Newton, N Platnauer, H Riley, I Rodgerson, W Ronson, A Saville, G Smith, SJ Smith (CC junior), K Summerfield, W Thirlaway, MR Thomas, J Vincent.

Also: Albert Lindon (Blues player, Cardiff scout), Fred Davies (Cardiff goalkeeper, Blues coach), Joan Hill (Commercial side of both clubs).

CARLISLE UNITED

Blues' playing record against the Cumbrians:

FOOTBALL LEAGUE

Venue	P	W	D	L	F	A
Home	9	6	1	2	16	9
Away	9	2	2	5	13	15
Totals	18	8	3	7	29	24

FA CUP

Venue	P	W	D	L	F	A
Home	1	1	0	0	4	0
Away	1	0	1	0	3	3
Totals	2	1	1	0	7	3

AUTO WINDSCREEN SHIELD

Venue	P	W	D	L	F	A
Neutral	1	1	0	0	1	0

The first time Blues and Carlisle met in the Football League was in season 1965-66 (Division 2). United won 1-0 at Brunton Park but Blues gained revenge with a 2-1 victory at St Andrew's when almost 15,000 fans saw Geoff Vowden and Malcolm Beard find the net in a 2-1 victory.

The following season United completed the double over Blues

and took three of the four points at stake in 1967-68 before Blues came good with a couple of wins in 1968-69, 3-2 away and 3-0 at home. Jimmy Greenhoff scored in both matches.

Blues played United in the First Division in 1974-75. They lost 1-0 at Brunton Park but won the return game 2-1 at St Andrew's when Trevor Francis and Kenny Burns found the net.

A record crowd at Brunton Park of 27,445 saw Blues draw 3-3 with United in a thrilling third round FA Cup-tie in January 1956. The home side came back from 3-1 down to earn a replay with hat-trick hero Alf Ackerman netting twice in the 84th and 88th minutes to stun Blues. Amazingly 56,000 spectators packed to see the replay - first FA Cup encounter under the St Andrew's floodlights. Blues won in style by 4-0 with Eddie Brown scoring twice.

Paul Tait's dramatic 103rd minute sudden death goal at Wembley in April 1995 gave Blues victory in the Auto Windscreen Shield Final over United in front of 76,663 spectators, around 40,000 of them supporting Barry Fry's men.

Players with both clubs include: J Bass, A Campbell, T Carter, AR Elliott, P Fitzpatrick, P Gorman, M Halsall, S Harland, R Hatton, RE Keating, R Knight, K Lowe, H Powell, M Prudhoe, GR Russell, CG Spencer (Blues reserve), W Wright.

Also associated: Ian Atkins (Blues player & assistant-manager, Carlisle manager).

CARROLL, Tommy

Capped by the Republic of Ireland on 17 occasions, Tommy Carroll was a footballing right-back and the first loan-signing to play for Blues at senior level. A steady, efficient player, he always tried to play his way out of defence rather than hoof the ball aimlessly downfield. Born in Dublin in August 1942, he played for Shelbourne in the European Cup and European Cup Winners Cup competitions and gained an Irish League championship medal in 1962. He then served with Cambridge City and Ipswich Town (126

Tommy Carroll in action against Millwall in 1968.

appearances) before joining Blues, initially on loan in October 1971, signing permanently the following month. Unfortunately after just 47 games for Blues he was forced to quit the game through injury in October 1973. Later, after returning to Ireland, he spent a short time in prison.

CELTIC

The Scottish giants Celtic have visited St Andrew's on three occasions.

Firstly they travelled down from Glasgow for a friendly match in March 1939 and in front of 6,000 fans were well beaten by relegation-threatened Blues 6-1, Charlie Wilson Jones scoring a hat-trick.

Their second visit was in November 1975 when they played Blues in the club's Centenary Match. A crowd of 14,670 saw Peter Withe score the only goal of the game to give Blues a 1-0 win.

And in July 1995 the Bhoys travelled south again for a pre-season friendly bringing with them 5,000 fans to boost the crowd to 11,381. Blues won by the same scoreline with Ian Muir on target 10 minutes after half-time.

Players with both clubs include: R Auld, P Hendrie (Celtic amateur), A Mulraney (Celtic junior).

Also: Lou Macari (Celtic player and manager of both clubs).

CHAMPIONSHIPS (see also Football League & Wartime)

Eleven members of Blues' Second Division championship winning squad in 1954-55
back row, left to right: T Smith, G Merrick, J Lane, R Warhurst, K Green.
Front row: G Astall, J Hall, L Boyd, P Murphy, A Govan, N Kinsey.

Blues have won six League championships, but as yet they have still to capture England's top prize!

Five of their successes so far have been achieved in the 'old' Division Two.

In season 1892-93 they had a point to spare over Sheffield United (36-35) after beating Ardwick (now Manchester City) 3-2 in the final match. But alas Blues lost one and drew one of two Test matches against Newton Heath (now Manchester United) and so missed out on promotion.

In 1920-21, after an end-of-season unbeaten run of eight matches, they edged out Cardiff City on goal-average (79-38 against 59-32) to climb into the First Division after both teams had chalked up 58 points.

In 1947-48, the championship was won by a margin of three points from runners-up Newcastle United, Blues obtaining 59 to United's 56.

In season 1954-55, under Arthur Turner's management, Blues' impressive goal-average of 92-47 gave them the edge over runners-up Luton Town and third-placed Rotherham United, all three teams having amassed 54 points. Blues clinched the title with an impressive 5-1 win at Doncaster on the final day of the campaign.

When winning the Second Division championship in 1994-95, Blues totalled 89 points (their highest tally ever). When the final curtain came down they had a four point lead over second-placed Brentford.

Blues' other 'championship' came in 1945-46 when they won the Football League (South) Division, pipping arch rivals Aston Villa on goal-average: 96-45 against 106-58. Both teams totalled 61 points.

CHAPLIN

The Reverend Ken Hawkins was the official Chaplin of Birmingham City football club in the 1990s.

CHARLTON ATHLETIC

Blues' playing record against the Addicks:

FOOTBALL LEAGUE

Venue	P	W	D	L	F	A
Home	22	13	6	3	33	18
Away	22	2	7	13	18	35
Totals	44	15	13	16	51	53

FA CUP

Home	1	1	0	0	1	0
Away	1	0	0	1	2	3

WARTIME

Home	1	1	0	0	1	0
Away	1	0	1	0	0	0
Totals	2	1	1	0	1	0

Blues first met Charlton in the Football League in September 1936 at The Valley (Division 1). A crowd of 35,000 that day witnessed the 2-2 draw. Four months later Charlton won 2-1 at St Andrew's.

A total of 15 goals were scored in the two Football League games involving Blues and Charlton in season 1938-39. The clash at The Valley ended in a 4-4 draw after Charlton had led 3-0 after half-an-hour. Fred Harris scored twice for Blues. The fixture at St Andrew's (on 4 February) saw Charlton win 4-3 despite a Fred Harris hat-trick on this occasion. Blues were 2-0 and 3-1 in front before the Addicks stormed back to take the points.

This was to remain Charlton's only League success at St Andrew's for some 57 years - until amazingly they won by the same score (4-3) in January 1996.

In February 1956 Eddie Brown netted a hat-trick in Blues' 4-0 home win over Athletic.

Charlton were relegated to the Second Division at the end of the 1956-57 campaign but they still managed to beat Blues 1-0 at The Valley!

Recommencing League duties in 1965-66, a crowd of 15,331 saw the 2-2 draw at St Andrew's, while 13,722 were present to see Charlton win 2-1 in London.

Blues won successive home League games by 4-0 over the Addicks - in November 1966 (two goals for Geoff Vowden) and in

May 1968 (two for Barry Bridges). It was 3-0 to Blues at St Andrew's in January 1970 and 4-1 on the same ground in September 1971 when Bob Latchford claimed a hat-trick.

Colin Todd was sent-off and Archie Gemmill scored the all-important goal when Blues beat Charlton 1-0 at The Valley in January 1980.

Blues and Charlton beat one another 2-1 in their respective home matches in 1984-85 and on the last day of the 1992-93 season a goal by Paul Moulden earned Blues three vital points as they beat Charlton 1-0 in front of 22,234 fans at St Andrew's. This victory kept Blues in the First Division!

And by coincidence Blues' opening match of the 1993-94 League programme took them to Charlton where they lost 1-0.

Blues needed to beat Charlton at home in the last League game of the 1997-98 season to secure a place in the end-of-season promotion play-offs. They drew 0-0, allowing Sheffield United to claim sixth and final spot.

Blues' FA Cup win over the Addicks was at St Andrew's in a fourth round tie in January 1934. Over 30,000 fans saw George Morrall score the all-important goal with eight minutes remaining.

Only 821 spectators saw the Charlton-Blues Full Members Cup encounter at Selhurst Park in November 1986 (the lowest for a competitive Blues game home or away since 1914).

In a transitional Wartime game between Blues and Charlton at St Andrew's in February 1946, Sam Bartram, the Londoners' goalkeeper, came up to take - and miss - a penalty (the ball hit the bar) and he had to race back towards his own goal as Blues launched a counter-attack. Blues won the game 1-0, Wilson Jones the scorer.

Players with both clubs include: D Bailey, S Bartram (Blues guest), G Breen (Charlton junior), A Campbell, A Curbishley (later Athletic manager), JM De Souza, M Hicks, M Jackson, AE Lindon (Athletic player-manager), J McDonough, DJ Madden, AA Millard, A Mulraney (guest), R Otto, G Poole, GS Scott, ET Watkins, C Whyte, P Williams.

Also: Joe Mallett and Ron Saunders (Charlton players, Blues managers).

Alan Curbishley

CHARSLEY, Chris

Goalkeeper Chris Charsley remained an amateur throughout his career and was the first Blues player to win a full cap - lining up for England against Ireland in February 1893, when his side romped to a 6-1 win. Born in Leicester in November 1864, he played for Stafford Rangers and guested for Aston Villa before joining Blues for the first of three separate spells in September 1886 (the others followed in December 1891 and December 1893-May 1894). He made a total of 83 appearances for Blues, helping them win the Second Division title in 1892-93. Tall and slim with a safe pair of hands and strong right-footed kick, he also served with West Bromwich Albion as well as being a policeman, later becoming Chief Constable of Coventry (August 1899). After retiring from the force in 1918 he moved to Weston-Super-Mare where he was elected to the town's council, taking over as deputy Lord Mayor in 1939-40, remaining in office until his death in January 1945.

- Chris's brother Walter Charsley made three first team appearances for Blues as a wing-half in the 1890-91 season.

CHELMSFORD CITY

Blues beat non-League Chelmsford 6-0 at St Andrew's in a 4th round FA Cup tie in January 1939. A crowd of 44,494 saw Fred Harris and Owen Madden both net twice that afternoon.

Former Blues forward Stan Davies was Chelmsford's trainer from April 1938 until May 1931.

Players with both clubs include: I Brown, S Davies (player & trainer Chelmsford), W Foster, C Phillips.

Also associated: Nigel Spink (City goalkeeper, Blues coach).

CHELSEA

Alex Govan (right) playing for Blues against Chelsea at Stamford Bridge in 1956

Blues' playing record against the Londoners:

FOOTBALL LEAGUE

Venue	P	W	D	L	F	A
Home	34	13	9	12	62	57
Away	34	6	10	18	39	63
Totals	68	19	19	30	101	120

FA CUP

Home	3	2	1	0	5	2
Away	5	3	0	2	8	4
Totals	8	5	1	2	13	6

LEAGUE CUP

Home	2	0	0	2	0	4

WARTIME

Home	1	1	0	0	5	2
Away	1	1	0	0	3	2
Totals	2	2	0	0	8	4

The first time Blues met Chelsea in the Football League was in season 1907-08 (Division 1). Both games finished level - 1-1 at St Andrew's and 2-2 at Stamford Bridge.

Blues' first win over the Pensioners followed in March 1911, when they triumphed 2-1 at home in front of 25,000 supporters.

Two goals apiece for Jack Elkes and Jack Whitehouse helped Blues to a 5-1 home League win over Chelsea in September 1921.

Nine years later (in 1930-31) Blues and Chelsea met four times (twice in the League, twice in the FA Cup).

At League level Blues won 6-2 at home but lost 1-0 in London, while in the Cup after a 2-2 draw at St Andrew's Blues went to Stamford Bridge for the 6th round replay and triumphed 3-0 in front of an amazing mid-week afternoon crowd of 74,365.

In April 1932 all Blues' goals in their 4-0 home win over Chelsea were scored by different players and five players shared the six goals when Chelsea beat Blues 4-2 at Stamford Bridge seven months later.

When Blues were relegated in the last pre-war season (1938-39) both League games with Chelsea were drawn but the teams met after the hostilities (1948-49) each won their home game, Blues by 1-0 thanks to Jackie Stewart's fine effort.

Chelsea won both matches by 3-0 in 1949-50 and when Blues came back into the top flight for the 1955-56 campaign they completed the double over the reigning League champions, winning 3-0 at home and 2-1 in London.

Chelsea romped to a 5-1 home win in August 1957 (two goals here for Jimmy Greaves) but in then return game at St Andrew's the scoreline ended all square at 3-3, Peter Murphy netting twice for Blues.

A year later, two goals by Johnny Gordon helped Blues to a 4-1 home win.

In November 1964 Blues were crushed at home by Chelsea 6-1 - their worst ever defeat at the hands of the London club for whom George Graham notched a hat-trick!

Nine goals were scored in the Blues-Chelsea League game at St Andrew's in December 1977. The Londoners finally won 5-4 despite two fine goals by Trevor Francis.

Both Blues and Chelsea were strong promotion candidates in 1979-80 and in the game at St Andrew's the Londoners were thrashed 5-1 as Blues produced their best attacking performance of the season to leap to the top of the Second Division table.

The last League game between the clubs took place at Stamford Bridge in April 1989 when Blues lost 3-1 in front of almost 14,800 fans.

Peter Bonetti, Chelsea's goalkeeper preparing to gather a high cross during the FA Cup-tie against Blues at St Andrew's in 1968.

Almost 46,000 fans saw Blues win a 5th round FA Cup-tie by 4-0 at Stamford Bridge in February 1953. The South African striker Ted Purdon scored twice.

A terrific 63rd minute goal by Fred Pickering was enough to beat Chelsea in the 6th round of the FA Cup at St Andrew's in March 1968. A capacity crowd of 52,500 saw the tie, realising record gate receipts of £14,400.

Players with both clubs include: J Argue (Blues reserve), T Aylott, E Barkas, M Bodley, B Bridges, M Dennis (Chelsea boys), K Downing (Chelsea trialist), P Furlong, A Godden, R Gregg, G Hall (Blues trialist), M Harford, A Hateley, WM Hughes, R McDonough, R McRoberts, F Mitchell, A Mulraney (guest), A Murray, E Newton, J Robertson, WH Robertson, AC Robinson, SJ Smith, D Speedie), J Windridge.

Also: Leslie Knighton (manager of both clubs), Peter Bonetti (Chelsea goalkeeper, Blues coach).

CHELTENHAM TOWN

A 58th minute goal by Simon Sturridge gave Blues a 1-0 home win over non-League Cheltenham Town in a first round FA Cup tie in November 1990. A crowd of under 8,000 saw Dean Williams (deputising for Martin Thomas) play a blinder in goal to 'save' Blues from defeat!

Blues beat Cheltenham 4-0 in a pre-season friendly in July 2000. Geoff Horsfield scored his first goal for the club in this game.

Players with both clubs include: J Crisp (Blues reserve), JM De Souza, W Finney, M Fox, DB Latchford, J Leonard, P Shearer, MR Thomas, WJ Wheeler, M Yates.

CHESTER CITY

Blues' playing record against Chester:
FOOTBALL LEAGUE

Venue	P	W	D	L	F	A
Home	4	3	1	0	5	2
Away	4	3	0	1	6	4
Totals	8	6	1	1	11	6

The first time Blues met Chester at League level was on 17 October 1989 when they crashed to a humiliating 4-0 defeat at Sealand Road in a Third Division contest, all the goals coming in the second-half. The meagre crowd of just 1,882 was the lowest to watch a Blues League match, at home or away, for 75 years - since September 1914 when barely 500 fans witnessed a Second Division tussle with Glossop.

When Blues beat Chester 1-0 at Moss Rose in November 1990 Nigel Gleghorn took over in goal from the injured Martin Thomas. Robert Hopkins scored the 87th minute winner that day in front of just 2,237 fans.

In November 1994 a Jonathan Hunt hat-trick helped Blues to an easy 5-0 home win over Chester and a month later that scoreline was almost repeated as Blues won 4-0 at The Deva Stadium in front of almost 4,000 fans. And this was Blues' ninth successive game without conceding a goal.

Robert Hopkins scored the only goal of the game to give Blues their first win over Chester at Macclesfield's Moss Rose ground the following season.

Players with both clubs include: I Atkins, F Barber, K Bertschin, H Fletcher (reserve), S Fox, W Horsman, K Langley, HH Lappin,

WR Meacock & T Neale (Blues reserves), W Smith, DP Weston, W Wright.

Also: Billy Hughes (Blues player, Chester scout), Doug Ellis (Chester junior, Blues Director).

CHESTERFIELD

Blues' playing record against the Spire-ites:

FOOTBALL LEAGUE

Venue	P	W	D	L	F	A
Home	7	4	3	0	12	5
Away	7	2	4	1	9	7
Totals	14	6	7	1	21	12

LEAGUE CUP

	P	W	D	L	F	A
Home	1	1	0	0	2	1
Away	1	0	1	0	1	1
Totals	2	1	1	0	3	2

WARTIME

	P	W	D	L	F	A
Home	1	0	1	0	2	2
Away	2	1	1	0	4	1
Totals	3	1	2	0	6	3

On 16 September 1899 Blues and Chesterfield met for the first time at League level - and Blues came out on top, winning a tremendous game 5-3 at Muntz Street in front of 8,000 spectators. Billy Bennett scored twice for Blues.

After losing 4-2 at The Recreation Ground in December 1908, just under 1,500 spectators attended Blues' return game with Chesterfield in April 1909 - one of the lowest crowds ever to assemble at St Andrew's. Blues won the game 3-0 with Arthur Mounteney claiming a hat-trick.

The last time Blues met Chesterfield in the League was in February 1951 when a near 35,000 crowd at St Andrew's saw Bob Brocklebank's Brummies win 2-1 with goals by Cyril Trigg and Jimmy Higgins.

Earlier that season Blues had drawn 1-1 at Chesterfield.

Players with both clubs include: K Bannister, P Barnes, W Beer, A Bloxham, F Bowden, T Capel, H Clutterbuck, J Crosbie, J Devine, W Halsall, G Haywood, P Ivey, R Martin, D Massart, T Neale (Blues reserve), S Ottewell, SE Phillips, H Powell, H Roberts, P Robinson, TE Robinson, F Sharp, C Thompson (Blues reserve), R Willis, WA Wragg, HR Yarnold (reserve).

Also: Bob Brocklebank (manager of both clubs), Paul Hart (Blues player, Chesterfield manager), Billy Harvey (Blues player & assistant-secretary, Chesterfield secretary-manager), Frank Barlow (Chesterfield player, Blues assistant-manager/coach), Charlie Elliott (Blues guest, Chesterfield player).

CHILDS, Gary

Childs was an England youth international midfielder who had a very useful playing career which saw him serve with three West Midlands clubs - West Bromwich Albion, Walsall and Blues - and also with Grimsby Town. He was born in Birmingham in April 1964 and went to The Hawthorns straight from School, turning professional in 1982. He switched to Fellows Park for £15,000 in 1983 and after over 150 appearances for the Saddlers signed for Blues for £50,000 in 1987. He did well at St Andrew's, scoring twice in 62 outings before ending his Football League career at Blundell Park, teaming up with the Mariners on a free transfer in July 1989. Under the managership of former Blues player Alan Buckley

Childs helped Grimsby rise from the Fourth to the Second Division in double-quick time while amassing in excess of 250 senior appearances for the Cleethorpes club. He did, however, have the tendency not to 'get stuck in' when the going got tough and was often criticised for this both at St Andrew's and at Blundell Park. Nevertheless, a useful footballer who later went into non-League soccer.

CHIRK

Billy Walton scored a hat-trick when Blues beat the Welsh non-League side Chirk 8-0 in an FA Cup first qualifying round tie at Muntz Street in October 1898.

Player with both clubs: S Davies

CHRISTMAS DAY

Peter Murphy - scored for Blues in their last League game on Christmas Day v Sheffield Wednesday in 1956.

Blues have played a total of 44 matches on Christmas Day. The first was in 1885, the last in 1956.

Here are the details of Blues' Festive Day fixtures:

1886	Mitchell v St George (H) 0-3
1889	Alliance v Birmingham St George (A) 1-4
1891	Friendly v Aston Villa (H) 0-3
1895	Division 2 v Walsall (H) 3-3
1896	Division 2 v Darwen (H) 5-1
1904	Division 1 v Middlesbrough (A) 0-1

1905   Division 1 v Manchester City (A) 0-1
1906   Division 1 v Manchester City (H) 2-1
1907   Division 2 v Stockport County (H) 4-2
1908   Division 2 v Glossop (A) 1-4
1910   Division 2 v Hull City (A) 0-4
1911   Division 2 v Barnsley (H) 3-1
1912   Division 2 v Glossop (H) 6-0
1913   Division 2 v Bury (H) 1-0
1916   Wartime PL v Sheffield Wednesday (A) 2-0
1917   Wartime PL v Leicester Fosse (H) 0-0
1918   Wartime PL v Leicester Fosse (H) 0-2
1919   Division 2 v Leicester City (A) 0-1
1920   Division 2 v West Ham United (A) 1-1
1921   Division 1 v Huddersfield Town (H) 0-0
1923   Division 1 v Arsenal (H) 2-1
1924   Division 1 v Tottenham Hotspur (H) 3-1
1925   Division 1 v West Ham United (A) 0-1
1928   Division 1 v Bolton Wanderers (H) 0-2
1928   Division 1 v Manchester United (A) 0-0
1929   Division 1 v Leeds United (H) 1-0
1930   Division 1 v West Bromwich Albion (A) 1-0
1933   Division 1 v Sheffield United (A) 1-2
1933   Division 1 v Sheffield Wednesday (A) 1-2
1934   Division 1 v Grimsby Town (A) 0-1
1935   Division 1 v Sunderland (H) 2-0
1940   Wartime FL v Walsall (A) 0-3
1942   Wartime FL v Wolverhampton Wds. (H) 1-0
1943   Wartime FL v Wolverhampton Wds. (A) 0-3
1945   Wartime FL v Leicester City (H) 6-2
1946   Division 2 v Swansea Town (H) 3-1
1947   Division 2 v Millwall (A) 0-0
1948   Division 2 v Newcastle United (H) 2-0
1950   Division 2 v Manchester City (A) 1-3
1950   Division 2 v Rotherham United (H) 4-0
1951   Division 2 v Plymouth Argyle (H) 4-0
1952   Division 2 v Notts County (H) 3-0
1953   Division 2 v Nottingham Forest (H) 0-1
1956   Division 1 v Sheffield Wednesday (H) 4-0

SUMMARY

P	W	D	L	F	A
44	20	6	18	68	55

CHRISTMAS DAY FACTS

- The First Christmas Day game at St Andrew's was attended by 20,000 fans who saw Blues beat Manchester City 2-1 in 1907.
- Fred Chapple scored all four goals when Blues beat Stockport at St Andrew's in 1908.
- Joe Bradford netted a hat-trick when Blues beat Spurs in 1925.
- A crowd of 42,000 - the best for a Christmas Day fixture at St Andrew's - saw Cyril Trigg and Harry Roberts give Blues a 2-0 win over Newcastle in 1948.
- Trigg netted a hat-trick against Walsall in the Wartime game in 1940. Guest Jack Rowley netted four times for the Saddlers.
- All five Blues forwards found the net in the 6-2 win over Leicester in 1945.
- The last Christmas Day game played by Blues in 1956 attracted a 24,380 crowd to St Andrew's where Eddie Brown, Peter Murphy, Gordon Astall and Alex Govan found the net in a 4-0 win over Sheffield Wednesday.

CLARIDGE, Steve

Steve Claridge driving in another shot!

A nomadic footballer, but a very good one, striker Steve Claridge began his playing career with non-League Fareham Town in 1982. Two years later he joined Bournemouth and then commenced his journey 'round the country' playing in turn for Weymouth, Crystal Palace (1988), Aldershot, Cambridge United (1990), Luton Town (signed for £160,000 in 1992), Cambridge United (again), Blues (bought for £350,000 in January 1994 and sold for £1.2 million in March 1996), Leicester City, Portsmouth (on loan), Wolves (on loan) and Portsmouth (permanently in August 1998 for £200,000). His often scruffy appearance, with socks seemingly always rolled down round his ankles, certainly belied the skill in his feet. He was exceptionally good on the ball, and despite having 13 different striking partners in 1994-95, he scored 42 goals in 120 outings for Blues, helping them win the Second Division title and Leyland DAF Trophy in 1995. He scored the dramatic 120th minute play-off winning goal against his old club Crystal Palace that took Leicester into the Premiership in 1996 and then a year later netted an extra-time winner for the Foxes in the Coca-Cola League Cup Final against Middlesbrough. During the course of the 1999-2000 season Claridge reached the personal milestone of 550 appearances at club level (over 160 goals scored).

- This is what Claridge said on leaving Cambridge United: "I knew I couldn't take anymore when, one day in training, a player shouted 'feet' meaning that's where he wanted the ball - and he was punished by being made to do 40 press-ups."
- Also during his time at The Abbey Stadium, Claridge was picked up by the police - for drunkenness! What happened is simple: One morning Claridge went out of the house to attend a training session having eaten just a bowl of corn flakes quite quickly! Feeling somewhat peckish, he called in at a local café for a fry-

up and a couple of chocolate bars. When he finally arrived at the ground his stomach was rumbling ten-fold, prompting him to pop into the nearest corner shop for some more chocolate. When training ended around 12.30pm - after some strenuous hill climbing - Claridge's stomach was churning over like nobody's business with eggs, bacon, beans and chocolates doing the rounds inside his body! He flaked out, totally exhausted in the back of the team's mini bus. A few hours later he got out, still feeling rather groggy, and started to walk around the Cambridge streets. A few residents thought him unfit to continue and called the police. They duly arrived on the scene....detained a wobbly-looking Claridge for what they thought was drunkeness. But thankfully no action was taken after the truth came out in more ways than one!

CLARKE, Wayne

Wayne Clarke, playing for Blues against West Bromwich Albion at snowbound St Andrew's in February 1986.

A former England Schoolboy and youth international and West Midlands representative player, Clarke was born in Willenhall in February 1961. A natural goal-poacher, like his three brothers Allan, Derek and Frank, he joined Wolves as a 15 year-old and turned professional in March 1978. He was transferred from Molineux to Blues for £80,000 in August 1984 and after scoring 43 goals in 105 games he left St Andrew's in March 1987 to join Everton for £500,000. Whilst at Goodison Park he gained a League Championship medal, but when Tony Cottee arrived at the club Clarke quickly departed to Leicester City in July 1989 for

£500,000. In January 1990 he moved to Manchester City and after loan spells with Shrewsbury Town, Stoke City and Wolves, he quit Maine Road to team up with Walsall (August 1992). He gave the Saddlers excellent service before returning to Shrewsbury for two seasons from July 1993. On pulling out of senior soccer he joined non-League Telford United as player-manager in August 1995, resigning his position in November 1996. All told Clarke, who suffered relegation with Wolves in 1984 and Blues in 1986, netted over 130 goals in more than 500 League appearances in an exceptionally fine career. In 1999 it was postman Clarke!

CLARKSON, Ian

Ian Clarkson - born in Solihull in December 1970 - was a very capable full-back who joined Blues on YTS forms in 1987, turning professional in December the following year. He went on to appear in 172 senior games during his five-year spell at St Andrew's before transferring to Stoke City for £50,000 in September 1993. He later played for Northampton Town (from August 1996). He won a Freight Rover Trophy medal with Blues in 1991.

CLEAN SHEETS

Goalkeeper Ian Bennett holds Blues' club record for most clean sheets in a League season - 21 - achieved in 1997-98.

He set the previous record of 19 in 1994-95 when he also remained unbeaten in seven consecutive matches.

Gil Merrick with 18 clean sheets in 1946-47, Dan Tremelling with 17 in 1919-20, Jeff Wealands, also with 17 in 1979-80 and Merrick (again) with 16 in 1948-49 have also done the business between the posts.

CLUB NAME

Originally called Small Heath Alliance (from the autumn of 1875), the name Alliance was dropped on 24 July 1888, leaving the club simply as Small Heath. The name was changed to Birmingham on 25 March 1905 and then City was added to Birmingham (to make Birmingham City Football Club) in the summer of 1943 (and not 1945 as previously thought). The official Blues home programmes for the 1943-44 season clearly show Birmingham City Football Club on the front cover.

COACHES
(masseurs, physiotherapists, trainers)

Among the scores of coaches employed over the years by Blues there have been several former players, not only having served for Blues but also for other clubs as well.

Here are some of the coaces/trainers/physiotherapists/masseurs who have been associated with the club: Ian Atkins, Jack Badham (former Blues player), Frank Barlow, Chic Bates (ex-Shrewsbury Town), Willie Bell (later Blues manager), George Blackburn (ex-Aston Villa forward), Norman Bodell (assistant-manager/coach), Ian Bowyer, Keith Bradley (ex-Aston Villa), Kevan Broadhurst, Tony Brown (West Bromwich Albion's record goalscorer and appearance-maker), Brian Caswell (ex-Walsall player), George Dalton (ex-Newcastle United player), former Wolves goalkeeper Fred Davies, Ray Devey (a former Blues player), Jack Eccles (trainer at St Andrew's either side of the Great War), Len Evans

(Blues' assistant-trainer 1934-35), Dave Fairhurst (once of Newcastle United and England who spent 15 years as a trainer at St Andrew's), Bobby Ferguson, Ken Fish, George Foster, Lil Fuccillo, Billy George (former Aston Villa goalkeeper), Bill Gibson (late 1930s trainer), Emilio Aldecoa Gomez (one-time Spanish international, trainer/coach), Harry Hampton (coach, 1934), Paul Heath, Peter Henderson, David Howells (under Barry Fry), Derek Jefferson, R Johnson, Tom Jones, Mike Kelly (ex-goalkeeper), Bill Kendrick, former striker Bob Latchford (coach in 1999-2000), Keith Leonard, Abvel Lowe (fitness coach), Neil McDiamond, John McMillan, Joe Mallett (assistant-manager & trainer/coach), Mick Mills, Trevor Morgan, Peter Murphy (albeit briefly in 1959), Ollie Norman (1890s West Bromwich Albion player), Ken Oliver, George Penfield (trainer 1886-87), John Pryce (appointed July 2000), Ray Shaw, Sid Scholey, Bill Shorthouse (1950s Wolves defender), Charlie Simms (who spent most 30 years on the Blues staff), Edwin Stein (with Barry Fry), Archie Taylor (1931 FA Cup Final trainer), Tony Taylor (late 1990s), ex-Blues goalkeeper Dan Tremelling, Kevin Walters (physio), Mark Ward (player-coach), Sid Wharton, physio Jim Williams and Alex Wilson (the first team trainer when Blues reached the 1956 FA Cup Final) and Chris Woods (goalkeeping coach).

Brian Ecstick was Director of Coaching at St Andrew's in 1999-2000.

● Since 1995 former Blues defender Pat Wright has organised soccer camps, academies and tours (abroad) for clubs, youth centres and schools from his Great Barr home in Birmingham - registered under Peershardy Soccer School & Academies 1995.

Mick Mills

Dave Fairhurst

COLCHESTER UNITED

Blues' playing record against the U's:

FA CUP

Venue	P	W	D	L	F	A
Away	1	1	0	0	2	0

LEAGUE CUP

	P	W	D	L	F	A
Home	1	1	0	0	2	1
Away	1	0	1	0	1	1
Totals	2	1	1	0	3	2

Blues' FA Cup win over the 'U's' was achieved in December 1989 at Layer Road, Nigel Gleghorn scoring both goals in front of 3,858 spectators.

The two League Cup encounters were staged in 1970-71 - the season Colchester United won the Watney Cup.

No League action yet!

Players with both clubs include: I Atkins (player-manager United), F Barber, D Barnett, J Birch, K Bremner, I Brown, P Bullock, J Cheesewright, M Ferguson, A Godden, J Hagan, R Hansbury, R Hopkins, JR Linford, R McDonough, S McGavin, TJ Morgan, I Rankin, JH Southam (United guest), S Whitton (player-manager United), M Yates.

Also: Jim Smith (United player-manager, Blues manager), Jimmy Allen (Blues guest, United manager: 1948-53), Mick Mills (United manager, Blues assistant-manager).

COLDWELL, Bill

Chief Scout Bill Coldwell acted as caretaker-manager of Blues for approximately three months - from June to August 1991 - following the departure of Lou Macari and before the appointment of Terry Cooper.

He did well in getting the majority of the senior players to re-sign for the club....in the end only defender and team captain Vince Overson decided against it (he moved to Stoke City).

COLOGNE SELECT

Blues met the German select side over two legs in a first round Inter Cities Fairs Cup tie in October/November 1958.

The first match in Germany ended in a 2-2 draw in front of 12,000 spectators, Dick Neal and Harry Hooper scoring for Blues.

For the return encounter the turn out was 20,266 and this time Blues won 2-0 (4-2 on aggregate) with strikes from Bunny Larkin and Brian Taylor.

COLOURS

When Blues (as Small Heath Alliance) first started to play football the club colours were dark blue shirts with a white sash and white shorts.

In 1883-84 they changed to wearing plain blue shirts and white shorts and in 1889-90 turned out in black shirts with gold colour and cuffs and white shorts.

The very next season (1890-91) the Blues players donned light blue shirts with a dark blue trim and white shorts and this design was to stay until 1914-15 when royal blue shirts with a central white 'V' replaced were introduced.

This held firm until 1927-28 when a plain royal blue shirt and white shorts came into being.

During the 1930s and '40s, Blues wore traditional white collared shirts with a button-up neckline, although before the War the colour blue was a fraction lighter than it was during the forties.

In the early to mid-1950s the club retained the blue shirt, white collar, white shorts design but in 1957-58 the 'V' neck was introduced - and remained so until 1963 when the round neck took over (Blues still wearing white shorts).

In 1965 the large white band round the neckline disappeared, to be replaced soon afterwards by a much thinner one when Blues also donned matching blue shorts. But it was back to plain blue shirts in 1968-69 (with blue shorts) and this theme continued until 1971 when the first penguin strip was seen.

In 1975 it was back to blue shirts with a white collar and white

Blues' players showing off the club's new kit in 1992-93.

shorts. The round neck was seen again in 1977 but in 1980 it was replaced with a 'V'.

A slight change in the overall design was effected during the early '80s (red socks were seen and there was a thin white strip visible on the shirt in 1984-85). A touch of red was forthcoming in the 1985-86 season (on the shoulder line) and in 1986-87 (for the very first time) Blues' shirts had a white band across the chest with white foldovers on the socks. Occasionally they also played in a lighter blue shirt with a dark blue band across the chest plus dark blue shorts.

In 1989-90 (under Dave Mackay) and with Mark One flashing across the front, the shirts comprised two broad flashes on each shoulder but it was soon done away with and back to blue shirts, white collars and cuffs and white shorts as the 1990s arrived.

A patterned blue shirt was seen in 1992-93 and a distinctive design on the sleeves appeared the following season before it was back to a traditional blue shirt with a small tucked in white band under the chin for the Barry Fry era. Then, when Trevor Francis came back to St Andrew's, Blues switched to a similar penguin-design shirt (like Francis and his colleagues wore in the early '70s) with a white body, blue sleeves and neckline and white shorts.

However it was back to blue shirts with white trimmings in 1997-98 and thereafter it has been a more plainer design with a designer-strip down each arm.

Blues' change strips over the years, have varied considerably with players wearing matching white shirts and shorts to white shirts and black shorts, all red, black and red halved shirts, red and black stripes with black (and sometimes white) shorts, all yellow, yellow shirts with black shorts, blue and yellow shirts and yellow shorts and even a green and yellow combination.

The blue shirt though, always stands out and one suspects that it will be Birmingham City's main colour for the next 125 years!
- When Blues played Crystal Palace at Selhurst Park in April 1967 they had to wear tangerine shirts!
- Shortly after the Second World War Aston Villa loaned Blues' home shirts for an FA Cup-tie against Burnley - and some Villa supporters refused to attend the match!

COMMERCIAL MANAGERS

The following have all held the position of either Commercial Manager or Promotions Manager of Birmingham City FC (listed in order of service): David Exall (first CM, appointed, 1968-69), Dennis Gilbert, Geoff Greaves (early 1970s), Dennis Shaw (mid/late 1970s), Des Blee, Ernie Adkins, Allan Robson, Joan Hill, David Teague, Mark Bowler and Simon Bradley.

Annie Bassett was the club's Chief Executive in the early 1990s.

CONNOLLY, John

A tall winger with excellent ball skills, Connolly scored nine goals in 63 appearances for Blues during his two seasons at St

Andrew's. A Scotsman, born in Barrhead, a suburb of Glasgow in June 1950, he became a professional with Perth club St Johnstone in 1968 and joined Everton four years later, switching to Blues in September 1976. Connolly then surprisingly left the club for Newcastle United in May 1978 and later assisted Hibernian, Gateshead (two spells) and Blyth Spartans (as player-manager) before becoming coach at Ayr United. He gained a Scottish League Cup runners-up medal with St Johnstone in 1970 and helped Hibs win the Scottish First Division title in 1981. He appeared in one full and two Under-23 internationals for his country

John Connolly

CONSECUTIVE LEAGUE SEQUENCE

- Longest sequence of wins: 13 from December 1892 to September 1893
- Longest sequence of defeats: 8 (achieved three times) from December 1922 to February 1923; from December 1978 to February 1979 and from September to November 1985
- Longest sequence of draws: 8 between mid-September and late October 1990 (five of them 1-1)
- Longest unbeaten run: 20 matches from 3 September 1994 to 2 January 1995 inclusive (previous best 18 in 1971-72).
- Longest unbeaten run from start of a season: 15 matches in 1900-01, followed by 12 in 1990-91.
- Longest unbeaten home run: 36 matches from 20 October 1970 to 15 April 1972 (Division 2).
- Longest unbeaten away run: 15 games between 13 December 1947 and 4 September 1948 (Divisions 1 & 2).
- Longest run of successive away defeats: 18 from 16 September 1978 to 1 May 1979 (Division 1). This is a Football League record for the longest run in any ONE season.
- Longest sequence without a win 17 matches between September 1985 and January 1986.
- Longest unbeaten home run: 36 matches from September 1970 to April 1972.
- Longest sequence of away wins: nine from 2 January to 18 September 1897. This is the joint second longest run in Football League history (shared with Doncaster Rovers). Tottenham lead with 10.
- Longest sequence without a home win: 11 matches, 1962-63
- Longest sequence with an away defeat: 15 matches, 1947-48
- Longest sequence without achieving an away win: 32 matches, 1980-82
- Longest sequence without a home win: 17 matches, 1902-03
- Longest sequence without an away win: 9 in 1897.
- Blues have remained unbeaten at home in a League season on three occasions - in 1892-93, 1902-03 (when they won all 17 matches) and 1971-72.
- Blues had suffered 11 consecutive League defeats (home & away) at the hands of Nottingham Forest (up to April 2000) when the Reds won at St Andrew's.

COOPER, Terry

A popular appointment as Blues manager in August 1991, the former Leeds United and England left-back succeeded Lou Macari in the hot seat at St Andrew's and he remained in office until December 1993 when he was replaced by Barry Fry. Cooper, who also became a Director at St Andrew's, guided Blues to promotion from Division Three in his first full season with the club, but after a close shave the following term when relegation was avoided by the skin of their teeth, he lost his job in favour of Fry. Born in Castleford in July 1944. Cooper spent 14 years at Elland Road (1961-75) making over 350 appearances, gaining League championship, League Cup and two Fairs Cup winners' medals plus runners-up prizes in the FA Cup and Fairs Cup. He scored only one goal in his career - the winner for Leeds in the 1968 League Cup Final v Arsenal. Cooper was capped 20 times by his country and on leaving Elland Road he joined Middlesbrough, later playing for and then managing Bristol City, acting as player-coach of Bristol Rovers, assisting Doncaster Rovers briefly in 1981-82 and manag-

Terry Cooper

ing Exeter City (before moving to St Andrew's). He got Bristol City promoted to Division Three in 1984 and led Exeter to the Fourth Division title in 1990. He returned to manage the Grecians for a second time in January 1994, staying at St James' Park until June 1995 when he was replaced by the former Stoke City goalkeeper Peter Fox.

Cooper's son, Mark scored five goals in 44 games for Blues between September 1991 and November 1992.

CORBETT, Walter

Capped by England on 18 occasions at amateur level and three times by the seniors, full-back Walter Corbett always carried a handkerchief in his withered left hand after suffering polio as a young lad. His career spanned twelve years (1904-15 inclusive) during which time he played exclusively as an amateur for Aston Villa (whose reserve team he helped win the Birmingham & District League title three seasons running), Blues (from July 1907 to June 1911 - making 48 first XI appearances) and Wellington Town. He also guested for Queens Park Rangers, skippered the Birmingham & District junior side against Scotland in 1905, toured with a joint amateur and professional party in 1906 (partnering Bob Crompton) and in 1908 won an Olympic soccer gold medal for Great Britain. Earlier in his life Corbett won four scholarships and played an occasional game of rugby. He became an expert linguist and was head of the Birmingham City Transport wages department during the Second World War.

Born in Wellington, Shropshire in November 1880, Corbett, a gentleman both on and off the field, died in Birmingham in 1955, shortly before his 75th birthday.

CORINTHIANS

On 7 January 1922 Blues played the famous amateur side the Corinthians in a friendly at St Andrew's. A crowd of 5,000 saw a rather one-sided contest end in 5-0 win for Blues, Harry Deacon (2), Jack Maker (2) and George Getgood the scorers.

In March 1925 the Corinthians returned to St Andrew's for a second time and on this occasion they were defeated 3-0

A further two friendly matches took place in March and April 1926. Blues lost 1-0 in London, but won the return fixture at St Andrew's by the same score, Joe Bradford the marksman this time.

CORK ATHLETIC

Blues beat Cork 5-2 in Ireland in a Festival of Britain game in May 1951. Cyril Trigg scored two of his side's goals that day in front of just 2,750 spectators.

Associated with both clubs: O Madden (Blues player, Cork player-manager)

COTON, Tony

Goalkeeper Tony Coton saved a penalty on his League debut for Blues against Sunderland at St Andrew's in December 1980, helping his side win the match 3-2. He went on to appear in a total of 114 senior games for the club before transferring to Watford for £330,000 in September 1984. He left Vicarage Road in a £1 million transaction for Manchester City in July 1990 (having been voted Hornets' Player of the Year on three occasions). He later played for City's arch-rivals Manchester United before joining Sunderland. But sadly he broke his leg in five places in 1997 while playing against Southampton in October 1997 and that was the end of his career. After retiring he became a coach. Born in Tamworth in May 1961, Coton (a Villa trialist) was spotted by Blues playing for Mile Oak Rovers and after serving his apprenticeship at St Andrew's he signed professional forms in October 1979. He was capped once by England at 'B' team level.

Tony Coton

In 1999-2000 Coton was appointed goalkeeping coach at Old Trafford.

COVENTRY CHARITY CUP FINAL (Lord Ma

In 1925-26 Blues and Coventry City played out a 2-2 draw in the Final of the Lord Mayor of Coventry Charity Cup Final. Each side held the trophy for six months.

COVENTRY CITY (Singers FC)

Blues' playing record against the Sky Blues:
FOOTBALL LEAGUE

Venue	P	W	D	L	F	A
Home	20	9	7	4	33	20
Away	20	7	5	8	27	28
Totals	40	16	12	12	60	48

FACUP

Home	1	1	0	0	5	1

LEAGUE CUP

Home	2	1	0	1	2	2
Away	1	0	1	0	1	1
Totals	3	1	1	1	3	3

FOOTBALL JUBILEE

Away	2	0	0	2	0	5

WARTIME

Home	12	6	1	5	22	15
Away	11	5	3	3	18	14
Totals	23	11	4	8	40	29

The first League meeting between Blues and City was on 13 September 1919. Blues won 4-1 at St Andrew's and a week later completed the double with a 3-1 victory at Highfield Road. Albert Millard scored twice in each game for Blues.

The following season (1920-21) Blues again did the double over

Coventry - on their way to winning the Second Division championship.

The first League match after the Second World War ended goalless at Coventry in October 1946 (Division 2). Blues won the return fixture 2-0 with both goals coming from Cyril Trigg.

A brilliant goalkeeping display by Gil Merrick and a 70th minute strike by Walter Aveyard gave Blues a 1-0 win at Coventry in August 1947 in front of 30,465 fans.

Blues lost a cracking Second Division match by 4-3 at Highfield Road in April 1966 when all seven goals came from different players. The attendance was just over 27,000.

Coventry climbed out of the Second Division (with Wolves) in 1966-67 but they couldn't beat Blues, both games ending in 1-1 draws.

The first-ever League meeting of the two 'Blues' in League Division One took place in October 1972 and again it finished 0-0 at Highfield Road. Blues were successful by 3-0 at St Andrew's five months later when Bob Hatton, Bob Latchford and Gordon Taylor found the net in front of 34,775 fans.

They were 3-2 victors at St Andrew's and comfortable 4-0 winners at Highfield Road.

When Blues lost 3-2 at Highfield Road in November 1975 (Division 1) Coventry had Donal Murphy sent-off.

Blues opened the 1980-81 season with a 3-1 home League win over Coventry, Alan Curbishley scoring twice, and on the same ground the following season (Boxing Day 1981) Tony Evans netted twice as Blues were held to a 3-3 draw at St Andrew's.

On 16 February 1986 - Blues' first ever competitive game on a Sunday - eight goals were scored in a thrilling 4-4 draw at Highfield Road. Andy Kennedy scored twice for Blues while both Dave Bennett and Kevin Kilcline (both penalties) did likewise for Coventry. The crowd, however, was a poor one, just 14,271.

Over 40,000 fans saw Fred Harris score a hat-trick in Blues' emphatic 5-1 home win over the Sky Blues in a third round FA Cup-tie in January 1935.

Coventry beat Blues 2-0 and 3-0 in two Jubilee Fund matches at Highfield Road in August 1938 and 1939.

Premiership side Coventry knocked Blues out of the League Cup in 1996-97, winning 1-0 at St Andrew's after a 1-1 draw at Highfield Road.

Peter Ndlovu is Coventry City's most capped player, winning over 30 caps for Zimbabwe before transferring to Blues.

Players with both clubs include: G Allen (CC amateur), HJ Bates, J Blyth, F Bowden, T Bowen (Blues reserve), S Bowser (Blues trialist), W Bradbury, G Breen, T Briggs, E Brown, J Brown, D Burrows, T Capel, A Chaplin, W Clark, R Craythorne (Blues reserve), J Crisp (Blues reserve), E Curtis, L Daish, G Daly, D Dearson, D Dorman, N Dougall (CC guest), J Dougherty, G Downs, K Drinkell, H Edwards, W Edwards, RO Evans, M Ferguson, P Furlong, J Gayle, J Godfrey, J Hagan, M Harford, A Hateley, F Hawley, W Holmes, W Hunter, L Jenkinson, JH Kearns, RD Latchford, A Leake, AE Lindon, A McClure, M McDonnell, A McIntosh, C Marsden, AA Millard, F Mitchell (CC amateur), F Mobley, WA Morgan, D Mortimer, P Murphy, P Ndlovu, N Platnauer, H Powell, J Randle, D Rennie, BL Roberts (also CC coach), AC Robinson, K Rowley, L Sealey (Blues N/C), P Shearer (CC junior), AH Sheldon & AR Smith (Blues reserves), B Smith, D Smith, W Smith, D Speedie, S Sutton, CH Tickle, C Trigg (CC trialist), HL Turner (reserve), WB Walker, S Whitton, C Whyte, R Woolhouse (Blues reserve).

Also: Harry Storer (manager of both clubs), Mick Mills (assistant-manager at both clubs), Joe Barratt, Caesar Jenkyns, Mike Kelly, Garry Pendrey & Ron Wylie (all Blues players and Coventry coaches), Charlie Elliott (Blues guest, Coventry player, scout & caretaker-manager), George Dalton (Blues coach, Coventry physio).

Peter Ndlovu

CREWE ALEXANDRA

Blues' playing record against the Alex:

FOOTBALL LEAGUE

Venue	P	W	D	L	F	A
Home	8	7	2	1	28	6
Away	8	4	3	1	17	9
Totals	16	11	5	2	45	15

FA CUP

	P	W	D	L	F	A
Away	1	1	0	0	2	1

LEAGUE CUP

	P	W	D	L	F	A
Away	1	0	0	1	1	2

FOOTBALL ALLIANCE

	P	W	D	L	F	A
Home	3	2	0	1	7	6
Away	3	1	0	2	6	12
Totals	6	3	0	3	13	18

In their last Football Alliance match Blues beat Crewe Alexandra 2-0 away on 20 April 1892.

Six months later, in October 1892, the first League meeting between the clubs ended in a 6-0 victory for Blues when all the goals came from different players. Blues achieved the double over the 'Alex' this season with a 3-1 win at Crewe.

The following season (1893-94) Blues scored 11 goals against the Alex. They won 6-1 at Muntz Street on 6 December and 6-3 at

Crewe on 13 January. Billy Walton, Frank Mobley and Tommy Hands scored in both games.

It was to be over 95 years before the teams met at League level again - and when they did - on 19 August 1989 - Blues continued where they had left off by winning 3-0 at St Andrew's, doubling up with a 2-0 success at Gresty Road in January 1990.

Jonathan Hunt's hat-trick in a 5-0 home win over Crewe in November 1994 was the first 'treble' by a Blues player in League football for nine and a half years - since David Geddis did the job in April 1985 against Portsmouth.

Over 24,000 fans saw five different players score for Blues when Crewe were beaten 5-0 at St Andrew's in August 1999.

Blues' FA Cup win at Crewe came in the third round in January 1998 (Paul Furlong scoring twice) while their League Cup defeat came 24 years earlier in September 1974.

Players with both clubs include: D Adebola, WA Bennett, A Box, H Butler, F Chapple, H Deakin, R Ferris, W Finney (Alex amateur), W Foster, A Goldie, J Greenhoff, FC Hodges, DWL Jones, JW Jones, HE King, T Lees, M McCarrick, M McDonnell, M Newell, M Regan, J Rothwell (Blues reserve), D Rowbottom, SJ Smith, P Tait, A Turner, R Warhurst.

Also: Arthur Turner (manager of both clubs), Ted Goodier (Alex player, Blues manager), Norman Bodell (Blues coach, scout, Alex player).

CRICKETING-FOOTBALLERS

Here is a list of Blues players and managers who were also very good cricketers in their own right at various levels:
- Alonzo Drake (Yorkshire all-rounder 1909-14 who played in 157 first-class matches, scored 4,816 runs for an average of 21.69 and took 480 wickets at 18 runs each. A left-hander, he twice scored 1,000 runs and took 100 wickets in a season and his best bowling return was 10-35 against Somerset).
- Charlie Elliott (Blues Wartime guest) scored over 11,000 runs for Derbyshire and became a test match umpire.
- Robert Owen Evans played for Derbyshire CCC.
- Arthur Foster (Warwickshire wicket-keeper)
- Freddie Goodwin (Lancashire second XI mainly)
- Bill Harvey (played for Warwickshire and Border Province, South Africa).
- Mike Hellawell (one County match for Warwickshire).
- Jack Higgins (middle-order batsmen and left-arm spinner with Worcestershire: 1912-30. In 121 matches, 223 innings, he scored 4.149 runs - average 19.57, And took a total of 30 wickets at 53.72. His best return was 5-72. He also took 59 catches).
- Stan Lazaridis played for the same side in Perth as Australian Test bowler Bruce Reid.
- Frank Mitchell (wanted to play Test Match cricket for Australia rather than become a professional footballer. He played 17 times for Warwickshire, 1946-48, taking 22 wickets for an average of almost 39. He also had trials with Kent and assisted both Cornwall and Hertfordshire).
- Arthur Mounteney (spent 13 years as a middle-order batsman for Leicestershire, scoring 5,306 runs, average 20.8).
- Gil Merrick was an excellent club cricketer who ran the Blues cricket side for many years.
- Ted Purdon (played in his home country of South Africa at a high standard and was 12th man for Warwickshire on one occasion).
- Dai Richards (played intermediate cricket in South Wales and the

Midlands for over 25 years).
- Harry Storer (played for Derbyshire: 1920-36, amassing 13,513 runs for an average of 27.63 - 18 centuries. He also took over 200 wickets and won a County Championship medal in 1936).
- Arthur Turner (scored five centuries for Silverdale cricket club).
- Fred Wheldon (played seven years for Worcestershire: 1899-1906. He notched almost 5,000 runs in 138 matches for an average of 22.54. He scored three centuries, took 95 catches, some as a wicketkeeper and was an occasional right-arm spin bowler who also played for the Carmarthenshire CC).
- Jimmy Windridge (played in seven matches for Warwickshire, scoring a total of 161 runs and taking 1-13 with the ball).
- Frank Womack (regular player in the Birmingham, Nottinghamshire and Leicestershire intermediate Leagues).
- Joe Barratt was a useful club cricketer who had trials for Warwickshire in the 1920s.
- Billy Guest was a very efficient cricketer in the Birmingham League with Moseley during the 1930s/40s.
- Mark Dennis and Keith Bertschin were also keen cricketers in their own right.

CRINGAN, Jimmy

Jimmy Cringan was a fine wing-half, a tenacious tackler, a battler to the end, who was also Blues' deputy goalkeeper! He scored 12 goals in 285 League and Cup appearances during his 12 years at St Andrew's. A Scotsman, born at Douglas Water in December 1904 and now deceased, he had trials with Sunderland, Bury and South Shields before joining Blues as a professional in November 1922. He played in the 1931 FA Cup Final before leaving St Andrew's in June 1934 to become player-manger of Boston United, later bossing Banbury Spencer (1935-36). Cringan's brother Willie played for Celtic and Scotland.

CROSBIE, Johnny

Johnny Crosbie

Another Scottish import, inside-right Johnny 'Peerless' Crosbie was signed from Ayr United in May 1920 for a then club record fee of £3,700. A very skilful footballer, he was a dignified craftsman as well as splendid marksman and provided Joe Bradford with heaps of opportunities to build up his goal-tally, often laying on chances for the England with a defence-splitting 40-yard pass. Born in the Gorballs district of Glasgow in June 1896, Crosbie had played in the Scottish League since 1913 and he remained at St Andrew's until July 1932 when he transferred to Chesterfield. He scored 72 goals in 431 appearances for Blues, helping them win the Second Division championship in 1921 and finish runners-up in the FA Cup Final ten years later. He won two full and one Victory international caps for his country. From Chesterfield he switched to Stourbridge where he became player-manager and for six months in 1933 he coached in Gothenburg, Sweden.

Crosbie was 85 when he died in February 1982.

CROWD DISTURBANCES

- In the Olympic Stadium, Rome back in October 1961, during the Inter Cities Fairs Cup Final second leg encounter with AS Roma, Blues' manager Gil Merrick and his counterpart, Luis Carniglia almost came to blows after incidents on the pitch. Several players embroiled in a punch-up and some over-zealous supporters also joined in the action. The whole incident lasted about five minutes before calm was restored both on and off the field. Blues eventually lost the game 2-0 and the final itself 4-2 on aggregate.

The Blues v Stoke City League game in February 1992 ends inside a deserted stadium

- Trouble erupted during Blues' Fairs Cup encounter in Italy against AS Roma in October 1961. Manager Gil Merrick had to step in and pull away some of his reserves after an ugly incident had developed out on the pitch.
- The Blues v Stoke City Nationwide League Division Three game at St Andrew's on 29 February 1992 was halted by a pitch invasion with barely a minute left on the watch. Blues were leading 1-0 courtesy of John Frain's penalty but a disputed late equaliser by Stoke's Paul Barnes following by a Stoke goal-line clearance that denied Blues a winner, several irate home supporters raced onto the pitch. Referee Roger Wiseman was seemingly attacked and he decided to take the players off, refusing to resume the game until the stadium had been cleared. His wish was granted and the remaining few seconds were played out at walking pace inside an empty St Andrew's. The game ended 1-1 and later Blues were fined £50,000 and ordered to play at least two future home matches behind closed doors - but these 'sentences' were both suspended! (This indirectly led to the Popplewell report being published).
- There was crowd scenes during the Blues v Leeds United on 11 May 1985 when 96 police officers (male and female) were hurt and one supporter killed when a wall collapsed at the Tilton Road End/Main Stand corner of St Andrew's.
- Crowd trouble flared up during Blues' 2-2 draw with Millwall at St Andrew's in November 1995 - and as a result a subsequent inquiry found Blues guilty of failing to control their fans, resulting in a suspended fine.
- In September 1996 there was crowd trouble involving a gang of so-called Blues fans at Maine Road when Manchester City won 1-0 in a League game in September 1996. Blues' owner David Sullivan referred to them as 'a mindless minority that ruined the good name of true supporters.'

CRYSTAL PALACE

Blues' playing record against the Eagles:

FOOTBALL LEAGUE

Venue	P	W	D	L	F	A
Home	15	9	2	4	23	17
Away	15	3	3	9	15	28
Totals	30	12	5	13	38	45

FA CUP

Home	2	1	1	0	5	2
Away	1	0	0	1	0	1
Totals	3	1	1	1	5	3

LEAGUE CUP

Home	1	0	1	0	1	1
Away	2	0	1	1	2	3
Totals	3	0	2	1	3	4

When Blues moved out of the Second Division (into the First) in 1921, so Palace rose from the Third Division to take their place (in a way).

The initial League game between Blues and Palace was on the opening day of the 1965-66 season at St Andrew's when a crowd of 19,205 saw Blues win a Second Division encounter 2-1, Dennis Thwaites netting both goals.

Palace reached the First Division themselves in 1970 and in doing so they completed the double over Blues, winning 3-2 at Selhurst Park and 1-0 at St Andrew's.

The first game between the clubs in the top flight was in August 1972 when more than 31,000 fans at St Andrew's witnessed the 1-1 draw.

Only 5,987 paying customers saw Blues beat Palace 4-1 at St Andrew's in a League game in October 1986.

Palace registered two successive 6-0 League wins over Blues in the space of six months during the years 1987 - beating them in March at Selhurst Park and in September at St Andrew's. John Trewick made his Blues' debut in the latter game.

The goals continued to flow and in August 1993 despite a brace from Paul Peschisolido, Blues still crashed to a 4-2 defeat at home to Palace.

Blues' were held 2-2 at home by Crystal Palace in a first round FA Cup-tie in 1914-15, but the London club agreed for the replay to be staged at St Andrew's and this time Blues won 3-0.

All three League Cup meetings were played in season 1991-92, Palace winning a third round second replay 2-1 at Selhurst Park.

At the end of the 1999-2000 season, the 36 games between the two clubs had produced 98 goals.

Players with both clubs include: T Aylott, D Bailey, L Bradbury, K Brown, S Claridge, M Dennis, L Donowa, A Evans, M Gabbiadini, R Huxford, R Hynd, DJ Madden, AA Millard, K Miller, WA Morgan, M O'Connor, GM O'Reilly, P Sansome (CP apprentice), R Strang (Blues reserve), L Thompson, C Whyte, J Williams, P Williams.

Also: Mike Kelly (Blues player, Palace assistant-manager, coach), Alec Leake (Blues player, Palace trainer), Tony Taylor (Palace player, Blues coach).

Blues' goalkeeper Jim Herriot saves Steve Kember's penalty during the 3-2 defeat against Crystal Palace in August 1968.

CULLIS, Stan

Stan Cullis had a marvellous playing career as a centre-half with Wolves (1934-47) and for England and after retiring he served as a manager at Molineux for another 16 years (1948-64) having spent one season 'learning the business' as assistant to Ted Vizard. He then had a brief spell out of football before returning in December 1965 to take over at St Andrew's, a position he held until retiring out of football in March 1970. He guided Blues to the League Cup semi-final in 1967 and the FA Cup semi-final twelve months later - and it was Cullis who signed Trevor Francis on apprenticeship forms for Blues in 1969. He was born in Ellesmere Port in October 1915 and was an amateur with Bolton Wanderers before joining the

playing staff at Molineux. He went on to appear in almost 200 games for Wolves (including Wartime) and skippered the side in the 1939 FA Cup Final defeat at the hands of Portsmouth. He won 12 full caps and 20 during the hostilities as well as representing the Football League. He skippered both Wolves and England and was one of the youngest international captains in May 1938 (aged 22 years, seven months). As Wolves manager he guided them to three League championships in the 1950s, steered them to two FA Cup Final triumphs in 1949 and 1960 and was in charge when all the great foreign club sides were beaten under the Molineux floodlights. Regarded as one of soccer's greatest managers, Cullis retired to Malvern where he still resides.

Stan Cullis

CURBISHLEY, Alan (L.C)

In May 1998, Alan Curbishley, as manager of Charlton Athletic, celebrated when Premiership football came to the Valley. As a midfield player himself Curbishley never reached the heights he had hoped for, although he did represent England at Schoolboy, youth and Under-23 levels. He made well over 600 senior appearances while serving with West Ham United (joining as an apprentice in 1973, turning professional in July 1975), Birmingham City (signed for £225,000 in July 1979), Aston Villa (bought for £100,000 plus Robert Hopkins in March 1983), Charlton Athletic (secured for £40,000 in December 1984) and Brighton & Hove Albion (a £32,000 capture in August 1987). He returned to Charlton as player/coach in July 1990, became assistant-manager three months later and was upgraded to team boss in June 1995 after four years as joint-manager with Steve Gritt. He then took Charlton into the Premiership for the first time in 1998 and then back there again in 2000. Earlier Curbishley had helped Blues win promotion from Division Two in 1980. He made 43 appearances for Villa (one goal scored) and 155 for Blues 155 (15 goals).

CURTIS, Ernie

Ernie Curtis

A Welsh international at Schoolboy and senior levels, Ernie Curtis appeared in almost 50 first-class games as an inside-forward for Cardiff City before joining Blues. Indeed, he was the youngest player on the field when the Welsh team shook the nation by beating Arsenal in the 1927 FA Cup Final at Wembley. He signed for Blues in a £3,000 deal in March 1928 and in no time at all was switched, with great effect, to the left-wing position. There he became an instant success, going on to score 53 goals in 180 senior games for Blues including another FA Cup final outing v West Bromwich Albion in 1931. Born in Cardiff in June 1907, Curtis became a professional at Ninian Park in 1925 and on leaving St Andrew's in November 1933 he returned there for a second spell which lasted until February 1935 when he moved back to the Midlands to sign for Coventry City. He then spent two years with Hartlepool United before the Second World War interrupted his routine. He retired straight away but during the hostilities he became a Prisoner-of-War, captured by the Japanese. Released safe and sound he eventually returned to Cardiff City as first team coach before becoming a publican in the City. Curtis died in November 1992, aged 85.

'D' CLUB

Founded in 1968 as a private members' club. It provided facilities and entertainment for its members to the benefit of Birmingham City Football Club.

DAISH, Liam

Solid defender, good in recovery, with strong heading ability, Liam Daish was born in Portsmouth in September 1968 and played his early football as both an apprentice and professional at Fratton Park. In July 1988 he moved to Cambridge United and in January 1994, after more than 180 appearances for the Abbey Stadium club, a fee of £50,000 brought him to St Andrew's. He went on to play in almost 100 games for Blues (six goals scored) before transferring to Coventry City for £1.5 million in February 1996. Capped by the Republic of Ireland at full, 'B' and Under-21 levels, injuries interrupted both the 1997-98 and 1998-99 seasons and he eventually left Highfield Road to sign for the Dr Martens Premier League side Havant and Waterlooville in 2000.

● Daish and his former Blues team-mate Michael Johnson were told to plead guilty to assault following the 'Battle of Ancona' affair in Italy in 1996 (see under Ancona and Anglo-Italian Cup).

DALE, Dicky

A former Tow Law Town player, chunky wing-half Dicky Dale arrived at St Andrew's in March 1922, Blues paying Stanley United just £200 for his services. Dale, perhaps a shade uncertain at times, did well and amassed exactly 150 appearances for Blues before joining neighbours West Bromwich Albion for £1,500 in November 1928. He spent three years at The Hawthorns (as reserve to Bill Richardson and Jimmy Edwards) and then played out his career

Dicky Dale

with Tranmere Rovers, Crook Town and his old club Tow Law before retiring in 1938. Dale played for the Staffordshire FA in 1925 - his only representative honour.

DALY, Gerry

Gerry Daly was a quality midfield player who had a fine career at both club and international level. Born in Cabra, Dublin in April 1954, he started out with the Bohemians club in Ireland before joining Manchester United in April 1973 for £20,000. He spent four years at Old Trafford, helping the Reds win the Second Division title in 1975 and finish runners-up in the FA Cup the following season. In March 1977 he switched to Derby County for £170,000. After two loan spells with the New England Tea Men in America he left the Baseball Ground to join Coventry City in a £310,000 deal in August 1980 and after another loan period, this time with Leicester City, he became a Blues player in August 1984. He scored twice in 76 appearances before leaving St Andrew's for Shrewsbury Town in August 1985, and after serving with Stoke City and Doncaster Rovers he quit League soccer to become player - manager of Telford United (July 1989) a position he held for four years. Capped 46 times by the Republic of Ireland, he also played for the Under-21 side and helped Blues win promotion from the Second Division in 1985.

DARLINGTON

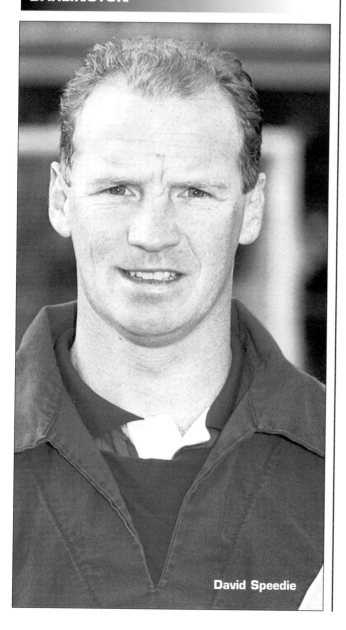

David Speedie

Blues' playing record against the Quakers:

FOOTBALL LEAGUE

Venue	P	W	D	L	F	A
Home	1	1	0	0	1	0
Away	1	0	1	0	1	1
Totals	2	1	1	0	2	1

FA CUP

Venue	P	W	D	L	F	A
Home	1	1	0	0	4	0

Blues met the Quakers for the first time in the Football League in 1991-92, winning 1-0 at home on 31 August (Simon Sturridge the scorer) and drawing 1-1 at The Feethams (Ian Rodgerson on target).

Jack Whitehouse scored a hat-trick in Blues' 4-0 FA Cup win over the Quakers in a second round tie at St Andrew's in January 1920 when the crowd topped 47,000. In an earlier round the Quakers had caused a major upset by beating Sheffield Wednesday 2-0.

Players with both clubs include: F Barber, M Gabbiadini, D Geddis, R Gregg, D Mason (reserve), I Muir, D Preece, M Prudhoe, R Sbragia, C Shutt, D Speedie, R Strang (Blues reserve - 170 League appearances for the Quakers), J Wealands.

DARWEN

Blues' playing record against the Lancastrians:

FOOTBALL LEAGUE

Venue	P	W	D	L	F	A
Home	4	4	0	0	21	4
Away	4	0	2	2	5	8
Totals	8	4	2	2	26	12

FACUP

Venue	P	W	D	L	F	A
Home	1	1	0	0	3	1

TEST MATCH

Venue	P	W	D	L	F	A
Neutral	1	1	0	0	3	1

FOOTBALL ALLIANCE

Venue	P	W	D	L	F	A
Home	2	1	0	1	9	6
Away	2	0	0	2	5	9
Totals	4	1	0	3	14	15

In the first ever League game against Darwen on 29 October 1892, Blues' left-back Fred Speller broke his right leg - an injury that effectively ended his career. Blues still managed to win the game 3-2.

Sadly, the return fixture this season resulted in a 4-3 reverse for Blues.

Blues rattled in five goals in successive home League games against Darwen in September 1896 and December 1897, the visitors knocking in just one in reply each time.

When Blues drew 1-1 at Darwen on 2 September 1897 it ended a club record run of nine successive away wins in the Football League.

Hot-shot Walter Abbott scored five goals (one a penalty) in Blues' 8-0 League win over Darwen at Muntz Street in November 1898. This win came just two weeks after hapless Luton Town had been crushed 9-0.

The crucial Test Match between Blues and Darwen at Stoke City's Victoria Ground was played in April 1894 and the 3-1 victory meant that Blues were promoted from the Second Division.

Associated with both clubs: Mick Rathbone (Blues player, Darlington Commercial Manager).

DAVENHAM

Blues beat Davenham 2-1 at Muntz Street in a fifth round FA Cup-tie in January 1886, Tommy Davenport scoring the all-important second goal.

DAVIES, Stan

Stan Davies

The versatile Stan Davies could play in any position, even goalkeeper. He was a tremendous footballer but it was as an inside or centre-forward where he did the damage! A Welshman, born in Chirk in April 1898, he had been in football twelve years before joining Blues from West Bromwich Albion in November 1927 for £1,500. His previous clubs included Chirk FC, Manchester United (as a trialist), Rochdale, Preston North End, Rochdale and Everton and he was at The Hawthorns for six years, scoring 83 goals in 159 games for the Baggies. He netted five times in his 17 outings for Blues before moving to Cardiff City in May 1928. Thereafter he was player-manager of Rotherham United, served briefly with Barnsley, Manchester Central, Dudley Town, Chelmsford City (as player-trainer) and the Rochester club Shorts as manager, finally quitting football in 1945 at the age of 47. He played in 18 full and one 'other' international for Wales occupying six different positions. He also toured Canada with the Welsh FA in June/July 1925. Davies died in Birmingham in January 1972.

DEARSON, Don

Initially a clever, scheming inside-forward, Welshman Don Dearson developed into a versatile footballer, able to occupy a variety positions from full-back, wing-half to centre-forward. Born in the village of Ynysybwl in May 1913, he had a fine career, starting out with Llanwit Major Juniors before joining Barry Town in 1932. From there he switched to St Andrew's (April 1934) and went on to score 17 goals in 136 peacetime games for Blues plus more than 25 in 166 Wartime matches, also guesting for Northampton Town, Nottingham Forest, West Bromwich Albion and Wrexham during the hostilities. He won a Football League (South) championship medal in 1946 before leaving St Andrew's for Coventry City for £6,000 in February 1947. He later played for Walsall, Nuneaton Borough and Bilston United, retiring in 1954. Dearson won four amateur and three senior caps for Wales as well as appearing in 15 Wartime internationals (he actually lined up in eight different positions for his country and missed a penalty in a wartime game against England at St Andrew's in 1941). After his footballing days were over he had a brief spell in the police force, worked for BSA, was employed by British Leyland and ran his own grocery business. He was 77 when he died in Sheldon, Birmingham on Christmas Eve 1990.

DEATHS

Don Dearson

Elias Ashurst was only 27 when he died.

Blues' left-half Billy McCourty, a great friend of Alec McClure, was killed in 1916 while serving in the Great War. He was only 32.

Three more Blues players - Tom Farrage, Dick Harris and Bill Taylor - all lost their lives while serving in HM forces during the Second World War.

Other Blues players who have suffered tragic deaths include: full-back Jeff Hall (a polio victim in 1959 at the age of 29), Alex Harley, Ian Handysides (brain tumour), Terry Hibbitt (August 1994), Trevor Hockey (heart attack) and Jack Jones (typhoid fever at the age of 29).

Elias Ashurst died after an eighteen-month illness in December 1927, three weeks before his 27th birthday.

John Johns died of typhoid fever at the age of 29 in 1904, having been a Blues player from 1894 to 1897.

And Wallace N Harris was only 33 when he died of ill-health in Switzerland in 1933.

DEBUTS

Bobby Thomson made his England debut at 19

A total of 25 players made their senior debut for Blues in season 1995-96.

All eleven players who lined up against Burslem Port Vale at Muntz Street on 3 September 1892 were making their Football League debuts for the club, namely Chris Charsley; Tom Bayley, Fred Speller; Billy Ollis, Caesar Jenkyns, Ted Devey; Jack Hallam, Harry Edwards, George Short, Fred Wheldon and Tommy Hands. And during the course of that 1892-93 season a total of nineteen players were utilised by the Blues' committee, all of course, having their first outings at League level for the club.

Likewise, the eleven players who beat Derby Town 4-1 on 14

October 1882, all made the FA (English) Cup debuts for Blues, the team being: Jack Bodenham; 'Father' Sam Gessey, Lawrie Summers, Tommy James, Victor Teychenne, Fred James; Walter Hards, Walter Rotherham, Arthur James, Jimmy Whitehead and Billy Slater.

Slater made history by scoring Blues' first goal at competitive level in this encounter and another record is that the three James brothers also played in this tie.

It was the same situation in the Football League Cup when Blues visited Park Avenue to play Bradford (PA) on 31 October 1960, the eleven players on duty that night all made a winning debut in the competition thanks to winger Mike Hellawell's deciding goal.

Blues' first venture into Europe took them to Italy to play Inter Milan in the Inter Cities Fairs Cup on 15 May 1956. The eleven players who made their 'Euro' debut earned a 0-0 draw.

Blues' youngest-ever debutant is Trevor Francis, who was just 16 years, four months and 16 days old when he came on as a substitute in a Second Division League game against Cardiff City on 5 September 1970.

One of the oldest players to make his 'debut' for Blues is the former Aston Villa goalkeeper Billy George who was over 37 years of age when he deputised for Horace Bailey in the 3-1 defeat by Barnsley at St Andrew's in September 1911.

Two more goalkeepers - Tony Coton and Gary Sprake - both saved penalties on their League debuts for Blues.

Peter Murphy scored a hat-trick on his League debut for Blues against Doncaster Rovers at Belle Vue in 1952.

Bobby Laing (at 5ft. 4in) scored twice on his Blues debut against Leeds United in February 1948.

Centre-half Trevor Smith conceded an own-goal on his debut for Blues at Derby in October 1953 (Blues still won the game 4-2).

And defender Paul Hart fractured his leg in a collision with his own team-mate Tommy Williams when making his debut for the club against Plymouth Argyle on New Year's Day 1987. That was his only outing for Blues.

In 1963 full-back Bobby Thomson (then of Wolves, later a Blues player) was still only 19 years of age when he made his full England debut.

DEFEATS

Here is a list of the most League games Blues have lost in a League season:

In 1985-86	29
In 1988-89	27
In 1978-79	26
In 1963-64	24
In 1909-10	23
In 1964-65	23
In 1938-39	22
In 1960-61	22
In 1975-76	22
In 1926-27	21
In 1949-50	21
In 1992-93	21
In 1993-94	21
In 1969-70	20

and a list of the fewest League defeats suffered in a season:

In 1892-93	3
In 1900-01	5

- Only 22 League games were played in 1892-93. The first time Blues played 42 games in a season was in 1919-20 and in 1988-89 they fulfilled a total of 46 for the first time.
- A record 14 home League defeats were handed out to Blues in 1985-86 when they dropped out of the First Division in 21st position. They lost a total of 29 matches that season.
- Thirteen home League games were lost in 1988-89.
- Blues suffered a club record 19 away League defeats when relegated to the Second Division in 1978-79 - eighteen in succession between 16 September and 1 May (this is also a Football League record for the longest run in any ONE season). It ended with a 3-1 win at QPR.
- In 1963-64 Blues lost 17 and won four of their 21 away First Division matches and the following season when they were relegated they suffered another 16 defeats on their travels.
- In 1975-76 they also lost 17 away games in the top flight.
- Blues lost 15 away League games (out of 19) in 1909-10 when they finished bottom of the Second Division. And in 1926-27 and again in 1938-39 they were beaten in 16 of their 21 away First Division matches.
- Blues suffered 10 home League defeats (out of 21 matches) in the First Division season of 1921-22.
- Blues lost only three away matches when winning the Second Division title in 1947-48. They were undefeated in 37 of the 42 League games completed during this season under skipper Fred Harris.
- Blues lost seven consecutive FA Cup-ties between January 1892 and October 1897.
- Blues have twice had eight-match League runs without recording a victory - in 1978-79 and again in 1985.
- In the first leg of the 2000 Division play-off semi-final v Barnsley at St Andrew's in May 2000, the 4-0 defeat suffered by Blues was one of the biggest by a home club since the play-off system was introduced in the mid 1980s.
  List of Blues' heaviest defeats (all competitions):
  1-9 v Blackburn Rovers, away (Football League) 5.1.1895
  1-9 v Sheffield Wednesday, away (Football League) 13.12.1930
  0-8 v Derby County, away (Football League) 30.11.1895
  0-8 v Newcastle United, away (Football League) 23.11.1907
  0-8 v Preston North End, away (Football League) 1.2.1958
  0-7 v Huddersfield Town, away (Football League) 25.10.1914
  0-7 v Hull City, away (Football League) 4.12.1909
  1-7 v Burnley, home (Football League) 10.4.1926
  1-7 v Burnley, away (Football League) 3.2.1962
  1-7 v Sunderland, away (Football League) 8.12.1894
  1-7 v Tottenham Hotspur, away (Football League) 18.9.1957
  1-7 v WBA, home (Football League) 18.4.1960
  2-7 v Sunderland, home (Football League) 13.4.1936
  2-7 v Wolverhampton W., away (Football League) 25.1.1896
  3-7 v Aston Villa, away (Football League) 7.9.1895

5-7 v Blackburn Rovers, away (Football League) 28.9.1929
0-6 v Crystal Palace, away (Football League) 14.3.1987
0-6 v Crystal Palace, home (Football League) 5.9.1987
0-6 v Norwich City, away (Football League) 15.4.1970
0-6 v Tottenham Hotspur, away (FA Cup) 12.4.1967
0-6 v West Bromwich Albion, home (Football League) 3.9.1958
0-6 v Wednesbury Old Athletic away (FA Cup) 17.10.1881
1-6 v Stoke, away (Football League) 19.10.1895
0-5 v Aston Villa, away (League Cup) 12.10.1988
0-5 v Tottenham Hotspur away (League Cup) 29.10.1986
2-5 v RCD Espanol, away (Fairs Cup) 11.11.1961

- The last three results are the heaviest in the named competitions.
  Blues were defeated by the winners of both the League Cup (QPR) and the FA Cup (Tottenham Hotspur) in those respective competitions in 1966-67.

DEFENSIVE RECORDS

In season 1947-48, when they won the Second Division championship, Blues conceded only 24 goals in their 42 games, 13 at home and only 11 away. A club record.

In 1900-01 Blues' defence also gave away 24 goals, but this time in 34 Second Division matches.

A total of 34 goals went past the Blues goalkeeper in 42 First Division fixtures in 1919-20, just 33 were conceded in their 42 First Division encounters in 1946-47 and 31 in season 1971-72 when they finished as runners-up in Division Two (42 matches played).

Blues' goalkeeper Ian Bennett kept 27 clean sheets (in 62 games) in the 1994-95 season. During that campaign he had a run of seven successive League games without conceding a goal.

Gil Merrick kept 20 clean sheets in League football in 1947-48 and 16 the following season.

DENNIS, Mark

A very talented left-back with a fiery temper, Mark Dennis scored one goal (v Ipswich at Portman Road in March 1983) in 145 appearances for Blues before leaving St Andrew's for Southampton in a £100,000 transaction in November 1983. Born in London in May 1961, he was associated with Chelsea as a schoolboy but found his way to Blues to sign apprentice forms in 1977, turning professional in August 19778. He made his debut for Blues in unusual circumstances, stepping in at the last minute after Jimmy Calderwood had cracked his head open after failing down in the Norwich City dressing room on 16 September 1978. The Canaries ruined his day by winning 4-0! Capped by England at youth and Under-21 levels, he left The Dell for Queens Park Rangers in May 1987 and later assisted Crystal Palace and Brighton & Hove Albion. Dennis was sent-off 14 times in various matches as a professional footballer and was often involved in unsavoury incidents both on and off the field as well as on the training ground and at a railway station!

DERBY COUNTY

Blues' playing record against the Rams:

FOOTBALL LEAGUE

Venue	P	W	D	L	F	A
Home	44	22	10	12	82	64

Away	44	6	16	22	45	87
Totals	88	28	26	34	127	151
FA CUP						
Away	4	2	0	2	9	7
Neutral	2	0	1	1	0	4
LEAGUE CUP						
Home	2	2	0	0	7	1
Away	2	1	0	1	4	3
Totals	4	3	0	1	11	4
SIMOD CUP						
Away	1	0	0	1	1	3
WARTIME						
Home	3	1	1	1	4	8
Away	3	1	0	2	6	8
Totals	6	2	1	3	10	16

The first ever League game between the clubs on 16 March 1895 resulted in a 5-3 home defeat for Blues. Derby then won the return fixture 4-1 a fortnight later when Blues centre-half Caesar Jenkyns was sent-off for brawling with a Derby player whom he alleged had spat at him! He never played for the club again!

Struggling Blues lost 8-0 to a rampant Derby side at The Baseball Ground in November 1895 but the great Steve Bloomer only managed one goal yet he did lay on five others for his colleagues, three scored by dashing right-winger John Paul.

Derby won 4-0 at St Andrew's in September 1911 (Bloomer scored a penalty this time) and in 1914-15 they doubled up over Blues before the war halted proceedings for four years!

Blues (up into the First Division) and Derby swapped places in 1921 and they didn't meet again at League level until October 1926 when 25,000 fans saw Blues win 1-0 at home.

Derby won 4-1 at The Baseball Ground in December 1927 and by the same score at St Andrew's in October 1928. They also gained a 4-2 victory on Blues' soil in April 1930 and a another 4-0 home victory in October 1933.

Billy Jones' hat-trick eased the pressure for Blues who gained a sweet 3-2 home win in March 1935 and in the last pre-war season of 1938-39 they achieved the double, winning 3-0 at home and 1-0 away.

Halfway through the 1949-50 season the Rams won 4-1 at The Baseball Ground as Blues struggled in a vain effort to avoid relegation.

Three goals in quick succession between the 11th and 23rd minutes helped Blues to a 4-2 home win over Derby County in a Second Division game in October 1953. Trevor Smith scored a spectacular own-goal for the Rams.

Ten goals were scored (five by each side) in a tremendously competitive Second Division game at St Andrew's in April 1966. Malcolm Beard scored twice for Blues - a year after he had netted a hat-trick in another 5-5 draw with Blackburn.

Over 38,000 fans at St Andrew's saw Blues beat the Rams 2-0 in February 1973 and Trevor Francis slotted home two penalties in Blues' 3-2 win on the same ground in September 1974.

In October 1976 future Derby player Kenny Burns was the Blues hero in their 5-1 home win over the Rams. He scored four times and also had a hand in the other goal.

When Derby beat Blues 4-1 in November 1995 it was their first League success at St Andrew's in 47 years, since their 1-0 victory back in October 1948. It also ended Blues' 15-match unbeaten run.

The Rams beat Blues 4-0 in an FA Cup semi-final replay at Maine Road in 1946 in front of 80,407 spectators. The first game had ended goalless at Hillsborough where the crowd was 65,013. Blues should have won this encounter as Harold Bodle missed a sitter in the last minute, shooting straight at County's 'keeper Vic Woodley in a one-on-one situation.

In the replay Blues defender Ted Duckhouse broke his leg early in extra-time while attempting to stop the second Derby goal and 10-men Blues couldn't keep out the rampaging Rams after that.

A crowd of 8,277 saw the Simod Cup-tie at Derby in November 1987, when Blues lost 3-1 after extra-time, John Trewick conceding an own-goal.

Players with both clubs include: G Ablett, HP Bailey, J Bradford (County trialist), K Burns, G Charles, GA Daly, P Doherty (Blues guest), H Edwards, K Francis, M Gabbiadini, A Gemmill, H Hampton (County guest), M Harford, A Hateley (County junior), F Hawley (County guest), T Hennessey, J Hunt, R Jones, R Knight (Blues loanee), M Kuhl, MA Lane, D Langan, M McDonnell, JS McMillan, T McMinn, R Martin, J Peart, D Preece, B Rioch, G Rowett, WG Steel, S Sutton, A Tinkler, C Todd, D Wassall, JC Whitehouse, P Wright.

Also: Jim Smith (manager of both clubs), Major Frank Buckley (Blues player, County manager), Dave Mackay and Harry Storer (Derby players, Blues managers), Johnny Newman (Blues player, County assistant and caretaker manager), George Foster (County player, Blues coach).

Ted Duckhouse broke his leg in the 1946 FA Cup semi-final replay

DERBY TOWN

Blues' first ever FA Cup-tie was against Derby Town at home on 17 October 1881. A crowd of 1,000 saw the contest which Blues won 4-1 with goals by Billy Slater (2), Walter Hards and Arthur James.

DEVEY, Ted

One of five footballing brothers, Ted was a tough-tackling, aggressive player who occupied the left-half position. He was born within throwing distance of Blues' Muntz Street ground in Small Heath in August 1862 and played for Birmingham Excelsior before joining Blues in April 1888. He remained with the club for six years during which time he scored six goals in exactly 100 first team matches, helping Blues win the Second Division title and gain promotion to the top flight in successive seasons. He left to join Burton Wanderers in October 1896 and died in Birmingham in September 1946, aged 84.

DICKS, Julian

Julian Dicks gives a helping hand to Lee Dixon then of Stoke, later of Arsenal.

Fiercely competitive left-back, Julian Dicks was born in the West Country in Bristol in August 1968 but moved to the Midlands as a youngster, eventually becoming an apprentice at St Andrew's in August 1984, turning professional twelve months later. He went on to play in 102 first team games, scoring two goals before transferring to West Ham United for £400,000 in March 1988. Five-and-a-

half years later he moved to Liverpool for £1.5 million but spent only one season at Anfield before returning to Upton Park for £1 million in November 1994. Injuries interrupted his performances with the Hammers but he still managed to reach a personal milestone of 450 appearances at senior level in 1999. Dicks helped West Ham win promotion in 1991 and he won four Under-21 and two 'B' caps for England. In 1999 Dicks quit football altogether to become a professional golfer and quickly made the grade!

DILLON, Kevin

A midfield player with some very neat and precise skills but a suspect temperament, Kevin Dillon scored 19 goals in 212 appearances for Blues, having joined the club as a junior in 1976 and turning professional in July 1977. He starred in the promotion-winning team of 1979-80 and gained one England Under-21 cap before leaving St Andrew's for Portsmouth in a £200,000 deal in March 1983. He scored a hat-trick of penalties for Pompey in a Full Members Cup-tie against Millwall in November 1986. He later played for Newcastle United, Reading, Newbury Town, Stevenage Borough and Yeovil Town. Dillon was born in Sunderland in December 1959 and represented Durham Boys as a teenager.

Dillon in his Newcastle shirt

DINAMO YUGOSLAVIA

Blues were well beaten by the Yugoslavian side 2-0 in a Festival of Britain game at St Andrew's in May 1951 when the attendance topped 12,000.

DINAMO ZAGREB

Blues played the Czechoslovakian club twice in the Inter Cities Fairs Cup competition in May 1959. A crowd of 21,411 saw Bunny Larkin give Blues a 1-0 first leg lead in a second round tie at St Andrew's. And after forcing a 3-3 draw in front of 50,000 fans in the return leg (Larkin scoring twice this time) Blues deservedly went through to the next stage, winning 4-3 on aggregate. Unfortunately late on in the second encounter Trevor Smith of Blues and Dvorvic of Dinamo were both sent-off for fighting.

MATCH SUMMARY

Venue	P	W	D	L	F	A
Home	1	1	0	0	1	0
Away	1	0	1	0	3	3
Totals	2	1	1	0	4	3

DIRECTORS

Walter W Hart

Birmingham City FC (Small Heath) was the first club in Great Britain to be registered as a Limited Company and introduce a Board of Directors. This happened as long ago as 24 July 1888 when Chairman Walter W Hart was appointed into office. Since that day Blues have always had a Directorate and the club has continued to be a limited company.

Several wealthy and important Birmingham-based businessmen were on the Board of Directors for long periods of time, especially between the two World Wars.

Among those in office before 1946 were WC Adams (also President), G Barlow, H Cant, PW Harlow, J Harris, WW Hart, W Hartley, S Howard, H Lattimer, H Morris senior, GE Muddyman, S Newey, H Rawson, RR Richardson, A Smith, D Stanley, W Starling, HS Thomas, T Turley, J Weston and DF Wiseman (later to receive the OBE).

Here are a number of Directors who have been associated with the club since 1946 (listed in A-Z order): Ald. N Bosworth LL.R., Karren Brady (Managing Director), H Brandham, R Burman FCA., WA Camkin, J Carrott, CC Coombs, CK Coombs B. Comm., DM Coombs, T Cooper, E Cox, H Dare, WH Dare, P Day, TWJ Edmonds, HD Ellis, B Gold, D Gold, R Gold, G Greaves, A Hones, AG Jones, BA. M.BA., B Kumar MA. B.Sc., R Kumar B. Sc., S Kumar BA., H Morris, LJ Morris, D Mortimer, HA Parkes, Sir A Ramsey, SFL Richards, BH Slater, BA (Honours), D Sullivan, A Ward, KE Wheldon, DF Wiseman, JF Wiseman, M Wiseman and J Woolman.

The following have also held the position of Chairman of the Board of Directors: H Cant, CC Coombs, CK Coombs, D Gold, WW Hart, S. Kumar, H Morris, KE Wheldon and JF Wiseman.

DONCASTER ROVERS

Blues' playing record against Rovers:

FOOTBALL LEAGUE

Venue	P	W	D	L	F	A
Home	7	4	2	1	23	7
Away	7	3	1	3	12	6
Totals	14	7	3	4	35	13

FA CUP

Venue	P	W	D	L	F	A
Home	1	1	0	0	2	1

LEAGUE CUP

Venue	P	W	D	L	F	A
Home	1	1	0	0	5	0

Celebrations as Blues clinch promotion (and the Second Division championship) with a 5-1 win at Doncaster in 1955.

Blues and Rovers met in the League for the first time on 13 December 1902. It wasn't a happy day for Blues who lost the away Second Division fixture 2-0. However, in the return clash at Muntz Street on 11 April 1903, Blues' equalled their biggest-ever League win by thrashing hapless Rovers 12-0. Arthur Leonard and Harry Melbourne Wilcox scored four goals apiece that day but there were only 8,000 fans there to see the action. Blues led 3-0 at half-time, all their five forwards found the net and Rovers' goalkeeper Jack Eggett was quite brilliant, saving at least another six goal-bound efforts!

On 16 March 1955 a crowd of just 5,621 at St Andrew's - the lowest for a League match at the ground since 1925 - saw Blues beat Rovers 4-1.

Two months later they secured promotion from the Second Division with a 5-1 victory at Belle Vue, Gordon Astall (2) leading the goal rush, followed by Eddie Brown, Peter Murphy and Alex Govan.

Three years earlier, in January 1952, Rovers had been hammered 5-0 at home when Peter Murphy, making his debut for Blues following his transfer from Tottenham Hotspur, scored a hat-trick.

Blues' 5-0 League Cup win over Rovers was achieved in season 1962-63, on their way to winning the trophy for the first time.

Players with both clubs include: J Aston, W Bennett (Blues reserve), S Black (Rovers reserves), H Bodle (Rovers trialist), J Cornforth, G Daly, J Deakin, P Doherty (Blues guest), A Drake, J Firth (Rovers amateur), P Holmes, RE Keating, BP Larkin, D Mangnall (Rovers amateur), P Mardon, J Morgan, M Newell, JL Price, M Prudhoe, A Reed, MJ Regan, J Sheridan, J Thorogood, D Williams, M Yates.

Also: Dave Mackay (manager of both clubs), Ian Atkins (Blues player, Rovers manager), Terry Cooper (Rovers player, Blues manager), Jackie Bestall (Blues coach/chief scout, Rovers manager/chief scout).

DONOWA, Louie

Scorer of 21 goals in 158 appearances for Blues between August 1991 and December 1996, Donowa was at times a crowd pleaser, a gifted winger with pace, good skills but an enigmatic nature. He had the distinction of being the first Blues substitute to be substituted himself . Born in Ipswich in September 1964, he made his League debut for Norwich City in the early 1980s and after a loan spell with Stoke City he moved to the Spanish club Deportivo La Coruna for £40,000 in February 1986. Two years later he joined the Dutch side Willem II before returning to England to sign for Ipswich Town in 1989. A year later, £50,000 took him to Bristol City from where he transferred to St Andrew's for a similar amount of money. Further loan spells with Burnley, Shrewsbury Town and Walsall preceded his departure from St Andrew's to Peterborough United in December 1996 before he was recruited on a full-time basis by the Saddlers in August 1997. Donowa won three England Under-21 caps and gained a League Cup winners medal with Norwich in 1985 and helped Blues to the Second Division championship and Freight Rover Trophy success ten years later. In 2000 Donowa joined Forest Green Rovers of the Nationwide Conference League.

DORMAN, Don

A determined footballer, inside-forward Don Dorman was a trier to the last. He scored six goals in 64 games for Blues before leaving St Andrew's for Coventry City in September 1951. Born in Hall Green in September 1922 he played for Shirley juniors as a youngster before at the tailend of the Second World War. A soldier in the 1st Airborne Division during the hostilities, he was wounded and captured after parachuting from a Dakota over Arnhem in August 1943. Taken Prisoner-of-War, he had to wait over twelve month before he could play football again - making his first team debut for Blues in a friendly in September 1944 whilst on leave. He finally got his chance at League level against Burnley at Turf Moor in January 1947. Dorman's never-say-die attitude saw him through a difficult period. After Coventry he played for Walsall, scoring 34 goals in 124 games for the Saddlers before retiring in 1957. He later returned to St Andrew's as a scout, rising to chief scout on the death of Walter Taylor. He later took up a similar position with Aston Villa. Dorman died in January 1997.

Don Dorman

DORRINGTON, Jack

Goalkeeper Jack Dorrington spent twelve seasons with Blues, during which time he made 111 first team appearances despite being first choice between the posts in only one full campaign (1908-09). Fearless, with a safe pair of hands, he was born in Smethwick in May 1881 and played briefly as an amateur for West Bromwich Albion before joining Bromsgrove Rovers and then Kidderminster Harriers. He moved to St Andrew's in July 1901 and although he had to fight for a first team place he was always a consistent performer when called into action. He saved two penalties from hot-shot Harry Hampton in a 5-2 Lord Mayor of Birmingham Charity Cup win over Aston Villa in September 1908. Dorrington was forced to retire through injury in May 1913. He died in Birmingham in January 1944 after a short illness.

DOUBLE WINNERS

In season 1994-95, under manager Barry Fry, Blues completed the 'double' by winning the Second Division championship and the Auto Windscreen Shield at Wembley.

Their League record as champions was an excellent one, reading:

Venue	P	W	D	L	F	A	Pts.
Home	23	15	6	2	53	18	51
Away	23	10	8	5	31	19	38
Totals	46	25	14	7	84	37	89

Their points tally was the highest in the club's history, so too was an excellent unbeaten run of 20 matches.

Steve Claridge top-scored with 20 League goals (25 in all) and the average League attendance at St Andrew's was over 17,000 - up by almost 2,700 on the previous season.

Neil Dougall, second left, with team-mates Jock Mulraney, Cyril Trigg (centre), Don Dorman and George Edwards in 1947.

DOUGALL, Neil

A red-haired inside-forward from a footballing family, Neil Dougall made an immediate impact at St Andrew's with his powerful shooting and purposeful displays. Born in Falkirk in November 1921, he was on schoolboy forms with Burnley before turning professional at Turf Moor in July 1940. After guesting for Coventry City during the War he was signed by Blues for just £2,750 in October 1945 and was instrumental in helping the team win the Football League South title that season and the Second Division championship in 1947-48. He went on to score 18 goals in 108 League and Cup matches for Blues before switching his allegiance to Plymouth Argyle in March 1949. He was converted into a wing-half at Home Park, displaying some excellent form. When he retired ten years later (after netting 26 goals in 289 outings for the Pilgrims) he took over as the club's assistant-trainer, rising to head trainer soon afterwards, a position he retained until 1968. In between times he also acted as first team coach and was the Devon club's joint-manager in 1960-61. He collected a Third Division (S) championship medal in 1952 and gained a Third Division championship medal in 1959. Dougall was capped once by Scotland at senior level and once in a Victory international.

DOUGHERTY, Jim

Initially a rugged, no-nonsense centre-half, Jim Dougherty developed into a constructive hard-working left-half displaying a neat wax moustache. Born in New Brighton in November 1878 he played for a series of clubs in and around his place of birth and signed for Blues from New Brighton Tower FC in September 1901. He remained at the club for seven years, making 136 senior appearances and scoring three goals before transferring to Coventry City in 1908. Later he assisted Stirchley United and Worcester City. Dougherty died in Liverpool.

DRAWS

Blues did not draw a single League game in season 1893-94.

They drew 18 of their 42 League matches in 1938-39 and equalled that record in 1971-72.

In season 1990-91 (between mid-September and late October) Blues drew eight League games in succession (four at home, four away). They drew 17 during the course of the campaign.

Blues' highest-ever competitive draw is 5-5 - achieved twice against Blackburn Rovers in a First Division League game in April 1965 and versus Derby County in a Second Division fixture twelve months later, both games at St Andrew's.

Blues have been involved in quite a few 4-4 scorelines in both major League and Cup competitions, one being a thrilling eight-goal encounter with Boldklub Copenhagen in an Inter Cities Fairs Cup clash in Denmark in November 1960.

DRUIDS

Blues beat the Welsh club 10-0 at home in the fourth qualifying round of the FA Cup in November 1898. Bob McRoberts scored a hat-trick that afternoon in front of 4,000 spectators at Muntz Street.

DUCKHOUSE, Ted

An amateur with West Bromwich Albion, Ted Duckhouse became a professional at St Andrew's in August 1938 and went on to score four goals in 139 senior appearances for Blues as well as having over 40 outings during the Second World War. Able to play as a full-back or centre-half, he was a solid, no-nonsense defender who unfortunately broke his leg in the 1946 FA Cup semi-final replay against Derby County attempting to prevent the Rams' second goal (scored by Peter Doherty in extra-time) in their 4-0 victory. He left St Andrew's in August 1950 for Northampton Town and later assisted Rushden Town (July 1952-May 1955). Duckhouse was born in Shelfield in April 1918 and died in Walsall in 1980.

DURHAM CITY

No competitive action between the two clubs as yet, but several players have been based in both camps, among them: M Briggs, H Bruce, J Bumphrey, W Clark and R Gregg.

EDMUNDS, WH 'Billy'

WH 'Billy' Edmunds

Wing-half Billy Edmunds, regarded as a 'good organiser' was the club's first honorary secretary (appointed in 1875) and the club's first official team captain, taking charge in 1877 at the age of 23. A local man, born in Bordesley Green on 3 September 1854, he played in Blues' first-ever game and remained with the club until 1884, when he handed over the secretary's job to former goalkeeper Will Edden. Edmunds once registered a hat-trick in the space of five minutes - scoring two goals for Blues, and the other for the opposition! In later life he became a successful businessman. Edmunds died in Birmingham in 1925.

EDWARDS, George

A former amateur with Swansea Town, George Edwards was spotted by Coventry City playing inside-left in an RAF team at Wellesbourne in 1938. He was quickly converted into a left-winger and in later years developed into a very positive and competent footballer, being fast and decisive and difficult to dispossess. He left Highfield Road for St Andrew's in July 1944 and went on to score nine goals in 97 senior appearances for Blues as well as scoring 17 times in 48 Wartime matches. He helped Blues win the Football League South title and reach the FA Cup semi-final in 1946 and two years later was a key member of the Second Division championship winning side. A fee of £12,000 took him from St Andrew's to Cardiff City in December 1948 and after retiring from the game in 1956 (having appeared in over 200 games for the Bluebirds) he became a Director at Ninian Park, holding office for over 20 years until 1977. He was also a well-respected broadcaster on BBC Radio Wales and a reporter for a Sunday newspaper. Edwards won 12 full caps for Wales and he also represented his country at Amateur level. He was a qualified teacher and in later life held a prominent position with a major oil company. He gained M.A. honours at Birmingham University, his thesis being 'A History of the Pembrokeshire Coalfields.'

He was born in Kilgetty, Treherbert in December 1920.

ELKES, Jack

Jack Elkes was born in Snedshill, Shropshire on New Year's Eve 1894 and played as an inside-right for two local amateur sides as well as Shifnal Town before joining Blues in January 1918. He spent four years at St Andrew's, scoring 18 goals in 35 League and Cup appearances before transferring to Southampton in March 1922. He scored twice on his debut for Saints and broke his collarbone in his second game. Then he started to attract the attention of the bigger clubs and in May 1923 he signed for Tottenham Hotspur for £1,000. For a tall man (6ft 2in) Elkes was a clever dribbler and at one time was regarded as one of the best in the country. He assembled a fine record with Spurs, netting 57 goals in 213 outings. He played in four international trials for England, represented the Football League XI on three occasions, toured Australia with the FA party in 1925 and lined up for the Professionals against the Amateurs in the FA Charity Shield game in that same year. He left White Hart Lane for Middlesbrough in August 1929; four years later he joined Watford and ended his career with spells at Stafford Rangers and Oakengates Town, retiring in 1937. Best known as a forward, in later years Elkes became a competent centre-half and after hanging up his boots he took up coaching, initially with the Ford Motor Works team at Dagenham. He died in Raleigh, Essex in January 1972.

EMMANUEL, Gary

Midfielder Gary Emmanuel scored six goals in 78 appearances for Blues during the 1970s. Born in Swansea in February 1954, he was educated in his home town and joined the apprentice staff at St Andrew's in 1970, turning professional in July of the following year. He was perhaps a shade too slow for First Division football, but after leaving St Andrew's he carved out a very useful career for himself. He amassed in excess of 300 first-class appearances while serving with Bristol Rovers (from December 1978 to July 1981), Swindon Town (to July 1984), Newport County (for a season), Bristol City as a non-contract player, Swansea City (from August 1985) and finally Barry Town.

His father Len Emmanuel also played for Swansea.

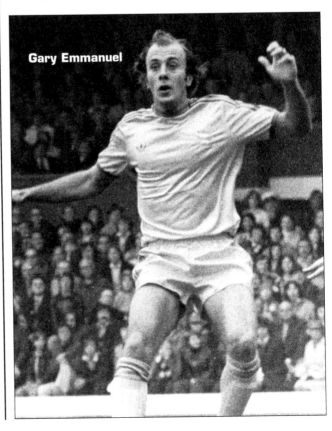

Gary Emmanuel

EVERTON

Blues' playing record against Everton:

FOOTBALL LEAGUE

Venue	P	W	D	L	F	A
Home	52	17	15	20	74	77
Away	52	6	12	34	60	123
Totals	104	23	27	54	134	200

FA CUP

	P	W	D	L	F	A
Home	2	1	1	0	4	2
Away	2	0	0	2	1	4
Totals	4	1	1	2	5	6

The first Blues-Everton League game was staged on Merseyside on 3 September 1894 - and it wasn't a happy day for Blues who crashed to a 5-0 defeat!

An eight-goal thriller at Muntz Street in November 1894 ended Blues 4 Everton 4 and nine years later, in November 1903, Blues suffered their heaviest home defeat of the season when losing 5-1 to the Merseysiders.

Blues completed the double over Everton in 1905-06 after the Liverpool-based club had done likewise over Blues in 1904-05.

The games were evenly matched during the 1920s although Everton did win 5-2 at Goodison Park in September 1927 only for Blues to go there and win 2-0 in January 1929.

In January 1937 Everton were beaten 4-0 by Blues at St Andrew's, with 5ft 7ins centre-forward George Haywood scoring a hat-trick.

Blues played superbly well to win 5-0 at Goodison Park in September 1948, Cyril Trigg (2) and Jackie Stewart (2) doing most of the damage in front of 49,199 fans.

Thanks to a hat-trick by Welshman Noel Kinsey, Blues beat Everton 6-2 at St Andrew's in a First Division game in December 1955. Twenty-four hours later, fielding the same team, they lost 5-1 at Goodison Park.

Johnny Watts played his last game for Blues in the 1-0 home defeat by Everton, the League champions-elect, in April 1963.

Later that year (October) Everton again defeated Blues on their own patch, this time by 2-0.

Malcolm Page made his League debut in Blues' 1-1 draw with Everton at Goodison Park in February 1965. He was a late replace-ment for the injured Terry Hennessey. Earlier that season Everton had won an eight-goal thriller by 5-3 at St Andrew's.

Back in the First Division in 1972-73 Blues beat Everton 2-1 at home and drew 1-1 away but the following season it was the Merseysiders who took the honours winning 2-0 at St Andrew's and 4-1 at Goodison Park when a certain Bob Latchford scored twice against his former colleagues!

Everton doubled up again in 1974-75 with victories of 3-0 at St Andrew's and 4-1 on Merseyside while in 1975-76 again Blues succumbed in both matches, losing 1-0 at home and 5-2 on Everton soil. Two more Everton doubles followed in 1978-79 and 1981-82.

The 100th League game between the clubs on 23 April 1983 saw Blues win a game at last - by a goal to nil, scored by Robert Hopkins at St Andrew's in front of 11,045 fans. This ended a run of 18 games without a win over the Merseysiders!

An aggregate attendance figure of more than 132,000 saw the two Blues v Everton FA Cup encounters in February 1939.

A never-to-be-beaten record crowd of 67,341 packed into St Andrew's to witness the 5th round clash and for the Goodison Park replay four days later the turn out was 64,789. The game at St Andrew's ended in a 2-2 draw with Owen Madden scoring both Blues' goals. Everton won the replay 2-1, their winning goal coming from the penalty spot after Don Dearson had handled.

At the time Blues were bottom of the First Division while Everton were on top! Ted Sagar, Joe Mercer and Tommy Lawton all played for the Merseysiders.

In January 2000 Blues succumbed 2-0 at Goodison Park in the fourth round of the FA Cup, both Everton's goals coming late on, the first a dubious penalty!

Players with both clubs include: G Ablett, W Abbott, A Ainscow, I Atkins, F Barber, M Branch (loan), D Burrows, W Clarke, J Connolly, A Cottee, M Ferguson, C Green, S Harland, J Harris, P Holmes, B Horne, M Jackson, GK Jones, T Jones, H Kendall (also manager of Everton), K Langley, RD Latchford, A Limpar, J McDonough, M McDonnell, T Myhre, M Newell, F Pickering, A Powell, B Rioch, G Rowett, V Samways, J Smith (Everton guest), SJ Storer, A Styles, C Todd, P Van Den Hauwe, M Ward, W Wright.

Also: Ron Saunders (Everton player, Blues manager), Tony Hateley (Blues player, Goodison Park ticket office clerk)

Everton goalkeeper Gordon West acrobatically saves a diving header from Blues striker Peter Bullock during the League game at St Andrew's in October 1963.

EXETER CITY

Blues' playing record against the Grecians:

FOOTBALL LEAGUE

Venue	P	W	D	L	F	A
Home	2	1	1	0	2	1
Away	2	1	0	1	3	2
Totals	4	2	1	1	5	3

LEAGUE CUP

	P	W	D	L	F	A
Home	4	2	0	2	9	6
Away	3	2	1	0	3	1
Totals	7	4	1	2	12	7

The first League encounters between the two teams took place only a decade ago in season 1990-91. Blues were held to a 1-1 draw at St Andrew's but won 2-0 at St James' Park with a brace from John Gayle. Martin Thomas saved a Tom Kelly penalty in this game.

Exeter won 4-1 at St Andrew's in a League Cup match in 1992-93 but Blues gained revenge in 1999-2000 ousting the Grecians from the same competition in the opening round with a 5-1 aggregate victory (3-0 at home, 2-1 away).

Players with both clubs include: N Blake (also Exeter City manager), K Bowker, L Bradbury, P Bullock, E Cameron, M Cooper, F Cornan, J Cornforth, J Dailey, E Dolan, R Dryden, A Evans, A Gosney, A Harris, S Hiley, R McDonough, K Miller, TJ Morgan, J Newman, F Okenla (Exeter trialist), SE Phillips, A Phoenix, H Riley, D Rowbotham (also Exeter assistant-manager), B Sharples, S Storer, K Summerfield, S Wigley.

Also: Terry Cooper (manager of both clubs), Alex Jackson (Blues player, Exeter lottery manager), George Foster (Exeter player, Blues coach).

EYRE, Edmund

'Ninty' Eyre was a positive outside-left, fast and tricky who assembled an excellent scoring record. Born in Worksop in December 1882 his first major club was Rotherham Town from where he moved to St Andrew's in March 1907. He netted 16 goals in 82 appearances for Blues before transferring across the city to Aston Villa in December 1908. After adding 31 outings and five goals to his tally he left Villa Park for Middlesbrough in April 1911 only to return to St Andrew's for a second spell in April 1914, having scored 15 times in 69 games during his stay at Ayresome Park. The Great War, however, disrupted his career and he retired in May 1919. Eyre died circa 1943.

FAIRHURST, Dave

Physiotherapist Dave Fairhurst spent over 35 years in football. He began his as a right-back with Walsall in 1927. At Easter 1929 he moved to Newcastle United and three years later gained an FA Cup winners medal when the Magpies beat Arsenal 2-1 at Wembley. In December 1933 he won his only international cap, helping England whip France 4-1 at Tottenham. He first took an interest in the treatment of players in 1937 and after some initial hard work duly completed his studies in PE and physiotherapy just prior to the outbreak of World War Two. A knee injury, however, ended his playing career and during the hostilities he served in the RAF and became a physical education instructor. In 1942 whilst over in India, he met up with Cyril Trigg - his first associa-

tion (in a way) with Birmingham City Football Club who at the time were looking for a trainer!

When Fairhurst and Trigg were repatriated in April 1946 they exchanged addresses - and in no time at all Fairhurst was taken on the backroom staff at St Andrew's under manager Harry Storer. In 1950-51 Fairhurst became full-time and senior physio at the club, and he did a terrific job with Blues for more than 15 years

FAMILY CONNECTIONS

Fred James, the Blues utility forward, showing off his 1886 FA Cup semi-final medal presented to him after Blues had been beaten 4-0 by West Bromwich Albion.

Several sets of brothers have represented Blues at various levels and they include the following - the Bremners (Des and Kevin), the Bullocks (Micky and Peter), the Charsleys (Chris and Walter), the Deveys (Edward and Will), the Eddens (George, Tom and Will), the Gesseys (George and Sam), the Godfreys (Bruce and Dan), the three James' of the 1870s/early 80s (Arthur, Fred and Tommy), the Latchfords (Bob and Dave), the Shorts (Charlie and George), the Stanleys (Eddy and Wilson) and of course, the Morris's (Harry senior and Harry junior, both as amateurs).

- The three James brothers all lined up together in Blues' first-ever FA Cup-tie against Derby Town in October 1881.
- Harry Morris and his two sons, Harry Morris junior and L. James Morris, all served on the Blues board, likewise three members of the Coombs family (CC, CK and DM), two of the Dares (H & WH), three Golds (B, D & R), three Kumars (B, R & S) and of course the Wisemans (David OBE, JF and M).
- Besides Ted and Will Devey playing for Blues, three other Devey brothers, Bob, Harry and Jack, all represented Aston Villa and another Latchford brother, Peter (also a goalkeeper like Dave) played for West Bromwich Albion and Celtic.
- Joe Bradford and his brother Jack were at Blues together in 1923. Jack went on to appear in over 300 games for Walsall (1926-36).
- Manager Terry Cooper (father) and player Mark Cooper (son) were at Blues together in 1991-92.
- Jack 'Soldier' Aston's brother, also named Jack, played for Wolves.
- Blues goalkeeper Harry Hibbs and his counterpart at West Brom, Harold Pearson were cousins. They lined up against each other in the 1931 FA Cup Final.
- Blues striker Wayne Clarke had four brothers, all of whom played at professional level and in the same position - Allan, Derek, Frank and Kelvin.
- Ned Barkas, Blues' 1931 FA Cup Final skipper, had four footballing brothers - Sam (an England international), Tommy, James and Henry. His uncle Thomas Jeffrey also played as a professional while his cousin Billy Felton did likewise.
- The Holdsworth twins, David and Dean, played against each other in the Blues-Bolton League game at The Reebok Stadium in September 1999.
- Blues' forward Danny Wallace had two brothers, Ray and

Two of the three Latchford brothers: Peter (left) and Bob (after a game against West Bromwich Albion).

Rodney - and all three were at Southampton together in 1988-89.

- Dave Regis (Blues) and his brother Cyrille played against each other on many occasions during the 1980s/90s.
- Tom Grosvenor (Blues) and his brother Percy (Leicester City) made almost 300 League and Cup appearances between them. Another Grosvenor brother, Cliff, was on Leicester's books as a junior.
- Gary Bull (a Blues player) is the cousin of Steve Bull, ex West Bromwich Albion and Wolves.

FAMILY OPEN DAY

Brian Farmer

The first official family open day at St Andrew's took place in August 1980. Around 6,000 supporters including mothers and fathers, sisters and brothers, the old, the middle-aged and the young, all flocked through the offices, dressing rooms, social clubs and executive boxes as well as walking round the perimeter of the pitch just to get a feel at what goes on behind the scenes of a major football club.

FARMER, Brian

Full-back Brian Farmer was a steady, efficient defender who got his chance of regular first team football with Blues following the tragic death of Jeff Hall in 1959. He went on to appear in 145 games for the club before transferring to Bournemouth in January 1962, retiring in May 1965 with almost 250 League appearances under his belt. Born in Wordsley, Stourbridge in July 1933, Farmer joined Blues as an amateur in 1950, turned professional in May 1954 and made his debut against Bolton Wanderers in October 1956. He played for Blues in the Fairs Cup Finals of 1960 and 1961. In later years he became a scout in the Midland region.

FENTON, Ronnie

Inside-forward Ronnie Fenton had a useful playing career which spanned almost fifteen years. Born in South Shields in September 1940, he played for Durham Boys before having a trial with West Bromwich Albion. He then assisted his hometown club and was an amateur at Turf Moor before signing professional forms with Burnley in September 1957. From there he ironically joined West Brom for £15,000 in November 1962 and in January 1964 arrived at St Andrew's, Blues' boss Joe Mallett paying £7,500 for his services. He did well with Blues, scoring eight goals in 39 first team appearances before moving to Brentford in January 1968, later assisting Notts County (1970-71). On retiring Fenton became a coach at Meadow Lane and after managing the Magpies for two years (1975-77) he was appointed assistant-trainer/coach under Brian Clough at Nottingham Forest, moving up to assistant-manager in 1987 after ten years service at The City Ground. In his playing career Fenton netted 62 goals in 212 senior games.

FERRIS, Ray

Irishman Ray Ferris was a red-haired half-back, possessing great determination, physical strength and the will-to-win. Born in Newry, County Down in September 1920, he had trials for Distillery, Glentoran and Newry Town before joining Brentford as an amateur in 1938. In the first Wartime season of 1939-40 he played for Cambridge Town and guested for Tottenham Hotspur and West Ham United during the hostilities before signing as a professional for Crewe Alexandra in 1945. Four years later he was recruited by Blues (March 1949) and over the next four years amassed 106 first team appearances and scored four goals. He was

capped three times by Northern Ireland and toured Canada with the Irish FA before joining Worcester City in September 1953. Ferris retired in May 1954 with a knee injury, suffered initially whilst on tour with the FA.

FESTIVAL OF BRITAIN

Blues played four games to celebrate the Festival of Britain in 1951. They lost twice at home - 5-3 to the Scottish club Airdrieonians and 2-0 to Dinamo Yugoslavia - but made amends by winning twice in Ireland, 2-1 against Home Farm and 5-2 versus Cork Athletic.

SUMMARY:

Venue	P	W	D	L	F	A
Home	2	0	0	2	3	7
Away	2	2	0	0	7	3
Totals	4	2	0	2	10	10

FIELD, Charlie

Charlie 'Oakey' Field was a slightly built footballer, with a good turn of speed who was able to play as an orthodox outside-left or as

Roy Ferris, extreme right facing the camera, in action during the local derby against Aston Villa at St Andrew's in April 1950 (2-2).

an inside-forward. A Yorkshireman, born in Hanwell in December 1879, he played a lot of junior football - and scored plenty of goals - before joining Brentford of the Southern League in August 1896. He started off in terrific fashion with the Bees, netting a hat-trick on his debut. In the 1897-98 season he scored over 30 goals including four more hat-tricks and a sixtimer. In the summer of 1898 he moved to Sheffield United and in 1901 helped the Blades reach the FA Cup Final, which they lost to Tottenham Hotspur.

He was recruited by Blues with team-mate Billy Beer in January 1902 but after suffering a serious leg injury early in the 1905-06 season he was forced to retire at the end of that campaign having scored 15 goals in 89 outings for Blues. Field died in Sheffield.

FILLINGHAM. Tom

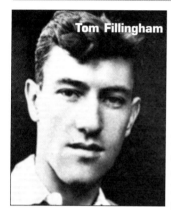

Tom Fillingham

Tom 'Tosher' Fillingham kept goal for Blues reserves before beginning his League career as a centre-forward, scoring twice on his debut in a 4-2 away win over Manchester City in April 1930. Tall, long-legged, strong and dominant in the air, he eventually reverted to a defensive position and replaced George Morrall at centre-half. He went on to make 192 first team appearances for Blues (nine goals scored) before transferring to Ipswich Town in June 1938, retiring the following year. Born in Bulwell, Nottinghamshire in September 1904, Fillingham - a former miner and dye house worker - played for several local clubs before joining Blues from Bromley United in August 1928. Besides his football, Fillingham also enjoyed his cricket and gained a 14 handicap at golf. He lost an eye late in life and died in Bulwell in May 1960.

FIRE

On 21 January 1942, the main stand at St Andrew's was completely gutted by a fire - started ironically by a Fire Officer who inadvertently threw a bucket of petrol (thinking it was water) over a smouldering brazier. The club's records (old programmes, minute books, player's files etc.) were all lost.

FIRSTS

Here is a list of some of the many 'firsts' in Blues' long history:
GAMES
- Football match v Holte Wanderers in November 1875.
- Football League v B.Port Vale (h) 3.9.1892 won 5-1 (Div 2)
- League Division Two v Walsall T.Swifts (a) 10.9.1892 won 3-1
- League Division One v Aston Villa (a) 1.9.1894 lost 1-2
- League Division One v Bolton Wanderers (h) 8.9.1894 won 2-0
- Third Division v Crewe Alexandra (h) 19.8.1989 won 3-0
- Third Division v Bristol City (a) 26.8.1989 lost 0-1
- Football Alliance v B'ham St George's (h) 7.9.1889 won 3-2
- Football Alliance v Walsall Town Swifts (a) 21.9.1889 drew 1-1
- FA Cup v Derby Town (h) 17.10.1881 won 4-1
- FA Cup v Wednesbury Old Athletic (a) 3.12.1881 lost 0-6
- League Cup v Bradford Park Avenue (a) 31.10.1960 won 1-0

Ronnie Fenton, Blues' first substitute to score.

- League Cup v Plymouth Argyle (h) 14.11.1960 drew 0-0
- Inter Cities Fairs Cup v Inter Milan (a) 15 May 1956 drew 0-0
- Inter Cities Fairs Cup v Zagreb Select (h) 3.12.1956 won 3-0
- Sunday game v Coventry C. (a) League Division 1, 16.2.1986, drew 4-4

INDIVIDUALS & CLUB
- League goalscorer - Fred Wheldon v B. Port Vale, 3.9.1892
- FA Cup scorer - Billy Slater v Derby Town on 17.10.1881
- League Cup scorer - Mike Hellawell v Bradford PA on 31.10.1960
- European scorer - Eddie Brown v Zagreb Select on 21.5.1956
- Full international - Caesar Jenkyns for Wales v Ireland 1891-92
- English international - Chris Charsley v Ireland 1891-92
- Scottish international - Johnny Crosbie v England 1921-22
- N.Ireland international - Jackie Brown v Scotland 1938-39
- Eire international - Jimmy Higgins v Argentina 1950-51
- U-23 international - Trevor Smith for England v Italy 1954-55
- U-21 international - Keith Bertschin for England v Scotland 1976-77
- England 'B' - Len Boyd v Holland 1951-52
- Hat-trick (League) - Billy Walton v Walsall Town Swifts (h) 17.12.1892
- Hat-trick (FA Cup) - Eddie Stanley v Burton Wanderers (h) 31.10.1885
- Hat-trick (League Cup) - Bob Hatton v Blackpool (h) 16.10.1973
- Hat-trick (Alliance) Will Devey v Nottingham Forest (h) 8.3.1890
- Manager (full time) - Bob McRoberts, appointed in July 1910
- Captain (official) - Billy Edmunds, appointed in 1877
- Sending-off - Caesar Jenkyns v Liverpool (H), League, 14.10.1893
- Penalty - scored by Fred Wheldon v Aston Villa (H), League 20.10.1894

- Penalty conceded - v Villa in the above match (Dennis Hodgetts scored)
- Black player - Carlos Francis (with Blues: 1979-84)
- Substitute (League) - Brian Sharples for Ron Wylie at PNE on 28.8.1965.
- 'Sub' to score - Ronnie Fenton v Bury (League) on 18.12.1965.
- First 'Cup' substitute: Fenton v Grimsby (FAC) on 26.10.1966 (scored).
- Chairman - Walter W. Hart, appointed on 24 July 1888, when Blues became the FIRST football club in the country to have a Directorate as a limited company.
- First secretary of Blues (Small Heath): Billy Edmunds in 1875.
- Fred Pentland was the first 'footballing' internee during World War One (see Pentland, Fred).
- The first club to score over 100 goals in a season of Second Division football was Birmingham (Small Heath) who achieved the feat in 1893-94 (total 103).
- Tommy Rae was the first player signed on loan by Blues. He joined the club in season 1965-66 but never appeared in competitive match. The first loanee to make a League appearance for the club was Irishman Tommy Carroll, who was signed in October 1971 from Ipswich Town. He made his Blues debut against Burnley in a Second Division game at Turf Moor.

FIRST GAME

Blues played their first game (under the name of Small Heath Alliance) at their Arthur Street ground on a bitterly cold afternoon in November 1875. In a 12-a-side contest, they drew 1-1 with Holte Wanderers from Aston. David Keys had the pleasure of scoring the club's first-ever goal.

Blues lined up with W. Edden (goalkeeper); A. Wright, F. James, T. James, G. Edden, W. Edmunds (captain), T. Edden, D. Keys, C. Barmore, C. Barr, J. Sparrow and R. Morris. The latter was recruited to the side at the last minute when it was seen that the Wanderers were fielding an extra player!

FIRTH, Jack

Jack Firth was reserve for Blues at Wembley for the 1931 FA Cup Final. Born in Doncaster in August 1907 he was an amateur with his hometown club before moving to St Andrew's, signing professional forms in August 1926 after a five-month trial period. Able to play as a wing-half or inside-forward and a player who was prepared to try his luck by shooting at goal from 30-40 yards range, he scored eight times in 98 senior appearances for Blues before moving to Swansea Town in August 1933, later assisting Bury (from May 1936). He played in more than 100 games for the Swans and was a very useful cricketer with Brodsworth Main. He died in Doncaster in December

FIRTH, Robert (Bob)

No relation to Jack (above) Bob Firth was a tram conductor when he signed for Blues in April 1909. Born in Sheldon in February 1887 and a pupil at Gower Street School Aston, he served in the 6th Battery Royal Field Artillery as an 18 year-old before taking to the buses! An outside-right, clever at times, he scored twice in 26 outings for Blues before leaving St Andrew's for Wellington Town in February 1911. Between October 1911 and

Bob Firth

March 1921 he scored 14 goals in 146 games for Nottingham Forest and after spells with Port Vale and Southend United he retired in May 1923.

FLOODLIGHTS

Floodlights were first erected at St Andrew's in 1956. Four pylons, standing 114 feet high, were placed in each corner of the ground with the two at the Tilton Road End slightly higher than the others.

They were officially 'opened' (switched on) on 31 October of that year when the German side Borussia Dortmund played Blues in a friendly match. A crowd of 45,000 witnessed an exciting 3-3 draw with Bryan Orritt (2) and Alex Govan scoring for Blues who fielded this team: Merrick; Farmer, Green; Watts, Newman, Warhurst; Astall, Orritt, Brown, Larkin, Govan.

Blues played Torquay United at Plainmoor in November 1954 in a game arranged to officially 'switch on' the south Devon club's new floodlights. Blues won 3-2.

In November 1961 Blues took a side to Scotland to play Stirling Albion in a game to officially 'switch on' the floodlights at Annfield Park.

And in April 1977 Blues visited non-League Alvechurch to officially open their new floodlights, likewise in September 1978 they played away at Brierley Hill in a floodlight-opening friendly (won 4-0).

FOOTBALL ALLIANCE

Blues spent three seasons playing Alliance League Football: 1889-92 inclusive.

THEIR FULL RECORD:

Venue	P	W	D	L	F	A	Pts
Home	33	19	5	9	99	52	43
Away	33	6	7	20	56	117	19
Totals	66	25	12	29	155	169	62

They finished 10th in 1889-90 and again in 1890-91 before taking third spot in 1891-92 prior to gaining entry into the newly-formed Football League Division Two.

Blues' biggest Alliance win was a 12-0 thrashing of Nottingham Forest (h) in March 1890. Their heaviest defeat was 9-1 - suffered on two separate occasions, at Sheffield Wednesday in December 1889 and away to Newton Heath (Manchester United) in April 1890.

Blues conceded 21 goals in five Alliance games between 22 November 1890 and 3 January 1891 and they also let in 30 goals in six successive away games: April-October 1890.

Will Devey notched a club record 35 Alliance League goals for Blues during the first two seasons of the competition. Fred Wheldon scored 34 goals in total with 21 in 1891-92.

Frank Speller with 64 out of a possible 66 made most appearances in the Football Alliance for Blues. Ted Devey played in 61 games.

Blues' best attendance for a home Alliance game was 5,000 - against Sunderland Albion on 13 September 1891, Walsall Town Swifts on 18 October that same year and Nottingham Forest on 28 February 1891.

The lowest home crowd was a mere 500 - versus Darwen on 15 February 1890 and Sheffield Wednesday on 10 January 1891

FA CUP

Blues' goalkeeper Harry Hibbs punches clear during the 1931 FA Cup Final against West Bromwich Albion at Wembley.

Blues first entered the FA (English) Cup competition in season 1881-82, winning a home tie against Derby Town by 4-1 to set the ball rolling.

Since then they have played a further 300 matches, a total that includes the third place play-off match v Stoke City in 1972-73.

Blues' full FA Cup record (to end of the 1999-2000 season):

Venue	P	W	D	L	F	A
Home	157	92	28	37	354	164
Away	125	40	27	58	169	198
Neutral	19	2	4	13	14	38
Totals	301	134	59	108	537	400

FA CUP FACTS

- The statistics include all ties that were 'switched' from home to an away venue and vice-versa. Also the drawn games at Liverpool in 1995 and the 3/4th place play-off match versus Stoke City in 1972 have both been included in the respective home and away 'draw' columns although both fixtures were decided via a penalty shoot-out.
- Neutral grounds include 2nd/3rd replays, semi-finals and finals.
- Blues have reached the FA Cup Final twice - in 1931 (beaten 2-1 by West Bromwich Albion) and 1956 (defeated 3-1 by Manchester City).
- Blues have also played in nine FA Cup semi-finals - once prior to the commencement of League Football (1886), four times as a Second Division club (1946, 1951, 1968 and 1972) and on four occasions whilst in the First Division (1931, 1956, 1957 and 1975).
- They have made the quarter-finals on 18 occasions.
- For reaching the 1886 semi-final against West Bromwich Albion, each Blues player received 2s 6d (13p)....5p for a cab to the ground and 8p for a meal! And when they reached the last four they eclipsed their arch rivals Aston Villa, who did not play in their first FA Cup semi-final until the following March when they played Glasgow Rangers!
- Blues failed to enter the FA Cup in 1921-22. The club secretary (Frank Richards) missed the deadline for applications - and this after Blues had won the Second Division championship the season before!
- Blues were disqualified from the 1890-91 FA Cup competition for fielding a match SHORT! The team for a second qualifying game of that season's tournament away to Wednesbury Old Athletic (won 2-0) contained an illegible player by the name of Charlie Short, ex-Unity Gas FC, who actually scored one of the goals. Despite pleading ignorance the club was reprimanded by the FA, but not fined! Blues had beaten Hednesford 8-0 in the opening round.
- Blues were knocked out of the competition at the first hurdle six seasons running: 1892-93 to 1897-98 inclusive.
- Blues scored 31 goals in the 1898-99 FA Cup competition.
- Joe Bradford netted at least one goal in every round of the FA Cup tournament in 1930-31, and he was the first player to net an equaliser in a Cup Final at Wembley, against West Bromwich Albion that season.
- Blues played all their Cup games away from St Andrew's in 1955-56.
- Blues lost 2-0 on penalties to Liverpool at Anfield in an FA Cup 3rd round replay in January 1995 (after 0-0 and 1-1 draws respectively).
- Blues' biggest FA Cup wins have been those of 10-0 v Druids (h) November 1898, 10-2 v Oswestry United (h) October 1899, 9-0 v Burton Wanderers (h) December 1888, 9-2 v Burton Wanderers, again, October 1885 and 8-0 v Chirk (h) October 1898.
- Their heaviest defeats have all been away - 0-6 (twice) to Wednesbury Old Athletic in December 1881 and at Tottenham Hotspur, April 1967; 2-6 (twice) against Stafford Road in November 1882 and Manchester United at Old Trafford in February 1969 and 0-5 versus Nottingham Forest at neutral Filbert Street in February 1959.
- The first FA Cup-tie at St Andrew's did not feature Blues! It was the semi-final clash between Arsenal and Sheffield Wednesday in March 1907.

- The first FA Cup encounter at St Andrew's involving Blues was against West Bromwich Albion on 15 January 1908 when the Baggies won a 1st round replay 2-1.
- Gil Merrick appeared in a record 56 FA Cup matches for Blues - and there weren't too many goalkeepers who starred in four semi-finals around the same time: Merrick did, in 1946, 1951, 1956 and 1957.
- Joe Bradford scored a record 18 FA Cup goals for Blues (in 31 matches).
- Alf Bond refereed Blues 3rd round FA Cup tie against Torquay United in January 1956 and then took charge of the Final against Manchester City three months later.

The 1956 FA Cup Final programme

FA YOUTH CUP FINAL

Blues reached the final of the FA Youth Cup in 1967. The contest against Sunderland was played over two legs, the first at St Andrew's on 17 May and the return at Roker Park a week later.

Blues lost their home leg 1-0, fielding this side: D. Latchford; Reynolds, Beckett; Lee, Saunders, Pendrey; Rushworth, Dorsett, R. Latchford, Bowker, Jones.

Blues were unchanged for the Roker Park clash and again they lost 1-0, losing the final 2-0 on aggregate.

Colin Suggett, Billy Hughes and goalkeeper Derek Forster were the stars of the Sunderland side.

Blues were defeated by Newcastle United in the FA Youth Cup semi-final in the 1984-85 season.

FOOTBALL LEAGUE

Blues' record in the Football League: 1892-2000 inclusive:

Venue	P	W	D	L	F	A
Home	1973	1021	486	466	3575	2194
Away	1973	466	486	1021	2211	3486
Totals	3946	1487	972	1487	5786	5680

Divisional Breakdown

Division	P	W	D	L	F	A	Pts.
1	2040	651	501	888	2776	3296	1845
1/2	1722	754	416	552	2752	2187	2101
2/3	184	82	55	47	258	197	301
Totals	3946	1487	972	1487	5786	5680	4247

LEAGUE FACTS

- Blues were founder members of the Football League Division Two in season 1892-93 and they won the championship at the first attempt with an impressive record of 17 wins and two draws from 22 matches. Their goal-average was 90 for and 35 against and they finished one point ahead of runners-up Sheffield United (36-35). But Blues did not gain promotion - they missed out by drawing 1-1 and losing 5-2 in two Test Matches against Newton

Heath (Manchester United).

- The following season though they did gain a place in the top flight by finishing second, eight points behind Liverpool (50-42), and then beating Darwen in a Test Match.
- Blues' highest-ever placing in the Football League was to finish sixth in season 1955-56 when they also reached the FA Cup Final for the second time.
- Blues won the 'old' Second Division title in 1892-93, 1920-21, 1947-48 and 1954-55. In 1994-95 they won the 'new' Second Division championship and they have also gained promotion as follows: from Division 2/1 in 1894, 1901, 1903, 1972, 1980 (in third place) and 1985 and from Division 3/2 in 1992.
- After finishing 4th, 6th, 8th and 3rd Blues finally regained their First Division status at the fifth attempt in 1900-01 as runners-up.
- It was a similar case in the early 1950s when Blues came 4th, 3rd, 6th and 7th before winning the Second Division title (and promotion) in 1954-55 by just 0.297 of a goal. The only time they topped the table was when they won at Doncaster on the last day of the campaign.
- From 1959-60 to 1964-65 Blues finished in the bottom six of the First Division before being relegated in last place!
- Blues made their best-ever start to a League season in 1900-01 (Division Two) when they were undefeated in their opening 15 matches (winning eight and drawing seven). They had won their last game of the previous season, giving Blues a 16-match unbeaten run.
- The club's best unbeaten League run, however, is 20 matches - from 3 September 1994 to 2 January 1995 inclusive. The previous record was 18 in 1971-72. Goalkeeper Ian Bennett kept seven successive clean sheets in that 20-match sequence in 1994-95.
- In season 1994-95 Blues amassed a club record 89 points. When it was two points for a win their highest total was 59 in season 1947-48.
- Blues played in the First Division from 1921 to 1939 (18 seasons)...the longest run on the top flight in the club's history. Their highest placing was 8th (in 1924-25) while they finished in the bottom six on eight occasions.
- In season 1972-73 Blues' League record in Division One was P42 W15 D12 L15 F53 A54 Pts 42.
- Blues' best League win is 12-0, achieved twice, against Walsall Town Swifts (h) in December 1892 and versus Doncaster Rovers (h) in April 1903.
- At the end of the 1999-2000 season Blues' goalkeepers and defenders between them had kept 1,068 clean-sheets in the 3,946 League games played by the club since 1892 (Test Matches and Play-off games not included). Blues' 1,000th clean sheet in League football came at Norwich (won 1-0) on 30 November 1996.
- Their heaviest League defeat has been a 9-1 drubbing at the hands of Sheffield Wednesday at Hillsborough in December 1930.
- Blues applied for membership of the First Division for the 1919-20 season when it was increased to 22 clubs. Unfortunately they received only two votes. Arsenal took the honours with 18 votes and they've been in the top flight ever since!
- After finishing 20th and bottom of the Second Division in 1909-10, Blues had to apply for re-election to the Football League. They were successful, obtaining 30 votes, four more than

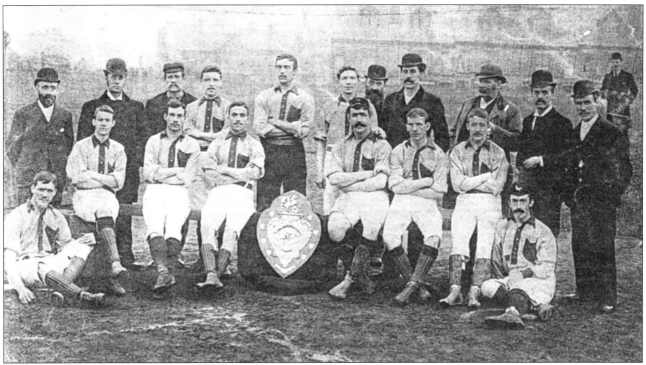

1893-94 (players only) back row (left to right): Jolly, Hollis and Devey. Seated, second row: Hallam, Pumphrey, Mobley, Jenkyns, Wheldon & Hands. On ground: Ollis & Lee (in cap).

Huddersfield Town, who were also re-elected. The clubs who challenged for a League place but missed out were Grimsby Town (17 votes), Darlington (7), Chesterfield (2), Hartlepool United (1) and Rochdale (1).

• If three points had been awarded for a win in 1937-38, Blues and NOT Manchester City would have been relegated to the Second Division. In 1946-47 it would have been Blues and NOT Burnley who would have been promoted to the First Division. In 1950-51

Blues would have climbed up into the top flight and NOT Cardiff City and in 1979-80 Chelsea and NOT Blues would have gained a place in the First Division.

• Blues have still to play the following present-day clubs at Football League level: Barnet, Cheltenham Town, Colchester United, Gillingham (due to meet in 2000-01), Halifax Town, Hereford United, Kidderminster Harriers, Rochdale and Scunthorpe United.

1921-22 Back row, left to right: W Kendrick (Assistant-trainer), Neil, Sharp, Getgood, Reddington, Tremelling, Hunter, Liddell, Jenkins, Brown, S Scholey (masseur), J Eccles (trainer). Second row: FH Richards (secretary), Burkinshaw, J Harris (director), Roulson, H Cant (chairman), WW Hart (director), T Turley (director), White, HS Thomas (director), S Richards (assistant-secretary). Third row: Booth, Whitehouse, Hampton, McClure, Womack, Barton, Elkes, Lane, Jones, Davies, Harvey. On ground: Cameron, Dixon, Crosbie, Linley, Bradford, Daws. The three trophies are the Birmingham Senior Cup, the Football League Division Two championship shield and the Lord Mayor of Birmingham Charity Cup.

- The longest trips Blues have made to play in a Football League game is approximately 226 miles.... to Sunderland. They have travelled 220 miles south to take on Plymouth Argyle and have also gone around 200 miles north to play Hartlepool and Newcastle United.

PLAY-OFFS

Blues have twice been involved in the First Division promotion play-offs - 1998-99 and 1999-2000 - and on each occasion they suffered disappointment! Watford beat them on penalties in May 1999 (after the two-legged semi-final had ended 1-1) and in May 2000 Barnsley prevented Blues from reaching Wembley with a 5-2 aggregate victory (winning 4-0 at St Andrew's but losing the return leg 2-1 at Oakwell).

Summary

Venue	P	W	D	L	F	A
Home	2	1	0	1	1	4
Away	2	1	0	1	2	2
Totals	4	2	0	2	3	6

TEST MATCHES

Blues were involved in end-of-season Test Match drama three times. In April 1893, after winning the Second Division championship at the first attempt, they did not gain automatic promotion, and had to play a two-legged Test match against Newton Heath (Manchester United) to decide who went up into the top flight. Blues crashed 6-3 on aggregate after drawing 1-1 at Stoke and losing 5-2 at Bramall Lane, Sheffield.

Their second venture followed in April 1894 when they played and beat Darwen 3-1 at Stoke to win promotion after finishing runners-up in Division Two.

And in April 1896 Blues were forced to play four Test Matches, this time to decide whether or not they stayed in the First Division! Unfortunately they were relegated after losing 4-0 at Liverpool and 3-0 at Manchester City and only drawing 0-0 at home with the Reds but thrashing the Mancunians 8-0.

TEST MATCH SUMMARY

Venue	P	W	D	L	F	A
Home	2	1	1	0	8	0
Away	2	0	0	2	0	7
Neutral	3	1	1	1	6	7
Totals	7	2	2	3	14	14

FOOTBALL LEAGUE CUP
(Coca-Cola Cup, Milk Cup, Worthington Cup)

Blues entered the Football League Cup competition at the outset in season 1960-61, winning their opening game 1-0 at Park Avenue against Bradford. Mike Hellawell was the goalscorer in front of 4,736 spectators on 31 October.

Since then Blues have played a further 145 games in the competition and this is their overall record up to and including the 1999-2000 season:

Stan Lynn and Trevor Smith with League Cup in 1963

Venue	P	W	D	L	F	A
Home	73	41	13	19	144	85
Away	72	20	23	29	80	110
Neutral	1	1	0	0	1	0
Totals	146	62	36	48	225	195

LEAGUE CUP FACT FILE

- Blues won the trophy in season 1962-63, beating neighbours and arch rivals Aston Villa 3-1 in the two-legged Final.
- Blues have also lost in two League Cup semi-finals - in 1966-67, beaten by Queens Park Rangers and in 1995-96, defeated by Leeds United.
- Blues' best League Cup victory is 6-0 - achieved twice against Manchester City in 1962-63 and versus Macclesfield Town in 1998-99. Both games were played at St Andrew's.
- On their way to winning the trophy in 1962-63 Blues beat Doncaster Rovers 5-0 and Barrow 5-1, both at home.
- Blues' heaviest League Cup defeat to date has been 5-0 - against Tottenham Hotspur (away) in 1986-87 and versus Aston Villa (also away) in 1988-89.
- Blues' worst League Cup defeat at St Andrew's has been 2-5 at the hands of Southampton in 1978-79. They also lost 1-4 to Q.P.R. in the 1966-67 semi-final first leg.
- A total of 22 of Blues' 35 drawn games in the League Cup competition have had a 1-1 scoreline.
- Blues were knocked out of the League Cup by Premiership opposition seven seasons running: 1992-93 to 1999-2000 inclusive. The teams involved were Aston Villa, Blackburn Rovers, Leeds United, Coventry City, Arsenal, Wimbledon and West Ham United.

FOOTBALL LEAGUE JUBILEE

Blues played Coventry City in two Football League Jubilee matches in August 1938 and August 1939, both at Highfield Road.

The first encounter ended in a 2-0 defeat in front of 12,133 fans and the second in a 3-0 reverse before 7,979 spectators. In the latter game two Blues players - Wilson Jones and Seymour Morris - left the field injured.

FOOTBALLER/PLAYER OF THE YEAR

Former Blues star Kenny Burns was voted PFA Footballer of the Year in 1977-78 when a Nottingham Forest player and defender Colin Todd, a future Blues player, received the same accolade in 1974-75 whilst with Derby County.

Dave Mackay, who was Blues manager from April 1989 to January 1991, was voted Scotland's 'Player of the Year' in 1957-58 when with Heart of Midlothian. In 1969 he received the FWA 'Player of the Year' award (jointly with Manchester City's skipper Tony Book) after leading Derby County to the Second Division championship.

FOREIGN BORN PLAYERS

Here is a list of some of the many foreign-born (overseas) players who have been associated with Blues down the years: Dele Adebola (Lagos, Nigeria), Jatto Ceesay (Gambia, trialist), Jose Dominguez (Portugal), Rui Esteves (Portugal), Bart Griemink (Holland), James Haarhoff (Lusaka), Tony Hey (Germany),

Lyndon Hooper (Guyana), Vasil Kalogeracos (Malaya), Hymie Kloner (South Africa), Stan Lararidis (Australia), Anders Limpar (Sweden), Tresor Luntala (France), Marcelo (Brazil), Thomas Myhre (Denmark), Peter Ndlovu (Bulawayo), Folorunso Okenla (Nigeria), John Paskin (South Africa), Paul Peschisolido (Canada), Paul Pezos (Australia), Sigurd Rushfeldt (Norway), Dan Sahlin (Sweden), Alberto Tarantini (Argentina), Pat Van Den Hauwe (Belgium), Jacques Williams (France), Christopher Wreh (Monrovia, Liberia).

Alberto Tarantini

FOREIGN OPPOSITION

Programme for the game v Czech Army in 1941 (Blues won 4-0).

Over the years Blues have met scores of foreign club sides, several at home, the majority away (see overseas tours).

Here are some of the teams that have visited St Andrew's: AC Sparta, A.I.K. Stockholm, Ajax Amsterdam (1978 when Blues won 1-0), Asanti Kotoko, AS Bari, AS Roma, Ascoli Calcio, Cesena, Czechoslovakian Army (1941), CF Barcelona, Bela Vista, Boldklub Copenhagen, Borussia Dortmund, Bratislava, Brescia Calcio, Cologne Select, Dinamo Yugoslavia, Dinamo Zagreb, Ferencvaros, Genoa, FC Groningen, FC Lucerne (Blues beat the Swiss side 10-1 in August 1980), Internazionale (Inter Milan), Lanerossi Vicenza, Los Angeles Aztecs (October 1979), FC Ominia, Real Madrid (1925), RCD Espanol, RCD Mallorca, Sampdoria, Slovan Bratislava, Sparta Prague (Athletic Prague), Tampa Bay Rowdies (October 1980), Ujpesti Dozsa, Union St Gilloise, Valencia, Willem II (also Tilborg Willem II) and Zagreb Select... and there are a few others! Even the Australian national team visited St Andrew's for a friendly in November 1976.

FORMATION OF CLUB

It is a well-known fact that Birmingham City football club was officially formed (as Small Heath Alliance) in late September or early October 1875.

Cricketing enthusiasts who were largely members of the Holy Trinity Church, Bordesley Green, determined to continue their sporting relationships during the winter months, decided, unanimously, to form a football team which they called Small Heath Alliance. It was as simple as that!

After a few kick-abouts on a stretch of waste land in Arthur Street, just off the main Coventry Road (not too far away from the present day St Andrew's ground) Blues played their first game - in November 1875 against Holte Wanderers from Aston. Today supporters and players alike owe an awful lot to those pioneers of 125 years ago.

FOSTER, Winston

Born during the War (in South Yardley, Birmingham in November 1941) hence his patriotic Christian name, Foster began his professional career as a long-legged, awkward-looking fullback. But injuries to Trevor Smith gave him the opportunity to establish himself at centre-half where he became much more at ease, producing some excellent performances for Blues until a knee injury interrupted his progress. He was signed in 1955 as a junior after representing the Birmingham County FA and turned professional in November 1958. He played in 170 senior games for Blues (two goals scored) and also had a loan spell with Crewe Alexandra before transferring to Plymouth Argyle in the summer of 1969, later assisting Chelmsford City and Bromsgrove Rovers, becoming assistant-manager of the latter club in 1973-74. Blues played a testimonial at Plymouth for Foster.

FRAIN, John

After forming a successful full-back partnership with Julian Dicks in the youth team at St. Andrew's John Frain surprisingly failed to impress at first in that position in the senior side. But after being converted into a midfield player also playing at full-back he did exceedingly well and went on to amass a total of 336 first-team appearances for Blues, scoring 26 goals. He skippered Blues on a number of occasions and starred at Wembley in the Freight Rover Trophy success over Tranmere Rovers in 1991. During his St Andrew's career Frain also played as a sweeper and was a terrific competitor, giving his all out on the pitch. In January 1997 he was transferred to Northampton Town and at the end of that season visited the Empire Stadium again - this time helping the Cobblers beat Swansea City in the Third Division play-off Final. During the second half of the 1999-2000 season Frain took his career appearance tally past the 450 mark.

John Frain - throwing in his lot with Blues!

FRANCIS, Kevin

Standing at 6ft. 7ins. in his bare feet, giant striker Kevin Francis is tallest player ever to appear in League football. He was born in Birmingham in December 1967 and played his early football with Mile Oak Rovers before becoming a professional with Derby County in February 1989. Francis made 17 senior appearances for the Rams (ten as a substitute in the Football League) before transferring to Stockport County for £45,000 in February 1991. He did exceptionally well at Edgeley Park, bagging 117 goals in less than 200 outings for the Hatters. Despite his awkward, ungainly and perhaps cumbersome style on the ground, he was extremely difficult to mark at set pieces and this clearly impressed Blues manager Barry Fry (and the club's Directors) who paid a record fee of £800,000 to bring the lanky striker to St Andrew's in January 1995. He quickly helped Blues win the Second Division championship and Auto-Windscreen Shield at Wembley and went on to net 21 goals in 94 outings for the club before leaving for Oxford United for £100,000 in February 1998. Two years later Francis returned to his former home at Edgeley Park.

FRANCIS, Trevor

Born in Plymouth in April 1954, Trevor Francis was an exceptionally talented teenage footballer who joined Blues as a junior in 1969 after playing for Plymouth Boys. He made rapid progress and before turning professional (in May 1971) he had already starred in 26 first team matches, scoring 16 goals, including a four-timer as a 16 year-old v Bolton Wanderers at St Andrew's in February 1971. The following season his 12 League goals helped Blues gain promotion from the Second Division.

Displaying electrifying speed over 25-35 yards, Francis was also a clever dribbler and brilliant finisher, possessing a powerful right-foot shot - and when he chose to shoot from distance he was often spot on target!

He went on to claim 133 goals in 329 appearances for Blues, scoring in eight successive League games between 6 February and 27 March 1971. He had the first of two decent spells in the NASL with Detroit Express prior to becoming the first £1 million footballer (£975,000 plus VAT & levy charges = £1.18 million) when he was transferred to Nottingham Forest in February 1979. Within three months of moving to The City Ground he scored the winning goal in the European Cup Final and after that his career got better and better! He gained 52 full caps for England (his first 12 won with Blues). He also appeared in five Under-23 internationals to go with the half-dozen youth caps he won as a teenager. He helped Forest win the League Cup in 1980 before moving to Manchester City for £1.2 million in September 1981.

From Maine Road he switched to Italy to play for Sampdoria (signing for £800,000 in July 1982), A year later, after collecting an Italian Cup winners medal, a £900,000 deal took Francis to Atalanta and in September 1987 he signed on a free transfer for Glasgow Rangers. Whilst at Ibrox Park he gained a Scottish League Cup winners medal before returning to the English game with Queens Park Rangers in March 1988, taking over as player-manager at Loftus Road in December of that same year.

He did not settle with Rangers and duly left the London club for Sheffield Wednesday in February 1990, taking over as player-manager at Hillsborough in June 1991, shortly after helping the Owls to a League Cup Final victory and promotion from the Second

Trevor Francis in action v Norwich City.

Division. He held that position for four years, retiring as a player in 1993. In May 1996 Francis returned 'home' to St Andrew's as manager, and on taking charge of Blues he said: "People will think I'm crackers. I'm voluntarily going back to the madhouse."

After coming through a difficult period he guided Blues into the First Division play-offs in succession seasons: 1998-99 and 1999-2000. Sadly, on both occasions, Blues failed at the death to make it to Wembley, losing, in turn, to Watford (on penalties after an aggregate 1-1 draw) and Barnsley (2-5 over two legs).

In his playing career Francis accumulated a total of more than 750 appearances at club and international level and scored over 220 goals.

NB - In August 1998 Francis signed a new one-year deal worth £4,000-a-week, making him the highest-paid person in the club's history.

FREEHOLD

The freehold of St Andrew's was bought in April 1921 for what is believed to have been less than £7,000.

FRIENDLY MATCHES

Programme cover from 1992 International Football Tournament

Before established competitive League and Cup football came to the forefront, most clubs up and down the country, Blues included, played several friendly matches during the course of a season - and this was the norm until the early 1900s.

Here are details of some of Blues' early friendly confrontations.

Blues' first ever game was a friendly, at home to Holte Wanderers in November 1875. The game ended in a 1-1 draw.

It is believed that Blues recorded their first victory over Nechells in September 1876, beating their near neighbours 2-0 in a home friendly match. Soon afterwards Aston Manor were eclipsed 5-0, also at home.

In 1877-78 Blues won all of the recorded 22 friendly matches. Their best win as a 10-0 triumph over St Luke's in April, a month after Walsall Swifts had been hammered 10-0. Lion Works were defeated 9-0 in mid-December and Coventry 8-0 (away) in January. In all Blues scored 108 goals for and conceded only 11.

Thereafter, until entering the Football Alliance in 1889, Blues played on average 20-30 friendly games a season plus various cup-ties.

It is understood that Blues' biggest friendly win on record is that of 18-1 over hapless Elwells (from the West Bromwich area) in October 1882. Blues, in fact, played with only 10 men for the last hour of this game following an injury to Sam Gessey after 29 minutes.

On 21 May 1888 Blues entertained Long Eaton Rangers at home in an end-of-season friendly. The visitors turned up with only eight players and had to make the numbers up by recruiting three spectators. Blues won the game 15-0.

Their heaviest defeat could well have been a 9-1 reverse at Stoke in February 1884. Blues also lost 8-1 at Aston Villa in March 1886 and 7-0 against the same team two months later. Villa also won 7-0 on Blues' soil in March 1887 - as they prepared for their FA Cup Final showdown against WBA.

A ten-goal thriller with Notts County in April 1885 ended all square at 5-5.

Blues beat Bolton 7-0, WBA 4-0, 5-0, 5-1 and 8-3, Woolwich Arsenal 4-3, Leyton 8-3, Liverpool 5-1 and Everton 6-2 all before 1900. They also lost heavily against Aston Villa 1-5 and 2-5, Newton Heath 2-7, Everton reserves 1-5, Millwall 1-9 (in London) and Hibernian 2-5.

Blues travelled to Norwich for a friendly in 1908 and lost 5-2 and four years later they lost 4-0 at Sheffield United.

During the Great War (September 1917) Blues beat an Army side 10-1 at the Rugeley Camp (Stevens scored five goals).

In January 1922 the famous Corinthians came to St Andrew's and lost 5-0 to Blues and three years later Blues were defeated 3-0 on Corinthians soil.

On their first overseas tour to Denmark in 1922 Blues were unbeaten and in May 1923 they played two matches in Spain, winning them both, 6-1 against CD Europa (in Barcelona) and 3-0 versus Real Madrid 3-0. This was the Blues team for both matches: Tremelling; Ashurst, Jones; Davies, McClure, Liddell; Harvey, Rawson, Bradford, Lane, Linley. Joe Bradford scored a hat-trick in the 6-1 victory.

Blues had defender Alec McClure sent-off during the match with Real Madrid (see under Sendings-off).

In the return 'friendly' at St Andrew's in September 1925, a strong Real Madrid side again lost 3-0 to Blues in front of 10,000 spectators.

Six months later (in March 1926) Glentoran from Ireland succumbed to an 8-2 home defeat when Joe Bradford scored four times.

During the 1930s and '40s only a handful of friendlies were played (sometimes none at all in any one season) but in the 1950s they increased in numbers as did Blues' trips abroad - and the team was involved in several interesting encounters.

Blues lost 2-1 to an Edinburgh Select side in August 1956, were beaten 3-0 in Valencia in March 1958 and crumbled to a 5-2 defeat against Dunfermline Athletic two days before Christmas, 1959.

Over 50 friendlies (including tour matches) were fulfilled in the 1960s; more than 60 were completed in the 1970s and close on 90 during the 'eighties with a further 60 or so following between 1990 and 2000.

In fact, in season 1980-81, a total of 23 home and away friendly matches were fulfilled by Blues' first XI.

Blues beat the Australian national side 4-1 at St Andrew's in November 1976 (Trevor Francis and Joe Gallagher scoring twice each). The Dutch side Ajax were Blues' visitors in a pre-season game in August 1978 and both Keith Bertschin and Archie Gemmill found the net twice when Blues whipped Ominia 5-0 in August 1979.

The last time Blues scored ten goals in a game was at home to FC Lucerne in a friendly in August 1980. The Swiss side were crushed 10-1 with Tony Evans (3), Gemmill (3) and Bertschin (2) the leading scorers.

Arsenal visited St Andrew's in 1988 and beat Blues 4-0 in a pre-season friendly.

In August 1992 an international tournament was staged at St Andrew's involving Blues, the Italian club Brescia Calcio, RCD Mallorca from Spain and Coventry City.

In recent years Blues have done reasonably well in several home friendlies, beating Manchester United 1-0 in August 1995. They have also lost a few, however, including a 4-0 home reverse against Chelsea in 1995 and a 6-0 drubbing at the hands of Aston Villa (see benefits) a year later.

FRY, Barry

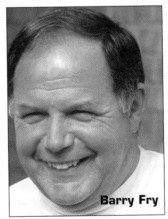

Barry Fry

Barry Fry, friendly, enthusiastic and vibrant had a terrific personality and brought sunshine to the drabbest of days! He was appointed Blues manager in December 1993 (in succession to Terry Cooper) and remained at the club until June 1996. After seeing Blues make a reasonable start under his control, Fry then started to pull his hair out as the team put together a run of 14 matches without a WIN. Relegation was staring Blues smack in the face but despite almost sorting things out with six wins and two draws from their remaining nine outings demotion could not be avoided.

In 1994-95 Fry used a staggering 41 players - but his switching and swapping around (mainly because of injury problems) worked as Blues stormed back into the First Division. They also won the Auto Windscreen Shield at Wembley when over 40,000 'Bluenoses' in the 76,663 crowd celebrated a 1-0 'golden goal' victory over Carlisle United.

The following season (1995-96) it was reported that Fry made tentative enquiries about every FOOTBALLER in the country as he again made changes galore to his team, using no fewer than 47 different players this time round - an all-time record for any club! Blues struggled hard and long to finish a disappointing 15th in the First Division. The Board wasn't too happy with what had transpired and after certain fans had lost their patience, Fry was dismissed just days after being given a 'vote of confidence' by his chairman!

Born in Bedford in April 1945, Fry was a player with Manchester United, Bolton Wanderers, Luton Town, Gravesend & Northfleet, Leyton Orient, Romford and Bedford Town - and he represented England at Schoolboy level.

His first managerial appointment came at non-League Dunstable Town (1972-76) and after further appointments with Hillingdon Borough (1976-77), his former club Bedford Town (1977-78), Barnet (1978-85) and Maidstone United (1985-86) he returned to Underhill and guided The Bees into the Football League in 1991 as GM Vauxhall Conference champions. Towards the end of their second League season (1992-93) just as Barnet were preparing to celebrate promotion from the Third Division, Fry took over the reins at Southend United but eight months later he was in charge at St Andrew's. After leaving Blues he eventually found his way to Peterborough United (appointed in May 1996) and four years later took Posh to Wembley for the Third Division play-off final after seeing his former club Barnet knocked out in the semi-final. Then a delighted Fry was 'over the moon' when his charges beat Darlington 1-0 to gain promotion, sending 25,000 supporters into raptures inside the Empire Stadium. Amazingly Fry walked out on Peterborough soon after that triumph - only to walk back into London Road 24 hours later saying :"They got it all wrong. I misunderstand what was said!"

Fry was certainly a man of words and among his many quotes as manager of Blues were the following:

- "Even if you are the worst manager in the world, you should at least win once in three months!"

- "There's a queue of people a mile long waiting for me to fail. I know that it they found me in the gutter they wouldn't help me up. I'd be smashed over the head with a cricket bat to make sure I stopped down."

- Talking about defender Liam Daish in 1995. "If a jumbo jet was coming towards our area, he'd try to head it clear."

- When Kidderminster Harriers were due to play at St Andrew's in an FA Cup-tie in 1994. He said: "It I was the Kidderminster boss, I would fancy my chances."

- Commenting about Blues' owner David Sullivan. "He doesn't know the a goal-line from a clothes-line."

- This was the message he left on his answerphone following his dismissal from Blues. "Kristine (his wife) has gone shopping as usual and I've gone to the job centre looking for new employment. Funny ol' game, innit?"

- After taking over at Blues: "I tried to come here (to St Andrew's) and use an attacking system, I have used the last 25 years. Even a blind man can see it was completely wrong."

- Contemplating a bad sequence of results: "I can understand the fans chanting 'Fry out'. In fact, the chants were led by my dad."

- Following twelve disastrous weeks with Blues: "I've made more mistakes in three months than in the last 30 years."

- After Blues had been relegated: "I'm gutted we went down. Looking back, I spread too much fear and panic when I first took over and we ended up not winning for 15 games after Boxing Day."

- On Portuguese winger Jose Dominguez: "Jose? There ain't been anyone as exciting in this country since George Best. I love him, the crowd love him, everybody loves him. But when you analyse it his final ball is ****. Full stop."

- On the brink of his dismissal: "I've told the players not to worry about me if I get sacked. I'll walk out that door into three other jobs - at Stourbridge, Nuneaton or Atherstone!"

FULHAM

Billy Rudd heading a goal against Fulham at Craven Cottage in September 1960....Blues lost the match 2-1.

Blues' playing record against the Cottagers:

FOOTBALL LEAGUE

Venue	P	W	D	L	F	A
Home	29	14	9	6	54	43
Away	29	8	9	12	34	48
Totals	58	22	18	18	88	91

FA CUP

Home	1	0	1	0	1	1
Away	3	3	0	0	6	3
Neutral	2	0	1	1	0	1

ANGLO SCOTTISH CUP

Away	1	1	0	0	5	0

WARTIME

Home	1	1	0	0	2	0
Away	1	0	0	1	2	3
Totals	2	1	0	1	4	3

Blues and Fulham first opposed each at League level in season 1908-09 (Division 2). After a 1-1 draw in London, Blues then lost at St Andrew's in the return fixture by 3-1.

Blues did not win any of the first eight meetings with Fulham. They finally broke their duck with a 2-1 victory at home in September 1912.

In the last season before the Great War Blues completed the double over the Cottagers, winning 3-2 (a) and 1-0 (h). Percy Barton scored the winner in the latter game.

When Blues crashed 5-0 at Fulham in March 1921, it was their heaviest defeat of their Second Division championship-winning season.

After that encounter Blues did not meet Fulham in the League for another 25 years. Then a goal by Cyril Trigg gave them a 1-0 win at Craven Cottage in November 1946. The double was completed later in the campaign with a 2-1 home win.

Fulham won 4-1 at St Andrew's early in the 1952-53 season, by 3-1 at Craven Cottage on 3 January and by 5-2, also in London, in February 1954.

Blues started their final charge for promotion in 1954-55 with a 3-2 home win over Fulham on 30 March - but the attendance at St Andrew's was just 7,000, the second lowest of the season.

The first game between Blues and Fulham in the top flight took place at St Andrew's on 24 October 1959. A crowd of 26,698 saw the visitors win 4-2, Johnny Gordon scoring twice for Blues.

Blues won 4-1 at home in September 1962 when Stan Lynn

almost burst the ball with a spot-kick and six goals were shared in a thrilling tussle at Craven Cottage in May 1963.

Stan Lynn also netted penalties against Fulham in August 1963 and August 1964.

A nine-goal bonanza in front of almost 27,400 fans at St Andrew's in October 1968, ended with Blues triumphant by 5-4 over Fulham in Division Two. Jimmy Greenhoff was the star of the show with a fourtimer (all his goals coming in succession) after Johnny Vincent had scored the first. Greenhoff also fluffed a 64th minute penalty!

In season 1979-80 Blues lost 4-3 at home to the Cottagers yet won 4-2 at Craven Cottage - 13 goals in two terrific Second Division matches. In the game at St Andrew's on 18 September, Blues were 3-0 ahead at half-time but 'blew up' after the interval!

Blues and Fulham met for the first time in Division Three in 1989-90 when the scores finished level at 1-1 at St Andrew's. Blues then won 2-1 in London later in the season.

Ian Rodgerson scored three goals against Fulham in 1991-92 - the winner (1-0) at Craven Cottage and a brace when Blues won 3-1 at St Andrew's.

Fulham beat Blues with a last minute goal (by John Mitchell) in the replay of the 1975 FA Cup semi-final at Maine Road after the sides had drawn 1-1 at Hillsborough.

Blues' 5-0 ASC win over the Cottagers was in 1979-80 when Keith Bertschin scored twice in front of less than 2,900 fans!

Geoff Horsfield became Blues' record signing when he joined the club from Fulham for £2.25 million in July 2000.

Jack Peart (ex-Blues) died in 1948 when manager of Fulham.

Players associated with both clubs include: D Bailey, J Birch, D Bremner, R Brennan, H Clutterbuck, M Cooper, H Crossthwaite, S Finnan, W Freeman, H Gayle, C Gordon, GM Horsfield, D Howell (Fulham app), G Johnston, C Kirby, G Leggatt, D Mangnall (Fulham guest), CH Millington, W Owen, J Peart, PP Peschisolido, TE Pike, ET Watkins.

Also: Pat Beasley (Fulham player, Blues manager), Mike Kelly (Blues player, Fulham assistant-manager)

FULL BACKS

Gary Ablett

Blues' duo of Cyril Trigg and Billy Hughes (both aged 18) were the youngest pair of full-backs in the Football League when they lined up as partners against Aston Villa on 28 March 1936.

England star Jeff Hall and Ken Green were superb full-back partners for Blues during the 1950s, appearing in some 200 competitive games together.

The full-back who has made most senior appearances for Blues has been Frank Womack who amassed a grand total of 607 (491 in the Football League, 24 in the FA Cup and 92 during the First World War). Ken Green played in 443 senior games.

Other outstanding full-back pairings for Blues have been: Fred Lester and Billy Pratt and Arthur Archer and Pratt (1890s); Jack Glover and Frank Stokes (early 1900s); Billy Ball and Frank Womack (1911-19); Womack and Jack Jones (1920s); George Liddell and Ned Barkas (early 1930s); Stan Lynn and Graham Sissons and then Lynn and Colin Green (1960s); Ray Martin with Bobby Thomson and Garry Pendrey (late 1960s/70s); Malcolm Page, Kevan Broadhurst and/or Mark Dennis; David Langan and Dennis; Ray Ranson and Julian Dicks (1980s); Ian Clarkson and John Frain (early 1990s) and thereafter Gary Rowett, Simon Charlton, Gary Ablett and Martin Grainger have all teamed up as partners.

Several international full-backs have been registered with Blues down the years, among them: Jeff Hall, Bobby Thomson and Nigel Winterburn (England), Colin Green and Billy Hughes (Wales) and Tommy Carroll and David Langan (Eire).

FULL MEMBERS CUP

Blues played in this competition in season 1986-87. They beat Brighton & Hove Albion 3-0 at St Andrew's, but lost to Charlton Athletic 3-2 at Selhurst Park where the attendance was just 821.

There was an own-goal scored for Blues in each game - by Kieran O'Regan (Brighton) and Peter Shirtliff (Charlton).

SUMMARY:

Venue	P	W	D	L	F	A
Home	1	1	0	0	3	0
Away	1	0	0	1	2	3
Totals	2	1	0	1	5	3

FURLONG, Paul

Paul Furlong

Paul Furlong scored twice for Enfield against Telford United in the FA Trophy Final replay at The Hawthorns in 1988 and he also gained five semi-professional caps for England. He has never looked back since. A native of Wood Green, London (born on 1 October 1968) he joined Coventry City for £130,000 in July 1991. Twelve months later he switched to Watford in a £250,000 deal and after scoring 41 goals in 92 appearances for the Hornets Furlong was snapped up by Chelsea for £2.3 million. He did well enough at the 'Bridge', netting another 17 goals in 84 outings and then, in July 1996, he moved to St Andrew's, joining Blues for £1.5 million. He helped Blues twice reach the First Division play-offs and when the 1999-2000 ended he had taken his club record to 55 goals in close on 140 senior appearances, and this despite suffering a few injury problems. In August 2000 Furlong joined QPR on loan.

GAINSBOROUGH TRINITY

Blues' League record against Trinity is:

Venue	P	W	D	L	F	A
Home	10	6	4	0	37	12
Away	10	4	3	3	13	8
Totals	20	10	7	3	50	20

A seven-goal thriller at Muntz Street in October 1897 went in favour of Blues by 4-3, Walter Abbott scoring twice, one a real gem from fully 25 yards. And it was in-form Abbott who was again the hero when Blues whipped Trinity 6-1 at home in April 1899 - this time with a hat-trick.

Blues achieved their best away win against Trinity in September 1899, winning 4-1 and they registered their best home victory later that season when rampaging to an 8-1 triumph at Muntz Street in January. Bob McRoberts was a hat-trick hero on this occasion and the same player also scored twice in September 1900 when Trinity were beaten 6-0.

Players with both clubs include: JT Bayley, W Bennett (Blues reserve), K Burns (Trinity, 1989), F Foxall, E Holmes, R Huxford, R McRoberts, BR Mills, B Pumphrey, A Saville, W Wigmore.

GALLAGHER, Joe

A very honest, brave and competitive centre-half, stylish and methodical, Joe Gallagher scored 23 goals in 335 appearances for Blues before transferring to Wolves in August 1981.

Born in Liverpool in January 1955, he was a junior at St Andrew's before turning professional on his seventeenth birthday. His initial outings for the first XI were at full-back, his debut coming in a Texaco Cup game against Stoke City in September 1973. But after taking over the No.5 shirt from Roger Hynd early in the 1974-75 season he became a dominant figure at the heart of the Blues defence. He suffered a fractured leg in 1977 (which kept him out of action for four months) and was capped by England 'B' against Australia at St Andrew's in 1980 before being sold for

Joe Gallagher

£350,000 to the Molineux club, thus allowing Blues to bank some much-needed cash!

Later he assisted West Ham United (for eight months), Burnley, Halifax Town and non-League Padiham before becoming manager of Coleshill Town in 1989 and later of Kings Heath (1991). For a brief spell in the early '90s Gallagher returned to St Andrew's as Blues' Community Liaison Officer.

GAMES PLAYED

In season 1994-95 Blues played a total of 63 competitive matces made up of 46 in the Football League, five in the FA Cup, four in the League Cup and eight in the Auto Windscreen Shield - a club record.

In 1990-91 they fulfilled 58 major League and Cup fixtures.

Ten years earlier, in season 1980-81, under Jim Smith's management, Blues' first XI took part in a staggering 73 games - 42 in the Football League, three in the FA Cup, five in the League Cup and 23 others (friendlies/tour etc).

Starting on 2 February and finishing on 28 March 1895 (55 days) Blues played seven home games on the trot - six in the League and one in the FA Cup. They won just one, defeating Burnley 1-0 in the Football League.

In the month of April 1946 Blues completed 10 Football League (South) matches.

The first XI participated in nine senior games during September 1961 (seven League, two League Cup) and nine more in September 1964 (eight League). Eight games were played in the months of September 1946, April 1960, September 1962, April 1963 and March 1990.

In all competitions (League, FA Cup, League Cup, European, sponsored tournaments, Wartime etc) Blues have played in more than 4850 games at first-class level (see under respective categories and playing record). And if one was to add to that tally all the friendlies, tour games etc. which the club has played in over the last 125 years, then the total number of fixtures in Blues' record files could well be around the 6,000 mark.

GATE RECEIPTS

Record gate receipts of around £260,000 (unconfirmed) were banked from the Blues v Wolverhampton Wanderers Nationwide League Division One game at St Andrew's on 1 April 2000.

This beat the previous record of £230,000 taken from the Blues v Aston Villa League Cup encounter at St Andrew's on 23 September 1993.

- Prior to that the St Andrew's receipts record had been bettered as follows:
  £116,372 v Nottingham Forest, FA Cup-tie, 20 February 1988.
  £110,450 v Watford, FA Cup, 10 March 1984.
  £48,505 v Aston Villa, Division One, 11 October 1980.
  £37,949 v Leeds United, FA Cup 29 January 1977.
  £29,379 v Middlesbrough, FA Cup, 8 March 1975.
  £19,587 v Leeds United, Division One, 29 December 1973.
- When Leicester City played Portsmouth in the 1934 FA Cup semi-final at St Andrew's, the 66,544 crowd realised record gate receipts of £5,978.
- When the record attendance of 67,341 was set at St Andrew's in February 1939 (Blues v Everton in the FA Cup) the receipts amounted to £4,556.

GAYLE, John

John Gayle

A big, hefty striker with terrific right-foot shot, John Gayle was the hero of Blues' 1991 Leyland DAF Trophy final victory over Tranmere Rovers at Wembley when he scored two stunning goals. Born in Birmingham in July 1964, he played initially for Highgate United and after spells with Mile Oak Rovers, Tamworth, Bromsgrove Rovers and Burton Albion he joined First Division Wimbledon in March 1989, switching to St Andrew's in November 1990. After scoring 14 goals in 55 outings for Blues and having a loan spell with Walsall, Gayle moved to Coventry City for £100,000 in September 1993. From Highfield Road he went to Burnley in August 1994 for £70,000 and the same amount of money took him to Stoke City in January 1995 (signed by Lou Macari, who had been his boss for a short time at St Andrew's). After another loan spell, this time with Gillingham, Gayle left the Potters to sign for Northampton Town and in July 1998 he found his way to Scunthorpe. During his spell with the 'Iron' he was sent-off twice in three weeks and served four separate bans in 1998-99 but he kept battling on and passed the milestone of 250 senior appearances as a professional footballer (50 goals scored). Gayle, a former Kings Heath printer, is 6ft. 4ins tall and weighed in at more than 15 stones.

GEDDIS, David

As a 20 year-old striker David Geddis played superbly well for Ipswich Town in the 1978 FA Cup Final and was immediately marked up as a star of the future. He never quite made it to the top although he did score plenty of goals at professional level. Born in Carlisle on 12 March 1958, he went to Portman Road as a 15 year-old and turned professional there in August 1975. A loan spell with Luton Town preceded his £300,000 move to Villa Park in September 1979. A second loan spell at Kenilworth Road (December 1982) followed before he was transferred to Barnsley for £50,000 in September 1983. From Oakwell, Geddis switched to St Andrew's, also for £50,000, in December 1984, and after a loan spell with Brentford (September 1986) he left Blues for Shrewsbury Town in a £25,000 deal in March 1987. In October 1988 he signed for Swindon and ended his League career with Darlington (1990-91). Geddis was capped by England at Youth and 'B' team levels and won both Youth Cup and FA Cup winners medals with Ipswich. His record with Villa was Villa 56 appearances and 16 goals. In 1999 Geddis took a job at Middlesbrough, working in the Community office.

GEMMILL, Archie

Archie Gemmill

Archie Gemmill was an all-action, dynamic, aggressive and courageous midfielder who had a marvellous footballing career which saw him appear in more than 650 first-class matches and win 43 full caps for Scotland. Born in Paisley in March 1947, he began with St Mirren in 1964. Three years later he joined Preston North End for £13,000 and in September 1979 moved to Derby County for £66,000. He helped the Rams twice win the First Division championship before transferring to Nottingham Forest in September 1977, being re-united with his former boss at the Baseball Ground, Brian Clough. A third League championship medal was gained in 1978 as well as League Cup and European Cup winners; medals before he joined Blues for £150,000 in August 1979. He went on to score 14 goals in 115 outings during his time at St Andrew's which ended in September 1982 when he signed as a non-contract player with Wigan following a spell in the NASL with the Jacksonville Teamen. He helped Blues win promotion from Division Two in 1980. After Wigan he returned to Derby (November 1982) and a year after leaving the Baseball Ground for a second time he went back to Nottingham Forest as a coach in 1985, later taking over as joint-manager with his former playing colleague John McGovern at Rotherham United (September 1994)

Gemmill had the honour of being the first substitute used in Scottish League football - for St Mirren against Clyde in August 1966.

GENOA

A then record Anglo-Italian Cup crowd for an English game (outside Wembley) of 20,430 saw Blues beaten 3-2 by the Italian side at St Andrew's on 5 September 1995. Blues led 2-0 after nine minutes, both goals coming from Jason Bowen, but Genoa turned on the style after that and drew level before half-time and then claimed the winner through Marco Nappi with just four minutes remaining. Nappi had earlier netted Genoa's equaliser after Mario Bortolazzi had scored on 19 minutes direct from a free-kick. Michael Johnson made his home debut - and this was only Blues' third home defeat in twelve months!

GILLINGHAM

Steve Castle

Blues' playing record against the Gills:

FA CUP

Venue	P	W	D	L	F	A
Away	1	1	0	0	3	0

LEAGUE CUP

Home	1	1	0	0	3	0
Away	1	1	0	0	1	0
Totals	2	2	0	0	4	0

AUTO WINDSCREEN SHIELD

Home	1	1	0	0	3	0

Blues and Gillingham were scheduled to play the first League match against each other in 2000-01.

Blues' 3-0 FA Cup win over the Gills was at The Priestfield Stadium in 1987-88 while their League Cup triumph was achieved in 1997-98 over two legs.

Blues beat the Gills at St Andrew's in the AWS in 1994-95 to set up a Southern Area quarter-final clash with Hereford United.

Players with both clubs include: A Archer, T Aylott, J Bass, A Blake, M Bodley, G Breen, K Brown, H Bruce, S Bruce, S Castle, H Clutterbuck, M Darrell, N Forster, J Gayle, J Glover, A Godden, C Gordon, J McDonough, F McKee, H Powell, HC Randle (Blues reserve), TE Robinson, A Roe, R Taylor, JE Travers, ET Watkins, J Wilson (Blues reserve).

Also: Billy Harvey and Johnny McMillan (Blues players, Gills managers), Ron Saunders (Gills player, Blues manager).

GIVENS, Don

Don Givens

In May 1969 Don Givens won the first of his 56 caps for the Republic of Ireland (19 goals scored) before he had played in a major League or Cup game. He was then a Manchester United player, having joined the Reds from Dublin Rangers in September 1965 as an apprentice, turning professional in December 1966.

His League debut finally arrived three months later and he went on to make just eight more appearances (one goal scored) before leaving Old Trafford for Luton Town in a £15,000 deal April 1970. After two seasons at Kenilworth Road (19 League goals in 83 outings) he switched to Queens Park Rangers for £40,000 and in his first season with the London club helped them win promotion to the First Division. In 1975-76 he was leading marksman for Rangers when they finished runners-up to Liverpool in the League championship. An aggressive, all-action utility forward, very useful in the air, Givens netted 76 goals in 242 League games for QPR and he reached the century of League goals with Blues, whom he joined in August 1978 for £165,000. He went on to net 10 goals in 54 games for Blues when he partnered at various times Alan Buckley, Trevor Francis and Keith Bertschin up front.

After a loan spell with Bournemouth, Givens moved from St Andrew's to Sheffield United on the transfer deadline in March 1981. Then six weeks later, with the very last kick of his English career, he missed a vital penalty for the Blades against Walsall and as result United were relegated to the Fourth Division!

From Bramall Lane Givens signed for the Swiss club Xamac Neuchatel and he helped them win their domestic League championship before retiring with an arthritic hip problem in May 1987 with well over 600 club and international appearances under his belt. Givens then stayed in Switzerland for eight years, coaching at various levels as well as acting as assistant-manager, before returning to Southern Ireland where he became manager/coach of the country's under 21 squad.

His record in the Football League was impressive - 113 goals in 408 games.

GLEGHORN, Nigel

Before joining Blues for £175,000 from Manchester City in September 1989, midfielder Nigel Gleghorn had only been in League football for four years, having started out with Ipswich Town prior to switching to Maine Road in August 1988. A former fireman, he was born in Seaham in August 1962 and was 23 before he made his League debut for the Portman Road club. With an excellent left foot he passed a ball precisely, long or short, and he went on to score 43 goals in 176 appearances for Blues, helping them win the Leyland DAF Trophy at Wembley in 1991. On leaving St Andrew's Gleghorn joined Stoke City for £100,000 in October 1992 and at the end of that season he had in his possession a Second Division championship medal. He made over 200 appearances for the Potters before switching north to Burnley, finally ending his Football League career in 1999 after loan spells Brentford and Gillingham.

GLENTORAN

On 27 March 1926 Blues beat the Irish League club Glentoran 8-2 in a friendly match at St Andrew's. Joe Bradford scored four of the goals and George Briggs two.

Players with both clubs include: T Briggs (player-manager Glentoran), R Ferris, A Leonard, W Purves (player-trainer Glentoran).

GLOSSOP (North End)

Blues' Football League record against North End:

Venue	P	W	D	L	F	A
Home	10	5	3	2	28	9
Away	10	3	1	6	12	21
Totals	20	8	4	8	40	30

Blues first met Glossop in the Second Division in season 1898-99, winning 2-1 away in mid-December with goals by Walter Abbott and Jimmy Inglis but drawing 1-1 at home four months later.

Blues completed the double in 1902-03 (after returning to Division Two) while Glossop themselves won both matches in 1908-09.

Blues' heaviest defeat of the eight suffered at the hands of Glossop was on Christmas Day 1909 when they lost 4-1 away.

Their biggest home victory was 11-1 on 6 January 1915 when Jimmy Windridge (5) and Andy Smith (4) led the goal-rush.

Glossop were also beaten 6-0 at St Andrew's on Christmas Day 1913, Billy Walker and Jack Hall both scoring twice in front of 25,000 spectators.

A total of 23 goals were scored in the four League games between Blues and Glossop during the last two pre First World War seasons, the other two results being a 4-1 reverse at Glossop on Boxing Day 1913 and a 3-3 draw also at Glossop, nine months later in September 1914.

Players with both clubs include: FW Hoyland, JS McMillan, A Phoenix, J Robertson.

GLOVER, Jack

Despite being on small side, Jack Glover developed into an excellent full-back, forming a splendid partnership with Frank Stokes during his time with Blues. Indeed, they played together for almost four years, Glover going on to amass 124 appearances for the club, scoring two goals - one a spectacular long-range effort in a 3-2 home win over Aston Villa in December 1906.

Born in West Bromwich in October 1876, he played a few games for Albion's reserve side before signing professional forms for Blackburn Rovers in

Jack Glover

May 1897. Two years later he joined New Brompton (Gillingham) for £100 and in October 1900 (after 24 Southern League outings) Liverpool paid £350,000 for his services to take him to Merseyside.

He helped the Reds win the League championship in his first season at Anfield and he also represented the Football League as well as appearing in two international trial matches for England. After 59 outings for Liverpool he moved to Blues for just £250 in January 1904. Four-and-a-half years later he went to Brierley Hill Alliance and retired in 1910. He represented Shropshire at county bowls level and later kept a pub in Dudley before his death in that town in April 1955.

GOALKEEPERS

Over the years Blues have been blessed with several fine goalkeepers who, during their respective careers, represented their country at senior level.

Here, in alphabetical order, is a list of the international 'keepers who have been associated with the club: Great Britain Olympic Gold Medal winner Horace Bailey (1910-13), Scotland's Jim Blyth (1982-85), Chris Charsley (1887-91 & 1891-94 - the first Blues player to win a full cap, doing so for England), Scotsman Jim Herriot (1965-71), Harry Hibbs of England (1924-40), Republic of Ireland 'keeper Jim McDonagh (1984), 1950s England custodian Gil Merrick (1938-60), Norway's Thomas Myhre (2000), Billy Robb of Scotland (1914-15), England's David Seaman (1984-86), Welsh stars Gary Sprake (1973-75) and Martin Thomas (1988-93) plus another England 'keeper Dan Tremelling (1919-32).

And we cannot forget the likes of Ian Bennett (1993 to date - who has now chalked up well over 250 senior appearances for Blues), Frank Clack (1932-39), Henry Clutterbuck (1897-99), Paul Cooper (1971-74 - who went on to do so well with Ipswich Town), Tony Coton (1977-84 - who saved a penalty on his League debut for Blues), Herbert Crossthwaite (1910-14), Jack Dorrington (1901-13), Neil Freeman (1978-81), Tony Godden (1987-89 - the former West Brom 'keeper), Roger Hansbury (1986-89 - who had a long career in the game), George Hollis (1891-94), Mike Kelly (1970-76), Dave Latchford (1964-77 - 239 games for Blues), Alan Miller (1991-92), Jim Montgomery (1977-79 - hero of Sunderland's epic 1973 FA Cup Final win over Leeds United), Mark Prudhoe (1984-86 - is still in the game as a professional), Nat Robinson (1898-1908 - over 300 games for Blues), Johnny Schofield (1950-66 - 237 outings for Blues), Les Sealey (1992 - who like Prudhoe also had a long and interesting career in League football), Ken Tewksbury (1929-31 - an England amateur interna-

Jim Montgomery

Gil Merrick

tional), Jeff Wealands (1979-83 - 119 appearances for the club) and Colin 'Tiny' Withers (1957-64 - 116 starts between the posts for Blues).

KEEPER FACTS

- Gil Merrick appeared in 551 League and FA Cup games for Blues plus 164 Wartime matches for a combined total of 715. A club record.
- Dan Tremelling made 395 first team appearances for Blues, Harry Hibbs 400 (including 12 in 1939-40) and Nat Robinson 306.
- Winger Steve Lynex (ex-Blues) was used as a third goalkeeper by Leicester City in an FA Cup-tie against Shrewsbury Town in March 1982.
- Luckless Francis Banks conceded 22 goals in three Football Alliance games for Blues in season 1889-90.
- Colin Withers had six goals put past him on his Blues debut against Spurs (away) in November 1960 (Division One).
- Billy Beel let in five goals in his only League game for Blues against Blackburn Rovers in April 1965 (5-5 draw).
- Ted Brueton conceded four goals in his only outing for Blues in

September 1894 v Preston (4-4).

- Gil Merrick conceded 666 goals in his 551 senior games for Blues. Nat Robinson let in 377 in his 306 outings while Harry Hibbs (389 games) and Dan Tremelling (395) were both beaten 556 times in League and Cup football. Johnny Schofield let in 433 goals in his 237 appearances for the club.
- Ritchie Blackmore saved two penalties after coming on as a substitute for Blues in their Texaco Cup game with Stoke City in October 1973. Blues won the contest 3-1 on penalties after a 0-0 draw. This was Blackmore's only outing for the club before going to play in Ireland.
- Robert Evans was Blues' first Welsh international goalkeeper (1913-14).
- Future Blues 'keeper Horace Bailey conceded 12 goals while playing for Leicester

Johnny Schofield

95

Fosse v Nottingham Forest in a League game in 1908.

- Both Billy George (Aston Villa, later Blues) and Harry Hibbs saved penalties for England, George against Ireland in 1902 and Hibbs (from Fred Keenor) v Wales in 1930.
- Ian Bennett kept a clean sheet in seven successive League games in 1994-95 and in all that season he was unbeaten in 27 of the 62 games he played in....a club record.
- In the 3,946 League games played by Blues between September 1892 and May 2000, no fewer than 1,068 ended without a goal being conceded.

GOALSCORING

Joe Bradford scored a club record 267 goals for Blues (249 in the Football League and 18 in the FA Cup). He also notched more than a dozen goals in various friendly and tour matches for the club.

No other player has come within 130 goals of Bradford's impressive tally - Trevor Francis being next in line with 133 (118 in the League).

Here are Blues' top 10 all-time champion goalscorers:

267	Joe Bradford
133	Trevor Francis
127	Peter Murphy
107	George Briggs
102	Billy Jones
92	Geoff Vowden
90	Eddie Brown
84	Bob Latchford
84	Fred Wheldon
82	Bob McRoberts

Top 10 League scorers:

249	Joe Bradford
118	Trevor Francis
107	Peter Murphy
99	Billy Jones
98	George Briggs
74	Eddie Brown
71	Johnny Crosbie
70	Bob McRoberts
68	Bob Latchford
67	Cyril Trigg

Top 10 FA Cup scorers:

17	Joe Bradford
17	Will Devey
14	Peter Murphy
13	Eddie Brown
10	Bob McRoberts
11	Eddie Stanley
11	Billy Walton
12	Fred Wheldon
8	George Briggs
9	Ernie Curtis

Top five League Cup scorers:

8	Ken Leek
8	Geoff Vowden
6	Mick Harford
6	Bob Latchford
5	Bob Hatton

Top five European scorers:

6	Johnny Gordon
5	Jimmy Harris
5	Harry Hooper
4	Bunny Larkin
4	Bryan Orritt

Top 10 Wartime scorers (1939-46):

87	Cyril Trigg
45	Wilson Jones

Peter Murphy, third top-scorer in Blues' history

Paul Moulden - 289 goals in 1981-82!

One of Eddie Brown's 90 goals for Blues in a crucial 5-1 win at Doncaster in 1955.

34	Jock Mulraney
30	Harold Bodle
23	Don Dearson
17	George Edwards
14	Dave Massart
11	Bob Bright
8	Jack Acquaroff
9	Neil Dougall

Top five Wartime scorers (1915-19):

48	Jack Whitehouse
23	Joe Godfrey
14	Billy Walker
8	Stan Stevens
9	Tom Butler

GOAL NETS!

- Walter Abbott, with 42 goals in 1898-99 (34 League, eight FA Cup) is Blues' champion marksman for one season.
- Five players - Walter Abbott (v Darwen 1898), Benny Green (v Middlesbrough 1905), Johnny McMillan and Bob McRoberts (both v Blackpool 1901) and Jimmy Windridge (v Glossop 1915) - all scored five goals in a League game for Blues. Some reports indicate that McMillan only scored twice against Blackpool in 1901 but I have now credited him with a record equalling five-timer after checking various sources and reading a couple of more match reports.
- Blues were the first club to have two players who scored more than 20 League goals in a season - Frank Mobley (24) and Fred Wheldon (22) in 1893-94 (Division 2).
- Blues scored a club record 103 Second Division goals in season 1893-94 (in only 28 matches).
- They conceded 96 goals in 42 First Division matches in 1964-65

- also a record.
- In 1947-48, when Gil Merrick and his defenders were in superb form, only 24 goals were given away in 42 Second Division matches. And 47 years earlier, in season 1900-01, 24 goals were conceded in 34 League games. Ian Bennett kept 27 clean sheets in 1994-95.
- In season 1948-49 Blues finished 17th in the First Division yet had the best defensive record of all 22 clubs - just 38 goals conceded in 42 games. In contrast Blues also had the worst attack in the Division during this campaign (36 goals for) and in 1949-50 they were the worst scorers again with just 31 this time round.
- Blues scored 35 goals without reply in four successive home matches in the space of a month in 1898. They beat Chirk 8-0 on 29 October in the FA Cup, crushed Luton Town 9-0 in a League match on 12 November, defeated Druids 10-0 in another cup-tie a week later and then accounted for Darwen 8-0 in the League on 26 November.
- Republic of Ireland international Jimmy Higgins scored the winning goal for Blues in their 6th round FA Cup-tie at home to Manchester United in February 1951 just 44 seconds after kick-off....one of the fastest on record by a Blues player.
- Paul Davlin netted after 16 seconds for Blues against Luton in April 1996.
- Trevor Francis scored in eight consecutive League games (13 goals in total) for Blues between 6 February and 27 March 1971.
- Joe Bradford scored in every round of the FA Cup in 1930-31 and in fact, he scored in each of his fifteen seasons of first team football with the club: 1920-21 to 1934-35 inclusive.
- Paul Tait scored the first 'sudden death' goal at Wembley - thirteen minutes into extra-time to earn Blues a 1-0 Auto Windscreen Trophy Final victory over Carlisle United in 1995.
- The 54 League goals scored by Blues in season 1933-34 were

distributed among 19 different players (three of them opponents). Fred Roberts was top marksman with eight.

- Jack Hallam scored five of Blues' 15 goals in the Midland (United) Counties League competition in season 1893-94.
- In 1985-86 Blues failed to score a single goal in 22 of their 42 League games - and between late October and the end of November they failed to find the net in six successive matches. They had similar six-match goalless runs in 1949-50 and 1988-89.
- Whilst a teenager in 1981-82 striker Paul Moulden scored a staggering 289 goals for Bolton Lads Club in just 40 matches. His best haul in one single game was 16 in a 28-0 win over Sharples. He also netted 15 times in a 25-0 victory over Atherton RR and 11 in a 16-0 triumph over St Williams. Moulden was a Blues player in the mid-1990s.
- Alf Chaplin apparently scored 24 goals in one junior game for Folesworth Great Heath earlier in his career. He joined Blues in 1903.

GOODIER, Ted

Born in Farnworth near Bolton in October 1902, Ted Goodier was a very useful wing-half in his playing days, serving with Huddersfield Town, Lancaster Town, Oldham Athletic (June 1925 to November 1931), Queens Park Rangers, Watford, Crewe Alexandra and Rochdale. He became player-manager of the latter club in September 1938, a position he held for six years before taking over the reins as caretaker-manager at St Andrew's in November 1944. He retained that position until May 1945, a month before Harry Storer was installed as team boss. Goodier then returned to Spotland and duly guided Rochdale to a 1-0 victory over Blackpool in the 1949 Lancashire Cup Final at Boundary Park before becoming manager of non-League Wigan Athletic (from June 1952 to May 1954), later taking the reins at Oldham Athletic (from May 1954 to June 1958). Goodier died in Farnworth in November 1967.

GOODWIN, Freddie

Freddie Goodwin

Freddie Goodwin was manager at St Andrew's from May 1970 (when he took over from Stan Cullis) until September 1975 (replaced by Willie Bell). In that five-year period Blues played almost 220 competitive games, 77 ended in victories and 75 in defeats. An excellent coach, Goodwin was always willing to try inventive ideas out on the pitch and off it (he once had his players doing yoga). It was he who developed Trevor Francis, the Latchford brothers (Bob and Dave) and Garry Pendrey among others.

He guided Blues to promotion from Division Two in 1972 and twice took them into the FA Cup semi-final. He never recovered from that bitter disappointment of losing to Fulham in the second of those semis in 1975 and soon after the start of the next season he had left the club.

A Lancastrian, born in Heywood near Bury in June 1933,

Goodwin joined Manchester United as a wing-half in 1953, acting initially as a reserve to Eddie Colman and Duncan Edwards. Seven years and 106 games later, having gained runners-up medals in the League championship and FA Cup Final (the latter in 1958 against Bolton Wanderers, the team he supported as a lad) he moved to Leeds United for £10,000. In December 1964 - seven months after helping Leeds win the Second Division title and having played in 120 games for the Elland Road club - he was appointed player-manager of Scunthorpe United, retiring as a player just as England won the Word Cup in 1966.

Goodwin remained with the 'Iron' until October 1967 when he left England to try his luck in America as coach of the New York Generals, returning to his homeland in October 1968 to take charge of Brighton & Hove Albion from where he switched to St Andrew's. After leaving Blues he had two further spells in the USA as coach to the Minnesota Kicks (1976-79 and 1980-81) and eventually retired to live in the States (his present home).

As a stock bowler on the cricket field, Goodwin also played in 11 county matches for Lancashire, taking 27 wickets.

NB - Quote from Goodwin during his managerial career: "It's tough at the top - it's hell anywhere else!"

GORDON, Johnny

An excellent goalscorer, Johnny Gordon was signed from Portsmouth by Blues manager Pat Beasley for £10,000 in September 1958. He remained at St Andrew's for two-and-half years during which time he netted 40 goals in just 115 first-class games, gaining a runners-up medal when Blues were defeated by Barcelona in the 1960 Inter Cities Fairs Cup Final.

The Fratton Park supporters loved Gordon and they were delighted when he returned 'home' in March 1961. He went on to take his tally of League appearances and goals with Pompey up to an impressive 443 and 105 respectively. Born within walking distance of the Portsmouth ground in September 1931, Gordon became a junior at Fratton Park in July 1947, turning professional there in January 1949. During his second spell at the club he gained a Division Two championship medal (1962).

Johnny Gordon

GOVAN, Alex

Alex Govan was a cracking left-winger, industrious, fast and tricky who regularly pushed the ball past his opponent and then beat him for speed before getting in a telling cross. Not a big man, he was never completely mastered by the burly defenders whom he came up against and quite often he found two men marking him!

Despite being born in Scotland Govan started his League career in the south of England with Plymouth Argyle, playing in the same team as Len Boyd and Gordon Astall at Home Park. Later, all three players linked up with Birmingham City and helped the Midlands club win the Second Division championship and reach the FA Cup Final in successive seasons. A consistent scorer throughout his career, Govan averaged a goal every three games at professional level and in 1956-57 set a club record for a winger by netting 30 times for Blues in all competitions, being the last player to reach this total in a season for the Midlands club.

He scored four hat-tricks during that campaign (three in four matches). He showed signs of slowing down in 1958 and was transferred to Portsmouth, later returning to his former club Plymouth before retiring in 1960.

- Govan is credited with bringing the club's anthem 'Keep Right On To The End Of The Road' to St Andrew's during the club's FA Cup run in 1956.

Alex Govan

GRAINGER, MARTIN

Signed from Brentford for £400,000 (plus George Parris) in March 1996, the uncompromising, strong tackling performances by Martin Grainger stood out like a beacon as Blues reached the play-offs in successive seasons of 1998-99 and 1999-2000. Born in Enfield on 23 August 1972, he was a trainee at Layer Road before becoming a professional with Colchester United in July 1992. In October 1993 he was transferred to Brentford for £60,000 and went on to make 124 appearances for the Bees before his move to St

Andrew's. After a difficult start with Blues he finally won the fans over with some excellent performances when occupying the left-back berth and a position wide left in midfield which he detests! Nevertheless, he is a very adaptable footballer, able to play 'anywhere' if asked although he does prefer defensive duties. Grainger passed the milestone of 150 senior appearances for Blues in the 1999-2000 season when he was also voted the club's 'Player of the Year.'

GREEN, Benny

Despite gaining a reputation of a trouble-maker, Benny Green was a bag of tricks on the field of play, a chunky, lively inside-forward who had the distinction of scoring the first-ever goal at St Andrew's for Blues against Preston North End in December 1906.

Twelve months earlier he had netted a five-timer when Middlesbrough were hammered 7-0 on Boxing Day. Those six goals helped Green register an impressive total of 46 in 198 first-class appearances for Blues made between

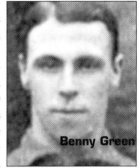
Benny Green

October 1903 (when he joined the club from Barnsley) and August 1911 (when he left to sign for Preston North End). A Yorkshireman, born in Penistone in February 1883, he started his professional career at Oakwell in August 1901 and after his time at Deepdale moved to Blackpool in December 1913, retiring during the First World War. He scored well over 125 goals (115 in the League) during his career. Green died in Yorkshire.

GREEN, Colin

Left-back Colin Green made his Football League debut for Everton in September 1960 against Blackpool at Goodison Park - his opponent for most of the game was Stanley Matthews. He came through with flying colours, helping the Merseysiders win 4-1.

Good on the overlap, Green defended well when he had to and went on to gain 15 full caps for Wales as well as representing his country in seven Under-23 internationals. He was born in the village of Brynteg near Wrexham in February 1942 and joined the staff at Goodison Park in July 1957, turning professional in February 1959. He left Everton for Blues in a £12,000 transfer in December 1962. During his time at St Andrew's he played in 217 competitive games, scored one goal, the winner in a 3-2 win at Carlisle in September 1968 - this after recovering from a broken leg suffered in 1966. He also helped Blues win the League Cup in 1963. After having a loan spell with Wrexham in January 1971, Green entered non-League soccer with Tamworth at the start of the 1971-72 season and after assisting Rhyl he duly retired in 1976 to concentrate on his garage business. He later became a sales representative for a veterinary medicine company.

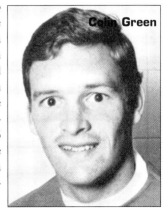
Colin Green

GREEN, Ken

Londoner Ken 'Slasher' Green was one of the most durable defenders in the game over the ten-year period: 1948-58. A canny full-back, he shared in most of Birmingham City's successes of the immediate post-war period and played in the FA Cup Final defeat of 1956.

He formed excellent partnerships with initially Dennis Jennings, then Jack Badham and finally with England international Jeff Hall. Able to occupy either the right or left-back berth, Green was serving in the Army when he wrote to the club asking for a trial. He impressed those watching and was immediately offered a contract in, of all places, the dressing room at Villa Park! He then spent sometime overseas before returning to England to establish himself in the Blues first XI, holding the right-back position unchallenged for five years before switching to the opposite side to accommodate Hall.

Green was a stern tackler, never erratic and after appearing in more than 400 games for Blues he retired in 1959 to take over a post office in Handsworth, Birmingham.

GREENHOFF, Jimmy

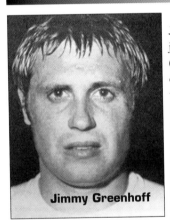
Jimmy Greenhoff

Leeds United transferred Jimmy Greenhoff to Blues for just £70,000 in August 1968 (signed by Stan Cullis). He had done well at Elland Road, netting 27 goals in 117 senior outings, but he simply couldn't command a regular first team place, despite the fact that he had starred in the 1968 League Cup-winning side. He also helped United to victory in the Fairs Cup Final that same year, having collected a runners-up prize in the same competition twelve months earlier. Born in Barnsley in June 1946 Greenhoff represented both Barnsley Schools and Yorkshire Boys before signing apprentice forms with Leeds in June 1961, turning professional two years later. He went on to claim 15 goals in only 36 outings for Blues (four coming in an incredible 5-4 win over Fulham) before he left St Andrew's to sign for Stoke City for £100,000 in August 1969.

He spent seven years at The Victoria Ground, scoring almost 101 goals for the Potters in 338 games. He was a star performer when they won the League Cup in 1972 and formed a terrific strike-force with big John Ritchie, ably assisted by Peter Dobing. In November 1976 Greenhoff moved to Old Trafford. United paid £120,000 for his signature and he quickly started to repay that with some sterling performances.

He helped United win the FA Cup in 1977 and reach the Final again two years later. He went on to score 36 goals in 122 outings for the Reds before joining Crewe Alexandra in December 1980. He later assisted Toronto Blizzard in the NASL (as player-coach) and then had a spell with Port Vale before spending a year as player-manager of Rochdale (March 1983-March 1984). He ended his footballing days as coach back at Vale Park.

Capped five times by England at Under-23 level, Greenhoff also played for the Football League XI and once for the 'B' team. He amassed an excellent record in the Football League - 146 goals in 571 appearances.

In later life Greenhoff coached the youngsters at various Butlin holiday camps while also working as an insurance broker. He now lives in Alsager, Stoke-on-Trent.

- Greenhoff scored in two FA Cup semi-finals for different clubs on the same ground - for Stoke City in 1972 and for Manchester United in 1979, both at Goodison Park. He also scored in a semi-final at Villa Park.
- Jimmy and his brother Brian played together in the same side at both Leeds and Manchester United.

GREGG, Bob

In 1931 Bob Gregg could well have become the hero of the City of Birmingham! At Wembley on 25 April in the FA Cup Final against West Bromwich Albion he had a first-half 'goal' ruled out for offside with the scoresheet blank. Had it been allowed to stand then who knows what might have happened on that wet and dismal Saturday afternoon in the capital? As it was the Baggies went on to win 2-1 and so deny Blues their first major trophy.

Gregg himself was a very useful inside-forward, who had played a significant part in helping Sheffield Wednesday win the First Division title in 1919. He left Hillsborough for St Andrew's in a £2,200 deal in January 1931 and within four months was starring in the Cup Final.

Despite struggling at times with injuries, he went on to score 15 goals in 75 appearances for Blues before leaving the club for Chelsea, who paid £1,500 for his services in September 1933. Gregg then assisted Boston United and Sligo Rovers prior to announcing his retirement in May 1944.

Born in Ferryhill, County Durham in February 1904 and now deceased, he played his early football with Ferryhill Athletic, Winlaton Juniors, Spennymoor United, Shilton Colliery and Durham City before having a second spell with Ferryhill. In September 1926 he was recruited by Darlington and moved to Hillsborough in May 1928. He scored seven goals in 37 outings for the Owls.

GRIMSBY TOWN

Blues' playing record against the Mariners:

FOOTBALL LEAGUE

Venue	P	W	D	L	F	A
Home	33	16	9	8	65	40
Away	33	7	8	18	35	46
Totals	66	23	17	26	100	86

FA CUP

Venue	P	W	D	L	F	A
Home	1	1	0	0	2	0
Away	1	0	0	1	1	2
Totals	2	1	0	1	3	2

LEAGUE CUP

Venue	P	W	D	L	F	A
Home	1	1	0	0	3	1
Away	2	1	1	0	5	3
Totals	3	2	1	0	8	4

FOOTBALL ALLIANCE

Venue	P	W	D	L	F	A
Home	3	2	0	1	7	3
Away	3	1	0	2	3	8
Totals	6	3	0	3	10	11

WARTIME

Home	3	2	1	0	7	1
Away	3	1	1	1	6	6
Totals	6	3	2	1	13	7

On their way to the Second Division championship in season 1892-93 Blues beat Grimsby Town 8-3 at Muntz Street in February - Billy Walton scored a hat-trick.

Blues registered their best win of the 1901-02 season when beating Grimsby Town 6-0 at home in late February.

In November 1913 Blues skipper Frank Womack was approached by a guy who offered him 55 guineas to 'fix' the result of a home Football League game against Grimsby Town at St Andrew's that same month. Womack quickly informed the club who in turn told the police. The so-called briber was arrested and later sentenced to a period of imprisonment at the local assize court. The game itself ended in a 2-1 win for the Mariners (the man wanted it end in a draw).

Blues were beaten 3-2 at St Andrew's by the Mariners in September 1935; it was 2-2 on the same ground a year later and then Charlie Craven scored his first goal for bottom of the table Blues in the 1-1 home draw with FA Cup semi-finalists-to-be Grimsby in February 1939.

The first time the teams met at League level after World War Two was in August 1951 when a crowd of 32,000 witnessed the 1-1 scoreline at St Andrew's. Welsh international Aubrey Powell scored for Blues.

A paltry St Andrew's crowd of just 4,457 saw Blues beat Grimsby 1-0 in May 1987. This was the lowest turnout for a senior game on Blues' soil for over 74 years, ironically since Grimsby were the visitors back in April 1913 (when the crowd was 3,000).

Blues defeated the Mariners by the same score (3-1) in a League game and then in a League Cup encounter at St Andrew's in the space of four weeks: September/October 1995. Steve Claridge scored in both matches.

On 1 March 1997 Blues (20th at the time) beat Grimsby (23rd) 2-1 in a crucial relegation match at Blundell Park. Blues' form improved ten-fold after this win and they finished 10th while the Mariners were relegated!

When Grimsby won 3-0 at St Andrew's in February 1999 it was their first triumph on Blues' ground for 63 years - since gaining a 3-2 victory back in September 1936 (Division 1).

Blues' biggest League Cup win over Grimsby is 4-2 at Blundell Park in 1966-67.

Blues gave a trial to the Gambian Jatto Ceesay in a friendly against the Mariners in August 1994 (3-3 draw).

Players with both clubs

Charlie Henderson

include: JM Beattie, W Bidmead, T Briggs, G Childs, H Clutterbuck, C Craven, K Drinkell, N Freeman, M Halsall, CG Henderson, W Hunter, D Jennings, HH Lappin, A Miller, A Mounteney, M North, M Prudhoe, A Rees, W Rudd, J Shaw, D Smith, W Wardle, T Williams, R Willis.

Also: Jackie Bestall (Town player, Blues coach), Alan Buckley, Johnny Newman and Frank Womack (all Blues players and Grimsby managers), Harry Storer (Grimsby player, Blues manager).

● Jackie Bestall scored 83 goals in 487 appearances for Grimsby and had a street named after him in that town. He was with Blues in 1938-39.

GROSVENOR, Tom

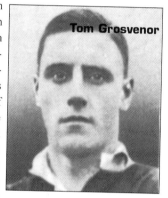

Tom Grosvenor

A Black Country, born in Netherton, Dudley in November 1908, Tom Grosvenor was a tall, long-legged footballer, able to occupy a number of positions including those of right-half and inside-right. Likened to the great Charlie Buchan, he played for several local teams before setting his stall out with Stourbridge. He moved to Blues from the Glassboys in March 1928, turning professional at St Andrew's six months later. Grosvenor who was plagued by injury during the first three years he was with Blues and again later on, was a creator of chances rather than a goalscorer himself. After taking over from Johnny Crosbie in 1931, he became instrumental in the centre of the field for Blues, going on to accumulate 115 appearances (15 goals). He eventually left St Andrew's for Sheffield Wednesday in February 1936 and rounded off his League career with Bolton Wanderers, finally hanging up his boots in 1943 after a brief spell with Dudley Town. Capped three times by England, Grosvenor also played for the Football League side. He died in October 1972.

● Tom's brother Percy was a professional footballer with West Bromwich Albion and and Leicester City another brother Cliff, was associated with Leicester.

GROUNDS

Blues have officially occupied four different 'home' venues:
76. Arthur Street (Bordesley Green)
1876-77 Ladypool Road (Sparkbrook)
1906. Muntz Street (Small Heath)
2000. St Andrew's (Bordesley Green)

They have also used the grounds for 'home' matches of Aston Villa, Leamington and Solihull.

GUEST PLAYERS

During the Wartime period of 1915-19 and again during World War Two (1939-46) Blues recruited several guest players to boost up their side - as did virtually every other club in the country!

Among the players who guested for the club during the Great War were Harry Hampton, who was later to join Blues, Harold Edgley, Charlie Wallace and Tom Weston all from Aston Villa,

Hubert Pearson, Jesse Pennington, Sid Bowser, Claude Jephcott and Sammy Richardson from West Bromwich Albion and Arthur Brooks, Sammy Brooks and Ernie Peers from Wolves.

Charlie Buchan (Sunderland) also had two outings in 1918-19.

- Among the long list of guest players to serve Blues during the seven year period from 1939 to 1946 were former player Billy Guest (from Blackburn Rovers), the Aston Villa sextet of Frank Broome, George Cummings, George Edwards, Bob Iverson, Alex Massie and Frank Moss, full-back Eddie Hapgood (Arsenal), goalkeepers Sam Bartram (Charlton Athletic) and Ted Ditchburn (Spurs), centre-forward Jack Acquaroff from Norwich City, Irish international inside-forward Peter Doherty from Manchester City and the Ipswich Town winger Jock Mulraney who actually joined Blues on a permanent basis in October 1945. In contrast quite a few Blues players guested for other clubs (see under respective clubs).

GUEST, Billy

Billy Guest

Black Country born and bred, outside-left Billy Guest was a very fine ball player who packed a powerful shot in both feet. He started out with Brierley Hill Juniors and after a short spell with their arch rivals Bromley Juniors from Kingswinford he joined Blues as a teenager in 1930, turning professional in February 1932. It took quite a while for him to get into the first XI (owing to the presence of Ernie Curtis and then Frank White). But he battled on gamely and went on to score 17 goals in 84 League and Cup appearances over the next five years including a marvellously struck hat-trick in a 7-3 win at Leicester in April 1934. In January 1937 Guest was transferred to Blackburn Rovers (in exchange for Jack Beattie) and at Ewood Park he did even better than he had done at St Andrew's, netting a goal every three games (32 in 94) up to August 1947 when he joined Walsall. He later assisted Peterborough United, Kidderminster Harriers, Lovells Athletic, Hinckley United, Bilston United and Brandwood Rovers where he was also a coach. He retired in 1956 and became a storeman at GEC, Witton. During World War Two Guest also played for Blues and West Bromwich Albion and gained a War Cup runners-up medal with Blackburn Rovers in 1940. He was born in Brierley Hill in February 1914 and died in the Lancashire cotton town of Darwen in November 1994.

GYPSY'S CURSE

The area of land where St Andrew's now stands was initially a dumping ground right next to a railway line. A band of gypsies lived there for quite some time and when they were asked to move off, a curse was placed on the club and the ground...and one feels it still hangs over the Blues to this day!

In the 1980s Blues' manager Ron Saunders did his best to remove the dreaded curse by hanging crucifixes to the floodlight pylons and arranging for the players' boots to be painted red! And

Barry Fry also had his own ideas as to how one should set about getting rid of the dreaded - and much talked about - gypsy's curse - by relieving the pressure!

HAGAN, Jim

Defender Jim Hagan played in 167 games for Blues and never scored a goal.

Born in Monkstown, Northern Ireland in August 1956, he was a booking clerk working for the Larne-Stranraer ferry service whilst playing for Larne Town at the age of 18. He was then persuaded to become a part-time professional with Coventry City, signing a full-term contract in November 1977. He never really got a break at Highfield Road and after a loan spell Torquay United and a few games with Detroit Express (NASL) and FC Seiko of Japan he moved to St Andrew's in June 1982. After five years with Blues he chose to try his luck in Spain with Celta Vigo (August 1987) but two years later he returned home to play for Larne. In October 1989 Hagan re-entered the Football League with Colchester United and after another short spell with Larne he signed for IFK Oddevold before going back to Ireland, becoming player-manager of Ballymena. His next move took him to Carrick Rangers (October 1993) and he finally settled once more in the capacity of player-boss of his beloved Larne (March 1994).

Capped six times by the Northern Ireland youth team, he was voted Ulster's Young Footballer of the Year in 1976.

HALIFAX TOWN

Blues' playing record against Halifax:

FA CUP

Venue	P	W	D	L	F	A
Home	1	1	0	0	2	0
Away	1	1	0	0	4	2
Totals	2	2	0	0	6	2

More than 18,000 fans saw Blues beat Halifax 4-2 in a third round FA Cup tie at The Shay in January 1968 - and six different players found the net.

Players with both clubs include: M Bullock (player and manager of Halifax), L Burkinshaw, T Capel, T Carter, J Gallagher, H Gayle, P Hendrie, GM Horsfield, K Langley, V Overson, FB Pentland, R Strang (Blues reserve).

Also: Jim Smith (Halifax player, Blues manager), Frank Worthington (Blues player, Halifax coach), Mick Rathbone (Blues player, Halifax physio), Norman Bodell (Blues coach, scout, Halifax player).

HALL, Jack

Over a seven-year period from 1906 to 1913 inside or centre-forward Jack Hall topped the scoring charts for each club he was associated with - Stoke, Brighton & Hove Albion, Middlesbrough, Leicester Fosse and Blues.

A terrific marksman, strong, mobile and very effective in the air despite being only 5ft 9ins tall, he moved to St Andrew's for what was described as a 'substantial fee' in December 1910 and stayed until 1915 when he joined Hucknall, the team of his birthplace. In that time he netted 48 goals in 103 appearances for Blues, forming a splendid partnership with Billy 'Bullet' Jones for a couple of seasons. From 17 December 1910 to 14 January 1911 Hall scored one

GUEST - HAMPTON

goal in seven successive League and Cup games for Blues and during his senior career he claimed more than 150 goals in total. Hall was born in July 1883 and had trials with both Nottingham Forest

1911 Hall scored one goal in seven successive League and Cup games for Blues and during his senior career he claimed more than 150 goals in total. Hall was born in July 1883 and had trials with both Nottingham Forest and Mansfield Town before signing for his first club Stoke. He died in Nottingham in 1938.

HALL, Jeff

Jeff Hall

Despite being on the small side, Jeff Hall was a very capable and efficient right-back, an England international who starred in 17 consecutive games for his country before losing his place to West Bromwich Albion's Don Howe in October 1957.

Perky, a strong defender and always a fighter, Hall took over the number 2 shirt at St Andrew's halfway through the 1952-53 season (when Ken Green moved across to left-back). He retained it competently thereafter, until being struck down with polio shortly after making his final League appearance at Portsmouth in March 1959. He was only 29 years of age - and proved a big loss to English football, especially to Birmingham City, his only club.

Hall was a member of Blues' Second Division championship-winning side of 1955 and twelve months later played at Wembley in the FA Cup defeat by Manchester City.

● A Jeff Hall Memorial scoreboard and clock can been seen at the City end of the St Andrew's ground.

HALLAM, Jack

Jack Hallam was a pint-sized outside-right, fast and clever who had an excellent scoring record with Blues - 67 goals in 157 first team appearances. Born in Oswestry in February 1869, he played initially for Oswestry Town before moving to Muntz Street in 1890 where he became an integral part of the dynamic Blues forward-

line of that era, forming a superb right-wing partnership first Charlie Short and then Billy Walton. He was instrumental in helping Blues win the Second Division championship in 1892-93 and take the runners-up prize the following season. From 1896 to May 1901 Hallam served with Swindon Town before retiring to work for the Great Western Railway Company in Swindon. He died in the Wiltshire town in March 1949.

Jack Hall

HAMPTON, Harry

'Appy' 'Arry' Hampton - the 'Wellington Whirlwind' - was a terror of a centre-forward, devil-may-care, robust and totally fearless. He certainly put the fear of God into many defenders and, indeed, goalkeepers with his all-action displays. He often charged into the opposing 'keeper and at times dived in head first. He once charged the 20-stone frame of the legendary soccer giant Billy Foulke into the back of the net (some feat). Amazingly Hampton suffered very

Harry Hampton (left) pictured with Johnny Crosbie

103

few injuries during his career which he ended playing as a right-half. Born in Wellington on 21 April 1885, he played for Shifnal Juniors and netted 54 goals in two seasons for Wellington Town before joining Aston Villa in May 1904. He formulated a brilliant record with Blues' arch rivals, scoring 242 goals in 376 appearances, helping them win the First Division championship in 1901 and the FA Cup in 1905 and 1913. He bagged two crucial goals against Newcastle United in the first of those Finals in front of 101,000 spectators at The Crystal Palace. He was top-scorer in each of his first eleven seasons at Villa Park and also played in four internationals for England (1913-14) and starred in three games for the Football League XI. A guest player with Blues, Derby County and Nottingham Forest during the Great War, he moved across Birmingham to St Andrew's in February 1920 and fired in 16 vital goals the following season to help Blues win the Second Division title.

Playing alongside another new signing, Joe Lane, he netted twice on his debut (in a 5-0 win at Barnsley) and all told secured nine goals in his first five outings for Blues.

He ended up with a total of 31 goals in just 59 games for Blues before moving to Newport County in September 1922. He retired in May 1923 at the age of 38, but surprised everyone by returning to action with his former club Wellington Town in January 1924. Hampton went on to score another 20 goals before finally hanging up his boots at the end of the 1924-25 season when he was appointed coach at Preston North End, a position he held for just six months. After a decade out of football (when he worked in a factory) Hampton returned to St Andrew's in October 1934 to coach the youngsters, leaving in April 1936 to run his own catering business in Rhyl. Late in life Hampton, querying his date-of-birth, visited Somerset House to check his birth certificate and found out he had actual name was Joseph! He died in Wrexham on 15 March 1963.

HANDS, Tommy

After leaving School at the age of 14 outside-left Tommy Hands played for a number of Small Heath teams before joining Blues in December 1890. He was born within 100 yards of the club's old ground Muntz Street on 4 January 1870 and was first choice in the first XI for six years, amassing 155 appearances and scoring 44 goals. As an ever-present he helped Blues win the Second Division championship in 1893 and finish runners-up in the same section the following season. Nicknamed 'Toddy', Hands had a terrific engine, always chasing backwards and forwards down the touchline but he dropped a bombshell in the summer of 1896 when he walked out on the club following a dispute. He later played for Kings Heath before retiring in 1900.

HANDYSIDES, Ian

Once described as the 'new' Trevor Francis, Ian Handysides never quite lived up to the reputation of his predecessor but he still gave Blues excellent service during his two spells at St Andrew's, scoring 12 goals in 133 first-class appearances. Born in Jarrow, County Durham on 14 December 1962, Handysides, who won youth caps for England, became an apprentice with Blues in 1978 and turned professional in January 1980. After four years trying to cope with First Division football Handysides moved to Walsall for £17,000 only to return to St Andrew's in March 1986. A loan spell with Wolves followed nine months later, but after scoring a hat-

Ian Handysides

trick for a Blues XI in a friendly win over Willenhall, Handysides complained of a headache and soon afterwards he and his family, and of course Blues, were stunned when a brain tumour was diagnosed. Handysides underwent intense treatment but the tumour spread dramatically to his spinal chord and he died in hospital at Solihull on 17 August 1990, aged only 27.

HARE, Charlie

Charlie Hare started his career with Warwick County, the club that provided several other quality footballers in the late 1880s, early '90s. A busy inside-forward, he next played for Birmingham United, then Aston Villa (from April 1891 - gaining a League championship medal in 1894) before having a decent spell with Woolwich Arsenal (August 1895 to November 1896). After Blues had recruited him from the Gunners he became a great favourite with the fans although his outings were interrupted continuously by niggling injuries. He scored 14 goals in 45 outings for Blues before transferring to Watford in July 1898, later assisting Plymouth Argyle (1903-04). Hare who made over 150 League and FA Cup appearances during his career, died in February 1934.

HARFORD, Mick

Nomadic striker Mick Harford drew up a magnificent record as a professional footballer, scoring over 230 goals in more than 700 senior appearances for no fewer than ten different clubs over a 20-year period. Born in Sunderland on 12 February 1959, he began his

Mick Harford

Stan Harland

career with Lincoln City in July 1977. He then played in turn, for Newcastle United (signed for £180,000 in December 1980); Bristol City (£160,000, August 1981); Blues (£100,000, March 1982); Luton Town (£250,000, December 1984); Derby County (£450,000, January 1990); Luton Town (again, £325,000, September 1991); Chelsea (£300,000, August 1992); Sunderland (£250,000, March 1993); Coventry City (£200,000, July 1993) and finally Wimbledon (£70,000, August 1994 - May 1997). His transfer fees totalled £2.25 million.

Capped twice by England at senior level (v Israel and Denmark in 1988-89) and once for the 'B' team, he won a League Cup winners' medal with Luton in 1988 and the following year collected runners-up medals in both the League Cup and Simod Cup with the Hatters, scoring at Wembley against Nottingham Forest in the League Cup. His record with Blues was a goal every three games - 33 in 109 outings - having been signed to take over the shirt previously worn by Frank Worthington. From 1997 onwards Harford has been coach and assistant-manager, even caretaker-boss for awhile at Wimbledon. He was with the Dons when they lost their Premiership status in May 2000.

• Harford's move from Newcastle United to Bristol City in 1981 was somewhat controversial. At the time of the deal the Ashton Gate club was on the verge of bankruptcy and could not meet the agreed instalments on his transfer fee. Newcastle appealed to the Football League who ordered Bristol City to return Harford to St James' Park on a free transfer. Rather than doing this, City immediately sold him to Blues, with the £100,000 fee involved going to Newcastle, leaving City with a balance of £60,000.

HARLAND, Stan

Before joining Blues in December 1971, left-half Stan Harland had made over 250 appearances for Swindon Town, skippering them to victory in the League Cup Final over Arsenal and to the Third Division championship in 1969 as well as lifting the Anglo-Italian Cup in 1970. After having trials with Burnley he then assisted New Brighton but missed out with Everton before moving to Bradford City in July 1961. From Valley Parade he switched to Carlisle United and arrived at The County Ground in August 1966. He was signed by Blues boss Freddie Goodwin to fill the vacancy left by first Dave Robinson and then Kenny Burns, but a lack of pace showed him up in the First Division and after 52 outings he quit in May 1973 to become player-manager of Yeovil Town. He later acted as assistant-manager at Portsmouth before taking charge of Gravesend & Northfleet. He returned to Yeovil as commercial manager in the mid-1970s and on leaving football ran a successful supermarket in the Somerset town.

Harland was born in Liverpool on 19 June 1940 and during his Football League career amassed 471 appearances and scored 33 goals.

HARRIS, Fred

Starting out as an inside-left and ending up as a wing-half Fred Harris played for Blues before, during and after World War Two. He made 312 League and FA Cup appearances for the club plus more than 90 during the hostilities, scoring well over 70 goals in total. Born in Solihull on 2 July 1913, he played for the Birmingham Transport team and Osborne Athletic before signing professional forms at St Andrew's in March 1933. He made his League debut against Aston Villa in front of 54,000 fans, scoring in a 2-1 win at St Andrew's in August 1934. He teamed up well with Charlie Wilson Jones before reverting to the wing-half position during the 1939-45 period. He skippered Blues to the Football League South championship in 1946 and the Second Division title in 1948, and he also represented the Football League side. On retiring from the game in May 1950 he qualified as a physiotherapist and chiropodist, later opening his own surgery in Acocks Green. Harris died in South Warwickshire in October 1998, aged 85.

Fred Harris

HARRIS, Jimmy

Jimmy Harris

Jimmy Harris was a sharp, fleet-footed forward whose greatest asset was his appetite for hard work. Born in Birkenhead on 18 August 1933 and a member of the district's highly successful Schoolboy team, he joined Everton as an amateur before making the transition to professionalism in September 1951. Four years later he made the first of 207 senior appearances for the Merseyside club (72 goals scored). He took over the centre-forward berth from Dave Hickson when he left Goodison Park for Aston Villa and within five months was capped by England at Under-23 level. When Hickson returned to Everton in the summer of 1957 Harris was switched to the right-wing. He scored a hat-trick at White Hart Lane in October 1958 but still finished on the losing side as Spurs won 10-4. A Football League representative, Harris left Everton for Blues in a £20,000 deal in December 1960. He continued to score regularly during his three-and-a-half years at St Andrew's, amassing a record of 53 goals in 115 appearances, mainly as a direct inside or centre-forward as strike partner to Johnny Gordon and then Ken Leek. He helped Blues reach the 1961 Inter Cities Fairs Cup Final against AS Roma and win the League Cup two years later. After leaving St Andrew's Harris played two seasons with Oldham Athletic (July 1964 to August 1966) and three months with Tranmere Rovers before joining non-League Rhyl Athletic in October 1966. He retired the following May to become steward of the Preston golf club.

HARRIS, Wallace

Outside-right Wally Harris replaced Billy Harvey in the Blues side following his transfer from Burton All Saints in November 1922. An England international trialist he went on to score 15 goals in 94 appearances in seven years at St Andrew's before joining Walsall September 1929. Born in Hockley on 22 February 1900, Harris retired prematurely through ill-health and he sadly died in a sanatorium in Davos, Switzerland in September 1933 after a short illness. He was a relative of Mr. J.T Harris, a former Director of Blues.

HARTLEPOOL UNITED

Blues' League record against the 'Pool:

Venue	P	W	D	L	F	A
Home	1	1	0	0	2	1
Away	1	0	0	1	0	1
Totals	2	1	0	1	2	2

These two encounters took place in season 1991-92 (Division Three). A crowd of 4,643 saw the game at The Recreation Ground on 21 September and 13,698 were present to see the return clash at

St Andrew's on 18 April when Trevor Matthewson and Nigel Gleghorn earned Blues a revenge victory.

Striker Andy Saville top-scored for both Hartlepool (13 goals) and Blues (seven goals) in the 1992-93 season.

Players with both clubs include: T Carter, E Curtis, K Dearden, WJ Hastings, K Lowe, J McCarthy, K Poole, M Prudhoe, A Saville, G Smith, J Trewick.

HARVEY, Billy

As a player Billy Harvey, possessing a heavy moustache, occupied the outside-right position before being superseded by his namesake 'Martin' Harvey. Although born in Netly near Freemantle in Hampshire on 12 April 1896 he was brought up in Yorkshire and after serving with the 2nd Battalion West Riding Regiment he joined Sheffield Wednesday as a professional in October 1919. He moved to St Andrew's in 1921 in readiness for Blues' first season back in the top flight after a break of 13 years. Capped three times by England as an amateur early in his career Harvey also toured South Africa with the FA in 1920. He scored once in 79 outings for Blues before joining Southend United in August 1925. A year later he returned to St Andrew's to take over as assistant-secretary and from March 1927 until May 1928 took over as team manager until Leslie Knighton came along. For six years from June 1932 to June 1938 Harvey was secretary-manager of Chesterfield, leading them to the Third Division North championship in 1936. He was in charge of Gillingham during the last pre-war campaign of 1938-39 but didn't figure in football after the hostilities, later choosing to emigrate to South Africa.

Harvey was also a very good cricketer, serving with Mitchell & Butlers and both Warwickshire and Border Province in South Africa. He was the first century-maker at Portland Road, scoring 115 not out for M&B against Moseley on 9 May 1931. He died in South Africa circa 1970.

HATELEY, Tony

Tony Hateley was a soccer nomad whose scoring record in League football was exceptional - 211 goals in 434 appearances...and all this after he had started out as a centre-half before being converted into a striker by the great Tommy Lawton who was his manager at Notts County.

Hateley, father of Mark (later to play for England) was born in Derby on 13 June 1941. He did well initially as a defender with Normanton Sports Club and after being on Derby County's books as a Schoolboy, he entered League soccer with Notts County, joining the Magpies in May 1956. Hateley then assisted, in turn, Aston Villa (signed for £20,000 in August 1963), Chelsea (bought from Villa for £100,000 in October 1966), Liverpool (£100,000 July 1967) and Coventry City (£80,000, September 1968) before signing for Blues for £72,000 in August 1969. After fifteen months at St Andrew's (six goals scored in 30 appearances)

Tony Hateley

Hateley moved back to Notts County for £20,000 in November 1970. Then he recommenced his merry-go-round antics by assisting Oldham Athletic (bought £5,000, July 1972), Bromsgrove Rovers (May 1974), Prescot Town (July 1975) and Keyworth United (from December 1978). He retired in August 1979. He later worked in the Everton lottery office and thereafter was employed by a brewery in Nottinghamshire. Tall and muscular, exceptionally strong in the air, Hateley helped Notts County win both the Third and Fourth Division championships in 1960 and 1971 respectively and was an FA Cup finalist with Chelsea in 1967.

HATTON, Bob

Bob Hatton

Like Hateley (above) Bob Hatton travelled the country scoring goals! Born in Hull on 10 April 1947, he began as a 15 year-old with Wath Wanderers (a junior side associated with Wolverhampton Wanderers). The following year he became an apprentice at Molineux, turning professional in November 1964. Thereafter as an inside or centre-forward with a knack of finding the net from anywhere within reason, Hatton played and scored for Bolton Wanderers (March 1967-October 1968), Northampton Town (to July 1969), Carlisle United (until October 1971), Blues (signed from Brunton Park for £20,000), Blackpool (July 1976), Luton Town (July 1978), Sheffield United (July 1980) and Cardiff City (December 1982 to May 1983). On retiring from first-class soccer he assisted Lodge Cotterill (a Birmingham Sunday side) and later became a match summariser on local radio while also working for an insurance company in the 1990s- and when time allowed he attended several matches at St Andrew's. In a total of 620 League matches Hatton scored 217 goals, with his Blues record reading 73 strikes in 218 senior outings. Playing alongside Trevor Francis and Bob Latchford, he netted 15 vital goals to help Blues win promotion from Division Two in 1972. Six years later he scored 22 goals for Blackpool but couldn't save them from being relegated to the Third Division.

HAT-TRICKS

Eddie Stanley (with four goals) had the distinction of scoring Blues' first ever hat-trick at competitive level, doing so against Burton Wanderers in a first round FA Cup-tie on 31 October 1885.

Billy Walton scored the first Football League hat-trick for Blues against Walsall Town Swifts on 17 December 1892.

Bob Hatton was the first hat-trick hero for Blues in a League Cup-tie, obliging against his future club Blackpool in October 1973. Bob Latchford quickly followed a month later v Ipswich and then Mick Harford became Blues' third 'League Cup' hat-trick hero with a treble against Derby County in 1983.

Will Devey (with six goals - a double hat-trick) was the first Blues player to grab a treble in the Football Alliance, doing so versus Nottingham Forest in March 1890. George Short also scored three goals in this game which Blues won 12-0.

Charlie Izon in a 4-0 win over Walsall Town Swifts at home in September 1893 (Division 1) and Peter Murphy in a 5-0 win at Doncaster Rovers in 19 January 1952 (Division Two) are the only Blues two players ever to score a hat-trick on their senior debuts for the club .

Vowden treble sets record for a substitute

By GRON WILLIAMS
Birmingham City 5, Huddersfield Town 1

Geoff Vowden went on in place of his skipper Ron Wylie for the second half and, as far as my researches tell me, created soccer history as the first Football League substitute to score a hat-trick since the substitute rule was adopted in 1965.

Vowden, 27, who has scored more goals for Blues than any other man on the staff, said afterwards: "In four years with the club I've never before been dropped and this was my first experience as a substitute.

Mick Harford (no. 9) hit a League Cup hat-trick against Derby County in 1983

Newspaper cutting of Vowden's hat-trick

Joe Bradford, with a total of 13 hat-tricks for Blues (12 in the League, one in the FA Cup) holds the club record for most trebles.

Bob McRoberts shares second spot with Abbott and Peter Murphy, all with six.

Bradford, in fact, netted three hat-tricks for Blues in September 1929 - all in the First Division against West Ham United, Newcastle United and Blackburn Rovers in that order. He also scored five times in an Inter League game that same month!

Between them Blues players scored a total of seven League hat-tricks in season 1893-94: Frank Mobley claimed four, including two (at home and away) against Northwich Victoria.

Mobley, in fact, registered a total of five League hat-tricks for Blues, the same number as Walter Abbott, who achieved the feat in 1898-99.

Abbott also scored three goals in an FA Cup-tie versus Burslem Port Vale in December 1898.

Fred Wheldon, with two Alliance trebles and three in the Football League, scored five hat-tricks for Blues at senior level.

Centre-forward Eddie Brown also weighed in with five trebles as did left-winger Alex Govan and Bob Latchford in the 1970s, while Trevor Francis notched four trebles and Kenny Burns three.

All of Govan's came in the same season (1956-57) including three in just 12 days during late August and early September against Portsmouth (away), Newcastle United and Preston North End (both at home).

Substitute Geoff Vowden replaced Ron Wylie in Blues' home League game with Huddersfield Town on 7 September 1968 and promptly scored a hat-trick in a 5-1 victory.

During the Great War period of 1916-19 Joe Godfrey scored four hat-tricks for Blues in Regional competitions and during the 1939-45 hostilities Cyril Trigg notched seven trebles to go with the two peacetime trebles he scored in Football League action in 1946 and 1951.

Over the years Blues players have so far scored more than 140 hat-tricks in major competitions - the 100th League treble being credited to Bob Latchford v Watford (home) on 28 September 1971.

Paul Furlong scored two League hat-tricks for Blues in January 1998 - the first in a 7-0 win at Stoke and the second in a 4-1 home victory over Stockport County.

Billy Edmunds scored a 'hat-trick' in just five minutes during a friendly game in 1879. Playing for Blues he scored twice for his own club and conceded an own goal for the opposition, Nechells, who won 4-3.

HEDNESFORD TOWN

Blues beat Hednesford 8-0 at Muntz Street in a first qualifying round of the FA Cup-tie in October 1890. A crowd of 1,500 saw Fred Wheldon (3) and Will Devey (2) lead the goal rush.

Blues' reserve side used Hednesford's Keys Park stadium during the 1990s.

Players with both clubs include: K Bertschin, J Birch, E Cameron, A McIntosh.

Also: Dick Neal (Blues player, Town manager).

HEIGHT

TALLEST

The tallest player ever to don a Blues jersey at senior level is believed to have been striker Kevin Francis, who was 6ft 7ins in height when registered at St Andrew's during the 1990s.

Centre-forward Albert Millard was another tall player at 6ft. 5in, as were goalkeepers Chris Charsley, Harry Crossthwaite and George Hollis, all standing around the 6ft 4in mark. Neil Freeman and reserve 'keeper George Yarnell from the early 1900s were also exceptionally tall Blues players.

Other tall players (over 6ft. 2in) include: Dele Adebola, Ken Armstrong, Archie Barton, Jimmy Bye, Tony Coton, Mick Ferguson, Joe Gallagher, John Gayle, Billy George, Andy Gosney, Tom Grosvenor, Mick Harford, Martin Hicks, Roger Hynd, Jackie Lane, Dave Latchford, Gil Merrick, George Morrall, Thomas Myhre, Jim Olney, Ryan Price, Nat Robinson, Mark Sale, David Seaman, Johnny Schofield, Brian Sharples, Jack Shaw, Trevor Smith, goalkeeper Paul Tomlinson and Colin Withers.

SMALLEST

Jose Dominguez, at 5ft 3ins tall, is one the smallest players ever to don a Blues shirt. The Portuguese international was at St Andrew's during the 1994-95 season.

Other relatively small players (5ft 5ins or under) to have worn the Blues colours include Bertie Auld, Johnny Berry, Alex Govan, Jimmy Haarhoff (5ft 4ins), Jack Hallam, Toddy Hands, Alec Jackson, Bobby Laing (5ft 4ins), Paul Peschisolido (5ft 4ins), Steve Robinson, Jackie Stewart, Simon Sturridge, Danny Wallace and Mark Ward.

HELLAWELL, Mike

Speedy outside-right who enjoyed hugging the touchline, Mike Hellawell was quick, very quick, over 25-30 yards. Exchanged for inside-forward Bill Finney, he moved to St Andrew's from Queens Park Rangers in May 1957 as a replacement for Gordon Astall and proceeded to score 33 goals in 213 outings for Blues over the next eight years. He was transferred to Sunderland in January 1965 and later returned to Huddersfield before rounding off his playing career with spells at Peterborough United (from December 1968) and Bromsgrove Rovers (1969-71). Born deep in the heart of

Rugby League territory in Keighley, Yorkshire - in the same town as Trevor Hockey - Hellawell began his career with Huddersfield Town but failed to make the grade at Leeds Road, switching south to London to join QPR in 1955. A Fairs Cup Finalist with Blues in 1960 and 1961, he gained a League Cup winners in 1963 when Aston Villa were defeated 3-1 over two legs and he also gained two England caps. Whilst with QPR he represented the Football League Division Three side.

After hanging up his boots Hellawell ran a shop for many years in his native Keighley. Besides being a fine footballer he was also a talented cricketer and represented Warwickshire in the County Championship.

Mike Hellawell

HENNESSEY, Terry

Terry Hennessey receiving the Midland Footballer of the Year award.

Born in Llay near Wrexham on 1 September 1942 and a pupil at Grove Park Grammar School, Terry Hennessey represented Wrexham & District Boys and was capped by Wales at Schoolboy level before joining Birmingham City as a junior, turning professional in 1959. He began his senior career as an attacking wing-half, but was later, perhaps controversially in some people's minds, switched to a sweeper.

During the early 1960s he was rated one of the best defenders in the game, producing some excellent performances for Blues, skippering the side on several occasions. With only a handful of League games under his belt, he was the star player when Blues beat Inter Milan in the semi-final of the 1961 Fairs Cup and although he battled hard and long before ending up on the losing side in the Final against AS Roma, two years later he was again a key figure when Blues defeated Aston Villa to win the League Cup.

Hennessey, strong, athletic and a fine passer of the ball, went on appear in 203 first-class games for Blues (three goals scored). He was an inspirational battler in several relegation campaigns before transferring to Nottingham Forest for a give-away price of £45,000 in 1965 - soon after Blues' demotion to the Second Division.

In February 1970, after 183 senior appearances for Forest, he surprisingly joined Derby County for £100,000, becoming the Rams' first six-figure signing. In 1972, he gained both League championship and Texaco Cup winners medals with the East Midlands club. Before leaving the Baseball Ground he took his tally of full international caps with Wales up to 39 - having gained his first as a Blues player against Northern Ireland in April 1962 when the Irish lost 4-0 in Cardiff (he helped set up two of John Charles' four goals). Hennessey also represented his country in six under-23 internationals.

In 1974, soon after undergoing an operation for appendicitis, Hennessey pulled out of competitive football to take over as man-ager of Tamworth. Three years later he took charge of Kimberley Town and then had a spell in the NASL as assistant-coach of Tulsa Roughnecks before returning to England in 1978 to coach Shepshed Charterhouse for two years. He then had a second spell with the Roughnecks in America, initially as a coach in 1980 then as chief scout from 1981 to 1983. His next appointment took him to Vancouver Whitecaps (as assistant-manager/coach to Alan Hinton). He then held a coaching position in Toronto before having season as boss of the Australian club Heidelberg (1987-88).

HEREFORD UNITED

Blues' playing record against United:

AUTO WINDSCREEN SHIELD

Venue	P	W	D	L	F	A
Home	1	1	0	0	3	1

LEYLAND DAF TROPHY

Home	1	1	0	0	1	0

Blues beat the Bulls in the Leyland DAF Trophy in 1989-90 and a record crowd of 22,352 (bigger than the Sheffield United v Manchester United FA Cup game on the same night) saw Blues narrow AWS victory in 1994-95 - on their way to a Wembley victory over Carlisle United.

Players with both clubs include: J Blyth, A Coton (Hereford reserves), K Downing (player/coach at Hereford), G Downs (United player-manager), A Elliott, C Francis, C Gordon, J Higgins, WM Hughes, G Johnston, MA Jones, SH King, EP O'Hara, BL Roberts, CR Robertson, P Robinson, I Rodgerson, D Rowbotham, FH Shell (Blues reserve), PM Starbuck, D Wassall.

Also: Johnny Newman (Blues player, Hereford manager), Ian Bowyer and Derek Jefferson (Hereford players, Blues trainer/coaches).

HERRIOT, Jim

Goalkeeper Jim Herriot was born in Chapelhall, Airdrie on 20 December 1939 and played for Douglasdale before gaining a Scottish Cup runners-up with Dunfermline Athletic in April 1965. The following month he joined Blues and became a big favourite with the St Andrew's fans, often daubing boot polish, American-football style, under his eyes to divert the glare of the floodlights during evening matches. An infuriating 'keeper at times, brilliant one minute, scary the next, he could produce a stunning save from one shot and then let in a silly goal from a rather weaker effort. Nevertheless Herriot went on to appear in 212 first-class matches for Blues after replacing Johnny Schofield between the posts. He left the club for Hibernian in August 1971 and at the end o his first season at Easter Road collected a second Scottish Cup runners-up prize, but made up for that disappointment twelve months later when he helped Hibs win the League Cup. In February 1975 Herriot transferred to Partick Thistle and after a loan spell with Greenock Morton he returned to his former club Dunfermline Athletic in 1976 before ending his playing career at Morton. Capped eight times by Scotland, Herriot became the first substitute for 61 years to come on the field of play during an international match at the Racecourse Ground, Wrexham when he replaced Liverpool's Tommy Lawrence against Wales in 1969. He also played for the Scottish League XI and today enjoys ever lasting fame following the adoption of his surname by the famous veterinarian author.

Jim Herriot in action against WBA in the 1968 FA Cup semi-final.

Terry Hibbitt

ings he returned to Newcastle in May 1978. He was made captain at Gallowgate and went on to push his total number of appearances for the Geordies up to 259 (13 goals) before quitting League football with a niggling knee injury. He did, however, find time to assist Gateshead (July 1982) first as a player before taking over as player-coach and then manager (August-October 1986). He ran a newsagent's shop and a pub in Newcastle before his tragic death on Tyneside on 5 August 1994, aged 46.

HIBBITT, Terry

Midfielder Terry Hibbitt scored a goal with his first kick in English football - for Leeds United against Nottingham Forest in February 1966 after coming on as a second-half substitute for Paul Madeley. Born in Bradford on 1 December 1947 and elder brother to Kenny Hibbitt (ex-Bradford Park Avenue, Wolves, Coventry City, Bristol Rovers etc.) Hibbitt was basically a squad member at Elland Road, contesting a first team place with Johnny Giles, Eddie Gray, Billy Bremner and company. In fact, he made only 53 senior appearances (9 goals scored) during his eight years with the Yorkshire club, collecting a runners-up medal in the 1968 Fairs Cup Final before transferring to Newcastle United for £30,000 in August 1971.

He spent four years at St James' Park, making over 150 appearances and obtaining a second runners-up medal, this time when United lost to Liverpool in the 1974 FA Cup Final but he did help the Magpies win a Texaco Cup. Hibbitt's precise left-foot set up heaps of chances for Malcolm Macdonald at Newcastle and at one time was marked down as a possible England candidate. But injury checked his career and when he regained full fitness there was another manager at the helm and was transferred to Blues for £100,000 in August 1975. Over the next three years Hibbitt was a key figure in the engine-room at St Andrew's but failed to win over the vociferous element of fans after netting 11 goals in 122 out-

HIBBS, Harry

One of the finest-ever goalkeepers in English football, Harry Hibbs had superb anticipation and although on the short side he had a remarkable temperament in crisis situations. He was never afraid to dive at the feet of onrushing forwards, was very capable when going for high crosses, often choosing to punch the ball rather than catch it and often made difficult ground shots look easy. He was a fitness fanatic and his agility meant that he could dive across his line to reach shots other 'keepers could not.

Born Henry Edward Hibbs in Wilnecote near Tamworth on 27 May 1906, he had family connections in football - his uncle Hubert Pearson and his cousin Harold Pearson both kept goal for West Bromwich Albion and another cousin Horace Pearson was Coventry City's last line of defence.

Hibbs attended and played for Wilnecote Holy Trinity School and also for Tamworth Castle FC before joining Blues in May 1924, the local vicar persuading him to go to St Andrew's instead of London to

Harry Hibbs

play for Arsenal! Hibbs spent 16-years with Blues (he retired in April 1940) and after eventually taking over from Dan Tremelling in 1929, he accumulated a grand total of 389 first-class appearances for Blues, 556 goals conceded (only two 'keepers have played in more matches: Gil Merrick and Tremelling). Hibbs also had 12 outings for the club during his last season at St Andrew's (1939-40) which culminated with a farewell benefit match against Aston Villa on 13 April in front of 15,000 fans (he received a cheque for £650). Hibbs won 25 England caps - his first in November 1929 when Wales were beaten 6-0 and his last in February 1936, also against Wales. England suffered only five defeats when he was in goal.

Hibbs also represented the Football League on three occasions and toured South Africa with the FA in the summer of 1929, playing in one game. He appeared in the 1931 FA Cup Final against WBA and played superbly well despite conceding two goals. He was a brave goalkeeper with tremendous reflexes whose positional sense at times was unbelievable. He was also courageous and once had six teeth knocked out after colliding with the Huddersfield Town centre-forward Joe Robson in a League game in 1930.

Four years after leaving St Andrew's Hibbs took over as manager of Walsall, a position he held until June 1951, having guided the Saddlers to runners-up in the League Three South Cup in 1946. He then signed as a permit player for the de Havillands club (February 1953-May 1954) playing his last game shortly before his 48th birthday. From August 1960 to 1962 he managed Ware Town and then ended his footballing career by taking charge of Welwyn Garden City (1962-64). Hibbs died at Hatfield on 23 May 1984.

HICKS, George

Outside-left George Hicks was a tall, slim player with good pace who, prior to joining Blues in October 1923, had scored 48 goals in 135 appearances for Manchester City, gaining an FA Cup runners-up medal in 1926 and a Second Division championship medal two years later. Born near Salford on 30 April 1902 (and now deceased) he started out with the Salford lads' club before playing regularly for Droylesden and then Manchester City, moving to Maine Road in November 1923. He had an excellent first season with Blues, netting 12 goals in 30 League outings, but then became a creator of chances rather than a goalscorer himself and after taking his overall record to 18 goals in 83 senior appearances, he left St Andrew's for Manchester United in January 1932. Unfortunately Hicks never got a game at Old Trafford and in August 1933 moved to Swindon Town, later assisting Rotherham United (from November 1933) and finally Manchester North End (September 1934-May 1935).

HIGGINS, Jimmy

A Republic of Ireland international centre-forward (one cap gained v Argentina at Dalymont Park in May 1951) Jimmy Higgins was born in Dundalk on 3 February 1926 and played for his home town club before joining Blues in November 1949 along with team-mate Eddie O'Hara. A bustling type-of-player, his stunning 44-second match-winner against Manchester United in a 6th round FA Cup-tie at St Andrew's took Blues into the semi-finals of the FA Cup in 1951. This is believed to be the fastest goal ever scored by a Blues player from kick-off at the start of a senior game. This was one of 14 goals Higgins scored in his 54 outings for Blues before he left to join Hereford United in July 1953, returning to his former club Dundalk in 1955.

HIGH SCORING GAME

Blues beat an International Select XI 12-8 at St Andrew's in Malcolm Beard's Testimonial match in November 1969. This the highest-scoring game involving Blues' senior side (20 goals).

● Twelve has been the most number of goals in a League and/or major Cup game involving Blues with scores of 12-0, 10-2 and 7-5 (see under wins, defeats).

HOCKEY, Trevor

Trevor Hockey

Yet another of football's journeyman, Trevor Hockey's professional career spanned almost 16 years during which time he amassed well over 600 senior appearances and played on all 92 League grounds which were being used when he was in action. He was an aggressive footballer who quite often was given the job of man-marking his opponent. And at times his aggressive nature often brought him into conflict with referees. Nevertheless he was a gritty performer, always giving 100 per-cent effort and very popular with the ladies, his beatle-style haircut having a big influence on that! Away from football he was quite a happy-go-lucky fellow, owning a pink piano which he played quite regularly. Hockey, in fact, made a record entitled 'Happy 'Cos I'm Blue' and he also appeared on stage at the Birmingham Town Hall. He was one of the first players to represent Wales on a parental qualification, going on to win nine full caps.

A Yorkshireman, born in Keighley on 1 May 1943, Hockey played Rugby League, Rugby Union and soccer at School. In the end he chose soccer and after starring for the West Riding under 19s and Keighley Central Youth club he joined Bradford City as an amateur in June 1958, turning professional at Valley Parade in May 1960. After that Hockey toured the country, playing in midfield or on the wing for Nottingham Forest (signed for £15,000 in November 1961); Newcastle United (£25,000, November 1963); Blues (£22,500, November 1965 - he made 232 appearances and scored 13 goals during his five-and-a-half years at St Andrew's); Sheffield United (£35,000, January 1971); Norwich City (February 1973); Aston Villa (signed for £38,000 in June 1973); Bradford City (again, June 1974); Athlone Town (as player-manager March 1976); San Diego Jaws (NASL, April 1976) and finally Stalybridge Celtic (manager, August 1977-78).

He later coached the British Army soldiers' children's soccer team on the Rhine and attempted to start a soccer School at Keighley rugby club. He also assisted San Jose Earthquakes and Los Angeles Quicksilvers during two more summer trips to America and collected a Second Division championship medal with Newcastle in 1965. Hockey sadly died of a heart attack shortly after taking part in a 5-a-side tournament in Keighley on 2 April 1987.

HODGETTS, Dennis

'Denny' Hodgetts scored 94 goals in 215 appearances for Aston Villa before moving across the City to join Blues in October 1896. A powerfully-built inside-left with an immaculate waxed moustache, he was born in Hockley on 28 November 1863 and had two separate spells with Birmingham St George's and another with Great Lever FC (Manchester) before signing as a professional with the Villa in February 1886. Over the next ten-and-a-half years Hodgetts gained two League championship medals (1894 and 1896), two FA Cup winners medals (1887 and 1895) and a Cup runners-up medal (1892). He won six England caps and also played for the Football League side. A clever footballer, he could shoot from any distance, was strong and effective in the air and could pass a ball with precision up to 30-40 yards. He played most of his football as an inside-left but occasionally ventured to the wing where he was just as good, if not better! He scored nine goals in 23 outings for Blues before retiring in May 1898 when he returned to Villa Park as a coach. He later became a publican (June 1910), initially taking over the licence at the Salutation Inn on Summer Lane, Aston. In June 1930 he was elected vice-president of Aston Villa Football Club, a position held with distinction until his death in Aston on 26 March 1945 (aged 81).

HOLLIS, George

Blues' goalkeeper when they won the Second Division championship in 1893, George Hollis was born near Kenilworth Castle in 1869 and joined the club in 1891 after two seasons with Warwick County. A swarthy player with heavy sideburns who used to keep his shorts up with a coloured cummerbund, he took over the number one spot from Chris Charsley, but when he returned to the club, Hollis was demoted to the reserves for a season. Over a three-year period he made just 33 first team appearances before being reinstated as an amateur in 1894 when he joined Bournbrook FC, retiring in 1897.

HOME FARM

Blues travelled to Ireland to meet and beat Home Farm 2-1 in a Festival of Britain game in 1951. Jackie Stewart and Johnny Berry scored the goals in front of 3,000 spectators.

HONOURS

Several people, who during their respective footballing careers served with Blues at various levels, have received honours for services to football in general. They include: assistant-manager Mick Mills MBE, manager and Director Sir Alf Ramsey and Director and president David Wiseman, OBE.

Other awards have gone to Syd Owen, voted 'Footballer of the Year' in 1959 after guiding Luton Town to the FA Cup Final in his last season as a player. Dave Mackay (then of Derby County) who was also named 'Footballer of the Year' in 1969 along with Manchester City's Tony Book. Colin Todd (Derby County) was honoured with the 'Footballer of the Year' title in 1975 and Kenny Burns (Nottingham Forest) also took the 'Footballer of the Year' prize in 1978.

Alan O'Neill was named Irish 'Young Footballer of the Year' in 1991-92.

The following Blues personnel - John Bond, Steve Bruce, Alan Buckley, Terry Cooper, Alan Curbishley, Barry Fry, Trevor Francis, Howard Kendall, Lou Macari, Dave Mackay, Bruce Rioch, Ron Saunders, Jim Smith and Colin Todd - all received 'Manager of the Month' (even 'Manager of the Year') awards with the respective clubs they managed.

And ex-Blues winger Gordon Taylor was first appointed secretary of the PFA in 1980 and later became that organisation's Chief Executive.

HOOPER, Harry

Harry Hooper

Dashing right-winger with flare and good scoring record, Harry Hooper enjoyed a fine career that spanned 13 years, took in over 320 senior appearances and saw him play for four different League clubs. Born at Pittington, County Durham on 14 June 1933, he was the son of former Hartlepool United, Nelson, Sheffield United defender, also named Harry, who skippered the Blades in the 1936 FA Cup Final against Arsenal.

Hooper junior kept goal for his junior School team, but became an outside-right when attending Neville's Cross High.

He then played for Hylton Colliery juniors - recognized at the time as one of the best junior teams in Britain - before representing Durham youths. He was on Sunderland's books as an amateur and joined West Ham United as a full-time professional in December 1950 - this after the Upton Park club had appointed his father to their training staff!

A former Durham youth sprint champion he scored 44 goals in 119 Second Division games for the Hammers, winning six England 'B' caps and two at Under-23 level as well as playing for the

Football League side. In March 1956 Wolverhampton Wanderers manager Stan Cullis paid £25,000 for him as a replacement for Johnny Hancocks and at the time it was the most money any club had forked out for a winger. Hooper, happiest on the right flank, scored 19 goals for the Wolves in 39 League games - all in 1956-57 - when he was leading marksman. But in December 1957, with Norman Deeley now established on the right-wing at Molineux, Hooper moved to St Andrew's, thus taking no part in Wolves' championship winning season. Blues paid £19,500 for his services and he netted 42 goals in 105 games and appeared in the 1960 Fairs Cup Final against Barcelona before being sold to Sunderland in September 1960 - a local boy going home if you like! Between them both Hooper and Astall switched wings frequently during the next two-and-a-half years but with the team going nowhere in terms of League success and with Mike Hellawell ready to move in, Hooper departed for Roker Park.

Hooper made a further 65 League appearances for the Wearsiders (16 goals) before joining Kettering Town in May 1963. He left football in 1967 and went into business in Kettering.

HOPE, Bobby

Bobby Hope was a masterful midfield player with terrific vision, splendid ball skills and strong shot. He scored 42 goals in 403 first-class games for West Bromwich Albion who he served for thirteen years before joining Blues. A Scotsman, born in the Stirlingshire town of Bridge of Allan on 28 September 1943, he signed for the Baggies in August 1959 with fellow countrymen Ken Foggo, Campbell Crawford and Bobby Murray soon after all four players had represented their country in three Schoolboy internationals earlier that year. Hope went on to win further caps at Under-23 and senior levels and gained both League Cup and FA Cup winners' medals in 1966 and 1968 respectively. He also scored Albion's first-ever goal in Europe v DOS Utrecht in 1966. Blues signed Hope in May 1972 for the unusual fee of £66,666. He went straight into the first XI, linking up in midfield with Malcolm Page and feeding the likes of Trevor Francis and Bob Latchford. Hope hit five goals in his 46 outings for Blues, and after playing in the NASL with Philadelphia Atoms (April-May 1975) he switched to Sheffield Wednesday in September 1976. He visited America twice again to serve with Dallas Tornadoes between April-August 1977 and April-August 1978. Later on he had two separate spells as manager of Bromsgrove Rovers, scouted for Albion and their arch rivals Wolves and played in more than 200 charity matches for the Albion All Stars (1979-95). Hope was appointed Albion's Youth Development Officer in July 1998, returning to The Hawthorns almost 40 years since he first set foot inside the ground as a 16 year-old, the age he made his League debut against Arsenal. Hope, who now resides in Walsall, has also owned a newsagents' shop in Boldmere and managed post offices in both Handsworth and Sutton Coldfield since retiring as a player.

HOPKINS, Robert

Robert Hopkins' early career was littered with disciplinary problems but he always gave total commitment while playing wide on the right of midfield, as a central midfield position and even as a full-back. Born in Hall Green, Birmingham on 25 October 1961 and a pupil at Pitmaston School, he joined Aston Villa as an apprentice after representing South Birmingham Schools and West

Midland County Boys. He turned professional at Villa Park in July 1979 and after scoring once in three games he left for St Andrew's in March 1983 in a deal that saw Alan Curbishley go in the opposite direction. After three-and-a-half years with Blues Hopkins was transferred to Manchester City in September 1986 for £130,000, but in March 1989 he returned to the Midlands to join West Bromwich Albion in a £60,000 deal involving Imre Varadi who moved to Maine Road in part-exchange. In March 1989, Blues boss Garry Pendrey brought Hopkins back to St Andrew's for £25,000 but after taking his club appearance record up to 205 (35 goals scored) in July 1991 he signed for Shrewsbury Town. After a spell in Hong Kong in 1992 with Instant Dictionary FC he enlisted with Solihull Borough and in February 1993 re-entered the Football League (albeit only briefly) with Colchester United before going back to Solihull Borough. Hopkins won an FA Youth Cup winners medal with Villa and helped Blues win promotion to Division One in 1985 and was a non-playing 'sub' for Blues when they lifted the Leyland DAF Trophy in 1991.

HOWARD, Pat

Pat Howard

Centre-half Pat Howard made 555 League appearances for five different clubs over a 17-year period: 1965-82. He also played in the NASL with Portland Timbers during the late 1970s. Born in Dodsworth, Yorkshire on 7 October 1947, his first club was Barnsley whom he joined as an apprentice before taking professional status in October 1965. From Oakwell he was transferred to Newcastle United for £21,000 in September 1971 and after gaining runners-up medals in the 1974 FA Cup Final and 1976 League Cup Final he moved south to Highbury. Signing for Arsenal in a £50,000 deal in September 1976. From there he switched to St Andrew's for £40,000 in August 1977 and played alongside first Tony Want and then Joe Gallagher in the Blues defence before moving on a free transfer to Bury in July 1979 - after his spell in the NASL. Howard later ran his own business in Bury.

HUDDERSFIELD TOWN

Blues' playing record against the Terriers:

FOOTBALL LEAGUE

Venue	P	W	D	L	F	A
Home	45	23	8	14	77	51
Away	45	8	18	19	36	70
Totals	90	31	26	33	113	121

FA CUP

	P	W	D	L	F	A
Home	3	2	0	1	4	3
Away	3	0	1	2	2	4
Totals	6	2	1	3	6	7

WARTIME

	P	W	D	L	F	A
Hom e	3	3	0	0	5	2
Away	3	0	0	3	3	7
Totals	6	3	0	3	8	9

Huddersfield gained entry into the Football League Division Two for the 1910-11 campaign and they made an impact right away!

Dave Mangnall

Blues lost 7-1 to the Terriers at their Leeds Road ground in April of that season and crashed 7-0 on the same pitch in October 1913 - each defeat being Blues' worst of that respective season.

Tommy Elliott scored a hat-trick and Billy Ball conceded a bizarre own-goal (the ball screwing over 'keeper Bert Crossthwaite off his posterior) in the October 1913 contest.

Town were one of the best club sides in the country during the 1920s (winning the First Division title three years running). They doubled up over Blues in 1923-24, claiming two 1-0 victories; triumphed 1-0 again at St Andrew's the following season; beat Blues 3-1 and 4-1 in 1925-26 and 3-1 on Blues' soil in January 1927.

In between times Blues did collect a few wins themselves, one of the best coming at St Andrew's in August 1927 to the tune of 3-1 when Joe Bradford scored twice.

Bradford also found the net twice when Huddersfield were defeated 4-1 on Blues territory in September 1929 and he netted once in another 2-0 home win for Blues in December 1930.

Blues raced to a 5-0 home victory in November 1931 (Bradford again on target) but Town gained revenge in December 1934 by whipping Blues 4-0 at St Andrew's.

Blues then registered successive home wins of 4-1 and 4-2 in the space of ten months (December 1935 and October 1936).

After the hostilities of World War Two Blues had to wait until November 1948 before meeting the Terriers again - and this time they won 1-0 at St Andrew's thanks to an own-goal by Hepplewhite.

Jack Wheeler, the former Blues 'keeper, starred in the Huddersfield team that won promotion to the First Division in 1952-53 but he was not in the side which crashed to a 5-0 defeat at St Andrew's in November 1955 when Eddie Brown scored twice.

Graham Leggatt was the star performer when Blues met Huddersfield at St Andrew's in December 1967. The Scottish international winger made three goals and scored one himself in a superb 6-1 victory.

Nine months later, when Huddersfield were defeated 5-1 in a Second Division match at St Andrew's on 7 September 1968, Blues' striker Geoff Vowden, who replaced skipper Ron Wylie for the second half, became the first substitute to score a hat-trick. All three of his goals were set-up by Johnny Vincent and came in the 71st, 74th and 89th minutes. Future Blues' star Frank Worthington netted Town's goal in this game.

There was no League action between the clubs during the 1970s (Blues replaced Huddersfield in the top flight in 1972) and it was not until September 1984 that the Terriers returned to St Andrew's, losing to a Robert Hopkins goal in front of almost 11,500 spectators.

In 1989-90 the teams met in the Third Division for the first time, Blues winning 2-1 at Huddersfield after losing 1-0 at St Andrew's!

Blues clinched their first League title (Division 2) for 40 years when they won 2-1 at the Alfred McAlpine Stadium against Huddersfield Town in May 1995. Steve Claridge and Paul Tait scored the goals that day in front of a record crowd of 18,775.

Bryan Hughes scored Blues' first competitive goal in the 21st century - the winner at home to Huddersfield in League Division One on 3 January 2000.

Huddersfield knocked Blues out of the FA Cup in 1970-71, winning a third round replay 2-0 at St Andrew's after the teams had played out a 1-1 draw at Leeds Road.

Players with both clubs include: E Barkas, P Barnes, JM Beattie, K Brown, N Brunskill, S Charlton, D Clarke, M Cooper, K

115

Dearden, P Doherty (Blues guest), AR Elliott, N Freeman, E Harvey (Town amateur), WH Harvey, M Hellawell, C Holland, B Horne, E Islip, D Jennings, A Johnson, FR Jones (trialist), J McDonough, D Mangnall, C Marsden, S Morris, P Moulden, M O'Grady, PJ Robinson, PM Starbuck, P Summerill, DP Weston, WJ Wheeler, P Withe, F Worthington

Also: Steve Bruce (Blues player, Town manager), Leslie Knighton (assistant-secretary/manager of Huddersfield, manager of Blues), Ted Goodier (Huddersfield player, Blues manager) Lou Macari (Blues manager, Town scout).

● Prior to the Blues-Huddersfield League game at St Andrew's on 13 April 1912, a minute's silence was held in respect of those who died when the Titanic sunk on its maiden voyage. Among those who lost their lives was a family of four from Yardley Wood, all ardent Birmingham supporters.

HUGHES, Billy

Billy Hughes was a ball-winning full-back, quick in recovery with a very useful long kick which enabled him to clear his lines safely. A Welshman, born in Carmarthen on 6 March 1918, he attended School in Llanelli and Swansea and played for Carmarthen, Archer Corinthians, Llanelli, Watcher's Celtic and Llanelli Town (1934) before having a loan spell with Swansea Town in March 1935. Two months later, after being spotted by an eagle-eyed Blues scout he was taken on the pay-roll at St Andrew's where he was to stay for the next twelve years. He went on to make 110 first team appearances plus a further 55 during the War, partnering initially Ned Barkas, then Cyril Trigg and later Don Dearson and Dennis Jennings (among others) in front of goalkeepers Harry Hibbs and Gil Merrick. Hughes made his senior debut as an 18 year-old and with Trigg (the same age) as his partner they were the youngest pair of full-backs in the Football League when they played against Aston Villa in the First Division on 28 March 1936. Hughes won 10 full and 14 Wartime/Victory international caps for Wales and in 1947 represented Great Britain against the Rest of Europe at Hampden Park - clearly indicating that he was by far the best left-back around in those days!

Hughes left St Andrew's for Luton Town in July 1947 and eight months later joined Chelsea for £12,000, eventually winding down his career with spells at Hereford United (from August 1951) and Flint Town (January 1954-May 1955 - helping them win the Welsh Cup at the end of his first season). Hughes later scouted for Chester and died in Birmingham on 16 June 1981.

HULL CITY

Blues' playing record against the Tigers:

FOOTBALL LEAGUE

Venue	P	W	D	L	F	A
Home	25	13	9	3	55	31
Away	25	8	6	11	21	38
Totals	50	21	15	14	76	69

FA CUP

Away	1	1	0	0	2	0

WARTIME

Home	3	3	0	0	11	4
Away	3	3	0	0	6	1
Totals	6	6	0	0	17	5

Blues and Hull first met in the Football League in November 1908 at St Andrew's. The visitors won 2-1 in front of 5,000 fans.

Just over a year later, on 4 December 1909, Blues were hammered 7-0 by Hull in a Second Division match at Anlaby Road - their heaviest defeat against the Tigers. Arthur Temple scored a hat-trick, two of his goals coming courtesy of defensive blunders!

Percy Barton, Johnny Crosbie (2) and Joe Lane (2) were on target when Blues beat Hull 5-1 at St Andrew's to gain their best League win of their Second Division championship-winning campaign in 1920-21.

Blues and Hull did not play against each other in League competition for almost 30 years - until the teams met in a Second Division match at Hull in November 1950. The Tigers won 3-2 that day, Cyril Trigg scoring both Blues goals. Blues gained revenge with a 2-1 home win four months later.

A seven-goal thriller in the fog at St Andrew's in November 1952 went in favour of Blues by 4-3. Leading 3-0 five minutes into the second-half Blues were pegged back by the Tigers before grabbing the 83rd minute winner through young winger Geoff Cox who was deputising for the injured Alex Govan.

Blues completed the League double over Hull at Easter 1967, winning 2-1 at home and 2-0 away, Bert Murray netting both goals at Boothferry Park.

Malcolm Beard (with a penalty) was among six different scorers as Blues slammed Hull 6-2 at home in September 1967 and just over a year later Phil Summerill scored a hat-trick in Blues' 5-2 home win over the Tigers.

As the Blues coach was making its way to Boothferry Park for the League game with Hull in March 1995 it was attacked by an unruly mob. The windows were smashed with bricks and a 'for sale' sign was used to batter the bus. The game ended goalless.

Players with both clubs include: J Acquaroff (Blues guest), G Ablett, W Bradbury, K Dearden, R Knight, L Jenkinson, BR Mills, J Needham, JG Roberts, A Saville, J Wealands.

Also: Bob Brocklebank (manager of both clubs), Major Frank Buckley (Blues player, Hull manager), Syd Owen (Blues player, Hull coach), Alf Wood (Tigers striker, Blues lottery salesman).

HYND, Roger

Centre-half Roger Hynd looked more like a heavy-weight boxer than he did professional footballer - but he was certainly a solid performer and never shirked a tackle, always giving full commitment each and every time he took the field. A Scotsman, born in Falkirk on 2 February 1942, and nephew of Bill Shankly, Hynd joined Glasgow Rangers on leaving Lanark Grammar School in 1961. He spent eight years at Ibrox Park, gaining a European Cup Winners Cup medal in 1967, before transferring to Crystal Palace for £12,000 in July 1969. From Selhurst Park he moved to St. Andrew's for a club record fee of £50,000 in July 1970. He scored five goals in 205 appearances for Blues over the next five seasons, helping them win promotion from the Second Division in 1972 when he partnered first Dave

Roger Hynd

Robinson and then Stan Harland at the heart of the defence.

After a loan spell with Oxford United (October 1975) he left St Andrew's for neighbouring Walsall whom he served from December 1975 to the summer of 1978, making a further 106 appearances for the Saddlers. He later managed Motherwell and after quitting football became a PE teacher in Wishaw (Scotland). Hynd is probably the only Blues footballer ever to play a trombone!

INJURIES

Colin Gordon

Fred Speller, the Blues left-back, fractured his right leg in a League game against Darwen in October 1892. The injury effectively ended his career, forcing him to retire in 1894 at the age of 29.

After suffering a horrific leg injury Billy Pratt was forced to retire in 1902, aged 28.

Blues goalkeeper Johnny Schofield suffered a fractured skull during a League game against Manchester United in November 1960 when he collided with the Reds' centre-forward Alex Dawson. He had a metal plate inserted in his head after this incident. Schofield also survived a pit explosion at the Baddesley Ensor colliery in 1957.

Striker Keith Bertschin broke the same leg twice during his career with Blues.

Fred Slater broke his leg ten minutes into his League debut for Blues against Huddersfield Town in November 1948.

Defender Paul Hart fractured his leg when making his debut for Blues on New Year's day 1987 at Plymouth - colliding with his team-mate Tommy Williams!

Ted Duckhouse broke his leg in the 1946 FA Cup semi-final replay against Derby County at Maine Road - trying to stop Peter Doherty from scoring the Rams' second goal in extra-time.

Winger Brian Taylor broke his leg playing for Blues against Union St Gilloise in the semi-final of the Fairs Cup in November 1959 and as a result missed the Final against Barcelona. Agonisingly he was injured again the following year and missed the 1961 Final with AS Roma.

Lee Jenkins broke an ankle when making his Blues debut against West Bromwich Albion in 1985 - and never had another game for the club.

Billy Garton (on loan to Blues in 1986) was forced to retire at the age of 25 through injury in 1990.

Goalkeeper Andy Gosney was badly injured following a two-footed lunge by Wolves' striker Steve Bull during a game at St Andrew's in September 1992 and was out of action for three months.

In September 1989, Blues inside-forward Colin Gordon was accidentally bitten on the arm by a Swansea City player. He missed the next match against Shrewsbury.

On leaving Blues in February 1986 defender Ken Armstrong broke his ankle in his first training session with Walsall and never played again.

Jon McCarthy broke the same leg twice in the same season. The first mishap came against Tranmere Rovers in November 1999 and the second in the crucial promotion/play-off encounter against Manchester City at Maine Road in April 2000.

Goalkeeper Ike Webb (a Blues player from 1898 to 1901) fractured his skull halfway through his professional career. He carried on playing for several months before the injury was diagnosed!

The long-legged Tom Grosvenor seemed to be injury-prone around Christmastime! In a reserve team game in 1929 he severely damaged a cartilage and was out of action for three months. In December 1931 he badly dislocated his elbow in a match against West Ham United (sidelined for two weeks) and on 23 December 1933 he broke his leg in a 0-0 draw at Huddersfield and didn't return to action until October 1934.

Gary Breen was mugged in London over Christmas 1996 and missed several matches following that incident and injuries received.

In October 1999 there were eleven members of Blues' first team squad receiving treatment - they were: Gary Ablett (knee), Simon Charlton (groin strain), Paul Furlong (knee), Martin Grainger (broken leg), Andrew Johnson (knee), Michael Johnson (back, knee), Stan Lazaridis (hamstring), Simon Marsh (back), Peter Ndlovu (ankle), Steve Robinson (knee) and Darren Wassall (heel).

INTER CITIES FAIRS CUP

Blues took part in the Inter Cities Fairs Cup competition on four separate occasions between 1958 and 1962. Their full record was:

Seasons 1956-58
Group 'B'
v Inter Milan (a) 0-0 (h) 2-1
v Zagreb Select (a) 1-0 (h) 3-0
Semi-final
v Barcelona (h) 4-3 (a) 0-1 (n) 1-2
Seasons 1958-60
Round 1
v Cologne Select (a) 2-2 (h) 2-0

Olympic stadium in Rome.

Round 2
v Dinamo Zagreb (h) 1-0 (a) 3-3
Semi-final
v Union St Gilloise (a) 4-2 (h) 4-2
Final
v Barcelona (h) 0-0 (a) 1-4
Season 1960-61
Round 1
v Ujpesti Dozsa (h) 3-2 (a) 2-1
Round 2
v Boldklub Copenhagen (a) 4-4 (h) 5-0
Semi-final
v Inter Milan (a) 2-1 (h) 2-1

Final
v Roma (h) 2-2 (a) 0-2
Season 1961-62
Round 1
v RCD Espanol (a) 2-5 (h) 1-0
SUMMARY OF RESULTS:

Venue	P	W	D	L	F	A
Home	12	10	2	0	29	11
Away	12	4	4	4	21	25
Neutral	1	0	0	1	1	2
Totals	25	14	6	5	51	38

Blues were unbeaten in their 12 home games.
Of the 51 goals scored Johnny Gordon netted seven, Jimmy

Waiting for a call (ready to come off the bench) in Spain.

Blues' boss Gil Merrick (centre) helps quieten things down in Rome!

Harris and Harry Hooper five apiece and Bunny Larkin and Bryan Orritt four each.

The goals were divided among 19 players, including the Inter Milan defender Balleri!

Trevor Smith appeared in most European games for Blues - 18. Brian Farmer and Johnny Watts each played in 17 matches.

The biggest crowd was that of 75,000 for the second leg of the Final against Barcelona in the Nou Camp Stadium in May 1960.

An audience of 60,000 witnessed the second leg of Blues' semi-final clash with the Spanish side in November 1957 and a similar crowd saw the RCD Espanol-Blues clash in November 1961.

The biggest attendance at St Andrew's was that of 40,524 for the first leg of the Blues v Barcelona Final in March 1960.

Surprisingly Blues had a total of four players sent-off during their Inter Cities Fairs Cup exploits - Trevor Smith, Johnny Gordon, Jimmy Harris and Bertie Auld (see Sendings-off).

INTERNATIONAL BLUES

List of players who won international honours for their respective country whilst associated with the Blues:

FULL INTERNATIONAL
AUSTRALIA
S Lazaridis (5)
England
G Astall (2), PH Barton (7), J Bradford (12), CC Charsley (1),WS Corbett (3), TJ Francis (12), AT Grosvenor (3), JJ Hall (17), MS Hellawell (2), HEHibbs (25), GH Merrick (23),T Smith (2), L Stoker (3), DR Tremelling (1).
Canada
L Hooper (5), PP Peschisolido (7)
Cayman Islands
M O'Connor (2)
Jamaica
M Johnson (7)
Nigeria
D Adebola (1)
Northern Ireland
RA Brennan (3), J Brown (3), RO Ferris (3), J McCarthy (5)
Republic of Ireland
E Barber (1), G Breen (6), TR Carroll (9), GA Daly (5), DJ Givens

(14), J Higgins (1), DF Langan (10).
Scotland
JA Crosbie (1), K Burns (8), A Gemmill (10), J Herriot (8), F McGurk (1).
Wales
ER Curtis (2), DJ Dearson (3), G Edwards (6), SVL Evans (1), CR Green (15), WT Hennessey (16), WM Hughes (10), CAL Jenkyns (4), CW Jones (2), FW Jones (1), N Kinsey (3), K Leek (5), A Legg (2), S Morris (5), ME Page (28), A Powell (1), AA Rees (1), D Richards (6), JG Roberts (15), G Sprake (5), WB Stevenson (4)
Zimbabwe
P Ndlovu (5)

UNDER 21
England
KE Bertschin (3), LC Curbishley (1), ME Dennis (3), KP Dillon (1), H Gayle (3), DA Seaman (10).
Wales
AA Rees (1)

UNDER 23
England
TJ Francis (5), J Greenhoff (4), RD Latchford (2), RM Neal (1), T Smith (15).
Scotland
K Burns (2), JR Calderwood (1)
Wales
JG Emmanuel (1), CR Green (4), WT Hennessey (6), B Orritt (3), ME Page (6)
England 'B'
L Boyd (1), JA Gallagher (1), K Green (2), JJ Hall (1), T Smith (2).
Great Britain
(v Rest of Europe)
WM Hughes (1)
United Kingdom (Olympic Games 1908)
WS Corbett (3)
Young England (v England)
JJ Hall (1), RM Neal (1), T Smith (4)

Gil Merrick
(England)

FOOTBALL LEAGUE

G Astall (1), J Bradford (5), J Glover (2), K Green (2), AT Grosvenor (1), F Harris (1), JJ Hall (3), HE Hibbs (3), H Hooper (1), JW Jones (1), WH Jones (1), A McClure (1), GH Merrick (11), WA Morgan (1), AC Robinson (2), T Smith (2), L Stoker (1), CH Tickle (1), DR Tremelling (2), SE. Wharton (1), GF Wheldon (2), W Wigmore (1), F Womack (1).

FOOTBALL LEAGUE XI

TJ Francis (1), GF Wheldon (1), F Womack (1)

ENGLAND YOUTH

M Beard, RP Bird, ME Dennis, KP Dillon, N Duce, AM Elliott, TJ Francis, AS Gibson, IR Handysides, PN Hawker, A Johnson, DW.L Jones, RD Latchford, S Parker, PJT Passey, SE Phillips, GS Potter, MJ Rathbone, J Roach, SJ Smith, PE Summerill, D Thwaites, JV Vincent, J Williams, N Winterburn.

FA YOUTH XI

R Martin (1)

NEW ZEALAND YOUTH

J Haarhoff

NORTHERN IRELAND YOUTH

F McKeown

FA XI

GH Merrick (1)

FOOTBALL LEAGUE XI

TJ Francis (1)

FA TOURS

JJ Hall 1955, WN Harris 1926, HE Hibbs 1931, W Smith 1951, KC Tewkesbury 1931, F Womack 1925.

FA OF IRELAND TOUR

R Ferris 1953 (to Canada).

WARTIME & VICTORY INTERNATIONALS
(1919-20 & 1939-46)
England
W Ball (1)
Scotland
DJ Dearson (15), G Edwards (2), WM Hughes (14)

UNOFFICIAL INTERNATIONALS
All Ireland
TR Carroll (1)
England
HE Hibbs (1), A Leake (1), FR Mitchell (1), WA Morgan (1), WH Smith (1), SE Wharton (1).
Scotland
C Dougall (1)

AMATEUR INTERNATIONALS
England
HP Bailey (4), WS Corbett (18), WH Harvey (3), S Hauser (2), J Slater (2), KC Tewkesbury (4)

INTERNATIONAL TRIALS
England (v The Rest)
PH Barton (1), J Bradford (1), AT Grosvenor (1). HE Hibbs (2)
The Rest (v England)
PH Barton (2), J Bradford (1), HE Hibb (1), L Stoker (2)
The North (v The South)
PH Barton (1), J Bradford (1), JW Jones (1), WH Jones (1), A Leake (1), AC Robinson (1), F Stokes (1), FJ Wilcox (1).
The South (v England)
PH Barton (2), F Womack (1)
The South (v The North)
F Womack (1)
Anglo Scots (v Home Scots)
JA Crosbie (3)
Professionals (v Amateurs)
J Bradford (1), WA Harris (1), AC Robinson (1), F Stokes (1), F Womack (1).
Possibles (v Probables)
L Stoker (1)
England Amateurs (North v South)
WS Corbett (3), T Pointon (1)

STAFFORDSHIRE COUNTY FA
GR Briggs, RA Dale, WH Edmunds, W Edden, A James,

Gerry Daly
(Republic of Ireland)

D Kayes, J Lee, JH Sparrow.
BIRMINGHAM ASSOCIATION
W Edden, W Edmunds, A James.
PLAYERS' UNION XI (V ENGLAND)
W Wigmore (1)

The following players all won FULL international honours with other clubs, either before or after joining Blues:
Argentina
A Tarantini
Australia
S Lazaridis
Canada
P Fenwick (Olympic Games), L Hooper, PP Peschisolido
Cayman Islands
I Rankine
England
WA Abbott, WC Athersmith, HP Bailey, RJ Barlow, JJ Berry, BJ Bridges, FC Buckley, G Charles, CC Charsley, J Conlin, A Cottee, TJ Francis, W George, H Hampton, MG Harford, D Hodgetts, RD Latchford, A Leake, LV Lodge, AW Morley, SW Owen, M O'Grady, FB Pentland, F Pickering, WV Rose, DA Seaman, J Smith, RA Thomson, C Todd, MA Towers, D Wallace, GF Wheldon, JE Windridge, N Winterburn, P Withe, FS Worthington.
Holland
BA. Brocken, AWMT Van Mierlo
Liberia
C Wreh
Nigeria
F Okenla
Northern Ireland
G Breen, RA Brennan, J Brown, O Madden, J McCarthy, JC McLaughlin, D Sonner.
Norway
T Myhre

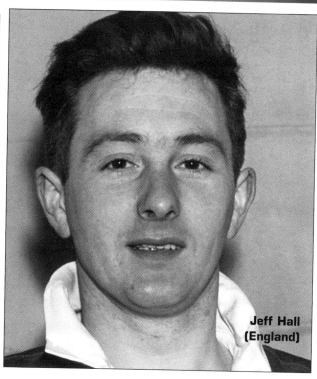
Jeff Hall (England)

Portugal
J Dominguez
Republic of Ireland
E Barber, J Brown, TR Carroll, GA Daly, S Finnan, DJ Givens, DF Langan, JM McDonagh, O Madden, J Sheridan.
Scotland
R Auld, JN Blyth, DG Bremner, D Bruce, K Burns, J Connolly, JA Crosbie, A Gemmill, RA Hope, A Johnson, WM Johnston, G Leggatt, BD Rioch, WR Robb, J Robertson, J Sheridan, DR Speedie.
Sweden
A Limpar
Wales
J Bowen, J Cornforth, E Curtis, S Davies, G Edwards, L Evans, RE Evans, D Giles, J Hallam, T Hennessey, T Hockey, B Horne, CAL Jenkyns, A Legg, N Kinsey, K Leek, C Phillips, A Powell, DA Richards, JG Roberts, G Sprake, B Stevenson, MR Thomas, P Van Den Hauwe.
Zimbabwe
P Ndlovu.

● These are other footballing personnel (not listed elsewhere in the international section) who have been associated with Blues in various capacities and gained full international recognition as players with other clubs:
Blues' managers Pat Beasley, Terry Cooper, Stan Cullis, Harry Storer and Sir Alf Ramsey (England) and Willie Bell, Dave Mackay and Lou Macari (Scotland). And coaches: Peter Bonetti, Tony Brown, Dave Fairhurst, Mick Mills, Nigel Spink, Chris Woods (all England) and Emilio Aldecoa Gomez (Spain).
Former Blues goalkeeper Mike Kelly was on the England coaching staff (1998-2000).

INTERNATIONAL SNIPPETS
● The first Blues player to be capped by his country was Caesar Jenkyns for Wales against Ireland at Bangor on 27 February 1892.

Harry Hampton (England)

Harry Hibbs
(England)

Jon McCarthy
(Northern Ireland)

- Goalkeeper Chris Charsley was the first Blues player to win an England cap v Ireland on 25 February 1893 at Perry Barr (Aston Villa).
- Johnny Crosbie was the first Scotsman to be capped whilst with Blues - versus England in 1921-22; the first player from Northern Ireland was winger Jackie Brown v Scotland in 1938-39 and the first from the Republic of Ireland to win a senior cap was Jimmy Higgins against Argentina in 1950-51.
- Blues' first under-23 international was Trevor Smith, capped for England v Italy in 1954-55 and the club's first under-21 international was striker Keith Bertschin who lined up for England versus Scotland in 1976-77.
- Blues' first England 'B' international player was skipper Len Boyd, who starred in a friendly against Holland in 1951-52.
- Malcolm Page has been Blues' most capped player, appearing in

28 full internationals for Wales during his time at St Andrew's.
- Harry Hibbs (with 25 appearances to his name) is Blues' most capped England international.
- Billy Smith scored 13 goals in five matches while on tour with the FA party in Australia in 1951.
- Don Dearson played in eight different positions for Wales and Stan Davies in six (including goalkeeper). Dearson also missed a penalty in a wartime game against England at St Andrew's in 1941.
- Fred Wheldon (when a Villa player) was on the winning side in each of his four international outings for England.
- During their careers Owen Madden and Jackie Brown won caps for both Northern Ireland and the Republic of Ireland!
- Blues' outside-right Wallace Norman Harris made 12 appearances for the FA XI on their North American tour in 1926, scoring six goals.
- Harry Hibbs made 10 appearances for the FA (England) side on tour to North America in 1931. He was accompanied over there by fellow goalkeeper Ken Tewksbury (then at Birmingham University and an amateur with Blues) who played in seven games.

INTERNAZIONALE (INTER MILAN)

On a sweltering April afternoon in 1961 Blues beat Inter Milan 2-1 in the San Siro Stadium in the semi-final first leg encounter of that season's Inter Cities Fairs Cup competition. It was no freak win for battling Blues who led 2-0 at half-time thanks to goals from Jimmy Harris and the Inter left-half Balleri who sliced the ball into his own net

The return leg at St Andrew's also ended in a 2-1 win for Blues, Harris and Bertie Auld the scorers this time.

BLUES' RECORD:

Venue	P	W	D	L	F	A
Home	1	1	0	0	2	1
Away	1	1	0	0	2	1
Totals	2	2	0	0	4	2

Trevor Smith
(England)

BIRMINGHAM CITY

Colin WITHERS

Brian FARMER 2   George ALLEN 3

Terry HENNESSEY 4   Trevor SMITH 5   Dick NEAL 6

Mike HELLAWELL 7   Jimmy HARRIS 9   Bryan ORRITT 11

Jimmy BLOOMFIELD 8   Jimmy SINGER 10

Referee: Mr. RAYMOND LESPINEUX (Belgium)

Linesmen: Mr. HUBERT BURGUET (Belgium) (Red Flag)
Mr. JOSEPH HANNET (Belgium) (Yellow Flag)

Mario CORSO 10   Bengt LINDSKOG 8

Egidio MORBELLO 11   Eddie FIRMANI 9   Mauro BICICLI 7

Costanzo BALLERI 6   Aristide GUARNERI 5   Bruno BOLCHI 4

Mauro GATTI 3   Armando PICCHI 2

Lorenzo BUFFON

INTER-MILAN

IPSWICH TOWN

Blues' playing record against Ipswich Town:

FOOTBALL LEAGUE

Venue	P	W	D	L	F	A
Home	27	11	9	7	35	26
Away	27	7	1	19	30	59
Totals	54	18	10	26	65	85

FA CUP

	P	W	D	L	F	A
Home	3	2	0	1	4	3
Away	1	0	0	1	0	1
Totals	4	2	0	2	4	4

LEAGUE CUP

	P	W	D	L	F	A
Home	2	2	0	0	4	2
Away	2	1	0	1	4	3
Totals	4	3	0	1	8	5

After beating League champions elect Wolves at Molineux in the 3rd round of the 1953-54 FA Cup competition, Blues went out at the next hurdle, beaten 1-0 at Portman Road by Third Division (S) side Ipswich.

The following season Blues and Ipswich met for the first time in the Football League. And all four Second Division points went to Blues who won 4-0 at home with goals by Noel Kinsey (2), Peter Warmington (on his debut) and Gordon Astall, and 2-1 away when Warmington again netted a beauty!

The first League clash in the top flight was staged at Portman Road in September 1961, Ipswich winning handsomely by 4-1. Blues gained revenge, though, by beating the Suffolk Punchers 3-1 at St Andrew's in January when Ken Leek netted twice in front of almost 27,000 fans.

A terrific performance by Blues in November 1962 saw them beat Ipswich, the reigning League champions, 5-1 at Portman Road. Leek (2) and Jimmy Harris (2) led the goal-rush.

Ronnie Fenton scored twice when Blues beat Ipswich 4-1 at St Andrew's in May 1966 but it was a different story seven years later (September 1973) when Ipswich won 3-0 on the same ground at a time when Blues were struggling to win a game....this was their ninth League match without a victory!

Paul Cooper

Nine goals were scored in the two games between the clubs in 1975-76. Ipswich won 4-2 at Portman Road while Blues took the honours with a 3-0 victory at St Andrew's, Trevor Francis almost bursting the net with his penalty!

Ipswich doubled up over Blues in 1976-77 and then raced to a 5-2 win at home in October 1977 and a 3-0 victory on the same ground in April 1979.

UEFA Cup champions elect Ipswich slammed Blues 5-1 at Portman Road in January 1981, having won 3-1 at St Andrew's three weeks earlier.

And it was Ipswich 4 Blues 0 in April 1989

Four players - Andy Edwards, Richard Forsyth, Ian Muir and Jason Bowen - made their debuts for Blues in a 3-1 home win over Ipswich in August 1995. Bowen figured on the scoresheet to mark the occasion.

Blues and Ipswich battled it out for a First Division play-off spot in successive seasons: 1998-99 and 1999-2000.

Players with both clubs include: I Atkins, F Barber, K Bertschin, J Brown, TR Carroll, P Cooper, L Donowa, T Fillingham, D Geddis, N Gleghorn, WS Havenga, J Hick (Blues reserve), A Legg, JR Linford, S McGavin, A Mulraney, D Sonner, JH Southam (Town guest), S Whitton.

Also: Sir Alf Ramsey (manager of both clubs), Mick Mills (Ipswich player, Blues assistant-manager), Derek Jefferson (Ipswich player, Blues trainer-coach).

Carroll was the first loan player to appear in a Football League or major Cup-tie for Blues, doing so in October 1971 (v Burnley, away).

THE ENCYCLOPAEDIA OF BIRMINGHAM CITY

IRISH CONNECTION

Jim McDonough

Personnel who have served with Blues and have also played, managed, and/or coached in Northern Ireland and the Republic of Ireland:

Eric Barber . . . . .Shamrock Rovers, Shelbourne
Dougie Bell . . . . .Portadown
Walter Bennett . . . . .Ballymena
Ritchie Blackmore . . . . .Dundalk, Galway United
Bobby Brennan . . . . .Distillery
Barry Bridges . . . . .St Patrick's (player-manager),
Sligo Rovers (manager)
Tommy Briggs . . . . .Glentoran (player-manager)
Jackie Brown . . . . .Belfast Celtic
Tommy Carroll . . . . .Shelbourne
John Cheesewright . . . . .Cobh Ramblers
Gerry Daly. . . . . .Bohemians
P Doherty* . . . . .Glentoran
Ray Ferris . . . . .Distillery, Glentoran, Newry Town
David Foy . . . . .Cobh Ramblers
Sean Francis . . . . .Cobh Ramblers
Bill Gildea . . . . .Belfast Celtic
Don Givens . . . . .Dublin Rangers
Brian Gray . . . . .Shelbourne
Bob Gregg . . . . .Sligo Rovers
Jim Hagan . . . . . . .Larne Town, Ballymena (player-manager),
Carrick Rangers, Larne (player-manager)
Jim Higgins . . . . .Dundalk
Trevor Hockey . . . . .Athlone Town
Eric Hogan . . . . .Cobh Ramblers, Shamrock Rovers,
College Corinthians
Billy Hume . . . . .Bangor City
Tommy Hunt . . . . .Drumcondra
Arthur Leonard . . . . .Glentoran
Steve Lynex . . . . . . .Shamrock Rovers, Sligo Rovers (trialist)

Jim McDonough . . . . .Galway United (player-manager)
Francis McKeown . . . . .Donegal Celtic
Owen Madden . . . . .Cork Athletic (player-manager),
Cork Hibs, Cork United, Sligo Rovers
Jock Mulraney .Sligo Rovers (trialist)
Tommy Neale. . . . . .Dundalk
Eddie O'Hara . . . . .Drumcondra, Dundalk, Sligo Rovers
Alan O'Neill . . . . .Cork City, Cobh Ramblers
Arthur Phoenix .Dublin Shelbourne
Billy Purves . . . . .Glentoran (player-trainer)
Martin Russell . . . . .Portadown
Mark Rutherford . . . . .Shelbourne
Tony Taylor . . . . .Athlone Town
Dean Williams . . . . .Cobh Ramblers
Frank Worthington . . . . .Galway United
* Blues Wartime guest

ISLIP, Ernie

Ernie Islip was a hard-shooting, dangerous inside or centre-forward who scored 52 goals in 172 appearances for Huddersfield Town before joining Blues for £1,500 in November 1923. A Yorkshireman, born in Packwood Springs, Sheffield on 31 October 1892, he played initially for Sheffield Douglas FC before becoming a professional at Leeds Road in June 1911. In 1919-20 he gained runners-up medals in both the FA Cup and Division Two but collected an FA Cup winners medal in 1922 when Huddersfield beat Preston North End. He was left out in the cold at St Andrew's following the emergence of George Briggs and in May 1927 he moved to Bradford City for £400. He only spent a season at Valley Parade before entering non-League soccer with Kidderminster Harriers. He later assisted Ashton National FC and then came back into the League with Wrexham in November 1928, retiring four months later. During the First World War Islip guested for Rotherham County, Sheffield Wednesday and West Ham United. He had the chance to join the Hammers and if he had agreed then he might well have appeared in the first Wembley Cup Final of 1923. He died in Huddersfield in August 1941.

JACKSON, Alec

Alec Jackson was an eager-beaver right-winger or inside-forward who gave West Bromwich Albion excellent service for ten years before joining Blues. A local lad who made good, 'Jacko' was born in Tipton, deep in the heart of the Black Country on 29 May 1937, and in a decade at The Hawthorns (May 1954 to June 1964) he scored over 50 goals in more than 200 first team appearances. A skilful ball player, he moved to The Hawthorns from W.G. Allen's FC and in 1962 represented the Football League v the Scottish League at Villa Park. He left Albion for St. Andrew's in a £12,500 deal and had 85 outings for Blues (12 goals scored) before assisting Walsall from February 1967 to August 1968. During his time with Blues he played either on the right-wing or inside and had a variety of partners including Mike Hellawell and Trevor Hockey.

After leaving the Saddlers Jackson served with a number of non-League clubs including Nuneaton Borough, Kidderminster Harriers, Warley, Oldbury Town, Warley Borough, Darlaston, Blakenhall and Rushall Olympic, finally hanging up his boots in 1990 after playing in some 150 Charity games for the Albion Old Stars. He currently lives and works in Tipton.

JENKYNS, Caesar Augustus Llewel

Caesar Jankyns

A big, burly footballer, Caesar Jenkyns was Birmingham's first-ever full international, capped for Wales against Ireland at Bangor in February 1892 (shortly before goalkeeper Chris Charsley made his debut for England).

A player with no little skill and a master of the shoulder charge - and more - he was reputed to have been fearsome on the field and often sent his opponent flying across the turf with one of his mighty chalwith one of his mighty challenges. He could head a ball - with power - up to a distance of 50 yards and once won a competition by kicking a dead ball 100 yards down field first bounce! Jenkyns, with his bone-shaking and muscle-bending challenges, was a great inspiration to the team. He skippered every club he served (and his country Wales) but was often in trouble with referees and occasionally with spectators! In March 1895 Blues decided to dispense with his services and suspended him for six weeks (until the end of that season) for brawling with a Derby player and also for attempting to assault two spectators. A few months later, having transferred to Woolwich Arsenal, Jenkyns refused to leave the field after being sent-off for foul play. He went eventually, drawing this comment from an Arsenal official: 'Jenkyns is a heavyweight and it is possible that gives him a character as a foul player he does not deserve.' In 1903 he was banned for taking part in an amateur match for Saltley whilst still holding professional status (with Coventry City). The ban was lifted two years later when he joined Walsall - but his career was nearing an end by then. Born in Builth on 24 August 1866, Jenkyns played his early football with Southfield, and then St Andrew's Sunday School team (of Small Heath). He then had a spell with Walsall Swifts and was on Blues' books in 1884 before serving with Unity Gas FC. In July 1888 he was taken on as a professional by Blues and remained with the club until May 1895. He scored 13 goals in 105 first team games for Blues, helping them finish third in the Football Alliance, take the Second Division League championship in 1893 and then gain promotion to the First Division as runners-up in 1894. From Arsenal he went to Newton Heath and then Walsall (November 1897), joining Coventry City as a player-coach in 1902. He had a second spell

with Unity Gas and also assisted Saltney Wednesday before hanging up his boots in 1905 after another brief spell with Walsall. He became a publican in Moxley (taking over the George Inn) and before the Great War joined the police force. His son, Octavius, had unsuccessful trials with Blues during the period 1912-13 while his brother Plato also served in the City of Birmingham police force for a number of years. Caesar Jenkyns died in Birmingham on 23 July 1941, aged 74.

JENNINGS, Dennis

Dennis Jennings appeared in every position for Blues except centre-half...yes, he even took over in goal on a couple of occasions during the 1940s! and he's the oldest player to serve the club (see Age)

Known as 'Mr Versatility' he lined up in 376 games for Blues (212 in League and FA Cup and 164 in various regional competitions during the Second World War) and scored 17 goals. Born in Habberley Valley near Kidderminster on 20 July 1910,

Dennis Jennings

he played his early soccer as a winger with Franche FC, St Barnabos, Foley Park, Stourport Swifts and Romsley Village before joining West Bromwich Albion as an amateur in 1928. He failed to make the grade at The Hawthorns and after a spell with Kidderminster Harriers (from July 1929) he became a professional with Huddersfield Town in October 1930. He scored five goals in 33 outings for the Terriers before joining Grimsby Town in September 1932. He stayed at Blundell Park until January 1936, netting 29 times in 102 games for the Mariners. Blues moved in and secured his services for £1,200, Jennings taking over the right-wing berth from Frank White. Jennings who possessed a brilliant cycle-kick (sometimes utilising it instead of a clearing with an easier header) became a firm favourite with the St Andrew's faithful. He helped Blues win the Football League South title in 1946 and the Second Division crown two years later, having helped win the same Division with Grimsby in 1934. He eventually became a full-back with Blues and he finally left St Andrew's in March 1951 to become player-coach of his former club, Kidderminster Harriers, a position he held until March 1953. He guested for Nottingham Forest during the War and was associated with Blues for more than fifteen years. He retired to live near Wadebridge in Cornwall, running a caravan park with his brother. Jennings died in March 1996, aged 85.

JOHNSON, Michael

Defender Michael Johnston played in almost 140 senior games for Notts County before transferring to Blues for £300,000 in September 1995. He made his debut in a 5-0 home win over Barnsley later that month and has been a resilient performer ever since, passing the personal milestone of 300 League and Cup appearances as a professional in the year 2000 (his Blues record is 222 games, 12 goals scored). Born in Nottingham on 4 July 1973, he joined the apprentice staff at Meadow Road in 1989 (on leaving

Michael Johnson

School) and developed rapidly. At St Andrew's he had to contest a first team place with the likes of Gary Ablett, Gary Breen and Steve Bruce but he stuck in there and is now a permanent fixture in the side. Nicknamed 'Magic' (for obvious reasons) he plays mainly on the left side of the defence and scored his first-ever goal on 22 February 1998 in a 2-0 win over Sheffield United. A very consistent performer and a firm favourite with the supporters, Johnson was capped by Jamaica in the 1999-2000 season.

● Johnson received a death threat in February 2000 from the neo-Nazi group Combat 18. Said Johnson at the time "The tone of the letter is deadly serious...it advises me to leave the country or be killed." Thankfully, nothing materialised after the police had been informed.

JOHNSTON, Willie

With devastating pace and the ability to beat his full-back on the outside, left-winger Willie Johnston was, without doubt, a terrific footballer - but one with a fiery temper which got him into trouble with authority far too often! Born in Glasgow on 19 December 1946, Johnston was signed by West Bromwich Albion boss Don Howe for a record fee of £138,000 from Glasgow Rangers in December 1972 just after he had served a record 67-day suspension. During his professional career Johnston was sent-off 19 times for clubs and country and was banished from Scotland's 1978 World Cup squad in Argentina following an allegation that he had used a stimulant. Before his move to The Hawthorns Johnston, who won 22 full caps for Scotland and two at Under-23 level, helped Rangers win the Scottish League championship, both domestic Cup competitions and the European Cup Winners Cup, gaining a few runners-up prizes as well! In 1971, after coming on as substitute in a League Cup-tie, he netted a hat-trick (including two penalties - his other goal coming from a spot-kick follow-up) for Rangers against St Johnstone.

On leaving Albion in March 1979 with a healthy record behind him of 28 goals in 261 outings, he joined the NASL club Vancouver Whitecaps for £190,000 and after helping them win the Super Bowl, Johnston spent five months on loan at St Andrew's (from October 1979 to February 1980). He appeared in 15 League games (18 in all) during that period as Blues prepared themselves for the

Second Division championship that season. After returning to Canada, he had a second spell at Ibrox Park, rejoining Rangers for £40,000 in August 1980. Then he willingly served with the Whitecaps for a third time (September 1982) and he also played for Heart of Midlothian and South China (Hong Kong) before becoming head coach at Tynecastle Park in 1983. Thereafter Johnston accepted coaching positions with East Fife (1985), Raith Rovers (March-June 1986) and Falkirk (1987) and nowadays he runs a pub in Kirkcaldy, deep in Rangers' territory!

Willie Johnston

JONES, Alfred

Alfred 'Inky' Jones, a manufacturer of scales, based in Birmingham, was employed by Blues in 1885, brought in to balance the books! He was given the title secretary-manager, a position he held until 1908 when he handed over the reins to Alex Watson. Jones, born locally, was well into his thirties when Blues engaged him as their first 'manager' and he did a very good job, guiding the team into the 1886 FA Cup semi-finals at the end of his first season in charge. He was at the helm when Blues gained entry into the Football League in 1892 and under his supervision the Second Division championship was won at the first attempt (1893), followed soon afterwards by promotion to the top flight of English football (1894). Although the team went through a bit of a yo-yo sequence after that (down in 1896 and 1902 and up in 1901 and 1904) he battled on, signed some excellent players and generally did a fine job. When he was replaced in office by Watson in 1908, Jones acted as a part-time accountant for the club until the outbreak of the First World War. In all he served Blues for 30 years.

JONES, Charlie Wilson

Charlie Wilson Jones

Jones was a pale-faced, red-haired, frail-looking footballer but what a terrific marksman! He netted 69 goals in 150 League and FA Cup games and another 40 in 65 Wartime matches for Blues between September 1934 (signed for £1,000 from Wrexham) and September 1947 (when he joined Nottingham Forest). Born in Pentre Broughton near Wrexham on 29 April 1914, Jones played for Brymbo Green and had trials with Blackburn Rovers and Bolton Wanderers before becoming a professional with Wrexham in August 1932. In the late 1940s he moved into non-League circles with Redditch United and then Kidderminster Harriers, retiring in June 1950. He guested for Blackburn, Huddersfield, West Bromwich Albion and Wrexham during the War and in 1946 helped Blues win the Football League South championship. He was capped twice by Wales against Ireland in 1935 and France in 1939, scoring a goal in his first international on his old hunting ground at Wrexham! He later became a licensee in Birmingham and died in the City on 9 January 1986.

JONES, Jack

Left-back Jack 'Cracker' Jones, a former miner, was a tough character, a formidable defender, rough and ready and a terrific partner to Frank Womack. Born in Rotherham on 8 February 1891, he was educated at Alma Road School and played for Allerton Bywater Colliery, Industry FC, Bird-in-the Hand and Maltby Main Colliery before enlisting in the armed forces where he also played football. In November 1914 he joined Sunderland and after six years at Roker Park, when he also played regularly during the Great War, he moved to St Andrew's for £2,000 in May 1920. He became a great servant with Blues, amassing 237 appearances and scoring one goal - against Manchester United in April 1926 in a 2-1 win. He helped the team win the Second Division championship in 1921 and represented the Football League side on one occasion. Jones used to play in dentures until he had them smashed during a Spanish tour game against CD Europa in Barcelona in May 1923. He put his hands up to protect his face, but the power of the shot did some damage (smashing his dentures) and his actions led to the referee awarding a penalty! Jones left Blues in May 1927 for Nelson, later assisting Crewe Alexandra (from March 1928) and Scarborough before retiring in 1931. He died in Rotherham on 20 July 1948, aged 57.

JONES, W.H. 'Bullet' Billy

Billy Jones

Despite his size (5ft. 6ins) 'Bullet' Jones - also known as the 'Tipton Slasher' - was a tough-nut, rip-roaring, dashing, wholehearted centre-forward who enjoyed shooting at goal - from any distance, with either foot. He could use his head to good effect as well and during his Blues days scored 102 goals in 253 senior appearances.

Born in Tipton on 12 April 1880, he played for his local team, Princes End and then Smethwick Town and Halesowen before joining Blues in August 1901 - missed by West Bromwich Albion, the team he supported as a lad!

In June 1909 after eight excellent years at the club, he was surprisingly sold to Brighton & Hover Albion, Blues believing he was past his best. But less than three years later he returned to St Andrew's and scored 16 goals in 33 League games in 1912-13 to show he still had something to offer! In November 1913 he went back to Brighton and after the War was given the job of trainer at The Goldstone Ground, a position he held until 1939.

Jones helped Blues win promotion in 1903 and Brighton lift the Southern League title in 1910. He also played for the Football League XI and appeared in an international trial match for England. He died in 1957.

KELLY, Mike

Mike Kelly had 18 years in football as a goalkeeper before moving into coaching and management. Born in Northampton on 18 October 1942, he played initially for Islington Boys and Chelsea juniors before signing amateur forms for Wimbledon (1960). After helping the Dons win the FA Amateur Cup at Wembley in 1963 he switched to the professional arena with Queens Park Rangers in March 1966 and four years later arrived at St Andrew's when Blues boss Jim Smith paid £18,000 for his signature in August 1970. Kelly, a very competent 'keeper with a rather loud voice (defenders were always aware when he was around) went on to make 74 first team appearances for Blues over the next six years, helping them win promotion from Division Two in 1972. He had Dave Latchford, Paul Cooper and then Gary Sprake to contend with for the number one spot but he stuck in there and did well. But one thought early in his career that Kelly would become a coach - and that's what happened when, after a spell as player-coach in the NASL with Minnesota Kicks in 1976 he returned to England to become reserve team manager and coach at Plymouth Argyle. In May 1977 he took over as manager at Home Park but left in February 1978 to become assistant-boss/coach at Craven Cottage, a position he held until 1981. Further coaching appointments followed at Crystal Palace, Portsmouth and West Bromwich Albion where he also acted as assistant-manager (1982-84). Since then he has been coach at the FA School of Excellence at Lilleshall, England's goalkeeping coach as well as doing a similar job with a handful of major clubs including Liverpool (1991-92).

One interesting point about Kelly is that he had an unusual pre-match ritual whereby he would kick the foot of both uprights and jump and touch the crossbar before the game got underway.

KENDALL, Howard

Although his uncle Harry Taylor played for Newcastle United, it was Howard Kendall's father who inspired him to become a footballer. After winning county and district recognition Kendall was selected to play for England against Wales in a Schoolboy international in 1961. He did well and almost immediately was signed as an apprentice by Preston North End. He turned professional two years later and in 1964, after skippering England youngsters to victory in the Little World Cup, he became the youngest player at that time to appear in an FA Cup Final, aged 17 years, 345 days (v West Ham United)...the youngest since 1879. His game got better and better, and after more than 100 League outings for the Deepdale club he was transferred to Everton for £80,000 in March 1967. He soon gained the first of six under 23 caps for his country (v Wales) but that elusive full cap always eluded him, despite him being regarded as one of the finest attacking midfielders in the country during the 1969-72 period. In 1968 he collected a second runners-up medal when Everton lost to West Brom in that year's FA Cup Final but in 1969-70 he was a key performer when the First Division championship came to Goodison Park, forming a terrific partnership in centre-field with Alan Ball and Colin Harvey. Kendall went on to score twenty nine goals in almost 270 senior games for the Merseysiders before moving to St Andrew's in March 1974 as part of a complicated £350,000 deal involving striker Bob Latchford. He had three-and-a-half excellent seasons with Blues, who entrusted him with the captaincy. His displays urged the players on and relegation was averted before he left the club to sign for Stoke City for £40,000 in August 1977. He spent two seasons as player-manager of Blackburn Rovers (July 1979 to May 1981) helping them win the Third Division title before returning to Goodison Park as a non-contract player-manager. He brought a great deal of success to Everton - two League championships in 1985 and 1987, FA Cup triumph in 1984 and runners-up spot a year later, European Cup Winners Cup glory in 1985 and a hat-trick of FA Charity Shield successes: 1984-85-86.

After that he tried his luck in Spain with Atletico Bilbao (June 1987 to November 1989) and had a brief spell in charge of Manchester City (December 1989 to November 1990) before surprisingly he went back to Everton for a third spell. This one lasted for three years and since then Kendall has managed FC Xanti, Notts County and Sheffield United (1995-97) as well as scouting for and coaching with a handful of other clubs.

During his League career as a player Kendall, who was born in Ryton-on-Tyne on 22 May 1946, starred in 613 games and scored 65 goals (his 600th came as player-manager of Blackburn Rovers in March 1981) - what more did he have to achieve to win a full cap?

Howard Kendall

KENNEDY, Andy

Scottish-born striker Andy Kennedy was a big favourite with the Blues supporters, helping the team win promotion in 1985. A hard-working forward he drew up a fine record during his time at St Andrew's, scoring 21 goals in 87 appearances between March 1985 and June 1988. Born in Stirling on 8 October 1964, he played initially for Sauchie Athletic and was recruited by Blues from Glasgow Rangers for £50,000. On leaving St Andrew's he joined Blackburn Rovers for an identical fee following a loan spell with Sheffield United. He had been on loan with FC Seiko (Japan) whilst at Ibrox Park. Later Kennedy played for Watford (from August 1990), had a loan spell with Bolton Wanderers (1991) and then assisted Brighton & Hove Albion and Gillingham, quitting League action in 1995.

KIDDERMINSTER HARRIERS

The GM Vauxhall Conference side from Aggborough caused a major shock by knocking Blues out of the FA Cup in the third round at St Andrew's in January 1994. A crowd of 19,668 saw Jon Purdie, ex-Wolves, score one of the Harriers' goals against a Blues side that had won only three of it's previous 12 League matches. Harriers' manager was Graham Allner, an ardent Blues' supporter!

Over 100 years earlier, on 12 April 1890, Blues had beaten Harriers 4-1 in a friendly at Muntz Street, Charlie Short scoring twice.

Harriers defeated Blues 5-0 in the Final of the Worcestershire Cup in 1932.

Players with both clubs include: D Barnett, J Bird, F Bowden, T Bowen (Blues reserve), C Brazier, R Craythorne (Blues reserve), J Dorrington, R Forsyth, G Getgood, W Guest, AW Hartwell, P Hawker, B Horne, D Isherwood, E Islip, A Jackson, D Jennings, C Kirby, JG Lane, F McKee, A Mulraney, E Pointer, S Robinson, BJ Taylor, M Yates.

- Horne was Harriers' boss Jan Molby's first signing (May 2000) after the Conference winners had gained entry into the Football League.

KINSEY, Noel

Welsh international inside-forward Noel Kinsey (seven caps gained) was described in one international programme as '...a grand little inside-right.' And so he was - a player who had a fine professional career that spanned over 20 years. Born in Treorchy, Glamorgan on Christmas Eve 1925, he played for his local team, Treorchy Amateurs before joining Cardiff City in March 1941. He stayed at Ninian Park for six years and then teamed up with Norwich City. He made over 243 appearances for the Canaries (65 goals) before transferring to Blues in June 1953. Three years later, having collected a Second Division championship medal in between times, he scored in the 1956 FA Cup Final defeat at the hands of Manchester City, thus becoming only the second Blues player to achieve that feat. He packed a fierce right-foot shot and often had a crack at goal from outside the area. Kinsey's record with Blues was impressive: 56 goals in 174 senior outings.

After leaving Blues he had a spell with Port Vale (February 1958-61) and then wound down his career with Kings Lynn and Lowestoft Town, the latter as player-coach: June 1962-64. He retired to live in Thorpe near Norwich.

Noel Kinsey

KNIGHTON, Albert Leslie

Manager Leslie Knighton guided Blues to their first-ever FA Cup Final in 1931. Born at Church Gresley near Burton-on-Trent in March 1884, his playing career was cut short by an ankle injury and in 1904 he broke into management with Castleford Town. Five years later he was appointed assistant-secretary manager of Huddersfield Town, moving in the same capacity to Manchester City in August 1912. He held that job for seven years and in May 1919 became manager of First Division Arsenal. He remained at Highbury for six seasons, but it is understood he never got on with the Gunners' chairman Sir Henry Norris who had instructed him to build a team that could win a trophy without spending too much money! Knighton did his best but the interfering Norris got on his back and eventually he was sacked. Knighton's next job was to manage Bournemouth for three seasons: July 1925-July 1928, before being engaged as Blues' manager for five years: July 1928-August 1933. He then bossed Chelsea right up to the outbreak of World War Two (the London club had made him an offer he couldn't refuse despite the Blues board requesting him to stay). After the hostilities had ceased he managed Birmingham League club Shrewsbury Town from August 1945 to December 1948 and in the 1950s he took over as secretary of a Bournemouth golf club, also managing Portishead FC briefly in 1952-53. He was given the nickname of football's 'lifeboatman'. Knighton died in May 1959

KUHL, Martin

Martin Kuhl

Midfielder Martin Kuhl's career began at St Andrew's in 1981 when he joined Blues as an apprentice. He turned professional on his 18th birthday in January 1983 and went on to score six goals in 132 senior appearances for the club before transferring to Sheffield United in March 1987, in a part-exchange deal involving Steve Wigley. An enthusiastic competitor, born in Frimley, Kuhl, who was a member of Blues' Second Division promotion-winning side in 1985, left Bramall Lane for Watford in February 1988 (a deal that involved Tony Agana). And after that he served, in turn, with Portsmouth, Derby County, Notts County and Bristol City. He made over 500 first-class appearances with his seven major clubs.

LADYPOOL ROAD

Blues' second ground was in Ladypool Road, Sparkbrook. They played here for just one season (1876-77) before moving to nearby Muntz Street.

The capacity of the ground was understood to be around 3,000 and the first match there is believed to have been between Blues and Nechells in September 1876 when Blues recorded a 2-0 victory in front of some 500 spectators who paid just 4s 3d (around 22p) at the gate!

LANE, James (Joe)

Born on 11 July 1892 in Hertford, centre-forward Joe Lane, a printer by trade, started playing football at competitive level whilst acting as player-coach to the crack Hungarian side Ferencvaros whilst working in Budapest. So well did he do (he scored twice in a friendly against Sunderland) that on his return to England in 1912 he signed professional forms for Watford, having previously been an amateur at Vicarage Road prior to going to Hungary. In 1913 he switched north to Sunderland, remaining on Wearside for barely two months before signing for Blackpool in the November. He scored 67 goals in 99 outings for the Seasiders (28 in the last season before the Great War and 28 in the first campaign after it) before leaving Bloomfield Road for St Andrew's, Blues paying out a club record £3,600 for his signature in March 1920. And he made an excellent start with his new club, scoring a penalty in a 2-2 draw at Lincoln. Playing alongside Harry Hampton in attack, Lane continued to hit the target, scoring 26 goals in 67 League and Cup appearances for Blues, helping them win the Second Division title. He was then, without prior notice, sold to Millwall in August 1922 for £2,000. He retired from League action in September 1924 and took a coaching job with the Spanish club Barcelona. He later returned to Watford (1935) to play casually for a local printing works, finally hanging up his boots in 1939 when he went to War with the Hertfordshire Yeomanry. A very wealthy man (some say he may well have been a millionaire) Lane tended to flaunt his money and never wore the same shirt TWICE, handing over his cast-offs to his team-mates. He died in Langley, Warley on 27 February 1959.

LANEROSSI VICENZA

Blues played the Italian club at home and away in the Anglo-Italian Tournament in June 1971. A crowd of around 3,000 witnessed the 0-0 draw in Italy while in stark contrast 23,642 spectators saw Blues win the return contest 5-3 at St Andrew's six days later when Bob Latchford (2), Trevor Francis, Bob Hatton and Gordon Taylor found the net.

LANGAN, David

David Langan

Republic of Ireland international right back, David Langan was recruited by Blues manager Jim Smith for a club record fee of £350,000 from Derby County in July 1980. A fine, attacking player he went on to make 102 appearances for Blues (two goals scored), winning the club's 'Player of the Year' award in 1981-82 before leaving St Andrew's on a free transfer to join Oxford United in August 1984, thus being re-united with his former boss (Smith). At The Manor Ground he helped the 'U's' win the Second Division championship in 1985 and the Milk Cup the following season. Loan spells with Leicester City and AFC Bournemouth preceded his move from Oxford to Dean Court in December 1987 and after a season with Peterborough United (1988-89) he moved into non-League soccer with Ramsey Town, later assisting Holbeach United, Rothwell Town and Mirlees Blackstone.

Born in Dublin on 15 February 1957, Langan joined Derby as a junior in 1974 and turned professional in February 1975. He made over 500 senior appearances as a professional, playing in all four divisions of the Football League. He was capped 25 times by Eire.

LANGLEY, Kevin

Born deep in the heart of Rugby League territory in St Helens on 24 May 1964, midfielder Kevin Langley opted for the round ball game and joined Wigan Athletic in June 1980, turning professional at Springfield Park in May 1982. Four years and almost 200 games later he was transferred to Everton for £100,000 (July 1986) but he never settled at Goodison Park, neither did he at his next club Manchester City and after a loan spell with Chester he moved to St Andrew's for £100,000 in March 1988. He became a vital cog in the Blues' engine-room and manager John Bond believed he was the player to help gain promotion back to the First Division. But Langley never looked comfortable when the pressure was on and in September 1990, after scoring twice in 88 outings for Blues, he returned to Wigan Athletic for £50,000. He retired from competitive football in 1994 after playing in a further 196 games for the Latics (12 extra goals) to finish with a career tally of 514 first-class appearances and 25 goals. He was a Freight Rover Trophy finalist with Wigan in 1986 and played for Everton soon afterwards in the FA Charity Shield match at Wembley.

LARKIN, Bunny

When he started his professional career Bunny Larkin was a cheerful, fair-haired wing-half, but after breaking his leg in a youth team match, his manager at Birmingham City Arthur Turner helped supervise his development into an exceptionally useful goalscoring inside-forward.

He netted 23 goals in the 1958-59 season and scored again in the following season's Inter Cities Fairs Cup semi-final against the Belgium side Union St Gilloise before a loss of form cost him his first team place at St Andrew's. Earlier he was dubbed 'Rip Van Winkle' after missing the team coach on the way to a vital Inter Cities Fairs Cup-tie.

On leaving Blues Larkin remained in League soccer for another five years, serving four more clubs: Norwich, Doncaster, Watford and Lincoln, doing well with them all while taking his overall tally of senior appearances at club level to past the 250 mark. He became the first Norwich City player to score on his debut in the Football League, League Cup and FA Cup. Moving from Sincil Bank in 1966 he entered non-League football with Wisbech Town and later assisted Nuneaton Borough and Stevenage Athletic before retiring to become a salesman in Norfolk. Larkin was born in Digbeth in January 1936, and scored 29 goals in 92 games for Blues (1952-66)

LATCHFORD, Bob

Over the years Brandwood School has produced quite a number of players but few, if any, have been better than centre-forward Bob Latchford. The bearded, swash-buckling striker, the main target man at St Andrew's for four years before his departure to Everton in 1974, was a big favourite with the fans. He was initially part of

Bob Latchford celebrates another goal, this one against Manchester City in 1974.

a formidable trio comprising himself, Trevor Francis and Phil Summerill and later with Bob Hatton and Francis. Strong and powerful, he was a sound header of the ball and could shoot with both feet. He scored some cracking goals, not only for Blues but also for his other League clubs and for England.

Born in Kings Heath on 18 January 1951, he joined Blues as an apprentice in May 1967 (having represented Birmingham & Warwickshire County Schools). He turned 'pro' in August 1968 (after gaining an FA Youth Cup runners-up medal) and finally established himself in the first XI at St Andrew's in 1970-71 when he scored 13 goals in 42 senior appearances. The following season he netted 30 times (in 52 matches), helping Blues reach the semi-final of the FA Cup and also gain promotion to the First Division. He followed up with another 20 goals (in 49 outings) in 1972-73 and weighed in with 18 more (in 36 games) in 1973-74 before his transfer to Goodison Park for a League record fee of £350,000, a deal that saw Howard Kendall and Archie Styles switch from Merseyside to St Andrew's. His record with Blues was excellent - 84 goals in 194 appearances.

The Everton fans took to him immediately and Latchford responded by scoring seven times in his first thirteen games. In 1977-78 he was presented with a cheque for £10,000 by a national newspaper after becoming the first player to register 30 goals in Division One for six years, clinching the money with a brace in the last match of the season against Chelsea.

He went on to net 138 goals in 289 appearances for Everton (the Merseyside club's highest post-war scorer at that time) before moving to Swansea City for £125,000 in July 1981. He enjoyed mixed fortunes at Vetch Field but still managed to tuck away another 32 goals in 1982-83. On receiving a free transfer in January 1984 he joined the Dutch club NAC Breda, but five months later he returned to England to sign for Coventry City. In July 1985 he switched to Lincoln City and after a loan spell with Newport County he finally drifted into non-League soccer in August 1986 with Merthyr Tydfil, gaining a Welsh Cup winners medal at the end of that season. He later became a Director of Alvechurch FC before returning to St Andrew's on the Community side during the late 1990s, taking over a coaching role in 1999-2000.

Capped 12 times by England at senior level (five goals scored) he also played in six under 23 and four youth internationals for his country and represented the Football League once. During an excellent career Latchford netted over 280 goals in more than 650 club and international appearances.

LATCHFORD, Dave

Bob Latchford's elder brother Dave was a goalkeeper - and very good one at that. He made 239 appearances for Blues during his thirteen years with the club. Born in Kings Heath on 9 April 1949, he was also a pupil at Brandwood School and represented South Birmingham Boys before joining the apprentice staff at St Andrew's in June 1964, turning professional in May 1966. England was called into the England youth squad as a teenager but failed to gain a place because of a certain Peter Shilton. Nevertheless he persevered at club level, gained an FA Youth Cup runners-up medal in 1967 (with his brother Bob) and became a regular in the Blues side in 1970, taking over the mantle from Jim Herriot.

Latchford despite his bulky 14 stone frame was surprisingly agile and handled the ball cleanly, making the occasional breathtaking save look easy! He helped Blues win promotion to the First Division in 1972 before leaving to join Motherwell in July 1977. Two years later he signed for Bury and was a non-contract player with Barnsley before drifting into non-League football with Redditch United in 1981, later assisting Cheltenham Town and East Worle. After some years as a funeral Director he became a Superintendent of Cemeteries based in Solihull whilst his son Oliver played for Solihull Borough.

• Dave and Bob's other brother, Peter, was a goalkeeper for West Bromwich Albion and Celtic.

Dave Latchford foiling an Aston Villa attack in 1977.

LEAKE, Alex

Football to Alex Leake was a pleasure! He regularly cracked a joke with an opponent while robbing him of the ball and quite often would burst out laughing just before a corner kick was being taken. He was a genuine 'Brummageem Button', a good humoured, easy-going defender whose temperament was second to none. A honest worker, tireless to the extreme, his stamina was unsurpassed. He never played to the gallery, always battling for his team; he never shirked a tackle and gave 110 per-cent effort every time he took the field. He was as safe as houses, never dallied on the ball and often came out best in the 50-50 challenges.

Born in Small Heath on 11 July 1871, he attended and played for Jenkins Street and Green Lane Schools in Bordesley Green before joining his weekend team Hoskins & Sewell. He then had spells with Kings Heath Albion, Saltley Gas Works FC, Singers, Hoskins & Sewell (again) and Old Hill Wanderers before joining Blues in July 1894. He went on to score 23 goals in 221 games over the next eight years (the last six as captain) before leaving Muntz Street for neighbours Aston Villa in June 1902. Three years later he starred for Villa when they won the FA Cup and during his five seasons at Villa Park he netted nine times in 140 senior games. He played for Burnley from December 1907 until the end of the 1909-10 season when he joined Wednesbury Old Athletic, and when he quit League soccer his record stood at 464 club appearances and 34 goals. Leake, with his dapper moustache and well-groomed hair, won five full England caps and also represented the Football League XI. In fact, he was chosen as reserve for his country in 1912 when fast approaching his 41st birthday (he was trainer at Crystal Palace at the time). Besides being a fine footballer he was also a very good swimmer who often dived to the bottom of the brine baths at Droitwich to retrieve a coin and was a very useful athletic, specialising in the 400 yards and hurdles events. He was a keen gardener and a blacksmith by trade. His cousin Jimmy Windridge also played for Blues.

Alex Leake

Leake died in Birmingham on 29 March 1938, aged 66.

LEEDS CITY

Blues' record against Leeds City is:

FOOTBALL LEAGUE

Venue	P	W	D	L	F	A
Home	7	4	1	2	16	13
Away	7	0	2	5	4	14
Totals	14	4	3	7	20	27

WARTIME

Venue	P	W	D	L	F	A
Home	3	2	1	0	8	4
Away	3	0	1	2	2	5
Totals	6	2	2	2	10	9

The first time Blues met the now defunct Leeds City was at Elland Road on 31 October 1908 (Division 2). City won 2-0 in front of 15,000 fans.

Jack Hall scored all Blues' goals when they beat Leeds 4-3 before a crowd of 10,000 at St Andrew's in September 1911.

Leeds gained sweet revenge for that defeat with a comprehensive 4-0 home victory in April 1913.

The last time Leeds City visited St Andrew's for a competitive League game was in October 1914 in the Second Division. Blues beat the Yorkshire side 6-3 with goals by Andy Smith (3), Percy Barton, Jimmy Windridge and Dick Gibson. The attendance was just 8,000.

Leeds completed two League doubles over Blues: 1909-10 and 1913-14.

All the wartime games were played between October 1916 and September 1918, Blues winning 4-2 at home in the last encounter.

Player with both clubs: J Robertson

Gill Merrick foiling John Charles against Leeds in August 1951.

LEEDS UNITED

Blues' record against United is:

FOOTBALL LEAGUE

Venue	P	W	D	L	F	A
Home	38	21	11	6	71	35
Away	38	6	12	20	23	56
Totals	76	27	23	26	94	91

FA CUP

Home	1	0	0	1	1	2
Away	1	0	0	1	2	3
Neutral	1	0	0	1	0	3

LEAGUE CUP

Home	1	0	0	1	1	2
Away	1	0	0	1	0	3

The first League game between Blues and United took place at St Andrew's on 18 December 1920 (Division 2). Blues won 1-0, Alec McClure scoring the deciding goal. A fortnight later (on New Year's Day) United won 1-0 at Elland Road to balance the books.

Joe Bradford scored a tremendous hat-trick when Blues beat Leeds 5-1 at St Andrew's in December 1928.

In the last game of the 1928-29 season (4 May) reserve right-winger Harry Riley played his one and only League game for Blues - in a 1-0 win over United at Elland Road.

A crowd of 21,566 saw Blues beat Leeds 4-0 in a First Division game at St Andrew's in September 1933, Tom Grosvenor scoring a superb goal.

Despite beating Leeds United 4-0 at home on the last day of the 1938-39 season Blues were still relegated to the Second Division. They finished 21st in the table, a point behind Chelsea who had drawn 1-1 in a crucial game at St Andrew's three days earlier. This game also marked the last League appearance of Blues' goalkeeper Harry Hibbs.

Two Scots celebrated St Valentine's Day 1948 as Blues beat Leeds United 5-1 in a Second Division game at St Andrew's. Jackie Stewart and Bobby Laing scored two goals apiece as Blues opened up a five-point gap at the top of the table. Laing, making his debut, netted his first after just four minutes to boost the home supporters in the 40,000 crowd.

Hymie Kloner made his only League appearance for Blues in the 3-0 defeat at Leeds in December 1950.

In April 1957 Alex Govan claimed his fifth hat-trick of the season in a 6-2 home win over Leeds.

Seventeen months later, in September 1958, it was Eddie Brown who did the damage, weighing in with four goals as Blues whipped the Yorkshire side 4-1, again at St Andrew's.

Gil Merrick played his last game in goal for Blues in the 2-0 home League win over Leeds in October 1959.

On the last day of the 1964-65 League season, just before they took on Liverpool in the FA Cup Final, Leeds were held to a 3-3 draw by Blues at St Andrew's.

A goal by Martin Kuhl gave Blues a 1-0 home win over Leeds on 11 May 1985 to celebrate promotion to the First Division!

Leeds beat Blues 4-0 at Elland Road in April 1987 and followed up with a 4-1 victory on the same ground seven months later (December 1987).

Leeds beat Blues 3-0 at Hillsborough in the FA Cup semi-final of 1972; won 3-2 at Elland Road in a 3rd round FA Cup encounter in 1998 and in between times, in season 1995-96, Blues lost 5-1 on aggregate to United in the two-legged League Cup semi-final. Kevin Francis scored a spectacular 30 yard goal past United 'keeper John Lukic in the first leg encounter at St Andrew's which Blues lost 2-1.

Blues have achieved four 'League' doubles over Leeds who have claimed exactly the same amount versus Blues!

Other players who made their debuts for Blues in games against have been (in order): Alec Leslie, Frank Clack Dave Mangnall, Ted Purdon, Bunny Larkin, Bryan Orritt, Bud Houghton, Jim Barrett, Paul Hendrie, Ricky Sbragia, Trevor Dark and Nicky Platnauer.

Players with both clubs include: N Blake, K Burns, W Clark, N Doherty (United trialist), J Greenhoff, P Hart, T Hibbitt, W Hutchinson (Blues reserve), FR Jones, J Kelly, D Mangnall, M O'Grady, A Powell, D Rennie, D Seaman, J Sheridan, C Shutt, G Sprake, WB Stevenson, DP Weston, C Whyte, F Worthington.

Also: Major Frank Buckley (Blues player, Leeds manager), Willie Bell, Terry Cooper and Fred Goodwin (Leeds players, Blues managers), Syd Owen (Blues player, Leeds coach), Brian Caswell (Leeds player, Blues coach).

LEEK, Ken

Ken Leek

Leek was a powerful, thrusting forward, able to shoot with both feet and with a knack of snapping up the half chances. Born next door to Don Dearson in Ynysybwl near Pontypridd on 26 July 1935, he played his first game of football at the age of 14 for Glyn Street juniors. He then did well with Pontypridd Youth Club and Ynysybwl Boys Club before joining Northampton Town in August 1952. He scored 26 goals in 71 League appearances for the Cobblers over the next six years before transferring to Leicester City in April 1958. He continued to do well at Filbert Street, notching a further 34 goals in 93 League outings but after being sensationally dropped for the 1961 FA Cup Final v Tottenham Hotspur (after scoring in every round) he left the club a month later joining Newcastle United in a £25,000 deal. He failed to settle down at St James' Park and after claiming half-a-dozen more goals in 13 starts for the Magpies he signed for Blues for £23,000 in November of that same year. His form continued at St Andrew's and in 1963 he helped Blues win their first major trophy, the League Cup, beating Aston Villa 3-1 in the two-legged final.

Leek scored a goal every two games for Blues - 61 in 120 appearances, including two in his last outing against Aston Villa and having a run of netting in each of seven successive League and Cup games between 2 December 1961 and 10 January 1962. He moved back to Northampton Town for £9,000 in December 1964 but less than a year later he was on the move again, this time to Bradford City for £10,000 in November 1965. He stayed at Valley Parade until August 1968 when he entered non-League soccer with Rhyl, later assisting Merthyr Tydfil and Ton Pentre before hanging up his boots in 1972. In his Football League career Leek scored close on 150 goals in almost 400 matches.

Leek who won 13 caps for Wales and also played in one under 23 international, was employed by the Ford Motor Company at Dagenham for many years after finishing with football.

LEEK TOWN

North Staffs side Leek Town were beaten 4-0 by Blues in an FA Cup third qualifying round tie at Muntz Street in November 1888. Caesar Jenkyns scored a brilliant goal in this game.

LEICESTER CITY (Fosse)

Blues' record against the Foxes is:

FOOTBALL LEAGUE

Venue	P	W	D	L	F	A
Home	57	31	9	17	107	73
Away	57	16	11	30	93	116
Totals	114	47	20	47	200	189

FA CUP

	P	W	D	L	F	A
Home	6	0	2	4	6	12
Away	4	1	1	2	10	9
Totals	10	1	3	6	16	21

WARTIME

	P	W	D	L	F	A
Home	16	10	4	2	39	16
Away	17	6	4	7	29	28
Totals	33	16	8	9	68	44

Blues and Leicester (Fosse) first met in the Football League on 27 March 1897 (Division 2). And it was Blues who took the points with a 1-0 away victory, Denny Hodgetts the scorer.

Three years later (in April 1900) Blues won 4-1 at home and then in season 1902-03 they put seven goals past Leicester, winning 4-3 at Filbert Street and 3-1 at Muntz Street. Former Leicester player Arthur Leonard scored twice against his former club in the latter game.

When Blues won 4-0 at home in October 1911, Jack Hall and Harry Graham both scored twice and in a 5-1 win for Blues in January 1913, Hall again found the net twice.

In between times Leicester salvaged some pride with a 5-2 win at Filbert Street (February 1912). That scoreline was to be repeated to a goal in August 1926.

Leicester (now City) were beaten 5-0 by Blues at St Andrew's in October 1920 - Joe Lane (2) and Harry Hampton (3) shared the goals.

On the last day of the 1929-30 season Blues beat Leicester 3-0 courtesy of a Joe Bradford hat-trick and a week after losing the 1931 FA Cup Final, Blues ended their League programme that season with a 2-1 home victory over Leicester, Joe Bradford notching the winner.

Leicester, in fact, registered 10 successive home League wins over Blues between 1914 and 1932.

One of Blues' best away wins in the Football League came in April 1934 when in a match they had to WIN to help their relegation fight, they defeated Leicester City 7-3 at Filbert Street. Billy Guest was the star that day with a stunning a hat-trick in front of 18,000 spectators. Blues led 3-1 at half-time and it was 3-3 after an hour before the home side caved in under pressure!

Blues' first home League game after World War Two (on 4 September 1946) saw them beat Leicester 4-0 with Wilson Jones (2), Jock Mulraney and Neil Dougall the scorers in front of 35,000 fans.

Blues completed an early double over Leicester in 1950-51, winning 2-0 at home and 3-1 away in August. Cyril Trigg and Billy Smith scored in each game.

Arthur Rowley grabbed a hat-trick when Leicester won 4-0 at Filbert Street in August 1951 and Peter Murphy copied the League's record marksman with a treble in Blues' 4-3 away win in January 1953.

Another hat-trick hero for Blues against Leicester was Robin Stubbs, in a 4-2 away win in March 1959 - this after Blues had won their home fixture 4-2 earlier in the season when debut boy Johnny Gordon scored in the 13th minute with his first shot at goal.

And in September 1961 - a few months after losing to Spurs in the FA Cup Final - Leicester cruised to a 5-1 League victory over Blues at St Andrew's.

Captains meet - Tony Towers (Blues) and Dennis Rofe (Leicester) with mascot and officials before a League game at St Andrew's in 1980.

In November 1964 eight goals were shared in a competitive 4-4 draw at Filbert Street. Bobby Thomson scored twice for Blues, one from the penalty spot.

Over a period of four years (April 1974 to April 1978) five League games between Blues against Leicester produced no fewer than 32 goals.

Kenny Burns scored a hat-trick in a 3-3 draw at Filbert Street in the first encounter. Four months later Blues lost 4-3 at home when Burns and Trevor Francis (2) found the net. It was 3-3 again on Leicester soil in August 1975 when Howard Kendall netted twice for Blues before Burns weighed in with another hat-trick in Blues' 6-2 victory at Filbert Street in December 1976. And to round things off Blues again took the honours with another convincing away win, this time by 4-1.

When Leicester beat Blues 3-0 at Filbert Street in April 1996, one of their scorers was former Brummie star Steve Claridge!

In 1891-92 in front of 1,000 fans, Blues beat Leicester 6-2 away in a qualifying round of the FA Cup and it took three games to decide the 1948-49 third round FA Cup-tie between the clubs, Leicester eventually winning 2-1 (after two 1-1 draws). City lost 3-1 to Wolves in the Final.

Leicester also reached the 1961 Final and in doing so they played TWO of their FA Cup games at St Andrew's! After a 1-1 draw in the fifth round, they duly won the replay 2-1 at Filbert Street where Ken Leek, later to join Blues, scored both his side's goals. This same season (on 27 March) Leicester beat Sheffield United 2-0 on Blues' soil in an FA Cup semi-final second replay - and Leek scored again but was then sensationally dropped for the Wembley Final against Tottenham Hotspur which City lost 3-1!

In January 1999 Leicester beat Blues 4-2 in a third round FA Cup-tie at Filbert Street. Tony Cottee, who also played for Blues, scored one of Leicester's goals that day in front of 19,846 fans.

Gary Rowett was Blues' record transfer 'out' when he joined Leicester in June 2000 for £3 million.

Players with both clubs include: HP Bailey, J Barratt, S Campbell, G Charles, S Claridge, W Clarke, P Cooper, A Cottee, J Crisp (Blues reserve), G Daly, H Edwards, P Fitzpatrick, C Gordon, H Graham, J Hall, A Harley, JK Henderson, D Hill (amateur), HE King, D Langan, K Leek, AR Leonard, WJ Lewis, S Lynex, JS McMillan, A Mounteney, A Mulraney (Leicester guest), M Newell, J Newman, M North, DW Pimbley (amateur), N Platnauer, K Poole, D Rennie, G Rowett, MC Russell, D Speedie, JE Travers, HM Wilcox, T Williams, F Worthington, W Wragg.

Also: Jimmy Bloomfield and Frank Womack (Blues players, Leicester managers), Willie Bell (Leicester player, Blues manager).

LEONARD, Arthur (Arthur Bamford)

An inside-right Arthur Leonard played under a pseudonym for the latter half of his career. His real name was Arthur Leonard Bamford but he decided to withdraw his surname from his title. Born in Leicester in 1874 he served with the 17th Leicestershire Regiment before becoming a footballer with Leicester Fosse in 1895. He failed to make the first XI and quickly 'disappeared'. He resurfaced a few months later with Rushden Town, playing next for Sheppey United and then Glentoran before joining Blues for £120 in November 1901 - this after starring in an Irish League game when representatives of both Blues and Leicester were present! The Leicester contingent identified him as their missing player (Bamford) and when approached Leonard denied the accusations, but again cleared off.

He later sent a telegram to his wife saying that he was in America! Later spotted in Bristol he was persuaded to return to St Andrew's to 'face the music'. Things were sorted out after he admitted that he was, in fact, Bamford and after Blues had paid out another £20 (to Leicester) he remained at the club until January 1904, making 75 first team appearances and scoring 26 goals. A bag of tricks, he was a big hit with the fans and was regarded and the star performer in the side. On leaving Blues he joined Stoke and after scoring three times in 14 outings for the Potters he left The Victoria Ground to sign for Clapton Orient, later assisting St Bernard's (in Scotland) and Plymouth Argyle. He died circa 1950.

LESLIE, Alec

A Scotsman born in Greenock in April 1902, Alec Leslie was primarily a defensive left-half, solid in the tackle and generally consistent. He played for his local junior team Greenock Wayfairers, then Houghton-le-Spring before joining Greenock Morton. A spell with St Mirren followed in 1924 before he ventured south to sign for Torquay United for £100 in August 1925. He left Plainmoor for St Andrew's in a £750 deal in April 1927 and spent the next five years with Blues before retiring with a knee injury in May 1932. A player who loved to toe-end the ball through to his forwards, he was a big influence in the Blues side after replacing Dicky Dale in the middle-line. He played for Blues against West Brom in the 1931 FA Cup Final and at one stage it looked as though he might challenge for an England place. He appeared in 143 senior games for Blues. In later life Leslie became landlord of the Freemason's Arms in Hawkes Street and he also worked for the Inland Revenue before returning to his native Scotland where he died in Greenock in 1974.

LEYLAND DAF TROPHY

Blues entered this competition twice in seasons 1989-90 and 1990-91 - winning the trophy at the second attempt!

They lost 3-0 at Aldershot and beat Hereford United 1-0 at home in the first season. Then Blues accounted, in turn, for Walsall (away) 1-0, Lincoln City (home) 2-0, Swansea City (home) 4-2 on penalties after a 0-0 draw, Mansfield Town (home) 2-0, Cambridge United (home) 3-1 in the Area semi-final and Brentford 3-1 on aggregate in the two-legged Area Final (2-1 at home, 1-0 away). They then took on and defeated Tranmere Rovers 3-2 at neutral Wembley in the Final itself, two goals coming from John Gayle, one a real beauty - the winner in the 86th minute! Around 40,000 Blues fans went to Wembley to boost the attendance figure up to 58.756.

For the final Blues had to wear their ordinary League shirts! A newly-designed set of jerseys was supposed to be available to take with them when Blues set off for their pre-Final destination, but no one could find them. It later transpired that the full set, with a specially-designed logo, had been delivered to the Blues club shop and had been sold to supporters!

SUMMARY OF MATCHES PLAYED:

Venue	P	W	D	L	F	A
Home	6	5	1*	0	10	2
Away	3	2	0	1	2	3
Neutral	1	1	0	0	3	2
Totals	10	8	1	1	15	7

*Penalty shoot-out.

LEYTON ORIENT (Clapton Orient, Orient)

Blues' record against Orient is:

FOOTBALL LEAGUE

Venue	P	W	D	L	F	A
Home	18	10	6	2	29	13
Away	18	4	7	7	22	26
Totals	36	14	13	9	51	39

FA CUP

Home	3	2	0	1	6	2
Away	2	2	0	0	5	0
Totals	5	4	0	1	11	2

LEAGUE CUP

Home	1	1	0	0	4	0

AUTO WINDSCREEN SHIELD

Home	1	1	0	0	1	0
Away	1	1	0	0	3	2
Totals	2	2	0	0	4	2

Celebrations (in the bath) after win at Orient in 1972.

On 24 October 1908 Blues met Orient for the first time and beat them 1-0 at home in a Second Division match, Jimmy 'Ginger' Williams the goalscorer in front of 10,000 fans.

Jack Hall's hat-trick helped Blues to a comfortable 4-0 home win over the Londoners in March 1912 and he was on the mark again in both League games in 1913-14.

Blues and Orient did not meet each other in League action between 1921 and 1962 - and when they did commence battle it was in the First Division. Orient forced a 2-2 draw at St Andrew's and it was the same scoreline at Brisbane Road in season 1962-63 - Orient's fleeting visit to the top flight!

A goal by Malcolm Page, his first of the season, earned Blues a 1-0 home win over Orient in November 1971 and four months later Trevor Francis and Phil Summerill netted at Brisbane Road to bring Blues the double.

After a bomb scare Blues won 1-0 at Orient on 2 May 1972 to clinch promotion back to the First Division. Bob Latchford scored the all-important goal in front of 10,000 Blues supporters in the 33,383 crowd - the best-ever for a League game at the London club's ground.

Keith Bertschin scored a hat-trick in Blues' 3-1 home win over Orient in February 1980.

On their way to the 1956 FA Cup Final, Blues beat Orient 4-0 at Brisbane Road in the fourth round and when they reached the semi-finals in 1968 they again accounted for the 'O's' 3-0 at St Andrew's at the same stage of the competition.

Blues' 4-0 League Cup win was achieved in 1975-76.

In the AWS competition of 1994-95 Blues beat Orient over two legs in the Southern Area semi-final. A then record crowd of 22,667 saw Peter Shearer score the winning goal in the first leg and Steve Claridge netted his 15th and 16th goals of the season in the return leg in London.

Players with both clubs include: J Bloomfield (player-manager of Orient), E Brown, M Bullock, S Castle, J Gill, R Hansbury, A Harris, I Hendon, HH Lappin, A Leonard, J Millington (Blues reserve), A Mulraney (Orient trialist), R Otto, D Purse, D Rowbotham, MA Smalley, RA Taylor.

Also: Barry Fry, Joe Mallett (Orient players, Blues managers), Ian Bowyer (Orient player, Blues coach).

LIDDELL, George

George Liddell extreme right, watching the ball bounce off the Blues crossbar during the 1931 FA Cup Final against West Bromwich Albion at Wembley.

George Liddell was born in County Durham on 14 August 1900. A pupil at Johnston Grammar School, he then received further education at the City of Leeds Training College and played for the Honourable Artillery Company side and for Duke of Wellington FC before enjoying a game of rugby whilst serving in the Army Regiment. He played next for Yorkshire Amateurs (1914) and South Shields (from 1915) before becoming a professional at St Andrew's in May 1920. A dapper player with smart moustache, Liddell used the ball well, trying to pass it rather than hoofing it downfield. He was originally a wing-half but was successfully converted into a right-back in 1928 (after Frank Womack's departure) and this was the turning point of his career as he went on to appear in 345 games for Blues, scoring six goals. A member of Blues' 1931 FA Cup Final side, Liddell, who combined the last three years of his playing days with that of a school-teacher (meaning that he missed quite a few mid-week away games) retired in April 1932. A year later, having hinted that he always wanted to become a League club manager, Liddell's wish was granted when Chairman Harry Morris placed him into the hot seat at St Andrew's, replacing Leslie Knighton who had moved to Chelsea. It was a big surprise to a lot of players and supporters, for he was not the most popular of men

in the dressing room! Nevertheless he got on with the job in hand but struggled to find success despite having a decent enough squad to choose from, although during his reign he did utilise some 70 players! He remained in office until May 1939 after Blues had been relegated to the Second Division.

After teaching at Leigh Road School, Washwood Heath and Cotteridge Infants School Liddell became headmaster at Handsworth Secondary Modern School before retiring to Hampshire.

LIMITED COMPANY

While at their Muntz Street ground, on 24 July 1888, Blues became Small Heath FC Limited (dropping the Alliance from their name). They were the first club in the country to be registered as a Limited Liability Company and at the same time was also the first club to have a Board of Directors.

Businessman Mr. Walter W. Hart was appointed the club's first chairman (in July 1888).

LINCOLN CITY

Blues' playing record against the Imps is:

FOOTBALL LEAGUE

Venue	P	W	D	L	F	A
Home	17	13	2	2	51	12
Away	17	9	6	2	29	20
Totals	34	22	8	4	80	32

FA CUP

	P	W	D	L	F	A
Home	1	1	0	0	2	1

LEYLAND DAF TROPHY

	P	W	D	L	F	A
Home	1	1	0	0	2	0

FOOTBALL ALLIANCE

	P	W	D	L	F	A
Home	1	1	0	0	4	0
Away	1	0	1	0	1	1
Totals	2	1	1	0	5	1

WARTIME

	P	W	D	L	F	A
Home	3	2	1	0	8	0
Away	3	0	1	2	5	7
Totals	6	2	2	2	13	7

Like Blues, Lincoln were one of the founder members of the League Division Two and the teams first met on 24 September 1892 at Muntz Street. Blues came out on top, winners by 4-1 with two-goal Fred Wheldon the star performer - just like he was in the return fixture later that season when he scored a hat-trick in Blues' 4-3 victory!

Frank Mobley emulated Wheldon's feat with a treble when Blues won 5-2 at Lincoln in November 1893 and in a 6-0 home canter soon afterwards Wheldon (2) and Mobley again found the net to make it four wins in a row for high-flying Blues over the Imps.

Bob McRoberts scored a hat-trick in Blues' easy 5-0 home League win over the Imps in October 1899 and Joe Lane followed suit when Blues beat Lincoln 7-0 also at home in March 1920. A week earlier the teams had drawn 2-2 at Sincil Bank, Lane having scored from a penalty when making his debut following his record transfer from Blackpool.

Blues did not meet Lincoln again at League level until the 1952-53 season when both games ended in draws before Blues doubled up with two hard-earned 1-0 victories the following season.

Six goals were shared in an exciting Second Division game at St

Andrew's in February 1955 when Peter Murphy scored twice in what was the last League clash between the teams.

The third round FA Cup-tie at St Andrew's in January 1969 attracted a crowd of 31,429. Blues just won through by 2-1 with goals by Fred Pickering and Dave Robinson.

The Leyland DAF encounter with the Imps at St Andrew's in November 1990 was seen by under 3,000 spectators. Simon Sturridge and Dave Clarke's own goal gave Blues a 2-0 win over the club placed 91st in the Football League!

Players with both clubs include: G Anderson, D Barnett, J Barratt, C Bosbury, C Brazier, FW Corbett (Blues reserve), J Cornforth, W Ellis, M Farmer, A Green, M Harford, JK Henderson, HR Houghton, FW Jones, JW Kirton, BP Larkin, RD Latchford, AR Linnecor, M McCarrick, R Matthewson, WR Meacock, R Neal, KI Neale, M North, N Platnauer, H Riley, TE Robinson, J Short, AE Sykes, RD Tremelling, J Wilson (Blues reserve), C Withers, M Yates.

Also: Willie Bell (manager of both clubs), Jim Smith (Lincoln player, Blues manager), George Foster (coach at both clubs), John Pryce (physio at both clubs), David Teague (programme editor at both clubs).

Eddie Brown (right) beaten by Lincoln goalkeeper Downie with Dick Neal (a future Blues player) looking on during a League game at St Andrew's in 1955.

LINLEY, Ted

An outside-left, balding, knock-kneed, Ted Linley gave Blues excellent service for six years during which time he appeared in 118 first-class matches and scored 11 goals. Born in East Retford on 26 September 1894, he played initially for Worksop Town before joining Blues in December 1920 for £800 plus Tom Pike. He fought off the challenges of several other wing forwards during his time with Blues and on leaving the club in 1926 he signed for Nottingham Forest, later assisting Sutton Town and then Mansfield Town, retiring in 1930. He helped Blues win the Second Division title in 1921.

LIVERPOOL

Blues' playing record against the Merseysiders is:

FOOTBALL LEAGUE

Venue	P	W	D	L	F	A
Home	43	19	10	14	68	43
Away	43	6	7	30	53	102
Totals	86	25	17	44	121	145

FA CUP

	P	W	D	L	F	A
Home	1	0	1	0	0	0
Away	6	1	1*	4	6	11
Totals	7	1	2	4	6	11

*Tie decided on penalties after 1-1 draw.

LEAGUE CUP

	P	W	D	L	F	A
Home	1	0	1	0	1	1
Away	2	0	0	2	1	6
Totals	3	0	1	2	2	7

TEST MATCHES

	P	W	D	L	F	A
Home	1	0	1	0	0	0
Away	1	0	0	1	0	4
Totals	2	0	1	1	0	4

Blues suffered their first-ever home League defeat when losing 4-3 to Liverpool on 14 October 1893 in front of 5,000 spectators at Muntz Street.

At one stage in this fixture Blues were looking good, leading the Reds with time running out, but then defender Caesar Jenkyns, who had already scored, was sent-off (the first Blues player to receive his marching orders) and after that Liverpool took control of the proceedings.

Earlier that season, Jenkyns had found the net in a 3-1 defeat on Merseyside - the first League meeting between the two clubs.

The first of Blues' 25 League victories over the Reds was achieved on 29 December 1894 when they eased to a 3-0 victory at Muntz Street with goals by Frank Mobley, Billy Walton and winger Bill Lewis.

Liverpool remained in the top flight of English football from 1905 to 1954. During that time games against Blues were always tight - with the odd exception!

Two goals by Arthur Mounteney in an exciting 4-3 win for Blues on Merseyside in September 1907 was witnessed by 20,000 fans and the same player found the net in the return game at St Andrew's which fizzled out into a 1-1 draw.

On their return to the First Division in 1921-22 Blues lost both games against Liverpool who then raced to a 6-2 win in a League game at Anfield in August 1923 - this defeat came just four days after Blues had beaten arch rivals Aston Villa 3-0.

Joe Bradford scored his first hat-trick for Blues in a superb 5-2 home win over Liverpool in November 1924 and Bob Gregg's only hat-trick for the club arrived in a 3-0 home win over the Reds in December 1932.

Blues lost a nine-goal thriller by 5-4 at Anfield in October 1934. Harold Booton (penalty) and Dave Mangnall (3) were Blues' scorers. And the entire Blues forward-line found the net when Liverpool were defeated 5-0 in a First Division game at St Andrew's in February 1937.

Liverpool won four games on the trot against Blues in 1948-49 and 1949-50 but then on a bone hard, frosty pitch at St Andrew's in December 1954, the Merseysiders suffered their heaviest defeat in League football to date, crashing 9-1 to a resilient Blues side.

Julian Dicks

The first goal arrived after just 48 seconds via Jackie Lane. It was 4-1 at half-time and 5-0 to Blues after the break! Eddie Brown (3), Gordon Astall (2), Peter Murphy (2) and Alex Govan rounded off the Blues scoring. It was a pity that only 17,514 hardy souls saw the goal rush!

Blues were promoted that season but Liverpool did not get out of the Second Division until 1962 and in their first 'top Division' clash with Blues for 12 years they came to St Andrew's and won 2-0, completing the double later that season with a resounding 5-1 win at Anfield!

Stan Lynn's penalty helped Blues beat Liverpool 3-1 at home in April 1964 to pocket two exceptionally valuable 'relegation' points but ten months later Liverpool, heading towards the FA Cup Final, won a seven-goal thriller at St Andrew's by 4-3 in front of almost 40,000 fans.

There was an identical scoreline at Anfield in December 1972 when the turnout was 45,407. This was a cracking match, goalmouth action and tension all down the line. Bobby Hope, Bob Latchford and Gordon Taylor scored for Blues, while Alec Lindsay (2), Peter Cormack and John Toshack were on target for the Reds who came back from 3-2 down to steal the points.

Taylor was again a scorer in Blues' 3-1 home victory in December 1974 before Liverpool won 4-1 at Anfield in February 1977 and 1-0 at St Andrew's seven months later. Blues then snatched a splendid 3-2 win on Merseyside in January 1978, Trevor Francis flashing in a dramatic penalty to stun the kop and the home fans in the 48,401 crowd.

The last time Blues met Liverpool in a League game they lost heavily - going down 5-0 at Anfield in April 1986 in front of 42,021

supporters. The unlikely figure of Gary Gillespie scored a hat-trick that day!

Liverpool dumped Blues out of the FA Cup twice at Anfield in five years in the early 1920s and many years later battling Blues lost 2-0 on penalties on Liverpool soil in a third round FA Cup replay in January 1995. Blues took 8,000 fans with them to Merseyside and the club received over £150,000 from the 36,275 gate.

The draw in one of their two Test Matches played at the end of the 1894-95 season against Liverpool helped Blues retain their First Division status.

Blues were beaten 1-0 at St Andrew's in the TNT Inter City Challenge Cup in July 1995. Ian Rush scored the goal on 73 minutes in front of 13,178 fans. Blues used 23 players in this game and Liverpool 15, including Britain's most expensive footballer, Stan Collymore.

Players with both clubs include: G Ablett, D Burrows, M Cooper ('Pool trialist), J Devlin, J Dicks, P Fitzpatrick ('Pool app), H Gayle, J Glover, A Goldie, M Halsall, W Halsall (Liverpool amateur), A Hateley, P Mardon ('Pool trialist), M Newell, M Prudhoe ('Pool on loan), W Smith (Anfield trialist), D Speedie, WG Steel.

Also: Mike Kelly (Blues player, Liverpool coach)

LONG EATON RANGERS

FOOTBALL ALLIANCE

Venue	P	W	D	L	F	A
Home	1	1	0	0	3	1
Away	1	1	0	0	2	0
Totals	2	2	0	0	5	1

In March 1888 Blues lost 7-3 away to Rangers in a friendly match.

Two months later Blues gained sweet revenge when they crushed Rangers 15-0, also in a friendly, this time at Muntz Street. Rangers arrived with only eight men. They made up the eleven with three spectators but Blues ran riot, scoring at will!

Later that same year (in October) Blues again defeated Rangers, this time by 6-2 in another home friendly. Will Devey scored a hat-trick. The two Alliance matches were in 1889-90.

LONG MATCHES

Blues have been involved in three cup matches that have gone to a fourth game (all totalling at least 420 minutes of playing time).

The Blues v Manchester United FA Cup-tie of 1903-04 went to a third replay. The first two encounters both ended in 1-1 draws, the second after extra-time. The second replay at Bramall Lane also went into extra-time and again finished level at 1-1 before United won the fourth encounter 3-1 at Hyde Road.

In 1983-84 Blues played Notts County four times in a League Cup tie. The first three matches ended 2-2 at St Andrew's, 0-0 at Meadow Road and 0-0 again on Blues soil before Blues won the fourth clash 3-1 at Nottingham.

The following season Blues met Norwich City four times in a third round FA Cup-tie. After a 0-0 draw at St Andrew's and a 1-1 scoreline in the Carrow Road replay, a further 1-1 draw ensued on Blues' ground before the Canaries finally went through with a 1-0 victory in East Anglia.

A Wartime game between Blues and Wolverhampton Wanderers on 14 April 1945 started at 3pm and ended at 5.45pm - 2 hours 33 minutes of actual playing time. Wolves won the game 1-0, the winning goal coming in the 63rd minute of extra-time! Following the scheduled hour and a half's normal time the referee and respective managers agreed to play on until a goal was scored!

LONG SEASONS

The 1946-47 League season started officially on 31 August and ended on 26 May - almost nine months. This was due to the arctic weather conditions that gripped Britain during mid-winter.

The 1939-40 season, severely disrupted by the outbreak of World War Two, started on 26 August and ended on 8 June - the longest period of time Blues have ever played football (in this country).

LONG SERVICE

David Wiseman

Mr David Wiseman, OBE, was on the Birmingham City Board of Directors for 48 years. He joined the Board in 1928 and after vacating his seat in 1976 he was appointed club President, a position he held until his death two years later (December 1978) at the age of 93. In all David Wiseman served Blues for almost close on 50 years.

Ray Devey also gave Blues supreme service. He joined the playing staff in 1937 and stayed with the club for ten years. He later returned as coach/trainer in 1950 and remained at St Andrew's until 1983 during which time he also acted as the club's physiotherapist and kit-man. He was a 'Bluenose' for a total of 43 years.

Director Harry Dare retired through ill health in July 1979 after giving Blues 40 years service.

Harry Morris, junior, followed his father (Harry senior) onto the St Andrew's Board of Directors in 1929. He became Chairman in 1933 and later took over as President in 1967, the year of his death, having served 38 years with the club.

Harry Morris, senior, was associated with Blues for 36 years. He was a player from August 1883 until May 1893 and then served as a Director from 1903 until 1929 when replaced by his son (above).

Walter Taylor spent more than 30 years on Blues' staff as assistant-scout and then chief scout from the early 1920s to the 1950s.

Charlie Simms spent well over 29 years with the club (from August 1884 until January 1914) first as a player until 1892, then as a trainer until 1905 and thereafter as groundsman. Dedicated to the last.

Alf 'Inky' Jones was secretary-manager of Blues from 1885-1908. After that he was employed as an accountant and served the club for a total of 30 years.

Harry Morris junior

Gil Merrick spent always 26 years with Blues - first as a player (he signed amateur forms in August 1938 and retired in May 1960) and then as a manager (from May 1960 until April 1964).

Full-back Frank Womack joined Blues in July 1908 and left St Andrew's in May 1928 - almost 20 years with Blues.

Here is a detailed list of other 'long serving' members of Birmingham City football club:

24 years Frank Richards . .1906-30's clerk/sec/sec-manager/director
23 years Alan Instone . . . . . .1960-83 assistant-secretary/secretary
19 years Cyril Trigg . . . . .1935-54 player
18 years John Edwards . . .1965-83 assistant-secretary/acting secretary
18 years George Liddell . . . .1920-32 & 1933-39 player/manager
18 years Dan Tremelling . . . . .1919-32 & 1936-41 player/trainer
18 years Fred Wilcox . . . .1950-68 groundsman, Elmdon ground.
17 years Percy Barton .1914-31 player
17 years Malcolm Beard . . . . . . .1957-71 & 1979-82 player/scout
17 years Fred Harris . . . . .1933-50 player
17 years Alec McClure . . .1912-23 & 1928-34 player/2nd XI manager
17 years Malcolm Page .1964-81 player
16 years Jack Badham . . . . .1934-60 player
16 years Ken Green . . . . .1943-59 player
16 years Harry Hibbs . . . . .1924-40 player
16 years Garry Pendrey . . . . .1965-79 & 1987-89 player/manager
16 years Johnny Schofield . . . . .1950-66 player
15 years Joe Bradford .1920-35* player
15 years Dennis Jennings . . . . .1936-51 player
15 years Billy Walton .1888-1903 player
15 years Dave Fairhurst . . . . .1946-61 physiotherapist
*Later worked part-time in the St Andrew's pools office.

Two former Blues players, goalkeeper Billy Robb and striker Trevor Francis, both had long careers in League football. Robb spent a total of 24 years, 66 days in League action while Francis had 23 years and 77 days in the game.

THE ENCYCLOPAEDIA OF BIRMINGHAM CITY

LONG THROW

In 1994 Andy Legg, the Blues midfielder, heaved the ball a distance of 41 metres from a throw in. At the time it was the longest throw ever recorded in League football. This was later beaten by Tranmere defender Dave Challinor who threw the ball over 45 metres in a game against Blues. The Blues 1930s trio of Lew Stoker, Tom Fillingham and Tom Grosvenor all had long throws.

LORD MAYOR of BIRMINGHAM CHARITY C

This trophy was first played for in 1881-82, Aston Villa going on to beat Walsall Swifts 4-1 in the final.

Blues entered the competition soon afterwards and fielding their first XI, won the Charity Cup outright on six occasions as follows:

1907	Blues 4	Aston Villa 0
1908	Blues 5	Aston Villa 2
1919	Blues 4	Aston Villa 1
1933	Blues 2	Aston Villa 0
1934	Blues 2	Aston Villa 1
1936	Blues 4	Aston Villa 2

- Blues were joint holders of the Cup with Aston Villa in 1904 (this game was abandoned after 50 minutes with Villa leading 1-0), with Villa again in 1906 (also 1-1), with West Bromwich Albion in 1921 (2-2), with Villa once more in 1924 (3-3), with Villa for the fourth time in 1937 (2-2) and with Coventry City in 1938 (1-1).
- They have also finished as runners-up on ten occasions: 1892, 1893, 1895 (beaten 5-3 by Aston Villa), 1903 (defeated 4-1 by Villa), 1910 (again defeated by Villa 2-1), 1922, 1925, 1927, 1928 and 1929. Blues lost to Villa in seven of these finals.
- In 1961-62 and 1963-64 the respective youth teams of Aston Villa and Blues contested the Birmingham Senior Cup Final and amazingly both matches ended in 4-4 draws, meaning that each club held the trophy for six months.
- Since 1965 this competition as been known as the Birmingham Senior Amateur Cup.
- In the 1908 Charity Cup Final Blues' goalkeeper Jack Dorrington saved two Harry Hampton penalties as Aston Villa were crushed 5-2.

LORD MAYOR OF COVENTRY CUP

On 12 April 1926 Blues met Coventry City in the Final of the Lord Mayor of Coventry Charity Cup. The game ended in a 2-2 draw, each club holding the trophy for six months.

LOUGHBOROUGH TOWN

Blues' playing record against 'Boro is:
FOOTBALL LEAGUE

Venue	P	W	D	L	F	A
Home	4	4	0	0	16	0
Away	4	2	1	1	5	4
Totals	8	6	1	1	21	4

In two successive home League games against Loughborough, Blues ran up a total of 12 goals, winning each match 6-0 - in January 1899 and February 1900. Walter Abbott in the first game

and Jack Aston in the second, both scored hat-tricks.

Blues only defeat (0-2) came a week before Christmas, 1896 - the first time the teams had met.

Player with both clubs: J Tebbs

LUCCHESE

Blues played the Serie 'B' club in the Anglo-Italian Cup competition in December 1992. Only 139 hardy supporters paid to see Blues beaten 3-0 in Italy - the lowest ever attendance for a Blues' first team game at competitive level.

LUTON TOWN

Blues' playing record against the Hatters reads:
FOOTBALL LEAGUE

Venue	P	W	D	L	F	A
Home	25	14	7	4	53	24
Away	25	11	8	6	32	29
Totals	50	25	15	10	85	53

FA CUP

	P	W	D	L	F	A
Away	2	1	0	1	2	2

LEAGUE CUP

	P	W	D	L	F	A
Home	2	1	1	0	4	3
Away	2	0	2	0	3	3
Neutral	1	1	0	0	1	0
Totals	5	2	3	0	8	6

WARTIME

	P	W	D	L	F	A
Home	3	3	0	0	12	7
Away	4	3	0	1	12	7
Totals	7	6	0	1	24	14

Blues won their first six League games against Luton (1897-1900).

The best of the 25 so far registered over the Hatters has been 9-0 at Muntz Street in November 1898. Six different players found the net with left-half Bill Robertson top-dog with a tremendous hat-trick. This is also Luton's heaviest League defeat to date.

Walter Abbott scored a hat-trick when Blues won 3-2 in March 1899.

Luton were out of the League from 1900 until 1919 and when they returned they entered the Third Division, eventually resuming competitive action against Blues in December 1946 when Cyril Trigg's hat-trick earned his side a 3-0 win at Kenilworth Road. Later that season Blues completed the double with a 1-0 home win and then won both Second Division matches the following season before claiming another success (3-0) in November 1950 to make in eleven successive League victories over the Hatters.

Blues went on to win 15 out of the first 17 encounters against Luton who finally broke the sequence with their first League victory - 2-0 at home on 9 September 1953 - just a week after Peter Murphy had scored a hat-trick in a 5-1 victory for Blues at St Andrew's. In that 'first' win for the Hatters in 55 years of trying , George Cummins netted his first goal for the Kenilworth Road club.

At the end of the 1954-55 season both Blues and Luton were promoted to the First Division and the initial meeting in the top flight ended goalless at St Andrew's on 17 September 1955. Later in the season Eddie Brown's goal gave Blues a 1-0 win at Luton.

On 29 August 1970 - ten years after last playing each other - Blues and Luton drew again at St Andrew's, this time 1-1.

142

Steve Phillips, 17 year old starter v Hatters

Steve Phillips made his first 'start' for Blues as a 17 year-old against Luton (away) in August 1971 (drew 0-0).

Trevor Francis' hat-trick gave Blues an easy 3-0 away win over the Hatters in October 1974 but with Luton fighting to avoid relegation from the First Division, they ran up a convincing 4-1 victory at St Andrew's towards the end of the season but still went down.

On 24 November 1979, it was Keith Bertschin's hat-trick which enabled Blues to beat Luton 3-2, also at St Andrew's.

Paul Devlin scored one of the fastest-ever League goals for Blues, just 16 seconds after the start of the League game with Luton Town at St Andrew's in April 1996 (won 4-0).

Blues met the Hatters three times in the League Cup competition in 1972-73. The first two games both ended in 1-1 draws before Blues won the second replay 1-0 at Northampton.

A crowd of 6,315 saw Blues' 100th game in the League Cup at Kenilworth Road against Luton in September 1991. The match ended all square at 2-2 but Blues went on to win the second leg 3-2.

Luton Town replaced Blues in the Wartime Midland Cup competition in December 1940.

Syd Owen (ex-Blues defender) made his last appearance of his career as skipper of Luton in the 1959 FA Cup Final against Nottingham Forest.

Players with both clubs include: T Aylott, F Barber, H Booton, R Brennan, J Brown (Associate Schoolboy with Town), S Claridge, R Cooke, D Geddis, D Givens, M Harford, R Hatton, WS Havenga, CG Henderson, A Hubbard, WM Hughes, JA Inglis, M Jackson, JL Loughran, JA Mitchell, M Newell, M North, S Ottewell, S Owen (also Luton manager), D Preece, B Rioch, F Roberts, CJ Russell, L Sealey (Blues N/C), B Small, S Sutton, W Thirlaway, RA Thomson, C Todd.

Also: Jimmy Bloomfield (Blues player, Luton scout), Sam Bartram (Luton manager, Blues guest), Alec McClure (Blues player, Luton trainer), Lil Fuccillo and Ed Stein (Luton players, Blues coaches).

LYNEX, Steve

Steve Lynex

Born in West Bromwich on 23 January 1958, winger Steve Lynex did well at youngster whilst playing for All Saints junior and Churchfields comprehensive Schools. He played weekend soccer for West Bromwich Town, Charlemont Farm Boys Club and Sandwell Rangers and had unsuccessful trials with both Aston Villa and Wolves before joining the apprentice staff at The Hawthorns in July 1974, turning professional with the Baggies in January 1977 (under Johnny Giles' managership).

Unable to gain a place in the first XI, Lynex moved to Shamrock Rovers, the Irish club, with Giles in July 1977, having previously had a trial with Sligo Rovers. He did well with the Dublin-based club, gaining European experience and after a trial period with QPR he joined Blues in April 1979, after the club had already been condemned to relegation.

He starred in his first full season at St Andrew's, helping Blues clinch promotion but after scoring 10 goals in 53 appearances he signed for Leicester City for £60,000 (February 1981). He proved to be an excellent purchase by the Foxes and over the next five-and-a-half years appeared in 240 competitive games for the Filbert Street club, scoring 60 goals, a third of them from the penalty spot.

An orthodox winger with good pace, he often moved inside and 'sniffed' for the half chance that came his way. He was a gritty footballer, always busy and a true competitor. He even kept goal for Leicester in an FA Cup-tie against Shrewsbury in 1982.

Before he left Leicester for his first club West Brom in March 1987, Lynex had another spell with Blues, this time on loan (October 1986). He netted another three goals in 13 outings and then added a few more to his tally whilst at The Hawthorns before joining Cardiff City on a free transfer in June 1988. He ended his League career in March 1990, having chalked up in excess of 400 appearances at senior level. He then played out his footballing days with first Telford United, then Trafford Park FC, Mitchells & Butlers and Ansells FC, the latter two being pub-minded teams with Lynex having become a licensee in 1990.

LYNN, Stanley

Stan Lynn putting in a challenge on his former Aston Villa team-mate Harry Burrows

A solidly built full-back with a kick like a mule, Stan Lynn was a terrific defender who was always totally committed. Born in Bolton on 18 June 1928 he joined Accrington Stanley in 1947 as a professional and in March 1950 was signed by Aston Villa for what turned out to be a bargain fee of just £10,000. Over the next eleven years he appeared in 324 games and scored 38 goals games for Villa, including a host of penalties and a hat-trick v Sunderland in January 1958. He helped them win the FA Cup in 1957 and the Second Division championship in 1960, and also starred in the first leg of the 1961 League Cup final. He left Villa Park for St Andrew's in October 1961 and two years later gained a League Cup winners' prize when Blues defeated his former club, Villa, in the two-legged final. Lynn, who left St Andrew's for Stourbridge in August 1966 after almost 150 games for Blues, was a keen golfer who later worked in the stores at Lucas and now resides in a residential home in Birmingham.

MACARI, Lou

Lou Macari was a busy little inside or centre-forward who buzzed around the penalty area, menacing defenders and scoring his fair share of goals.

He found it all too easy to win honours with Celtic and decided to try his luck in the Football League with Manchester United - and he succeeded to do the business south of the border just like he had done previously in Scotland.

Born to Italian parents in Edinburgh on 4 June 1949, Luigi (his Christian name) Macari played his first serious football with St Michael's Academy and then Kilwinning FC before joining Kilmarnock Amateurs. He next served with Kilwinning Rangers and in 1966 signed professional forms for Celtic, determined to be a great success at both club and international level.

He went on to win 24 full caps for Scotland, also adding two more to his collection with the under 23 side as well as representing his country at both schoolboy and youth team levels. With the Bhoys he starred in two League championship-winning sides (1970 and 1972); in two Scottish Cup winning teams (1971 and 1972) and in two victorious Scottish League Cup finals (1972 and 1973). He

also collected a handful of League Cup runners-up medals. And above all he scored plenty of goals!

After seven years at Parkhead Macari was one of several Scotsmen signed by manager Tommy Docherty shortly after he had taken over the reins at Manchester United, Macari moving to Old Trafford in January 1973 for £200,000.

From the glory days at Celtic he found it tough going for a time in the First Division of English football, a bit of a culture shock, and at the end the 1973-74 season he tasted relegation for the first time in his career!

United bounced back quickly, though, and in 1976 they reached the FA Cup Final only to be beaten by Southampton. The following year United were back at Wembley and this time - after Macari's shot was deflected into the net by Jimmy Greenhoff - they went one better and beat Liverpool 2-1 to win the trophy for the fourth time. In 1979, however, Macari was a loser again (when United were beaten in the last minute by Arsenal).

Macari went on to score 97 goals in exactly 400 senior appearances for United before he left Old Trafford to become player-manager of Swindon Town in July 1984. He was sacked in April 1985 after a row with his assistant and former Manchester United goalkeeper Harry Gregg, but was reinstated by the club six days later. Macari then steered Swindon from the Fourth to the Second Division in two seasons. The Robins captured the Fourth Division crown with a massive 102 points in 1986 and twelve months later beat Gillingham in the 1987 play-off final. Two years on and Swindon again reached the play-offs, but this time they lost out to Crystal Palace. From The County Ground Macari was given the manager's job at West Ham (July 1989). He held firm at Upton Park for just 28 weeks, leaving in February 1990 after seeing his side walloped 6-0 by Oldham Athletic in a League Cup semi-finalencounter at Boundary Park

A month earlier the FA had charged Macari and his former Swindon chairman, Brian Hillier, of unauthorised betting on a League game involving Swindon Town.

Macari returned to management in February 1991 when he took over from fellow Scotsman Dave Mackay at St Andrew's. He guided Blues to victory in the Leyland DAF Final at Wembley over Tranmere Rovers but surprisingly resigned shortly afterwards,

Lou Macari

saying that the club lacked ambition!

Macari was soon offered the gaffer's job at Stoke City and he took them to the Third Division play-offs at the end of his first season in charge but they lost to Stockport County on aggregate. Three days later he gained sweet revenge when the same opponents were beaten in the Autoglass Trophy at Wembley.

Stoke comfortably took the Second Division title with 93 points in 1993 when tremendous support boosted the team. However, Macari became unsettled and in November 1993 took the manager's job at his former club Celtic, only to return to the Potteries for a second stint with Stoke in October 1994, holding office this time until May 1997. Stoke played 250 League games under his charge (winning 108). In 1999 Macari was appointed Huddersfield's European scout.

MACCLESFIELD TOWN

Blues' playing record against the Silkmen is:
LEAGUE CUP

Home	1	1	0	0	6	0
Away	1	1	0	0	3	0
Totals	2	2	0	0	9	0

Blues defeated the Silkmen 9-0 over two legs in a second round League Cup-tie in September 1998, winning 3-0 at Moss Rose and 6-0 at St Andrew's. Gary Rowett and Chris Marsden scored in both legs....and this is an aggregate scoring record for Blues at competitive level. Only 3,443 fans saw the game at St Andrew's (the lowest for a major League, FA Cup, League Cup or Fairs Cup match on the ground since April 1913 - 65 years) while just 2,275 hardy souls turned out at Macclesfield.

The first meeting between the clubs was in March 1888 when Blues won a home friendly encounter 3-2.

Players with both clubs include: R Knight, T Neale (Blues reserve), R Price, B Sedgemore.

McCLURE, Alec

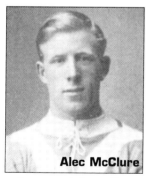

Alec McClure

Alec McClure was a solid defender with superb positional sense who served with five major Midland clubs between 1911 and 1928. Born in Workington on 3 April 1892, he played initially for Grangemouth Juniors in Cumbria before joining Blues in January 1912. He became the fulcrum of the defence at St Andrew's and for almost twelve seasons was like a rock, accumulating a fine record of 198 senior appearances and scoring four goals.

A sailor in World War One, McClure participated in the Zebrugge Affair (one of the great military actions) and after the hostilities had ended he returned to St Andrew's and helped Blues win the Second Division championship (1921). In May 1923 while on tour with Blues in Spain, he was sent-off against Real Madrid for telling his goalkeeper Dan Tremelling where to stand (right by an upright) when facing a penalty kick!

McClure joined Aston Villa in December 1923 and ten months later, in October 1924, He was transferred to Stoke. Two years after that he moved Coventry City and after ending his playing days with

Walsall (March-May 1928) he took a job training the colts at Luton Town. Brief spells with Bromsgrove Rovers and Market Harborough followed before he returned to St Andrew's as trainer of Blues' junior team (the third XI which came into being at the time of McClure's return). He retained that position until 1932 when he was appointed assistant-manager to Leslie Knighton, later assuming the same role under boss George Liddell. McClure left Blues in 1934 to work for Rudge Motor Cycles and later ran a very successful haulage business in Small Heath. McClure died in Birmingham in August 1973.

● There was a strong link with football within the McClure family. Alec's brother Sammy played for Blackburn Rovers and his nephew Joe for Everton. His daughter now lives in Droitwich.

McMILLAN, Johnny

Jimmy McMillan and his strike partner Bob McRoberts both scored five goals in Blues' 10-1 win over Blackpool in March 1901. He was an excellent marksman, left-footed who complimented every centre-forward and left-winger he played with during his senior career which saw him net well over 150 goals in major League and Cup competitions with 25 coming in just 52 appearances for Blues.

Born in Port Glasgow on 16 February 1871, he played for Port Glasgow Athletic and then St Bernard's of Edinburgh before joining Derby County in December 1890. He was joined by England ace Steve Bloomer in 1892 and together they formed a lethal partnership, McMillan going on to register 50 goals for the Rams, including another fivetimer in a 9-0 win over Wolves in his seventh outing for the club. He remained a front line player at Derby until 1896 when he moved to Leicester Fosse with whom he stayed for four-and-a-half seasons before signing for Blues in January 1901. He again did well at Filbert Street, netting another 48 goals in 131 outings. Leading by example, he prompted Fosse to its first serious promotion challenge in 1899 and took a club benefit from a friendly with Notts County before he left for Birmingham. With Blues he experienced promotion, relegation and promotion again during an eventful stay. Towards the end of his time with the club he was severely handicapped by injury and he left Blues for Bradford City in May 1903. He was made skipper at Valley Parade for their inaugural League season and as time went on he gradually prepared himself for management, taking his first job with Glossop in May 1906, while also being registered as a player. He returned to Blues as first team trainer in August 1909, a position he held right up until the outbreak of the Great War. After the hostilities had ended he returned to management, this time with Gillingham (1919-22), initially earning £7-a-week plus bonuses. He later became a licensee in Derby. McMillan died in Birkdale on 3 November 1941.

● His Leicester-born son, Stuart, was also a player with Derby County, Wolves, Chelsea, Clapton Orient and Bradford City and he managed Derby in the 1946 FA Cup Final win.

McROBERTS, Bob

Bob McRoberts was Birmingham's first full-time manager, being appointed into the St Andrew's 'hot seat' in July 1910. As a player McRoberts had been a great favourite with the Blues supporters. He was an elegant, ball-juggling utility forward who preferred to score his goals with precision rather than using a booming shot or nudge-over-the-line. Born in Coatbridge, Scotland in July

1874, he played for his home town club before joining Airdrieonians in 1893. He then had a spell with Albion Rovers and entered the Football League with Gainsborough Trinity in August 1896. Two years later (August 1898) Blues secured his services for £150 and over the next seven seasons he scored 82 goals in 187 first team matches, helping Blues win the Second Division championship in 1901 at the first attempt.

Occasionally he was criticised for holding the ball too long - indeed, quite often he over-elaborated to the extreme by trying to beat an extra player rather than having a shot at goal or passing to a colleague. Nevertheless, he was a terrific footballer, somewhat eccentric at times, and it was something of a surprise in some quarters when he left St Andrew's to join Chelsea in August 1905 for £100, becoming the London club's first-ever signing! He spent four years at Stamford Bridge, helping Chelsea consolidate their position in the Football League. He played in their first-ever League game against Stockport County and during his time at the 'Bridge' he was also used as a centre-half.

Bob McRoberts

His management days with Blues lasted five years, up to August 1915. During that time the team had mixed results, although they did finish third in the Second Division 1913, missing promotion by seven points.

McRoberts died in Birkenhead on 27 February 1959, aged 84.

- In April 1905 McRoberts was presented with an illuminated address in recognition of five years magnificent service to the club.

MACKAY, Dave

As a footballer Dave Mackay was one of the greatest of his era. He won just about every honour in the game during his long and distinguished playing career that spanned 20 years. A barrel-chested, hard-tackling wing-half, he started out with Heart of Midlothian in April 1952, having learnt the game with Slateford Athletic and Newton Range Star in Edinburgh where he was born on 14 November 1934.

A driving force behind the attack he had a tough, no-nonsense approach to the game and was totally committed, never shirking a tackle, going in where it hurt and often coming out on top.

During his seven years at Tynecastle Park, Mackay won the first of his 22 full international caps and represented the Scottish League XI. He also gained a League championship medal (1958), two Scottish League Cup winners' medals (1955 and 1959) and a Scottish Cup winners' medal (1956). He joined Tottenham Hotspur in March 1959 and at White Hart Lane he slotted into a 'footballing machine' run by Bill Nicholson. With Danny Blanchflower occupying the right-half berth and John White aiding and abetting from the inside-right position, the Spurs midfield was the best in the country. This was clearly emphasised when the double was won in 1960-61, the FA Cup retained the following season and victory achieved in the European Cup Winners Cup Final in 1963, although Mackay missed the latter triumph with a stomach injury.

He won a third FA Cup winners' medal with Spurs in 1967 and when he left the London club for Derby County in July 1968 he had amassed an exceptionally fine record of 364 appearances and 63 goals.

At the end of his first season at The Baseball Ground (under Brian Clough) Mackay was voted joint PFA 'Footballer of the Year' (with Manchester City's Tony Book) as the Rams swept to promotion from the Second Division. In May 1971 he was appointed player-manager of Swindon Town; in November 1972 he took charge of Nottingham Forest and returned to his former club Derby County as their boss in October 1973, a position he held until November 1976. A spell out of the game preceded his appointment as Walsall boss in March 1977, but after a year with the Saddlers, Mackay decided to try his luck in the Far East, taking charge of Al-Arabi Sporting Club in Kuwait. Eight years later he was handed the manager's job at Alba Shabab (Dubai) but in December 1987 he returned to England to take over the reins of struggling Doncaster Rovers. He stayed at Belle Vue until March 1989 and the following month was given the Blues job in succession to Garry Pendrey, being officially appointed by the Kumars.

He held his position until January 1991 when ironically after being given a vote of confidence by the Kumars, Mackay handed in his resignation.

Blues had finished a respectable seventh in the Third Division at the end of Mackay's first full season in charge. Overall though he had a mediocre record at St Andrew's, Blues winning only 34 and

Dave Mackay

had a mediocre record at St Andrew's, Blues winning only 34 and losing 30 of the 91 League and Cup games played under his control. He signed almost £800,000 worth of players with Nigel Gleghorn at £175,000 the dearest buy. His sales/transfers 'out' amounted to just under £600,000, with £500,000 coming in from one source, Kevin Ashley, sold to Wolves.

After leaving St Andrew's Mackay's last major appointment took him to Egypt as manager-coach of FC Zamalek in September 1991.

● As a player Mackay appeared in 36 FA Cup-ties for Spurs and was on the losing side just three times. Unfortunately he missed four major Cup Finals through injury!

MALLETT, Joe

Joe Mallett came to St Andrew's having already proved his worth as an excellent technical coach. He was handed the Blues manager's job in July 1964, following the departure of Gil Merrick, but failed to translate his coaching skills from training ground to match play and during his eighteen months in charge Blues won only 15 of 64 fixtures played.

Born in Gateshead on 8 January 1916, Mallett was a wing-half with Charlton Athletic, Queens Park Rangers, Fulham and West Ham United (as a Wartime guest) and Leyton Orient before becoming a coach at Nottingham Forest in August 1954. He initially moved to St Andrew's as a coach but was quickly offered the managers' job which he accepted without hesitation.

From December 1965 Mallett acted as assistant-boss to Stan Cullis. In March 1970 he became coach of the Greek club Panionios (Athens) and after six months coaching rivals Appollon, he returned for a second spell with Panionios (1973-74) before going to the States to coach New York Cosmos. He later held two separate scouting positions with Southampton and coached again in the NASL with San Jose Earthquakes.

MANAGERS

Blues' managers from 1892 when they entered the Football League: (Prior to 1892 team affairs were placed in the hands of a committee).

July 1892-June 1908 . . . . .Alfred Jones
July 1908-June 1910 . . . . .Alex Watson
July 1910-May 1915 .Bob McRoberts
May 1915-May 1923 .Frank Richards
May 1923-March 1927 . . . . .Billy Beer
March 1927-May 1928 . . . . .Bill Harvey
August 1928-May 1933 . . . . .Leslie Knighton
July 1933-September 1939 . . . . .George Liddell
October 1939-November 1944 . . . . .William A. Camkin
November 1944-May 1945 . . . . .Ted Goodier
June 1945-November 1948 . . . . .Harry Storer
January 1949-October 1954 . . . . .Bob Brocklebank
November 1954-September 1958 . . . . .Arthur Turner
February 1958-May 1960 . . . . .Pat Beasley
May 1960-April 1964 . . . . .Gil Merrick
July 1964-December 1965 . . . . .Joe Mallett
December 1965-March 1970 . . . . .Stan Cullis
May 1971-September 1975 . . . . .Freddie Goodwin
September 1975-Sepotember 1977 . . . . .Willie Bell
September 1977-March 1978 . . . . .Sir Alf Ramsey
March 1978-February 1982 . . . . .Jim Smith
February 1982-January 1986 . . . . .Ron Saunders
January 1986-May 198 .John Bond
May 1987-April 1989 .Garry Pendrey
April 1989-January 199 . . . . .Dave Mackay
February 1991-June 1991 . . . . .Lou Macari
August 1991-December 1993 . . . . .Terry Cooper
December 1993-May 1996 . . . . .Barry Fry
May 1996 to date . . . . .Trevor Francis

Photograph showing manager George Liddell (centre) with his Blues side from 1936.

MANAGERIAL NOTES

- Chief Scout Bill Coldwell was Blues' caretaker-manager for three months, prior to the appointment of Terry Cooper.
- The playing side of the club was run by a selected committee for almost 17 years: from September 1875 until June 1892.
- Alfred 'Inky' Jones was the club's first 'manager' assuming that title along with that of secretary. He held office for 16 years, having been secretary in 1885, taking over from WH 'Billy' Edmunds.
- Jones, Alex Watson and Frank Richards all held the joint position of secretary-manager of Birmingham City Football Club (Small Heath).
- Richards was certainly more of an administrator than a team manager and, in fact, he did not have the final say in the formation or selection of the team! He took over the reins during the Great War and held the position for eight years. It was Richards who failed to enter Blues in the 1921-22 FA Cup competition.
- Pat Beasley and Arthur Turner were joint managers at St Andrew's for seven months from February-September 1958.
- Eight ex-players have returned (or stayed on) to manage Birmingham City football club. They are Bob McRoberts, Billy Beel, Bill Harvey, George Liddell, Gil Merrick, Arthur Turner, Garry Pendrey and Trevor Francis.
- The man who has remained in office for the longest period of time has been George Liddell - a fraction over six years: 1933-39.
- Ex-Blues star Howard Kendall (with Everton in 1985) and former Blues boss Ron Saunders (twice with Aston Villa in 1975 and 1981) were both honoured with the 'Manager of the Year' award.
- Trevor Francis when boss of QPR said: "I am not difficult to get on with....I'm just difficult to get to know." And as Sheffield Wednesday's manager Francis lost both the 1993 League Cup Final and FA Cup Final at Wembley.
- Barry Fry, when given the sack as Blues manager, left this message on his answerphone: 'Kristina (his wife) has gone shopping and I'm at the job centre looking for employment. Funny old game, isn't it."
- Sir Alf Ramsey managed England to victory in the 1966 World Cup Final, took them to the quarter-finals as holders in 1970 and saw them gain third place in the European championships.
- Manager Harry Storer signed Martin O'Donnell three times for three different clubs. Initially he secured his services for Blues (May 1947), then Coventry City (October 1949) and finally Derby County (July 1955). They weren't related!
- Ex-Blues forward Jack Peart died in 1948 when manager of Fulham.
- Bob Brocklebank sold, transferred, released over 40 players during his five years in charge at St Andrew's.
- After Stan Cullis had left Blues in March 1970 the club began to search for his replacement. First choice was Brian Clough (no joy). Next it was Don Revie (no luck) and thirdly they went for Ronnie Allen (again nothing doing). Blues eventually secured the services of Freddie Goodwin.

PLAYER TO MANAGER

Here is a list of Blues players who went into soccer management:
Senior Level
Jimmy Allen * . . . . .Colchester United
Ian Atkins . . .Cambridge United, Carlisle United, Chester City, Colchester United, Doncaster Rovers.
Bertie Auld . . . .Dumbarton, Hamilton Academical, Hibernian, Partick Thistle
Billy Beer . . . . .Birmingham (City)
Noel Blake . . . . .Exeter City
Harold Bodle . . . . .Accrington Stanley
Tommy Briggs . . . . .Glentoran
Steve Bruce . . . . .Huddersfield Town, Sheffield United
Alan Buckley .Walsall, West Bromwich Albion, Grimsby Town

Arthur Turner and Pat Beasley flanked by reserve team trainer Tom Jones (left) and senior trainer Ken Fish (right)

Frank Buckley . . .Blackpool, Hull City, Leeds United, Norwich City, Notts County, Walsall, Wolverhampton Wanderers
Micky Bullock . . . . .Halifax Town
Alan Curbishley . . . . .Charlton Athletic
Stan Davies . . . . .Rotherham United
Neil Dougall . . . . .Plymouth Argyle
Greg Downs . . . . .Hereford United
Charlie Elliott* .Coventry City
Ronnie Fenton . . . . .Notts County
Trevor Francis . .Sheffield Wednesday, QPR, Birmingham City
Archie Gemmill . . . . .Rotherham United
Jimmy Greenhoff . . . . . .Crewe Alexandra, Port Vale, Rochdale
Paul Hart . . . . .Chesterfield
Bill Harvey . . . . .Birmingham (City), Chesterfield, Gillingham
Terry Hennessey . . . . .Heidelberg
Harry Hibbs . . . . .Walsall
Mike Kelly . . . . .Plymouth Argyle
Howard Kendall . . . . .Athletic Bilbao, Blackburn Rovers, Everton, Manchester City, Notts County
George Liddell .Birmingham City
Albert Lindon . . . . .Charlton Athletic, Merthyr Town (Tydfil)
Roy McDonough . . . . .Colchester United
John McMillan . . . . .Gillingham
Bob McRoberts . . . . .Birmingham (City)
Dave Mangnall . . . . .QPR
Gil Merrick . . . . .Birmingham City
Johnny Newman .Exeter City, Grimsby Town, Hereford United
Syd Owen . . . . .Luton Town
Jack Peart . . . . .Fulham
Garry Pendrey .Birmingham City
Mick Rathbone .Halifax Town
Bruce Rioch . . . . .Arsenal, Bolton Wanderers, Middlesbrough, Millwall, Torquay United
Ray Shaw . . . . .Walsall
Billy Steel . . . . .Airdrieonians, Third Lanark
Colin Todd . . . . .Bolton Wanderers, Middlesbrough, Swindon
Arthur Turner . . . . .Oxford United, Birmingham City
Jack Wheeler . . . . .Notts County
Peter Withe . . . . .Wimbledon
Frank Womack . .Grimsby Town, Leicester City, Notts County, Oldham Athletic, Torquay United
Frank Worthington . . . . .Tranmere Rovers
Ron Wylie . . . . .West Bromwich Albion
*Blues Wartime guest

Intermediate (Non-League) Level

Jack Badham	Alec McClure*
Ned Barkas	Jim McDonagh
Keith Bowker	Owen Madden
Barry Bridges	Dennis Mortimer
Kevan Broadhurst	Jock Mulraney
Eddie Brown	Dick Neal
Kenny Burns	Sid Ottewell
Wayne Clarke	Steve Phillips
John Connolly	John Roberts
Johnny Crosbie	Craig Russell
Gerry Daly	Johnny Schofield
Joe Gallagher	Geoff Scott
Billy Garton	Joe Smith
Tony Godden	Bobby A Thomson

Micky Halsall	William Baird Walker
Terry Hibbitt	Syd Wallington
Trevor Hockey	Jack Whitehouse
Bobby Hope	Steve Whitton
Graham Leggatt	Pat Wright

* Managed Blues' colts side.

MANCHESTER CITY (Ardwick)

Blues' playing record against City:

FOOTBALL LEAGUE

Venue	P	W	D	L	F	A
Home	58	36	11	11	130	70
Away	58	9	10	37	53	111
Totals	116	45	21	48	183	181

FA CUP

	P	W	D	L	F	A
Home	6	5	0	1	17	5
Away	1	0	0	1	0	4
Neutral	1	0	0	1	1	3
Totals	8	5	0	3	18	12

LEAGUE CUP

	P	W	D	L	F	A
Home	1	1	0	0	6	0

TEST MATCHES

	P	W	D	L	F	A
Home	1	1	0	0	8	0
Away	1	0	0	1	0	3
Totals	2	1	0	1	8	3

FOOTBALL ALLIANCE

	P	W	D	L	F	A
Home	1	1	0	0	4	0
Away	1	0	1	0	2	2
Totals	2	1	1	0	6	2

WARTIME

	P	W	D	L	F	A
Home	1	0	1	0	0	0
Away	1	0	0	1	0	1
Totals	2	0	1	1	0	1

Blues clinched the Second Division championship with a hard-earned 3-2 home win over Manchester City (then known as Ardwick) on 1 April 1893.

Earlier that season - the first game between the clubs - saw Fred Wheldon's goal give Blues a 1-0 away win.

Blues' best League win over City followed soon afterwards when they comfortably recorded a 10-2 success at Muntz Street in March 1894 - on their way to the runners-up spot in the Second Division. Frank Mobley led the goal feast with a hat-trick. Fred Wheldon and Jack Hallam both scored twice.

Blues' last League game before leaving Muntz Street for St Andrew's saw them lose 1-0 at Manchester City on Christmas Day 1906.

The first time Manchester City played at St Andrew's was against Blues on 29 March 1907. A crowd of 10,000 saw Blues canter to a 4-0 win with Percy 'Putt' Gooch scoring his only goal for the club.

In season 1925-26 Blues completed the double over relegated City, winning 1-0 at home and 4-2 away, George Briggs netting twice at Maine Road in front of 60,000 spectators.

Blues netted seven League goals against City in 1928-29 - winning 4-1 at St Andrew's on the opening Saturday and 3-2 at Maine Road in late December.

Another seven goals were claimed the following season as Blues won 3-0 at home and 4-1 away, Tom Fillingham netting twice in the latter contest.

149

1956 FA Cup Final action: German-born goalkeeper Bert Trautmann and centre-half Dave Ewing (Manchester City) thwart Eddie Brown (Blues).

Blues were defeated 4-2 by City away and then 5-1 at St Andrew's in the space of fourteen months during the early 1930s and, in fact, up until 1938 Blues were second best in most matches against City.

When Blues lost 1-0 at Maine Road on 8 September 1948 it brought to an end a club record run of 15 away League games without defeat.

When the teams met again a week later, dynamic Scotsman Jackie Stewart scored all Blues' goals in their emphatic 4-1 home win over City in front of 40,000 fans at St Andrew's.

And then over 30,000 spectators saw Blues crash 4-0 to City at Maine Road in November 1949 while a similar crowd witnessed Blues 1-0 home win in March - but at the end of the day both clubs were relegated to the Second Division that season!

Manchester City's infamous 'M' Plan (revolving round Don Revie) was ripped apart by attack-minded Blues at St Andrew's in October 1957 to the tune of 4-0, Peter Murphy grabbing a hat-trick this time.

On Boxing Day 1958 Blues raced to a convincing 6-1 home League win over City with both Alex Jackson and Bunny Larkin scoring twice.

Terry Hennessey made his League debut for Blues in a 3-2 home win over Manchester City in March 1961 when he helped mark Scottish international Denis Law, scorer of both City's goals!

Bob Latchford scored his first hat-trick for Blues in a 4-1 home win over City in September 1972 (Division 1).

In October 1980 an 89th minute penalty, converted by Archie Gemmill after Alan Ainscow had been tripped inside the area, gave Blues a 1-0 win at Maine Road and nine years later a Tony Evans hat-trick earned Blues a 3-0 home win over City (September 1981).

A vital promotion encounter at Maine Road ended in a 1-0 defeat for Blues in April 1999. Winger Jon McCarthy unfortunately broke his leg for the second time that season in this match.

City were whipped 5-0 by Blues at St Andrew's in a fifth round FA Cup-tie in February 1947, Cyril Trigg scoring two of the goals in front of 50,000 fans. Both Trigg and Jock Mulraney had outstanding games.

In March 1955 a sixth round FA Cup-tie attracted a crowd of 58,000 to St Andrew's. Manchester City won 1-0 with an 88th minute goal by Johnny Hart whose deflected effort from Roy Clarke's free-kick struck Blues' keeper Gil Merrick on the right wrist and head before entering the net.

Roy Warhurst, later to move to Maine Road, said: "It was the biggest fluke in football I ever saw."

Noel Kinsey's goal was not enough as Blues were defeated 3-1 by City in the 1956 FA Cup final at Wembley. Bert Trautmann Manchester's German-born goalkeeper, played on despite fracturing his neck in a collision with the Blues' striker Peter Murphy.

There were two own-goals and a penalty (hammered in by Stan Lynn) in Blues' emphatic 6-0 home League Cup win over City in December 1962. This is Blues' joint biggest League Cup victory (home or away).

Despite beating City 8-0 at Muntz Street in the last of four end-of-season Test Matches in April 1896, Blues failed to hold on to their First Division status. They were relegated having earlier lost 3-0 away to Manchester City, crashed 4-0 at Liverpool and drawing 0-0 with the Merseysiders at home.

Two players, Jack Jones and Fred Wheldon, both scored hat-tricks in that eight-goal romp.

Players with both clubs include: J Beckford, J Beresford, W Blyth, L Bradbury, F Buckley, T Capel, F Carrodus, W Clarke, J Conlin, T Cooke, P Cooper, FW Corbett (Blues reserve), A Coton, P Doherty (Blues guest), G Dorsett (Blues trialist), R Dryden, T Francis, N Gleghorn, J Godfrey, A Harley, G Hicks, S Hiley, R Hopkins, K Langley, P Moulden, A Mulraney (MC guest), W Mumford (MC apprentice), R Ranson, J Sheridan (MC junior), C Shutt, AW Smith (MC guest), R Taylor, J Thorogood (MC trialist), A Towers, A Wallace, M Ward, W Wardle, R Warhurst, D Wassall, JS Watson, J Wilson (Blues reserve).

Also: John Bond and Ron Saunders (managers of both clubs), Howard Kendall (Blues player, MC manager), Leslie Knighton (MC assistant-secretary-manager, Blues manager), Ian Bowyer (MC player, Blues coach), Alf Wood (MC striker, Blues lottery salesman).

MANCHESTER UNITED (Newton H...

Blues' playing record against the Reds is:

FOOTBALL LEAGUE

Venue	P	W	D	L	F	A
Home	40	15	15	10	62	53
Away	40	9	8	23	34	60
Totals	80	24	23	33	96	113

FA CUP

Home	4	1	2	1	5	6
Away	4	0	2	2	4	9
Neutral	1	0	0	1	0	2
Totals	9	1	4	4	9	17

TEST MATCHES

Neutral	2	0	1	1	3	6

FOOTBALL ALLIANCE

Home	3	2	1	0	6	4
Away	3	0	1	2	5	15
Totals	6	2	2	2	11	19

WARTIME

Home	1	1	0	0	3	1
Away	1	0	1	0	1	1
Totals	2	1	1	0	4	2

Blues joint heaviest defeat in the Football Alliance was 9-1 - suffered at the hands of Manchester United (Newton Heath) away from home on the last day of the 1889-90 season.

The first Football League meeting between the clubs took place at the Bank Street ground, Manchester on 10 October 1896. It ended 1-1 in front of 7,000 spectators. Six weeks later Blues won the return fixture 1-0 with a goal by Jack Jones.

United's first visit to St Andrew's in March 1907 ended in a 1-1 draw and their first win at the ground followed eight months later in November when a seven-goal thriller went in their favour by 4-3.

Only 8,948 paying customers - one of the smallest crowds ever to attend a competitive game between the two clubs - witnessed the 2-1 home win for Blues in April 1926.

Eleven goals were scored in the two League games in 1938-39. United won 4-1 at Old Trafford before taking a point from a 3-3 draw at St Andrew's.

In November 1948 FA Cup holders United beat Blues 3-0 at Old Trafford in front of 45,482 fans but at the same venue the following season Blues turned the tide with a 2-0 scoreline, Johnny Berry, later to join United, scoring one of the goals.

When Blues returned to the top flight in 1955 they opened their League programme at St Andrew's with a 2-2 draw against the Busby Babes and the following season the fixture was reversed as Blues drew their opening game 2-2 at Old Trafford.

The last time Blues met United before the Munich air disaster was at St Andrew's in December 1957. A crowd of almost 36,000 witnessed a 3-3 draw. And in the penultimate League match of that season goals by Harry Hooper and Ken Green (only his second for the club) gave Blues an unexpected 2-0 win at Old Trafford - as United had their minds on the FA Cup Final!

On 29 November 1958 Blues lost 4-0 at Old Trafford - a week after they had won 4-0 at Tottenham! And there was another heavy loss, 4-1 again on United soil in April 1961.

An excellent 2-0 Blues win at United six months later was followed with a fine 3-1 home victory over the FA Cup winners elect in May 1963.

When Blues won 2-1 at Old Trafford in front of 44,695 fans in January 1964, Geoff Anderson made his one and only first team

Steve Bruce

appearance for the club and 17 year-old Micky Bullock scored one of his side's goals.

Over 52,000 spectators saw Blues lose 1-0 to United in Manchester in October 1972 and there were 51,278 spectators present to see Blues win the return fixture that season by 3-1, Alan Campbell sealing victory with a penalty.

Alan Buckley scored twice when bottom-of-the-table Blues beat Manchester United 5-1 at St Andrew's in a First Division encounter in November 1978 - this after more than 56,000 fans had witnessed United's opening day 1-0 win at Old Trafford.

The last League game between Blues and United took place on 29 March 1986 when a crowd of 22,551 at St Andrew's saw Ian Handysides score in the 1-1 draw.

Blues were beaten by United 2-0 in the 1957 FA Cup semi-final at Hillsborough.

After holding United to a 2-2 draw at St Andrew's in a fifth round FA Cup-tie in February 1969 Blues travelled to Old Trafford for the replay and crashed 6-2 in front of 61,934 fans. A crowd of 51,685 had witnessed the first match.

A crowd of 13,330 saw defender Chris Whyte score the only goal for Blues in a friendly against United at St Andrew's in August 1995.

The two Test Matches took place in April 1893. Blues drew 1-1 at Stoke and lost 5-2 at Bramall Lane, results that saw them relegated from the First Division. Players with both clubs include: J Berry, R Bonthron, S Bruce, F Buckley, W Carrier (United junior), T Cooke, A Coton (later United coach), C Craven, G Daly, S Davies (United trialist), JW Fall, W Garton, R Gibson, D Givens, J Greenhoff, G Hicks, FC Hodges, CAL Jenkyns, W Johnston (United trialist), FW Jones, HH Lappin, J Merrick (Blues & United reserve), RS Morton, W Rudd (United amateur), MC Russell, L Sealey (Blues N/C), S Sutton (United trialist), JE Travers, D Wallace, J Wealands.

Also: Freddie Goodwin and Lou Macari (United players, Blues managers), Syd Owen (Blues player, United coach).

Martin Buchan (United) shields the ball away from Trevor Francis during Blues' 1-0 win at St Andrew's in March 1974.

MANGNALL, Dave

Strong, hard-shooting inside or centre-forward Dave Mangnall scored 15 goals in 39 appearances for Blues between February 1934 and March 1935. Signed as a possible long-term replacement for Joe Bradford, he never really settled in the Midlands (despite his excellent strike record) and on leaving St Andrew's he joined West Ham United for almost £3,000.

Born in Wigan on 21 September 1907, he played his early football in Yorkshire and did well with Maltby New Church (for whom he scored 52 goals in one season) and Maltby Colliery FC (35 goals in one campaign) before having trials with Rotherham United and Huddersfield Town.

He joined Doncaster Rovers as an amateur in August 1923, but stayed only a season with the newly-elected Third Division (N) side. In fact, he quit the game for a while and was working down the mine when, in November 1927, he signed professional forms for Leeds United.

After scoring 10 goals for United's intermediate League side in a 13-0 win over Stockport County in September 1929, he made his senior debut four days later. But he never fitted in at Elland Road and moved to the club that rejected him, Huddersfield Town, for £3,000 in December 1929, replacing George Brown (sold to Aston Villa).

He was a star performer (at times) for the Terriers and netted a club record 42 goals in 1931-32 only to be relegated to the reserves the following season! His final record with Huddersfield was impressive - 73 goals in 90 senior appearances. He then left to join struggling Blues.

After Blues he grabbed 28 goals in 35 Second Division outings for the Hammers before transferring to neighbours Millwall in May 1936. Two years later he skippered the Lions to the Third Division (S) title, top-scoring with 18 goals, having earlier led Millwall against Sunderland in the 1937 FA Cup semi-final. A row over terms saw him leave The Den in May 1938, but he returned to League soccer with QPR just before the outbreak of World War Two. He was appointed manager at Loftus Road in 1944 and guided Rangers to the Third Division (S) championship in 1947-48. But when the London club suffered relegation in 1952 Mangnall's footballing career ended. He retired to live in Penzance where he died on 10 April 1962.

MANSFIELD TOWN

Blues' playing record against the Stags is:
FOOTBALL LEAGUE

Venue	P	W	D	L	F	A
Home	2	1	1	0	4	1
Away	2	1	0	1	4	6
Totals	4	2	1	1	8	7

LEAGUE CUP

Home	1	0	0	1	0	1
Away	2	0	1	1	3	4
Totals	3	0	1	2	3	5

LEYLAND DAF TROPHY

Home	1	1	0	0	2	0

WARTIME

Home	1	1	0	0	4	1
Away	1	0	0	1	1	4
Totals	2	1	0	1	5	5

The first League meeting between Blues and the Stags was at St Andrew's on 3 March 1990. Blues won 4-1 but a month later at Field Mill, Mansfield gained sweet revenge with a 5-2 victory, making it 12 goals in 180 minutes of action-packed football!

The League Cup-tie at St Andrew's was played in 1965-66, while the two-legged contest in the same competition in 1987-88 saw Blues beaten 3-2 on aggregate by the Stags.

Amazingly both Second World War encounters ended in 4-1 home wins!

Players with both clubs include: G Anderson, S Barrowclough, J Daws, R Devey, A Green, TW Grice (reserve), J Hall, J Herriot, EA Liney, JW Morfitt, TJ Morgan, J Needham, SC Ottewell, D Peer, A Phoenix, N Platnauer, HC Randle (Blues reserve), D Rowbottom, B Sedgemore, F Shaw, FH Shell (Blues reserve), MA Smalley, SJ Storer (Stags YTS), S Sutton, N Whatmore, F White (guest).

Also: Johnny Newman (Blues player, Stags chief scout), George Foster (Town player, Blues coach).

MARTIN, Ray

Ray Martin

Full-back Ray Martin scored one goal for Blues in 374 senior appearances - against Hull City in April 1970.

But scoring was certainly not his game - he was a defender, and a good one at that, who gave Blues excellent service and at the end of the day thoroughly deserved his testimonial. Born in Wolverhampton on 23 January 1945, he represented South East Staffs Boys before joining Aston Villa as a junior, moving across the City to St Andrew's as an apprentice in June 1961, signing professional forms in May 1962.

He was carefully nurtured by Blues and after representing the FA XI youth side he duly made his senior debut on his 19th birthday. Martin never looked back after that. Occasionally the victim of abuse from the terraces, he battled on became was a much-loved

full-back, honest, consistent, resilient. He helped Blues win promotion in 1972 and was twice voted the club's 'Player of the Year' in 1970 and again in 1971.

He left St Andrew's for Portland Timber (NASL) in the summer of 1976 and three years later he retired to become a soccer coach at Oregon State University, a position he held well into the 1990s.

● One interesting fact: during a training session with Villa Martin accidentally broke manager Joe Mercer's toe. Did this lead to his departure?

MATTHEWSON, Trevor

As a central defender and an occasional over-lapping full-back Trevor Matthewson made well over 500 senior appearances as a professional during a 15-year career at League level. Born in Sheffield on 12 February 1963, he was an apprentice at Hillsborough before turning professional with Wednesday on his 18th birthday. Thereafter he played, in turn, for Newport County (from October 1983), Stockport County (1985), Lincoln City (1987), Blues (signed for £45,000 in July 1989, left in August 1983), Preston North End (until 1994), Bury and finally Hereford United, retiring in 1997. He skippered Lincoln to the GM Vauxhall Conference title in 1988 and was a member of the Blues team that lifted the Leyland DAF trophy in 1991, one of his 203 appearances for the club (13 goals scored). A very reliable performer who was the first player to appear in 46 League games in a season for Blues.

MEDALS

Bertie Auld won 14 winners' medals at club level between 1963 and 1970 and he also gained three runners-up medals. His winners' prizes came with Blues (1963 League Cup) and Celtic (Scottish League championship 1966, 1967, 1968 and 1970; Scottish FA Cup 1965, 1967 and 1969; Scottish League Cup 1967, 1968, 1969 and 1970: European Cup 1967; World Club championship 1968). And his runners-up medals were collected with Blues (1961 Fairs Cup) and Celtic (Scottish Cup 1970, European Cup 1970).

Auld also won three full caps for Scotland and represented the Scottish League on two occasions.

Charlie Athersmith, before joining Blues in 1901, won five League Division One championship and two FA Cup winners' medals with Aston Villa and he also added an FA Cup runners-up medal to his tally as well.

Fred Wheldon, another Villa player, won three League championships and an FA Cup winners medal before adding a Second Division championship and a runners-up medal to his collection with Blues (1890s).

● Other Blues personnel who gained a hatful of League and Cup medals as players include Scottish-born managers Lou Macari and Dave Mackay, while Stan Cullis, before taking charge of Blues collected honours galore with Wolves both as a player and manager. Ron Saunders also achieved honours as a manager before bossing Blues, while Trevor Francis before returning to St Andrew's as manager in 1996, gained medals at club level both in the UK and in Italy. Howard Kendall, too, gained several medals in various competitions both as a player and manager after leaving St Andrew's. Bruce Rioch has also gained a few medals, likewise goalkeepers David Seaman and Gary Sprake, defenders Steve Bruce, Pat Van Den Hauwe and Nigel Winterburn, Jimmy Greenhoff and striker Peter Withe.

MERRICK, Gil

Gill Merrick

Regarded as one of the best goalkeepers in Great Britain during the early 1950s, Gil Merrick had the misfortune to be between the posts when the Hungarians put 13 goals past England in home and away internationals in 1953 and 1954. He was hardly to blame for that barrage and soon afterwards played in the World Cup finals in Switzerland - but for years he was still remembered as 'Mister 13'.

It is said that Merrick - who never wore a cap (the one given to him by his father was stolen in Argentina) - copied the style of Harry Hibbs, his illustrious predecessor in the Birmingham goal. Certainly there were many similarities between the two keepers, Merrick being calm, unspectacular with a technique all of his own, that of tremendous positional sense. He also used the whole framework of his body to stop shots as well as having a massive pair of hands.

A powerfully built man with dapper moustache, Merrick made 713 appearances for Blues (551 in League, FA Cup and Fairs Cup competitions and 162 during World War Two). He actually conceded only 666 goals in his major League and Cup games - a remarkable achievement. He helped Blues win the Football League South title in 1946, conceded only 24 goals in 41 League matches when the Second Division championship was won in 1955 and then he did his utmost to prevent Manchester City from winning the FA Cup the following year. Over a period of eight years from 1946 Merrick was very rarely absent from League action, international duties and the occasional injury disrupting his progress.

After being replaced by Johnny Schofield, Merrick announced his retirement as a player in 1960. He was immediately appointed Blues manager, leading them to the Inter Cities Fairs Cup Final at the end of his first season in charge. Two years later he saw Blues win the Football League Cup, defeating Aston Villa 3-1 over two legs in the Final. He held that position for four years and then went on to manage Bromsgrove Rovers and Atherstone Town during the late sixties.

Merrick was born in Sparkhill on 26 January 1922 and attended Acocks Green Council School. An Aston Villa supporter, he repre-

sented Birmingham Boys in the English Shield and Acocks Green in the South Birmingham Schools League before joining Shirley Juniors and then Solihull Town, playing briefly under former Blues defender Ned Barkas. From here he switched to Blues just before the outbreak of the Second World War. His first game for Blues was in the 'A' team against Wolves in a Birmingham Combination match on Jack Mould's ground. The Blues' side included Reg Foulkes (later to play for Walsall and Norwich City) and Dave Massart, while in the Wolves line-up there was Ted Elliott (goal), Billy Wright and Alan Steen.

During the hostilities Merrick started playing basketball (seriously) when serving as an infantryman in the Royal Warwickshire Regiment. He later joined the APT (PE) Corps and had his own gymnasium based in Oswestry. He had entered the services as a goalkeeper but came out as a centre-forward, having performed well in that position for the Western Command side at Shrewsbury and also against the Southern Command at Wrexham, scoring twice in the latter game. He played in attack after breaking a finger as a goalkeeper following impressive displays between the posts for the British Army against the French Army in Paris, versus the Belgian Army in Brussels and v the BAOR in Germany.

Merrick was the first Blues player to write a book: 'I See It All' published in 1954 by Museum Press. He also coached (soccer) at one of the biggest private schools in the country during the late 1940s, Greenmore College.

Merrick's father played for Nuneaton Borough for many years and Harry Clutterbuck, Birmingham's goalkeeper in the 1890s and later trainer at Moor Green, lived in the same street as Merrick - Fenton Road, Acocks Green.

MIDDLESBROUGH

Blues' playing record against 'Boro:

FOOTBALL LEAGUE

Venue	P	W	D	L	F	A
Home	41	21	13	7	74	45
Away	41	10	15	16	47	59
Totals	82	31	28	23	121	104

FA CUP

	P	W	D	L	F	A
Home	3	3	0	0	6	1
Away	2	1	1	0	1	0
Totals	5	4	1	0	7	1

LEAGUE CUP

	P	W	D	L	F	A
Home	2	2	0	0	5	2
Away	2	0	2	0	2	2
Totals	4	2	2	0	7	4

Blues were Middlesbrough's first League opponents on the Linthorpe Road ground on 9 September 1899. Blues won 3-1 and Bob McRoberts scored a hat-trick.

On Boxing Day 1905 Benny Green scored five goals as Blues beat Middlesbrough 7-0 in a League game at Muntz Street.

Twelve months later on Boxing Day 1906

Picture of old ball used in first game at St Andrew's.

Middlesbrough put on a much better display when they held Blues to a 0-0 draw in the first League game ever to be staged at St Andrew's. Around 32,000 fans were present in bitterly cold, snowy conditions to see the ground officially opened.

After gaining promotion to the First Division, Blues took three points off 'Boro in 1921-22, drawing 1-1 on Teeside and then winning 4-3 at St Andrew's, Joe Bradford and Harry Hampton both finding the net.

Two seasons later, in 1923-24, Blues completed the 'League' double over 'Boro.

Having spent a brief spell out of the top flight 'Boro returned to hammer Blues 5-1 at Ayresome Park in February 1930 and in October 1932 they raced to a convincing 4-1 victory at St Andrew's.

In between times Ernie Curtis netted two penalties in Blues' 3-0 home win over Middlesbrough in March 1932.

Another double for Blues arrived in 1934-35, both Frank White and Wilson Jones scoring two goals each in a 4-2 victory at St Andrew's, and another Blues double followed the very next season (2-0 away, 1-0 at home).

Blues failed to win any of the first four League games between the clubs after the Second World War. They finally broke through with an excellent 5-2 victory at Ayresome Park in April 1955 and followed up with a 3-0 home win 72 hours later.

In September 1967 Johnny Vincent, later to play for 'Boro, found the net with a crackerjack as Blues beat the Teesiders 6-1 at St Andrew's.

And on the last day of the following season Phil Summerill netted twice as Blues won 3-1 at St Andrew's.

'Boro claimed two 3-0 wins in 1974-75 under manager Jack Charlton's leadership and in the later seventies Trevor Francis scored his fair share of goals against the Teesiders, including two braces both at Ayresome Park.

Blues doubled up over 'Boro in 1980-81, winning both games 2-1

George Smith

(Frank Worthington netting twice at Ayresome Park) and it was Canadian international Paul Peschisolido who netted twice on 'Boro soil when Blues earned a point from a 2-2 draw in October 1993.

In season 1932-33 Blues battled to earn a 0-0 draw in a 5th round FA Cup-tie at Middlesbrough and then pulled out all the stops to win the replay 3-0 before losing in the quarter-finals to West Ham.

Blues reached the semi-final of the FA Cup in 1974-75 with a 6th round win over Middlesbrough, Bob Hatton scoring the tie's only goal in front of 47,260 fans at St Andrew's.

Blues beat 'Boro 5-4 on aggregate (after extra-time) in a second round League Cup-tie in September/October 1986. Steve Whitton scored in both games for Blues - but only 4,978 fans saw the second leg at St Andrew's.

In the same competition in 1995-96 Blues drew 0-0 at Middlesbrough in the fourth round and won the replay 2-0 at St Andrew's to enter the quarter-finals.

Players with both clubs include: W Clark, J Elkes, E Eyre, J Hall, A Miller, R Neal, B Orritt, FB Pentland, K Poole, MC Russell, GS Scott, G Smith, MR Thomas, J Vincent, FJ Wilcox, J Windridge.

Also: Malcolm Beard (Boro' coach), Terry Cooper (Boro' player, Blues manager), Bruce Rioch (Boro' assistant-manager & manager), Colin Todd (Boro' coach, assistant-manager and manager), David Geddis (Blues player, 'Boro Community officer), Mike Kelly (Blues player, 'Boro coach), Alf Wood (Boro' striker, Blues lottery salesman).

MIDDLESBROUGH IRONOPOLIS

Blues' playing record against Ironopolis is:

FOOTBALL LEAGUE

Venue	P	W	D	L	F	A
Home	1	1	0	0	2	1
Away	1	0	0	1	0	3
Totals	2	1	0	1	2	4

These two Second Division games took place in 1893-94, the first on Teeside on 25 November and the second at Muntz Street on 23 December when Billy Walton scored one of the goals that helped pocket two promotion points.

Player with both clubs: JS Oliver

MIDLAND (UNITED) COUNTIES LE...

In season 1893-94 Blues entered the locally organised Midland (United) Counties League. They played in the first of two groups along with Stoke, West Bromwich Albion and Wolverhampton Wanderers.

Here are details of Blues' six games:

11 December v Wolves (H) drew 3-3
17 February v Wolves (A) won 2-1
24 February v WBA (H) lost 4-5
26 February v WBA (A) lost 1-3
2 April v Stoke (H) won 3-0
9 April v Stoke (A) lost 1-2

SUMMARY OF MATCHES

Venue	P	W	D	L	F	A
Home	3	1	1	1	10	8
Away	3	1	0	2	4	6
Totals	6	2	1	3	15	14

Blues failed to qualify for the final, West Bromwich Albion winning the group.

Jack Hallam top-scored with five goals; Frank Mobley netted three times and both Billy Walton and Fred Wheldon notched two apiece.

The appearances made and goals scored by the players who took part in these six matches have been included in their respective career records.

MILLINGTON, Charlie

A decidedly quick, willing outside-right, Charlie Millington had an appetite for hard work and during his 20 years in the game gained hundreds of admirers for his professionalism and all-action performances. Never a great goalscorer (he netted only 13 times in 87 games for Blues) but he created chances galore for his colleagues.

Born in Lincoln on 25 April 1884, he played his early football with Grantham (1901). He then assisted Ripley Athletic (from January 1905) before transferring to Aston Villa at the end of that year. He netted 14 goals in 38 outings during his time at Villa Park which ended when he moved to London to join Fulham for £400 in October 1907. From Craven Cottage he switched back to the Midlands to sign for Blues for £600 (August 1909) and after three fine seasons at St Andrew's he entered non-League soccer with Wellington Town (August 1912). He later played for Brierley Hill Alliance and Stourbridge before hanging up his boots in May 1920 when he went to work in an iron foundry in Lincoln where he died on 13 June 1955, aged 71. Millington was also a useful cricketer, playing for Lincolnshire in the Minor Counties.

His cousin Ben played for Fulham while his son, Charlie junior, was a trialist with Blues.

MILLWALL

Blues' playing record against the Lions:

FOOTBALL LEAGUE

Venue	P	W	D	L	F	A
Home	13	8	3	2	21	9
Away	13	3	3	7	14	23
Totals	26	11	6	9	35	32

FA CUP

Away	1	1	0	0	4	1

LEAGUE CUP

Home	1	1	0	0	2	0
Away	1	0	1	0	1	1
Totals	2	1	1	0	3	1

WARTIME

Home	1	1	0	0	4	0
Away	1	0	0	1	1	5
Totals	2	1	0	1	5	5

A crowd of 25,000 at St Andrew's saw Blues beat Millwall 4-0 in the first League meeting between the two clubs. Cyril Trigg scored twice that day.....26 October 1946.

In the 20th away game that season Blues duly completed the double over the Lions with a 2-0 victory at The Den. Blues then took three points off the London club the following season.

After a longish break of not playing against each other, the Lions resumed the action with a 3-1 home win in October 1966, only for

Kevin Bremner

Blues to gain revenge four months later with a 2-0 victory at St Andrew's.

Blues were slammed 6-2 by Millwall at the Den in March 1969 - their heaviest defeat at the hands of the Lions!

Both games ended goalless in 1992-93 while each team won its home fixture the following season.

Blues played superbly well at The Den when beating Millwall 4-1 in a 5th round FA Cup-tie in front of 41,000 fans in February 1957, Noel Kinsey scoring twice and making another.

The League Cup matches were played in 1998-99 and Dele Adebola scored in both legs for Blues.

Players with both clubs: A Archer, T Aylott, J Beckford, A Bloxham, K Bremner, B Bridges, K Brown, T Carter, K Green (Millwall amateur), R Huxford, DWL Jones, JC Lane, IG Lea, CA Leatherbarrow, D Mangnall, SH Moffatt, A Mulraney (Millwall guest), P Murphy, AW Oakes, P Sansome (Blues' loanee), P Summerill, JG Sykes, P Tait, J Thorogood, D Wallace.

Also: Jim Barrett (Blues player, Millwall coach), Bruce Rioch (Blues player, Millwall manager), Nigel Spink (Millwall player, Blues coach), Alf Wood (Lions' striker, Blues lottery salesman).

MISSED (Players)

Over the years several useful players have passed through Birmingham City's hands and have gone on to make the grade elsewhere. Loan players and wartime guests have not been included, but among the 'missed' players we have the following:
- Nigel Winterburn - 192 games for Wimbledon and over 500 appearances for Arsenal. He was also capped by England.
- Steve Phillips scored over 200 goals in almost 600 senior appearances in 13 years with other clubs after leaving Blues.
- Reg Foulkes, released in 1945, made 160 League appearances

for Walsall and 216 for Norwich City.

- Jimmy Argue, a Blues reserve in 1932-33, made 125 appearances for Chelsea (35 goals scored).
- George Binks played over 100 games for Walsall in the 1920s.
- Tommy Bowen, released in 1921, appeared in more than 175 games for Walsall, Wolves and Coventry up to 1930.
- Sid Bowser, a trialist in 1907, went on to play over 300 games for WBA (1908-24) and he also represented England.
- Another trialist (in 1900) George Dorsett, scored 22 goals in 100 games for WBA and 65 in 211 outings for Manchester City.
- Reuben Woolhouse, a second XI player in 1927-28, made 250 senior appearances while serving with Southend, Bradford City, Coventry, Walsall and Swindon Town.
- Richard Strang, a reserve in 1923, made 300 League appearances while assisting Crystal Palace, Halifax Town, Northampton Town and Darlington before retiring in 1938.
- Centre-forward Sam Small, signed in 1934, made only six first team appearances before scoring 39 goals in 118 matches for West Ham.
- Jack Travers had two games for Blues (1907-09) and later played over 250 games for Aston Villa, QPR, Leicester City, Barnsley, Manchester United, Swindon Town, Millwall, Norwich City and Gillingham.
- Billy Wragg played once for Blues in 1900-01 but either side his stay at Muntz Street he amassed almost 150 senior appearances with Nottingham Forest, Leicester Fosse, Watford, Chesterfield and Brighton.
- Herbert Randle, a Blues reserve in 1931, went on to accumulate in excess of 230 major appearances with Mansfield Town, Gillingham, Accrington Stanley and Southend United.
- Harry Riley was released after one appearance for Blues in 1928-29. He went on to make 213 at League level while playing for Accrington Stanley, Lincoln, Notts County, Cardiff, Northampton and Exeter City.
- Herbert Lewis Turner, signed by Blues as a squad player in 1919, was not given a chance at St Andrew's but after leaving the club he went on to play in 144 League games for Merthyr Town, 30 for Coventry City, 36 for Torquay United and nine for Bristol Rovers. He also assisted Bournemouth.
- Sid Wallington had just two senior outings by Blues in 1931-32 before leaving the club. He later made almost 100 first team appearances for Bristol Rovers (1933-36).
- Ernie Watkins had eight games for Blues (1922-23) and later amassed over 200 appearances for Southend United, Brentford, Millwall, Fulham, Gillingham and Charlton Athletic (1923-32).
- Jack Wheeler, reserve goalkeeper to Gil Merrick, made 12 appearances for Blues and later starred in 182 matches for Huddersfield (from 1948).
- Another goalkeeper, Billy Robb, made 40 appearances for Blues during the last two seasons before World War One. Then, after the hostilities and having left St Andrew's, he played in well over 600 League and Cup matches (1919-38) when he was regarded as one of the finest 'keepers in the United Kingdom.
- Greg Farrell had five games for Blues (1960-64) and then played in a further 200 for Cardiff and Bury before emigrating to South Africa.
- Fred Pentland, an England international, had one game for Blues versus Portsmouth in the FA Cup in 1902. After leaving the club he played for Blackpool, Blackburn, Brentford, QPR,

Middlesbrough, Halifax and Stoke City, amassing more than 300 appearances at various levels.

- Billy Peplow made 17 appearances for Blues in 1907-08 and then had 216 for Bristol Rovers (scoring 42 goals).
- John Price had one outing for Blues in 1898-99 and followed up with almost 100 for Watford and Doncaster Rovers.
- Bernard Pumphrey played 11 games for Blues (1892-94) before starring in over 120 for Gainsborough Trinity (1894-1901).
- Harry Deacon had three games for Blues (1920-22) and then went on to spend ten years with Swansea, scoring 88 goals in 319 outings and helping the Welsh club win the Third Division (South) title in 1925.
- Goalkeepers David Seaman and Paul Cooper, 'given away' by Blues, both went on to amass tremendous League appearance records, the former also gaining England recognition on numerous occasions.
- James Quinn, after just four outings for Blues in the early 1990s, went on to play in over 180 games for Blackpool, more than 100 for West Brom and was also capped more than 20 times by Northern Ireland.

MITCHELL, Frank

Although born in Goulborn, New South Wales on 3 June 1922, Frank Mitchell left his native Australia as a teenager to come to England where, in fact, he wanted to play cricket and joined the Warwickshire Club and Ground as a 15 year-old.

He took up football in the winter (as a full-back) and in 1941 signed amateur forms for Coventry City, guesting for Blues, as well as Arsenal, Northampton Town and Portsmouth during the War. So impressive was he during his brief spell with Blues that he was

Frank Mitchell

offered professional status in August 1943. He went on to star in 166 League, Cup and regional Wartime games for the club, scoring 10 goals, after being converted into a very classy left-half of international quality, although he never gained a cap.

Cool under pressure, he was a fine passer of the ball and was an expert at taking free-kicks, always planting the ball into the danger-zone. And he wasn't a bad penalty-taker either, always hitching up his shorts before stepping up to strike the ball.

He helped Blues win the Football League (South) championship in 1946 and the Second Division title two years later. He also represented the FA XI.

On leaving St Andrew's in January 1949 Mitchell moved to Chelsea. In August 1952 he transferred to Watford and spent six years at Vicarage Road before hanging up his boots with well over 400 appearances at club level behind him.

Mitchell also served in the Royal Navy during WW2 and after retiring from football he was in charge of the sports grounds and coaching facilities at Kynoch's for many years.

As a cricketer Mitchell played in 17 county matches for Warwickshire (1947 and 1948), taking 22 wickets at an average of 38.9. He also had trials with Kent CCC and assisted both Cornwall and Hertfordshire as well as Knowle & Dorridge CC, becoming secretary of the latter club for whom he scored a century at the age of 47.

He died in Lapworth, Warwickshire on 2 April 1984.

MITCHELL ST GEORGE'S

Blues were beaten 3-1 at home by local side Mitchell St George's in a first round FA Cup-tie in October 1886. A crowd of 5,000 saw the action.

Players with both clubs include: JE Roberts, C Simms.

MOBLEY, Frank

Despite his height (5'8") Frank Mobley was fast and fearless centre-forward with a big heart. He also packed a powerful right-foot shot and scored 67 goals in 109 appearances for Blues between April 1892 and May 1896.

He would often charge the goalkeeper (and ball) over the line and at least a dozen of his goals came that way. Born in Handsworth on 21 November 1868, he played initially for Hockley Belmont FC and then Singer's (of Coventry) before moving to Muntz Street. He was signed after an efficient Blues scout, sent to watch another Singers player, Harry Edwards, recommended Mobley as well! (Edwards was also signed).

At the end of his first full season with Blues Mobley gained a Second Division championship medal. On leaving the club he joined Bury and later assisted Warmley (Bristol) before retiring in April 1898. He returned to Birmingham where he went into business. He died in 1940.

MONTGOMERY, Jim

After making more than 600 League and Cup appearances in goal for Sunderland whom he helped win the 1973 FA Cup Final against Leeds United (remember his terrific double-save) Jim Montgomery left Roker Pak for St Andrew's in February 1977 (following a loan spell with Southampton). He later assisted Nottingham Forest and then returned to Blues as a temporary goal-

keeping coach: July-August 1989, before going back to Sunderland as reserve team player and club coach: August 1980-82. Born in Sunderland on 9 October 1943, he went to Roker Park as a junior and turned professional in October 1960. He won England caps at both youth and under 21 levels but never made the full international side (kept out by Gordon Banks). A great shot-stopper, he made 73 appearances for Blues before handing over the gloves to Neil Freeman.

Jim Montgomery

MORGAN, Bill

Outside-left Bill Morgan was born in the Black Country at Old Hill on 3 November 1891. He played for Cradley St Luke's before joining Blues in November 1912. After scoring 13 goals in 69 senior outings for the club he was transferred to Coventry City in the summer of 1920. He later played for Crystal Palace (1922-25) before returning to Cradley St Luke's where he ended his footballing career. Rather chubby for a winger, Morgan was a 'bulldozing' type of player who always gave a good account of himself.

MORRALL, George

George 'Lofty' Morrall stood well over six feet tall, weighed 13 stones and was like a rock at the heart of the Blues defence. A fine figure of a man, a centre-half, he was resolute, solid, mobile when he had to be and significantly dependable. Born in Smethwick on 4 October 1905 he played for several minor teams in the area before having a trial with West Bromwich Albion, the club he supported as a lad. He didn't impress The Hawthorns management and in March 1927 was taken on as a professional by Blues. He stayed at St Andrew's until June 1936 when he moved to Swindon Town, retiring in 1940. In his nine years with Blues Morrall amassed 266 senior appearances and scored seven goals. He played against WBA in the 1931 FA Cup Final. George, who died in Birmingham on 15 November 1955, was the uncle of Terry Morrall, the former Aston Villa player.

MORRIS, Harry

Harry Morris

Harry Morris senior was associated with Blues for 36 years. He was a player for ten years and then served as a Director for 26.

As a footballer he was able to play as a wing-half or centre-forward and scored four goals in 69 first team appearances for Blues between August 1883 and May 1893. Born in Birmingham on 11 April 1866, he joined the club soon after leaving Small Heath Council School whilst engaged as an apprentice plumber for a company not too far from Muntz Street. After 10 years excellent service he established himself in business and then set about finding Blues' new home - St Andrew's - having become a Director of the club in 1903, a position he held until 1929. His two sons, Harry junior and Len, both followed him onto the Blues board.

Harry Morris senior died in June 1931 - two months after Blues had lost the FA Cup Final - and 45 years after he, himself, had starred against WBA in the 1886 FA Cup semi-final.

• A shrewd businessman Morris was one of the first men in Birmingham to see the potential of talking pictures and at the time of his death he was already linked with several local cinemas in the Midlands area.

MORRIS, Seymour

Seymour Morris was a rather frail looking left-winger with good ball skills and a fair amount of pace. A Welshman, born in the village of Ynyshir in the Rhondda Valley on 15 February 1908, he played for the local Schools select XI and then went to work down the pit. After narrowly escaping serious injury when a roof collapsed down a mine-shaft, he joined the army, becoming a drummer boy with the Welsh Regiment. Whilst stationed at Maindy Barracks near Cardiff he began turning out for the local junior side Aberaman in the Welsh League. He developed quickly and was induced to quit the army to sign professional forms. In March 1933 Huddersfield Town from the First Division secured his services for £2,000. He spent two seasons with the Terriers (making only five League appearances because of an enormous playing staff) before transferring to Blues in March 1935. Likened in some quarters to Stanley Matthews, he was top-scorer at St Andrew's in 1936-37

and in this same season he won the first of his five peacetime international caps for Wales, scoring direct from a corner against England at Cardiff. He later added a Wartime cap to his collection.

Three separate knee operations in 1939 put him out of action for quite some time but when he regained full fitness the Second World War broke out. Morris serviced aircraft at Elmdom during the hostilities, playing the occasional regional game for Blues. After retiring from soccer in 1944 (having scored 30 goals in 84 League and FA Cup games for Blues) he returned to Wales to take up a coaching position. In the early 1950s he and his wife opened a children's home in Glynoch which they continued to run successfully for over 20 years.

MOUNTENEY, Arthur

Inside-forward Arthur Mounteney scored a goal every three games for Blues - 30 in 97 senior appearances for the club, amassed over a four-year period between April 1905 and April 1909. Born in Belgrave, Leicester on 11 February 1883, he played initially for Leicester Imperial before joining Leicester Fosse (then at their lowest ebb) in November 1903, making his League debut against Bolton Wanderers in January 1904. Nicknamed 'Pecker' he netted 21 goals in only 34 outings for the Foxes (10 coming in four cupties, including a stunning hat-trick in a 5-2 win at West Brom). His efforts went unnoticed by the First Division clubs and it was Blues who secured his signature towards the end of the 1904-05 season. A big, burly footballer, he was often criticised for not throwing his weight around inside the penalty area but nevertheless he was a very capable marksman, quick, alert and decisive when it came to scoring goals (he had the pleasure of grabbing the last at Blues' old Muntz Street ground). He left St Andrew's for Preston North End and after two years at Deepdale had a brief spell with Grimsby Town (July 1911-December 1912). He then served with Portsmouth and ended his playing days with a season at Hinckley Athletic (1914-15), retiring during the War. Mounteney besides being an excellent soccer player was also a very capable cricketer, representing his native Leicestershire for 13 years during which time he scored 5,306 runs (including six centuries) for an average of almost 21. He died in Leicester on 1 June 1933.

MULRANEY, Ambrose

Jock Mulraney was a fast-raiding winger who could occupy both flanks. A Scotsman, born in Wishaw near Motherwell on 18 May 1916, he had trials for Scotland at schoolboy level and turned out for a variety of local clubs as a teenager including Wishaw White Rose and Carluke Rovers. He also had unsuccessful trials with Heart of Midlothian, Celtic, Hamilton Academical, Blackpool, Sligo Rovers and Clapton Orient before joining Dartford in August 1935, a year after having represented the Scottish Alliance XI. Twelve months later he signed for Ipswich Town and had the pleasure of scoring the Portman Road club's first-ever League hat-trick against Bristol City in April 1939. During the Second World War (when on leave from the RAF where he attained the rank of Flight Sergeant, PT Instructor) Mulraney guested for Blues, Blackburn Rovers, Brentford, Charlton Athletic, Chelsea, Hibernian, Leicester City, Manchester City, Millwall, Third Lanark and Wolves. In fact, he scored 41 goals in 118 games for Blues during the hostilities, helping them win the Football League South championship and reach the FA Cup semi-finals in 1946, having signed as a full-time professional at St Andrew's for £3,750 in October 1945. After netting 16 times in 41 senior games for Blues he was transferred to Shrewsbury Town in July 1947. In July 1948 he switched his allegiance to Kidderminster Harriers only to return to the second City with Aston Villa two months later. He spent the remainder of that season at Villa Park and then left competitive League soccer to become player-manger of Cradley Heath. He later took charge of Brierley Hill Alliance (1952-53) and retired from the game in 1954 to concentrate on his carpentry work in Kinver where he still resides, having overcome a major heart attack in 1968.

MUNTZ STREET

Old stand at Muntz Street

Blues used Muntz Street as their home ground from 29 years - from early September 1877 until late December 1906.

The club initially paid £5 a year to rent the ground, known locally as the 'celery trenches'. This rose to £200 by 1891 and when Blues left there in the winter of 1906 the rent had risen to £300 per annum.

The ground itself was built on land owned by 'Father Sam' Gessey who played four first team games for Blues as a defender during the 1877-84 period.

The record crowd at Muntz Street was estimated at 34,000 for a mid-week third round FA Cup replay against Tottenham Hotspur on 28 February 1906.

The biggest League attendance was almost 30,000 for the visit of Aston Villa in September 1905, although it was reported that another 4,000 fans could well have entered the ground without paying!

Blues' first home game at Muntz Street was a friendly against Saltley College on 11 September 1877. They won the contest 5-0 in front of just a handful of spectators, the gate receipts amounting to just 6s 8d (34p).

In their first season at Muntz Street Blues were undefeated in 22 matches.

The last game at Muntz Street was staged on 22 December 1906 when a crowd of 10,000 saw Blues defeat Bury 3-1 - and Arthur Mounteney had the pleasure of scoring the last goal at the ground.

Four junior internationals were staged at Muntz Street in 1898, 1900, 1904 and 1906 between a Birmingham representative side (featuring players from Aston Villa, Blues and WBA) and a Scotland XI. England won 5-2 in the first game, lost 2-1 in the second and won the last two by 2-1 and 2-0 respectively.

Two Inter Association matches between Birmingham and London were played at Muntz Street in 1887 and 1890. Birmingham won them both: 3-0 and 6-1 in that order.

In 1897 Blues purchased an old stand from neighbours Aston Villa for just £90, transferring it in sections from Perry Barr to

Muntz Street. It was re-erected as a terrace cover behind one of the goals.

Action from Blues v Sheffield United at Muntz Street in January 1905.

MURPHY, Peter

Peter 'Spud' Murphy was a trialist with Middlesbrough, an amateur inside-forward with both Coventry City and Birmingham City and played as a guest for Millwall during the War before signing professional forms at Highfield Road in 1946. After four excellent years with the Sky Blues he was transferred to Tottenham Hotspur for £18,500 (a healthy sum in those days) and helped the London club win the Second Division championship in 1951 by scoring nine goals in 25 matches as deputy for Les Bennett.

He became unsettled in London and left White Hart Lane for St Andrew's where he joined Billy Wardle on the left-wing, getting off to a flying start by netting a hat-trick on his Blues debut (at Doncaster) in January 1952. Scotsman Alex Govan then took over the left-wing position as Blues went on to win the Second Division championship, Murphy weighing in with 20 goals. The following season he scored another 17 including five in the FA Cup as Blues went through to Wembley where they lost to Manchester City. Murphy was the player who accidentally collided with Bert Trautmann, the City goalkeeper, causing the German to fracture his neck.

Murphy's phenomenal left-foot shooting from 30-40 yards out often caused problems for opposing goalkeepers and such was his marksmanship that he topped the scoring charts on four occasions during his time with Blues. He officially retired in 1959 and was

Peter Murphy

handed a coaching job at St Andrew's but with Blues battling against relegation the following season he came back to help them avoid the drop.

A supreme marksman, Murphy ended his career with more than 150 goals to his credit in just under 400 League appearances made with three clubs. In 1960-61 he guided Rugby Town to promotion to the Southern League Premier Division and later returned to Highfield Road to manage Coventry's 'A' team. He died on 7 April 1975.

MURRAY, Bert

During his Football League career Bert 'Ruby' Murray occupied every position in the team, even goalkeeper (a role he filled whilst at Chelsea and Blues). Originally a right-winger, he was lightly built but quick and decisive, and scored his fair share of goals at competitive level. Born in Shoreditch near Hoxton on 22 September 1942, he joined the junior ranks at Stamford Bridge as a 16 year-old and turned professional in May 1961. Honoured at both schoolboy and youth team levels by England, he later added six under 23 caps to his tally whilst at Stamford Bridge and also gained a League Cup winners prize in 1965 before transferring to St Andrew's for £25,000 in August 1966. Three months later, when Ray Martin was injured, he took over the right-back berth and did a splendid job for the next 18 months. He went on to net 23 goals in his 162 first team outings for Blues in his four-and-a-half years with the club, helping them reach two Cup semi-finals in successive seasons. On leaving St Andrew's in February 1971, he signed for Brighton & Hove Albion and later assisted Peterborough United (from September 1973). Murray retired in May 1977 having scored 108 goals in almost 600 League appearances for his five clubs. Soon afterwards he went into the licensing trade, taking over as mine host at The White Horse Inn at Market Deeping, Cambridgeshire.

Bert Murray

NAMES

Here are details of Blues players with the shortest and longest names and also some unusual names associated with Blues at senior level. Wartime guests/trialists have not been included.

SHORTEST SURNAME

Arthur Box (goalkeeper 1909-10), Jimmy Bye (wing-half 1937-44), Geoffrey Cox (winger 1950-57), Matt Fox (centre-back 1993), Steve Fox (winger 1970s), David Foy (midfielder 1989-91), Antoine Hey (midfielder 1990s), George Lea (right-half 1932-37), John Lee (forward 1893-95), Simon Rea (defender 1990s) and Arthur Roe (forward 1919-20).

The player who has represented Blues with the least number of letters in his whole name (letters of one Christian and surname added together) has been Coventry-born Simon Rea (eight letters in total).

LONGEST SURNAME (not including double-barrel names)

Goalkeeper Charlie Leatherbarrow followed by fellow 'keeper Harry Clutterbuck, defender John Cornelius Sleeuwenhoek and striker Frank Worthington.

- If we should add a foreigner to this category then surely the Dutchman Antonius Wilhelmus Matthias Theodore Van Mierlo would head the charts for the name with most letters (42).

UNUSUAL NAMES (not including foreign-born players)

William Naismith Blyth

Edgar Underwood Bluff (1907-08), William Naismith Blyth (1929-301), Alonzo Robson Drake (1907-08), Crosbie Gray Henderson (1910-11), Caesar Augustus Llewellyn Jenkyns (1888-95), Ezekiel Kingston (1881-83), Conyers Kirby (1906-07), Wilton Lines (1898-99), Frederick Beaconsfield Pentland (1900-03) and Theophilus Enos Pike (1928-30).

THE NAME GAME

Arthur Ralph Leonard also played football under the name of Arthur Leonard Bamford.

Dr Ian Smith also played as Ian Leslie Taylor-Smith.

NDLOVU, Peter

Born in Bulawayo, Zimbabwe on 25 February 1973, Peter Ndlovu began his Football League career with Coventry City in 1991 following his £10,000 transfer from the Highlanders club in his home country. He did very well at Highfield Road, scoring 41 goals 197 senior appearances before moving to St Andrew's for £1.6 million in July 1997. Ndlovu enjoys playing wide on the left (or even right) and gives defenders plenty to think about with his electrifying pace, ball skills and work-rate. Unfortunately injuries interrupted his game over the last year or so but he is still a vital member of the Blues and Zimbabwean national squads and at 27 still has a lot to offer. He has now made well over 100 senior appearances for Blues, 25 goals scored.

Jumping high, Peter Ndlovu against Port Vale.

NEAL, Dick

Neal Dick

Wing-half Dick Neal spent six years with Wolves - initially joining the club's nursery side Wath Wanderers in 1948, turning professional in March 1951 and leaving in July 1954 without making a first team appearance. He then served with Lincoln City and moved to St Andrew's in April 1957 in a deal worth £18,000 plus Albert Linnecor. Born in Dinnington on 1 October 1933, he was a well-built defender, physically strong who tackled hard but fair, although occasionally he did get a finger-waving from the referee for some over zealous play! He made 197 appearances for Blues (18 goals scored) before losing his place in the side to Terry

Hennessey. He played for the Young England XI (v England) and gained four under 23 caps as well as lining up in the 1960 Fairs Cup Final during his time at St Andrew's. He also skippered Blues in 1960-61 before leaving for Middlesbrough in October 1961, later rejoining Lincoln City (August 1963). He ended his senior career in 1965 with 415 League appearances under his belt. A spell with Rugby Town preceded his appointment as manager of Hednesford Town in August 1968, a position he held for a couple of years before becoming a publican in Birmingham and then in Penkridge (Staffs).

● Neal's father Dick senior, was a professional with Accrington Stanley, Blackpool, Bristol City, Derby County and Southampton before the Second World War.

NEUTRAL GROUNDS

Here is a list of the neutral grounds on which Blues have played competitive matches:

Aston Lower Grounds . . . . . .FA Cup semi-final v WBA 6.3.1886
Bramall Lane . . . . .Test Match v Newton Heath 27.4.1893
Bramall Lane . .FA Cup 1st rd, 2nd replay v Man.Utd. 21.12.1903
County Ground . .League Cup 2nd rd, 2nd rep v Luton 19.9.1972
Elland Road . . . . .FA Cup semi-final v Sunderland 14.3.1931
Filbert Street .FA Cup 5th rd, 2nd replay v Nottm. For. 23.2.1959
Goodison Park . .FA Cup semi-final replay v Blackpool 14.3.1951
Hillsborough . . . . .FA Cup semi-final v Derby County 23.3.1946
Hillsborough . . . . . . .FA Cup semi-final v Sunderland 17.3.1956
Hillsborough . . .FA Cup semi-final v Manchester Utd. 23.3.1957
Hillsborough . . . . . .FA Cup semi-final v Leeds United 15.4.1972

Hillsborough . . . . .FA Cup semi-final v Fulham 5.4.1975
Hyde Road, Manchester . . .FA Cup 1st rd, 3rd replay v Man Utd. 11.1.1904
Maine Road . . . .FA Cup semi-final replay v Derby Co. 27.3.1946
Maine Road . . . . .FA Cup semi-final v Blackpool 10.3.1951
Maine Road . . . . . .FA Cup semi-final replay v Fulham 9.4.1975
Molineux . . . . . .FA Cup 6th rd 2nd replay v Tottenham 9.3.1953
St Jacob Stadium . . . .Basle Fairs Cup semi-final rep. v Barcelona 26.11.1957
The Victoria Ground . . . . .Test Match v Newton Heath 22.4.1893
The Victoria Ground . . . . .Test Match v Darwen 28.4.1894
Villa Park . . . . .FA Cup semi-final v WBA 27.4.1968
Wembley Stadium . . . . .FA Cup Final v WBA 25.4.1931
Wembley Stadium . . . .FA Cup Final v Manchester City 5.5.1956
Wembley Stadium . . . .Leyland DAF Final v Tranmere 26.5.1990
Wembley Stadium . .Auto Windscreen Shield v Carlisle 23.4.1995

During the Second World War Blues used the grounds of Jack Moulds' and Leamington's for reserve, intermediate and 'A' team games in 1939-40 and Villa Park for various regional League and Cup matches. And in March 1944 they played Manchester United at Maine Road in a League Cup North game.

Due to building work being carried out at St Andrew's, the Bescot Stadium (home of Walsall) was hired by Blues for a pre season friendly against Notts County in August 1994 (lost 2-0).

Blues have also played Charlton Athletic at Selhurst Park and in recent years the club's second XI has utilised Cross Keys (home of Hednesford Town).

NEW BRIGHTON TOWER

Blues' playing record against New Brighton:

FOOTBALL LEAGUE

Venue	P	W	D	L	F	A
Home	3	3	0	0	9	2
Away	3	0	2	1	2	6
Totals	6	3	2	1	11	8

The six games all took place in Division Two during seasons 1898-99, 1899-1900 and 1900-01.

Blues' only defeat was a 4-0 battering in the very first match played on 22 October 1898. They gained revenge with an identical scoreline in the last meeting on 12 January 1901 when two Scotsmen, Bob McRoberts and Walter Main both netted twice.

NEWCASTLE UNITED

Blues' playing record against the Geordies is:

FOOTBALL LEAGUE

Venue	P	W	D	L	F	A
Home	41	21	7	13	73	53
Away	41	7	14	20	44	80
Totals	82	28	21	33	117	133

FA CUP

Venue	P	W	D	L	F	A
Home	1	0	1	0	2	2
Away	1	0	0	1	0	3
Totals	2	0	1	1	2	5

LEAGUE CUP

Venue	P	W	D	L	F	A
Home	2	1	1	0	4	2
Away	1	1	0	0	1	0
Totals	3	2	1	0	5	2

TEXACO CUP

	P	W	D	L	F	A
Home	2	0	1	1	2	5
Away	3	0	2*	1	3	5
Totals	3	0	2	1	3	5

* Includes one abandoned game

The first Blues-United League match was played on 28 October 1893 on Tyneside. Blues won 2-0 with goals by Frank Mobley and Fred Wheldon.

Surprisingly the return fixture ended in a 4-1 victory for United!

Blues then conceded a total of eight goals in two successive League visits to Newcastle - losing 4-3 in September 1896 and 4-0 in November 1897.

Newcastle beat Blues 8-0 at St James' Park in November 1907. This was Blues' heaviest defeat of that season and their worst in the League since November 1895 (beaten by the same score at Derby).

On returning to the top flight in 1921-22 Blues lost 4-0 at home to United but won 1-0 at St James' Park.

Joe Bradford scored twice in a 4-1 home win for Blues against the FA Cup Finalists in April 1924 but seven months later they were whipped 4-0 on Tyneside. United also won their home game in November 1926 by 5-1.

In September 1929 - a week after scoring a hat-trick in a 7-5 defeat at Blackburn - Joe Bradford again claimed a treble when Blues beat Newcastle 5-1 at St Andrew's.

Blues ran up two impressive wins in 1931-32 (the season United won the FA Cup). They triumphed 4-1 at St Andrew's and 3-0 at St James' Park, Bradford netting in both matches.

Over 100,000 fans saw the two second Division matches between the clubs in 1946-47 when Blues won 2-0 at home and drew 2-2 away, and there was an aggregate attendance figure of almost 86,800 for the two clashes in 1947-48 when United won 1-0 at home and drew 0-0 in Birmingham.

Blues took three points off the FA Cup holders United at the start of the 1955-56 season, winning 3-1 at St Andrew's and drawing 2-2 in the north-east.

In September 1956, hot-shot left-winger Alex Govan scored a hat-trick in Blues' excellent 6-1 home in over United. And seven goals were scored as Blues won 4-3 over United in a First Division match at St Andrew's in August 1959.

Bobby Hope scored his first goal for Blues in a 3-2 home win over United in August 1972 and Archie Styles netted his first home goal for the club when United were clipped 3-0 in October 1974.

Blues lost 4-0 at St James' Park in April 1976, 3-2 on United soil in October of that same year and then went down 2-1 at St Andrew's in April 1977.

In April 1986 United's 4-1 home win earned them the double over Blues that season

A Trevor Francis penalty in extra-time earned Blues a third round League Cup replay win at St James' Park in November 1973.

A crowd of almost 20,000 saw First Division Blues beat Premiership side Newcastle 2-0 in a third round League Cup-tie at St Andrew's in October 1999.

The second round second leg Texaco Cup-tie between Blues and Newcastle at St James' Park

Texaco Cup s/f programme

in November 1973 was abandoned after 100 minutes through bad light.

The following season Blues were knocked out of the Texaco Cup by United in the two-legged semi-final, losing 5-2 on aggregate.

Blues met United seven times in 1973-74 - twice in the League, twice in the League Cup and three times in the Texaco Cup. They played each other four times the following season, when Blues completed the double in the League. That made it eleven clashes in two seasons.

Players with both clubs include: S Barrowclough, J Beresford, N Brunskill (United trialist), J Connolly, T Daykin (United trialist), J Devine, K Dillon, A Fraser (United reserve), H Gayle, M Harford, CG Henderson, T Hibbitt, C Holland, P Howard, R Jones, RE Keating, J Kelly, K Leek, D Mason (Blues reserve), J Peart, R Ranson, G Smith, MR Thomas, J Trewick, D Williams (United trialist), P Withe , E Wood

Also: Jim Smith (manager of both clubs), George Dalton (Newcastle player, Blues trainer), Dave Fairhurst (United player, Blues physio), Ken Oliver (coach at both clubs).

Jimmy Dailey goes close with a header during Blues' home League game with United in April 1950. The visitors won 1-0.

NEWMAN, Johnny

Wing-half Johnny Newman helped Blues win the Second Division title in 1954-55 and had played in just 14 League games in 1955-56 when, surprisingly, he was named in Blues' FA Cup Final side against Manchester City in place of the injured Roy Warhurst. Preferred to the more experienced Jack Badham, he performed well enough against an attack-minded side but to no avail as Blues crumbled to a 3-1 defeat.

Born in Hereford on 13 December 1933 Newman attended a Welsh School, played for Hereford United juniors and gained a

Welsh junior international cap before linking up with Blues' adopted youth team St Andrew's Athletic in 1949. He was taken on the professional staff in March 1951 and developed into a resolute, hard-tackling defender. He remained at the club until November 1957 when he switched to the East Midlands to join Leicester City for £12,000. Stepping straight into the centre-half berth at Filbert Street, he had a disastrous debut as City crashed 7-3 at Burnley. But when Ian King returned, Newman switched to right-half and stood firm as the Foxes battled to consolidate their position in the First Division. He stayed with Leicester until January 1960, leaving after a young Frank McLintock had been introduced to League soccer. Newman then went on to appear in over 300 games for Plymouth Argyle whom he served and captained up to October 1967 when he was transferred to another Devon club, Exeter City, for £8,000 (plus another player). In a League Cup-tie against Aston Villa, Newman took a penalty but tapped the ball only a few yards forward, allowing a colleague to run in and crack the ball into the net (the game ended 3-3). In April 1969, Newman was appointed player-manager at St James' Park. He retired as a player in 1972, but remained in charge of the Grecians for another four years before taking the reins at Grimsby Town (December 1976-July 1979), steering the Mariners to the Fourth Division runners-up spot in his last season at Cleethorpes.

On leaving Blundell Park he stepped right into the assistant-manager's seat (under Colin Addison) at Derby County and between January and November 1982 he was boss at The Baseball Ground.

From November 1983 until September 1987 Newman managed Hereford United, leading the Bulls to promotion in 1985. He then became assistant to manager John Barnwell at Notts County (July 1988) and briefly held the position of caretaker-manager at Meadow Lane when Barnwell left. His next job, later in the year, was that of assistant-manager of York City, before he became a coach and chief scout of Mansfield Town in 1991.

Johnny Newman

NEWPORT COUNTY

Blues' playing record against the Welsh club is:

FOOTBALL LEAGUE

Venue	P	W	D	L	F	A
Home	1	0	1	0	1	1
Away	1	1	0	0	3	0
Totals	2	1	1	0	4	1

WARTIME

Home	2	2	0	0	8	4
Away	2	1	1	0	3	2
Totals	4	3	1	0	11	6

The two League fixtures took place in 1946-47 (Division Two). A crowd of 20,000 saw Harold Bodle salvage a point for Blues in the 1-1 draw at St Andrew's on 21 September, while Bodle (2) and Neil Dougall clinched a 3-0 win at Somerton Park on the last day of the season (26 May) in front of 14,000 sun-drenched spectators.

Players with both clubs include: T Carter, M Darrell, E Edwards,

G Emmanuel, H Fletcher (reserve), H Hampton, G Johnston, RD Latchford, T Lees, T Matthewson, DJ Singer, JH Southam.

Also: Albert Lindon (Blues player, County scout)

NICKNAMES

Several footballers world-wide have nicknames and here are some belonging to Blues players:

George 'Nosey' Anderson, Jack 'Soldier' Aston, Robert 'Bertie' Auld, Bill 'Kosher' Ball, Fred 'Sticker' Banks, James 'Young Jim' Barrett, 'Gentleman Joe' Bradford, Gary 'Alderbreeny' Breen, George 'Nippy' Briggs, Frank 'Clitterty' Clack, Wayne 'Sniffer' Clarke, Charlie 'Swerver' Craven, Johnny 'Peerless' Crosbie, LC 'Alan' Curbishley, Paul 'Dev' Devlin, 'Pouncer' Will Edden, Richard 'Handsome Dick' Elliman, Edmund 'Ninty' Eyre, Tommy 'Tot' Farnall, Tom 'Tosher' Fillingham, Kevin 'Big Man', 'Inch', 'Sir' Francis, JC 'Cammie' Fraser, 'Father Sam' Gessey, George 'Good Man' Getgood, DJ 'Don' Givens, PG 'Putt' Gooch, Ken 'Slasher' Green, WG 'Salty' Halsall, 'Appy Arry' Hampton (also known as the Wellington Whirlwind), Thomas 'Toddy' Hands, Wilbert 'Fay' Harrison, Charles 'Soldier' Harvey, Edmund 'Martin' Harvey, George 'Abie' Haywood, Dennis 'Denny' Hodgetts, William 'Harry' Holmes, Robert 'Hoppy' Hopkins, Brian 'Bud' Houghton, Billy 'Sailor' Hunter, Alec 'Jacko' Jackson, John 'Jimmy' James, Andrew 'AJ' Johnson, Michael 'Magic' Johnson, Willie 'Bud' Johnston, Edwin 'Teddy' Jolly, Billy 'Bullet' Jones (also known as the 'Little Bloodhound'), Jack 'Cracker' Jones, John 'Bristol' Jones, James 'Joe' Lane, GA. 'Ginger' Leatherbarrow, Andy 'Leggy' Legg, AJ 'Alec' Leslie, Stan 'The Wham' Lynn, JM 'Seamus' McDonough, Kevin Clifton 'Ted' McMinn, Robert 'Roy' Martin, Bertie 'Paddy' Mills, George 'Kid' Moore, Richie 'Whoopie' Moran, George 'Lofty' Morrall, Arthur 'Hetty' Morris, Arthur 'Pecker' Mounteney, Ambrose 'Jock' Mulraney, Peter 'Spud' Murphy, Albert 'Ruby' Murray, Peter 'Nuddy' Ndlovu, Dick 'Ticker' Neal, John S. 'Dowk' Oliver, Bryan 'Orrible' Orritt, Garry 'Gazza' Pendrey, Paul 'Pesch' Peschisolido, Cuthbert 'Charlie' Phillips, Theo 'Tot' Pike, Carroll 'Carl' Richards, David 'Dai' Richards, Brian 'Harry' Roberts, Arthur 'Nat' Robinson, Dave 'Sugar' Robinson, Charlie 'Bowie' Simms, John 'Tulip & Slogger' Slueewenhoek, Arthur 'Nipper' Smith, George 'Sconnie' Southall, Gary 'Mother' Sprake, Ron 'Mickey' Stainton, Alf 'Eddy' Stanley, John 'Jackie' Stewart, Simon 'Studger' Sturridge, JE 'George' Travers, Dan 'The India Rubberman' Tremelling, John 'Tucker' Trewick, Cyril 'Triggy and Trigger' Trigg, David L 'Danny' Wallace, Billy 'Mother' Walton, Isaac 'Ike' Webb, Freddie 'Diamond' Wheldon, Colin 'Tiny' Withers and Francis 'Frank' Womack.

An early team captain, Arthur James, was called the 'People's Pet' and 1880s secretary Alf Jones was nicknamed 'Inky'. And one cannot forget Blues' boss Jim 'Bald Eagle' Smith, earlier manager Leslie Knighton who was called football's 'Lifeboatman' and Barry 'Baz' Fry.

And we can't really omit Birmingham City's or the diehard supporters' nicknames can we - The Blues and Bluenoses!

NON-LEAGUE OPPOSITION

Since becoming a Football League club in 1892, Blues have encountered non-League opposition on 18 occasions in the FA Cup competition. The teams (in A-Z order) have been Altrincham, Brighton & Hove Albion, Chelmsford City, Cheltenham Town,

Chirk, Crystal Palace, Darlington, Druids, Kidderminster Harriers, Oswestry United, Peterborough & Fletton United, Portsmouth (three times), Slough Town, Southend United, Stevenage Borough and Wrexham.

● See under respective clubs for further match details.

NORTHAMPTON TOWN

Blues' playing record against the Cobblers is:

FOOTBALL LEAGUE

Venue	P	W	D	L	F	A
Home	2	2	0	0	7	0
Away	2	0	1	1	3	4
Totals	4	2	1	1	10	4

WARTIME

Venue	P	W	D	L	F	A
Home	10	5	2	3	21	14
Away	12	3	1	8	17	23
Totals	22	8	3	11	38	37

Graham Potter

Johnny Vincent scored twice in Blues 3-0 home win over the Cobblers on Boxing Day 1966 and when the teams met at St Andrew's again in October 1989 Nigel Gleghorn was a two-goal hero as Blues romped to a 4-0 victory.

Players with both clubs include: I Atkins (also Town manager), M Bodley, R Bonthron, K Bowker, I Brown, S Bryant, I Clarkson, D Dearson (Town guest), N Doherty, E Duckhouse, P Fitzpatrick, M Fox, J Frain, S Francis, N Freeman, M Gabbiadini, A Garrett, J Gayle, N Gleghorn, R Hatton, I Hendon, MI Kendall, HE King, K Leek, G Merrick (Town guest), F Mitchell (Town guest), D Peer, L Phillips, SE Phillips, K Poole, G Potter, H Riley, JG Roberts, P Robinson, TE Robinson, GS Scott, B Sedgemore, WH Smith, JH Southam, R Strang (Blues reserve), S Sturridge, P Tait, J Wealands.

Also: Jason Beckford (Blues player, Town assistant-manager), Tony Godden (Blues goalkeeper, Cobblers' coach), Tony Taylor (Cobblers player, Blues coach).

● Blues played Luton Town in a League Cup second replay at Northampton's old County Ground in 1972.

NORTHWICH VICTORIA

Blues' playing record against the 'Vics' is
FOOTBALL LEAGUE

Venue	P	W	D	L	F	A
Home	2	2	0	0	14	2
Away	2	2	0	0	13	0
Totals	4	4	0	0	27	2

As you can see the four Second Division League games produced a total of 29 goals. Blues won 6-2 at home and 6-0 away in the 1892-93 season and 8-0 at home and 7-0 away the following year. Fred Wheldon netted four times in that eight-nil victory while Frank Mobley scored a hat-trick in the seven-goal romp.

Fred Wheldon also scored a hat-trick in the first home game.

Players with both clubs include: D Adebola, M McCarrick, P Sproson, P Tait, M Ward.

NORWICH CITY

Blues' playing record against the Canaries:
FOOTBALL LEAGUE

Venue	P	W	D	L	F	A
Home	21	12	4	5	38	23
Away	21	3	9	9	25	44
Totals	42	15	13	14	63	67
FA CUP						
Home	2	0	2	0	1	1
Away	2	0	1	1	1	2
Totals	4	0	3	1	2	3
LEAGUE CUP						
Home	2	2	0	0	5	2
Away	3	0	2	1	2	4
Totals	5	2	2	1	7	6
TEXACO CUP						
Home	1	0	0	0	3	1

The first League match between Blues and the Canaries took place at St Andrew's on 9 October 1965. Alec Jackson scored the game's only goal to earn Blues a 1-0 victory in front of 11,622 fans.

Norwich beat Blues 6-0 at Carrow Road in the last League game of the 1969-70 season...this after Blues had won 3-1 at St Andrew's in mid-September.

There were three successive 2-2 draws between the clubs before Blues beat Norwich 4-0 at home in March 1972, Bob Hatton scoring twice in front of almost 41,000 fans who were sensing promotion at the time - for both clubs! Mike O'Grady, on loan from Wolves, made his debut for Blues in this game.

The following season - in the First Division - Blues doubled up over struggling Norwich, winning their home game 4-1 with rare goals from Garry Pendrey and Tony Want.

Norwich slammed luckless Blues 4-0 at Carrow Road in September 1978 but a Don Givens goal at St Andrew's later in the season enabled Blues two gain sweet revenge.

Blues suffered another heavy defeat in Norfolk in September 1982, going down 5-1. Norwich also won 4-0 at St Andrew's that season and repeated the dosage with another win on Blues' territory in December 1983 (1-0).

Jonathan Hunt scored a terrific hat-trick in Blues' 3-0 win over the Canaries at St Andrew's in August 1995 - and immediately manager Barry Fry placed a price tag of £28 million on the midfielder's head!

Keith Bertschin

In 1996-97 both teams won their respective away game in the League. Midfielder Martyn O'Connor crashed in Blues' second-half winner at Carrow Road to give his side a 1-0 scoreline - and this result was the 1,000th League game Blues had played without conceding a goal (3,771 fulfilled up to that time).

Blues beat the Canaries 2-1 in a League Cup replay at St Andrew's in January 1996 and so progressed into the semi-finals of this competition for the first time since 1967. Liam Daish scored a dramatic 88th minute winner.

Blues' scorers in their convincing 3-1 Texaco Cup win over the Canaries on 10 August 1974 were Alan Campbell, Trevor Francis and Bob Hatton. The attendance was 14,847.

Following the transfer of Percy Gooch from Norwich to Blues in March 1907, a friendly was arranged between the two clubs - the Canaries won it in style by 5-2.

Players with both clubs include: J Acquaroff (Blues guest), A Archer, K Bannister, E Barkas (Norwich amateur), K Bertschin, R Brennan, K Brown, S Bruce, L Donowa, G Downs, K Drinkell, R Foulkes (Blues amateur), P Gooch, R Hansbury, T Hockey, T Hunt (Blues reserve), M Jackson, RE Keating, N Kinsey, BP Larkin, O Madden, J Mullett, TE Pike, CJ Russell, MC Russell, J Short, J Smith, CG Spencer (Blues reserve), RA Taylor, JE Travers.

Also: John Bond and Ron Saunders (managers of both clubs), Major Frank Buckley (Norwich manager), Bruce Rioch (Blues player, Norwich manager), Chris Woods (Canaries goalkeeper, Blues coach), Fred Davies (Norwich trainer-coach, Blues coach).

NOTTINGHAM FOREST

Blues' playing record against Forest is:

FOOTBALL LEAGUE

Venue	P	W	D	L	F	A
Home	40	16	9	15	69	55
Away	40	11	12	17	45	52
Totals	80	27	21	32	114	107

FA CUP

Venue	P	W	D	L	F	A
Home	3	0	2	1	1	2
Away	3	2	1	0	4	1
Neutral	1	0	0	1	0	5
Totals	7	2	3	2	5	8

Trevor Francis (right) in action for Nottingham Forest against Blues.

LEAGUE CUP

Home	2	1	0	1	4	4
Away	1	0	0	1	1	2
Totals	3	1	0	2	5	6

FOOTBALL ALLIANCE

Home	3	2	1	0	17	4
Away	3	1	1	1	5	6
Totals	6	3	2	1	22	10

WARTIME

Home	9	6	2	1	18	10
Away	9	3	2	4	14	11
Totals	18	9	4	5	32	21

The first time Blues met Forest in the Football League was on 22 December 1894 at Muntz Street. The visitors won 2-1 and soon afterwards completed the double with a 2-0 victory by the River Trent!

A crowd of 10,000 saw a thrilling 3-3 draw between the teams at Muntz Street in September 1903 and a little over two years later, a hat-trick by Freddie Wilcox enabled Blues to beat Forest 5-0 in a home League game in December 1905.

Blues completed 'League' doubles over Forest in 1911-12 and 1919-20. A crowd of 15,000 saw Forest hammered 8-0 at St Andrew's in that latter season when Harry Hampton (4 goals) and Joe Lane (2) were both making their home League debuts for Blues.

There was no action between the teams during the 1930s but immediately after World War Two Blues raced to a 4-0 home win over Forest (October 1946) and the following season completed another double as they headed towards the First Division.

Forest bounced back and beat Blues 5-0 at St Andrew's in November 1952 to end Blues' five-match unbeaten run.

Blues scored a scintillating 7-1 victory at Forest in March 1959, Gordon Astall (2) and Robin Stubbs (2) leading the goal glut. This was to remain Blues' best away win until their 7-0 romp at Stoke in January 1998.

In that season of 1958-59 Blues and Forest (the eventual FA Cup winners) met each other five times with 20 goals being scored in the process.

Forest won an FA Cup fifth round second replay 5-0 at neutral Filbert Street just a fortnight before taking that seven-goal beating at The City Ground!

Ten goals were scored in the two League meetings in 1963-64. A crowd of 18,158 watched a 3-3 draw at St Andrew's and just 14,000 attended the City Ground to see Forest win 4-0 at a time when Blues were fighting for their First Division lives!

The 1964-65 opened with Forest beating Blues 4-3 at St Andrew's in front of more than 26,000 fans. Stan Lynn cracked in a penalty for Blues - his fourth success from the spot in eight matches.

Forest had a terrific 1977-78 League season - they were unbeaten at home and lost only three times away. Blues were defeated 2-0 at St Andrew's and forced a draw at The City Ground on the last day in front of 37,625 fans.

Two goals from Neil Whatmore helped Blues beat Forest, the reigning European Cup holders, 4-3 in a cracking League game at St Andrew's on 5 September 1981.

With Blues cascading rapidly towards the Second Division, they were hammered 5-1 by Forest at The City Ground on 21 April 1984.

Forest completed the double over Blues in the space of four weeks during the 1993-94 season and when Blues were battling to stay in contention for automatic promotion in 1999-2000 Forest came to St Andrew's at a crucial time in the season and won 1-0 - their 11th successive victory over Blues!

Three of the five meetings between Blues and Forest in 1958-59 were in the FA Cup 5th round. After two 1-1 draws at St Andrew's and The City Ground, Forest finally came good with that thumping 5-0 second replay victory at Leicester.

Forest beat Blues 5-3 on aggregate in a second round League Cup-tie in October 1981. The two 'Ws' - Whatmore and Worthington - scored for Blues in the game at St Andrew's which Blues lost 3-2.

Will Devey scored six goals (a double hat-trick) when Blues beat Forest 12-0 in a Football Alliance game at Muntz Street in March 1890.

Blues met Forest in a 'championship celebration' match at St Andrew's in May 1995. A crowd of 10,742 saw Forest win 4-1 and Liam Daish collect the Second Division trophy.

Players with both clubs include: FW Banks, J Barrett, A Buckley, G Bull, K Burns, J Bye (guest), T Capel, G Charles, R Firth, T Francis, A Gemmill, J Godfrey (reserve & guest), J Hall (Forest trialist), H Hampton (Forest guest), P Hart (Forest player and coach), F Hawley (Forest guest), T Hennessey, T Hockey, CW Jones, EA Linley, WP Meates (trialist), G Merrick (Forest guest), J Montgomery, S Ottewell, J Sheridan, MA Smalley, PM Starbuck, L Stoker, S Sutton, C Todd, C Trigg (Forest guest), G Vowden, D Wassall, S Wigley, P Withe, W Wragg.

Also: Dave Mackay (manager of both clubs), Ronnie Fenton (Blues player, assistant-manager Forest), Joe Mallett (Blues manager, Forest coach), Ian Bowyer (Forest player, Blues coach).

- Goalkeeper Steve Sutton appeared in 199 games for Forest (1979-82) and had just six outings for Blues (1996-97).

NOTTS COUNTY

Blues' playing record against the Magpies:

FOOTBALL LEAGUE

Venue	P	W	D	L	F	A
Home	26	15	6	5	44	25
Away	26	5	8	13	26	48
Totals	52	20	14	18	70	73

FA CUP

Home	2	0	0	2	1	4

LEAGUE CUP

Home	4	1	2	1	5	6
Away	2	1	1	0	3	1
Totals	6	2	3	1	8	7

WARTIME

Home	6	3	1	2	15	15
Away	7	2	3	2	12	15
Totals	13	5	4	4	27	30

Blues first met County (away) at League level on 3 February 1894 (Division 2). The Magpies won 3-1 in front of 6,000 spectators. On the last day of that season Blues gained revenge with a 3-0 victory at Muntz Street.

When Blues lost 6-1 at Meadow Lane in December 1901 it turned out to be their heaviest League reverse of that season.

In February 1906 two goals by Billy Jones helped Blues to a 4-2 home win over County while both games in 1907-08 (played over

Paul Barnes

Christmas) ended in 0-0 draws.

Blues doubled up with two 1-0 wins over County in 1924-25 and the following season relegated County completed the double over Blues!

It was 1950-51 before the teams met again in the Football League and honours were fairly even, Blues winning 1-0 at home but losing 4-1 at County.

When the Magpies beat Blues 5-0 in front of 24,360 spectators at Meadow Lane in a Second Division match on 19 April 1952, four of their goals were scored by Ron Wylie, later to become skipper at St Andrew's. This defeat didn't help Blues' promotion cause - they eventually missed out on goal-average!

Soon afterwards, in February 1953, Cyril Trigg netted with two booming penalty kicks as Blues beat County 3-2 at St Andrew's.

There were no League meetings between the clubs for 26 years, from 1953 until 8 December 1979 when Blues drew 1-1 in Nottingham (Steve Lynex the scorer).

By drawing 3-3 at home with County on the last day of that season (3 May 1980) Blues duly clinched promotion to the First Division, finishing in third place. A best-of-season crowd of 33,863 celebrated in style!

Blues ended a disastrous League record of 32 away games without a win when they whipped County 4-1 at Meadow Lane on 1 May 1982. Tony Evans scored twice that day.

In season 1983-84 Blues met County on six occasions - twice in the League and four times in the League Cup third round. Each side

recorded a win apiece with four draws (three in the League Cup).

Players with both clubs include: K Armstrong, FW Banks (County trainee), P Barnes, D Bruce, K Burns, R Catlin, R Craythorne (Blues reserve), J Daws, W Devey, P Devlin, K Downing, R Dryden, R Fenton (also coach and manager of County), S Finnan, P Gooch, P Harding, R Harper, P Hart (County player-coach), A Hateley, I Hendon, W Holmes, M Johnson, A Jones, M Kuhl, JG Lane, A Legg, J McDonough, C Marsden, J Millington (Blues reserve), BR Mills, A Morley (County trialist), E Newton, DW Pimbley, N Platnauer, D Regis, I Richardson, H Riley, PJ Robinson, BW Rushton, F Shaw, J Short, J Smith (County guest), KC Tewksbury, P Van Den Hauwe, TW White, R Wylie.

Also: Major Frank Buckley, Howard Kendall and Frank Womack (Blues players, County managers), Johnny Newman (County assistant-manager), Jack Wheeler (Blues player, County trainer & caretaker-manager), Peter Doherty (Blues guest, County joint advisor), Frank Broome (County player/Blues guest)

NUMBERING OF PLAYERS

Numbers on the shirts of the Blues' players were first seen in August 1938 - when Coventry City were their opponents in a Football League Jubilee fund game at Highfield Road.

OFFSIDE RULE

The offside rule, as we know it today, was introduced for the 1925-26 season. Blues' first match under the new rule was against Sunderland at Roker Park on 29 August 1925 when the home side won 3-1 in front of 25,000 spectators.

OLDBURY TOWN (United)

Blues won 3-1 at Oldbury in an FA Cup second qualifying round tie in October 1889. Will Devey scored twice in front of 1,000 spectators.

Players with both clubs include: A Jackson, AH Sheldon (Blues reserve)

Also: D Robinson (Blues player, Oldbury manager).

OLDHAM ATHLETIC

Blues' playing record against the Latics:
FOOTBALL LEAGUE

Venue	P	W	D	L	F	A
Home	12	4	4	4	15	13
Away	12	4	3	5	12	21
Totals	24	8	7	9	27	34

FA CUP

	P	W	D	L	F	A
Home	3	0	2	1	4	5
Away	3	1	0	2	3	4
Totals	6	1	2	3	7	9

The first League clash between Blues and the Latics took place at Boundary Park on 17 October 1908 and in front of 20,000 fans, the Latics won 2-0.

Billy Beer scored both goals when Blues won the return fixture by the same score at St Andrew's in February.

The first game in the top flight was at Oldham on 3 December 1921 and on this occasion Blues won 1-0 and quickly doubled up with a 3-1 home victory a week later.

The Latics completed their first double over Blues in 1922-23 and it was another 30 years before the teams met again, Blues gaining two Second Division points with a 3-2 win at Boundary Park in November 1953.

Later in the season Peter Murphy and Len Boyd scored to give Blues a 2-1 home win.

There was no further action at League level between the clubs for 26 years, until 21 December 1979 when a Second Division match ended in favour of the Latics 1-0 at Boundary Park. Blues won the return fixture 2-0, Archie Gemmill and Alan Ainscow the scorers.

Both teams won away 1-0 in 1984-85 (Division 2) and in successive seasons after that - in November 1986 and March 1988 - the Latics ran up two 3-1 wins at St Andrew's. In October 1987, however, Blues recorded their ONLY League win on plastic, beating the Latics 2-1 at Boundary Park.

In September 1988 Oldham walloped Blues to the tune of 4-0, also on their plastic pitch to gain revenge!

Blues' conceded two own-goals (by Gary Poole and Kevin Francis) when they again crashed 4-0 at Boundary Park in December 1995.

Peter Murphy scored a hat-trick when Blues defeated the Latics 3-1 in a third round FA Cup-tie at Boundary Park in January 1953.

Players with both clubs include: N Brunskill, J Devlin, J Harris, A Hateley, P Mardon, P Moulden, J Shaw, J Sheridan, J Shufflebottom, J Slueewenhoek, GB Waddell, M Ward, R Warhurst, JS Watson, J Wealands.

Also: Frank Womack (Blues player, Latics manager), Ted Goodier (Latics player, Blues manager).

Kevin Francis (highest) in action for Blues against the Latics in the mid-1990's

OLLIS, Billy

Billy Ollis

Right-half Billy Ollis played in the same middle line with Jenkyns and Devey, and was a very capable and reliable defender. Born within shooting distance of Blues' Muntz Street ground on 12 August 1871, Ollis played for Newall Juniors and Southfield FC before moving to the more established Warwick County in 1890. He switched to Blues in April 1891 and took over the captaincy from Caesar Jenkyns (when he was sacked). Ollis helped Blues win the Second Division championship in 1892 and went on to score twice in 118 first-team outings for the club before transferring to Hereford Thistle in February 1896. He retired through injury three years later and died in Birmingham in May 1940.

ORRITT, Bryan

The only Welsh-speaking professional footballer in the game during the 1950s-60s, Bryan Orritt was born in Carmarthen on 22 February 1937 and he is believed to be the only player to enter the professional game having previously starred for Llanfairpwllgwyngyllgogerychwyrndrowllllantysiliogogogoch (shortened for obvious reasons to Llanfair FC). He joined Blues in January 1956 (from Bangor City) and during his six years at St Andrew's scored 27 goals in 119 senior appearances, helping Blues

Bryan Orritt

reach both the 1960 and 1961 Fairs Cup Finals. He also gained three under 23 caps for Wales. His best spell at the club came in 1957-58 when, after replacing Welsh international Noel Kinsey, he netted 11 times in 25 First Division matches. But after that he was in and out of the side and eventually lost his place to Johnny Gordon, transferring to Middlesbrough in March 1962. He later played for Johannesburg Rangers in South Africa (1966-67) and then became a prominent figure in Soweto where he coached black youngsters.

OSWESTRY UNITED

Blues' record against Oswestry:
FA CUP

Venue	P	W	D	L	F	A
Home	1	1	0	0	10	2

Four players each scored twice in this 10-2 FA Cup win at Muntz Street in a qualifying round tie in October 1899.

Players with both clubs include: A Bloxham, J Hallam, JG Roberts (United player-manager), VH White.

OVERSEAS CONNECTIONS

Marco Gabbiadini

Here are details of players/managers who served with Blues and also had connection/associations with clubs other than those in Great Britain.

- Alan Ainscow . . . . .Eastern FC (Hong Kong)
- Eric Barber . . . . .Chicago Spurs, Kansas City Spurs, Weiner Sportsklub
- Dave Barnett . . . . .Edmonton Oilers
- Malcolm Beard . . . . .Coach in Saudi Arabia
- Willie Bell . . . . . . .Soccer coach at Campus Crusade of Christ, Liberty College (Virginia, USA)
- Keith Bertschin . . . . .Jacksonville Teamen
- Fred Bowden . . . . .French League football
- Colin Brazier . . . . .Jacksonville Teamen
- Barry Bridges . . . . .Highland Park (South Africa)
- Bud Brocken . . . . .SV Willem II, Groningen, BVV Den Bosch
- Steve Bryant . . . . .Australian League football
- Kenny Burns . . . . .IF Elfsborg
- Jimmy Calderwood . . . . .SV Willem II, Roda JC, SC Heracles, Den Ham, FC Zwolle (assistant-manager/coach), SC Cambuur, FC Leeuwaardden (assistant-manager)
- Bob Catlin . . . . . .Apia Leichardt, Marconi Fairfield (Australia)
- Gary Charles . . . . .Benfica
- Johnny Crosbie . . . . .Coach in Sweden
- Gerry Daly .New England Teamen
- Jimmy Devlin . . . . . . .Brooklyn Wanderers (USA), FC Zurich
- Jose Dominguez . . . . .Benfica, Real Madrid (trial), Sport Uniao Sintrense
- Louie Donowa . . . . .Deportivo La Coruna, SV Willem II
- Greg Downs . . . . .Connecticut Bicentennials
- Rui Esteves . . . . .Real Benfica, SC Olhansense, Louletano DC, Spor Sporting Club Farense, Scu Torriense, Vitoria Setubal St Benfica
- Len Evans . . .Reserve player-trainer of Svenborg FC (Sweden)

- Paul Fenwick . . . . .Edmonton Oilers, Hamilton Steelers, Toronto Blizzard, Winnepeg Fury
- Paul Fitzpatrick .Hong Kong football
- Trevor Francis . . . . .Detroit Express, Sampdoria, Atalanta
- Lil Fuccillo . . . . . . .Tulsa Roughnecks, player/coach in Malta
- Marco Gabbiadini . . . . .Panionios (Greece)
- Howard Gayle . . . . .Dallas Sidekicks
- Archie Gemmill . . . . .Jacksonville Teamen
- Don Givens . . . . .Xamac Neuchatel (player & coach and assistant- manager), also coach in Switzerland
- Freddie Goodwin . . . . . . .Coach New York Generals, manager Minnesota Kicks
- Jimmy Greenhoff .Toronto Blizzard
- Bart Greimink .WK Emman FC
- Christophe Gronlin . . . . .Toulouse
- Jimmy Hagan . . . .Detroit Express, FC Seiko, Real Celta Vigo, IFK Oddevold
- Roger Hansbury . . . . .Eastern FC (Hong Kong)
- Paul Hendrie . . . . .Portland Timbers
- Terry Hennessey . . . . . . .Assistant coach & chief coach Tulsa Roughnecks, assistant coach Vancouver Whitecaps, manager of Heidelberg (Australia).
- Antoine Hey . . . . .Fortuna Cologne
- Trevor Hockey . . .Dan Diego Jaws, San Jose Earthquakes, Los Angeles Quicksilver
- Lyndon Hooper . . .Eastern Ontario All Stars, Ottowa Pioneers, Montreal Supra, Toronto Blizzard
- Bobby Hope . . . . .Philadelphia Atoms, Dallas Tornadoes
- Robert Hopkins . . . . .Instant Dictionary (Hong Kong)
- Pat Howard . . . . .Portland Timbers
- Billy Hume . . . . .Hakoah (Australia)
- Steve Isoifidis . . . . .South Melbourne
- Paul Ivey . . . . .Karlskrona, Kalmar, AIK, Vasalund
- Lee Jenkins . . . . . .Rovaniemen Palloseura, Finnainan Palloilij
- Alan Johnson . . . . .FC Rennes
- Willie Johnston . . . . .Vancouver Whitecaps, South China (Hong Kong)
- Gary Jones . . . . .Fort Lauderdale Strikers
- Johnny Jordan . . . . .Juventus
- Vasil Kalogeracos . . . . .Malaysia
- Mike Kelly . . . . .Player/coach Minnesota Kicks, coach in Switzerland
- Howard Kendall . . . . . . .Manager Athletic Bilbao, FC Xanthi (manager)
- Andy Kennedy . . . . .FC Seiko (Hong Kong)
- Hymie Kloner . . .Marist Brothers (South Africa), Transvaal FC
- Joe Lane . . . . .Player-coach Ferencvaros Torna, coach Barcelona
- Bob Latchford . . . . .NAC Breda
- Stan Lazaridis . . . . .West Adelaide (Australia)
- Terry Lees . .Sparta Rotterdam, Rhoda JC, Kerkerade (Holland)
- Graham Leggatt . . . . .Manager of Toronto Star
- Anders Limpar . . . . .Cremonese (Italy), Swedish football
- John Linford . . . . . .DS79 Doredrecht, Den Haag, NAC Breda, Zurich, Fortuna Sittard, FC Utrecht, Go Ahead Eagles
- Ivor Linton . . . . .Kasko IK, IK Kraft Naipes
- Kenny Lowe . . . . .Spearwood Dalmatic (Australia)
- Tresor Luntala . . . . .FC Rennes, French Football Academy
- Mark McCarrick . . . . .FC Koprait
- Jim McDonough . . . . .Wichita Wings

171

- Duncan McDowell . . . . .Liberty College FC (Virginia)
- Ted McMinn . . . . .FC Seville
- Dave Mackay . . . . . .Manager Al Shahab (Dubai) & Al Arabi (Kuwait), coach of Zamalek, Egypt.
- David Madden . . . . .Los Angeles Lazers
- Joe Mallett . . . . .Manager of Panionios, Greece
- Marcelo Cipriano . . . . .Del Aleves (Brazil)
- Roy Martin . . . . .Portland Timbers, coach at Oregon State University
- Richie Moran . . . . .FC Fujita
- Trevor Morgan . . . . .Sydney St George, Happy Valley, South China
- Tony Morley . . . . .FC Seiko, Den Haag, Tampa Bay Rowdies, Hamrun Spartans (Malta), New Zealand football
- Ronnie Morris . . . . .Nuvo Pistoiese
- Thomas Myhre . . . . .FC Moss, Viking Stavenger
- Peter Ndlovu . . . . .Highlands FC (Bulawayo)
- Foley Okenla . . .Leventis United & Julius Berger FC (Nigeria), FC Zion, Montreal Impact
- Bryan Orritt . . . . . . .Johannesburg Rangers, coach in Soweto
- John Paskin . . . . . . .Hellenic, Toronto Blizzard, South China, FC Seiko, KV Kortrijk (Belgium)
- Fred Pentland . . .Coach in Germany, France & Spain (Athletic Bilbao)
- Paul Peschisolido . . . . . .Toronto Blizzard, Kansas City Comets
- Arthur Phoenix . . . . .Racing Club de Paris
- Ted Purdon . . . . .Marist Brothers (South Africa), Polish White Eagles (Toronto)
- Sir Alf Ramsey . . . . .Panathinaikos (Technical Director)
- Bruce Rioch . . . . .Seattle Sounders
- Billy Ronson . . . . .Baltimore Blast, Detroit Rockers, Tampa Bay Rowdies
- Billy Rudd . . . . .New York All Stars
- Sigurd Rushfeldt . . . . .FC Tromso
- Guy Russell .Kemin Palloseura (Finland)
- Mickael Sabathier . . . . .Toulouse
- Dan Sahlin . . . . .Hammarby
- Vinny Samways . . . . .Las Palmas
- Danny Sonner . . . . .Preussen Kolm
- Alberto Tarantini . . . .Boca Juniors, Talleres Cordoba, River Plate, Bastia (Corsica),Toulose, Urania, FC Geneva, Platense
- Gordon Taylor . . . . .Vancouver Whitecaps
- Bobby A. Thomson . . . . .Hartford Bi-Centennials, Connecticut Bi-Centennials, Memphis Rogue
- Colin Todd . . . . .Vancouver Whitecaps
- Tony Towers . . . . .Montreal Manic, Tampa Bay Rowdies, Vancouver Whitecaps
- Tony Van Mierlo . . . . .Kraarwogals, SVV Eindhoven, RWD Molenbeek, MVV Maastricht, AA Ghent, Racing Club Harelbeke VV Venlo
- Johnny Vincent .Connecticut Bi-Centennials
- Geoff Vowden . . . . .New York Cosmos, Saudi Arabia (coach)
- Alex Wallace . . . . .Baltimore FC
- Tony Want . . . . .Minnesota Kicks, Philadelphia Fury
- Neil Whatmore . . . . .Coach of Mannin Rangers (South Africa)
- Steve Whitton . . . . .Halmstad BK
- Chris Whyte . . . . .Los Angeles Lazers, Detriot Neon
- Jacques Williams . . . . .Bordeaux, French Football Academy
- Peter Withe . . . . .Port Elizabeth, Arcadia Shepherds, Portland Timbers

- Colin Withers . . . . .Go Ahead Eagles
- Chris Woods . . . . .Colorado Rapids (USA)
- Frank Worthington . . . . . . .Philadelphia Fury, Tampa Bay Rowdies, Capetown Spurs
- Christopher Wreh . . . . .AS Monaco, AC Milan, Monrovia IFC, Guincamp
- Pat Wright . . . . .Coach in Dubai, Saudi Arabia, UAE & Zambia

Bart Griemink

Kenny Lowe

OVERSEAS TOURS

Blues' first official tour took them to Denmark in 1922 where they played three matches (all won). The King of Denmark attended every one and had no guards near him! Indeed, he used to walk round the streets daily, chatting to the local people who used to take off their hats and bow to him. He did likewise in return.

In the summer of 1923 Blues visited Spain where they played two matches, the first against Real Madrid (won 3-0) and the second versus CD Europa in Barcelona (won 6-1). In the latter fixture the home side, 5-0 down at half-time, refused to come out for the second period -and it took 10 minutes of gentle persuasion before they left the dressing room! Joe Bradford scored a cheeky backheeler in this game and so annoyed and frustrated was the Spanish 'keeper that he grabbed Joe by the throat and all but strangled him!

In May 1930, en-route to Denmark, Blues stopped off in Holland and defeated Sparta Rotterdam 2-1 before going on to lose 2-0 and then beat a Copenhagen Select side 2-1 in the Danish capital. Soon afterwards they accounted for a Denmark XI by 5-4 when both Joe Bradford and George Hicks each netted twice and on the homeward journey they stopped in Germany to hammer a Berlin Select 5-0 when the same two players again netted braces.

Blues' first post Second World War tour took them to Sweden in May 1946 where they played four games, winning three, including a 2-1 victory over a strong AIK Stockholm side that included six internationals.

In May 1948 a five-match tour to Switzerland resulted in four wins and a draw for Blues, their best victory being a 5-0 demolition of Basle.

Four years later, in May 1952, Blues visited Germany, Denmark and Holland. They played six matches, winning them all with a goal average of 23-7. Their best victory was 6-2 v Flensburg while Armenia Bielgeld were beaten 5-0.

Another tour to Switzerland and Austria in 1959 ended with a 7-0 win over FC Schaffhausen after Blues had started off with a 5-2 win in Lucerne.

Blues played both Atletico Madrid and Seville in Spain in 1960 and in May/June 1961 they took part in an international soccer tournament in North America (see under USA Tournament).

Blues visited Austria and Germany in May 1964, playing three matches, winning two of them: 6-3 v Rheindalen and 5-1 against Wuppertal.

Since then several short tours to various parts of the world have taken place, mainly pre-season and these include trips to Holland (many times, starting in 1970), Australia and Tahiti (winning all four matches in May 1973), Switzerland (again and again), France (in 1974 - when they didn't conceded a goal in three matches), Spain (three times including the La Linea tournament in August 1978), USA & Canada (once more in July 1972 - when they beat Baltimore 7-2 in their opening game), Norway (twice), Belgium, Denmark (twice) and even South America (playing in Peru, Honduras, Columbia and Guatamala in May 1981).

Blues line-up before a tour game in Sweden in 1946.

OVERSON, Vince

Vince Overson

No-nonsense centre-half, a battling, totally committed predominantly right-footed defender, Overson skippered Blues to victory in the Leyland DAF Final at Wembley in 1991 and made 212 senior appearances and scored five goals during his five years at St Andrew's (June 1986 to August 1991). Born in Kettering on 15 May 1962, Overson played Kingswood Boys, Corby Town and Long Buckby FC before joining Burnley as an apprentice in June 1978, turning professional in November 1979. An

England youth international, he helped the Clarets win the Third Division championship in 1982 and made almost 250 appearances during his time at Turf Moor before his £235,000 transfer to St Andrew's.

A big favourite with the fans, Overson served Blues well before departing with others to rejoin his manager Lou Macari at Stoke City for a tribunal set fee of £55,000. He quickly picked up two more winners' prizes with the Potters with triumphs in the Autoglass Trophy in 1991 (at Wembley) and the Second Division title in 1993. He went on to amass 216 first-team appearances for

Stoke prior to completing a full circle when he returned to Burnley for a second spell in August 1996. He took his career appearance tally to past the 700 mark in 1997-98 following a loan spell with Shrewsbury Town. Later he assisted Halifax Town and Padiham.

● Overson played alongside his brother Richard in five League games for Burnley in 1979-80.

OWN GOALS

Centre-half Trevor Smith conceded an own-goal on his League debut for Blues against Derby County on 31 October 1953 - but still finished on the winning side (4-2).

Blues gave away two own-goals in their 4-0 League defeat at Oldham in November 1995.

Blues goalkeeper Martin Thomas stepped back over the line with the ball in his hand to concede an own-goal against Shrewsbury Town in a League game at St Andrew's on 27 March 1989. Blues lost 2-1.

Goalkeeper Gary Sprake, prior to joining Blues, threw the ball into his own net playing for Leeds United against Liverpool in December 1967 - a classic own goal!

Kevin Lock scored for both Blues and Fulham in a League game at Craven Cottage in November 1979.

OXFORD UNITED

Blues' playing record against United is:

FOOTBALL LEAGUE

Venue	P	W	D	L	F	A
Home	13	4	6	3	13	8
Away	13	6	3	4	17	11
Totals	26	10	9	7	30	19

The first Blues-Oxford League game took place on 2 November 1968 at St Andrew's. Almost 23,500 fans turned out to see United win 1-0.

In early January, though, Blues gained revenge with a 2-1 win at The Manor Ground, Fred Pickering and Phil Summerill the scorers.

Oxford doubled up over Blues in 1969-70 and won one of the two clashes the following season while Blues gained a 1-0 home victory in 1971-72.

With the teams in different Divisions, there was no action for twelve years (until 1984-85) and then it was Blues who came out on top, winning 3-0 at St Andrew's after a 0-0 draw at Oxford.

When Blues beat Oxford 1-0 at The Manor Ground in February 1986, it ended a run of 17 League games without a victory. Wayne Clarke was the goalscoring hero!

When Blues won 7-1 at Oxford in December 1998 they led 4-0 at half-time. This was their biggest win over the 'U's' and equalled their third highest away victory at League level. Gary Rowett and Paul Furlong both scored twice.

Colin Todd is Oxford's oldest player - aged 35 years, 4 months in 1984.

Players with both clubs include: T Aylott, M Bullock, K Dearden, K Francis, M Gabbiadini, A Harris, D Hill, HR Houghton, R Hynd, R Knight, D Langan, DW Liney, S Marsh, E Newton, M Page, L Phillips, D Purse, C Todd, J Trewick, N Whatmore, C Whyte.

Also: Arthur Turner (Blues player and manager of both clubs), Jim Smith (manager of both clubs), Ken Fish (Blues reserve and coach, Oxford trainer).

PAGE, Malcolm

Malcolm Page

Malcolm Page was born just inside the Welsh border at Knucklas, Radnorshire during the arctic winter of 1947 (5 February) when his mother, who was visiting an aunt, was stranded, unable to return to her home in England.

Encouraged to play soccer rather than rugby by his father, Bill, a South Shropshire League referee, Page was spotted by Birmingham City scout Don Dorman playing for the Radnorshire County XI.

He was signed as an apprentice in July 1964 and upgraded to the professional ranks by Blues' manager Gil Merrick within two months of his arrival at St Andrew's.

Page developed fast and made his senior debut two days after his 18th birthday (against Everton). Blues were relegated at the end of his first season with the club but Page had already shown what he could do. A versatile player, able to occupy a variety of positions (including that of goalkeeper) he was at his best as a defender where his consistent performances earned the respect of his fellow professionals. He had the ability to man mark the most talented players in the game and perhaps his best display in a Welsh jersey came in 1975 when Hungary were defeated 2-1 in Budapest as Wales swept into the quarter finals of the European Championships.

Page appeared in 28 full internationals for his country - making him Blues' most capped player. He had his first outing against Finland in Helsinki in May 1971 (three days before his wedding) and his last against West Germany eight years later.

He never asked for a transfer and went on to spend over 17 years at St Andrew's, amassing almost 400 senior appearances and helping Blues win promotion from the Second Division in 1972 and reach two FA Cup semi-finals (1968 and 1975).

After leaving Blues he had a year or so with Oxford United before retiring in 1972 to start work for a large insurance company based in Birmingham.

PEER, Dean

Peer in action v Walsall, March 1990

Born in Wordsley, Stourbridge on 8 August 1969, midfielder Dean Peer played for Lye Town and Stourbridge Falcons before joining Blues on the YTS in July 1985, turning professional two years later. With his distinctive gangling style the 6ft. 2in. Peer initially played wide on the right but was later switched to the centre. A hard-working performer he scored 12 goals in exactly 150 first team outings for Blues, collecting a Leyland DAF Trophy winners' medal in 1991. After loan spells with both Mansfield Town and Walsall he was eventually transferred to the Saddlers in November 1993 and quickly scored a hat-trick in a 5-2 win over Lincoln City. In August 1995 Peer left the Bescot Stadium for Northampton Town and made over 150 appearances for the Cobblers up to 2000 when he joined Shrewsbury.

PENALTY KICK

The penalty kick was first introduced to the Football League in September 1891, the Irish FA having featured it the previous season.

Fred Wheldon scored the first spot-kick for Blues in a 2-2 home draw with Aston Villa on 20 October 1894.

Billy Beer scored 7 times (in 7 attempts) from the penalty spot for Blues (1902-10). Billy Wright netted 12 times for Blues from 'twelve yards' in his three years at the club (1983-86).

Blues were the first team to be involved in a penalty shoot-out in the FA Cup. It was against Stoke City in a match to decide the third place in the competition on 5 August 1972. The game was played at St Andrew's and after a 0-0 draw in normal time, Blues beat the Potters 4-3 on penalties, Alan Campbell, Bobby Hope, Stan Harland and Trevor Francis netting from the spot.

Ritchie Blackmore saved two penalties after coming on as a sub-

Wolves and England international Ron Flowers brings down Blues' striker Ken Leek inside the area during the First Division League game at St Andrew's in March 1963.

stitute for Blues in their Texaco Cup game with Stoke City in October 1973. Blues won the contest 3-1 on penalties after a 0-0 aggregate draw over two legs.

Stoke are the only team Blues have so far met in two penalty shoot-outs.

Blues' goalkeeper Gil Merrick saved a penalty from his England team-mate Bill Eckersley in a Second Division game in April 1952 but the Blackburn Rovers left-back recovered quickly to head home the rebound - one of the few occasions a 'penalty' has been scored with the head!

Centre-forward Joe Lane scored a penalty on his League debut for Blues in the 2-2 away draw with Lincoln City in March 1920.

Stan Lynn netted a penalty for Blues in both League games against his former club Aston Villa in 1963-64.

The following season Lynn scored from the spot in three successive games for Blues.

Alex Stepney scored a penalty to give Manchester United a 1-0 home League win over Blues in October 1973. It was his second spot-kick success.

Len Davies of Cardiff City had his penalty kick saved by Blues' goalkeeper Dan Tremelling during the final League game of the 1923-24 season. The result was a 0-0 draw and if Cardiff had won they would have taken the First Division championship!

Billy Walker, the England international, netted two penalty kicks for Aston Villa in a 3-0 home win over Blues in March 1923.

Both Gary Sprake and Tony Coton saved penalties on their debuts for Blues.

Blues lost 7-6 on penalties to Watford in the First Division play-off semi-final at St Andrew's in May 1999. The scores were level at 1-1 after the two legs before the game went a shoot out to decide who went through to Wembley. The Hornets stung the Blues and

went on to gain a place in the Premiership.

Blues were beaten 4-1 on penalties by West Bromwich Albion in the Anglo-Italian Cup semi-final at St Andrew's in January 1996. Former Blues player David Smith netted the clinching spot-kick for the Baggies. The game had ended 2-2 in normal playing time.

The three spot kicks fluffed by Blues' players at the end of this game made it 14 misses out of 24 kicks in double quick-time! And when Steve Claridge failed with his spot-kick in the second leg of the League Cup semi-final against Leeds United soon afterwards it was 15 misses out of 25!

Blues' goalkeeper Jack Dorrington saved two penalties, both taken by Aston Villa's Harry Hampton, during a 5-2 Lord Mayor of Birmingham Charity Cup victory in September 1908.

Former Blues midfielder Kevin Dillon scored a hat-trick of penalties for Portsmouth in a Full Members Cup-tie against Millwall in November 1986.

And Willie Johnston, before joining Blues, scored a hat-trick for Rangers against St Johnstone in a Scottish League Cup-tie in 1971. Two of his goals came from penalties, his third was a follow-up after his spot-kick had been saved!

Don Dearson (Blues) missed a penalty for Wales in the Wartime international against England at St Andrew's in October 1941 and Trevor Francis (ex-Blues) did likewise for England!

Goalkeepers Billy George (then of Aston Villa, later Blues) and Harry Hibbs, both saved penalties in full internationals for England, George against Ireland in 1902 and Hibbs (from Fred Keenor) against Wales in 1930.

Nigel Winterburn, former Blues left-back, missed a penalty for Arsenal in the 1988 League Cup Final against Luton Town at Wembley - one of only a handful of players to miss from the spot at the Empire Stadium.

Don Givens (ex-Blues) missed a penalty with his last kick in English football - and it sent Sheffield United into the Fourth Division for the first time in the club's history. It happened on the final day of the 1980-81 season when the Blades lost 1-0 at home to Walsall - Givens' penalty could have earned them the vital point which would have kept them up!

On 5 September 1981 Nottingham Forest 'keeper Peter Shilton saved a twice-taken penalty from Blues midfielder Archie Gemmill. The two had played together at The City Ground.

Gerry Daly (then of Coventry) had a twice-taken penalty saved by each time Notts County's 'keeper Raddy Avranovic in September 1981.

Stan Lynn netting a penalty for Blues against his former club Aston Villa at St Andrew's in 1962

PENDREY, Garry

Garry Pendrey

Garry Pendrey gave Blues terrific service as a player - amassing 360 appearances and scoring five goals. A West Bromwich Albion supporter as a lad, he joined the apprentice ranks at St Andrew's in July 1965 after doing well with Stanley Star and Harborne Lynwood in local junior football. He became a professional in October 1966 and at the end of that season played in the FA Youth Cup Final defeat by Sunderland. In 1972, having established himself in defence, he helped Blues win promotion from the Second Division. He remained at St Andrew's until the summer of 1979 when, after his testimonial match against neighbours West Brom, he moved to The Hawthorns to strengthen the Baggies defensive squad. During the early 1980s Pendrey assisted Torquay United and Bristol Rovers and in July 1982 was named player-coach of Walsall, later acting as assistant-manager to former Blues striker Alan Buckley (1983-86). His next appointment took him to Molineux as coach in November 1986. He then had an eventful two-year spell as manager of Blues from June 1987 to April 1989 before returning to Molineux to take up his coaching duties for a second time. Pendrey later became coach under Gordon Strachan at Premiership club Coventry City.

Born in Lozells, Birmingham on 9 February 1949, Pendrey was Blues' youngest captain when in 1969 he skippered the side at the age of 20 years, six months.

PERUGIA

On 11 October 1994 Blues beat Perugia 1-0 in Italy in the Anglo-Italian tournament. Just 1,500 fans saw Steve Castle score the game's only goal in the 51st minute.

PESCHISOLIDO, Paul (Paulo Pesqu...

Paul Peschisolido

Paul Peschisolido, Canadian international striker, who is married to Birmingham City's Managing Director Karren Brady, had two spells with Blues - the first lasted from November 1992 until August 1994 and his second from March to July 1996. Born in Scarborough, Ontario on 25 May 1971, he played for Toronto Blizzards (twice) and Kansas City Comets before moving to St Andrew's first time round, his original purchase being financed by 'Blues Society' Scheme. In between his spells with Blues he starred for Stoke City (sold for £400,000 to help finance the purchase of Mike Newell) and after leaving in 1996 he moved across the Midlands to neighbouring West Bromwich Albion, this time for £600,000. The Baggies then sold him to Fulham for £1.1 million in October 1997. He helped the Cottagers win the Second Division championship two years later and in 2000 his total number of full international caps with Canada reached 35.

Standing only 5ft. 4ins. tall, Pesch is a nippy, all-action striker who scored 18 goals in his 57 outings for Blues.

PETERBOROUGH UNITED (Fletton U

Blues' playing record against Posh is:
FOOTBALL LEAGUE

Venue	P	W	D	L	F	A
Home	4	2	2	0	7	1
Away	4	1	1	2	5	6
Totals	8	3	3	2	12	7

FA CUP
Home	1	1	0	0	4	3

AUTO WINDSCREEN SHIELD
Away	1	1	0	0	5	3

TEXACO CUP
Away	1	0	1	0	1	1

In season 1991-92 after a 1-1 draw at St Andrew's (the first League game between the two clubs), Blues won 3-2 at London Road with a fine Trevor Matthewson goal proving decisive.

Two goals by Gary Bull helped Blues to an excellent 4-0 home win over Posh on 18 September 1994. Seventeen year-old Mark Taylor made his debut for Posh in this game.

In a third round FA Cup-tie at St Andrew's in January 1928 non-League Peterborough looked like causing a major upset when they led Blues 3-1 at half-time. But Blues fought back to win the contest 4-3 thanks mainly to a fine hat-trick by top-scorer Joe Bradford. There were 4,000 Posh fans in the 38,000 plus crowd. This was, in fact, Blues' 100th game in the competition.

When Jonathan Hunt scored a hat-trick in a 5-3 AWS victory at London Road in September 1994 he became the first Blues player to achieve that feat for nine years. Ryan Price, making his Blues debut, conceded a goal after just 55 seconds!

Players with both clubs include: K Ashley, F Barber, M Bodley, G Breen, K Bremner, S Castle, K Charlery, G Cooper, J Cornforth, M Darrell, K Dearden, JM De Souza, A Edwards, H Forinton, R Forsyth, N Freeman, A Godden, M Gorman, B Griemink, W Guest, M Halsall, M Hellawell, D Langan, A Legg, I Linton, A Murray, M O'Connor, R Otto, SE Phillips, M Prudhoe, S Rea, A Rees, CL Richards, S Robinson, RP Scott, D Seaman, B Sedgemore, G Sissons, A Styles, R Willis.

Also: Barry Fry (manager of both clubs), Lil Fuccillo (Posh player and manager, Blues coach).

• Fry led Posh to victory in the Third Division play-off final at the end of the 1999-2000 season.

Ricky Otto

PHILLIPS, Charlie

Cuthbert Phillips, who was always known as Charlie, was born in Victoria, Monmouthshire, on 23 June 1910 and won Welsh schoolboy honours while working as a boilerman and playing Welsh League football for Ebbw Vale in 1925. Several clubs wanted to sign him and he had offers from Plymouth Argyle, Torquay United and Cardiff City before signing professional forms for Wolves in August 1929. He was a speedy forward, mostly at home on the right wing, and that is where he played the majority of his 200 plus senior games for Wolves. He was capped ten times for Wales while at Molineux, and he helped Wolves win the Second Division championship in 1931-32, scoring 18 goals. Phillips netted on his international debut v Northern Ireland at Wrexham in 1931 and captained his country on six occasions. At Christmas 1935 he was sent-off whilst skippering Wolves against Bolton and a month later, in January 1936, he was transferred to Aston Villa for £9,000. He was capped three more times as a Villa player, but made only 25 appearances for the Birmingham club and although he scored on his debut (in a 3-1 win at Derby) he could not save them from relegation. When they returned as Second Division champions in 1937-38 he managed only a handful of games before moving across the City to join Blues in March 1938. In 1939 - after netting 10 goals in 25 outings - Phillips went into non-League football with Chelmsford City. He then guested for several clubs until retiring at the end of the War. Phillips was a fine all-round sportsman who also excelled at cricket, golf, tennis, rugby union and various athletics events. He was later a licensee in Bushbury and Lichfield, dying in the latter City on 21 October 1969.

PICKERING, Fred

Fred Pickering

Scorer of 32 goals in 88 games for Blues, centre-forward Fred Pickering had a fine career in League football. He ventured around the country playing in turn, for Blackburn Rovers (FA Youth Cup winners in 1959), Everton, Blues (signed from Goodison Park for £50,000 in August 1967), Blackpool (transferred from St Andrew's in June 1969), Blackburn Rovers (again) and finally Brighton & Hove Albion as a trialist in 1972. Capped by England on three occasions, he scored a hat-trick on his debut in a 10-0 win over the USA, but unfortunately he missed out on England's glory year of 1966 and was an absentee from Everton's FA Cup Final victory over Sheffield Wednesday that same year. Besides his senior caps Pickering also represented his country in three under 23 internationals and played for the Football League XI. During a fine career he netted a total of 168 goals in 354 League games. After quitting football Pickering became a fork lift truck driver.

PHYSIOTHERAPISTS

Blues training session in 1931

Certainly up until the 1950s a professional club, Birmingham City included, did not employ a physiotherapist as such. The injuries were treated by the trainer or coach, even the assistant-manager or medical officer (commissioned by the club). The trainer used to take the players for morning training sessions, unlike the physio of today, and it was common practice for the trainer (physio) to be deeply involved with the fitness and general welfare of the players.

(See under Coaches)

PLASTIC PITCHES

Blues have played a total of nine League matches on artificial surfaces, all away from home. Their full record on plastic is:

P	W	D	L	F	A	Pts
9	1	2	6	0	21	4

Their first encounter was at Loftus Road against QPR on 19 November 1983. They lost 2-1, Mick Harford having the pleasure of scoring Blues' first 'plastic-covered' goal!

Blues' single victory came at Boundary Park on 31 October 1987 when they beat the Latics 2-1 with goals from John Frain and Steve Whitton (penalty).

They drew 2-2 with Oldham the previous season.

Blues also lost 3-1 to QPR in September 1985, 2-0 at Luton in November 1985, 4-0 at Boundary Park in September 1988 and twice at Deepdale against Preston, 2-0 in March 1991 and 3-2 April 1992, having earlier drawn 2-2 with North End in April 1990.

PLAYERS

Blues manager Barry Fry utilised a total of 47 players in competitive matches during season 1995-96 - a club record. This beat his previous 'best' tally of 41 in 1994-95. Darwen (45) held the previous record for players back in season 1897-98.

When Blues lost 1-0 at home to Liverpool in the TNT Inter City Cup in July 1995 manager Barry Fry used 23 players. Liverpool utilised 15 - good value for the 13,178 fans!

A year earlier for a pre-season friendly against Walsall at the Bescot Stadium in July 1994 Fry called on the services of 21 players in Blues' 2-1 victory.

PLAYERS' UNION (PFA)

Walter Wigmore (Blues) represented the Players' Union Select team against England in 1898-99. And 100 years later former Blues winger Gordon Taylor was a key figure within the Professional Footballers' Association.

PLAYING RECORD

Blues' first-class playing record in all major League, Cup and senior wartime competitions. Abandoned matches not included.

Competition	P	W	D	L	F	A
Anglo-Italian Cup	17	8	5	4	28	24
Anglo-Scottish Cup	6	2	3	1	9	7
Autoglass Trophy	2	0	0	2	1	4
Auto-Windscreen Shield	8	8	0	0	22	8
Football Alliance	66	25	12	29	155	169
FA Cup	301	134	59	108	537	400
Football League	3946	1487	972	1487	5786	5680
League Play-offs	4	2	0	2	3	6
League Test Matches	7	2	2	3	14	14
Football League Cup	146	62	36	48	225	195
Full Members Cup	2	1	0	1	5	3
Inter Cities Fairs Cup	25	14	6	5	51	38
Leyland DAF Trophy	10	8	1	1	15	7
M.Counties League	6	2	1	3	15	14
Texaco Cup	12	2	8	2	14	12
Wartime (1st)	106	57	20	29	221	142
Wartime (2nd)	215	107	39	69	428	335
Totals	4879	1921	1164	1794	7529	7058

Also:	P	W	D	L	F	A
TNT Challenge	1	0	0	1	0	1
Football League Jubilee	2	0	0	2	0	5
Festival of Britain	4	2	0	2	10	10

PLYMOUTH ARGYLE

Blues' playing record against the Pilgrims is:

FOOTBALL LEAGUE

Venue	P	W	D	L	F	A
Home	12	7	3	2	27	11
Away	12	5	4	3	17	15
Totals	24	12	7	5	44	26

LEAGUE CUP

Home	5	3	1	1	9	3
Away	5	3	0	2	6	6
Totals	10	6	1	3	15	9

ANGLO-SCOTTISH CUP

Away	2	0	2	0	2	2

WARTIME

Home	1	0	0	1	0	1
Away	1	1	0	0	3	2
Totals	2	1	0	1	3	3

Harold Bodle scored a hat-trick in Blues' 6-1 home win over Argyle in December 1946 - the first League meeting between the clubs and Blues' best-ever win over the Pilgrims.

Blues completed the double this season by winning 2-0 at Home Park.

The kick-off time for the Blues v Plymouth Argyle Second Division game at St Andrew's on Christmas Day 1952, was delayed because the Argyle captain John Porteous couldn't be found! He was eventually located by a member of the Blues' staff...celebrating the festive season somewhat early! He didn't play in Argyle's next two matches! Blues won the game 4-0 and two members of the

Argyle side - Gordon Astall and Alex Govan - were soon to become Brummies.

Jackie Lane, a stand-in centre-forward, scored a tremendous goal when Blues played Argyle in April 1955. He received the ball near the halfway line and raced past four non-plussed defenders before finding the net in a 3-1 win.

Nineteen years after the clubs had first met, Argyle gained revenge for that 1946 scoreline by defeating Blues by exactly the same margin (6-1) at Home Park in September 1965 (Division 2). Mike Trebilcock (soon to star in an FA Cup Final for Everton) scored a hat-trick for the Pilgrims that day; Blues goalkeeper Jim Herriot had a 'stinker' and Terry Hennessey was out in the cold playing as a sweeper!

That defeat was soon forgotten, though, when Bobby Thomson's goal gave Blues a 1-0 victory in the return fixture five months later!

Blues and Argyle did not meet at League level for almost 19 years (from April 1968) and then it was Blues who came good, winning 3-2 at home in New Year's Day 1987 when midfielders Martin Kuhl and Dennis Mortimer both figured on the scoresheet.

On 3 September 1994 Dave Regis scored twice in Blues' 4-2 home win over the Pilgrims while in South Devon in April 1995 Steve Claridge netted a couple of goals as Blues completed the double with a 3-1 victory.

Goalkeeper Colin Withers made his senior debut for Blues in a League Cup game at St Andrew's against Argyle in November 1960 (result was a 0-0 draw).

Blues beat Argyle 5-1 on aggregate (4-1 at home, 1-0 away) in a second round League Cup-tie in 1984-85. They repeated the act in

Darren Rowbotham

1993-94, winning 3-2 over two legs (3-0, 0-2) and then completed the treble with a 3-1 aggregate victory in 1995-96 (1-0 at home, 2-1 away).

The first-ever competitive game between the clubs was in the Football League (South) in March 1946 when Argyle won 1-0 on Blues' soil.

Players with both clubs include: G Astall, J Bloomfield, L Boyd, K Bremner, G Briggs, T Briggs, K Brown, S Castle, G Cox, N Dougall, R Dryden, H Forinton, W Foster, A Govan, CB Hare, AJ Jackson, H Lane, A Leonard, A Miller, J Newman, C Phillips (Argyle trialist), G Poole, D Regis, D Rowbotham, L Sealey (Blues N/C), WH Smith, K Summerfield, D Smith, HM Wilcox.

Also: Mike Kelly (Blues player, Argyle reserve team coach and manager), George Foster (Argyle player, Blues coach).

- Trevor Francis was born in Plymouth and watched Argyle as a youngster at Home Park.

POINTS

The most League points gained by Blues in a season (with three available for a victory) has been 89 in 1994-95. They amassed 59 under the 2 points for a win rule in 1947-48.

The least Blues have collected (3 points for a win) is 29 in 1985-86 and under the 2-point law it was 22 in 1938-39.

POOLE, Gary

Gary Poole

Gary Poole took over the right-back berth from Scott Hiley in the Blues side in the mid 1990s. Born in Stratford (London not Warwickshire) on 11 September 1967, he started his professional career with Tottenham Hotspur in 1985 but failed to make the first XI at White Hart Lane. In August 1987 he was transferred to Cambridge United; in March 1989 he switched to Barnet and in June 1992 found his way to Plymouth Argyle. From Home Park Poole moved to Southend United in July 1993 (under manager Barry Fry) and it was Fry who brought him to St Andrew's in September 1994. On leaving Blues in November 1996 Poole signed for Charlton Athletic but unfortunately he suffered a serious knee injury with the Addicks which forced him to quit the game in February 2000 after lengthy spells of physiotherapy covering almost two years. He made only 16 appearances for Charlton, having earlier amassed 102 for Blues (three goals scored). Poole helped Barnet win the GMVC title in 1991 and was in Blues' Second Division and Auto Windscreen Shield winning sides of 1995.

POOLE, Kevin

Goalkeeper Kevin Poole had already made 240 League appearances before he joined Blues (as cover for Ian Bennett) in August 1997. Born in Bromsgrove on 21 July 1963, Poole played initially for Aston Villa (1981-84) and after spells with Northampton Town,

Middlesbrough and Hartlepool United (the first and last on loan) he had almost 200 first-class outings for Leicester City, gaining a League Cup winners' medal in 1997. Sound on crosses and a specialist penalty-saver (it is believed Kevin has stopped a dozen spot kicks in open play) he kept nine clean sheets for Blues in 1998-99. Poole has now amassed over 60 appearances for Blues (as Bennett's deputy).

PORT VALE (Burslem)

Murphy scoring against Vale in the 7-2 win in 1954.

Blues' playing record against the Valiants is:

FOOTBALL LEAGUE

Venue	P	W	D	L	F	A
Home	14	11	1	2	45	14
Away	14	6	2	6	18	23
Totals	28	17	3	8	63	37

FA CUP

Venue	P	W	D	L	F	A
Home	5	4	0	1	16	4
Away	1	0	0	1	1	2
Totals	6	4	0	2	17	6

WARTIME

Venue	P	W	D	L	F	A
Home	1	1	0	0	4	0
Away	1	0	0	1	0	3
Totals	2	1	0	1	4	3

Blues' first ever game in the Football League was at home to (Burslem) Port Vale on 2 September 1892. A crowd of 2,500 at Muntz Street saw Blues race to a 5-1 win against the ten men of Vale (Billy Beats was their missing player, having failed to get on the train at Stoke). Vale arrived at the ground half-and-hour late and the kick-off was delayed for an hour, the game eventually starting at 4.30pm. Fred Wheldon claimed Blues' first League goal while

Wallace Bliss was the first opponent to score against Blues at League level. (This was also Vale's first ever League match).

Blues also won in the Potteries later that season by 3-0, Billy Walton scoring twice.

Vale gained revenge with a 5-0 home win in September 1893 but Blues went one better at Muntz Street six months later, romping to a 6-0 victory, Walton (2) and Frank Mobley (2) the top marksmen.

Another big Blues home win followed in January 1903, Vale going down 5-1 with Jimmy Windridge a two-goal hero this time round.

On 2 May 1921 Blues beat Port Vale 4-0 at St Andrew's and five days later they won 2-0 on Vale soil to complete the double. These four points gained duly brought the Second Division championship to St Andrew's.

There was a break of more than 33 years before the teams did battle again in the Football League and when they did Vale lost 7-2 to Blues at St Andrew's in November 1954. This was the first time the Potteries' club had conceded that many goals in a League game for 17 years. Peter Murphy scored a hat-trick for Blues, while future Vale player Noel Kinsey netted twice. Vale won the return fixture 2-0 in front of almost 25,000 fans - at a time when Blues were surging towards the Second Division championship!

There followed another lengthy break of 40 years before the teams met again - this time on 29 October 1995 when Blues won 2-1 at Vale Park, Paul Tait and Steve Claridge the goalscorers.

Walter Abbott scored a hat-trick when Blues beat the Vale 7-0 in an FA Cup fifth qualifying round tie at Muntz Street in December 1898, having lost 2-1 in the same competition in the Potteries the previous season. This is Vale's heaviest defeat in any major cup competition.

In November 1905 Blues beat Vale 7-0 in a Birmingham cup-tie.

Players with both clubs include: G Anderson, W Aveyard, D Barnett, J Beckford, A Box, R Firth, S Fox, J Greenhoff, G Haywood, LR Jenkins, FW Jones, N Kinsey, T Lees, J McCarthy, S Moreland, I Osborne, J Peart, N Platnauer, CG Spencer (Blues reserve), P Sproson, F Stokes, PJ Taylor, A Richards (Blues junior), RA Thomson.

Also: Andrew Waterhouse and John Westmancoat (secretaries of both clubs).

● When he was transferred to Blues in September 1997, winger Jon McCarthy became Vale's most expensive 'outgoing' player.

PORTSMOUTH

Blues' playing record against Pompey is:

FOOTBALL LEAGUE

Venue	P	W	D	L	F	A
Home	35	22	7	6	72	39
Away	35	11	10	14	49	51
Totals	70	33	17	20	121	90

FA CUP

Venue	P	W	D	L	F	A
Home	6	4	0	2	8	8
Away	2	0	1	1	1	2
Totals	8	4	1	3	9	10

WARTIME

Venue	P	W	D	L	F	A
Home	1	1	0	0	1	0
Away	1	1	0	0	4	3
Totals	2	2	0	0	5	3

The first Blues-Portsmouth League game was played at Fratton Park on 26 November 1927 when 14,000 fans witnessed the 2-2 draw, Johnny Crosbie scoring twice for Blues.

Blues won the return fixture 2-0 five months later in front of a 30,000 crowd at St Andrew's.

A week before the 1929 FA Cup Final Blues beat finalists Pompey 1-0 at home, Joe Bradford the scorer. And there was a repeat scoreline on the same ground twelve months later when Tom Fillingham's goal decided the outcome. Tom Grosvenor netted twice in Blues' 4-0 home win over Pompey on Christmas Eve 1932 and a month before the 1934 FA Cup Final, Portsmouth lost 3-1 at St Andrew's (Ned Barkas slamming in a penalty) and then succumbed 2-1 to Manchester City at Wembley.

In 1935-36 Blues scored seven goals without reply against Portsmouth, winning 4-0 at home and 3-0 away. And in the last season before the Great War when again Portsmouth reached the FA Cup Final (this time ending up as winners) Blues lost 2-0 at Fratton Park having won by the same score at St Andrew's.

Nicky Platnauer

Barry Horne

Football League champions-elect Portsmouth were defeated 3-0 by Blues at St Andrew's in April 1949 in front of 30,000 fans. But then as champions, Pompey came back to the same ground six months later and reversed that scoreline before a 38,000 gate.

When Blues beat Pompey 5-0 at Fratton Park in a First Division match in October 1955, Eddie Brown scored a hat-trick. Blues took the lead after just 35 seconds and were 4-0 up at half-time.

Blues triumphed 4-3 at Portsmouth at the start of the 1956-57 season thanks to an Alex Govan hat-trick and later on they completed the double with a 3-1 win at St Andrew's.

A crowd of almost 24,000 saw full-back Ken Green play his last League game for Blues in the 2-2 draw with Pompey at St Andrew's in November 1958. Brian Taylor scored his first goal for Blues in this same match.

In August 1966 a nine-goal classic at Fratton Park resulted in a 5-4 win for Blues, Geoff Vowden heading the scorers list with two. Six days later Blues completed the double with a 3-0 win at St Andrew's when Vowden was again on target.

On 8 January 1972 Blues crushed Pompey 6-3 at St Andrew's in a League game; the following the month Blues won 3-1 in the FA Cup and Messrs Hatton and Latchford, the two Bobs, scored seven of those nine goals between them.

In 1986-87 Portsmouth achieved the double over Blues as they powered into the First Division, and another Pompey double in 1992-93 saw them win 4-0 at Fratton Park and 3-2 at St Andrew's.

Pompey (from the Southern League) beat Blues 5-2 at St Andrew's in a first round FA Cup-tie in January 1909 in front of 18,813 fans.

Gil Merrick saved a penalty from Portsmouth's Duggie Reid in the FA Cup game at St Andrew's in January 1946 when Blues won 1-0 on aggregate.

Players with both clubs include: J Allen (Blues guest), J Beresford, N Blake, L Bradbury, S Bryant, S Claridge, L Daish, K Dearden, K Dillon, J Gordon, A Gosney, A Govan, I Hendon, S Hiley, B Horne, R Jones, M Kuhl, S Claridge, W McCafferty, F Mitchell (Pompey guest), A Mounteney, J Shufflebottom, G Smith, B Squires (Pompey trialist), A Styles, GF Wheldon, S Wigley, HM Wilcox.

Also: Jim Smith (manager of both clubs), Ron Saunders (Pompey player, Blues manager), Malcolm Beard (Blues player, Pompey coach), Stan Harland (Blues player, Pompey assistant-manager), Tony Taylor (Pompey player, Blues coach), Pat Wright (Blues player, Pompey coach & chief scout).

POSTPONED MATCHES

The 1962-63 Birmingham City-Bury third round FA Cup-tie was postponed no fewer than 14 times. It was scheduled to take place initially on Saturday 5 January 1963 but owing to the bad weather (snow, ice, frost) it was called off 14 times before finally getting the go-ahead on 5 March. Even then the game ended 3-3 at St Andrew's before the Shakers won the replay 48 hours later 2-0 at Gigg Lane.

During the 'Icelandic' winter Blues did not play a single game (League or Cup) between 23 December and 4 March.

In the 1946-47 winter, when the weather was just as bad, Blues played only two games between 29 December and 31 January. And in 1978-79 they did not fulfil a single League fixture between 31 December and 2 March, although they did lose an FA Cup-tie at home to Burnley on 6 January.

PRATT, Billy

Left-back Billy Pratt was born in Highgate, Birmingham in June 1872 and joined Blues at the age of 22 from the Birmingham Works League side Hoskins & Sewell in August 1894. He went on to appear in 139 first-class matches for the club before retiring through injury in May 1902. He could use both feet and was strong in defence, often committing fouls in dangerous situations!

PRESTON NORTH END

Blues' playing record against the Lillywhites is:

FOOTBALL LEAGUE

Venue	P	W	D	L	F	A
Home	36	22	8	6	70	36
Away	36	4	11	21	32	74
Totals	72	26	19	27	102	110

FA CUP

Home	2	2	0	0	3	1

LEAGUE CUP

Home	1	1	0	0	2	1
Away	1	1	0	0	1	0

The second League meeting between the clubs on 29 September 1894 produced an eight-goal thriller that finished all square at 4-4 - the first such scoreline in Blues' League history. A week earlier

Eddie Brown

Blues had won 1-0 at Deepdale, Tommy Hands the scorer.

Two excellent goals by Fred Wheldon helped Blues beat Preston 5-1 at home in November 1895 - six weeks after North End had won their home game 3-2.

Blues recorded their first League win at St Andrew's on 29 December 1906 when they defeated Preston North End 3-0. In opening the scoring in this game Benny Green also had the distinction of becoming the first player to claim a goal at the ground, sliding through the snow to put Blues ahead.

Blues completed the double over Preston in the space of seven days in March 1923, Albert Rawson scoring in both games.

Another Blues double was claimed in 1934-35 with a 1-0 win at Deepdale and a 3-0 victory at St Andrew's, Frank White netting a hat-trick in the latter game.

It was White who scored both goals in Blues' 2-2 home draw with FA Cup Finalists Preston in 1936-37 and he found the net against North End the following year as well. This led him to joining the Deepdale club in December 1938, six months after they had won the FA Cup!

Blues crashed to a 5-0 defeat at Preston in January 1939 - just two weeks after they had conceded six goals at Stoke!

A crowd of 44,500 saw Alex Govan score a cracking hat-trick (his fifth of the season) when Blues beat North End 3-0 at St Andrew's in a First Division game in September 1956. The little Scot netted a total of 13 goals in the first seven games of this season - a record for a winger.

On 1 February 1958 Blues went down 8-0 at Preston (their heaviest League defeat since 1930). It made it 20 goals conceded in five matches.

Six goals were shared at 3-3 when Blues visited Preston for a Second Division game in August 1965 and in this fixture Blues called on their first ever substitute when Brian Sharples replaced Ron Wylie.

On 15 March 1980 Archie Gemmill made his 500th appearance in the Football League - for Blues against Preston - having made his first for Preston against Norwich in August 1967.

The first games between Blues and North End in Third Division took place in 1989-90 - Blues won 3-1 at home and drew 2-2 away on plastic! Dennis Baily scored both goals in the latter game and he also found the net in the first encounter.

In 1979-80 Blues beat North End 3-1 on aggregate in a second round League Cup-tie. Steve Lynex scored the decisive goal in the second leg at Deepdale.

Players with both clubs include: J Blyth, C Bosbury, JW Bradford (Blues reserve), E Brown, S Davies, J Devlin, P Fitzpatrick, A Garrett, A Gemmill, A Godden, B Green, C Holland, M Jackson, H Kendall, T Matthewson, A Morley, A Mounteney, M Rathbone, M Sale, GH Smithies, GB Waddell (also assistant trainer & coach at Preston), J Wealands, F White, HM Wilcox, F Worthington.

Also: Harry Hampton (Blues player, PNE coach), Norman Bodell (Blues coach, scout, PNE coach), Peter Doherty (Blues guest, PNE assistant-manager).

PROFESSIONALISM

In 1885 and Blues, along with scores of other clubs up and down the country, adopted professionalism - because the players could not afford to lose money by taking time off work to play on a Saturday afternoon (or indeed in mid-week).

PROGRAMMES

The first official Blues matchday programmes appeared on a regular basis soon after the First World War.

Prior to that either a single-card or team-sheet had been the order of the day as far as a programme was concerned in the Blues camp.

During the 1920s and 1930s the club's programmes were exceptionally well produced, containing a lot of news, statistics, club information etc.

During the Second World War the Blues News was reduced to four pages and a much smaller size, but gradually during the late 1940s/early fifties the page content was increased - and a splash of colour was added to the front cover.

The size was enlarged in the mid 1950s and gradually the content was increased as well. A picture of the St Andrew's ground was first featured on the cover in 1956 (initially with a touch of colour - the green pitch). However, the Blues News around this time, was not regarded as a top-line production.

This style remained until the end of the 1965-66 season (when the Blues programme also carried a supplementary Soccer Review).

For the 1966-67 season again the programme became much smaller (12mm wide by 18mm deep).

For the following two seasons the programme doubled in size (up to 17mm x 24mm approximately) and the price was increased.

An extra two pages were added in 1967-68 and eight more in 1968-69.

In 1969-70, for the fourth time since 1965 Blues had in a different sized programme - a tall upright publication, 15mm x 26mm (approx.)..

In 1970-71 punters received a 'free' copy of the Football League review with their programme - making the whole magazine itself well worth the 8p cover price.

The Blues News went up to 7p (still with the League review) for the 1971-72 season.

For each of the 1972-73 and 1973-74 seasons the Blues News (as it was now officially called) changed in style once more - this time to a much squarer publication (21mm x 20mm). And the 'free' Football League Review disappeared.

From August 1974 to May 1978 - four complete seasons - the Blues News was an 18mm x 24mm standard production with 16 pages initially, rising to 20 (for two seasons) and then 24. The price also increased gradually: 10p to 15p to 20p, so too did the design on the front cover.

All colour to the front outer cover was introduced for the first time on a regular basis for the 1975-76 season.

In 1978-79 the Blues News came down in size to a smaller version (15mm x 21mm). Again the front cover carried a coloured photograph and a small amount of spot colour appeared on the inner pages. A charge of 20p was made for the 24 page programme.

From 1979 to 1982 (three seasons) Peerless Press (West Bromwich) designed and printed the Blues News and their efforts were rewarded with some excellent sales and a handful of prizes!

The size changed (yet again) to a square programme at 21mm x 21mm. More colour was brought in, and although the price rose to 30p, on the whole the magazine was regarded 'good value for money'.

Maybank Press Ltd (Ilford, Essex) looked after the Blues programme for the 1982-83 season and they changed the design and size again - upping the price to 40p for 28 pages, including a 4-page supplement.

In 1983-84 it was all change again for the Blues News with regards to printing and design, this time the onus was put on Sports Projects (Birmingham) who also did the Aston Villa programme.

Plain, simple and efficient, it was a worthy production at 40p for 24 pages. However, it was a one-off for 'Sports' and the Blues News went back to Peerless Press for the next four seasons: 1984-88.

At first, the square magazine was re-introduced and the price went up to 50p for 24 pages including the front and back covers.

The size of the Blues News for the next three seasons was 14mm to 21mm. Smart, compact, several interesting articles, plenty of pictures, news and statistics - it was a good club programme - and the price was now 60p for 32 pages.

That cover price was retained for 1988-89 when the production and publishing of the programme was taken over by Pemandos Advertising & Marketing (Lichfield). It went back to 24-pages and was described as one of the best publications made for/by Blues up to that time.

For the following season (1989-90) the price rose to 70p. The programme improved slightly, retaining most of the previous year's contents, likewise the following season.

In 1991-92, with David Teague installed as editor, the Blues News went to new printers, Archway, Panbourne, and it reverted back to a standard B5 size (17mm x 24mm). The price rose to £1 (for 32 pages) and the average fan appreciated that it was perhaps just about value for money with an array of general (some basic) and historical articles.

Windmill Print & Design (Cradley Heath) competently looked after the Blues programme during the 1992-93 and 1993-94 sea-

sons although the cover price did go up again, firstly to £1.20 (for 40 pages) and then to £1.50 (also 40 pages).

With plenty of colour around by now (and advertising) the programmes became more like magazines - but to compensate for more pages, more reading material, more photographs and indeed more editorial on the whole, the cover price went up again!

From 1994-98 Colourplan, based in St Helens, Merseyside looked after the Blues News. It proved to be a worthwhile read but never really changed in style although the price did remain static at £1.50.

The last two season of the 20th century saw PFP, from Brislington, Bristol, publish and print the Blues programme. But during the summer of 2000 they lost the contract and the club reverted back once more to Colourplan.

Programme Facts:
- Probably the oldest matchday card seen, featuring Blues (Small Heath) was the one issued for the semi-final of the FA Cup (against West Bromwich Albion) at The Aston Lower Grounds on 6 March 1886.
- Another old one in circulation is from the away friendly against Marlow on 26 December 1893.
- And there is also a programme in existence covering the first League game at St Andrew's - Blues against Middlesbrough on Boxing Day 1906.
- Blues issued a double-match programme in 1993, covering the TNT Inter City Challenge Cup match v Liverpool on 28 July and the home friendly with Norwich City on 7 August.

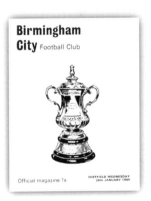

Blues News Countdown

Seasons	Pages	Price	Publishers/Printers
1921-39	12	2d	Moody Bros, Livery St. Birmingham
1940-45	4	1d	Parkes & Mainwarings, Coleshill St, Birmingham
1946-54	8	2d	Parkes & Mainwarings, Coleshill St, Birmingham
1954-65	10	3d	Studio Press/PM Advertising, Birmingham
1965-66	8	6d/3p	Studio Press/PM Advertising, Birmingham
1966-67	16	6d/3p	Studio Press/PM Advertising, Birmingham
1967-68	18	1s/5p	Studio Press/PM Advertising, Birmingham
1968-69	24	1s/5p	Studio Press/PM Advertising, Birmingham
1969-71	24	1s/5p	West Midlands Press Ltd, Walsall
1971-72	24	7p	SPBL, Lozells, Birmingham
1972-73	24	8p	Studio Press, Elkington St, Birmingham
1973-74	24	10p	Studio Press, Elkington St, Birmingham
1974-75	16	10p	Midland Sports Magazines/CT Printers, Leicester
1975-77	20	15p	Midland Sports Magazines/CT Printers, Leicester
1977-78	24	20p	Midland Sports Magazines/CT Printers, Leicester
1978-79	24	20p	Peerless Press, Spon Lane, West Bromwich
1979-80	24	25p	Peerless Press, Spon Lane, West Bromwich
1980-81	24	30p	Peerless Press, Spon Lane, West Bromwich
1981-82	24	35p	Peerless Press, Spon Lane, West Bromwich
1982-83	20	40p	Maybank Press Ltd, Ilford, Essex
1983-84	24	40p	Sports Projects/Hemmings & Capey, Leicester
1984-85	24	50p	Peerless Press, Spon Lane, West Bromwich
1985-86	32	60p	Peerless Press, Spon Lane, West Bromwich
1986-88	24	60p	Peerless Press, Spon Lane, West Bromwich
1988-89	24	60p	Pemandos Advertising & Marketing, Lichfield
1989-90	32	70p	Pemandos Advertising & Marketing, Lichfield
1990-92	32	£1.00	Archway, Panbourne Press Ltd, Dorset
1992-93	40	£1.20	Windmill Printing, Cradley Heath
1993-94	40	£1.50	Windmill Printing, Cradley Heath
1994-98	40	£1.50	Colourplan, St Helens, Merseyside
1998-00	48	£2.00	PFP, Brislington, Bristol
2000-01	48	£2.00	Colourplan, St Helens, Merseyside

Programme Notes

- The Football League Review was inserted in the matchday programme from 1966 to 1974. Five years later, in 1979-80, the Blues News contained 'Programme Plus' (another floating insert) and in the late 1990s, a further insert, the 'Nationwide Review' was made available. The latter two were only short-term publications!
- Occasionally, for minor Cup matches etc, the size and the number of pages have been reduced accordingly along with the cover price. And for certain games a large format (A4) programme has been printed.
- For The Anglo-Italian Cup competition in 1971-72 a specially-designed brochure/magazine was produced to cover the whole of the Group matches in England.

PROMOTION AND RELEGATION

Blues have gained promotion from their respective Division on eleven occasions while they have also been relegated the same number of times!

The promotion campaigns: 1893-94*, 1900-01, 1902-03, 1920-21, 1947-48, 1954-55, 1971-72, 1979-80, 1984-85, 1991-92 and 1994-95.

The relegation seasons: 1895-96*, 1901-02, 1907-08, 1938-39, 1949-50, 1964-65, 1978-79, 1983-84, 1985-86, 1988-89 and 1993-94.

* Blues' fate decided by Test Matches

PURDON, Ted

The blond figure of centre-forward Ted Purdon bearing down on goal during the 1950s was an awesome sight for the supporters at St Andrew's. It was a pity the South African powerhouse didn't stay longer at the club! Born in Johannesburg on 1 March 1930, Purdon played for the Marist Brothers club in his homeland before joining Blues in August 1950. At 6ft tall and weighing over 13 stones he had all the requirements for the rough and tumble of English League football and he did the business, scoring 30 goals in 70 games for Blues before leaving St Andrew's to join Sunderland in January 1954. He later played for Workington and Barrow, Bath City, then Bristol Rovers, Toronto City and Polish White Eagles (both in Canada) before retiring in 1963 to concentrate on a business venture. Purdon was also a very useful cricketer and was selected as 12th man for Warwickshire during his time with Blues. He scored 87 goals in 228 League games for his five English clubs.

QUEENS PARK RANGERS

Blues' playing record against Rangers is:

FOOTBALL LEAGUE

Venue	P	W	D	L	F	A
Home	19	14	4	1	33	10
Away	19	4	7	8	22	29
Totals	38	18	11	9	55	39

FA CUP

Venue	P	W	D	L	F	A
Home	1	0	0	1	1	2
Away	1	0	0	1	0	2
Totals	2	0	0	2	1	4

LEAGUE CUP

Home	1	0	0	1	1	4
Away	2	0	0	2	1	5
Totals	3	0	0	3	2	9

Blues first met QPR at League level in season 1950-51 (Division Two). The game at St Andrew's ended all-square at 1-1, while at Loftus Road Rangers won 2-0.

Blues recorded their first League win over the London club the following season, on 24 November 1951 (also in Division Two), Tommy Briggs and Billy Smith the scorers in a 2-0 victory.

A single goal by Cyril Trigg earned Blues the double when the teams met at St Andrew's five months later in mid-April.

As reigning League Cup holders and Third Division champions, Rangers lost 2-0 to Blues at St Andrew's in December 1967 but won the return fixture by the same score five months later.

The first time Blues and Rangers opposed each other in the top flight of English football was in season 1973-74. The games ended 2-2 in London and 4-0 to Blues at St Andrew's when Gordon Taylor, Trevor Francis (2) and Howard Kendall found the net in front of more than 39,000 fans.

Francis was again on target when Blues registered a 4-1 home in March 1975 and that completed the double for the season follow-

Don Givens

ing a 1-0 win on Rangers' soil in September (Joe Gallagher the scorer).

In 1978-79 Blues completed another double over QPR - winning both matches 3-1. Alan Buckley scored three of the six goals, two coming at Loftus Road on the last day of the season when victory ended a League record sequence for Blues of 18 successive away defeats!

The following season Blues gained promotion from the Second Division and on the way they beat Rangers 2-1 on an icy pitch at St Andrew's to celebrate the New Year in style.

Blues played their first League game on a plastic pitch on 19 November 1983, losing 2-1 at Loftus Road.

When Blues beat QPR 2-0 in March 1986 it was their first home League win for six months - since beating Leicester in September 1985 - a run of 10 matches!

Rangers defeated Blues 7-2 on aggregate in the 1967 League Cup semi-final. They won 4-1 at St Andrew's and followed up with a 3-1 victory at Loftus Road.

Players with both clubs include: A Archer, D Bailey, B Bridges, G Cooper, WS Corbett (Rangers guest), M Dennis, J Devine, A Drake, W Finney, T Francis (also manager of both clubs), P Furlong, D Givens, AW Hartwell, F Hawkley, M Hellawell, WH Guest (Rangers guest), M Jackson, M Kelly, S Lynex (Rangers trialist), D Mangnall (also Rangers manager), J Merrick and S Morris (Blues reserves), IJ Muir, D Seaman, AR Smith, J Thorogood, JE Travers, GF Wheldon.

Also: Jim Smith (manager of both clubs), Ted Goodier and Joe Mallett (Rangers players, Blues managers), George Smith (Blues player, Rangers coach), Chris Woods (QPR goalkeeper, Blues coach).

RCD ESPANOL

Blues' last game in a major European tournament was against the Spanish side in the 1961-62 Inter Cities Fairs Cup competition. A crowd of 60,000 witnessed the first round, first leg encounter in Spain on 15 November which Blues lost 5-2. And there were 16,874 fans present for the return fixture at St Andrew's on 7 December when four players were sent-off (Bertie Auld and Jimmy Harris of Blues, Sanchez and Rivas for Espanol). Auld, though, did have the pleasure of scoring Blues' last 'European' goal (to date) to earn them a 1-0 victory. Espanol however, still won the tie 5-3 on aggregate.

RAMSEY, Sir Alf

Knighted in 1967, a year after he had guided England to victory in the World Cup final at Wembley, Alf Ramsey's record as manager of his country was impressive: 113 games in charge, 69 wins, 27 draws and 17 defeats.

As a player himself - a solid, efficient and reliable right-back - he started off his senior career with Southampton and then helped Tottenham Hotspur win successive Second and First Division championships in the early 1950s. After retiring he repeated that double as manager with Ipswich Town in the early 1960s.

Born in Dagenham on 22 January 1920, Ramsey was on Portsmouth's books as an amateur before moving to The Dell, initially in 1943 and turning professional in August 1944. He moved to White Hart Lane for £21,000 in 1949 and remained with the London club until May 1955 when he retired to take over as manager of Ipswich Town, a position he held until January 1963 when he was named England boss. He had earlier won 32 full caps for his country (his debut came in 1948 in a 6-0 win over Switzerland) and had also played at 'B' team level and represented the Football League side on five occasions. He captained his country in the absence of Billy Wright and played in that disastrous 1-0 World Cup defeat by USA in Bela Horizonte in 1950. Ramsey scored eight goals for Southampton in 90 League outings and added another 250 senior appearances to his tally with Spurs (24 goals - 20 of them penalties).

As England manager Ramsey started off very well and slowly built up a tremendously competitive team. In 1966 he was acclaimed the Messiah as the World Cup was won for the first and only time (so far) but four years later England lost their crown in Mexico 1970 when they slipped out of the World Cup in the heat to arch rivals West Germany. After failing to qualify for the 1974 World Cup Finals he lost his job. Two years later Ramsey became a Director of Birmingham City (January 1976) and in September 1977 he became the first knight to manage a Football League club when he took over the reins at St Andrew's, holding the fort until March 1978. Blues achieved very little under his guidance before he was forced to relinquish his position owing to ill-health. His last soccer appointment took him to Greece where he acted as Technical Director of Panathinaikos, a position he held for just a few months before retiring from football to live in Ipswich where he died on 28 April 1999, aged 79.

RANDLE, Jack

Jack Randle, an ex-miner, was a tremendously aggressive and wholehearted left-back who appeared in 116 senior games for Blues, scoring one goal - a penalty in a 3-1 FA Cup win over Wrexham in 1928. Born in Bedworth on 23 August 1902, he played his early football with Exhall Colliery FC and Bedworth Boys before joining Coventry City in 1922. He spent five years at Highfield Road and once scored a hat-trick of own-goals! He moved to St Andrew's in November 1927 and stayed until April 1933 having lost his place to George Liddell. He joined Southend United on leaving the Midlands and later assisted both Bournemouth and Guildford City before retiring in 1936. After the War Randle became a groundsman while working at Newdegate Colliery in Nuneaton. He died in Bournemouth in 1990.

RANSON, Ray

Following his bargain £15,000 transfer from Manchester City right-back Ray Ranson made 158 first team appearances for Blues between November 1984 and December 1988, having earlier amassed in excess of 200 for the Maine Road club. Born in St Helens (deep in Rugby League country) on 12 June 1960, he joined the apprentice ranks at Maine Road in June 1976 and became a professional twelve months later. An FA Cup winner with City in 1981, he made eleven under 21 appearances for England and also represented his country at both schoolboy and youth team levels before joining Blues. On leaving St Andrew's he went to Newcastle United for £175,000 (good business here on Blues' behalf) and after a loan spell with his former club Manchester City he rounded off his senior career with a season at Reading (1993-94). Ranson made a total of 444 Football League appearances with his four clubs (only two goals scored).

READING

Blues' playing record against the Royals is:

FOOTBALL LEAGUE

Venue	P	W	D	L	F	A
Home	8	3	4	1	14	8
Away	8	2	5	1	9	8
Totals	16	5	9	2	23	16

FA CUP

	P	W	D	L	F	A
Away	1	0	0	1	0	1

WARTIME

	P	W	D	L	F	A
Home	1	1	0	0	2	0
Away	1	1	0	0	2	0
Totals	2	2	0	0	4	0

The first time Blues met Reading in the Football League was in season 1986-87 (Division Two). Both games ended all square - 1-1 at St Andrew's and 2-2 at Elm Park.

Blues registered their first win over the Royals in October 1987 - a crowd of just 6,147 attending at St Andrew's to see Steve Whitton and Andy Kennedy give them a 2-1 victory.

Blues' first win at Elm Park came in November 1989 when goals by Simon Sturridge and Reading defender Martin Hicks (later to move to St Andrew's) earned them a 2-0 victory in the Third Division. Reading then gained revenge with a last-match win at St Andrew's (1-0).

Barry Fry's last game as Blues' manager was against Reading at St Andrew's on 5 May 1996 - and he went out on a winning note (2-1).

Paul Devlin scored twice (one a penalty) when Blues beat the Royals 4-1 at St Andrew's in January 1997.

In the League game at St Andrew's in August 1997 Reading had Francis Benali sent-off as Blues won 3-0 and when the teams met for the return fixture Blues had both Chris Marsden and Paul Furlong dismissed as they lost 2-0.

The FA Cup-tie between the clubs took place at Elm Park on 15 November 1992 (Round 1) in front of 7,667 fans.

Blues won 2-0 at Reading in the Wartime League Cup competition in 1940.

Players with both clubs include: E Bluff, J Bowen, K Bremner, K Brown, H Bruce, K Dillon, N Forster, G Getgood, C Gordon, H Graham, T Green, M Hicks, A Jones, FW Jones, A Legg, W McCafferty, DJ Madden, AW Oakes, N Platnauer, G Potter, R Ranson, WH Smith, F Stokes, S Sutton.

Also: Chris Woods (Reading 'keeper, Blues coach).

READING FOOTBALL CLUB, Ltd.

READING v. BIRMINGHAM

Elm Park, Saturday, May 11th.

Official Team Sheet.
ONE PENNY. Nº 919

Programme from 11 May 1940.

REAL MADRID

Whilst touring Spain in the summer of 1923, Blues beat Real Madrid 3-0 in a friendly match in Madrid and in the process had centre-half Alec McClure sent-off ...simply for telling his goal-keeper (Dan Tremelling) where to stand after Real had been awarded a second-half penalty. The spot-kick was given for handball by Blues' full-back Jack Jones who, in fact, was protecting his face (his dentures)! McClure,   so annoyed, instructed Tremelling to stand right next to an upright and let the Spanish penalty-taker to score without any fuss! The referee though kept on saying 'ready, are you ready' to Tremelling who refused to move from his position. At that point the irate official turned round and said to McClure 'buzz off.' After the game the referee admitted he was wrong to award a penalty in the circumstances and the Spanish officials made him apologise in the local newspaper!

Two years later Blues repeated that scoreline, beating Real 3-0 in a return friendly match at St Andrew's on 2 September 1925. The referee for this game was Ted Lines of Birmingham and he had no such problems in front of 10,000 fans.

Programme from 11 May 1940.

REDCAR

Blues defeated Redcar 2-0 at home in the quarter-finals of the FA Cup in February 1886. Tommy Davenport scored both goals in front of 6,000 spectators.

REES, Tony

Tony Rees netted 16 goals in 111 appearances for Blues, but during a fine career in English soccer he accumulated an overall record of 60 goals in 337 League and Cup games, serving also with Aston Villa (no senior outings), Peterborough United, Shrewsbury Town, Barnsley, Grimsby Town and West Bromwich Albion (his last major club: 1994-96).

Born in Merthyr on 1 August 1964, he signed professional forms for Aston Villa on his eighteenth birthday and moved to St Andrew's in July 1983. After loan spells at both London Road and Gay Meadow he was transferred to Oakwell in March 1988. Capped once by Wales at senior level, Rees also represented his country at schoolboy, youth, 'B' and under 21 levels. A niggling hamstring injury effectively ended his

RESERVES

Blues have had a reserve side since 1879. The second string participated in friendly matches until 1893 when they gained entry to the Birmingham & District League..

They raced away with the title in 1914-15, winning 26 and drawing seven of their 34 matches for a total of 53 points. The team scored a staggering 160 goals 'for' and conceded only 39.

Directly after the Great War Blues were not members of the Central League but they quickly gained a place for the 1921-22 campaign.

Programme from Blues reserves v Everton reserves at Hednesford in 1996

They didn't compete in 1945-46, returned in 1946-47, but were then replaced by Barnsley in 1947-48. At that juncture Blues' second string joined the Football Combination.

They remained in this competition throughout the fifties, sixties, seventies and early eighties before joining the Midland Senior League and also the long-established Central/Pontins League.

Blues' second XI has regularly participated in the Birmingham Senior Cup from the late 1940s to date. In April 1992 a team including four YTS players were beaten by VS Rugby 3-0 in the Final at The Hawthorns.

Facts

- When Blues won the Birmingham & District League title in 1914-15, sharpshooter Charlie Duncan scored 52 goals. Amazingly he made just 24 senior appearances for Blues (nine goals scored).
- Around 23,000 fans saw Blues beaten by Aston Villa 6-3 in a Central League game at Villa Park in 1928. The big crowd turned out to see the home club's new signing, Tom 'Pongo' Waring, who scored a hat-trick!
- In Blues' Central League game against Leeds United in 1934 centre-forward Dave Mangnall netted 10 goals.
- Johnny Schofield was 'reserve' to Gil Merrick for practically nine

years (from 1950) before establishing himself as Blues' number one goalkeeper in 1959-60. He made well over 200 second XI appearances for Blues.

- In the mid-1990s Blues agreed to play their 'home' reserve matches at Hednesford Town's Keys Park ground.

RICHARDS, Dai

'Dai' Richards was born in Abercanaid near Merthyr on 31 October 1906 and his early clubs were River Field, Bedlingog and Merthyr Town, who were then a Third Division South side, before he signed for Wolverhampton Wanderers in August 1927 for £300. Originally a full-back, Richards was converted to a scheming wing-half and occasionally inside-forward by Major Frank Buckley. He remained at Molineux for nine seasons, making 229 appearances and helping Wolves to the Second Division championship in 1931-32. He won 11 of his 21 full Welsh caps as a Wolves player. In November 1935 he was transferred to Brentford for £3,500 who were in their first-ever season in Division One, but although Richards earned some excellent reports, he never settled in London and in March 1937 moved to Birmingham in the most extraordinary circumstances. Richards woke up one Saturday morning expecting to play for Brentford against Birmingham but was transferred before the start of the game and when kick-off time came around he was opposing his former colleagues. In July 1939, after scoring twice in 66 games for Blues he joined Walsall on a free transfer, but the new season was only three games old when War was declared. Richards played a few times in the early Wartime seasons, but by 1945 was serving with Sedgley at the age of 39. His trade was a builder and contractor and he was also a good cricketer and keen motorist. His younger brother, Billy, made 31 senior appearances for Wolves from 1927 to 1929. Richards died at Yardley, Birmingham on 1 October 1969.

RICHARDS, Frank

Frank H Richards was secretary-manager at St Andrew's from May 1915 to May 1923. He was in charge of the side for almost 170 competitive matches of which 76 were won and 36 drawn. He steered Blues to the Second Division championship and into the top flight in 1920-21 and signed some excellent players in the process. A superb tactician, he certainly improved the team as a whole, morale-wise and on the field of play. He did, however, drop one major clanger - he failed to enter Blues in the 1921-22 FA Cup competition! "I completely forgot all about it" said a red-faced Richards. Born in Handsworth, Birmingham circa 1880, he attended Hockley County School before going to work in the jewellery quarter (1904-06). He joined the office staff at St Andrew's a month after the ground was opened (January 1907) and became assistant-secretary in 1910 and club secretary in 1911, adding the position of team manager to his title four years later. He retained the position of Blues secretary/manager until the end of the 1922-23 season when he handed over the managerial duties to Billy Beer, retaining his position as club secretary. In May 1925 Richards left St Andrew's to become secretary-manager of Preston North End, a position he held with dignity until July 1927 when he returned for a another spell as club secretary of Blues, this time under manager Billy Harvey. On this occasion he held office, however, for just twelve months, up until July 1928, when Leslie Knighton took charge, also assuming the title of secretary-manager. Richards' last

job in football was that of secretary-manager of Bournemouth (July 1928-June 1930). Richards who later spent five years on the Board at St Andrew's, died in Birmingham in 1963, aged 83. He served Blues for a total of 24 years.

ROBB, Billy

Goalkeeper Billy Robb is in the record books as being the player with third longest gap between League games - 17 years, four months. Harry Kinghorn (18 years, 72 days: 1911-28) and Septimus Atterbury (18 years: 1902-20) played longer. He starred in his last game for Blues in April 1915 and his next League outing came with Aldershot in August 1932. He actually played League football for almost a quarter of a century: 24 years 66 days. Born in Rutherglen, Glasgow on 20 March 1895, Robb played his early soccer with Rutherglen Welfare, Lanarkshire Boys' Club and Kirkintillock Rob Roy before joining Blues as a professional in January 1914. He made 45 senior appearances during his time at St Andrew's that ended in 1915 when he moved to Armadale. After guesting for Third Lanark in 1916-17 he signed for Rangers in January 1920. He did well during his seasons at Ibrox Park, amassing 200 appearances and winning four Scottish League championship medals and two Scottish cup runners-up prizes. After a four-year spell with Hibernian (1926-30) he returned to League action in England with Aldershot, initially joining the 'Shots for £100 in 1930. He later played for Guildford City from 1937 and retired in May 1939, aged 44!

Capped twice by Scotland, Robb, safe, reliable and daring, also represented the Scottish League XI. He died in Aldershot on 18 February 1976, aged 80.

ROBERTS, Brian 'Harry'

Brian Roberts

Defender Roberts was christened Brian but called Harry after the famous gangster of the late 1960s. He had a fine professional career which began with Coventry City in May 1974 (having spent two years on the apprentice staff prior to that). He stayed with the Sky Blues for 12 years, accumulating almost 250 senior appearances, scoring one goal - a beauty against West Ham United, away, in December 1982 (won 3-0). After this effort a badge was produced saying 'I saw Harry score a goal.' He became a Birmingham City player in March 1984, the £10,000 transfer fee being raised via a 'Buy a player Fund.' He gave Blues excellent service, amassing another 213 first-class appearances but didn't find the net, albeit not for the want of trying! In June 1990, he left St Andrew's for Wolverhampton Wanderers on a 'free' and passed the personal milestone of 500 senior appearances during his time at Molineux. In the summer of 1992 he returned to Highfield Road as reserve team coach and later did a similar job at the Knightlow School, Stretton-on-Dunsmore. 'Harry' who occupied every defensive position at both Coventry and St Andrew's, was born in Manchester on 6 November 1955.

ROBERTS, John

John Roberts

John Roberts a Welsh international central defender, strong, wholehearted and forever a battler, was born in Abercynon, Glamorgan on 11 September 1946. After doing well with his local side Abercynon Athletic he joined Swansea Town in July 1964 and played three years at The Vetch Field before moving to Northampton Town in November 1967 (under the Welsh team manager Dave Bowen). From the Cobblers he switched to Arsenal for £45,000 in May 1969 and three years later moved to St Andrew's for a record £140,000 (October 1972). He appeared in 79 League and Cup games for Blues (one goal scored) before transferring to Wrexham for £30,000 in August 1976. He rounded off his senior career with Hull City (August 1980-May 1982, linking up with, once again, the Welsh team boss, this time Mike Smith). He then acted as player-manager of Oswestry Town before quitting football in 1983. Capped 22 times by his country (1971-76 - the last 15 whilst with Blues) Roberts was once a railway fireman and started off as a free-scoring centre-forward before developing into an international-class centre-half. He also won one under 21 and five under 23 caps. As a tower of strength at the back he helped Wrexham win the Fourth Division championship in 1977-78. On leaving football Roberts worked briefly as a salesman for a stationery company before becoming a driving instructor in Chester.

ROBINSON, Arthur

'Nat' Robinson always wore two goalkeeping jerseys, no matter how cold or warm the weather! One of the game's characters, when annoyed he used to stand on his line or by an upright whistling! Yet he was a fine custodian - one of the best in the country during the early part of the twentieth century. Born in Coventry on 28 February 1878, he played for Allesley FC, Coventry Stars and Singers FC (now Coventry City) before joining Blues in August 1898. He took over the number one spot from Harry Clutterbuck and remained first choice at the club for almost 10 years before losing his place to Jack Dorrington. He helped Blues twice win pro-

motion from Division Two (1901 and 1903) and gained two full England caps as well as twice representing the Football League. Described in some circles as 'all arms and legs' he used to 'windmill' his arms around catherine-wheel style when an opponent was racing towards him. A real character, he often raced some 40 yards out of his area to clear the ball. On leaving St Andrew's in July 1908 Robinson signed for Chelsea. Two years later he moved to Coventry City and retired before the Great War to become a licensee, taking over the Red House Inn, Barrass Cross, Coventry. He died in Coventry on 15 May 1929, aged 51.

Arthur Robinson

- 'Nat' Robinson used to have a pet dog called ninety - after the number of minutes in a game!

ROBINSON, Dave

Dave 'Sugar' Robinson was a very useful defender, a no-nonsense performer who was a 100 per-cent competitor. He scored four goals in 127 appearances for Blues during his nine years with the club. Born in Bartley Green on 14 July 1948, he represented Birmingham and Warwickshire District Schools before joining the apprentice ranks at St Andrew's in June 1964, turning professional in July 1966. A former England schoolboy trialist he was a West Brom fan as a lad and started out as an inside-forward before establishing himself in the middle-line. He made his Blues debut in the local derby against Aston Villa in September 1968 and never looked back after that. When he signed Robinson on pro-forms, Blues manager Stan Cullis admitted that he had saved the club at least £80,000!

On leaving Blues in February 1973 'Sugar' joined Walsall with whom he stayed for three years before becoming player-manager of non-League Chelmsley Town, later playing for Tamworth (from November 1978) and managing Oldbury United (1980-82).

RODGERSON, Ian

Able to fill the roles of an attacking right-back, right-sided midfielder or even the anchorman in the engine-room, Ian Rodgerson - regarded as one of the country's first wing-backs - had a fine career which began in earnest with Hereford United in June 1985 after earlier service with Pegasus Juniors. Born in Hereford on 9 April 1965, he left his home town club for Cardiff City in a £7,000 deal in August 1988 and found his way to St Andrew's in December 1990, initially signing on loan. He became a permanent fixture with Blues in January 1991 and went on to play in 116 games for the club, scoring six goals before transferring to Sunderland in July 1993, having missed Blues' success in the 1991 Leyland DAF Trophy Final at Wembley through injury.

Unfortunately, before he could play his first game for the Wearsiders he was badly injured in a car crash. He later returned to action and rejoined Cardiff City in July 1995, going back home to play for Hereford United (again) in the Conference.

- Ian's brother Alan played as an inside-forward for Middlesbrough.

ROTHERHAM UNITED (Town, County...)

Blues' playing record against the Millermen is:

FOOTBALL LEAGUE

Venue	P	W	D	L	F	A
Home	13	10	1	2	39	18
Away	13	5	5	3	22	20
Totals	26	15	6	5	61	38

FA CUP

Venue	P	W	D	L	F	A
Home	1	1	0	0	4	0

WARTIME

Venue	P	W	D	L	F	A
Home	3	2	0	1	5	3
Away	3	1	0	2	4	9
Totals	6	3	0	3	9	12

Blues and Rotherham (known at the time as Town) first played each other in the Football League on 4 September 1893 at Muntz Street. A crowd of 3,000 saw seven goals scored, Blues winning 4-3. Later in the season Blues completed the double with a 3-2 victory in Yorkshire. Jack Hallam and Fred Wheldon scored in both games for Blues.

Rotherham lost their League status in 1896 and they did not face Blues again until November 1919 (Division 2) by which time Town had been changed to County. After a 2-2 draw at St Andrew's Blues went to Millmoor seven days later and won 3-2, giant centre-forward Albert Millard netting twice.

The following season Blues took another three points off the Millermen on their way to winning the Second Division title. They triumphed 3-2 at home (Scotsman Johnny Crosbie scored twice) and drew 1-1 away when Percy Barton cracked in a beauty!

It was another 30 years before Blues met Rotherham again and this time for the Christmas Day encounter at St Andrew's in 1951 the Yorkshire club had replaced County with United. A crowd of 28,000 saw Blues claim a 4-0 victory, Billy Smith weighing in with a hat-trick. Twenty-four hours later Jack Badham found the net as Blues completed the double with a 2-1 win at Millmoor.

Twelve months later almost to the day (20 December 1952) Blues repeated that 4-0 scoreline at St Andrew's, Cyril Trigg, (penalty), Peter Murphy, Billy Wardle and Ted Purdon the scorers this time.

United doubled up over Blues in 1953-54 but when promotion was gained the following season Blues won 3-1 at home and 2-0 away, Alex Govan netting in both matches.

With both teams in different Divisions it was 12 years before they resumed battle, Blues losing 3-2 at home and away in September 1966. They quickly gained revenge however, whipping United 4-1 at St Andrew's in October 1967 (three goals here for Barry Bridges) and drawing 1-1 away.

Very few matches have been played since then but in October 1989 Blues crashed 5-1 at Rotherham - their heaviest defeat to date at the hands of the Millermen

The League match at Rotherham in March 1991 saw two penalties awarded in 55 seconds. John Frain scored for Blues but straightaway Clive Mendonca then missed for United. The game ended 1-1.

Jimmy Singer scored twice when Blues beat the Millermen 4-0 at St Andrew's in a fourth round FA Cup-tie in January 1961. The attendance was almost 32,000.

Players with both clubs include: H Bodle, L Burkinshaw, S Davies, H Deacon, A Drake (United trialist), H Draper, E Eyre, J Godfrey (reserve), G Hicks, H Howard (United trialist), L Jenkinson, CA Leatherbarrow, G Leggatt, J McDonough, D Mangnall (United trialist), M O'Grady, H Powell, W Quinton, BJ Taylor, C Thompson (Blues reserve), PC Watson, DP Weston, AR Wilson, P Wright (United player-coach).

Also: Jackie Bestall (Rotherham player, Blues coach/chief scout), Archie Gemmill (Blues player, United joint-manager), Arthur Turner (Blues player and manager, United chief scout).

ROULSON, Joe

A Yorkshireman, born in Sheffield in 1890, right-half Joe Roulson was as hard as nails, rugged, determined, competitive and a player who never shirked a tackle. He worked in a steel works in Scotland and played for Cammell Laird FC before joining Blues in August 1912. He went on to appear in 125 senior games (4 goals scored) over the next 11 years, although the Great War certainly disrupted his progress quite considerably. He played his part in bringing the Second Division championship to the club in 1921 (appearing in 22 games). Indeed, at one stage he looked set for international honours but injuries crept in when last expected! After leaving St Andrew's in the summer of 1923 he spent two seasons with Swansea Town.

ROWETT, Gary

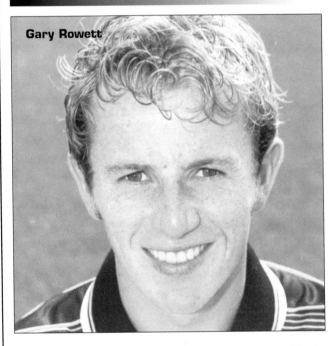

Gary Rowett

Named in the PFA Nationwide League Division One side for 1999-2000, Gary Rowett was a sterling performer for Blues throughout that campaign.

A tremendous competitor, he was a trainee with Cambridge United before turning professional at The Abbey Stadium in September 1991. In May 1994 a £200,000 move took him to Everton but he never settled on Merseyside and after a loan spell with Blackpool he was transferred to Derby County for £300,000 in July 1995. After 120 appearances for the Rams he was snapped up by Blues manager Trevor Francis for £1 million in August 1998. An impressive tackler, he played in over 50 first-class matches for Blues in 1999-2000 and amassed a total of 103 appearances for the club before his record £3 million transfer to Premiership side Leicester City in June 2000.

Initial site of St Andrew's in 1905.

ST ANDREW'S

The area of land where St Andrew's now stands was initially a dumping ground right next to a railway line.

A band of gypsies lived there for quite some time and when they were asked to move off, a curse was placed on the club and ground…and one feels it still hangs over the Blues to this day!

Blues Director Harry Morris, with his charisma and charm, convinced his fellow board members that this piece of wasteland near St Andrew's church was without doubt the right place to build a new stadium. In the autumn of 1905 papers were drawn up and after Blues had agreed and duly signed a 21-year lease (in February 1906) twelve months of hard labour followed.

Former art student, Harry Pumfrey, a carpenter living nearby, was the man asked to formulate the plans. He was the cheapest Blues could find to do the job!

His design was accepted and the first job was to put in the kop. This was raised to almost 50 feet thanks mainly to the general public who were asked to despatch their unwanted refuge on the land so that it could be utilised to good effect.

Secondly a large stand was assembled (said to be the second biggest in the country at the time) and slowly but surely the ground began to take shape.

The terracing was made up of old railway sleepers; wooden boards were placed proportionately around the perimeter of the playing area and the turf itself was laid at the end of the summer of 1906. It took another four months (from the end of August to mid-December) to get the whole ground ready for the official opening on Boxing Day 1906 - when a crowd of 32,000 saw Blues held to a 0-0 draw by Middlesbrough in a First Division League game. Sir John Holder officially opened the ground on a bitterly cold snowy afternoon. In fact, scores of volunteers, club officials, anyone wishing to help, spent three hours clearing the pitch of snow before the game could take place.

At that time it was said that 75,000 spectators (6,000 seated, 22,000 under cover) could be accommodated at St Andrew's (?).

True or false, we shall never know. But over the next 33 years or so a lot of building and construction work was carried out at the ground and the official capacity was put at 68,000 at the start of the 1938-39 season. And in February 1939 a never-to-be-bettered record crowd of 67,341 assembled there to watch an FA Cup-tie against Everton.

At this juncture there was now a roof covering the back-end of the Tilton Road End of the ground and another smallish one keeping the elements off the fans at the Railway End. Also two wing-stands introduced either side of the latter.

There was a mini problem from time to time whereby smoke from the passing trains would often engulf part of the ground. But Blues and the fans got used to this consequential discomfort.

During the Second World War the Chief Constable of Birmingham closed St Andrew's in fear of enemy air-raids.

But local MP's raised the matter in Parliament despite the Home Secretary refusing to overrule the Chief Constable's decision. But as the ground was the only one to be closed during the early part of the conflict, the ban was lifted on 23 March 1940 when Walsall were beaten 2-1 in a regional game in front of 12,000 fans.

St Andrew's in the early 1960's.

In mid-January 1942 the main stand at St Andrew's was completely destroyed by fire - not from German bombs I might add, but by petrol!

A member of the National Fire Service (which was using the ground as a local auxiliary fire station) tried to put out a small fire in a brazier. He picked up a bucket thinking it was full of water - it wasn't - and the petrol sparked off a major incident. The fire caused several thousands of pounds worth of damage and all the club's records went up in smoke! And to make matters worse the German Luftwaffe scored a direct hit on the grandstand in that same year!

With St Andrew's looking in a sorry state with steelwork twisted in all directions and cratered terraces, Blues sought another ground to play their matches. They chose that of Leamington and also played occasionally at nearby Villa Park.

When the War had ended Blues, having added City to their name (believed to be in 1943 as the club's programme had Birmingham City Football Club printed on it) they set about raising funds to rebuilt the damaged sections of the ground.

Work on a new main stand was started in 1951. That was soon completed and in 1956 floodlights were installed - Blues played the German side Borussia Dortmund in a friendly match to officially switch them on.

The Kop, situated opposite the Main Stand, ran from corner flag to corner flag and was able to house around 40,000 spectators - making it one of the biggest areas of terracing in the country. But for a number of years it was the centre of a political wrangle in Birmingham.

The Asda Supermarket chain desperately wanted to develop a large open stretch of land behind the Kop. They offered to share the cost of building a new stand to replace it, similar to what hap-

pened at Selhurst Park and Boothferry Park and later at Burnden Park and to a certain extent at Molineux.

The arguments hotted up, simply because the Co-op also wanted to build a supermarket not too far away. No one gave way, a supermarket was NOT built and eventually the Kop had a roof put completely over it.

A replica of the Main Stand was erected at the Railway End as the ground was re-shaped during the late 1950s and early '60s.

In 1963 the capacity inside St Andrew's had been reduced to 43,204. There were almost 9,300 seats situated entirely in the Main Stand and behind one of the goals (the Railway End).

Twenty-five years later, in 1988, the ground could house 5,000 fewer spectators, 10,000 of them seated, 2,500 in a family enclosure in the Railway End stand.

Then, after the tragedies at Valley Parade and Hillsborough, the subsequent Taylor Report of 1992 resulted in the capacity of St Andrew's being reduced again, this time to 26,000 (for safety reasons). This was increased however, to 28,235 a year later, but it now it was thought that the time had come to completely revamp the whole stadium.

Under the new regime of millionaire David Sullivan, the Gold brothers and Karren Brady, initial plans were put forward and quickly approved.

But just before work was about to start the already agreed plans were quickly rehashed after Karren Brady had seen what had been achieved at Old Trafford!

The first phase of the redevelopment of St Andrew's commenced soon after an emotional home game against Bristol City on 16 April 1994 when the ardent fans waved goodbye the their beloved Tilton Road End stand and the famous Kop. As momentoes they took

St Andrew's in the year 2000.

home anything from a screw to a girder, from a bolt to a stanchion, even a simple letter from the old scoreboard!

The 1970s trio of Trevor Francis, Bob Hatton and Bob Latchford officially set the building work in motion.

The £4.5 redevelopment project encompassed a 7,000 all-seater Tilton Road stand, which was ready for occupation for the first home game of the 1994-95 season against Chester City on 20 August. A massive flag was draped over the seats saying 'Thank You David Sullivan' and 12,188 fans saw Louie Donowa give Blues a 1-0 win. The Kop, with its 9,500 seats, was opened for the Blues v Blackburn Rovers Coca-Cola Cup encounter on 4 October.

The 'new' all-seater St Andrew's stadium was officially opened on 15 November 1994 when Blues entertained their old rivals Aston Villa in a friendly. A crowd of almost 20,000 turned out to witness the 1-1 draw.

Baroness Trumpington, spokeswoman for the department of national Heritage in the House of Lords, unveiled a plaque and she also presented a cheque for £2.5 million to Blues' Chairman Jack Wiseman (a grant from the Football Trust).

Work followed soon afterwards on assembling another 9,500 all-seater stand at the Railway End and when the turn of the century arrived St Andrew's was one of the most compact ground outside the Premiership with a capacity of just over 29,000.

Other matches at St Andrew's:

- Two major internationals have been staged at the ground - England 1 Scotland 1 in April 1922 when the crowd was 20,020, and England 2 Wales 1 on 25 October 1941 when the turn out was 25,145
- An Inter-League game in February 1919 finished: Football League 3 Scottish League 1. A crowd of 21,990 saw the action.
- Two 'B' internationals saw England beat Scotland 4-1 in February 1957 in front of almost 40,000 fans and in November 1980 England defeated Australia 1-0 in front of just 3,292 spectators.
- In 1962 England demoralised Greece 5-0 in an Under 23 international (att. 20,530) and in 1968 England drew 2-2 with Holland, also in an Under 23 encounter (24,258).
- In April 1920, May 1952 and April 1962 England met Scotland, Wales and Ireland respectively in schoolboy internationals.
- There have been three Birmingham County FA v Scottish FA junior games at St Andrew's: 1-1 in 1910, 1-0 to England in 1923 and 2-1 to Scotland in 1933.
- London beat Birmingham 3-1 in an Inter Association match at St Andrew's in 1911 and in 1913 at the same venue Birmingham gained revenge with a 5-1 victory.
- In March 1958 the RAF met the Royal Navy in an annual friendly at St Andrew's and six years later (February 1964) an FA XI played the Universities Athletic Union on Blues' soil.
- England played Belgium on Blues' territory in a Youth International in April 1983, and the following month England met Scotland in the UEFA Youth tournament.
- Several other major Cup matches have also been held at the ground, and these include Blues v Barcelona and Blues v AS Roma in respective Fairs Cup Finals in 1960 and 1961 and the 1963 Football League Cup Final between Blues and Aston Villa.
- There have been nine FA Cup semi-final matches staged at St Andrew's: 1907 Arsenal 1 Sheffield Wednesday 3 (att.35,940), 1909 replay Bristol City 2 Derby County 1 (att. 27,600), 1911 Chelsea 0 Newcastle United 3 (att. 40,264), 1913 replay

The main stand at St Andrew's.

Sunderland 3 Burnley 2 (att. 45,000), 1924 Manchester City 0 Newcastle United 2 (att. 50,039 - receipts £3,733), 1934 Leicester City 1 Portsmouth 4 (att. 66,544 - receipts £5,973 - both ground records), 1957 replay Aston Villa 1 West Bromwich Albion 0 (att. 58,067), 1959 replay Luton Town 1 Norwich City 0 (att. 49,488) and 1961 second replay Leicester City 2 Sheffield United 0 (att. 37,190).

- The Arsenal-Sheffield Wednesday clash in March 1907 was, in fact, the first FA Cup game to be played at St Andrew's.
- The first FA Cup game involving Blues followed in January 1908 when West Bromwich Albion won 2-1 in a 1st round replay in front of almost 25,000 spectators.
- In April 1950 the Air Training Corps International semi-final replay between England and Wales was staged on Blues' ground.
- A vital play-off encounter at St Andrew's in May 1987 ended Charlton Athletic 2 Leeds United (att. 15,841).
- Two FA Amateur Cup semi-finals ended Hendon 2 Skelmersdale 2 in 1967 and Sutton United 4 Whitley Bay 2 in 1969.
- The Amateur FA Senior Challenge Cup Final between Boldmere St Michael's and Cambridge Town was played at St Andrew's in 1948.
- Six FA Cup games (replays) not involving Blues have taken place at St Andrew's: 1926 Kettering Town 1 Worcester City 0; 1956 Burnley 2 Chelsea 2; 1958 Aldershot 2 Worcester City 0; 1970 Cardiff City 1 York City 3; 1970 Nuneaton Borough 1 Tamworth 3; 1972 Alvechurch 0 Oxford City 0.
- A Football League Cup replay in October 1976 saw Bolton Wanderers defeat Fulham 2-1.

- In a representative match, Birmingham beat the FA of Ireland 3-1 in 1959 (crowd 2,500). In April 1970 an 'old' England XI played an 'old' Scotland XI in an international charity match and three years later, in October 1973, a similar game took place between an England XI and a 'old' European side.
- England met Spain in a Youth international in September 1957 and a Blues under 18 side played England's youth team in November 1966.
- An Inter County schoolboy match between Birmingham and London took place at St Andrew's in April 1956 and in January 1957 a Youth representative match saw England meet The Rest.
- St Andrew's has not always staged soccer matches - on 28 December 1960 a Midlands Counties XV took on the South African tourists in a Rugby Union friendly match.

Ground facts
- The biggest attendance at St Andrew's (since the ground was redeveloped) is 29.050 v Wolves (League) on 1 April 2000.
- St Andrew's at 123 metres above sea level, is the sixth highest League ground (above sea level) in the country, behind WBA (The Hawthorns at 165 metres), Port Vale (Vale Park, 160), Oldham Athletic (Boundary Park, 155), Rochdale (Spotland, 145) and Wolves (Molineux, 131).
- The HRH the Prince of Wales visited St Andrew's on his official tour of Birmingham in the summer of 1980. And the legendary Mohammad Ali, the undisputed World Heavyweight Boxing champion, paid a visit to Blues' ground on 5 May 1984 (when Blues met Liverpool in a First Division game).

St Andrew''s of the 1950s.

St Andrew''s of the 1980s.

197

SAMPDORIA

Blues played the Italian Serie 'A' side Sampdoria twice in the Anglo-Italian Cup tournament in June 1971. After losing 2-1 away in front of 15,000 fans Blues won the return fixture 2-0 at St Andrew's in front of 19,510 spectators but still failed to qualify from the English Group.

Player with both clubs: T Francis.

SAUNDERS, Ron

Ron Saunders

A hard-shooting 1950s centre-forward with Everton, Tonbridge, Gillingham, Portsmouth, Watford, and Charlton Athletic, Ron Saunders then became a positive, award-winning and pretty successful manager, serving with Yeovil Town, Oxford United, Norwich City, Manchester City, Aston Villa (1974-82), Birmingham City (1982-86) and West Bromwich Albion (1986-87). As a striker he scored well over 200 League goals in almost 400 appearances, his best set of figures coming with Portsmouth (145 goals in 236 games). Born in Birkenhead on 6 November 1932, he started his career as a junior at Goodison Park in 1948 and signed professional in 1951, making his League debut three years later. He kicked his last ball in earnest in 1967 with Charlton. As a manager he won plenty of prizes, and taking them in order they were, with Norwich: Second Division champions 1972, League Cup runners-up 1973; with Manchester City: League Cup runners-up 1974; with Villa: League Cup winners 1975 and 1977, League champions 1981, Second Division runners-up 1975; with Blues: Second Division runners-up 1985. Occasionally Saunders was strong in his approach but he knew the game and although at times he was never the fans' favourite manager, he did the business, perhaps not with West Brom though, especially as he sold Steve Bull to Wolves saying that his first touch wasn't good enough....Bull went on to score over 300 goals for Wolves!

SAVILLE, Andy

A much-travelled striker, born in Hull on 12 December 1964, Andy Saville started his League career at Boothferry Park, signing for the Tigers as a professional in September 1983. Thereafter he played (and scored) for Walsall, Barnsley and Hartlepool United before joining Blues for £155,000 in March 1993. He remained at St Andrew's for a shade over two seasons during which time he netted 18 goals in 65 appearances. After a loan spell with Burnley he moved to Preston North End for £100,000 in July 1995 and since then has served with Wigan Athletic, Cardiff City, Hull City (again) and Scarborough (March 1999). He helped PNE win the Third Division title in 1995-96 and scored in excess of 135 goals in more

Andy Saville

than 500 competitive matches.

Saville was top-scorer for both Hartlepool and Blues in 1992-93. He Joined Gainsborough Trinity in 1999 - 2000.

SCHOFIELD, Johnny

Daring, big-hearted and extremely loyal and dedicated goalkeeper who made 237 appearances for Blues during his 16-year stay at the club. Born in Atherstone on 8 February 1931, Johnny Schofield played for Nuneaton Borough reserves before becoming a full-time professional with Blues in February 1950. He understudied England international Gil Merrick for several years before making the number one position his own in 1959-60. During his career he certainly suffered his fair share of injuries. He fractured his skull against Manchester United in 1960 when the foot of centre-forward Alex Dawson sickeningly thudded into his head; he damaged his shoulder, ruptured various muscles, twisted both knees and dislocated and/or broke a number of fingers. But he always bounced back, came up smiling and very rarely let the side down. He also survived a pit explosion at the Baddesley Ensor colliery in 1957. Schofield helped Blues win the Second Division title in 1955 (making 15 appearances), he played in both the 1960 and 1961 Fairs Cup Finals and collected a League Cup winners' prize in 1963. He left St Andrew's after Jim Herriot had bedded himself between the posts and spent two years with Wrexham (1966-68) before entering non-League soccer as player-manager of Atherstone Town. He then assisted Bromsgrove Rovers, Tamworth and Atherstone (again, also as manager from July 1972). Schofield later ran a very successful wine and spirits business in Atherstone and for many years was a season ticket-holder at St Andrew's. A terrific servant to Birmingham City football club - not only as a player!

Johnny Schofield in action against Sheffield United in 1961

SCOTTISH CONNECTION

Personnel who have served with Blues and also with Scottish club(s):

Ken Armstrong . . . . .Kilmarnock
Bertie Auld . . . . . . .Celtic, Dumbarton, Hamilton Acc., Hibernian
Jim Ballantyne . . .Dumfries, Kilmarnock, Rangers, Vale of Leven
Dave Barnett . . . . .Dunfermline Athletic
Dougie Bell . .Aberdeen, Clyde, Elgin City, Hibs, Partick Thistle, Rangers, St Mirren
Willie Bell . . . . .Queens Park
Noel Blake . . . . .Dundee
Albert Bloxham . . . . .Raith Rovers
Robert Bonthron . . . . .Dundee, Leith Athletic
Des Bremner . . . . .Hibernian
Kevin Bremner . . . . .Dundee, Keith
Danny Bruce . . . . .Perth FC, Rangers, Vale of Leven
Kenny Burns . . . . .Rangers (schoolboy forms)
Ted Cameron . . . . .Clydebank
Jimmy Conlin . .Airdrieonians, Albion Rovers, Falkirk, Hibernian
John Connolly . . . . .Hibernian, St Johnstone
Johnny Crosbie . . . . .Ayr United
Jim Dailey . . . . .Third Lanark
Jimmy Devlin . . . . . . .Aberdeen, Kilsyth Rangers, Third Lanark
Kevin Drinkell . . . . .Falkirk (player-coach), Rangers, Stirling Albion (player- coach)
Charlie Duncan . . . . .Clyde, Dunfermline Athletic
Tom Dunlop . . . . .Dundee Harp, Port Glasgow (trial)
Bobby Ferguson . . . . .Kilmarnock
Paul Fitzpatrick .Hamilton Academical
Trevor Francis . . . . .Rangers
Adam Fraser . . . . .Glasgow Nomads, Glasgow Northern

Cammie Fraser . . . . .Dunfermline Athletic, Falkirk
Archie Garrett . . . . .Airdrieonians, Heart of Midlothian
Archie Gemmill . . . . .St Mirren
George Getgood . . . . .Ayr United, Bo'ness
Bill Gildea . . . . .Falkirk
Archie Goldie . . . . .Clyde
Mick Good . . . . .Airdrieonians
Paul Gorman . . . . .Gretna Green
Harry Graham . . . . .St Bernard's, Heart of Midlothian
Alex Harley . . . . .Dundee, Third Lanark
John Henderson . . . . .Dumfries
Paul Hendrie . . . .Celtic (amateur), Kilsyth Rangers, Kirkintillock Robroy
Jim Herriot . . . .Dunfermline Athletic, Hibernian, Morton, Partick Thistle, St Mirren
Frank Hodges . . . . .St Mirren (guest)
Billy Hume . . .Berwick Rangers, Dunfermline Athletic, St Mirren
Roger Hynd . . . . .Motherwell (manager), Rangers
Jimmy Inglis . . . . .Airdrieonians
Leigh Jenkinson . . . . .St Johnstone
Alan Johnson . . . . .Heart of Midlothian
Willie Johnston . . . . .East Fife (coach), Heart of Midlothian, Raith Rovers (coach), Rangers
Andy Kennedy . . . . .Rangers
Jack Kidd . . . . .St Johnstone
Bobby Laing . . . . .Falkirk
Dave Latchford . . . . .Motherwell
Graham Leggatt . . . . .Aberdeen
Arthur Leonard . . . . .St Bernard's
Alec Leslie . . . . .Morton, St Mirren
John Logan . . . .Edinburgh Emmett, Musselburgh, Partick Thistle
Lou Macari . . . . .Celtic (player and manager)
Dave Mackay . . . . .Heart of Midlothian
Bill McCafferty . . . . .Celtic
Frank McGurk . . . . .Blantyre Celtic, Clyde
Alex McIntosh . . . . .Hearts of Bleith
Frank McKee . . . . .Dundee United
John McMillan . . . . .Port Glasgow Athletic, St Bernard's
Ted McMinn . . . . .Queen of the South, Rangers
Bob McRoberts . . . . .Airdrieonians, Albion Rovers
Walter Main . . . . .Airdrieonians, St Bernard's
John Morgan .Edinburgh Emmett
Jock Mulraney . . .Celtic (trialist), Hamilton Academical (trialist), Heart of Midlothian, Hibernian (guest), Third Lanark (guest)
Jim Murray . . . . .Ayr United, St Augustine's
Thomas Myhre . . . . .Rangers
Peter Neil . . . . .East Fife, Heart of Midlothian
Peter Neilson . . . . .Airdrieonians
Mike Newell . . . . .Aberdeen
John Paskin . . . . .Dundee United (trialist)
David Preece . . . . .Aberdeen
Ernie Richardson . . . . .Vale of Leven
Billy Robb .Armadale, Eastern Burnside, Hibernian, Kirkintilloch Rob Roy, Rangers, Royal Albert, Third Lanark, Vale of Leven
George Robertson . . . . .Clyde
Jim Robertson . . . . .Glasgow United, Partick Thistle
Jim E. Robinson . . . . .Dundee, Kilmarnock, Lochee United
Peter Shearer . . . . .Dundee United
Billy Steel . . . . .Airdrieonians (trainer & manager), St Johnstone, Third Lanark (manager)

Jackie Stewart . . . . .Raith Rovers
Tony Taylor . . . . .Morton
Ian Taylor-Smith . . . . .Heart of Midlothian, Queen of the South, Queens Park (amateur)
Bobby Thomson . . . . .Airdrieonians, Albion Rovers
George Waddell . . . . .Fraserburgh, Hamilton Academical, Kilmarnock, Rangers
Jock Wilson . . . . .Edinburgh St Bernard's
Chris Woods . . . . .Rangers
Ron Wylie . . . . .Clydesdale Juniors
● Joe Devine . . . . .refereed in the Highland League

Ken Armstrong (no. 5) in action v WBA in 1985.

SCOUTS

Walter Taylor, Don Dorman, Norman Bodell and Malcolm Beard have been the four most prominent of Blues' scouts down the years. Taylor was responsible for bringing several star players to the club during the 1930s and '40s, while Dorman recruited the likes of Kenny Burns, Trevor Francis, the Latchfords, Garry Pendrey and Malcolm Page among others when he was based at the club.

SCUNTHORPE UNITED

Blues' playing record against the 'Iron' is:

FA CUP

Venue	P	W	D	L	F	A
Home	1	0	1	0	0	0
Away	1	1	0	0	2	1
Totals	2	1	1	0	2	1

Blues knocked the 'Iron' out if the FA Cup in the second round in December 1994, winning a replay with goals by Steve McGavin and Gary Cooper in front of 6,280 fans. This defeat - seen live on Sky TV - was United's first at home by a League side in 10 years of FA Cup football.

Players with both clubs include: G Bull, C Calladine, D Foy, J Gayle, R Huxford (United app), T Lees, J Millington (Blues reserve), BR Mills, M North, S Ottewell, N Platnauer, H Roberts.

Also: Freddie Goodwin (United player, Blues manager).

SEAMAN, David

David Seaman made 84 appearances in goal for Blues between October 1984 and August 1986. Then, during the next 14 years he became one of the finest 'keepers in the world, winning honours galore with Arsenal and starring in more than 60 internationals for England, also representing his country in 10 under 21 matches and six 'B' internationals. A Yorkshireman, born in Rotherham on 19 September 1963, Seaman joined Leeds United as a junior and turned professional at Elland Road in September 1981. Surprisingly he failed to make a single first team appearance for Leeds and left for Peterborough United in a moderate £4,000 transfer deal in August 1982. From London Road he switched to St Andrew's for £100,000 and on leaving Blues he joined Queens Park Rangers for £225,000, switching to Highbury for £1.3 million in May 1990. Over the next decade Seaman, tall, commanding, a fine shot-stopper with terrific reflexes, amassed 450 appearances for the Gunners, gaining seven medals for various competitions. At competitive level alone Seaman ended the 1999-2000 campaign with more than 800 appearances under his belt...and he still looks fit and eager to play on until he tops the 1,000 mark!

SECRETARIES (of Blues)

The following have all held the position of secretary (and/or secretary-manager) of Birmingham City (Small Heath) football club: WC Adams (late 1945 to 1964), WA Camkin (1941-44), W Edden (1884-85), WH Edmunds (1875-84), WH Grady (1933-41), AG Instone (1964-83), A 'Inky' Jones (1885-1908) AG Jones BA, MBA (1993 to date), L Knighton (1928-33 as secretary-manager), F Richards (three spells between 1911 and 1928, one as secretary-manager: 1915-23), S Richards (briefly in the mid-1920s), A Waterhouse (1983-88) and J Westmancoat FAAI, MBIM (1988 to 1993).

● Billy Edmunds was the club's first secretary (1875-85). Alf Jones followed him, holding office for 23 years before Frank Richards was initially appointed as secretary in 1911. Alan Instone was assistant to Walter Adams before becoming Blues' secretary, a position he held for 19 years until his death in February 1983.

Alan Instone   **John Westmancoat**

SENDINGS-OFF

Martyn O'Connor, sent-off in the local derby with Wolves in 2000.

- Welsh international defender Caesar Jenkyns was the first Blues player to be sent-off in a competitive match. He took an early bath after being dismissed in the League Division One game v Liverpool on 14 October 1893. He had already scored for Blues who eventually lost the game 4-3 at Muntz Street.
- The tough-tackling Jenkyns, in fact, was banished for an early bath on four occasions whilst with Blues and seven times during his career. In March 1895 Blues decided to dispense with his services and suspended him for six weeks (until the end of that season) for brawling with a Derby player and also for attempting to assault two fans. A few months later, having been transferred to Woolwich Arsenal, Jenkyns refused to leave the field after being sent-off for foul play (he did leave eventually).
- Percy Barton was sent-off four times during his career, three of his dismissals coming as a Blues player.
- Gary Cooper also received three red cards as a Blues player - versus Watford (Division 1) in January 1994, v Brighton & Hove Albion (Division 2) in April 1995 and v Tranmere Rovers (League Cup) in October 1995.
- Colin Todd was sent-off twice in London during the second half of Blues' 1979-80 promotion-winning season - first at Charlton in February and then against West Ham (with Billy Bonds) in April. After this dismissal against the Hammers Todd received 20 penalty points, appeared before the FA Disciplinary Committee and was suspended for one match.
- Darren Wassall was sent-off in successive months for Blues against Sheffield United at Bramall Lane in a League game in September 1997 and against Arsenal at Highbury in a Coca-Cola

League Cup-tie in October. Crowe (Arsenal) was also dismissed in the latter game.
- Mick Harford was dismissed twice and Robert Hopkins once in season 1983-84.
- Both Paul Furlong and Chris Marsden received red cards in Blues' away League game with Reading in January 1998 (lost 0-2). In the game at St Andrew's at the start of that season, Andy Bernal of Reading was sent-off in Blues' 3-0 win.
- Malcolm Beard had the misfortune to be sent-off in his last game for Blues, a League fixture at Millwall in December 1970.
- Garry Pendrey was ordered from the field twice as a Blues player.
- Midfielders Martyn O'Connor and Bryan Hughes were both sent-off during the last ten minutes of Blues' vital home League game against Wolves on 1 April 2000.
- Gary Poole was red-carded in the home League Cup quarter-final encounter against Norwich City in 1996.
- Peter Ndlovu was sent-off by referee Rob Styles for 'diving' in Blues League game with Huddersfield at St Andrew's in October 1998. The decision was later changed!
- Mark Dennis is the only Blues player to be sent-off TWICE against the same opponents in the same League season - dismissed versus Wolves at St Andrew's and Molineux in 1978-79. Peterborough's David McDonald suffered the same fate for Posh against Blues in 1993-94.
- Blues had four players sent-off in Fairs Cup football. They were centre-half Trevor Smith (with Dvorvic of Dinamo Zagreb) on 24 May 1959 in Zagreb; striker Johnny Gordon v Ujpesti Dozsa of Hungary in Budapest on 26 October 1960 and both Jimmy Harris and Bertie Auld against RCD Espanol on 7 December 1961 at St Andrew's. Two Espanol players - Abel Sanchez (fighting with Harris) and Vidour Rivas (fisticuffs with Auld) - were also dismissed in this same game. And all four went off in the second half.
- When Blues won 5-0 at Barnsley in September 1995, two home players were sent-off (goalkeeper David Watson and defender Charlie Bishop).
- Four players were sent-off in the last 15 minutes of the Birmingham Senior Cup Final between Blues and Aston Villa at St Andrew's in May 1996. They were John Cornforth, Ian Jones and Paul Peschisolido (Blues) and Ben Petty (Villa).
- Blues defender Alec McClure was sent-off during a Spanish tour game against Real Madrid in May 1923 - for telling his goalkeeper (Dan Tremelling) where to stand after the home side had been awarded a penalty for handball against Jack 'Cracker' Jones who, in fact, was protecting his false teeth! The referee later printed an apologetic letter in the newspaper admitting he had made a mistake!
- Blues full-back Mark Dennis was sent-off 14 times in his professional career while Willie Johnston, who was at St Andrew's during the 1979-80 season, was dismissed on 19 occasions (possibly a record at professional level). He was banished once playing for Scotland, four times each with both Vancouver Whitecaps and West Brom, three times with Hearts and on seven occasions with Rangers.
- Ex-Blues defender Julian Dicks was sent-off eight times during his interesting career, once in the local derby for West Ham United against Arsenal in September 1995.
- Bertie Auld was ordered off five times as a professional footballer, once in the World Club championship for Celtic against Racing Club Buenos Aries in Argentina in November 1967. He

was one of four Celtic players to be dismissed along with two Argentinians, but somehow Auld himself stayed on the pitch until the final whistle!

- Striker Roy McDonough also had a wretched disciplinary record as a professional, being sent-off seven times during his career (once as a manager). He was with Blues between 1974 and 1978.
- Martin Kuhl also had a short temper and he too has received a number of dismissals during his playing career.
- Sometime earlier (in the late 1920s/early '30s) Bertie Mills (a Blues player in 1929) often lost his temper with his team-mates and the referee and was sent-off five times in five years for misconduct!
- Before joining Blues from Leeds United, defender Byrom Stevenson had the misfortune to be sent-off playing for Wales against Turkey in 1979 for violent conduct. He was subsequently banned from international football for four years.
- Ex-Blues loanee midfielder Vinny Samways quickly gained a reputation as the hard man of Spanish soccer after receiving 12 red cards and 55 bookings in the first two years with the Canary Island club Las Palmas whom he joined for the 1998-99 season. It appears that rivals opponents (and supporters) wind him up by calling him 'El Brando", the 'whimp.'
- Ex-Blues star Eric Barber was sent-off in th FA Cup Final when playing for Shelbourne in 1973.
- Paul Tait left the pitch early in the League Cup game against Aston Villa in October 1993.

SHEFFIELD UNITED

Blues' playing record against the Blades is:

FOOTBALL LEAGUE

Venue	P	W	D	L	F	A
Home	46	25	9	12	82	45
Away	46	11	8	27	62	100
Totals	92	36	17	39	144	145

FA CUP

	P	W	D	L	F	A
Home	3	3	0	0	7	2
Away	2	0	2	0	2	2
Totals	5	3	2	0	9	4

LEAGUE CUP

	P	W	D	L	F	A
Away	1	0	0	1	2	3

WARTIME

	P	W	D	L	F	A
Home	3	3	0	0	13	2
Away	3	1	1	1	4	4
Totals	6	4	1	1	17	6

Sheffield United inflicted upon Blues their first-ever League defeat, beating them 2-0 at Bramall Lane on 17 September 1892.This was also the first League meeting between the two clubs.

Blues claimed their first victory over the Blades at Muntz Street in December 1894, winning 4-2 with inside-forward Charlie Leatherbarrow grabbing a hat-trick. Blues completed the double with a 2-0 win at Bramall Lane on the last day of the season.

Blues beat United 5-1 at home in October 1901 and followed up with a 4-1 victory in Sheffield four months later. Scotsmen Johnny McMillan and Bob McRoberts both scored two goals apiece out of the total of nine.

United ended Blues' run of nine successive home League victories when they won 2-1 at Muntz Street on 5 September 1903.

Between 1903 and 1934 Blues and United met 36 times in the Football League - and it was the Yorkshire club who came out on top, winning 19 times to Blues' 12. In fact, Blues lost 10 games in a row at Bramall Lane (1923 to 1933) when they conceded a total of 37 goals.

Blues' heaviest League defeat of the 1922-23 season was suffered on United soil where they crashed 7-1 on 17 February, Harry Johnson scoring four times. In this game United netted five goals in the first 18 minutes and David Mercer set up his team's last five. This wasn't a happy debut for Blues' centre-forward Albert Rawson, who had left Bramall Lane three days before the game - although he did mark his return to Yorkshire with a goal! Amazingly just over three weeks later Blues turned the tables completely by beating United 4-2 at St Andrew's, Rawson scoring twice on this occasion.

Other United home wins in this emphatic spell included 4-3, 4-1, 4-3, 3-1, 3-2, 4-2 and 3-1. Among Blues' better performances were two 4-1 home wins, a 4-2 victory and another at 3-1. George Briggs scored a hat-trick in the 4-1 triumph in March 1928.

There was a break of 14 seasons before the Blues and the Blades played each other again at League level and when they did it was the Yorkshire side who came out on top, winning both First Division matches in 1948-49 by 2-1 at St Andrew's and 4-0 at Bramall Lane.

Blues' first post Second World War win over United came at St Andrew's in April 1951 when future Blades player Roy Warhurst was among the scorers in a 3-0 victory.

Peter Murphy netted twice as Blues repeated that scoreline in March 1952 and it was 3-0 again to Blues, this time at Bramall Lane, in a First Division match in August 1955.

In April 1962 Blues secured yet another 3-0 League win over United, Jimmy Harris netting twice this time in front of 19,476 fans at St Andrew's.

Amazingly on 25 April 1964 Blues once again beat United 3-0 at home - and this result kept them in the First Division! Bertie Auld, Trevor Smith and Stan Lynn (penalty) were the scorers in front of 26,191 fans.

In December 1969 Blues were slammed 6-0 by United at Bramall Lane in a Second Division game, Colin Addison scoring twice for the Blades. And when United won 2-1 at St Andrew's on the opening day of the 1972-73 season, they ended Blues' excellent run of 36 home League games without defeat.

Blues scored eight goals and conceded four in the two League games against united in 1984-85. Robert Hopkins, David Geddis, Wayne Clarke and Gary West (own-goal) netted in a 4-3 win at Bramall Lane, while Clarke (2), Gerry Daly and Andy Kennedy were on target in their 4-1 home win at St Andrew's.

On 19 December 1986, a crowd of 5,007 - the lowest for a League game at St Andrew's for more than 61 years - saw Blues beat United 2-1.

In August 1996 Blues were 2-0 up then 2-4 down before forcing a 4-4 draw with the Blades at Bramall Lane.

Over 33,000 fans saw Blues beat United 3-1 at St Andrew's in a third round FA Cup-tie in January 1934 and there was an identical scoreline for Blues in a fourth round replay on the same ground in February 1953 when Peter Murphy notched a couple of goals.

Billy Wright scored a penalty in each of Blues' two third round encounters with United in January 1984. Blues eventually won their home replay 2-0 after a 1-1 draw in Yorkshire.

Players with both clubs include: G Ablett, K Bremner, W Beer, E Bluff, S Bruce (player-manager of United), Cipriano (Marcelo),

P Devlin, A Drake, C Field, G Gallimore, D Givens, R Hansbury, R Hatton, F Hawley, T Hockey, D Holdsworth, B Horne, H Howard, J Hunt, A Kennedy, M Kuhl, C Marsden, D Mortimer, J Peart, AN Rawson, B Rioch, P Starbuck, P Tomlinson, R Warhurst, F White (United guest), S Wigley, W Wigmore, P Withe.

Also: Howard Kendall (Blues player, United manager), Jim Smith (United player, Blues manager), Geoff Vowden (Blues player, United coach), Frank Barlow (Blades player, Blues assistant-manager/coach)..

Paul Devlin

SHEFFIELD WEDNESDAY

Blues' playing record against the Owls is:

FOOTBALL LEAGUE

Venue	P	W	D	L	F	A
Home	35	17	14	4	53	25
Away	35	8	6	21	49	94
Totals	70	25	20	25	102	119

FA CUP

Home	1	1	0	0	2	1
Away	2	0	1	1	2	4
Totals	3	1	1	1	4	5

FOOTBALL ALLIANCE

Home	3	1	2	0	10	4
Away	3	0	1	2	7	18
Totals	6	1	3	2	17	22

WARTIME

Home	3	3	0	0	12	4
Away	3	3	0	0	5	0
Totals	6	6	0	0	17	4

Having played against each other in the Football Alliance, Blues and Wednesday first met in the Football League in season 1894-95 (Division One). The Owls came out on top, winning 2-0 at home and drawing 0-0 at Muntz Street.

After losing 4-0 at Sheffield in October 1899, Blues gained their first League win over Wednesday the following February, beating them 4-1 at Muntz Street in front of 9,000 spectators. And then after suffering a 4-2 reverse on Wednesday soil in December 1905, Blues gained revenge with a pulsating 5-1 home victory in April 1906 when Charlie Tickle netted a hat-trick.

Blues completed the League double over the Owls in 1907-08, winning their home game 4-1 in late April. Alas, it mattered not because Blues were relegated to the Second Division.

When Blues won promotion to the top flight in 1920-21, they again doubled up over Wednesday, winning 4-0 at home and 2-0 away. And when First Division football resumed between the two clubs (in 1926-27) both games ended in draws, 0-0 at St Andrew's and a thrilling 4-4 tussle at Hillsborough where seven different players figured on the scoresheet. George Liddell scored a rare goal for Blues.

There was another double for Blues in 1927-28 and a 4-1 home victory in February 1929 before a First Division encounter at Hillsborough on 13 December 1930 saw Blues crash to embarrassing 9-1 defeat - their joint heaviest in League football in terms of goals conceded and goals difference.

In November 1932 Blues returned to Hillsborough and this time lost 5-1!

Wednesday won the FA Cup in 1935 and that season they also got the better of Blues, taking four points off them in the League with a 2-1 home win and a 4-1 victory at St Andrew's over the Christmas holiday period.

Wilson Jones scored a hat-trick when Blues took the honours with a 4-1 win at St Andrew's in April 1936 and when Blues won 3-0 on the same ground a year later, Wednesday were staring relegation in the face. In this game former St Andrew's star Tom Grosvenor missed a penalty for the Owls (saved by Harry Hibbs) when the score was 1-0 before Dai Richards netted Blues' second goal from fully 50 yards!

After the War Blues and the Owls played in the Second Division before the Yorkshire club began its yo-yo act between the top two flights.

First Division action resumed in 1956-57, Blues charging to a 4-0 home win in their last-ever fixture on Christmas Day!

A thumping 5-1 Wednesday win at Hillsborough in August 1961 was followed thirteen months later by a 5-0 demolition of Blues on the same ground and in October 1964 the Owls again went to town with a 5-2 home victory!

Six goals were shared in an eventful Second Division clash at Sheffield in February 1971 when Trevor Francis netted twice for Blues in front of 13,138 fans.

Wednesday had a spell in the Third Division prior to meeting Blues back in the top flight in 1985-86 and then it was the Owls who won hands down at Hillsborough, Blues succumbing to a 5-1 defeat as they slithered towards the Second Division.

Blues were drawn at home to Wednesday in the second round

proper of the FA Cup in 1891-92, but they forfeited the advantage, accepted £200 compensation and played the tie at Owlerton where they lost 2-0 in front of 4,000 spectators. Soon afterwards the Wednesday ground was closed for 14 days following crowd disturbances!

Blues knocked the Owls out of the FA Cup in the fourth round in 1969, winning the replay 2-1 at St Andrew's after a 2-2 draw at Hillsborough.

The combined attendance figure for these two games was a massive 103,525.

Blues joint heaviest defeat in the Football Alliance (1-9) was suffered at the hands of Wednesday in December 1889 - but there was a reason! Blues fielded only NINE players at Owlerton.

The Owls were walloped 7-1 by Blues at Muntz Street in an Alliance encounter in January 1891 - reasonable revenge for that earlier massacre!

Players with both clubs include: W Aveyard, S Bryant, L Burkinshaw, M Burton, J Dailey, H Deacon (Owls amateur), F Foxall, T Francis (Owls player-manager), A Godden, R Gregg, T Grosvenor, P Hart (also Owls' coach), R Hope, H Howard (Owls trialist), G Hyde, JW Jordan, T Matthewson, T Neale (Blues reserve), J Sheridan, C Shutt, D Sonner, JC Whitehouse, S Whitton, P Williams, AR Wilson.

Also: Chris Woods (Owls player, Blues coach), Charlie Elliott (Blues guest, Owls amateur), Bobby Ferguson (Wednesday goalkeeper, Blues assistant-manager/coach), Derek Jefferson (Owls player, Blues coach), F Barlow (coach at both clubs).

SHORT CAREERS

Malcolm Briggs may well hold the record for having the shortest career in English professional football! He came on as an 87th minute substitute for Blues in their away League game at Manchester City in May 1979. This was his only first team appearance at any senior level.

Ian Brown played just 12 minutes in Blues' first team - as a late substitute in a Football League Cup encounter away at West Bromwich Albion in November 1984. And it understood he didn't even touch the ball during that time!

SHREWSBURY TOWN

Joyous scenes in the St Andrew's dressing room after Blues had beaten Shrewsbury to clinch promotion in April 1992.

Blues' playing record against the Shrews is:

FOOTBALL LEAGUE

Venue	P	W	D	L	F	A
Home	9	3	2	4	5	6
Away	9	1	3	5	4	10
Totals	18	4	5	9	9	16

LEAGUE CUP

Venue	P	W	D	L	F	A
Home	2	2	0	0	6	1
Away	2	0	1	1	2	3
Totals	4	2	1	1	8	4

The Shrews are one of Birmingham City's bogey teams!

In a shade over five years - September 1986 and October 1991 - there were eleven League games between the two teams; Shrewsbury won seven and the other four were drawn (three of them in a row by 0-0).

Bobby Hope

Blues claimed their first win over the Shrews at the twelfth attempt and in doing so clinched promotion from the Third Division with a 1-0 success at St Andrew's on 25 April 1992, Nigel Gleghorn's goal doing the trick in front of almost 20,000 spectators.

The first League meeting took place at Gay Meadow on 13 December 1986 (Shrewsbury winning 1-0) and in October 1990 Blues crashed to their heaviest defeat so far at the hands of Shrewsbury, going down 4-1 at Gay Meadow. Former Blues star Wayne Clarke scored a hat-trick for the Shrews in 29 minutes (20-49). This defeat was also Blues' first in the League that season and it ended an unbeaten run of 12 matches from the start of a campaign (the club's best since 1900 when they went 15 matches without losing).

Blues' first win at Gay Meadow was achieved on 5 November 1994 when Gary Bull and Jonathan Hunt found the net in a 2-0 triumph in front of 5,942 fans...2,000 supporting Blues!

Blues beat the 'Shrews' 5-2 on aggregate in a second round League Cup-tie in 1982-83. Alan Curbushley scored twice in the 4-1 second leg victory at St Andrew's after Ian Handysides' strike had earned a 1-1 draw at Gay Meadow.

When Blues lost 2-1 at Shrewsbury in a League Cup first round first leg encounter in August 1994, former St Andrew's striker Wayne Clarke scored for the home side.

Players with both clubs include: J Argue (Blues reserve), AW Atkins, I Atkins, WJ Beel, DK Bell, N Blake, M Burton, F Castle, W Clarke, J Cornforth, G Daly, L Donowa, N Forster (Town amateur), M Fox, F Foxall, D Geddis, G Getgood, P Gorman, AW Hartwell, C Harvey, R Hopkins, MA Jones, TT Jones, A Morris, R Morris (Town trialist), A Mulraney, J Paskin, D Peer, W Quinton, A Rees, MJ Regan, H Roberts, CR Robinson, D Rowbotham, MR Rutherford, RP Scott, AH Sheldon (Blues reserve), K Summerfield, BJ Taylor, P Wright.

Also: Leslie Knighton (manager of both clubs), Chic Bates (Town player, assistant-manager & player-manager, Blues coach & assistant-manager), Fred Davies (Shrewsbury manager, Blues coach), Alf Wood (Shrews' player, Blues lottery salesman).

SIMOD CUP

Blues played in this short-lived competition in 1987-88. They lost both games - 3-1 at Derby on 25 November and 6-0 at neighbours Aston Villa on 9 November when the attendance was just 8,324. Villa were 5-0 in front at half-time!

Summary

Venue	P	W	D	L	F	A
Away	2	0	0	2	1	9

SIX-A-SIDE

Blues twice won the National Six-A-Side Tournament, first in 1982 and then as holders in 1983 to retain the trophy.

SLOUGH TOWN

Blues were drawn away to non-League Slough Town in the first round of the FA Cup in November 1994 but were handed home advantage by the underdogs. Blues won the game 4-0 in front of 13,394 spectators, Peter Shearer and Steve McGavin both scoring twice to see off the underdogs.

This was Blues' seventh successive win (League and Cup).

SMITH, Billy

A Blues player from February 1950 to December 1952, wing-half or inside-forward Billy Smith scored 23 goals in 62 first team appearances for the club. And overall he did very well, netting over 50 goals in more than 250 as a 'pro'. Born in Plymouth on 7 September 1926, and a rugby union player at school, he joined his home town club Plymouth Argyle as a centre-half in readiness for the start of the 1945-46 transitional Football League season. In August 1947 he switched to Reading and in the summer of 1948 teamed up with Northampton Town. From The County Ground he moved to St Andrew's. On leaving Blues he joined Blackburn Rovers and after filling every position on the field for the Ewood Park club he became player-coach and captain of Accrington Stanley (July 1960). He lent the Peel Park club valuable experience as a player and also as joint caretaker-manager (with H Hubbick) during Stanley's final months in the Football League before the club resigned its position in Division Four in March 1962. Smith actually played in Stanley's last-ever Football League game - a 4-0 defeat at Crewe on 2 March 1962. He didn't stay in football after that. He played for an England XI v Australia in 1951-52

SMITH, Jim

Jim 'Bald Eagle' Smith completed a novel managerial record in April 1986 by becoming the first manager to visit all 92 League club grounds (being utilised at the time) for competitive matches. He achieved the feat with Colchester United, Blackburn Rovers, Blues, Oxford United and QPR.

Jovial Jim as he was sometimes called, was born in Sheffield on 17 August 1940. As a player (a left-back with biting tackle) he served with Sheffield United (as an amateur and professional from 1959), Aldershot, Halifax Town, Lincoln City and Boston United, becoming player-manager of the latter club in 1968. In 1972 he took up a similar position with Colchester United, retiring as a player in 1973. A year after guiding Colchester into the Third Division he became boss of Blackburn Rovers - a post he retained until March 1978 when he took over the reins from Sir Alf Ramsey at St Andrew's. Smith, one of the most affable of managers in League football, did Blues proud. He signed some fine players but had the misfortune (if you can call it that) of being relegated in 1979 only to bounce straight back the very next season with a team comprising some tremendous footballers, Alan Curbishley, Frank Worthington, Archie Gemmill, Joe Gallagher, Kevan Broadhurst and Colin Todd among them. He was an adventurous manager, admired and much liked by the St Andrew's faithful. He did bring in a few perhaps weaker players and some 'risky' ones (Willie Johnston, Alan Buckley and Alberto Tarantini were three who all cost pretty big transfer fees). But generally speaking he was a good manager and he continued to be so despite being sacked by Blues in February 1982 (to let in Ron Saunders). At this juncture Smith took over at Oxford United and he held the fort at The Manor Ground until June 1985 when, twelve months after leading Oxford to the Third Division championship, he was named boss of QPR. In 1986 he strode out at Wembley with the London club only to see his charges lose the League Cup Final to his former club Oxford United! In December 1988 Smith moved away from Loftus Road to manage Newcastle United where he stayed until March 1991. At that point he left football management to become coach at Middlesbrough, but lasted only three months at Ayresome Park before being engaged as manager at Portsmouth. At Fratton Park he was short on players and money but had an excellent first season there, taking the club to the semi-finals of the FA Cup where they lost to Liverpool in a penalty shoot-out at the end of the second replay. In 1992-93 Pompey's and Smith's luck deserted them again when they missed automatic promotion to the Premiership after a great late run almost saw them leap over West Ham. They eventually lost in the play-offs to Leicester City.

After Portsmouth came Derby County, the Rams appointing Smith as their new manager in August 1995 - and over the last five years he has done exceedingly well with the East Midlands club, guiding the Rams into and consolidating them in the Premiership after steering them there in 1996.

Smith celebrated 40 years in football in 1997 and 30 years in management in 1998. And there's a lot more to come from the grand old Yorkshireman.

Jim Smith

SMITH, Trevor

As a teenager Trevor Smith looked out of place as he occupied a defensive position in the Brierley Hill schoolboys side behind the solid figure of Duncan Edwards, soon to become a superstar with Manchester United. But Smith worked hard at his game and built up his physique in the gym, quickly developing into a muscular centre-half with Birmingham City whom he served supremely well for thirteen years, initially as an amateur before turning professional at the age of 17. In fact, he made his senior debut straightaway and conceded an own goal to mark the occasion!

Weighing 13-and-a-half stone, he was a colossus at the heart of the Blues defence, helping them win the Second Division championship in 1955 and reach the FA Cup Final the following year. He skippered the team on several occasions, including their appearance in the 1960 Fairs Cup Final against Barcelona and when they lifted the Football League Cup in 1963. He also won two England caps.

Trevor Smith

After suffering an injury during the early part of the 1964-65 season, Smith was replaced at centre-half by Winston Foster. He later moved to Walsall but Blues were called cheats for selling an injured player, for Smith only appeared in 13 matches before retiring from first-class football in February 1966. Smith later worked as a manager for Thresher's Wine Stores, first in the Bull Ring and then in Essex.

SOUTH SHIELDS (Gateshead)

Blues' playing record against South Shields:
FOOTBALL LEAGUE

Venue	P	W	D	L	F	A
Home	2	1	1	0	5	1
Away	2	0	0	2	0	4
Totals	4	1	1	2	5	5

FA CUP

Venue	P	W	D	L	F	A
Away	1	0	0	1	1	2

Blues lost their first League game against the North-East club 1-0 away at Horsley Hill in September 1919, but they quickly gained revenge winning their home match 4-0 nine days later.

The following season after losing 3-0 away, Blues were held to a 1-1 draw at St Andrew's.

The FA Cup-tie was in the fourth round and took place in South Shields in January 1926, Blues losing by the odd goal in three in front of 20,000 fans.

Players with both clubs include: J Connolly, T Daykin, D Dixon, T Hibbitt (also player-manager of Gateshead), GM Liddell (amateur with SS), K Lowe, J Robertson, A Roe, W Thirlaway, J Trewick.

Also: George Smith (Blues player, Gateshead manager), Ken Oliver (South Shields player 1960s, Blues coach).

SOUTHAMPTON

Blues' playing record against Saints is:

FOOTBALL LEAGUE

Venue	P	W	D	L	F	A
Home	14	4	6	4	16	15
Away	14	4	1	9	10	18
Totals	28	8	7	13	26	33

FA CUP

Venue	P	W	D	L	F	A
Home	1	1	0	0	2	1
Away	2	1	0	1	4	4
Totals	3	2	0	1	6	5

LEAGUE CUP

Venue	P	W	D	L	F	A
Home	2	0	1	1	3	6
Away	1	0	0	1	0	3
Totals	3	0	1	2	3	9

WARTIME

Venue	P	W	D	L	F	A
Home	1	1	0	0	4	0
Away	1	0	1	0	1	1
Totals	2	1	1	0	5	1

Blues and Saints first met at League level on 28 September 1946 at The Dell (Division 2). Almost 25,000 fans saw Saints win 1-0 with a goal by Jack Bradley.

However, two goals by Cyril Trigg earned Blues a 3-1 home when the teams met for the return fixture at St Andrew's in February 1947.

Trigg was again on target on the same ground in 1950-51 when Blues completed the League double over Southampton, winning 2-0 at The Dell and 2-1 in the return fixture.

Both teams won their respective 'away' games against each other by 1-0 in 1965-66 as Saints surged into the First Division, But it wasn't until October 1972 that the two antagonists met for the first time in the top flight. Then in front of 30,757 spectators at St Andrew's, Welsh international defender John Roberts salvaged a point for Blues in the 1-1 draw.

Two goals by Stewart Barrowclough (one a penalty) enabled Blues to force a 2-2 draw with Saints at St Andrew's in April 1979.

Blues' final League game in each of seasons 1982-83 and 1983-84 was against Saints - first at The Dell where they won 1-0 (Mick Harford on target) and then at St Andrew's a year later (0-0).

The last time Blues and Saints met in the Football League was on 19 April 1986 at St Andrew's. A meagre crowd of 5,833 saw the visitors win 2-0 as Blues slithered harmlessly towards the Second Division.

Saints beat Blues 5-2 at St Andrew's in a second round League Cup-tie in August 1978. A crowd of 18,464 saw Phil Boyer and Ted MacDougall both score twice for the Saints who went on to reach the Final at Wembley where they lost to Nottingham Forest.

Danny Wallace, later to play for Blues) became Saints' youngest-ever player, aged 16 years 313 days when he made his League debut against Manchester United in 1980.

Players with both clubs include: K Armstrong, J Barrett, J Beresford, E Bluff, C Bosbury, J Bowen, E Brown, G Bull, S Charlton, M Dennis, R Dryden, J Elkes, R Fairman, F Foxall, G Getgood, G Hall (Blues trialist), H Haynes, S Hiley, B Horne, DJ Madden, C Marsden, J Montgomery, G Potter, D Speedie, D Wallace, JM Wilcox, F Worthington.

Also: Joe Mallett and Sir Alf Ramsey (Saints players, Blues managers), Chris Woods (Saints goalkeeper, Blues coach).

Mick Bodley

SOUTHEND UNITED

Blues' playing record against the Shrimpers is:

FOOTBALL LEAGUE

Venue	P	W	D	L	F	A
Home	5	4	1	0	10	3
Away	5	0	1	4	4	13
Totals	10	4	2	4	14	16

FA CUP

Venue	P	W	D	L	F	A
Home	1	1	0	0	2	1
Away	1	1	0	0	6	1
Totals	2	2	0	0	8	1

The first time Blues met the Shrimpers at League level was in season 1990-91. The teams drew 1-1 at St Andrew's when the visitors had David Martin sent-off and at Roots Hall, Southend won 2-1 with Martin netting the equaliser.

Blues lost 4-0 at Roots Hall in January 1993, having won 2-0 at

St Andrew's four months earlier.

Two smartly taken goals by Steve Claridge earned Blues a 2-0 League win over Barry Fry's ex-club United in October 1995 when more than 17,000 flocked to St Andrew's.

Blues beat the Shrimpers 6-1 at Roots Hall in a fourth round FA Cup-tie in January 1957. Alex Govan scored a hat-trick that afternoon in front of 30,000 spectators.

Players with both clubs include: W Bennett (Blues reserve), M Bodley, R Booth, K Brown, P Bullock, JH Burton, K Charley, J Cheesewright, M Cooper, G Davies, JM De Souza, D Dixon, A Edwards, E Edwards, F Firth, N Freeman, P Harding, A Harris, M Harrison, WH Harvey, G Haywood (United trialist), HR Houghton, D Howell, J Hunt, H Lane, JR Linford, R McDonough, S McGavin, D Mangnall (United guest), J Martin, JW Morfitt, R Otto, SE Phillips, TE Pike, G Poole, M Prudhoe, W Quinton, HC Randle (Blues reserve), J Randle, D Regis, P Sansome (Blues loanee), W Smith, W Thirlaway, MR Thomas, C Thompson (Blues reserve), ET Watkins, R Willis, R Woolhouse (Blues reserve), P Wright.

Also: Barry Fry (manager of both clubs), Lil Fuccillo (United player, Blues coach), Ed Stein (assistant-manager & coach both clubs), Tony Taylor (United player, Blues coach).

SPELLER, Fred

Born in Marlow, Essex in the winter of 1864, full-back Fred Speller played for Great Marlow for five years before joining Blues as a professional in 1888. He remained with the club for six years before retiring through injury in 1894. A very competitive player, he always tried to pass the ball to a colleague rather than hoof it downfield. He made well over 100 appearances for Blues in his six years at Muntz Street (97 in senior football) before a broken leg (suffered in a League game at Darwen in October 1892) effectively ended his career, although he did attempt a comeback the following season. Speller died in Birmingham in 1940.

SPONSORSHIP

Here are some of the companies who, in recent years, have been deeply involved in sponsorship with Birmingham City Football Club: Auto Windscreens, Co-op, P.J. Evans, Evans Halshaw, Mark One, Triton (Showers) and Sentinel Telecom.

STAFFORD ROAD

Blues' playing record against the Wolverhampton railway works side is:

FA CUP

Venue	P	W	D	L	F	A
Home	1	0	1	0	3	3
Away	1	0	0	1	2	6
Totals	2	0	1	1	5	9

The works side defeated Blues in a preliminary round of the FA Cup in 1882-83. At the time Stafford Road FC were on par with their arch-rivals the Wolves!

STAFFORDSHIRE CUP

Blues reached the Final of the Staffordshire Cup on nine occasions, winning the trophy twice.

Details of the nine Final appearances:

1914	Blues 4 Wolves 0
1915	Blues 6 West Bromwich Albion 2
1908	Aston Villa 5 Blues 0
1911	Burlsem Port Vale 2 Blues 0
1912	Aston Villa 2 Blues 0 (after 1-1 draw)
1914	Blues 1 Aston Villa 0
1919	Port Vale 1 Blues 0
1926	Walsall reserves 2 Blues 1
1936	Wolves reserves 4 Blues 1

● Blues fielded their reserve side in the 1908, 1909, 1912, 1913, 1915, 1927 and 1937 finals.

After World War Two the competition was basically for non-League clubs, the likes of Aston Villa, Blues, Walsall, West Bromwich Albion and Wolves fielding their reserve sides when they participated.

STEEL, Billy

Billy Steel

Scotsman Billy Steel made 91 first team appearances for Blues between March 1935 and February 1939. A real solid performer, strong in every department of defensive play, he was a footballing right-back signed from Liverpool for £5,000 to replace Harold Booton, but the following season he was switched to left-back with Ned Barkas moving across to the right. Born in Blantyre on 6 February 1908, and now deceased, Steel was reluctant to use the 'big boot' always trying to play the ball to a team-mate.

The fans didn't take to him at first but he soon won over the St Andrew's hecklers and gave Blues excellent service until leaving the club for Derby County seven months prior to World War Two. After the hostilities Steel became trainer for Airdrieonians (April 1950), taking over as manager of the Scottish club in April 1954. Between January 1963 and June 1964 he was in charge of Third Lanark. He also acted as masseur to the Scotland national team on a number of occasions during the early 1950s.

STEVENAGE BOROUGH

Blues beat the Conference non-League side 2-0 in a third round FA Cup-tie in January 1997 - this after Borough had agreed to switch their 'home' game to St Andrew's for a larger attendance which was 15,365! Kevin Francis and Paul Devlin (penalty) scored for Blues.

Player with both clubs: K Dillon, BK Larkin.

STEVENSON, Byron

Born in Llanelli on 7 September 1956 and an apprentice at Elland Road before turning professional with Leeds United in September 1973, Byrom Stevenson moved to St Andrew's in March 1982 in a player-exchange deal that took Frank Worthington to the Yorkshire club. Ron Saunders' first signing, he was a very capable and workmanlike defender, who went on to appear in 91 first-class games for Blues (three goals scored) over the next two-and-a-quarter years before transferring to Bristol Rovers in July 1985. From there he dropped down a peg, signing for non-League Garforth Miners' Welfare in 1988, the club he later managed. Capped by Wales on 15 occasions at senior level, Stevenson also represented his country at both youth and under 21 levels and was being groomed by Leeds to take over from Norman Hunter. This never really happened, hence his move to Blues. Stevenson had the misfortune to be sent-off playing for Wales against Turkey in 1979 for violent conduct and was banned from international soccer for four years. On retiring from football in 1990 he took over the Angel Hotel in Rothwell, Yorkshire.

STEWART, Jackie

A former miner, Jackie Stewart, 5ft. 5ins tall, was a fast-raiding, purposeful outside-right who scored goals as well as making them. A Scotsman, born in Lochgelly, Fife on 4 September 1921 (just after Blues had won the Second Division title) he played junior football north of the border with Lochgelly Welfare and Donibristle Youth club before joining Raith Rovers in August 1939. Unfortunately the War disrupted his progress considerably and after all sorts of adventures around Europe he came back to Britain and rejoined Raith before transferring to St Andrew's in January 1948, brought in to replace Goodwin. During the following season Stewart was switched inside to accommodate Johnny Berry but when he moved to Manchester United Stewart was given back the right-wing berth - and how well he performed. He scored 55 goals for Blues (including a fourtimer against Manchester City in September 1948) in 218 appearances. He gained a Second Division championship medal in 1948 but injuries began to affect his performances and he eventually left the club in February 1955, just prior to Blues clinching another Second Division championship success. Stewart returned to his first love, Raith Rovers who later engaged him as trainer at Stark's Park. He remained in Scottish football until 1963 when he went into business in Cowdenbeath.

STOCKPORT COUNTY

Blues' playing record against the Hatters is:

FOOTBALL LEAGUE

Venue	P	W	D	L	F	A
Home	16	12	2	2	36	12
Away	16	4	3	9	15	24
Totals	32	16	5	11	51	36

FA CUP

	P	W	D	L	F	A
Home	3	3	0	0	6	2

LEAGUE CUP

	P	W	D	L	F	A
Home	1	1	0	0	4	1
Away	1	0	0	1	1	2
Total	2	1	0	1	5	3

Boxing Day 1900 saw Blues and County meet for the first time in League competition - and in front of 7,000 fans at Muntz Street, Bob McRoberts and Jack Aston scored to give Blues a 2-0 victory.

Two years later Blues repeated that scoreline on the same ground and then doubled up with a 2-1 win at Stockport in March 1903.

Fred Chapple may well have earned himself a massive bonus, a

huge Christmas present in fact, by scoring all Blues' goals in their 4-2 home League win over County on 25 December 1908.

Blues began their 1913-14 League programme with a 3-2 home win over County, Yorkshireman Arthur Reed scoring twice in front of 15,000 fans.

When Blues won the Second Division championship in 1920-21 they scored eight goals in their two League games against Stockport, winning 3-0 at Edgeley Park and 5-0 at St Andrew's in the space of seven days in December.

Johnny Crosbie, Jack Whitehouse and Joe Lane scored in both matches with Lane netting twice in that 5-0 victory which drew a 30,000 pre-Christmas crowd to St Andrew's.

It was another 70 years, ten months before the teams met again at League level and on this occasion - in October 1991 - Blues won again, this time by 3-0 also at St Andrew's.

Blues met County eight times over the course of two seasons - three clashes came in the 1996-97 campaign while the other five were staged in 1997-98

The five games in the latter season produced 21 goals, Blues winning home League and League Cup games by the same score of 4-1. They also won their home FA Cup-tie 3-1.

Players with both clubs include: H Bodle, K Charlery, K Francis, P Cooper, P Hart, P Hendrie, RE Keating, C Marsden, T Matthewson, J Quinn, RG Thomson, F Worthington.

Chris Marsden

STOKE CITY

Blues' playing record against the Potters is:

FOOTBALL LEAGUE

Venue	P	W	D	L	F	A
Home	40	20	9	11	54	42
Away	40	6	8	26	41	71
Totals	80	26	17	37	95	113

FA CUP

	P	W	D	L	F	A
Home	3	1	1*	1	3	3
Away	4	1	2	1	5	7
Totals	7	2	3	2	8	10

* Game decided by penalty shoot-out.

TEXACO CUP

	P	W	D	L	F	A
Home	1	0	1*	0	0	0
Away	1	0	1	0	0	0
Totals	2	0	2	0	0	0

ANGLO ITALIAN CUP

	P	W	D	L	F	A
Away	1	0	0	1	0	2

AUTOGLASS TROPHY

	P	W	D	L	F	A
Away	1	0	0	1	1	3

FOOTBALL ALLIANCE

	P	W	D	L	F	A
Home	1	1	0	0	5	1
Away	1	0	0	1	2	4
Totals	2	1	0	1	7	5

MIDLAND COUNTIES LEAGUE

	P	W	D	L	F	A
Home	1	1	0	0	3	0
Away	1	0	0	1	1	2
Totals	2	1	0	1	4	2

WARTIME

	P	W	D	L	F	A
Home	5	4	1	0	14	4
Away	5	1	2	2	5	11
Totals	10	5	3	2	19	15

Blues registered their best home League victory over Stoke as far back as November 1894 when they triumphed 4-2 at Muntz Street - the second meeting between the two clubs.

The first match had ended in a 2-2 draw at The Victoria Ground three weeks earlier and was played in a continual downpour in front of 1,500 hardy spectators. Willie Naughton put the Potters ahead while the Blues players were confronting the referee about not awarding them a penalty! Frank Mobley, though, scored twice in quick succession, his second goal a brilliant header, to edge Blues in front, before Jack Farrell equalised to save the Potters a point!

There were 3,000 fans present for the return fixture at Muntz Street. Caesar Jenkyns was a tower of strength in the Blues defence and found time to set up two of his side's goals. Billy Walton, Frank Mobley, Fred Wheldon and Jack Hallam scored for Blues who may well have won more convincingly had the Stoke 'keeper George Clawley not been in such terrific form.

A year later Blues lost 6-1 at Stoke in October 1895, their heaviest League defeat at the hands of the Potters. Joey Schofield scored a hat-trick for the home side in this game.

In 1906-07 Stoke lost their First Division status but they still managed to beat Blues 3-0 at The Victoria Ground!

Having had a spell outside the Football League altogether, Blues and Stoke resumed battle in 1919-20 and it was Blues who took the honours, completing the double with a 1-0 win in the Potteries and a 2-1 victory at St Andrew's. And when Blues took the Second

Division title the following season they again doubled up over Stoke, winning 2-1 away and 3-0 at home, Harry Hampton scoring both goals on Stoke soil.

Blues first met up with Stanley Matthews in a First Division game at St Andrew's in March 1934. The Potters won the game 1-0, Tommy Sale the goalscorer after good work by Matthews!

Blues' heaviest home League defeat against Stoke is 5-0 - in September 1935 when that man Stanley Matthews scored a rare hat-trick. Poor old Billy Steel, the Blues left-back, was given a roasting!

Twelve months later Stoke won 4-2 on Blues' soil and this time Freddie Steele scored a hat-trick while Matthews netted just once. And on 14 January 1939 Blues lost 6-3 at Stoke - their heaviest defeat of the season in terms of goals conceded. Goal-machine Steele netted four times for the Potters that day, three of them courtesy of Matthews' genius!

The first League game between the teams after the Second World War saw Blues win 2-1 at St Andrew's in September 1948, Neil Dougall and Fred Harris the scorers in front of almost 50,000 fans.

Just after beating Liverpool 9-1 and three weeks after hammering fellow Potteries side Port Vale 7-2, both at St Andrew's, Blues then accounted for Stoke by 2-0 to gain revenge for an opening day defeat at The Victoria Ground.

With Blues in the First Division and Stoke in the Second it was not until season 1963-64 that the teams met again - and this time Stoke took the glory, winning 4-1 at home and 1-0 at St Andrew's.

Stoke won both matches the following season as Blues slipped into the Second Division.

Stoke v Blues at The Victoria Ground in 1934.

Blues had not won a League match at The Victoria Ground in 13 attempts (from 1922) before Bob Latchford ended that sequence by netting both goals in a 2-1 First Division victory in November 1972. And then Malcolm Page, Trevor Francis and Bob Hatton found the Stoke net in a 3-1 triumph at St Andrew's six months later.

Stoke 5 Blues 2 was the result of a First Division game at The Victoria Ground in November 1973 and in December 1974 it was Blues 0 Stoke 3 at St Andrew's. Stoke also won 4-1 on Blues' territory in September 1982 and 3-1 at The Victoria Ground in January 1988.

Blues crashed through the Second Division trap door at the end of the 1988-89 season, having lost both matches against Stoke 1-0. But it was Blues' turn to celebrate in 1990-91 when they won both matches, 1-0 at Stoke (Nigel Gleghorn the scorer) and 2-1 at St Andrew's (Trevor Matthewson and Robert Hopkins on target).

After a dramatic game at St Andrew's in February 1992, the last minute was played inside an empty stadium! Earlier a crowd of 22,162 had seen the Third Division promotion clash go to 1-1 but incensed Blues' fans charged onto the pitch after Paul Barnes (Stoke) scored a dubious late equaliser. Referee Roger Wiseman ordered the 22 players to the dressing room, told the police to clear the stadium and then allowed the remaining 60 seconds to be played at walking pace before he blew the final whistle.

There were six former Blues players in the Stoke City squad for the League game at St Andrew's in September 1995 (1-1 draw).

Blues' 7-0 win at The Britannia Stadium on 10 January 1998 equalled the club's best away record in the Football League. Bryan Hughes scored twice in the opening nine minutes; it was 3-0 at the interval and then Paul Furlong weighed in with a second-half hat-trick. The crowd was 14,940.

Freddie Steele was once again a worry to Blues as he slammed in a hat-trick in Stoke's 4-1 FA Cup win over Blues in January 1937.

The FA Cup match played in August 1972 decided the 3rd and 4th places in the competition from the previous season and after a 0-0 draw Blues won the penalty shoot-out 4-3.

In the Texaco Cup competition of 1973-74, Blues beat the Potters 3-1 in a penalty shoot-out after both matches had ended goalless.

Stoke, in fact, are the only team Blues have met TWICE in penalty shoot-outs.

In the Autoglass Trophy clash at The Victoria Ground in December 1991, Blues fielded an under strength side and were defeated comfortably by 3-1.

Both the Midland Counties League games between the two clubs were played in April 1894.

Cyril Trigg netted five of Blues' goals in their emphatic 6-2 Wartime win over Stoke in a Regional League game in November 1940.

Players with both clubs include: H Bailey, P Barnes, J Beckford, K Bertschin, N Blake, A Box, P Bullock, W Clarke, I Clarkson, S Cole (Stoke amateur), G Daly, L Donowa, K Downing, R Dryden, W Finney, R Forsyth, M Gabbiadini, G Gallimore, H Gayle, J Gayle, N Gleghorn, J Greenhoff, W Haines, J Hall, A Jones, R Jones, H Kendall, T Lees, AR Leonard, K Lowe, A McClure, V Overson, J Peart, FB Pentland G Potter, PP Peschisolido, G Potter, M Prudhoe, D Regis, WH Robertson, PJ Robinson, M Sale, GS Scott, B Siddall (non-contract with Blues), B Small, AW Smith, S Sturridge, S Sutton (Potters trialist), A Turner (also Blues

manager).

Also: Lou Macari (manager of both clubs), Mick Mills (Stoke player & manager, Blues assistant-manager), Chic Bates (assistant-manager/coach of both clubs), Brian Caswell (coach at both clubs), Peter Henderson (physio at both clubs), Alan Ball senior (Blues reserve player, Stoke coach).

* Four players, later to join Stoke, top-scored for Blues between 1980 and 1991 - Keith Bertschin, Howard Gayle, Wayne Clarke (twice) and Nigel Gleghorn.

STOKER, Lew

An attack-minded half-back who was always looking to assist his forwards, Lew Stoker was described as 'an excellent feeder of the attack' and gave Blues splendid service, appearing in 246 senior games and scoring two goals. Born in County Durham on 31 March 1910, he played for Bearpark FC and West Stanley before becoming a professional with Blues in September 1930 (after a brief trial period). He became a regular member of the first team in 1931 and during his

Lew Stoker

time at St Andrew's gained three England caps - and played for the Football League representative side. He left St Andrew's in May 1938 for Nottingham Forest, retiring during the War. He later worked as a charge-hand in Wimbush's bakery, a stone's throw from the Blues ground. Stoker's younger brother Bob played for Bolton Wanderers and Huddersfield Town during the 1930s. Lew himself died in May 1979 aged 68.

STOKES. Frank

Full-back Frank Stokes scored just one goal for Blues (in 213 first-class games) - a screaming left-footer from fully 25 yards against Notts County in a 2-0 League win at St Andrew's in October 1906.

Stokes, a dedicated footballer, didn't even play in his own Testimonial Match, choosing to turn out for the reserves instead in a crucial game.

Born deep in the heart of the Potteries (at Burslem) on 7 June 1881, he played for both Burslem Port Vale and Reading

Frank Stokes

before joining Blues in October 1903. Over the next seven years Stokes, a tremendously effective full-back, played positively and never looked out of sorts always battling to the last, hardly ever having a poor game. An England trialist in four games between 1902 and 1906, he retired in August 1910 with a serious knee injury. Stokes died in 1945 at the age of 64.

Harry Storer (extreme right) with his team in 1946.

STORER, Harry

When the subject of football managers is on the agenda (not necessarily concerning those who have been in charge of Blues) the name of Harry Storer regularly crops up during the course of the conversation - for he was the personification of the 'olde worlde' qualities of discipline, economy and common-sense.

Born in West Derby, Liverpool on 2 February 1898, he came from good sporting stock. His father, Harry senior, and his uncle Bill were both Derby County players and Derbyshire county cricketers. Harry himself joined the playing staff at the Baseball Ground for £2,500 in 1921 after trials with Notts County and two years with Grimsby Town. He spent almost eight years with the Rams, amassing a record of 63 goals in 274 League and Cup appearances. His normal position was in centre-field, but he often was used as an out-and-out forward and had a lot of success in the attack, securing 24 goals in 1923-24. He was also capped by England against France at the end of that season.

After leaving Derby for Burnley in a £4,250 deal in February 1929, he spent two seasons at Turf Moor before being appointed manager of Coventry City in June 1931. He continued to play cricket until 1936, amassing almost 13,500 runs (average 27.63), scoring 17 centuries and taking over 200 wickets for Darbyshire. He led Coventry to promotion from Division Three (S) in 1936 and they were still in the Second Division when he left Highfield Road for St Andrew's in June 1945. He guided Blues to the FA Cup semi-finals in 1946 and to victory in the Football League (S) that same season. Two years later Blues gained promotion to the top flight with a remarkable defensive record of just 24 goals conceded in 42 League games.

In November 1948 he moved back to Highfield Road as team manager and quickly sold ex-Blues star and Welsh international Don Dearson to Walsall. In December 1953 he left Coventry and had two years out of the game before returning to League management with Derby County in June 1955 at a time when the Rams had nose-dived into the Third Division (North). His first signing was

Reg 'Paddy' Ryan from West Bromwich Albion and with the Irishman in midfield, Derby not only won the Third North championship but before he retired in May 1962 Storer had also reduced the club's overdraft by half! He acted as a scout for Everton in the mid-1960s. A fierce tackler himself, Storer was as keen as mustard both on and off the field, having a firmness in defence as good as any player in the country. It is on record that Storer had a 'sharp tongue, a heart of gold and a fantastic knowledge of the game.' He suffered from ulcers after ending his playing career and they effected his health for long periods, especially his eating!

He died in Derby on 1 September 1967.

STUBBS, Robin

Robin Stubbs, tall and thin, didn't look like a centre-forward at first glance - but he certainly proved his worth in that position, scoring 20 goals in 70 appearances for Blues and a total of 122 in 238 League games during his career. Born in Quinton on 22 April 1941, he joined Blues as a junior and turned professional in April 1958. Unfortunately he never quite had the appetite for First Division football and he left Blues for Torquay United in August 1963, later playing for Bristol Rovers and Torquay (again) before retiring in 1974. His wife, Anthea Redfern, left him to marry television celebrity Bruce Forsyth. Stubbs now works as a salesman in Torquay.

Robin Stubbs

STURRIDGE, Simon

Striker Simon Sturridge, fast and elusive, scored 38 goals 186 senior games for Blues whom he served between July 1988, when he signed professional, and September 1993, when he moved to Stoke City for £75,000. Born in Birmingham on 9 December 1969, he had to contend with several niggling injuries during his time at St Andrew's and was continuously visiting the treatment room during his time with the Potters. But he always bounced back. He helped Blues win the Leyland DAF Trophy in 1991 and before being released by Stoke City in May 1999 he netted 15 goals in 93 outings for the Britannia Stadium club as well as netting once in five outings on loan with Blackpool. In season 1999-2000 Sturridge helped Northampton Town gain promotion from the Third Division. His brother Dean has played for Derby County and Torquay United.

SUBSTITUTES

Blues' first ever substitute (to come off the bench) was defender Brian Sharples, who replaced the injured Ron Wylie during the League game at Preston on 28 August 1965.

The first 'sub' to score for Blues was Ronnie Fenton against Bury on 18 December 1965.

Geoff Vowden came on as a substitute for Blues against Huddersfield Town in a League game at St Andrew's in September 1968 and promptly scored a second-half hat-trick in a 5-1 win.

Blues used 29 substitutes in 1978-79 and the same number again in 1985-86 when only one had to be named.

When the team sheet was required to have two substitutes listed, Blues called up 77 in season 1994-95 and when the three-sub ruling was introduced, manager Trevor Francis sent on no fewer than 113 in 1997-98, 137 in 1998-99 and a staggering 152 in 1999-2000.

Kevin Francis was a used 'sub' on 18 occasions in 1994-95, likewise Jose Dominguez in 1997-98, but in 1998-99 striker Nicky Forster was called off the subs' bench a club record 29 times. In 1999-2000 striker Dele Adebola almost reached that figure with no fewer than 25 substitute appearances (21 in the League). Forster, in fact, played in 76 games for Blues, 47 of them as a substitute.

In comparison, Malcolm Briggs appeared in just one senior game for Blues, away at Manchester City in the First Division in May 1979 - coming on as substitute for the last three minutes...this is

Brian Sharples - Blues' first League substitute in 1965

believed to be the shortest League career in history (certainly with Blues).

David Linney was another 'late' substitute for Blues at home to Stoke City in 1982, replacing Neil Whatmore with barely five minutes remaining. This was his only game at senior level.

Ian Brown also made one first-class appearance for Blues, also as a substitute, against West Bromwich Albion in a League Cup encounter at The Hawthorns in 1985. He was on the pitch for the last 12 minutes of the 3-1 defeat and it is

believed he never touched the ball during that time!

Dan Sahlin's only appearance for Blues was a substitute in November 1995 v Leicester City in a League match. He touched the ball just four times whilst on the pitch!

Another 'one sub' appearance-maker for Blues was Neil Sproston in October 1987 v Middlesbrough (home). He received a nasty cut eye into the bargain!

Adam Wratten made one appearance for Blues - as a substitute against Wolves in an Anglo-Italian cup-tie at St Andrew's in 1993 - and he scored twice in the 2-2 draw.

Ritchie Blackmore saved two penalties after coming on as a substitute for Blues in their Texaco Cup game with Stoke City in October 1973. Blues won the contest 3-1 on penalties after a 0-0 draw. This was Blackmore's only outing for the club.

Louie Donowa was one of the first Blues substitutes to be substituted! Future Blues midfielder Archie Gemmill was the first player to be used as a substitute in Scottish League football - coming on for St Mirren against Clyde in August 1966.

Trevor Francis was named as substitute ten times by England.

Future Blues' players Graham Leggatt and Bruce Rioch were the first substitutes used in League games by Fulham (v Chelsea) and Luton (v Aldershot) respectively in August 1965. Ex-Brummie Bryan Orritt was Middlesbrough's first 'sub' v PNE in September 1965.

Keith Bertschin made his history when he scored with his first kick in League football - as a substitute for Ipswich Town against Arsenal at Highbury in April 1976. He joined Blues from Portman Road the following year.

When Blues' Scottish international goalkeeper Jim Herriot replaced Liverpool's Tommy Lawrence between the posts during the game against Wales in 1969, he was the first substitute to be called into action at The Racecourse Ground, Wrexham for 61 years. Back in 1908 David Davies (Wales) had replaced Dr Leigh Richmond Roose during the match against England.

SULLIVAN, David

Multi-millionaire publisher David Sullivan who runs Britain's biggest soft porn empire as well as owning the Daily Star and Sunday Sport newspapers, bought Birmingham City Football Club from the receivers for an estimated £1.7 million in March 1993. He immediately appointed Karren Brady as managing-director at St Andrew's.

Sullivan made it publicly known that he was prepared to spend a lot of money in order to bring success to the club. But despite millions of pounds being splashed out on players by the respective managers since 1993, all Blues have to show for their efforts is gaining promotion from the Second Division, the winning of the Auto Windscreen Shield and two play-off semi-final appearances (both lost).

Sullivan, born in 1949 and who grew up in Cardiff where he played 50-a-side football matches on a housing estate as a youngster, is Blues-mad.

He now lives in a £7 million Georgian-style stately mansion (themed on a Roman villa), some 120 miles away from Birmingham, situated in 12 acres of land overlooking the Epping Forest deer park in Essex. It is believed to be the biggest private house built in Britain since the Second World War.

Although a fair distance away from St Andrew's, he never fails to keep in contact with the club, receiving and sending fax messages daily to find out what's happening on the football front.

A bachelor and racing fanatic (he once had a stable of 30 horses but in 1994 reduced that number to 20) Sullivan owned a £120,000 powder blue K-Reg Bentley turbo limousine, plus other vehicles and simply wants to see Blues playing in the Premiership.

SUMMERILL, Phil

Phil Summerill

Phil Summerill, tall and slender looking, began his career as winger but developed into a fine inside or centre-forward who conjured up a very useful record in terms of goals scored! Born in Erdington on 20 November 1947, he joined the St Andrew's apprentice staff in June 1963 (having watched the League Cup Final as a Villa fan). He turned professional eighteen months later and went on to net 52 times in 131 first team outings for Blues, helping them win promotion in 1972. In January 1973, almost 10 years after moving to St Andrew's, Summerill joined Huddersfield Town; he switched to Millwall in November 1974, and played for Wimbledon from September 1977 until May 1979. He then wound down his career with Highgate United, Atherstone Town, Redditch United and Highgate (again) finally retiring in 1986, having taken a part-time job of coaching at a youth centre in Sparkhill. He was also a painter and decorator and later worked for the Birmingham Council's Football Development and Coaching Department. He attends as many Blues homes games as he possibly can.

SUNDAY FOOTBALL

Sunday football first came into the English game on a regular basis in the mid 1970s and nowadays each and every team, no matter what level they are playing at, enjoy a Sunday afternoon game of soccer, Blues being no exception!

Their first Sunday game at competitive level was in 1984 v Coventry City (League Division 1) at Highfield Road.

SUNDERLAND

ORRITT SPURS THE BLUES TO A GOAL GALLOP
by Alan Lake
Sunderland 1, Birmingham City 6

Four goals in 14 minutes—Blues were off to a great start and never looked back in this relegation struggle at Roker Park. Sunderland threw everything at Blues, but Trevor Smith did a grand job in checking the wild rushes of 'Rhino' Kichenbrand. The Blues forwards also had a joy day, switching the ball about in the mud and always looking too good for the shaky Sunderland rearguard.

Blues' playing record against Sunderland is:

FOOTBALL LEAGUE

Venue	P	W	D	L	F	A
Home	47	22	11	14	66	54
Away	47	7	7	33	49	102
Totals	94	29	18	47	115	156

FA CUP

	P	W	D	L	F	A
Home	1	1	0	0	3	1
Away	2	1	0	1	2	2
Neutral	2	2	0	0	5	0
Totals	5	4	0	1	10	3

ANGLO-ITALIAN CUP

	P	W	D	L	F	A
Away	1	1	0	0	1	0

On 8 December 1894 Blues and Sunderland met for the first time in the Football League - and if the truth is known, it was game Blues would rather forget! They lost 7-1 to the Wearsiders.

The following season Sunderland completed their first double over Blues.

Billy Jones scored twice when Blues won 4-1 at Sunderland in November 1904 but that scoreline was reversed in March 1907 when Blues came under the hammer again,

After a spell in the Second Division, Blues were reunited with Sunderland in the top flight in 1921-22 and after losing at Roker Park 2-1 they quickly gained revenge with a 1-0 victory at St Andrew's thanks to Jack Whitehouse's goal.

Sunderland got the better of an eight-goal thriller in December 1922, winning 5-3 at home and they ran up a 4-0 win at Roker Park in September 1924. Blues though had their successes as well with three home wins in the mid-1920s.

Blues played their first League game under the present day offside law against Sunderland on 29 August 1925 and were beaten 3-1 at Roker Park in front of 25,000 fans.

A hat-trick by Joe Bradford gave Blues an exciting 4-3 win at Sunderland in September 1928 - Blues having lost on the same ground by 4-2 twelve months earlier.

Three more rapid home wins for Blues (1928-31) was followed by an excellent 3-2 victory at Sunderland (September 1931) but in

March 1934 the Wearsiders raced to an emphatic 4-1 victory and followed up nine months later by winning 5-1, also at Roker Park.

Blues were annihilated 7-2 at St Andrew's by a brilliant Sunderland side in April 1936. England's Raich Carter was in sparkling form for the Wearsiders along with Bobby Gurney who scored four goals.

Sunderland also won 4-0 at Roker Park in December 1936 and completed the double over Blues in the last pre-war season of 1938-39.

Games were evenly matched during the late 1940s and when Blues re-entered the top flight in 1955-56 they were beaten twice by Sunderland in the League but won a crucial semi-final encounter in the FA Cup.

In April 1958 Blues put on a tremendous performance at Roker Park, beating Sunderland 6-1 in front of 34,184 fans. All five Blues forwards found the net as the Wearsiders were given a real hiding as they headed towards the Second Division. Four of Blues' goals came in a pulsating opening 14 minutes, Bryan Orritt netting twice.

There was another seven-goal cracker at St Andrew's in December 1964 but on this occasion it was a much closer contest, Blues winning 4-3 with Brian Sharples scoring his first goal for the club. At the time Sunderland hadn't lost on Blues' soil in eight visits and led through a Dominic Sharkey goal halfway through the first-half. Bobby Thomson equalised before Dennis Thwaites edged Blues in front only for Sharkey to balance things up. Straightaway Brian Sharples scored a third for Blues but McNab levelled again for the visitors with ten minutes left. Blues though, had the last laugh, Alec Jackson snatching the winner after a frantic goal-mouth melee. The three goals conceded in this game made it 23 'against' for Blues in just six matches!

There was no League action between the clubs from 1965 until 1976 and then Blues walked tall with a 2-0 win at St Andrew's (11 December).

The first Second Division meeting involving Blues and Sunderland was staged at Roker Park on 22 August 1979 and in front of 25,877 fans the Wearsiders won 2-0. The return fixture at St Andrew's in October 1979 attracted almost 19,000 fans and those present saw winger Steve Lynex win the game for Blues (1-0).

Blues, in fact, recorded four successive home wins over Sunderland before losing 1-0 at St Andrew's in November 1983.

Another hat-trick of home wins for Blues followed shortly afterwards but Sunderland responded with a double over Blues (in 1995-96) as they challenged for and eventually gained Premiership status.

Blues defeated Sunderland in both the 1931 and 1956 FA Cup semi-finals. In the former they triumphed 2-0 at Elland Road in front of 43,570 fans (recs. £3,930). Both goals came from Ernie Curtis, the first on the half-hour mark, the second in the 87th minute. In the latter game Blues won 3-0 at Hillsborough with Peter Murphy (10 minutes), Gordon Astall (70) and Eddie Brown (83) the marksmen in front of 65,107 fans.

Wilson Jones netted a brilliant goal when Blues beat Sunderland 3-1 in the second leg of a 5th round FA Cup-tie in February 1946. The first leg at Roker Park resulted in a 1-0 win for the Wearsiders.

Three players - Roy McDonough (1977), Jeff Wealands and Willie Johnston (the latter two in 1979) - all made their Blues debuts against Sunderland.

Players with both clubs include: I Atkins (also assistant-manager of Sunderland), K Bertschin, R Bonthron, C Buchan (Blues wartime guest), T Carter, T Cooke, J Cornforth, J Coxford,

J Cringan (Sunderland trialist), T Daykin, J Devine, W Ellis, M Gabbiadini, H Gayle, M Harford, M Hellawell, H Hooper, R Hope (Sunderland trialist), H Isherwood, A Johnson, JW Jones, JW Kirton, JC Lane, J McDonough, F McKeown (junior), J Montgomery, JS Oliver, M Prudhoe, E Purdon, I Rodgerson, W Threlfall, C Todd, A Towers, I Webb, F Worthington.

Also: Tony Coton and Roger Jones (Blues players, Sunderland coaches), Ian Bowyer and Chris Woods (Sunderland players, Blues coaches), Mick Ferguson (Blues player, Sunderland Community officer), Peter Doherty (Blues guest, Sunderland assistant-manager).

John Cornforth

SUNDERLAND ALBION

Blues' playing record against Albion is:

FOOTBALL ALLIANCE

Venue	P	W	D	L	F	A
Home	2	0	0	2	1	6
Away	2	0	0	2	1	10
Totals	4	0	0	4	2	16

Blues' two heaviest Alliance defeats at the hands of 'Albion' were 6-1 (in October 1889) and 4-0 (in March 1891) both away.

Player with both clubs: GE Anderson.

SUPPORTERS' CLUB (founder)

Harry Smith, a Yorkshireman, born in Bridlington 1894, moved to Birmingham at the age of 18 to work in the Austin car factory where he stayed for 35 years. He was solely responsible for forming the Birmingham City FC Supporters Club, circa 1930, initially from his home. Harry, who started following Blues as soon as he moved to the Midlands in 1912, served with the 1st Royal Warwickshire Regiment during the Great War and later worked in the Pools Office at St Andrew's for ten years up to 1969 when he 'retired' aged 75. His son, Ken Smith, became Chairman of the Northfield branch of the Blues' supporters club (1960s).

SWANSEA CITY (and Town)

Blues' playing record against the Welsh club is:

FOOTBALL LEAGUE

Venue	P	W	D	L	F	A
Hom	13	8	3	2	28	10
Away	13	6	3	4	14	11
Totals	26	14	6	6	42	21

FA CUP

Venue	P	W	D	L	F	A
Away	1	0	0	1	0	3

AUTO WINDSCREEN SHIELD

Venue	P	W	D	L	F	A
Home	1	1	0	0	3	2

LEYLAND DAF TROPHY

Venue	P	W	D	L	F	A
Home	1	0	1*	0	0	0

WARTIME

Venue	P	W	D	L	F	A
Home	1	1	0	0	5	0
Away	1	1	0	0	4	2
Totals	2	2	0	0	9	2

* Blues won on penalties

Blues and Swansea first did battle for League points in season 1946-47 (Division 2). The initial contest took place at St Andrew's on Christmas Day and in front of 33,000 fans Blues won 3-0 - only to lose the return fixture 1-0 at the Vetch Field 24 hours later.

On 16 December 1950 Cyril Trigg powered in a hat-trick as Blues beat Swansea 5-0 in a Second Division League game at St Andrew's.

When Blues beat the ten men of Swansea 8-0 in a Second Division game at St Andrew's in August 1953, a crowd of 27,000 saw Peter Murphy score a fine hat-trick. The Swans line-up included Cliff Jones, Terry Medwin and Ivor Allchurch.

A year or so later in October 1954, Blues' famous forward-line of Astall, Kinsey, Brown, Murphy and Govan played together for the first time when Swansea were defeated 2-0 also at St Andrew's in another Second Division game. It was Eddie Brown's debut, but Murphy stole the show again with two more goals.

No action between the clubs for 24 years until 1979-80 when it was Blues who took the honours, winning 2-0 at St Andrew's (20 October) and 1-0 in Swansea (25 February). Steve Lynex scored in both matches and Colin Todd made the 500th League appearance of his career in the initial game.

The first-ever contest in the top flight of English football was staged at Swansea in November 1981 and in front of 15,097 fans Blues went down 1-0. They recovered, however, and duly won the return fixture later in the season 2-1 with Kevan Broadhurst and Mick Harford the scorers.

The following season both matches ended in draws before the Swans slowly disappeared down the Divisions!

When they resumed confrontations with Blues, Swansea won 1-0 at St Andrew's (with 10 men) in March 1995 and ended a run of 20 League games without defeat for the Brummies.

Blues defeated Swansea 3-2 with a 97th minute 'sudden death goal' by Paul Tait in the AWS Southern Area semi-final encounter at St Andrew's in January 1995 - on their way to glory in the Final at Wembley. A crowd of 20,326 saw Stave Claridge and Kevin Francis score Blues' other goals.

After a 0-0 draw in a Leyland DAF Trophy game at St Andrew's in 1989-90, Blues made progress after winning a penalty shoot-out against the Swans 4-2.

Players with both clubs include: R Booth, J Bowen, J Cornforth, H Deacon, G Edwards (Swansea (amateur), G Emmanuel, R Firth, T Greer, F Hoyland, WH Hughes, RD Latchford, A Legg, J Millington (Blues reserve), A Powell, EW Richardson, JG Roberts, J Roulson, G Smith, L Thompson.

Also: John Bond (manager of both clubs), Fred Davies (coach at both clubs).

● Scotsman Tom Greer (ex-Blues) had the distinction of scoring Swansea Town's first-ever senior hat-trick in the Southern League in 1913-14.

SWINDON TOWN

Blues' playing record against the Robins is:

FOOTBALL LEAGUE

Venue	P	W	D	L	F	A
Home	10	5	3	2	20	13
Away	10	4	3	3	14	13
Totals	20	9	6	5	34	26

FA CUP

Venue	P	W	D	L	F	A
Away	1	0	0	1	0	2

LEAGUE CUP

Venue	P	W	D	L	F	A
Home	1	0	1	0	1	1
Away	1	0	0	1	0	2
Totals	2	0	1	1	1	3

The first of the twenty League games so far played between the two clubs took place at St Andrew's on 8 November 1969 (Division 2). A crowd of 28,167 saw Blues win 2-0, Geoff Vowden and Bert Murray the scorers.

Later in the season the Robins gained revenge with a 4-1 win at The County Ground.

Blues completed the double in 1970-71 (winning both matches 2-1) and when they took the Second Division title the following year they drew 1-1 at Swindon and won comfortably by 4-1 at St Andrew's, Bob Latchford netting twice in front of almost 28,000 spectators.

With the teams in separate Divisions, there was no League action from 1971 until September 1987 when Blues won 2-0 at The County Ground.

Only 4,026 supporters saw relegation-threatened Blues lose 2-1 at home to the Robins in a Second Division game in April 1989.

Blues were leading Swindon Town 4-1 in a League game at St Andrew's on Bank Holiday Monday in April 1993. The near 18,000 crowd anticipated more goals - they duly arrived alright, but all were scored by Swindon who went on to win an amazing match by 6-4.

Dele Adebola suffered a hairline fracture of the leg during Blues' 1-1 home draw with Swindon in November 1999.

Players with both clubs include: R Barlow (Town trialist, guest), G Bull, M Carrick, H Cope (Blues reserve), K Dearden, J Devlin, G Emmanuel, A Evans, D Geddis, C Gordon, B Griemink, G Hall (Blues trialist), J Hallam, S Harland, F Hawley, G Hicks, S Moreland, G Morrall, IJ Muir, JF Olney, D Preece, C Thompson (Blues reserve), JE Travers, J Wilson & R Woolhouse (Blues reserves).

Also: Lou Macari and Dave Mackay (managers of both clubs; Macari also Town player), Cold Todd (Blues player, Town manager), Tony Taylor (Swindon player, Blues coach), Chic Bates (Swindon player, coach, assistant-manager, Blues coach), Albert Lindon (Town scout).

TAIT, Paul

Unusually tall for a midfield player, Paul Tait stands an inch over six feet and has put his height and physique to good use as a professional footballer.

trainee and turned professional in August 1988. He amassed a fine record of 211 appearances and 18 goals for Blues, helping them win the Auto Windscreen Shield Final at Wembley in 1995 with his classic 'sudden death' winner in extra-time against Carlisle United. He also assisted the club in winning promotion that same season. He was loaned out to Millwall in February 1994, Bolton Wanderers at the start of the 1994-95 season and then Northampton Town in December 1997 before moving on a free transfer to Oxford United in January 1999.

Paul Tait

TARANTINI, Alberto

Blues manager Jim Smith signed the 1978 Argentinian left-back Alberto Tarantini for £295,000 just four months after he had gained a World Cup winners medal. He then made his Football League debut against Tottenham Hotspur in London, lining up opposite two of his fellow countrymen and World Cup winners Ossie Ardiles and Ricardo Villa. Tarantini, with mop of curly hair, was an excellent footballer but, if the truth be known, he never really settled in England and played only 24 games for Blues, scoring one goal - to earn Blues a home draw against Bristol City in only his seventh League game. Born in Buenos Aires on 3 December 1955, Tarantini played for Boca Juniors before moving to St Andrew's and on leaving Blues in May 1979 he joined the Spanish club Talkers Cordoba before returning to Argentina to sign for River Plate (1980). He later assisted Bastia (Corsica), Toulouse (France), Urania Geneva (Switzerland) and finally Platense (Argentina) in 1989-90. Capped 59 times by his country, Tarantini now travels round the district of Buenos Aires, coaching youngsters at various schools and youth clubs.

TAYLOR, Gordon

Gordon Taylor once scored 97 goals in a season playing junior football during his last year at school. As an inside-right he starred for Hurst Weslyans and Curzon Ashton before playing for Bolton Wanderers 'B' and 'A' teams, and the Trotters' reserve side. Born in Ashton-under-Lyne on 28 December 1944, he was eventually taken on the professional pay-roll at Burnden Park in January 1962 and spent almost nine years playing on the left wing for Bolton before transferring to Blues for just £18,000 in December 1970. He did very well at St Andrew's, making 203 appearances for Blues and scoring 10 goals. He starred in the team's Second Division promotion-winning campaign of 1971-72 and no doubt made heaps of scoring chances for the likes of Francis, Hatton, Latchford and company.

He moved from Blues to Blackburn Rovers in March 1976 and after a loan spell in the NASL with Vancouver Whitecaps (June-August 1977) he ran down his career with Bury, retiring in 1980 having appeared in 622 League games after serving with four clubs all beginning with the letter 'B'.

Taylor became secretary of the PFA within months of hanging up his boots, having joined the committee whilst at Gigg Lane. He is now chief executive of the PFA - making him one of the most influential men in English football.

Gordon Taylor

TELEVISION

The first time Blues appeared 'live' on TV was on 5 May 1956 for the FA Cup Final against Manchester City at Wembley.

The first time they starred on 'Match of the Day' was on 28 December 1964 when they were defeated 2-1 by West Ham United at Upton Park, Brian Sharples scoring City's goal.

TEXACO CUP

Blues entered this competition in 1973-74 and again in 1974-75 and by coincidence they were defeated by Newcastle United each time.

In their first challenge they beat Stoke at the second attempt on penalties after two 0-0 draws and then following a 1-1 scoreline at St Andrew's and a similar result at St James' Park when the match had to be abandoned after 100 minutes, United went through 3-1.

When they tried again, Blues drew 0-0 at West Bromwich Albion, 1-1 at Peterborough and beat Norwich City 5-1 in their group. They than accounted for Ayr United 3-0 on aggregate before losing 5-2 in the two-legged semi-final to Newcastle.

SUMMARY

Venue	P	W	D	L	F	A
Home	5	2	2	1	10	6
Away	7	0	6	1	4	6
Totals	12	2	8	2	14	12

THOMAS, Martin

At times goalkeeper Martin Thomas was brilliant; on a few occasions he was erratic and unsure - once conceding a stupid own goal against Shrewsbury Town in March 1989 which resulted in a 2-1 defeat for Blues!

Born in Senghenydd, near Caerphilly, Wales on 28 November 1959 and a product of the 'Welsh' nursery at Bristol Rovers, Thomas was voted Pirates' 'Player of the Season' in his first full year as a professional at Eastville (1976-77). He went on to appear in more than 160 League games for Rovers and also played for Wales at youth and under 21 levels. He had loan spells with Cardiff City, Tottenham Hotspur, Southend United and Newcastle United before transferring to St James' Park on a permanent basis in July 1983 for £35.000. He won his only senior cap with the Magpies (versus Finland in 1987...he was always in the shadow of Neville Southall) and after 115 League outings with the Gallowgate club and yet another loan spell, this time with Middlesbrough, he moved south to St Andrew's in October 1988 for a bargain fee of £75,000. Three years later Thomas helped Blues win the Leyland DAF trophy at Wembley and went on to appear in 176 first-class games before leaving St Andrew's Cheltenham Town in August 1993. Thomas played in over 400 League games between 1976 and 1993.

THOMSON, Bobby A.

Born in Smethwick on 5 December 1943, Bobby Thomson emerged as a classy right-back, who went on to play for his country at both under 23 and senior levels (winning eight full caps). He joined Wolverhampton Wanderers as a youngster in June 1959 on leaving Lyndon High School and turned professional at Molineux in July 1961. He made his first team debut in an FA. Cup-tie against West Bromwich Albion the following January and thereafter gave

Wolves excellent service, amassing 300 appearances up to March 1969 when he moved to Blues for £40,000. Over the next three years with injuries creeping in here and there, he made 69 appearances for Blues before switching to Luton Town in July 1972. After that Thomson played in turn for Hartford Bi-Centennials in the NASL (April 1976), Port Vale (from October 1976 to April 1977), Connecticut Bi-Centennials (as player-coach), Worcester City, Stafford Rangers (player-manager, August 1979-1981), Memphis Rogues (NASL), Brewood, Solihull Borough and finally Tipton Town. For a number of years he ran a sports shop in Sedgley near Wolverhampton and during the 1980s Thomson played in several Charity matches in and around the Midlands area.

THOMSON, Bobby G.

Bobby G Thomson

Scottish inside-forward Bobby Thomson had a splendid career after leaving Molineux in June 1959. Born in Dundee on 21 May 1937, he represented Dundee and Dunblane Schools and was an amateur with both Albion Rovers and Airdrieonians (August 1952) before joining Wolves as an amateur in 1953, turning professional in August 1954. Unable to gain a first team place he left Molineux for Aston Villa for £8,000 in June 1959 and here his career took off. He went on to net 70 goals in 171 appearances in four seasons with Villa, helping them win the Second Division title in 1960 and the League Cup in 1961 as well as gaining a runners-up medal in the latter competition in 1963 against his future club Blues. As hard as nails, the chunky, wavy-haired Thomson left Villa Park for St Andrew's in September 1963. He stayed four years with Blues, hitting another 25 goals in less than 130 games before ending his League duties with Stockport County (December 1967 to May 1968). He had a two-year spell with Bromsgrove Rovers (1968-70) and then kept himself fit by playing squash and tennis.

TICKLE, Charlie

Inside-right Charlie Tickle was a fast and clever dribbler who had the tendency to over-elaborate at times! Nevertheless he still gave Blues useful service, appearing in 91 competitive games and scoring 15 goals. Born locally in Northfield in 1884 he played initially for Selly Oak St Mary's FC and Bournbrook before joining Blues in January 1902. He spent six years with the club, leaving in 1908 (after his best-ever season) to sign for Coventry City. Tickle ended his major playing career with Worcester City (1913-15) and thereafter worked on the trams, playing for the Birmingham Tram department's football team and also for Redditch Town. He later became secretary of Birmingham Trams.

TODD, Colin

Born in Chester-le-Street, County Durham on 12 December 1948, Colin Todd represented the town's schoolboy team before joining Sunderland as a 16 year-old, turning professional at Roker

Park in December 1966 - seven months before helping the Wearsiders with the FA Youth Cup. He spent the next four years with Sunderland before transferring to Derby County for £180,000 in February 1971. Seven-and-a-half years later, in September 1978, he moved from The Baseball Ground to Everton for £350,000 and twelve months after that he became a Blues player for £350,000. In August 1982 Todd switched to Nottingham Forest for £70,000 and in January 1984 he signed for Oxford United before trying his luck in the NASL with Vancouver Whitecaps (May-October 1984). He then returned to England to assist Luton Town, retiring in the summer of 1985 to take over as manager of Whitley Bay (near his home in the North-east). In May 1986 Todd became reserve team coach at Middlesbrough; four months later he was given the position of chief scout/assistant-manager to Bruce Rioch, and then when Rioch left, he became manager there in March 1990, retaining that position until May 1991. Twelve months later Todd was given the assistant-manager's job at Bolton Wanderers (again under Rioch) and in January 1995, with Roy McFarland, he became joint-manager of the Trotters, taking over the reins himself when McFarland left for Cambridge United in November 1996. Todd left The Reebok Stadium in 1999 and in April 2000 became manager of relegated Swindon Town.

A man who has certainly seen it all and done it all in the world of football, Todd amassed more than 700 appearances at club and international level, having 293 Football League outings for Derby and 173 for Sunderland. His Blues record was 108 first team appearances. A powerful, determined footballer able to occupy the right-back, wing-half, centre-half or midfield positions, he won 27 full caps for England as well as representing his country at youth and under 23 levels. He also played for the Football League side. He won two League championship medals with Derby in 1972 and 1975; helped Blues gain promotion from the Second Division in 1980 and was voted 'Footballer of the Year' in 1975. As manager he took Bolton up to and down from the Premiership. He is the oldest player ever to appear in a League game for Oxford United - 35 years, four months.

TORQUAY UNITED

Blues' playing record against United is:

FOOTBALL LEAGUE

Venue	P	W	D	L	F	A
Home	1	1	0	0	3	0
Away	1	1	0	0	2	1
Totals	2	2	0	0	5	1

FA CUP

Venue	P	W	D	L	F	A
Away	2	1	0	1	7	4

Blues and United first met in the Football League in season 1991-92. Just under 9,500 fans saw Blues win 3-0 at St Andrew's on 2 November and there were just 2,448 fans present at Plainmoor to see Blues complete the double with a 2-1 victory in late March.

Blues defeated United 7-1 in a third round FA Cup-tie at Plainmoor in January 1956 - as they set in style off on the road to Wembley. Eddie Brown scored a hat-trick that day in front of 18,739 fans

It wasn't such a happy day out, however, in 1991-2 when Torquay knocked Blues out of the FA Cup in the first round, beating them 3-0 at their Devon home.

Blues officially 'opened' the Plainmoor floodlights, beating United 3-2 in a friendly on 22 November 1954.

Players with both clubs include: G Allen, G Astall, A Bloxham, K Bowker, H Bruce, W Clark, AW Clarke, J Cooper (Blues reserve), FW Corbett (Blues reserve), G Cox, G Downs, TW Grice (Blues reserve), J Hagan, P Holmes, W Hunter, J James, A Leslie, WR Meacock, G Pendrey, SE Phillips, A Phoenix, B Rioch (player-coach Plainmoor), D Rowbotham, M Sale, J Slueewenhoek, R Stubbs, HL Turner (Blues reserve), T Wolstenholme.

Also: John Bond (manager of both clubs), Frank Womack (Blues player, Torquay manager), George Foster (United player, Blues coach).

TOTTENHAM HOTSPUR

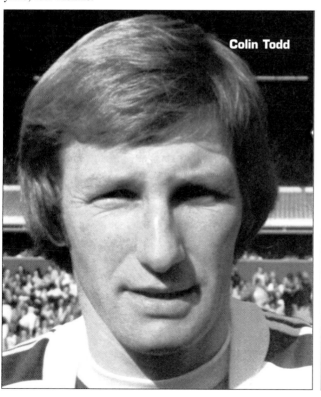

Colin Todd

Blues goalkeeper Dan Tremelling in action at White Hart Lane in 1925.

Blues' playing record against Spurs is:

FOOTBALL LEAGUE

Venue	P	W	D	L	F	A
Home	34	16	6	12	46	37
Away	34	7	6	21	30	73
Totals	68	23	12	33	76	110

FA CUP

	P	W	D	L	F	A
Home	3	1	2	0	6	4
Away	4	0	2	2	6	10
Neutral	1	0	0	1	0	1
Totals	8	1	4	3	12	15

LEAGUE CUP

	P	W	D	L	F	A
Away	1	0	0	1	0	5

WARTIME

	P	W	D	L	F	A
Home	1	1	0	0	8	0
Away	2	1	0	1	1	1
Totals	3	2	0	1	9	1

The first of the 68 League games between the two clubs was played on 26 April 1920 at White Hart Lane when a crowd of 35,000 witnessed the 0-0 draw. Five days later (1 May) 39,000 fans attended St Andrew's to see Spurs, the Second Division champions, win 1-0.

Blues joined Spurs in the top flight for the 1921-22 campaign but they had no joy against the Londoners, losing both matches, 3-0 at home, 2-1 away.

Blues registered their first League win over Spurs in April 1923 - succeeding 2-1 at St Andrew's - and they followed up with a 3-2 win on the same ground in January 1924.

Joe Bradford - a thorn in so many defences over the years - scored a hat-trick in Blues' 3-1 home win over Spurs on Christmas Day 1925 - just 24 hours after Blues had lost 2-1 in London!

Almost a year later - in October 1926 - Spurs did the business in style, beating Blues 6-1 at White Hart Lane with Jimmy Seed and Jimmy Dimmock the star performers.

After a sojourn in Division Two, Spurs reclaimed their First Division place in 1933 and beat Blues 3-2 at White Hart Lane, before losing the return fixture 2-0 in April 1934. This latter victory set Blues off on a run of 10 undefeated League matches v. Spurs (ending in December 1956).

On 31 August 1946, Blues and Spurs played their first Football League game for seven years - and it was Blues who came out on top, winning the Second Division match 2-1 at White Hart Lane in front of 51,256 fans. Wilson Jones scored both goals. Four players made their League debuts for Blues in this game - Gil Merrick, Frank Mitchell, Jock Mulraney and Neil Dougall.

Blues later completed the double over the London club, winning 1-0 at St Andrew's in front of 44,000 fans, Mulraney the scorer.

Over 31,000 fans saw Blues beat Spurs 3-0 at home in October 1955 and more than 26,000 witnessed a 1-0 victory in London where Gordon Astall scored the winner.

Spurs were quite brilliant, however, when slamming Blues 7-1 at home in September 1957. Alf Stokes scored five times that day and missed another three!

There weren't too many sides who won in style at White Hart Lane during the 1950s and early '60s - but two goals by Bunny Larkin helped Blues whip Spurs 4-0 on their own patch in a First Division match in November 1958.

And to add salt to the wound, Blues won the return fixture at St Andrew's that season (in April) by 5-1, when Larkin was again on target.

Double-chasing Spurs, however, gained revenge with a convincing 6-0 win at White Hart Lane in November 1960 in front of a 46,000 plus crowd, Cliff Jones and Terry Dyson both scoring twice past debutant goalkeeper Colin Withers! Earlier that year (in January) Spurs recorded their 700th win in the Football League when they defeated Blues 1-0 at St Andrew's.

In October 1963 Spurs went on the rampage yet again, beating Blues 6-1 in London. Jimmy Greaves scored a hat-trick this time! The return game also went in Spurs' favour by 2-1.

Spurs then won 4-1 at home in September 1964 but lost to a Malcolm Beard goal at St Andrew's in January 1965.

Two interesting points are (1) Spurs won 10 successive League games versus Blues between 2 January 1960 and 5 September 1964 and (2) Jimmy Greaves scored in each of the last six consecutive matches from 28 April 1962.

On 17 April 1976 Spurs conceded their 2,000th 'away' in the Football League goal (scored by Trevor Francis) when losing 3-1 to Blues at St Andrew's.

Spurs were relegated to the Second Division at the end of the 1976-77 campaign but not after doubling up over Blues, who had won both games (by 3-1) over the Londoners the previous season.

There were 1-0 away wins for each side in 1983-84 and then, in 1985-86 (the last time Blues and Spurs have met at League level) almost identical crowds of 9,394 and 9,359 respectively saw the Londoners win 2-1 at St Andrew's and 2-0 at White Hart Lane as Blues slipped out of the top flight.

It took Spurs three attempts to knock Blues out of the FA Cup in 1952-53. They eventually won a second replay 1-0 at Molineux.

Over 109,000 spectators witnessed the two third round FA Cup clashes between Blues and Spurs in January 1962.

A crowd of 46,096 saw the exciting 3-3 draw at St Andrew's when Blues fought back from 3-0 down to earn a replay against the FA Cup holders.

Jimmy Greaves (7 minutes), Cliff Jones (29) and Greaves again (32) seemed to have given Spurs an easy victory - but resilient Blues never gave in and sixty seconds after Spurs' third goal had gone in, Jimmy Harris reduced the deficit. Four minutes into the second-half it was 3-2 when Harris headed home from close range. The fans invaded the pitch with joy - and they were back again five minutes later when Welsh international Ken Leek notched the equaliser. The headline in the Sports Argus that evening said it all: 'Great Blues in a Thriller of Season'.

There were 62,917 fans present to see the replay at White Hart Lane - a game Spurs won by four goals to two. Harris and Leek again scored for Blues while Terry Medwin (2), Les Allen and Greaves (once more) netted for the Londoners - who went on to retain the trophy that season.

Clive Allen, Glenn Hoddle and Chris Waddle were among the scorers when Spurs hammered Blues 5-0 in a League Cup-tie at White Hart Lane in October 1986.

Blues' biggest-ever win over Spurs came in the transitional Wartime season on 1945-46 when they romped to an 8-0 home victory on 6 October when Ted Duckhouse featured on the scoresheet, netting from fully 50 yards!

Players with both clubs include: P Barton (Spurs guest), J Cheesewright, R Cooke, K Dearden, E Ditchburn (Blues guest), J Dominguez, J Elkes, R Ferris (Spurs guest), I Hendon, D Hill, WH Hughes (Spurs guest), J Jones, JW Jordan, P Murphy, GM O'Reilly, G Poole, V Samways, P Van Den Hauwe, A Want.

Also: Dave Mackay and Sir Alf Ramsey (Spurs players, Blues

managers), Len Thompson (Blues player, Spurs reserve team manager).

TOWERS, Tony

After doing very well with Manchester City and Sunderland, midfielder Tony Towers was somewhat disappointing during his four years with Blues, making 103 appearances and scoring four goals. Born in Manchester in 13 April 1952, he became an apprentice at Maine Road in 1967 and turned professional in April 1969. After helping City win the League Cup in 1970 (v WBA) he moved north to Roker Park for £100,000 (plus Mick Horswell) in March 1974. He switched to St Andrew's in a £140,000 deal in July 1977 and left Blues for Montreal Manic in March 1981. Later Towers assisted Tampa Bay Rowdies and Vancouver Whitecaps before rejoining the Football League with Rochdale on a non-contract basis in February 1985, retiring from competitive football the following year. Capped three times by England at senior level, Towers also played in eight under 23 internationals and represented his country at both schoolboy and youth team levels. He skippered Blues on a number if occasions when his performances were much better!

TRANMERE ROVERS

Blues' playing record against Rovers is:

FOOTBALL LEAGUE

Venue	P	W	D	L	F	A
Home	9	4	4	1	9	7
Away	9	3	1	5	10	16
Totals	18	7	5	6	19	23

LEAGUE CUP

	P	W	D	L	F	A
Home	1	0	1	0	1	1
Away	1	1	0	0	3	1
Totals	2	1	1	0	4	2

LEYLAND DAF TROPHY

	P	W	D	L	F	A
Wembley	1	1	0	0	3	2

Blues and Rovers met each other for the first time in the Football League on 16 September 1989. A crowd of 8,604 at St Andrew's saw Blues win 2-1, Colin Gordon and Dennis Bailey the scorers.

Rovers eased through the return fixture at Prenton Park in February, winning hands down by 5-1 (no comment) and in October 1992 they again went on the rampage with a 4-0 victory.

Blues had to travel to Prenton Park on the last day of the 1993-94 season knowing they had to win to stand any chance of remaining in the First Division. Either they or West Bromwich Albion (away at Portsmouth) would be relegated. Blues, backed by 7,000 fans, beat Rovers 2-1 but cheers turned into groans as news filtered through that the Baggies had won at Fratton Park and by doing so sent Blues down!

Jon McCarthy broke his leg playing for Blues against Rovers in the 3-1 League win in November 1999.

Big John Gayle scored two goals, one a cracker, to help Blues beat Rovers 3-2 in the Leyland DAF Trophy Final at Wembley in May 1991.

Players with both clubs include: C Curtis (Blues reserve), R Dale, P Fitzpatrick (Rovers' app), J Harris, M McCarrick, WR Meacock, IJ Muir, F Worthington (Rovers player-manager), Doug Ellis (Rovers colt, Blues Director).

TRANSFERS

Wayne Clarke

Bob Latchford

On 10th July 2000 Trevor Francis broke the Birmingham City transfer record when he paid £2.25 million for the Fulham striker Geoff Horsfield.

The fee was £400,000 more than Francis had paid for the Irish international right-winger Jon McCarthy from Port Vale three years earlier.

Here is a breakdown on Blues' record signings:

£2.25m . . . . .Geoff Horsfield from Fulham July 2000
£1.85m . . . . .Jon McCarthy from Port Vale September 1997
£1.6m . . . . .Peter Ndlovu from Coventry City July 1997
£1.5m . . . . .Paul Furlong from Chelsea July 1996
£800,000 . . .Kevin Francis from Stockport County January 1995
£800,000 . . . . .Ricky Otto from Southend United December 1994
£350,000 . . .Neil Whatmore from Bolton Wanderers August 1981
£350,000 . . . . .David Langan from Derby County July 1980
£300,000 . . . . .Colin Todd from Everton September 1979
£259,000 . . .Alberto Tarantini from Boca Juniors September 1978
£180,000* Howard Kendall + player from Everton February 1974
£140,000 . . . . .John Roberts from Arsenal October 1972
£80,000 . . . . .Bob Hatton from Carlisle United October 1971
£70,000 . . . .Alan Campbell from Charlton Athletic October 1970
£70,000 . . . . .Jimmy Greenhoff from Leeds United August 1968
£55,000 . . . . .Barry Bridges from Chelsea May 1966
£25,000 . . . . .Harry Hooper from Wolves December 1957
£20,000 . . .Peter Murphy from Tottenham Hotspur January 1952
£20,000 . . . . .Bobby Brennan from Luton Town July 1949
£5,000 . . . . .Billy Steel from Liverpool March 1935
£4,000 . . . .Ned Barkas from Huddersfield Town December 1928
£3,700 . . . . .Johnny Crosbie from Ayr United May 1920
£3,600+ . . . . .Joe Lane from Blackpool March 1920
£1,000 . . . .Alonzo Drake from Sheffield United December 1907
£700 . . . . .Billy Beer from Sheffield United January 1902
£120 . . . . .Arthur Leonard from Glentoran November 1901
£100 . . . . .Danny Bruce from Notts County November 1895
*The Kendall deal involved Bob Latchford (to Everton) and A . . Styles (to Blues) and the whole transaction amounted to £350,000....a British record at that time.
+The sale of Joe Lane from Blackpool to Blues in 1920 was a British record transfer fee at the time.

Other signings upwards from £300,000 include:
£1.2m . . . . .Stan Lazaridis from West Ham United July 1999
£1.2m . . . .David Holdsworth from Sheffield United March 1999

£1m . . . . .Gary Rowett from Derby County August 1998
£1m . . . . . .Dele Adebola from Crewe Alexandra February 1998
£775,000 . . . . .Darren Purse from Oxford United February 1998
£750,000 . . . . . .Mike Newell from Blackburn Rovers July 1996
£750,000+ . . . . .Bryan Hughes from Wrexham March 1997
£700,000 . . . . .Nicky Forster from Brentford January 1997
£600,000 .Chris Holland from Newcastle United September 1996
£500,000+ . . .Martyn O'Connor from Peterboro' November 1996
£500,000 . . .Chris Marsden from Stockport County October 1997
£500,000 . . . . .Marcelo from Sheffield United October 1999
£500,000 . . . . .Mark Ward from Everton August 1994
£450,000 . . . . .Andy Edwards from Southend United July 1995
£400,000 . .Gary Breen from Peterborough United February 1996
£400,000 . . . . .Ken Charley from Chelsea July 1995
£400,000 . . . . . .Paul Peschisolido from Stoke City March 1996
£400,000 . .Martin Grainger + player from Brentford March 1996
£390,000 . . . . .Gary Ablett from Everton August 1996
£375,000 . . . .Paul Barnes + player from York City March 1996
£350,000 . . . . .Jason Bowen from Swansea City July 1995
£350,000 . . . .Ken Charley from Peterborough United July 1995
£350,000 . .Steve Claridge from Cambridge United January 1994
£350,000 . . . . . .John Cornforth from Swansea City March 1996
£325,000 .Ian Bennett from Peterborough United December 1993
£300,000 . .Michael Johnston from Notts County September 1995

Blues' record transfers out in sequence:

£3m . . . . .Gary Rowett to Leicester City June 2000
£2.5m . . . . .Gary Breen to Coventry City January 1997
£1.5m . . . . .Liam Daish to Coventry City February 1996
£1.18m . . . . .Trevor Francis to Nottingham Forest February 1979
£350,000 . . . . .Joe Gallagher to Wolves August 1981
£350,000* . . . .Bob Latchford + player to Everton February 1974
£100,000 . . . . .Jimmy Greenhoff to Stoke City August 1969
£45,000 . .Terry Hennessey to Nottingham Forest November 1965
£25,000 . . . . . .Johnny Berry to Manchester United August 1951
£19,500 . . . . .Bobby Brennan to Fulham June 1950
£12,000 . . . . . .George Edwards to Cardiff City December 1948
£6,000 . . . . .Don Dearson to Coventry City February 1947
£1,500 . . . . .Bob Gregg to Chelsea September 1933
£1,500 . . .Dicky Dale to West Bromwich Albion November 1928
£350 . . . . .Fred Wheldon to Aston Villa June 1896
*This deal involved Howard Kendall and Archie Styles moving from Everton to St Andrew's for what was then a British record fee, beating the previous best of £250,000 paid by Derby County to Leicester City for David Nish in August 1972.

Other sales of £300,000 and upwards include:

£1.3m . . . . .Jose Dominguez to Sporting Lisbon May 1994
£1.2m . . . . .Steve Claridge to Leicester City March 1996
£800,000 . . . . . . .Chris Marsden to Southampton February 1999
£600,000 . . . . . . .Paul Peschisolido to West B. Albion July 1996
£500,000 . . . . .Jonathan Hunt to Derby County May 1997
£500,000 . . . . .Steve Claridge to Leicester City March 1996
£500,000 . . . . .Kevin Ashley to Wolves September 1990
£400,000 . . . . .Paul Peschisolido to Stoke City August 1994
£400,000 . . . . . . .Paul Mardon to West B. Albion September 1993
£400,000 . . . . . . .Julian Dicks to West Ham United March 1988
£300,000 . . . . .Wayne Clarke to Everton March 1987
£300,000 . . . . .Steve Finnan to Notts County October 1996

Transfer Talk...

- Trevor Francis became Britain's first £1million footballer when he transferred from Blues to Nottingham Forest in 1979.
- Joe Lane was a record signing by Blues from Blackpool in March 1920 - £3,600.
- On 31 August 1991 Blues signed Robert Taylor from Norwich City. Less than two months later, on 21 October, he was sold to Leyton Orient. In 1994 Taylor moved to Brentford for £500,000; four years later he switched to Gillingham for the same amount of money and two-thirds of the way through 1999-2000 a £1.5 million transfer took him to Maine Road where he helped Manchester City reach the Premiership, Taylor then joined Wolves. After leaving Blues Taylor has scored 120 goals!
- Blues transferred Billy 'Bullet' Jones to Brighton twice - first in 1909 and again in 1913.
- Tommy Carroll (Ipswich Town) was the first loan player to appear in a League game for Blues, doing so against Burnley at Turf Moor in October 1971.
- Barry Fry signed 41 players permanently for Blues at a cost of almost £7.8 million. He also took 14 players on loan or on short-term contracts. Fry sold or released 46 players for a cost of £5.6 million and struck 15 deals to loan players out to other clubs.
- In December 1995 manager Barry Fry placed 14 Blues players on the 'open to transfer' list.

Here are the 'buys and sales' involving fees that Fry made when he was manager at St Andrew's (December 1993 to May 1996):
Players who came in:

Paul Barnes (York City) £375,000
Steve Barnes (Welling United) £70,000
Dave Barnett (Barnet) £150,000
Ian Bennett (Peterborough United) £325,000
Jason Bowen (Swansea City) £350,000
Steve Castle (Plymouth Argyle) £225,000
Ken Charley (Peterborough United) £400,000
Steve Claridge (Cambridge United) £350,000
John Cornforth (Swansea City) £350,000
Liam Daish (Cambridge United) £50,000
Paul Devlin (Notts County) £275,000
Miguel De Souza (Wycombe Wanderers) £25,000
Neil Doherty (Barrow) £40,000
Jose Dominguez (Benfica) £150,000
Andy Edwards (Southend United) £450,000
Steve Finnan (Welling United) £75,000
Richard Forsyth (Kidderminster Harriers) £100,000
Kevin Francis (Stockport County) £800,000
Martin Grainger (Brentford) £400,000
Paul Harding (Notts County) £40,000
Michael Johnston (Notts County) £300,000
Andy Legg (Notts County) £225,000
Steve McGavin (Wycombe Wanderers) £150,000
Ian Muir (Tranmere Rovers) £125,000
Ricky Otto (Southend United) £800,000
Paul Peschisolido (Stoke City) £400,000
Ryan Price (Stafford Rangers) £20,000
Ian Richardson (Dagenham) £60,000
Peter Shearer (Bournemouth) £55,000
Mark Ward (Everton) £500,000
Roger Willis (Watford) £60,000

Gary Ablett, Paul Furlong and Steve Bruce behind Barry Horne and Mike Newell - all signed just before the start of the 1996-97 season for a combined total of £3 million.

Players who went out::

Steve Claridge (Leicester City)	£1.2m
Liam Daish (Coventry City)	£1.5m
Miguel De Souza (Wycombe Wanderers)	£100,000
Jose Dominguez (Sporting Lisbon)	£1.3m
Richard Dryden (Bristol City)	£200,000
Scott Hiley (Manchester City)	£200,000
Steve McGavin (Wycombe Wanderers)	£140,000
Ted McMinn (Burnley)	£150,000
Kevin Miller (Watford)	£260,000
Ian Richardson (Notts County)	£200,000
Andy Saville (Preston North End)	£125,000

223

Ben Sedgemore (Peterborough United) £60,000
Carl Shutt (Bradford City) £75,000
David Smith (West Bromwich Albion) ....£90,000.

Fry was also involved a number of exchange or part-exchange deals. The players who came in via this method were Kenny Lowe and Dave Regis (from Stoke City), Jonathan Hunt and Gary Poole (from Southend United) and Gary Breen (Peterborough United), and those who went out were Gary Bull (York City as part of the Barnes transaction), Ken Charlery (Peterborough United), George Parris (Brentford as part of the Grainger deal), Paul Peschisolido and Graham Potter (both to Stoke City) and Dave Regis and Roger Willis (to Southend United).

His loan 'signings' were Mick Bodley (Southend United), Gary Bull (Nottingham Forest - later signed on a free), Rui Esteves (Vitoria Setubal), Ian Hendon (Leyton Orient), Danny Hill (Tottenham Hotspur), Richard Huxford (Barnet), David Preece (Derby County), Sigurd Rushfeldt (Tromso), Dan Sahlin (Hammarby), Vinny Samways (Everton), Paul Sansome (Southend United), John Sheridan (Sheffield Wednesday), Bryan Small (Aston Villa) and Paul Williams (Crystal Palace).

The players Fry loaned out were Steve Castle (Gillingham), Neil Doherty (Northampton Town), Louie Donowa (Shrewsbury Town), Scott Hiley (Manchester City, later to sign for the Maine Road club), Kenny Lowe (Carlisle United), George Parris (Brentford), Simon Rea (Kettering Town), Ian Richardson (Notts County, later to join the Magpies), Steve Robinson (Kidderminster Harriers and Peterborough United), Paul Tait (Millwall) and Chris Whyte (Coventry City).

The players Fry signed on a free transfer were Fred Barber (Luton Town), Ken Charlery (Southend United), Gary Cooper (Peterborough United), Bart Griemink (Emmen) and Jae Martin (Southend United).

And those given frees from St Andrew's were Jason Beckford (to Millwall), Keith Downing (Stoke City), Paul Fenwick (Dunfermline Athletic), Lyndon Hooper (Canadian football), Vasil Kalogeracos (Malaysia), Kenny Lowe (Gateshead), Paul Moulden (Rochdale), George Parris (Brighton & Hove Albion), Darren Rogers (Walsall), Richard Scott (Shrewsbury Town), Danny Wallace (Wycombe Wanderers), Mark Ward (Huddersfield Town) and Chris Whyte (Charlton Athletic).

The following were released without going to another club immediately: Fred Barber, Robert Bloxham, James Bunch, Gary Cooper, Neil Doherty, Paul Hiles, Lee Hughes, Ian Jones, Steve Round, Richard Steadman, Jason Thomas, Richard Weston and Adam Wratten.

- Regarding players who had two separate spells with the club, see under Two Spells.

TRAVELLING MEN

- Frank Worthington played competitive League football for 21 years: 1966-87. In that time he served with 11 different League clubs covering all four Divisions: Huddersfield Town, Leicester City, Bolton Wanderers, Blues, Leeds United, Sunderland, Southampton, Brighton & Hove Albion, Tranmere Rovers, Preston North End and Stockport County. He also assisted Philadelphia Fury and Tampa Bay Rowdies (NASL), Cape Town Spurs in South Africa and Galway United. And at non-League level he turned out for Chorley, Stalybridge Celtic, Weymouth, Radcliffe Borough, Guiseley and Hinckley Town and ended up

as a coach with Halifax Town for whom he played in two reserve team games. Overall Worthington turned out for 22 different clubs at various levels and standards.

- Goalkeeper Mark Prudhoe, who played in five first team matches for Blues between 1984 and 1986, served with 14 different Football League clubs during his 19-year professional career (1981-2000). The clubs concerned were Sunderland, Hartlepool United (two spells), Blues, Walsall, Doncaster Rovers, Grimsby Town, Bristol City, Carlisle United, Darlington, Stoke City, Peterborough United, Liverpool, York City, Bradford City and Southend Utd.

- Striker Mike Newell is another nomadic footballer who between 1981 and 2000 assisted 12 clubs - Liverpool (juniors), Crewe Alexandra, Wigan Athletic, Luton Town, Leicester City, Everton, Blackburn Rovers, Birmingham City, West Ham United, Bradford City, Doncaster Rovers and Blackpool.

- Nicky Platnauer had 11 League clubs as a professional (1982-93): Bristol Rovers, Coventry City, Blues, Reading, Cardiff, Notts County, Port Vale, Leicester, Scunthorpe, Mansfield and Lincoln City in that order. He also played for Bedford Town.

- Another 11-club man was David Speedie who assisted, in turn, Barnsley, Darlington, Chelsea, Coventry, Liverpool, Blackburn Rovers, Southampton, Blues, WBA, West Ham United and Leicester City (1978-93).

- Another goalkeeper, Fred Barber, spent 16 years as a professional footballer, serving 10 different clubs: Darlington, Everton, Walsall, Peterborough United (three spells), Chester City (two spells), Blackpool (twice), Colchester United, Luton Town, Ipswich Town and finally Birmingham City (1996 - one game). He amassed 385 League appearances.

- Midfielder Kenny Lowe played for Hartlepool United, Scarborough, Barrow, Barnet, Barrow (again), Stoke City, Blues (1993-94), Carlisle United, Hartlepool (for a second time) and Darlington up to 1996. He also served with Billingham, Spearwood FC (Australia), Gateshead and Morecambe.

- Listed among the other nomadic footballers who have been registered with Blues we have three strikers, namely Mick Harford (10 clubs), Tony Hateley (8) and Bob Hatton (9) plus midfielder Trevor Hockey (7 League clubs, one in Ireland and three in the NASL).

TREMELLING, Dan

Dan Tremelling

Affectionately known as the 'India Rubberman' because he used to bounce around on his line, Dan Tremelling was a tremendously consistent goalkeeper who gave Blues sterling service as a player for thirteen years (May 1919 to May 1932). During that time he amassed 395 first team appearances (conceding only 556 goals) and only Gil Merrick has made more first team appearances as a goalie for Blues (551).

Born in Mansfield Woodhouse on 12 November 1897, Tremelling, once a full-back who took up goalkeeping by accident, joined Blues from Lincoln

City where he had been since 1918.

He helped Blues win the Second Division championship in 1921 and gained one full England cap, also representing the Football League.

On leaving Blues Tremelling joined Bury but returned to St Andrew's as assistant-trainer in 1936 (having held that same position for a while at Gigg lane). He held that position until 1941, giving him a total of 18 years with the club.

In later life Tremelling became a licensee, taking over the Old Lodge public house near St Andrew's. He died in Birmingham on 15 August 1978.

NB - Tremelling was not superstitious….he joined Blues on the 13th on the month, left on the 13th of the month, spent 13 years with the club and played in 13 FA Cup matches…and without confirmation he faced 13 penalties!

TRIGG, Cyril

Cyril Trigg served Blues as a player for a total of 19 years. Born in Measham, Leicestershire on 8 April 1917, he joined the St Andrew's staff as an amateur from Bedworth Town in August 1935, turning professional three months later. A former Coventry City trialist, he made 291 first-class appearances for the club, scoring 72 goals. During his time at St Andrew's he witnessed relegation, promotion, success and failure. He saw many changes take place within the club. 'Triggy' or 'Trigger' as he was called, enjoyed playing at full-back and centre-forward (he starred in both positions) and during the War he was a star marksman, netting a staggering 88 goals in only 95 regional matches for Blues. He helped the team win the Football League (S) title in 1946 and become Second Division champions two years later. He was asked to stay on at Blues (possibly to become manager) but he declined the offer and left St Andrew's in May 1954 to become player-coach of Stourbridge United, quitting football in 1957. During the hostilities Trigg also guested for Blackpool and Nottingham Forest when time allowed from his duties with the RAF in Burma and India.

He died in Birmingham on 9 April 1993, a day after his 76th birthday.

Cyril Trigg

TURNER, Arthur

Born in Chesterton, Staffs on 1 April 1909 and a former West Bromwich Albion trialist, Arthur Turner made his name as Stoke City's centre-half during the 1930s when he played in the same team as Stanley Matthews, Freddie Steele, Joe Johnson and such likes. He went on to score 17 goals in 317 games for the Potters having had one excellent run of 118 consecutive League outings and gaining a Second Division championship medal in 1932-33. He moved from The Victoria Ground to St Andrew's in February 1939 and almost immediately saw the team relegated before the War disrupted his progress with Blues. Nevertheless he battled on and appeared in 53 first-class games for the club as well as making another 176 regional appearances during the hostilities, before joining Southport in February 1948 - just as Blues were heading for the Second Division championship! He retired as a player in May 1949 and became Crewe Alexandra's manager for the start of the next season, a position he held for barely twelve months before becoming assistant-manager at his former club, Stoke City. From there Turner, jovial and witty, took over the reins at St Andrew's (November 1954). He remained in office for over four years, guiding Blues back into the top flight of English football and to the 1956 FA Cup Final. He left Blues in January 1959 to take charge of Oxford United whom he took into the Football League and then later to promotion from the Fourth Division and also the Third Division championship - this after guiding the 'U's' to successive Southern League title triumphs in 1961 and 1962. He became general manager at the Manor Ground in February 1969 but was sacked when the club admitted they couldn't afford the luxury of employing a man for that position! Turner left Oxford very disillusioned and shortly afterwards he became chief scout for Rotherham United, later taking a similar position with Sheffield United (1980-81). A fine cricketer as well as a footballer and manager, Turner played for the Silverdale club for many years, scoring over 3,000 runs and hitting five centuries. He died in Sheffield on 12 January 1994, aged 84.

Arthur Turner

TWO SPELLS

The following personnel all had at least two spells with Birmingham City Football Club and the year given is when they joined the club (guests, trialists not included):

Walter Abbott . . . . .1896 player, 1910 player
Ian Atkins . . . . .1988 player, 1991 assistant-manager
Jack Badham .1934 player, 1958 coach
Malcolm Beard . . . . .1957 player, 1979 scout
Billy Beer . . . . .1902 player, 1923 manager
Kevan Broadhurst . . . . .1975 player, 1993 coach
Gary Bull . . . . .1994 player, 1995 player
Chris Charsley . . . . .1886 player, 1891 player, 1893 player
Ray Devey . . . . .1937 player, 1950 trainer
Don Dorman . . . . .1945 player, 1954 scout
Bob Fairman .1907 player, 1912 player
Trevor Francis . . . . .1969 player, 1996 manager
Joe Gallagher . . . . .1970 player, 1990 community officer
Ian Handysides . . . . .1978 player, 1986 player
Bill Harvey .1921 player, 1926 manager
Robert Hopkins . . . . .1983 player, 1989 player
Billy Jones . . . . .1901 player, 1912 player
Bob Latchford . . . . . .1964 player, 1998 community officer/coach
George Liddell . . . . .1920 player, 1933 manager
Steve Lynex .1979 player, 1986 player
Alec McClure . . . . .1912 player, 1928 colts manager
Bob McRoberts . . . . .1898 player, 1910 manager
Jim Montgomery . . . . .1977 player, 1980 coach
Harry Morris .1883 player, 1903 Director
Ian Muir . . . . .1983 player, 1995 player
Peter Murphy . . . . .1944 amateur, 1952 player
Syd Owen . . . . .1945 player, 1975 assistant-manager
Garry Pendrey . . . . .1965 player, 1987 manager
Paul Peschisolido . . . . .1992 player, 1996 player
Frank Richards 1906 clerk, 1911 secretary-manager, later Director
Bill Robertson . . . . .1896 player, 1902 player
Charlie Short .1889 player, 1890 player
Joe Tatton .1880 player, 1888 Director
Arthur Turner . . . . .1939 player, 1954 manager
Jimmy Windridge . . . . .1899 player, 1914 player
Peter Withe .1975 player, 1987 player

UJPESTI DOZSA

Blues played the Hungarian club in two Inter Cities Fairs Cup games in October 1960. A crowd of 23,381 saw Blues win the first leg of a first round tie at St Andrew's by 3-2 with Johnny Gordon netting twice and there were 25,000 present to see the Hungarians defeated on their own patch in the return leg as Blues went through 5-3 on aggregate. Gordon was sent-off in the 83rd minute of the return leg.

UNION ST GILLOISE

Blues met - and defeated - the Belgium outfit 8-4 on aggregate in the two-legged Inter Cities Fairs Cup semi-final in 1960. The first game took place in Belgium on 7 October and in front of a 20,000 crowd Blues won 4-2 with Johnny Gordon, Harry Hooper, Jim Barrett and Bryan Orritt their scorers.

The return clash at St Andrew's on 11 November drew a 14,152

crowd and by coincidence Blues repeated the scoreline, again winning 4-2 with Gordon (2), Bunny Larkin and Hooper (penalty) on target.

USA TOURNAMENT

In May and June 1961 Blues participated in an international soccer tournament staged in the North American and Canada. They played nine games as follows:

May 17 v Third Lanark in New York, lost 1-4
May 21 v Montreal Cantalia in Montreal, lost 0-1
May 25 v Hamilton Steelers in Hamilton, won 4-2
May 27 v Third Lanark in Toronto, won 3-2
May 30 v Calgary All Stars in Calgary, won 11-2
June 3 v Third Lanark in Vancouver, drew 1-1
June 7 v Victoria All Stars in Victoria, won 5-1
June 10 v British Columbia All Stars in Vancouver, won 5-2
June 14 v FC Rheims in Toronto, won 2-1

SUMMARY OF MATCHES:

P	W	D	L	F	A
9	6	1	2	32	16

VAN DEN HAUWE, Pat

Left-back Van Den Hauwe played in four FA Cup Finals in the space of six years - three with Everton (1985, 1986 and 1989) and Tottenham Hotspur (1991). He gained just one winners medal - with Spurs.

Born in Dendermonde, Belgium on 16 December 1960, Van Den Hauwe joined Blues as an apprentice in 1976 and turned professional in August 1978. A ferocious tackler, his only goal in 143 appearances for Blues came in a 2-1 home win over Arsenal in March 1983. He left St Andrew's for Everton in September 1984 for a fee of £100,000 (signed by former Blues player Howard Kendall) and at the end of his first season at Goodison Park played at Wembley against Manchester United in the FA Cup Final and collected a League championship medal. A year later Van Den Hauwe claimed a League runners-up medal and then added a second First Division championship prize to his collection in 1987.....and by this time he had also won the first of 13 full international caps for Wales (despite not being born in that country).

He was on the verge of being called up into the Belgium national side by manager Guy Thees after he had seen him in action against Manchester United at Old Trafford in 1985. After pencilling him in as an over-age player for the under 21 match against Spain, Thees found out that Van Den Hauwe had unwittingly signed away his birthright by opting out of national service.

This, of course, led to press speculation as to which of the British nations would pursue him and eventually he teamed up with Everton colleagues Kevin Ratcliffe and Neville Southall in the Welsh side, making his debut in a World Cup qualifier against Spain at Wrexham. In August 1989 Van Den Hauwe, after 190 appearances for Everton, moved to Tottenham Hotspur for £595,000 and two years later, at long last, he got his hands on an FA Cup winners' medal. In September 1993 (after more than 100 outings for Spurs) he moved across London to sign for Millwall and ended his career with Notts County (February-May 1995). His father Rene kept goal for Belgium.

VINCENT, Johnny

Johnny Vincent

Born in West Bromwich on 8 February 1947 and a Baggies supporter as a lad, Johnny Vincent played for Brierley Hill Schoolboys

He joined Blues as a 15 year-old apprentice in 1962 and turned professional in February 1964. Recalled Vincent: "In those days I had to get up around 7 o'clock, get a bus, then a train and jump on another bus (the number 53) which got me to St Andrew's for 9 o'clock - to start my day's duties."

After bedding himself in at the club, Vincent gained England youth honours (winning five caps in total) and duly made his Football League debut as a 17 year-old against Blackburn Rovers, replacing the injured Jimmy Bloomfield in midfield in the 2-2 draw.

He soon established himself in the first XI, and quickly became one of Blues' most respected players during the late 1960s. A strong running player, very consistent, Vincent used to glide past opponents, triggering off many attacks with a sweeping pass or a powerful forward run. He went on to scored 44 goals in 194 senior outings for Blues.

Eventually, and not to the agreement of the supporters, manager Freddie Goodwin traded Vincent in for the more robust George Smith of Middlesbrough in March 1971 (both players being rated

at £40,000). From Ayresome Park he switched to Cardiff City for £35,000 in October 1972 and after a spell with Atherstone Town (1975-77) he spent a season in America, playing for Connecticut Bi-Centennials where he brushed shoulders with the Brazilian star Pele. On his return to England Vincent became a publican, running pubs in Oldbury and Northfield. He later moved to Allesley, Smith of Middlesbrough in March 1971 (both players being rated at £40,000). From Ayresome Park he switched to Cardiff City for £35,000 in October 1972 and after a spell with Atherstone Town (1975-77) he spent a season in America, playing for Connecticut Bi-Centennials where he brushed shoulders with the Brazilian star Pele. On his return to England Vincent became a publican, running pubs in Oldbury and Northfield. He later moved to Allesley, Coventry.

VOID MATCHES

In 1939, just prior to the outbreak of the Second World War, Blues played three games in the Second Division of the Football League, all of which were later declared null and void. Here are the details of those games:

    25 August v Tottenham Hotspur (A) 1-1 Brown
    30 August v Leicester City (H) 2-0 Farrage, Sharman (og)
    2 September v Burnley (H) 2-0 Dearson, Duckhouse

• These games were repeated in order at the start of the 1946-47 season. This time Blues beat Spurs 2-1 and Leicester 4-0 but lost 2-0 to Burnley.

VOWDEN, Geoff

A Yorkshireman, born in Barnsley on 27 April 1941, Geoff Vowden started his playing career in Jersey before joining Nottingham Forest as an amateur in 1958, turning professional at The City Ground in January 1960. He developed into a fine marksman and went on to score over 150 goals in under 500 competitive matches over 14 years. After hitting 40 goals in 90 League games he moved from Forest to St Andrew's in October 1964 for £25,000 and he duly paid that money back with huge dividends by netting another 95 goals in 253 appearances for Blues. In March 1971 he switched across the City to join Aston Villa for £12,500 and immediately helped them win the Third Division championship. In 1974 Vowden became Kettering Town's player/assistant-manager before spending a few months in the NASL with New York Cosmos. He later coached in Saudi Arabia (late 1970s) as well as at local youth clubs in the Nottingham area. In 1980 he became assistant reserve team manager with Sheffield United, a position he held for barely a year. Vowden was the first substitute to come off the bench and score a hat-trick, achieving the feat for Blues against Huddersfield Town in September 1968.

Geoff Vowden

WALSALL (Town Swifts)

Blues' playing record against the Saddlers is:

FOOTBALL LEAGUE

Venue	P	W	D	L	F	A
Home	10	9	1	0	37	7
Away	10	5	1	4	17	15
Totals	20	14	2	4	54	22

FA CUP

Venue	P	W	D	L	F	A
Home	4	3	1	0	7	1
Away	3	0	1	2	0	3
Totals	7	3	2	2	7	4

AUTOGLASS TROPHY

Venue	P	W	D	L	F	A
Home	1	0	0	1	0	1

AUTO WINDSCREEN SHIELD

Venue	P	W	D	L	F	A
Home	1	1	0	0	3	0

LEYLAND DAF TROPHY

Venue	P	W	D	L	F	A
Away	1	1	0	0	1	0

FOOTBALL ALLIANCE

Venue	P	W	D	L	F	A
Home	3	1	0	2	4	4
Away	3	1	1	1	7	9
Totals	6	2	1	3	11	13

WARTIME

Venue	P	W	D	L	F	A
Home	9	8	1	0	32	10
Away	10	5	2	3	19	19
Totals	19	13	3	3	51	29

Blues registered their first away win in the Football League by beating the Saddlers 3-1 at The Chuckery on 10 September 1892. In this game - also the first between the clubs at League level - Walsall defender Alf Pinches became the first player to concede an own-goal against Blues.

Three months later, on 17 December, in front of just 2,000 spectators, Frank Mobley and Billy Walton both scored their first League hat-tricks in Blues' crushing 12-0 home win over luckless Walsall.

On 2 September 1893 Blues opened their Second Division League programme with a 3-1 win at Walsall in front of 5,000 spectators. A fortnight later the Swifts were beaten 4-0 at Muntz Street when Charlie Izon scored a hat-trick on his Blues debut.

In October 1896, Blues won 6-1 on Walsall soil (their best away win of the season) and in December 1897 they claimed an impressive 6-0 victory, also on Saddlers' territory. In between times (December 1896) the teams had drawn 3-3 at Muntz Street...making it nineteen goals in three successive League meetings.

Following Blues' 2-1 home win over Walsall in April 1901, it was to be another 87 years and four months before the teams met again at League level! This time Blues were embarrassingly beaten 5-0 at Fellows Park in September 1988...their heaviest reverse against the Saddlers.

The 1999-2000 season was

HARRY HIBBS Blues goalkeeper, Walsall manager.

crucial for both clubs - and after losing at Bescot Stadium, Blues gained revenge by beating the Saddlers 2-0 at St Andrew's. At the time Blues were attempting to consolidate their position in the play-offs while Walsall were fighting - in vain - to stay in the First Division.

Walsall were beaten 4-0 by Blues in an FA Cup fourth qualifying round tie at Muntz Street in December 1889. Will Devey was the star player with a smartly taken hat-trick in front of 2,000 spectators.

Blues knocked Walsall out of the FA Cup 1-0 in a 3rd round replay at St Andrew's in January 1983. Kevin Summerfield scored the winning goal, having just returned from a loan spell with the Saddlers.

Just 5,239 loyal supporters witnessed the Autoglass Trophy game between Blues and Walsall at St Andrew's in January 1992. The Saddlers won 1-0.

Cyril Trigg scored three hat-tricks for Blues against Walsall in various regional games during World War Two (December 1940, April 1944 and December 1944).

Alan Buckley is Walsall's champion marksman of all-time with a total of 204 goals for the Saddlers in all competitions.

Manager Barry Fry used 21 players during Blues' friendly against Walsall at the Bescot Stadium in July 1994 (won 2-1).

Ex-Blues midfielder Des Bremner is the oldest player to don a Walsall shirt, aged 37 years, 240 days in 1990.

Players with both clubs include: K Armstrong, J Aston, G Banks (Blues reserve), D Barnett, HJ Bates, JT Bayley, JM Beattie (Walsall guest), K Bertschin, W Bidmead, J Bird, N Blake, T Bowen (Blues reserve), S Bowser (Blues trialist), JW Bradford (Joe's brother, Blues reserve), C Brazier, D Bremner, K Broadhurst, A Buckley (also manager of Walsall), P Bullock, W Bunch, C Cameron, G Childs, W Clarke, J Cochrane, J Cooper (Blues reserve), D Dearson, W Devey, J Devlin, D Dorman, A Evans, H Evans, W Felton, R Foulkes (Blues amateur), N Freeman, W Freeman, J Gayle, A Godden, C Gordon, TW Grice (reserve), W Guest, I Handysides, WN Harris, P Hart, P Hawker, H Haynes, T Hedges, J Hirons, W Hunter, R Hynd, C Izon, JL Jenkins, CAL Jenkyns, G Johnston, MA Lane, CA Leatherbarrow, F Lester, A McClure, R McDonough, D Massart, J Merrick (reserve), J Metcalfe, T Morgan, A Morley (Walsall trialist), M O'Connor, C Pearson (reserve), D Peer, G Pendrey, TS Pointon, D Preece, M Prudhoe, A Richards (Blues junior), DT Richards, D Robinson, D Rogers, A Saville, R Sbragia, R Shaw (Walsall amateur, later manager), G Sissons, SJ Smith, T Smith, HE Stalby (reserve), K Summerfield, BJ Taylor, KC Tewksbury, RA Thomson, R Woolhouse (Blues reserve).

Also: Major Frank Buckley and Harry Hibbs (Blues players, Walsall managers), Dave Mackay (manager of both clubs), Alec Leake (Blues player, Walsall trainer), Alf Wood (Saddlers player, Blues lottery salesman), Jim Southam (Blues player, Walsall assistant-trainer), Ken Wheldon (chairman/Director of both clubs), Tom WJ Edmonds (Director of Blues & Walsall) and John Westmancoat (secretary of both clubs).

Phil Hawker

WALSALL CUP

Blues won the first ever trophy in season 1882-83 when they lifted the Walsall Cup, beating the host town Walsall Swifts 4-1 in the Final, Eddy Stanley scoring two of their goals and making another.

WALTON, Billy

During his 15 years with Blues Billy 'Mother' Walton certainly gave the fans something to cheer about! He was a brilliant footballer, possessing clever on-the-ball ability, a powerful shot and an extremely hard-worker, always there to help his team-mates (thus his nickname!) Born in Hockley Brook, Birmingham on 15 October 1871, he was playing for Hockley Belmont FC in the Handsworth League when spotted by Blues who secured his services as a professional in August 1888. He went on to score 65 goals in 204 first team appearances for Blues, helping them win the Second Division championship in 1893 and gain promotion in 1894 and again in 1901. A workaholic wing-half or inside-forward, Walton as a supporter, helped clear the snow from the Perry Barr pitch prior to Blues' FA Cup semi-final showdown with West Bromwich Albion back in 1886, unknowing at the time that he would soon be wearing his favourite teams colours! He left Blues for Dudley in May 1903 but three-and-a-half years later he was a guest of the club when St Andrew's was officially opened. He also attended both the 1931 and 1956 FA Cup Finals while working as a silversmith in the jewellery quarter. He died in Dudley Road hospital, Winson Green on 10 February 1963, aged 91.

WARD, Mark

Mark Ward

Diminutive midfield dynamo Mark Ward began his footballing career with Northwich Victoria before embarking on the Football League circuit with Oldham Athletic in July 1983. Over the next 16 years he served with West Ham United, Manchester City, Everton, Blues (March 1994 to March 1996), Huddersfield Town and Wigan Athletic (non-contract). He accumulated a fine individual record of 463 League appearances and 51 goals. For Blues he netted eight times in 82 outings and was named player-coach before leaving St Andrew's.

Born in Huyton on 10 October 1962, Ward gained semi-professional honours for England with the Vics. On moving from Boundary Park to West Ham in 1985, the fee involved was £250,000 and when he switched from Upton Park to Maine Road the transfer money this time was four times that amount at £1 million. He joined Everton for £1.1 million and became a Blues player for £500,000 - eventually signing for Huddersfield Town on a 'free'.

WARHURST, Roy

Roy Warhurst, who was born in Sheffield in September 1926, started out as a winger but developed into a stocky, wavy-haired wing-half with a bone-crunching tackle, a destroyer of the highest degree. He never shirked a tackle, was totally committed and always gave 110 per-cent each and every time he took the field. When he first joined Birmingham City in 1950, after spending six years as a professional with Sheffield United during which time he made only 17 League appearances, Warhurst played on the left-wing. But when he was switched into the half-back line to partner Len Boyd and Trevor Smith, Blues began to produce the goods.

With Warhurst instrumental the Second Division championship

Roy Warhurst

was won in 1954-55 and the following season Blues reached the FA Cup Final at Wembley. But sadly after starring in each of the first four matches leading up to the semis, the unfortunate Warhurst missed out on the big occasion through injury, his place going to Johnny Newman. Some say his absence was a crucial factor as Blues lost 3-1 to Manchester City.

It was a surprise to a lot of people, certainly the fans at Maine Road, when iron-man Warhurst was transferred to Manchester City in the summer of 1957 after he had made almost 240 appearances for Blues. He spent almost two years with City and rounded off his career with a season at Oldham Athletic. He amassed in well over 300 League appearances during his playing days.

After leaving the football scene Warhurst became a scrap metal dealer.

WARTIME FOOTBALL

This is Blues' record in Wartime football:
WORLD WAR ONE (1915-19)

P	W	D	L	F	A
106	57	20	29	221	142

WORLD WAR TWO (1939-46)

P	W	D	L	F	A
215	107	39	69	428	335

The 10 FA Cup games played in 1945-46 have not been included but three void League game in 1939 have been inserted in the full statistics.

FACTS & FIGURES
- Frank Womack (92) and Jack Whitehouse (87) made most appearances for Blues during the Great War, while Whitehouse (48) and Jack Godfrey (27) were the top marksman.
- Arthur Turner (186), Dennis Jennings (174), Gil Merrick (172) and Don Dearson (166) were the leading appearance-makers for Blues during WW2 (all games) while Cyril Trigg (88), Charlie Wilson Jones (45) and Jock Mulraney (41) were the leading scorers. Trigg top-scored in three seasons: 1940-41 with 20 goals, 1943-44 with 35 and 1944-45 with 22.
- Blues biggest win during the 1915-19 period was 7-0 v Barnsley (h) on 30 November 1918. Notts County were beaten 7-2 (h) on 12 January 1918.
- Blues' two heaviest First World War defeats were at the hands of Rotherham County (a) on 25 December 1916, lost 2-8 (not a very nice Christmas present) and 0-7 at home to Notts County on 11 January 1919.
- Blues did not play any competitive matches in 1916-17.
- In World War Two, the biggest win registered by Blues was 8-0 against Tottenham Hotspur (h) on 6 October 1945. They also defeated Walsall 8-1 at home on 8 June 1940 and Bradford 6-0 at St Andrew's in an FA Cup match on 9 March 1946.
- Blues' heaviest WW2 defeat (in terms of goals conceded in regional matches) was a 6-1 demolition by West Bromwich Albion on 24 February 1940 at The Hawthorns. They suffered a 5-0 bashing at Stoke City on 9 October 1940, at home to Derby County on 12 September 1942 and away to Aston Villa on 10 March 1945. They also crashed 6-2 away at Wolves on 9 December 1939 and 6-3 at Walsall on Christmas Day 1940.
- Blues did lose 7-0 in a friendly encounter, away to Aston Villa on 15 November 1941. This season they did not play any competitive regional League or Cup matches.

- Blues fielded two 'first' teams in friendly matches on 14 October 1939. They lost them both - 0-1 at Wolves and 2-3 at Stoke City.
- Blues and Wolves were involved in one of the longest matches of all-time in April 1945. The League Cup (North) encounter kicked off at 3pm and finally finished at 5.45pm when Bill Morris scored the only goal of the game in the 153rd minute (in the 63rd minute of added time).
- Blues recorded a run of 18 consecutive home wins in 1945-46, commencing on 3 September through to 9 March inclusive.
- Blues won the Football League (South) championship in 1945-46, beating arch rivals Aston Villa on goal-average. Each team finished with 61 points but Blues' goal-average of 96-45 was better than Villa's 106-58 by 0.206 of a goal. Charlton were third on 60 points.
- The biggest single attendance for a home game for Blues during World War Two was 56,615 v Charlton Athletic in February 1946. There were 63,820 spectators present for the away game against rivals Aston Villa a month earlier. These were the two biggest attendances, other than those which saw the FA Cup semi-final encounters with Derby County in 1946, that Blues played in front during the hostilities.

WATFORD

Blues' playing record against the Hornets is:
FOOTBALL LEAGUE

Venue	P	W	D	L	F	A
Home	11	5	3	3	18	11
Away	11	2	1	8	9	19
Totals	22	7	4	11	27	30

LEAGUE PLAY-OFFS

	P	W	D	L	F	A
Home	*1	1	0	0	1	0
Away	1	0	0	1	0	1
Totals	2	1	0	1	1	1

* Watford won 7-6 on penalties
FA CUP

	P	W	D	L	F	A
Home	3	2	0	1	9	3
Away	3	2	0	1	3	2
Totals	6	4	0	2	12	5

Harry Wilcox

The first League meeting between Blues and Watford was in November 1969 when a Second Division encounter ended in a 3-2 win for Blues at Vicarage Road.

Bob Latchford scored a hat-trick when Blues stung the Hornets 4-1 at St Andrew's in September 1971.

The first encounter in the top flight was staged St Andrew's in October 1982, Kevin Summerfield scoring for Blues in the 1-1 draw. Later that season Watford won 2-1 at Vicarage Road.

Goals by Micky Halsall and Robert Hopkins earned Blues a 2-0 home win in September 1983 while in season 1985-86 Watford completed the double with a 3-0 home victory and a 2-1 win at St Andrew's.

After winning 1-0 at home in October 1993, Blues crashed to a 5-2 defeat at Watford three months later and had Gary Cooper sent-off in the process. This is the Hornets biggest win of the 14 recorded so far over Blues.

After the 1998-99 play-off semi-final between Blues and Watford had finished level after two legs and extra-time, the Hornets broke the hearts of the St Andrew's faithful by winning the penalty shoot-out 7-6.

Jock Mulraney was in brilliant form when Blues beat Watford 5-0 in the first leg of a fourth round FA Cup-tie at St Andrew's in January 1946. He scored twice in a minute early in the game and after hitting both uprights in the next minute, he went on to claim his only hat-trick for the club in the second half. In fact, Mulraney could well have created an all-time record in this tie - a hat-trick in less than two minutes.

The last knockout match between the clubs saw Blues beat Premiership side Watford 1-0 in a 3rd round FA Cup-tie at Vicarage Road in December 1999 - Gary Rowett the scorer.

Players with both clubs include: D Bailey, K Charlery, A Coton, N Doherty, H Edwards, J Elkes, H Evans, T Farnall, F Foxall, P Furlong, W Gadsby, M Good, P Harding, CB Hare, WJ Hastings, D Hill, D Holdsworth, A Kennedy, M Kuhl, RS Laing, JC Lane, BP Larkin, K Miller, F Mitchell, JA Murray, J Shaw, J Short, HM Wilcox, R Willis, WA Wragg.

Also: Ted Goodier (Watford player, Blues manager), Allan Robson (Commercial Department at both clubs).

WATSON, Alexander

After Alfred Jones had successfully managed Blues for 23 years, Alex Watson was given the difficult task of following him in the same capacity. He was appointed in the summer of 1908 but remained at the club as secretary-manager for just two seasons before handing over the mantle of team manager to former player Bob McRoberts. It is believed that Watson was born in Birmingham, the son of a wealthy businessman. He supported the club as a junior but never played football himself.

WATTS, Johnny

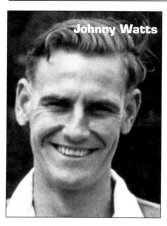

Johnny Watts

Johnny Watts played his last season at St Andrew's under manager Gil Merrick, who had been Blues' goalkeeper in the same side during the 1950s. Merrick then became manager of Bromsgrove Rovers and one of his first jobs was to secure the services of the ever-reliable Watts.

Born in Vauxhall, Birmingham on 13 April 1931, Watts was a tremendously dedicated footballer who gave his all each and every time he took the field. He was spotted by eagle-eyed Blues scout Walter Taylor while playing Sunday football for Saltley Old Boys on Glebe Farm recreation ground and was signed by the club as a 'highly rated' 17 year-old junior in August 1948. He did well in the intermediate and second teams before turning professional in August 1951.

A versatile wing-half who could play as a full-back, Watts took five years before establishing himself in the Blues first XI (two of which were spent on national service). He eventually took over the right-half berth from Len Boyd in 1956 and went on to amass 248

senior appearances (three goals scored), helping Blues reach the Fairs Cup Final in successive years (1960 and 1961), having earlier played in 10 League matches when promotion was gained in 1955. He possessed a terrific sliding tackle and this was not well appreciated by the fussy referees on the European circuit when Blues played in the Fairs Cup. He was replaced in the middle-line by Terry Hennessey and in July 1963 was re-united with Gil Merrick at Bromsgrove, retiring in 1969 at the age of 38.

WEALANDS, Jeff

Jeff Wealands

Born in Darlington on 26 August 1951, goalkeeper Jeff Wealands started his career as a professional with Wolverhampton Wanderers. He had a loan spell with Northampton Town before moving to his home town club at The Feethams in 1970. From there he switched to Hull City (1972) and after making over 250 first team appearances for the Tigers he served with Blues from July 1979 to May 1983. In his four years at St Andrew's the capable if unspectacular Wealands made 119 senior appearances, helping Blues to promotion in 1979-80. Following a loan spell with Manchester United (February 1983) he eventually moved to Old Trafford on a permanent footing and thereafter had an interesting end-of-League-career with loan spells at Oldham Athletic and Preston North End before playing at a lower level with Altrincham. He kept goal for the non-League side when they knocked Blues out of the FA Cup in 1985 at St Andrew's. In May 1987 Wealands switched to Barrow (also in the Conference) before returning to Altrincham as a Director. Now a successful property developer in Wilmslow, Cheshire he has in recent years helped out various clubs as a goalkeeping coach, including Bury.

WEATHER

On 1 September 1906 Blues played Preston North End at Deepdale in temperatures touching 90 degrees Fahrenheit. Two days later the temperature gauge had dropped by five degrees when Blues entertained Bristol City on Bank Holiday Monday.

When they visited Australia and Tahiti in May 1973 Blues encountered temperatures well into the upper '90s and the temperatures were again sky high when Blues visited the South American countries (Peru, Columbia etc) in May 1981.

Blues' two Fairs Cup encounters against Barcelona in Spain in November 1957 and May 1960 respectively, were both played in temperatures touching 90 degrees and it wasn't much cooler when they travelled over to Italy for two matches in the Anglo-Italian Cup competition in June 1971.

On the cold front, Blues battled in temperatures below freezing during the winters of 1946-47, 1962-63 and 1978-79, while in February 1969 the gloves were out when Blues played Manchester United in a 5th round FA Cup replay at Old Trafford when the gauge again dropped well below freezing point.

WEDNESBURY OLD ATHLETIC

Blues' record against the Athletic is:

FA CUP

Venue	P	W	D	L	F	A
Home	1	1	0	0	5	1
Away	1	1	0	0	2	0
Totals	2	2	0	0	7	1

Blues were disqualified from the FA Cup competition after their 2-0 win on Wednesbury soil in December 1890 - for fielding an unregistered player, namely Charlie Short, ex Unity Gas FC, who actually scored one of the goals.

Players with both clubs include: F Barlow, E Kingston, A Leake, C Partridge, V Teychenne, S Webb, VH White.

WEIGHT

Three of the heaviest footballers to have donned a Blues shirt have been 1880s defender Charlie Simms at 14 stones 1911-12, goalkeeper Billy George who weighed 14 stones, 6 lbs and 1990s striker Kevin Francis who tipped the scales at a massive 16 st 10lbs at one time.

The heaviest player to appear against Blues in a competitive game has been 22 stone goalkeeper Billy 'Fatty' Foulke of Sheffield United.

WELSH CONNECTION

Jack Peart

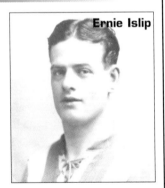
Ernie Islip

Personnel who have served with Blues and have also played for, managed, and/or coached football clubs in Wales:

Alan Ainscow . . . . .Flint Town
Keith Bannister . . . . .Wrexham
Joe Barratt . . . . .Pontypridd
Keith Bertschin . . . . .Barry Town
Albert Bloxham . . . . .Rhyl Athletic
John Bond .Blues & Swansea manager
Robert Booth . . . . .Merthyr Town, Swansea Town
Jason Bowen . . . . .Cardiff City, Swansea City
Kevin Bremner . . . . .Wrexham
John Burton . . . . .Cardiff City
Alan Campbell . . . . .Cardiff City
Bill Carrier .Merthyr Town (junior)
Frank Carrodus . . . . .Wrexham
Tim Carter . . . . .Newport County
Wallace Clark . . . . .Connah's Quay
Terry Cooke . . . . .Wrexham
John Cornforth . . . . .Swansea City
Ernie Curtis . . . . .Cardiff City player & coach

Micky Darrell . . . . .Newport County
Fred Davies . . . . . . .Cardiff City, Blues & Swansea Town coach
Stan Davies . . . . .Cardiff City, Chirk
Harry Deacon . . . . .Swansea Town
Kevin Dearden . . . . .Wrexham
Don Dearson . . . . .Barry Town, Llanwit Major
Dave Dixon . . . . .Rhyl Athletic
Greg Downs . . . . .Merthyr Tydfil
Ernie Edwards . . . . .Merthyr Town, Newport County
George Edwards . .Cardiff City player/Director, Swansea amateur
Gary Emmanuel . . . . .Barry Town, Haverfordwest, Llanelli, Newport County, Swansea City
Tony Evans . . . . .Cardiff City
Robert Evans . . . . .Wrexham
Sid Evans . . . . .Aberdare Athletic, Barry Town, Cardiff City, Cardiff Corinthians, Lovells Athletic, Merthyr Town
Greg Farrell . . . . .Cardiff City
Jack Firth . . . . .Swansea Town
Harry Fletcher . . . . .Newport County reserve
Steve Fox . . . . .Wrexham
George . . . . .Getgood Aberdare
Joe Godfrey . . . . .Merthyr Town
Colin Green . . . . .Wrexham
Tom Greer . . . . .Swansea Town
Harry Hampton . . . . .Newport County
Roger Hansbury . . . . .Cardiff City
Paul Harding . . . . .Cardiff City
Jimmy Harris . . . . .Rhyl Athletic
Seymour Harris . . . . .Aberaman
Bob Hatton . . . . .Cardiff City
Danny Hill . . . . .Cardiff City
Barry Horne . . . . .Wrexham
Fred Hoyland . . . . .Swansea Town,
Bryan Hughes . . . . .Wrexham
Billy Hughes . . . . . .Archer Corinthians, Carmarthen, Flint Town, Llanelli Town, Swansea Town
Ernie Islip . . . . .Wrexham
George Johnston . . . . .Caerau, Cardiff City, Newport County
C Wilson . . . . .Jones Wrexham
Fred Jones . . . .Carmarthen Ironopolis, Chirk, Llandudno Swifts, Llanrwst Major
Mark Jones . . . . .Merthyr Tydfil
Reg Keating . . . . .Cardiff City
Noel Kinsey . . . . .Cardiff City, Treorchy Amateurs
Hubert Lappin . . . . .Chirk
Bob Latchford . . .Merthyr Tydfil, Newport County, Swansea City
Alec Leake . . . . .Merthyr Town manager
Ken Leek . . . . .Rhyl Athletic, Ton Pentre
Terry Lees . . . . .Newport County
Andy Legg . . . . .Cardiff City, Swansea City
Albert Lindon . . . . .Cardiff scout, Merthyr Town p/manager, Newport scout
Steve Lynex . . . . .Cardiff City
Trevor Matthewson . . . . .Newport County
Albert Millard . . . . .Cardiff City
John Millington . . . . .Swansea Town
Seymour Morris . . . . . . .Aberaman, Cathays FC, Lovells Athletic
Eddie Newton . . . . .Cardiff City
Alf Oakes . . . . .Rhyl Athletic
Bryan Orritt . . . . .Bangor City, Llanfair PG FC

John Paskin	Wrexham
Jack Peart	Ebbw Vale player/manager
Charlie Phillips	Ebbw Vale
Arthur Phoenix	Colwyn Bay
Nicky Platnauer	Cardiff City
Aubrey Powell	Cwm Wanderers, Swansea Town
Dai Richards	Belingoed, Merthyr Town, Riverford FC
Ernie Richardson	Swansea Town
Harry Riley	Cardiff City
John Roberts	Abercynon Town, Swansea City, Wrexham
Ian Rodgerson	Cardiff City
Kevin Rogers	Merthyr Tydfil, Rhyl Athletic, Wrexham
Billy Ronson	Cardiff City, Wrexham
Joe Roulson	Swansea Town
Andy Saville	Cardiff City
Johnny Schofield	Wrexham
Alfred Sheldon	Wrexham
Jimmy Singer	Hengoed FC, Newport County
George Smith	Cardiff City, Swansea Town
Sam Smith	Cardiff City junior
Jim Southam	Newport County
Kevin Summerfield	Cardiff City
Bill Thirlaway	Cardiff City
Martin Thomas	Cardiff City
Len Thompson	Swansea Town
Herbert Turner	Merthyr Town
Johnny Vincent	Cardiff City
William B Walker	Merthyr Town
Don Weston	Bethesda, Wrexham
Frank White	Wrexham (guest)
Edmund Wood	Rhyl Athletic

John Paskin

WEMBLEY STADIUM

Blues have visited Wembley Stadium on four occasions.

They lost both the 1931 and 1956 FA Cup Finals there to West Bromwich Albion (2-1) and Manchester City (3-1) respectively. But then they triumphed twice in the 1990s, beating Tranmere Rovers 3-2 in the Leyland DAF Trophy final in 1990 and Carlisle United 1-0 in the Auto Windscreen Shield final in 1995. The only players to have scored goals for Blues at Wembley are Joe Bradford, Noel Kinsey, Simon Sturridge, John Gayle and Paul Tait.

Joe Bradford, actually, became the first player to net an equaliser at Wembley in an FA Cup Final (1931).

Trevor Francis played 19 times at Wembley while Colin Todd had 13 games inside the Empire Stadium.

WEST BROMWICH ALBION

Blues' playing record against the Baggies is:

FOOTBALL LEAGUE

Venue	P	W	D	L	F	A
Home	51	16	14	21	60	70
Away	51	13	15	23	53	70
Totals	102	29	29	44	113	140

FA CUP

	P	W	D	L	F	A
Home	3	0	0	3	4	7
Away	2	1	1	0	2	1
Neutral	3	0	0	3	1	8
Totals	8	1	1	6	7	16

LEAGUE CUP

	P	W	D	L	F	A
Home	1	0	1	0	0	0
Away	1	0	0	1	1	3
Totals	2	0	1	1	1	3

TEXACO CUP

	P	W	D	L	F	A
Away	1	0	1	0	0	0

ANGLO-ITALIAN CUP

	P	W	D	L	F	A
Home	1	0	1*	0	2	2

MIDLAND COUNTIES LEAGUE

	P	W	D	L	F	A
Home	1	0	0	1	4	5
Away	1	0	0	1	1	3
Totals	2	0	0	2	5	8

WARTIME

	P	W	D	L	F	A
Home	10	7	1	2	27	9
Away	14	5	3	6	25	31
Totals	24	12	4	8	52	40

*Lost 1-4 on penalties

The first time Blues and Albion opposed each other at Football League level was in season 1894-95 (Division 1). And it was the Throstles who came out on top, winning 4-1 at Stoney Lane and 2-1 at Muntz Street.

A Division apart for quite a while, Blues' first League success over their near neighbours arrived in March 1904 when they triumphed 1-0 at home, Benny Green the scorer.

Albion, though, had by far the better of the next 14 exchanges, completing the double on three occasions and winning seven times with seven draws, four of them goalless.

The goals flowed again in 1925-26 (when the present day offside law was introduced). Blues at long last won 3-0 at home while the Baggies romped to a 5-1 victory at The Hawthorns.

Blues claimed their first double in 1926-27 and then gained some revenge for their FA Cup Final defeat by winning 1-0 at The

1931 at The Hawthorns: Blues' 'keeper Harry Hibbs guides an effort round the post in his side's 1-0 win.

Hawthorns on Christmas Day 1931 and then doubling up again with an identical score 24 hours later when almost 58,000 fans crammed into St Andrew's.

It was tit-for-tat during the 1930s before Albion were relegated in 1937-38 despite a plucky 4-3 home win over Blues in their 39th match of that campaign.

After the War over 43,000 fans saw Jackie Stewart score twice when Blues beat Albion 4-0 at home in March 1948 - on their way to the Second Division title. This was to remain Blues' best-ever League win over the Baggies until they equalled it to a goal on the same ground in March 1999 when Dele Adebola scored twice.

In three successive visits to St Andrew's, Albion scored a total of 18 League goals against Blues - winning 5-3 in December 1957, 6-0 in September 1958 and 7-1 in April 1960. Both Ronnie Allen and Derek Kevan scored hat-tricks in that third victory which is also Blues' heaviest reverse against the Baggies in any major competition.

Blues tossed aside those set-backs by completing the double over Albion in 1960-61 but Albion bounced back with a double themselves in 1963-64.

Brothers Pete (Albion) and Bob (Blues) played against each other in a 2-2 First Division draw at The Hawthorns in August 1972 (Bob scoring once).

There were two more Albion doubles in 1976-77 and 1977-78 and a run of five successive draws before Blues won 2-1 at St Andrew's in November 1982.

One of those drawn games turned out to be a real thriller. After leading 1-0 (through an Archie Gemmill goal) then trailing 3-1 after a Cyrille Regis hat-trick, Blues stormed back to salvage a point from a 3-3 draw at St Andrew's in October 1981.

Again Albion won both League games against Blues in 1987-88 and they carved out a 4-1 victory at St Andrew's in October 1988

and a 3-0 success on the same ground in February 1992.

In December 1993, a crowd of 28,228 - the biggest of the season and the highest at St Andrew's for eleven years - saw Blues beat Albion 2-0...just after Barry Fry had taken charge.

Five months later, in April 1994, Blues won a vital relegation battle at The Hawthorns by 4-2 ...but still suffered relegation at the end of that season (the Baggies stayed up - see under Tranmere Rovers).

Michael Johnson's 96th minute goal gave Blues a 1-0 home League win over Albion in March 1998 in front of 23,280 fans.

Blues won 3-1 on Baggies' soil in November 1998 and 3-0 in March 2000.

In the drawn League game at St Andrew's in September 1999 (1-1) Blues' Martin Grainger broke his leg.

Albion beat Blues 2-1 at a rain-soaked Wembley Stadium to win the 1931 FA Cup Final. Joe Bradford scored for Blues that afternoon but the scoreline might well have been different had Bob Gregg's headed 'offside' goal been allowed to stand!

Blues lost the 1886 FA Cup semi-final 4-0 to West Bromwich Albion at the snow-covered Aston Lower Grounds, and some 82 years later, in 1968, they were again beaten by the Baggies at the same stage in the same competition, this time losing 2-0 at Villa Park.

Peter Murphy's excellent goal on a snow-covered Hawthorns pitch gave Blues a 1-0 victory in a 5th round FA Cup clash over Albion in 1956 - on their way to the final.

The two League Cup encounters took place in season 1984-85 (with the first game at St Andrew's).

Blues were beaten 4-1 on penalties by West Bromwich Albion in the English semi-final of the Anglo-Italian Cup at St Andrew's in 1997-98. Former Blues' player David Smith netted the clinching spot-kick for the Baggies.

1960 at The Hawthorns: Blues' 'keeper Johnny Schofield foils another Albion attack.

Fred Wheldon, later to play for Albion scored twice in Blues' 5-4 Midland Counties League defeat by Albion in February 1894.

Blues and Albion have played against each other in two friendly matches on the island of Guernsey - drawing 1-1 in February 1979 and Blues winning 2-1 in January 1982.

The first-ever Blues v Albion match was a friendly on 5 May 1883 at Muntz Street which Albion won 5-1.

Dave Massart netted two hat-tricks in successive matches (home and away) for Blues against Albion in Wartime games in May 1945.

Players with both clubs include: J Acquaroff (WW2 guest for both clubs), R Barlow, D Barnett (WBA reserve), S Bowser (Blues trialist), W Bowser, D Burrows, H Butler (guest), J Bye (guest), C Charsley, G Childs, D Clarke, J Crisp (Blues reserve), RA Dale, S Davies, P Doherty (WW2 guest for both clubs), J Dorrington (WBA amateur), G Dorsett (Blues trialist), E Duckhouse (WBA amateur), E Edwards (Blues amateur), R Fenton, J Glover (WBA reserves), A Godden, T Green (snr), P Hawker, P Holmes, R Hope, R Hopkins, A Jackson, D Jennings (WBA junior), W Johnston, A Lindon (WBA reserve), S Lynex, M McCarrick (WBA reserves), P Mardon, G Merrick (WBA guest), A Miller, A Morley, G Morrall (WBA trialist), R Morris (WBA trialist), HSM Oliver (Blues reserve), J Paskin, G Pendrey, PP Peschisolido, G Potter, J Quinn, A Rees, D Rogers, AW Smith, D Smith, J Smith, W Smith, JH Southam (WBA guest), D Speedie, K Summerfield, G Tranter (Blues reserve), J Trewick, A Turner (WBA amateur, also Blues manager), I Webb, GF Wheldon, N Whitehead, C Whyte, HM Wilcox, C Withers (WBA amateur).

Five Albion players who all won League championship medals in 1919-20, guested for Blues during World War One. They were S Bowser, AC Jephcott, H Pearson, J Pennington and S Richardson.

Also: Ron Saunders (manager both clubs), Alan Buckley and

Ron Wylie (Blues players, Albion managers), Bob Brocklebank (Blues manager, Albion scout), Tony Brown (WBA player, Blues coach), Dennis Mortimer (Blues player, Albion assistant-manager/coach), Mike Kelly (Blues player, Albion coach), Keith Leonard (coach at both clubs), John McGowan and Graham Doig (physios at both clubs), John Westmancoat (secretary of both clubs), Tom Jones (trainer at St Andrew's and The Hawthorns), Ollie Norman (WBA player, Blues trainer), Fred Barber (Blues goalkeeper, Albion gk. coach), Keith Smith (Albion player, Blues lottery staff), N Spink (Albion player, Blues coach), Tom Hedges (Blues player, WBA Director), Brian Harris (groundsman at The Hawthorns and St Andrew's), Ernie Adkins (Commercial Department at both clubs).

Albion 'keeper Pete Latchford gathers the ball safely as Blues' midfielder Alan Campbell waits for a slip. The 1972 League game ended in a 2-2 draw.

WEST HAM UNITED

Blues' playing record against the Hammers is:

FOOTBALL LEAGUE

Venue	P	W	D	L	F	A
Home	37	22	7	8	68	36
Away	37	13	9	15	49	70
Totals	74	35	16	23	117	106

FA CUP

	P	W	D	L	F	A
Home	1	1	0	0	3	0
Away	2	0	0	2	2	8
Totals	3	1	0	2	5	8

LEAGUE CUP

	P	W	D	L	F	A
Home	2	0	0	2	3	5
Away	1	0	1	0	1	1
Totals	3	0	1	2	4	6

WARTIME

	P	W	D	L	F	A
Home	1	0	0	1	0	1
Away	2	0	0	2	4	7
Totals	3	0	0	3	4	8

Blues and the Hammers met for the first time in competitive League action on 25 October 1919 (Division 2). That day a St Andrew's crowd of 25,000 saw the visitors record a 1-0 win. A week later in London the outcome was reversed as Blues took the points with a 2-1 victory, Jack Short and Albert Millard the scorers in front of 20,000 fans.

A crowd of 37,000 saw Joe Bradford score his first goal for Blues in a 1-1 draw at West Ham on Christmas Day 1920.

The return fixture 48 hours later drew a record crowd of more than 60,000 to St Andrew's when Blues won 2-1, Harry Hampton netting both goals.

The first meeting between the clubs in the top flight took place at Upton Park on 3 November 1923 and this time, despite a splendid Joe Bradford goal, Blues crashed to a 4-1 defeat. Like before, however, seven days later Blues gained revenge with a 2-1 home victory, Bradford again on target.

In all, Bradford netted 17 goals for Blues against the Hammers, including a brilliantly executed hat-trick in a 4-2 home win in September 1929. Blues completed the double over the London side that season, Bradford netting the only goal of the game at Upton Park.

Another double was achieved in 1931-32, Blues winning 4-1 at home and 4-2 away. Bradford (2) and Ernie Curtis (2) found the net at St Andrew's while George Briggs was a two-goal hero on Hammers soil.

Blues won ten and drew one of the first twelve League meetings between the clubs after World War Two, doubling up over the Hammers on five occasions, in seasons 1946-47 (4-0 at home, 3-0 away), 1950-51, 1951-52, 1952-53 and 1953-54.

West Ham's first post-war League victory over Blues was registered at St Andrew's on 26 March 1955 (2-1).

Between 1958 and 1965 a further fourteen League games took place, Blues winning eight and losing five.

In 1960-61 thirteen goals were scored in the two encounters, Blues winning 4-2 at home and losing 4-3 away.

In October 1962 Blues lost 5-0 at Upton Park in a First Division match and this scoreline was repeated to a tee eighteen months later (April 1964) when Blues were battling to stay up!

In between times, when Blues beat the Hammers 3-2 at St Andrew's on May Day 1963, they ended a club record run of 13 home League games without a victory.

Kenny Burns scored twice in Blues' 3-1 home win in December 1973 and on 1 November 1975, West Ham visited Birmingham and won hands down to the tune of 5-1 -Trevor Francis netting Blues' consolation goal against the FA Cup holders.

In winning promotion in 1979-80, Blues took three points off the Hammers. They were held to a 0-0 draw at St Andrew's but claimed a crucial 2-1 victory at Upton Park in front of 36,167 fans in their 40th League game of that season. Colin Todd (Blues) and Billy Bonds (Hammers) were sent-off for fighting in this game.

In September 1982 Blues crashed to their third 5-0 defeat at Upton Park when two defenders (Ray Stewart and Alvin Martin) both found the net.

The last League game of the 74 played saw Blues lose 2-1 at home in April 1993.

A crowd of 44,233 was present to see the Hammers beat Blues 4-0 at Upton Park in an FA Cup quarter-final tie in 1933.

When Blues beat the Hammers 3-0 in a fifth round FA Cup encounter at St Andrew's in February 1984, their goals came from Robert Hopkins, Tony Rees and Billy Wright (penalty). The crowd was almost 30,000.

The Hammers came back from 2-1 down to snatch two goals in the last four minutes to win 3-2 and so knock Blues out of the League Cup in November 1999.

Players with both clubs include: J Barrett (WHU 'A' team player-manager), J Bloomfield, F Bowden, K Brown, D Burrows, JH Burton, M Carrick, G Charles, A Cottee, LC Curbishley, J Dicks, E Dolan, F Fairman, R Ferris (WHU guest), J Gallagher, H Hooper, WH Hughes (WHU guest), S Lazaridis, D Mangnall, M Newell, G Parris, L Sealey (Blues N/C), S Small, D Speedie, W Thirlaway, C Thompson (Blues reserve), M Ward, S Whitton, N Winterburn.

Also: John Bond (WHU player, Blues manager), Lou Macari (manager of both clubs), Bobby Ferguson (Hammers' goalkeeper, Blues assistant-manager/coach).

Mark Ward

WHARTON, Sid

Sid Wharton was a short, stocky, bouncy outside-left with good pace, silky skills and powerful shot (in both feet). Born in Birmingham in June 1876, he played his early football with Smethwick Weslyan Rovers before joining Blues as a professional in November 1897. He remained with the club for six years, retiring through injury in May 1903. He remained at Muntz Street for a short time after hanging up his boots, coaching the second team. Wharton scored 25 goals (and made dozens more) in 167 senior games for the club, He twice helped Blues win promotion from the Second Division (1901 and 1903) and represented England in the unofficial international match against Germany in 1902, as well as playing for the Football League XI. He was always involved in the action and loved a challenge, often getting too involved with his opponents! Some years after ending his footballing life Wharton became a celebrated and much-respected master of ceremonies especially in the boxing ring. He died in his native Birmingham in 1951.

WHELDON, Fred

Inside-forward Fred 'Diamond' Wheldon, the youngest in a family of ten children, was born in Langley Green, Oldbury on 1 November 1869. He attended Chance's Infants and Langley St Michael's senior schools before playing weekend football with first Rood End White Star and then Langley Green Victoria. After unsuccessful trials with West Bromwich Albion in the summer of 1898, some eighteen months later, in February 1890, he signed for Blues. He became a quite brilliant footballer, an exceptional talent, a tremendous goalscorer who went on to great things with club and country.

Often seen wearing a pair of golfing stockings (instead of the footballing type), he scored 84 goals in 134 games for Blues, helping them win the Second Division championship and win promotion in successive years (1893, 1894). In fact, Wheldon notched Blues' first-ever Football League goal against Burlsem Port Vale in a 5-1 in on 3 September 1892 and he scored the club's first penalty in the 2-2 home draw with Aston Villa at Muntz Street in October 1894. But he wanted a bigger stage and in June 1896 he moved across the City to sign for Aston Villa for £350 (around £3.5 million on today's price-scale!). He impressed all and sundry with his performances with the Villa, being instrumental in three League championship triumphs (1897, 1898 and 1900) and in the 1897 FA Cup Final which was the year, of course, the double was achieved. Wheldon played in four international matches for England (it should have been far more) and he also starred in four Inter League games. He participated in 138 League and Cup games for Villa, scoring 74 goals. That gave him an overall record of 156 goals in 267 first-class outings for the two second City clubs. He left Villa Park for West Bromwich Albion in August 1900, playing in the first League game at The Hawthorns and thus becoming the first professional to appear at competitive level for three central West Midland clubs. However, he struggled to find his form with his third major club and in December 1901, eight months after the Baggies had been relegated from the top flight, he moved to Queens Park Rangers. He switched to Portsmouth in 1902 before finally calling it a day after a spell with Worcester City (May 1904-06). Besides being a splendid footballer, Wheldon was also a very useful cricketer, scoring almost 5,000 runs in 138 matches for

Worcestershire between 1899 and 1906. He averaged over 22.5 at the crease and hit three centuries into the bargain as well as claiming 95 catches, some as a wicketkeeper. He also played cricket for Carmarthenshire and later became a publican in Worcester where he died on 13 January 1924. Wheldon's brother Sam also played for West Brom.

● An unusual incident occurred early in Wheldon's playing career whereby one of his booming shots struck the referee on the pocket of his jacket. The pocket contained a box of matches, used to light the official's pipe! The box burst into flames and the ref's jacket was ruined!

WHITE, Frank

Frank White at front of line during a Blues training session. The players behind him are left to right: Wilson Jones, Harry Hibbs, Lew Stoker and Billy Guest

A goal every three games for Blues (50 in 156 senior appearances) was Frank White's record during his seven years with at the club (September 1931-December 1938). A very efficient outside-right or left, born at Wilnecote, near Tamworth on 14 November 1911 (not too far away from Harry Hibbs who came from the same village) White played for Tamworth before joining Blues' beaten FA Cup Final squad. He quickly slotted into his new surroundings but didn't establish himself in the first XI until October 1933 when he took over from Ernie Curtis. He switched to the opposite flank halfway through the 1934-35 campaign, teaming up well with Fred Harris. One or two injuries caused him to miss a handful of games in 1936 and after regaining full fitness he was transferred to Preston North End (December 1938). He guested for Aldershot, Mansfield Town, Sheffield United and Wrexham during the hostilities but when League football returned in 1946 he opted to join Redditch United (teaming up with Wilson Jones) before retiring in 1950. He later coached his former club, Tamworth.

WHITEHOUSE, Jack

A Smethwick man, born on 4 April 1897, Jack Whitehouse could play in any of the main three central striking positions and what a fine job he did, not only for Blues but for Derby County as well! A squat, pugnacious footballer, he gained a reputation for being one of the game's 'hard men', never pulling out of a tackle, always giving as good as he got and never adverse to 'mixing it' with his opponents (he was quite often in trouble with referees during his time with Blues and indeed, with Derby).

He joined Blues from Redditch in August 1916 and had a decent spell during the three War years, scoring 48 goals in 87 matches. He continued to hit the net after the hostilities and between 1919 and May 1923 when he moved to Derby, he rattled in another 35 goals in 115 League and FA Cup games for Blues, helping them win the Second Division title in 1921. He stayed with the Rams for six seasons, notching a further 86 goals in exactly 200 senior appearances before joining Sheffield Wednesdday. He never settled down at Hillsborough (only 10 outings for the Owls) nor at Bournemouth and he eventually rounded off a very effective career with spells at Folkestone Town (1933-34) and Worcester City (player-manager 1934-35). Whitehouse died in Halesowen on 3 January 1948.

WHITTON, Steve

A strong, willing and adaptable utility forward, Steve Whitton's League career spanned 17 years during which time he played for seven different clubs yet only ever gained one medal - when Ipswich Town won the Second Division title in 1992. A Cockney, born in East Ham on 4 December 1960, he joined the apprentice ranks of Coventry City before becoming a professional at Highfield Road in September 1978. In July 1983 he was sold to West Ham United (the team he supported as a lad) for £175,000 and in January 1986 was loaned out to Blues, eventually signing permanently at St Andrew's for £75,000 seven months later. He went on to score 35 goals in 119 appearances for Blues before moving to Sheffield Wednesday for £275,000 in March 1989....a very handsome profit. After an excellent loan spell in Sweden with Halmstad BK in 1990 where he top-scored in Swedish football, he went from Hillsborough to Ipswich Town (January 1991) and then in March

1994 signed as player-coach for lowly Colchester United, taking over as player-caretaker manager two months later. He ended his senior career at Layer Road in 1998 (after suffering a back injury) having scored 117 goals in 531 competitive games in England.

WHYTE, Chris

Born in Islington, London on 2 September 1961, central defender Chris Whyte began his professional career with Arsenal in December 1979 having spent two years at Highbury as an apprentice. He remained a registered Arsenal player until transferring to West Bromwich Albion in August 1988 having in between times played on loan with Crystal Palace and in America with Los Angeles Lasers. He made almost 100 appearances for the Baggies before leaving The Hawthorns to join Leeds United for £400,000 in June 1990. Two years later he collected a First Division championship medal and after switching to Blues for £250,000 in August 1993 he added a Second Division championship medal to his collection in 1995. Whyte, strong and resilient with good heading ability, starred in 90 games for Blues (one goal scored) and then left St Andrew's for Charlton Athletic in March 1996 (after a loan spell with Coventry City). He later assisted Detroit Neon, Oxford United and Leyton Orient (1997) before entering non-League soccer with Rushden & Diamonds. Whyte amassed a grand total of 488 League and Cup appearances in English football (24 goals scored) and at one time it looked as if he might become a full England international, having won four caps at under 21 level. But that was not to be.

WIGAN ATHLETIC

Blues' playing record against the Latics is:

FOOTBALL LEAGUE

Venue	P	W	D	L	F	A
Home	3	0	3	0	3	3
Away	3	0	1	2	1	5
Totals	6	0	4	2	4	8

FA CUP

Home	1	1	0	0	4	0

Just 2,600 fans saw the first League game between Blues and Wigan at Springfield Park on 1 December 1980. Blues lost 1-0.

A six-goal thriller between Blues and the Latics at St Andrew's ended all-square at 3-3 in October 1991 (Division 3).

Keith Bertschin and Trevor Francis both scored twice for Blues when they beat the Latics 4-0 in a third round FA Cup-tie at St Andrew's in January 1978. The attendance was 29,202.

Players with both clubs include: W Bradbury (Athletic player-coach), E Brown, T Cooke, A Gemmill, L Jenkinson, K Langley, M Newell, A Saville, D Sonner, SJ Storer.

Also: Ted Goodier (Athletic player, Blues manager), John Bond (Blues manager, Wigan coach), Bruce Rioch (Blues player, Wigan manager).

WIGLEY, Steve

Steve Wigley was a very effective and enterprising winger, possessing good pace and crossing ability. He scored five goals in 98 appearances for Blues during his two years with the club: March 1987 to March 1989.

Born in Ashton-under-Lyne on 15 October 1961, he played for

Curzon Ashton before becoming a professional under Brian Clough's management at Nottingham Forest in March 1981. From The City Ground he was transferred to Sheffield United (October 1985) and he arrived at St Andrew's in a player-exchange deal involving midfielder Martin Kuhl almost eighteen months later. He left Blues for Portsmouth for £50,000, switched to Exeter City in August 1993, moved on to Bognor Regis Town in 1994 and in March 1995 teamed up with Aldershot Town.

Steve Wigley

WIGMORE, Walter

Walter Wigmore was a powerfully built footballer. Initially an inside-forward and later a centre-half and stand-in right-back, he was able to use both feet to good effect and was also a sound passer of the ball. He gave Blues splendid service over a period of thirteen-and-a-half years, during which time he scored 25 goals in

355 first-class appearances. Born in Chipping Sodbury on 25 February 1873, he joined Sheffield United in 1895 and then played for Worksop Town and Gainsborough Trinity before teaming up with Blues in March 1899 for just £180. He formed a fine partnership in attack with Bob McRoberts and after moving into the middle-line (following an injury to Alex Leake) he performed magnificently alongside the various partners he lined up with. Even when asked to play at full-back he still came up trumps with some outstanding displays. Occasionally he found himself in trouble with referees - for he would rarely head the ball, getting his leg up high to bring it down. This annoyed opponents and referees who thought it to be 'dangerous play' but he was hardly ever booked, the officials finally agreeing that there was no malice in his actions! Wigmore, who helped Blues twice win the Second Division championship (1901 and 1903), also represented the Players' Union and the Football League. He moved to Brierley Hill in March 1912 before retiring the following year. He died in Worksop on 8 September 1931, having been a guest at that year's FA Cup Final (Blues v West Bromwich Albion).

Walter Wigmore

WILCOX, Freddie

Freddie Wilcox was an all-action inside or centre-forward, regarded by many as one of the finest dribblers of his day. He was a consistent performer both at home and away and scored 32 goals in his 84 games for Blues between March 1903 and March 1906. Born in Bristol on 7 July 1880, he played for Bristol Rovers from 1901 before moving to Muntz Street and on leaving Blues he went north to team up with the great Steve Bloomer at Middlesbrough. Unfortunately he wasn't the same player after moving from the Midlands and scored only 12 goals in 110 games for Boro'. A former England trialist, Wilcox, retired in the summer of 1910 after seriously damaging his right knee when he collided with an upright. He later returned to his native Bristol where he died in 1954.

WIMBLEDON

Blues' playing record against the Dons is:
FOOTBALL LEAGUE

Venue	P	W	D	L	F	A
Home	1	1	0	0	4	2
Away	1	1	0	0	2	1
Totals	2	2	0	0	6	3

FA CUP

Home	1	0	0	1	0	1

LEAGUE CUP

Home	1	0	0	1	1	2

The first League meeting between Blues and the Dons was on 1 September 1984 at St Andrew's (Division 2). A crowd of almost 10,500 saw Blues win comfortably by 4-1, Wayne Clarke (2), Mick Ferguson and Robert Hopkins the goalscorers..

The Dons beat Blues 2-1 in a League Cup-tie at St Andrew's in 1998-99 - ten years after the Dons, as FA Cup holders, had won 1-0 in a third round FA Cup-tie at St Andrew's.

239

Players with both clubs include: G Allen, J Gayle, C Gordon, M Harford (also Dons coach, assistant and caretaker manager), M Kelly, F Okenla (Dons trialist), P Summerill, N Winterburn (Blues reserve).

Also: Peter Withe (Blues player, Dons manager)

WINDRIDGE, Jimmy

Jimmy Windridge

Inside-forward Jimmy Windridge had two spells with Blues - the first from 1899 to 1905 and the second from 1914 to 1916. Overall he scored 19 goals in 61 League and Cup games. Born on 21 October 1882 in Small Heath - within walking distance of both Muntz Street and St Andrew's - he played initially for Small Heath Alma before joining Blues for his first spell.

He left the club for less than £200 in 1905 for Chelsea who had just started their first-ever season in the Football League, and then he assisted Middlesbrough from 1911 before coming back to the Midlands. Windridge, who netted seven times in eight internationals for England whilst away from Blues, created a fine record whilst at Stamford Bridge: 58 goals in 152 outings and although well past his best when he returned to Blues he still managed to bang in a fivetimer against Glossop in 1915. Windridge, besides being a quality footballer, was also a capable cricketer, who scored 161 runs for Warwickshire (avg. 14.6) and took 13 wickets. His cousin was Alex Leake.

He died in Small Heath on 23 September 1939.

WINS

Blues' top 20 home victories at competitive level:

13-0 v Coseley (Birmingham Senior Cup) 11.11.1886
12-0 v Doncaster Rovers (Football League) 11.4.1903
12-0 v Nottingham Forest (Football Alliance) 8.3.1889
12-0 v Walsall Town Swifts (Football League) 17.12.1892
11-1 v Glossop (Football League) 6.1.1915
10-2 v Ardwick (Football League) 17.3.1894
10-2 v Oswestry United, (FA Cup) 28.10.1899
10-1 v Blackpool (Football League) 2.3.1901
10-0 v Druids, (FA Cup) 19.11.1898
9-0 v Burton Wanderers (FA Cup) 27.10.1888
9-0 v Luton Town (Football League) 12.11.1898
9-1 v Liverpool (Football League) 11.12.1954
9-2 v Burton Wanderers (FA Cup) 31.10.1885
8-0 v Chirk (FA Cup) 29.10.1898
8-0 v Darwen (Football League) 26.11.1898
8-0 v Hednesford Town (FA Cup) 4.10.1891
8-0 v Manchester City (Test Match) 27.4.1896
8-0 v Northwich Victoria (Football League) 2.12.1893
8-0 v Nottingham Forest (Football League) 10.3.1920
8-0 v Tottenham Hotspur (Wartime) 6.10.1945
8-1 v Walsall (Wartime) 8.6.1940

Blues' biggest away wins (competitive level):

7-0 v Northwich Victoria (Football League) 6.1.1894
7-0 v Stoke City (Football League) 10.1.1998
7-1 v Nottingham Forest (Football League) 7.3.1959
7-1 v Oxford United (Football League) 12.12.1998
7-1 v Torquay United (FA Cup) 7.1.1956
7-3 v Leicester City (Football League) 28.4.1934

Other 'big' wins in friendly/benefit/tour matches:

18-1 v Elwells 1882
16-0 v Darlaston All Saints 1881*
15-0 v Long Eaton Rangers 1888
12-8 v International XI 1969
11-0 v Scarblaka IF 1980
11-2 v Calgary All Stars 1961
10-0 v Oldbury Town 1888
10-0 v St Luke's 1878
10-1 v FC Lucerne 1980
10-1 v The Army XI 1917
10-2 v Walsall Swifts 1878
9-0 v Burton Swifts 1888
9-0 v Lion Works 1877
8-0 v Coventry 1878
8-0 v Weymouth 1981
8-3 v Ex-Blues XI 1979

* See abandoned games.

Blues won all 17 home League games in Division Two in season 1902-03 when they were promoted to the top flight as runners-up.

Blues recorded five double-figure scoring wins in League matches (all in Division 2) before World War One.

Blues won successive home games by 9-0 and 8-0 in November 1898.

WISEMAN, David F. OBE.

When David Wiseman died in December 1978 at the age of 93, the game of football, and indeed, Birmingham City Football Club, lost one of its greatest personalities.

A lifetime of achievement saw him grow up from a boy into a wealthy and much-respected businessman in his native Birmingham where he was born on 15 August 1885. He initially pushed a plumber's handcart around the area near to Blues' old Muntz Street ground and became a top man in both worlds.

He founded the family plumbing and building contracting business, subsequently taken over by one of the giants of the trade.

In football he was a Director of Birmingham City FC for 48 years (1928-76) and for a short time before his death he held the position of club President, having previously acted as vice-Chairman at St Andrew's since 1945 under a variety of Chairmen, including both Clifford and Keith Coombs.

His influence quickly spread from the club scene to the wider field of soccer administration. His service to both the Football Association and the Football League was such that he was made a Life Member of both bodies.

From the many posts he filled the one which gained most public attraction was that of Chairman of the FA Challenge Cup Committee in which he was known as 'the Voice' on cup draw day.

A sportsman himself in his younger days, he was very good at golf, a game he played until well into his eighties. But incredibly there was another side of David Wiseman. In addition to being head of a closely-knit family and football-mad (Birmingham City of course), he was, especially in his early days, a very popular figure around the music halls with his Charlie Chaplin style walk, tap dancing technique and comedy act drawing full houses on many occasion. Even in later life he could liven up the party with a turn or two! There was never a dull moment when David Wiseman was around.

There are many stories of his favourite 'rhyming slang' ways of taking. His close friend, Frank Carter, was always Barclay (for Barclays Bank); Aston Villa were the 'Jolly Miller' and one son AD (Alan) Wiseman was always 'Sadie'. David himself was referred to by his other son, Jack, as an affectionate 'Curley.'

David Wiseman - who received the OBE in August 1970 - certainly led a champagne life though vintage drink entered his life rather late! He first took to bubbly in the 1970s when his doctor told him to have a glass of the sparkling wine to perk him up following a brief illness!

Never a man to spurn advice David Wiseman thereafter enjoyed half-a-bottle of champers for his elevenses each day! To ensure that the important event was never overlooked he had a watch with a bell set to chime at the appropriate time.

The Grand Old Man of Soccer in general and Birmingham City in particular he lived life to the full. There will, one suspects, never be another David Wiseman.

WITHERS, Colin

Colin Withers

Colin 'Tiny' Withers - 6ft. 3ins. tall - conceded six goals on his League debut for Birmingham City at Tottenham in November 1960, but after that crushing experience his form improved greatly and throughout his career he put in some supreme performances for both Blues and Villa. Withers was born in Erdington on 21 March 1940 and after gaining an England schoolboy cap at the age of 15, he played for West Bromwich Albion as an amateur in 1956-57 and signed professional forms with Blues in May 1957. After seven-and-a-half seasons and 116 games he left St Andrew's for Aston Villa for just £18,000 in November 1964. He did very well there amassing a further 163 League and Cup appearances before moving to Lincoln City in June 1969. A spell in Holland with Go-Ahead Eagles (Deventer) followed in 1970 before he rounded off his career by keeping goal for Atherstone Town. He retired in 1974 to take over a hotel on Osborne Road, Blackpool and later became a licensee in Bridgnorth.

WOLVERHAMPTON WANDERERS

Action at Molineux 1905 (Blues in white shorts)

Blues' playing record against the Wolves is:

FOOTBALL LEAGUE

Venue	P	W	D	L	F	A
Home	53	20	16	17	75	73
Away	53	11	6	36	54	104
Totals	106	31	22	53	129	177

FA CUP

Home	1	0	1	0	1	1
Away	3	1	0	2	4	5
Totals	4	1	1	2	5	6

LEAGUE CUP

Home	2	1	0	1	1	2
Away	1	0	0	1	2	3
Totals	3	1	0	2	3	5

ANGLO-ITALIAN CUP

Home	1	0	1	0	2	2

MIDLAND COUNTIES LEAGUE

Home	1	0	1	0	3	3
Away	1	1	0	0	2	1
Totals	2	1	1	0	5	4

WARTIME

Home	8	4	2	2	8	5
Away	11	3	2	6	18	24
Totals	19	7	4	8	26	29

The first League meeting between Blues and Wolves took place in October 1894 (Division One). Wolves won 2-1 at Molineux - but three weeks later Blues gain ample revenge with a 4-3 victory at Muntz Street - this after Wolves had taken a 3-0 half-time lead!

In January 1896 Blues crashed 7-2 at Molineux to an attack-minded Wolves side whose scorers included England international Harry Wood.

Blues' best League win over Wolves has been 4-1 - recorded on three separate occasions: in February 1905, January 1914 and November 1920.

In February 1912 Jack Hall scored a hat-trick (including a penalty) in Blues' 3-1 home win over Wolves.

Percy Barton scored with a 35 yard header in Blues' 4-1 League win over Wolves on 13 November 1920 - this after his defensive partner Alec McClure had netted in the game at Molineux the previous week when Blues won 3-0.

After spells in the Second and Third Division (N) Wolves joined Blues back in the top flight of English football for the 1932-33 season, drawing 0-0 at St Andrew's and winning 1-0 at Molineux.

Wolves, in fact, had the better of the exchanges during the 1930s, Blues winning only twice: 2-0 in November 1937 and 3-2 in March 1939, both at St Andrew's.

August 1959 at St Andrew's, Wolves' winger Micky Lill firing in a shot at goal as Blues' defenders George Allen (3) and Dick Neal attempt to close him down.

Aerial battle at St Andrew's in August 1993 between David Kelly (Wolves) and Chris Whyte (Blues).

Blues' first League game following Blues' promotion in 1947-48 saw them draw 2-2 with Wolves at Molineux in front of 54,361 fans - the biggest-ever turn-out for a League game between the two clubs.

In May 1950 Wolves sent Blues back to the Second Division after hammering them 6-1 at Molineux on the final day of the season.

Returning to the top sector in 1955-56, Blues lost 1-0 at Molineux and drew 0-0 at St Andrew's. The following season it was 3-0 to Wolves on their home patch and 2-2 on Blues' territory.

In season 1957-58, League champions-elect Wolves, completed the double over Blues, beating them 5-1 both at home and away. Jimmy Murray scored four of the ten goals for the Wanderers including a hat-trick at Molineux.

Another 5-1 victory for Wolves followed in March 1961 when Ted Farmer scored four of his side's goals.

Seven months later (in October 1961) nine goals flew into the respective nets when Blues lost 6-3 to Wolves in a ding-dong League encounter at St Andrew's in front of 29,000 fans. And in March 1963 Wolves again came out on top winning 4-3 in another tremendous contest at St Andrew's. Stan Lynn slammed in two penalties for Blues in this game.

The following season (March 1964) Wolves won 5-1 at Molineux, Alex Harley scoring Blues' consolation goal.

Both Blues and Wolves were relegated together in April 1965 and although Wolves gained promotion in 1966-67, they got nothing from Blues that season - losing 2-1 at home and 3-2 away. This was Blues' first double over their Midland rivals for 46 years and they came back from 2-0 down with barely 20 minutes remaining of the pre-Christmas clash at St Andrew's.

Blues had previously failed to win a League game at Molineux in 13 attempts since March 1939.

Stan Cullis started his first full season as Blues' manager by returning to his old hunting ground at Molineux for the opening League game of that 1966-67 campaign, And, thanks to two goals by Bert Murray, Blues gave him a winning start.

Blues strikers Robin Stubbs (8) and Ken Leek (10) attacking the Wolves goal at St Andrew's in March 1963.

Between 1958 and 1966, two Wolves players - George Showell and David Woodfield - scored for both sides in League games.

Wolves recorded League doubles over Blues in 1972-73 and 1975-76 before Blues won both matches in 1977-78.

Full-back Mark Dennis had the unusual - if unwanted - distinction of being sent-off in both League games against Wolves in 1978-79 (the first Blues player to suffer this embarrassment).

Two of the lowest-ever crowds to attend Blues-Wolves derbies assembled for the First Division clashes in 1984-85. Just 12,698 spectators witnessed Blues' 2-0 win at Molineux and 10,230 were present to see Wolves beaten 1-0 at St Andrew's.

In September 1992 Blues were thrashed 4-0 at home by Wolves for whom Darren Roberts scored a hat-trick.

Ex-Wolves midfielder Chris Marsden netted Blues' winner in their 1-0 win at St Andrew's in October 1997 and later that season two goals by Peter Ndlovu helped inflict a 3-1 defeat on the Wanderers at Molineux.

Both Blues and Wolves were battling it out for a play-off spot when, during a crunch game at St Andrew's on 1 April 2000, two Blues players, Martyn O'Connor and Bryan Hughes, were both sent-off in the last ten minutes. Blues held on to win 1-0 - after Keith Curle had missed an early penalty for Wolves. David Holdsworth headed the vital goal.

Second Division Blues caused a major shock when knocking First Division champions-elect Wolves out of the FA Cup in the third round at Molineux in January 1954. They won 2-1 in front of almost 37,000 fans. Ex-Wolf Ken Rowley scored the winning goal!

Jonathan Hunt missed a penalty in Blues' 2-1 FA Cup replay defeat at Molineux in January 1996.

One of Blues' lowest home attendances this century - just 2,710 - saw the Anglo-Italian Cup-tie against Wolves in September 1993. This was the game when substitute Adam Wratten came off the bench to score both goals for Blues on his senior debut in the 2-2 draw.

Bill Morris scored a dramatic goal in the 63rd minute of 'added time' to give Wolves a 1-0 win over Blues in a Regional League Cup tie at Molineux in April 1945. The game started at 3pm and finished at 5.45pm!

When Blues played Wolves in a Wartime game on 16 March 1940 the average age of the Wolves side was just 19 years, seven months. When Blues beat Wolves 3-2 in a friendly in 1939, two of their goals were scored by Villa players, George Edwards and Frank Broome.

Blues lost 8-2 to Wolves in a Birmingham Senior Cup encounter in 1896-97.

In October 1896 Blues beat Wolves 2-0 in a friendly at Crystal Palace - a game arranged to help boost the funds of the London club!

Blues beat Wolves 3-0 in the 'unknown' Marsh Cup Final in April 1910!

Players with both clubs include: A Ainscow, K Ashley, J Acquaroff (guest for both clubs), D Barnett (Wolves apprentice), JM Beattie, W Booth (reserve), T Bowen (Blues reserve), M Branch (Blues on loan), C Brazier, A Brooks & S Brooks (Blues wartime guests), J Brown, W Bunch, B Caswell (also coach), S Claridge, W Clarke, R Coy (Blues junior), J Dailey (Wolves amateur), W Devey, K Downing, W Ellis (Wolves junior), A Evans, J Gallagher (also Blues Community officer), G Getgood, A Godden (Wolves trialist), I Handysides, R Hansbury, R Hatton, H Haynes, H Hooper, T Hunt (Blues reserves), R Iverson (Blues guest), T Jones (Wolves amateur), A Kay (Blues guest), DB Latchford (Wolves reserves),A McIntosh, S Mardenborough (Blues reserves), C Marsden, A Mulraney (Wolves guest), R Neal (Wolves reserves), J Needham, M O'Grady, J Paskin, E Peers (Blues guest), C Phillips, A Potts (guest), BL Roberts, P Robinson, WC Rose (Blues reserves), K Rowley, V Samways, J Shelton (Blues guest), J Smith, B Squires (Wolves amateur), S Storer (Wolves apprentice), R Taylor, RA Thomson, RG Thomson, T Trevellyan Jones (reserves), JE Travers (Wolves reserves), G Waddell, P Withe

Also: Major Frank Buckley (Blues player, Wolves manager, Stan Cullis (player and manager of Wolves, manager of Blues), Garry Pendrey (Blues player and manager, Wolves assistant-manager); Bill Shorthouse (Wolves player, Blues coach); Jim Barron, Fred Davies and Derek Jefferson (Wolves players, Blues coaches); Ian Ross (Wolves reserve and caretaker-manager, Blues coach), Tony Evans (Blues player, Wolves Community officer), Mel Bird (Blues and Wolves ticket office clerk), Kevin Walters (physio with both clubs), Doug Ellis (Director of both clubs).

WOMACK, Frank

Frank Womack

Frank Womack appeared in more Football League games than any other Blues player - 491 - and only Gil Merrick (551) has starred in more first-class games for the club than the tough-tackling, resourceful full-back who totalled 515 senior appearances for Blues between 1908 and 1928. Womack also had 92 outings for the club during the First World War, giving him a total in excess of 600 games overall. A fine record for a very fine footballer.

Born in the village of Wordley near Attercliffe on the outskirts of Sheffield on 16 September 1888, he played for Rawmarsh FC before moving to St Andrew's. After a season 'breaking himself in' he deputised for Frank Stokes at left-back during the 1909-10 campaign before establishing himself in the first XI the following season. He skippered Blues for seventeen successive years - from 1911 - leading them to the Second Division championship in 1921. It was a pity that Jesse Pennington of West Bromwich Albion was

around at the same time as Womack, for he would surely have gained a full England cap in any other era. His only honours were to play for the Football League XI and have three international trials. He was named twice as reserve for his country (no consolation though).

In November 1913, Womack was approached by a seedy-looking guy, who offered him 55 guineas to fix the result of a game between Blues and Grimsby Town. Womack, wise and honest, immediately informed the club who in turn contacted the police. The briber was arrested and later sentenced to imprisonment. Womack, a dedicated club man, was bitterly disappointed when Blues released him in the summer of 1928 after giving the club such splendid service. At the time he was the oldest player ever to don a Blues shirt in a competitive match - aged 39 years, 207 days - later bettered by Dennis Jennings. Nevertheless life had to go on and he duly became the first player-manager to take charge of a Birmingham League side when appointed by Worcester City, quickly leading them to the championship of their respective Division at the end of his first season at St George's. This set him up for bigger things and in July 1930 he became manager of Torquay United. He bossed Grimsby Town from May 1932 to May 1936, was in charge at Leicester City from October 1936 to September 1939, managed Notts County from July in 1942 to March 1944 and did likewise at Oldham Athletic from February 1945 to April 1947.

He then had a second spell in the hot seat at Grimsby (as caretaker-manager) for four months early in 1951 before retiring to live in Caister, Lincolnshire where he died on 8 October 1968, aged 80

WORTHINGTON, Frank

Frank Worthington

Frank Worthington lined up in 757 League matches during a splendid career, firmly establishing himself in the top 12 of all-time appearance-makers in English football.

A flamboyant character, an original happy-go-lucky centre-forward who brought a sparkle to the game, Worthington, with his cavalier approach and swash-buckling displays, was a personality in his own right. His charismatic humour, his style, his arrogant ball control, his popularity all made his one of the country's likeable footballers.

A Yorkshireman to the core, he was born in Halifax on 23 November 1948 and on leaving school joined Huddersfield Town as an apprentice, taking professional status in November 1966. In August 1972 he was transferred to Leicester City for £70,000 and during his five years at Filbert Street he scored 78 goals in 239 senior outings - his best spell with any of his major clubs. On leaving the Foxes in September 1977 he moved to Bolton Wanderers for £87,000 and was both the Wanderers' and the First Division's top-scorer in 1978-79 with 24 goals despite his team finishing 17th in the table. Following a loan period in the States with Philadelphia Fury Worthington arrived at St Andrew's in November 1979, Blues manager Jim Smith paying £150,000 for his services. Worthington certainly contributed greatly in helping Blues gain promotion and then consolidate their position in the First Division. When he left, after scoring 33 goals in only 88 senior appearances, the club had lost one its finest post-war players. From Blues, following a loan spell with Tampa Bay Rowdies (NASL), Worthington switched to Leeds United in March 1982 in a part-exchange deal involving Welsh international Byrom Stevenson. Nine months later, after failing to settle at Elland Road, he teamed up with Sunderland, diverting due south to The Dell in June 1983 to sign for Southampton. In May 1984, one of soccer's nomadic journeymen was on the move again, this time to Brighton & Hove Albion from where he switched his attention to Tranmere Rovers in July 1985, taking over as player-manager at Prenton Park. In February 1987 Worthington was off again, this time to Preston North End (as a player); in September of that same year he moved to Stockport County and in April 1988 went over to South Africa to play for Cape Town Spurs. Soon afterwards he returned to England to sign for non-League Chorley and thereafter his 'interesting' career saw him serve, in turn, with Stalybridge Celtic, Galway United in Ireland, Weymouth, Radcliffe Borough, Guiseley, Hinckley Town (as player-manager) and finally Halifax Town (part-time coach 1991-92). Even after that Worthington still turned out in various charity matches, finally hanging up his boots in 1998 to concentrate on his 'after dinner speeches.' He was granted a benefit by the PFA in 1991. The game was played at St Andrew's and over 7,000 attended to say 'thank you.'

Capped by England on eight occasions, he also represented his country in two under 23 internationals and played once for the Football League side and he helped both Huddersfield Town and Bolton Wanderers win the Second Division title in 1970 and 1978 respectively.

Statistics don't always tell the story, but in Worthington's case they certainly do.

- He scored in League football in each of 21 consecutive seasons: 1966-67 to 1987-88 inclusive, amassing a total of 234 goals (in 757 games).
- In all competitions (League, FAC, LC, internationals, in America, etc) he netted close on 300 goals in 905 appearances - some record! And there is no doubt that he scored some real

beauties - remember the one at Bolton?

Worthington's two brothers, Dave and Bob, both started their professional careers as full-backs with Halifax Town....the club Frank never played for! And his nephew Gary started out with Manchester United (1984).

WREXHAM

Johnny Vincent scoring for Blues against Wrexham in the League Cup encounter at The Racecourse Ground in 1970.

Blues playing record against the Welsh club is:

FOOTBALL LEAGUE

Venue	P	W	D	L	F	A
Home	2	2	0	0	7	2
Away	2	0	1	1	1	2
Totals	4	2	1	1	8	4

FA CUP

Venue	P	W	D	L	F	A
Home	2	1	0	1	7	4
Away	1	1	0	0	3	1
Totals	3	2	0	1	10	5

LEAGUE CUP

Venue	P	W	D	L	F	A
Home	1	0	1	0	3	3
Away	1	1	0	0	3	2
Totals	2	1	1	0	6	5

The first League game between the two clubs was played at Wrexham's Racecourse Ground on 13 October 1979 in front of 13,693 spectators. Sadly Blues lost 1-0 - but four months later in the return fixture at St Andrew's the Welsh side were defeated 2-0 before a 19,306 crowd. Kevin Dillon and Tony Evans scored for Blues.

Two goals by Kevin Francis helped Blues defeat Wrexham 5-2 in the second League game at St Andrew's in February 1995. In fact, Blues netted three times in five minutes straight after half-time.

When Blues beat Wrexham 6-1 at Muntz Street in an FA Cup fourth qualifying round tie in November 1899, Bob McRoberts led the goal rush with a hat-trick.

In January 1928 it was perhaps appropriate that Welsh international Stan Davies should score twice when Blues beat Wrexham 3-1 in an away fourth round FA Cup encounter. Jack Randle netted Blues other goal from the penalty spot - his only goal for the club.

An upset occurred at St Andrew's in February 1997 when lowly Wrexham booted Blues out of the FA Cup, beating them 3-1 in a fifth round tie in front of 21,511 spectators. Steve Bruce scored for Blues.

In August 1970 Blues beat Wrexham 3-2 at The Racecourse

Ground in a first round League Cup replay (coming back from 2-0 down)…this after the teams had fought out a 3-3 draw at St Andrew's. Johnny Vincent and Geoff Vowden scored in both games for Blues while Eddie May did likewise for Wrexham.

Players with both clubs include: K Bannister, K Bremner, F Carrodus, T Cooke, K Dearden, RO Evans, S Fox, C Green, E Islip, B Horne, B Hughes, CW Jones, J Paskin, JG Roberts, K Rogers, W Ronson, J Schofield, AH Sheldon (Blues reserve), DP Weston, F White (Wrexham guest).

WRIGHT, Billy

Billy Wright

Billy Wright was a stocky, compact, hard-tackling centre-half whose career spanned 15 years (1974-89) during which time he amassed well over 400 senior appearances and around 500 in all games. Born in Liverpool on 28 April 1958 he signed as an apprentice for Everton at the age of 16, turned professional in January 1977 and after almost 200 senior outings for the Merseysiders he moved to St Andrew's in June 1983 on a free transfer. He became captain and chief penalty-taker with Blues and accumulated a total of 137 appearances (14 goals scored, 12 of them penalties) before switching to Carlisle United in August 1986, five months after completing a loan spell with Chester City. A big favourite with the fans, he developed weight problems during his last year with Blues and although it was sad to see him leave, 'Wrighty' knew that his career was slowly drawing to a close. He ended his playing days with Morecambe in 1989. Capped twice by England 'B' and on six occasions at under 21 level, Wright helped Blues win promotion from the Second Division in 1985.

WYCOMBE WANDERERS

Blues' playing record against the Wanderers is:

FOOTBALL LEAGUE

Venue	P	W	D	L	F	A
Home	1	0	0	1	0	1
Away	1	1	0	0	3	0
Totals	2	1	0	1	3	1

When Blues lost 1-0 to Wycombe at home on 30 August 1994 (the first League meeting between the clubs), the Regis brothers Dave (Blues) and Cyrille (Wanderers) played against each other.

Blues' first away win in the League in the year 1995 was 3-0 against Wycombe at Adams Park on 18 March and full-back Gary Poole figured on the scoresheet!

Wanderers' record buy has been Steve McGavin from Blues in 1995 for £140,000.

Players with both clubs include: G Ablett, T Aylott, M Cooper, J Cornforth, JM De Souza, I Hastie, S McGavin, G Potter, B Squires, D Wallace.

WYLIE, Ron

Ron Wylie

Barrel-chested midfielder Ron Wylie appeared in more than 700 senior games during an excellent professional career that spanned 20 years. A Scotsman, born in Glasgow on 6 August 1933, he played initially for Clydesdale Juniors and won two Scottish international schoolboy caps before joining Notts County as an amateur in April 1948, turning professional at Meadow Lane in September 1950. After doing well with County - playing alongside Tommy Lawton for a short while - he was signed by Aston Villa for £9,250 in November 1958 and two years later, after suffering relegation, helped win back the team's First Division status. The following year he was a League Cup winner and after 244 outings in the claret and blue strip (28 goals scored) he was perhaps surprisingly transferred to Blues in July 1965 - after having been voted 'Midland Footballer of the Year.' Said to be past his best at the time of his move Wylie went on to play in almost 150 games for Blues, skippering the team to both the 1967 League Cup and 1968 FA Cup semi-finals. He announced his retirement in May 1970 when he returned to Villa Park as a coach, later taking up a similar position with Coventry City, where he also acted as assistant-manager. After serving as a soccer adviser in Cyprus, Wylie then became manager of West Bromwich Albion (July 1982 to February 1984). After leaving The Hawthorns he went back to Villa Park to look after the second team (to May 1987) and thereafter scouted for several clubs up and down the country before in August 1990 his appointment as Community Officer at Villa Park in August 1990. Wylie then assumed the position of Villa's Community Liaison Officer in 1995.

YORK CITY

Blues' playing record against the Minstermen is:
FOOTBALL LEAGUE
Venue	P	W	D	L	F	A
Home	1	1	0	0	4	2
Away	1	0	0	1	0	2
Totals	2	1	0	1	4	4

FA CUP
Venue	P	W	D	L	F	A
Away	1	0	0	1	0	3

Blues played the Minstermen for the first time at League level in January 1995, winning 4-2 at St Andrew's in front of almost 15,000 fans. Kevin Francis scored the opening two goals in the 9th and 10th minutes.

The Minstermen knocked Blues out of the FA Cup in comprehensive style in the third round in January 1958, winning 3-0 at Bootham Crescent in front of 24,000 fans. Arthur Bottom, who had done so much in helping York reach the semi-final stage in 1955, scored one of his side's goals against Blues.

Players with both clubs include: P Barnes, G Bull, W Ellis, M Gabbiadini, A Gosney, R Jones (also York coach), J McCarthy, J Metcalfe, G Potter, M Prudhoe, W Rudd, R Sbragia (also York youth coach), F Slater, T Wolstenholme.

ZAGREB SELECT

Blues' record against the Select XI is:
INTER CITIES FAIRS CUP
Venue	P	W	D	L	F	A
Home	1	1	0	0	3	0
Away	1	1	0	0	1	0
Totals	2	2	0	0	4	0

Blues' first-ever European home game was against a Zagreb select side from Czechoslovakia in Group 'B' of the Inter Cities Fairs Cup competition on 3 December 1956.

Having won the away game 1-0 six months earlier on 21 May with a goal by Eddie Brown, a crowd of 40,144 turned out to see if Blues could complete the 'double'. And those who attended weren't at all displeased as Blues romped to a 3-0 win, Bryan Orritt, Peter Murphy and Brown (again) the scorers.

STOP PRESS.........................

- It was confirmed before the start of the 2000-01 season that Ian Bennett, David Holdsworth, Martin Grainger, Bryan Hughes and Michael Johnson had all signed new contracts with Blues.
- After a series of hard-fought friendlies, Blues commenced their League programme with a worthy 0-0 draw at Queens Park Rangers before almost 14,000 spectators. New signing Geoff Horsfield made his Blues' debut.
- In mid-August a swap-deal involving Nottingham Forest's midfielder Andy Johnson and Blues' Zimbabwean international Peter Ndlovu was put 'on ice.'
- Fulham, one of the favourites to win promotion, then came to St Andrew's and defeated Blues 3-1 before an audience of 21,659. Danny Sonner scored on his home debut. At this juncture Blues were 16th in the First Division.
- The initial win of the season was gained in the Worthington Cup, Blues easily accounting for hapless Southend United 5-0 in the 1st round, 1st leg encounter at Roots Hall. Nicky Eaden (with his first goal for the club), Marcelo, Michael Johnson, Dele Adebola and Bryan Hughes found the net in front of 3,694 hardy supporters.
- A trip to The City Ground, Nottingham on 26 August, saw Blues register their opening League win of 2000-01 when they beat Forest 2-1 before a crowd of 18,820. Marcelo and Eaden were again on target and three points gained shot Blues up to 14th in the table.
- Forty-eight hours later Barnsley visited St Andrew's but the Tykes left with their tail between their legs after Blues had recorded a convincing 4-1 victory in front of a Bank Holiday Monday crowd of 17,160. Peter Ndlovu, Martin Grainger, David Holdsworth and Hughes found the net this time and Blues were now 5th.
- Suprising, after Blues' nap-hand at Roots Hall, the return leg of their Worthington Cup-tie with Southend failed to produce a single goal - much to the disappointment of the 9,507 paying customers. Both Andy Johnson and Jacques Williams came on as substitutes for Blues in the second-half.
- A penalty by Martyn O'Connor gave Blues their third League win of campaign when Sheffield United lost 1-0 before a St Andrew's crowd of 21,493 on 9 September. Blues were now lying sixth in the Division with 10 points.
- Newly-promoted and in-form Preston North End were Blues' next victims, beaten 3-1 at St Andrew's on 12 September in front of 16,464 spectators. Ndlovu, Johnson and O'Connor (penalty) fired in the goals after Mark Rankine had given the visitors a first-half lead. Blues were now 4th in the table with 13 points.
- The local derby with West Bromwich Albion followed on the Sunday (17 September) and despite the fuel situation and live TV coverage, a crowd of almost 20,000 saw the 1-1 draw.
- In the second round of the Worthington Cup Blues were paired with Wycombe Wanderers, a team they had met just twice before in League competition Blues won the first leg 4-3 away.
- This game was followed by a home fixture with Tranmere Rovers (on 23 September) before Blues travelled to play Watford and then Crewe Alexandra prior to taking on Crystal Palace and Stockport County, both at home, on 14 and 17 October respectivly.
- At St Andrew's, on 24 October 2000, Blues scheduled to play Gillingham for the first time in a League game.
- Saturday 11 November 2000, the probable date of Birmingham City football club's 125th birthday.

DIARY

AUGUST 2000

SEPTEMBER 2000

OCTOBER 2000

NOVEMBER 2000

DECEMBER 2000

FEBRUARY 2001

249

JANUARY 2000

MARCH 2001

DIARY

APRIL 2001

MAY 2001

JUNE 2001

JULY 2001

AUTOGRAPHS

CELEBRATION/PRESENTATION

Ever wanted to see a friend or loved one go onto the pitch at St Andrew's in front of 20,000 plus fans meeting the Star of the Day, be presented with a signed shirt and have a framed photo to commemorate the moment?

Well you can! Just like Andy Wiedman, pictured here with Nicky, Josh and Luke, celebrating his 35th birthday with Blues star Geoff Horsfield.

Nicky arranged all this, without Andy even knowing, until he was called onto the pitch, she had simply phoned Promotions Manager Bob Matthews on:

0121 772 0101 Ext. 1228

and he did the rest!

We can also arrange for a signed ball to be presented before the kick off, also by the Star of the Day together with Beau Brummie plus a photo. This is aimed at the younger members of the family, once again just contact Bob Matthews.

Walkway Of Fame

The walkway is proving very popular with our fans and your dedication can be put on display in front of the Directors Entrance on the Kop side of the ground.
What's more this will last a lifetime.

Madeline and Peter Kinsella, both dedicated Bluenose Fans, decided to mark the birth of their son Daniel, by having a brick installed in the Walkway of Fame. A sure way to be certain that Daniel will always follow the Blues.

We also have a memorial area where fans can place a brick for a loved one who passed away, these bricks are blue with gold lettering and are against the Stadium wall away from the general walkway.

Application forms can be picked up from Reception, Ticket Office and the Club shops.

DANIEL KINSELLA
D.O.B. 04.03.91
BLUES FOREVER